North-Eastern England
during the
Wars of the Roses

NORTH-EASTERN ENGLAND DURING THE WARS OF THE ROSES

Lay Society, War, and Politics
1450–1500

A. J. Pollard

CLARENDON PRESS · OXFORD

1990

Oxford University Press, Walton Street, Oxford OX2 6DP
Oxford New York Toronto
Delhi Bombay Calcutta Madras Karachi
Petaling Jaya Singapore Hong Kong Tokyo
Nairobi Dar es Salaam Cape Town
Melbourne Auckland
and associated companies in
Berlin Ibadan

Oxford is a trade mark of Oxford University Press

Published in the United States
by Oxford University Press, New York

British Library Cataloguing in Publication Data
Pollard, A. J. (Anthony James) 1941–
North-eastern England during the Wars of the Roses: lay
society, war and politics, 1450–1500.
1. England. North-east England, 1399–1485
I. Title
942.804
ISBN 0-19-820087-0

Library of Congress Cataloging in Publication Data
Pollard, A. J.
North-eastern England during the Wars of Roses: lay society, war,
and politics, 1450–1500/A. J. Pollard.
p.   cm.
Includes bibliographical references and index.
1. Great Britain—History—Wars of the Roses, 1455–1485.   2. Great
Britain—History—Henry VII, 1485–1509.   3. England, Northern-
History.   I. Title.
DA250.P64   1990
942.04—dc20   90-7275
ISBN 0-19-820087-0

Typeset by Rowland Phototypesetting Ltd
Bury St Edmunds, Suffolk
Printed and bound in
Great Britain by Bookcraft Ltd
Midsomer Norton, Bath

For Sandra

Preface

FIFTEEN years ago Bill Chaytor first showed me his book. In the Clervaux Cartulary I 'discovered' part of a receiver's account of the lordship of Middleham. The roll had been cut so that the names of all the gentry receiving fees charged to the lordship at the end of the life of Richard Neville, earl of Salisbury were preserved and sewn into the cartulary. It was in effect a roll-call of the Richmondshire gentry; friends and relatives of its compiler, Richard Clervaux, put there, one suspects, as a permanent memento of his social world. Such was my introduction to the same provincial society. This book is the outcome of fifteen years spent exploring it. The search began on the Tees, at Croft; but it has extended since then into many different corners of north-eastern England, and has taken in many other documents. The reader may nevertheless notice that the river Tees and its valley remain at the heart of what follows. I make no apology. I have lived and worked for twenty years on its banks. Studying the history has been part and parcel of the process of getting to know and appreciate my adopted home. In this respect this work is an 'inside job'; and I hope that familiarity with the region today has helped in my understanding of its past.

I find too that I have gone the way pointed recently by Colin Richmond: 'Bruce McFarlane never went into provincial society, but is it not the place to go for those of us who come after him?'[1] I have made a slightly different journey. Dr Richmond directed us to the gentry. And the gentry have been visited; but provincial society involves far more than the gentry—it includes the great nobility, the clergy, the yeomanry, burgesses, husbandmen, and many other humble persons. I have sought to visit all lay society, not just one group. It is, however, only lay society. I have but tentatively and fleetingly peered into cloister or chapter. The ecclesiastical history of the fifteenth-century north-east lies in other, more capable hands.

[1] C. F. Richmond, 'After McFarlane', *History* 68 (1984), 60.

It is hoped too that this book fills a gap or two. Although much has been written recently on Yorkshire in the second half of the fifteenth century, the rest of the north-east has been neglected by contemporary historians. Durham between 1450 and 1500, in particular, has tended to be overlooked. That history is here. It is not treated separately: the reader will find that it has been subsumed in the history of the region as a whole. Secondly, despite the prominence given in the last decade to the association between Richard III and the north, it was still possible in 1986 for a study of 'Yorkshire since AD 1000' to omit all reference to the last Plantagenent.[2] The significance of this provincial society in the politics of the kingdom in the later fifteenth century is still under-appreciated.

The historian of the north-east is fortunate in being able to call upon the work of generations of dedicated antiquaries and scholars. Not only am I following in the footsteps of Hutchinson, Surtees, and Whitaker (above all Whitaker, whose *Richmondshire* is a triumph of the antiquary's art); but also I have been able to call upon the long series of documents published under the auspices of the Surtees and Yorkshire Archaeological Societies. These published sources have been augmented by central government records in the PRO, Durham palatine records, and the many collections of family and corporate papers deposited in local archives. There are some sources that have eluded me; no doubt, as it will be pointed out, more than should have. But there is always one more document to consult; if the attempt had been made to run every source down, the book would never have been completed.

That it has been completed owes much to the generous and unselfish assistance of many bodies, friends, and colleagues. I would like to thank the staff of the following institutions: Alnwick estate office; the Borthwick Institute of Historical Research; the British Library; Cumbria Record Office; the Department of Palaeography and Diplomatic at the University of Durham, both at the College and the Prior's Kitchen; Darlington Local History Library; Durham County Record Office; Essex County Record Office; Lancashire County Record Office;

[2] D. Hey, *A Regional History: Yorkshire from AD 1000* (1986), 103–4. See also F. B. Singleton and S. Rawnsley, *A History of Yorkshire* (Chichester, 1986), 49 where similarly Richard III is noticeable by his absence.

The Library of Congress; Middlesbrough Central Reference Library; the National Register of Archives (Scotland); North Yorkshire County Record Office; the Pierpont Morgan Library; the Public Record Office; and the Yorkshire Archaeological Society.

I owe special debts of gratitude to Margaret Condon, who has searched out documents for me at the Public Record Office, and to Carol Arnold, Lorraine Attreed, Michael Bennett, Barrie Dobson, Keith Dockray, Bill Hampton, Michael Hicks, Rosemary Horrox, Richard Hoyle, Michael Jones, Jenny Kermode, Robin Storey, Anthony Tuck, and Geoffrey Wheeler, who have generously and unselfishly shared their knowledge by making available to me transcripts of documents, photocopies, unpublished papers, and other information. Over the years I have received encouragement from and the benefit of stimulating discussion with many other fellow-historians, but especially Ian Arthurson, Anne Curry, Chris Dyer, Ralph Griffiths, David Palliser, Christine Newman, Carole Rawcliffe, and Colin Richmond. And finally there remains a lasting debt to the late Charles Ross, who first started me down this road.

I am extremely grateful to Jill Wren, and to Marlene Melber, Pauline Wayne, Jean Connell, Margaret Couhig, and Beryl Wilkinson of the Data Preparation section of the Computer Centre at Teesside Polytechnic for their assistance in preparing the manuscript for publication; to the staff of Teesside Polytechnic library for handling an unending stream of inter-library-loan requests; to Ivon Asquith and Anthony Morris for their encouragement and assistance through the press; and to Enid Barker and David Phelps, whose painstaking copy-editing significantly reduced the number of errors and inconsistencies in the text. I gratefully acknowledge too the financial support of Teesside Polytechnic, who also granted me a sabbatical year for research, and the British Academy, who provided a generous award to fund it.

Others not professionally involved have in different ways, and in some cases without realizing it, helped me get on with the work. In particular I would like to thank John Carthew, Bill Chaytor, Chris Emery, Monica Sturrock, Paul Weightman, and Guy Whitburn. Above all this book owes most to the patience, support, and constant encouragement of my wife, to whom it is dedicated with love.

Hurworth-on-Tees   A. J. P.
April 1989

Contents

List of Maps

Abbreviations

Add. Ch.	British Library, Additional Charter
Add. MS	British Library, Additional Manuscript
Arch. Ael.	*Archaeologia Aeliana*
BI	Borthwick Institute of Historical Research, York
BIHR	*Bulletin of the Institute of Historical Research*
BJRL	*Bulletin of the John Rylands Library*
BL	British Library
C	Public Record Office, Chancery
Campbell, *Materials*	*Materials for a History of the Reign of Henry VII*, ed. W. Campbell, 2 vols. (Rolls Series, 1873–7)
CCR	*Calendar of Close Rolls*
CDRS	*Calendar of Documents Relating to Scotland preserved in the Public Record Office*, ed. J. Bain, 4 vols. (Edinburgh, 1881–4)
CFR	*Calendar of Fine Rolls*
CIM	*Calendar of Inquisitions Miscellaneous (Chancery) preserved in the Public Record Office*, 7 vols., 1916–68
CIPM	*Calendar of Inquisitions Post Mortem*
Coles, 'Middleham'	G. M. Coles, 'The Lordship of Middleham, especially in Yorkist and Early Tudor Times' (unpublished University of Liverpool MA thesis, 1961)
CP	Public Record Office, Common Pleas
CP	G. E. Cokayne, *The Complete Peerage, of England, Scotland, Ireland, Great Britain and the United Kingdom*, ed. Gibbs *et al.*, 12 vols. (1910–50)

CPR	*Calendar of Patent Rolls*
Crowland Chronicle	*The Crowland Chronicle Continuations, 1459–1486*, ed. N. Pronay and J. Cox (Gloucester, 1986)
DL	Public Record Office, Duchy of Lancaster
DNB	*Dictionary of National Biography from the Earliest Times to 1900*, ed. Sir Leslie Stephens, 21 vols. (1885–1900)
Durh.	Public Record Office, Durham
Durham	University of Durham, Department of Palaeography and Diplomatic
Dur. RO	Durham County Record Office
E	Public Record Office, Exchequer
Econ. HR	*Economic History Review*
EETS	Early English Texts Society
EHR	*English Historical Review*
Ellis, *Original Letters*	*Original Letters Illustrative of English History*, 1st series, 3 vols. (1823); 2nd series, 4 vols. (1827); 3rd scries, 4 vols. (1846)
Hardyng, *Chronicle*	*The Chronicle of John Hardyng*, ed. H. Ellis (1802)
Harleian MS 433	*British Library Harleian Manuscript 433*, ed. R. E. Horrox and P. W. Hammond, 4 vols. (1979–83)
HMC	Historic Manuscripts Commission
Hutchinson, *Durham*	W. Hutchinson, *The History and Antiquities of the County Palatine of Durham*, 3 vols. (Durham, 1817)
JEH	*Journal of Ecclesiastical History*
KB	Public Record Office, King's Bench
North Country Wills	*North Country Wills*, ed. J. W. Clay, Surtees Society, vol. cxvi (1908)
NH	*Northern History*
NYCRO	North Yorkshire County Record Office
NYCROJ	*North Yorkshire County Record Office Journal*
Paston Letters	*Paston Letters and Papers of the Fifteenth Century*, ed. N. Davis, 2 vols. (Oxford, 1971–6)

Plumpton Correspondence	*Plumpton Correspondence*, ed. T. Stapleton (Camden, os, iv, 1839)
Pollard, *Henry VII*	*The Reign of Henry VII from Contemporary Sources*, ed. A. F. Pollard, 3 vols. (1913)
PP	*Past and Present*
PPC	*Proceedings and Ordinances of the Privy Council*, ed. N. H. Nicolas, 7 vols. (Record Commission, 1834–7)
PRO	Public Record Office
RO	Record Office
Rot. Parl.	*Rotuli Parliamentorum*, ed. J. Strachey, 6 vols. (1767–77)
Rot. Scot.	*Rotuli Scotiae*, 2 vols. (Record Commission, 1814–19)
RS	Rolls Series
Rymer, *Foedera*	T. Rymer, *Foedera, Conventiones, Litterae, et Cuiuscunque generis Acta Publica*, 20 vols. (1704–35)
SC	Public Record Office, Special Collection
Somerville, *Duchy of Lancaster*	R. Somerville, *History of the Duchy of Lancaster, 1265–1603*, vol. i
SR	*Statutes of the Realm*, ed. A. Luders, 11 vols. (Record Commission, 1810–28)
SS	Surtees Society (Durham and London)
Surtees, *Durham*	R. Surtees, *The History and Antiquities of the County Palatine of Durham*, 4 vols. (1816–40)
Test. Ebor.	*Testamenta Eboracensia*, ed. J. Raine, Parts 2–5, Surtees Society, vols. xxx, xlv, liii, lxxix, (1855, 1865, 1869, 1884)
TRHS	*Transactions of the Royal Historical Society*
VCH	*Victoria History of the Counties of England*
Warkworth, *Chronicle*	J. Warkworth, *A Chronicle of the First Thirteen Years of the Reign of King Edward the Fourth*, ed. J. O. Halliwell (Camden, 1839)
Wedgwood, *Biographies*	*History of Parliament: Biographies of*

	Members of the Commons House, 1439–1509, ed. J. C. Wedgwood (1938)
Wills and Inventories	*Wills and Inventories Illustrative of the History, Manners, Language etc. of the Northern Counties of England,* ed. J. Raine, Surtees Society, vol. ii (1835)
YAJ	*Yorkshire Archaeological Journal*
YAS, RS	Yorkshire Archaeological Society, Record Series (Leeds)
YCR	*York Civic Records*, ed. A. Raine, vol. i (1939), vol. ii (1941), Yorkshire Archaeological Society, Record Series, nos. xcviii and ciii
Yorks. Deeds	*Yorkshire Deeds*, ed. W. Brown, C. T. Clay, vols. i–vi; Yorkshire Archaeological Society, Record Series, vols. xxxix, l, lxiii, lxv, lxix, lxxvi (1909, 1914, 1922, 1924, 1926, 1930)

The spelling and punctuation of English prose texts have been modernized; quotations of fifteenth-century English verse have been left in their original form. All books are published in London unless otherwise stated. Full references are only given at first mention. Short titles can be identified by reference to the Bibliography.

I

Introduction

IN 1436 Aeneas Sylvius Piccolomini, the future Pope Pius II, travelled home through England from an embassy in Scotland. He spent his first night on English soil in the borders. Alarmed when his male hosts took shelter in the local peel for fear of a Scottish raid, and unwilling to accept the consolation offered by two young women, he spent instead an uncomfortable night with heifers and nanny-goats as companions in a stable. It was, he later wrote, a rude and uncultivated country, unvisited by the winter sun.[1] Piccolomini thus inaugurated a long tradition of uncomplimentary comment on northern England in the fifteenth century which has continued to the present day. It was, according to this tradition, remote, backward, barbarous, superstitious, lawless, and rebellious. The north, wrote R. R. Reid in 1921 'remained almost untouched by the economic, social and intellectual changes which were breaking up medieval society in the south'.[2] According to W. K. Jordan several decades later, Yorkshire, even after 1480, 'lying far to the north, remote, suspect and badgered by the Tudors, . . . was thinly populated, poor and backward'.[3] The north-east, according to the author of a recent geographical study of the region, was, before the Industrial Revolution, 'both a peripheral and relatively poor part of the English economy'. 'The power of the Prince Bishop of Durham, the exploits of the Percy family, the romantic if brutal feuds, and Scottish incursions into Redesdale were all indicative of the March-land status of the North East.'[4] But perhaps the most colourful expression of this traditional view belongs to the youthful Lord Dacre, who described the county palatine of Durham in the early sixteenth century as 'an economic

[1] *Memoirs of a Renaissance Pope: The Commentaries of Pius II*, ed. L. C. Gabel (1960), 35.
[2] R. R. Reid, *The King's Council in the North* (1921), 6.
[3] W. K. Jordan, *The Charities of Rural England* (1961), 18.
[4] K. Warren, *North East England* (Oxford, 1973), 10. cf. F. W. Brooks, *The Council of the North* (Historical Association, 1966), 4.

back-water, a savage and infertile country', in which the
merchants of Newcastle alone 'in a barbarous country among
illiterate and boorish squireens, constituted a single element of
civilization . . . separating them from their elder brothers who
bit their fingernails in draughty castellated farmhouses and
murdered each other over the bitting of a greyhound or even less
important matters of dispute'.[5]

The second half of the fifteenth century in the north-east has a
further dimension: the close association with the notorious
Richard III. Although this was never made explicit in traditional
historical writing, Richard III stood as a typical product of the
region. As far as A. F. Pollard was concerned, the north in 1485
was one of the feudal and more backward parts of the realm,
indifferent to the commercial and national growth offered by
Henry VII.[6] James Gairdner affirmed that 'The middle ages
passed away with Richard III. Their order had long been breaking down, their violence and lawlessness increasing. The martial government which feudalism properly required, instead of
preserving peace and progress, had culminated in tyranny,
usurpation and regicide.'[7] The north and Richard III were at one
in offering not only an outmoded but also a dangerous path for
England to follow at the end of the fifteenth century. The
association of 'The Regicide' with the region reinforced the idea
that the north was barbarous. In some hands the association was
a source of embarrassment to be passed over quickly. Francis
Drake could not avoid the evidence before him of the city of
York's support for Richard III. 'This place,' he commented, 'he
seemed, if the hypocrite could ever be sincere, to pay an extraordinary regard to.'[8] William Hutchinson, fifty years later, in his
history of Durham, resorted to denial. 'The dreadful machinations by which Richard duke of Gloucester was opening his
passage to the throne, do not seem to have had any particular

---

[5] H. L. Trevor Roper, 'The Bishopric of Durham and the Capitalist Reformation', *Durham University Journal*, 38 (1945–6), 45, 47.

[6] Pollard, *Henry VII*, pp. i, xviii–xx.

[7] J. Gairdner, *The History of the Life and Reign of Richard the Third*
(Cambridge, 1898), 252.

[8] Francis Drake, *Eboracum or the History and Antiquities of the City of York*
(1736), 116. See also the comments by D. M. Palliser, 'Richard III and York' in
R. E. Horrox (ed.), *Richard III and the North*, Hull Studies in Regional and Local
History, 6 (Hull, 1986), 69–70.

influence on the northern parts of the kingdom.'[9] Neither was willing to follow George Buck, who in the early seventeenth century enthusiastically, if inaccurately, endorsed Richard III as a noble son of the north:

For the most part the employment of this duke of Gloucester was in the north parts, where he much lived and did good service according to his charge and duty. For he was Lord Warden of all the marches, eastern, middle and western, and earl and governor, or captain (as they then said) of Carlisle. And he liked well to live in those parts of the north for sundry good causes. For [besides that] Yorkshire was his native country . . .

And [for that] they were the native country both of the duke his father and of the duchess his mother, [and] by whom he had most noble alliance and very many great friends, and much love in those parts. And certainly he was generally well beloved and honoured of all the north-ern people, his countrymen, not only for his greatness and alliance, but also (and chiefly) because he was a valiant, wise, and a bountiful and liberal prince, and a good and magnificent housekeeper, and the which bringeth not the least love of the people, but rather the most and greatest good will, for they and all men love and admire liberality and good hospitality. And thirdly he liked best to live in these parts because his appanage and patrimony was there chiefly and he had besides goodly possessions and lordships by hereditary right of the duchess his wife in the north parts . . . And for these many good causes, he was so much in the good liking of the north countries as that he desired only to finish his days there and in the condition of a subject and a servant to the king.[10]

   In more recent times Buck's pride in the northern connection with Richard III has received a powerful romantic gloss. It is first to be observed in Caroline Halsted's two-volume study. This early-nineteenth-century panegyric by the wife of the rector of Middleham owes much to her awareness of the particular connection between her home town, her husband's living, and her hero.[11] But perhaps the most complete expression of the

[9] Hutchinson, *Durham*, i. 443.

[10] G. Buck, *The History of King Richard III (1619)*, ed. N. A. Kincaid (Gloucester, 1979), 20–1.

[11] C. A. Halsted, *Richard III as Duke of Gloucester and King of England* (2 vols.; 1844).

romantic, Gothic, attachment to Richard III is to be found in the pages of P. M. Kendall's famous biography:

Wensleydale was less subdued to man than the softer countryside which Richard had known in the south: a land of scattered castles and abbeys, their villages and fields huddled about them amidst the great wild sweep of moor. The hills seemed to have been rounded by the stamp of Roman legions and of Celtic Kings. The earth was gigantic, elemental; leading men's thoughts to God, teaching men the necessity of human ties; confirming men in their feeling for old ways and old things. The people were directly swayed by their instincts, quick to take arms in a quarrel, slow to shift loyalties, earnest in their convictions. Here young Richard, in those impressionable years between nine and thirteen, discovered the native country of his spirit, a country which half created, half affirmed the kind of man he was to be.[12]

The native country of Richard III's spirit has become the romantic vision of the Middle Ages. Rather than remote, backward, and barbaric, it is unspoilt, uncomplicated, and clean. It is Merrie England; it is the lost garden. It is the same country, but its faults have become its virtues. It has become, for the twentieth century, a land to which one can withdraw to enjoy 'the quality of life'. Thus notions of the fifteenth-century (and twentieth-century) north have a close correspondence with the conflicting historiographical perceptions of Richard III: the region reflects either the vices or the virtues of the monarch.

Recent writing, while shedding some of the romantic attachment, has nevertheless continued to stress the northernness of Richard III, and a division in England which he represented between a developing south and a more conservative north.[13] Cautiously expressed by Charles Ross in his study of Richard III,[14] it has taken a more forceful form elsewhere. 'Then, as now,' one recent historian has written, 'England was two nations, and the events of Richard III's reign are best seen in focus through the perspective of north versus south.'[15] Commenting on the 1984 miners' strike Professor Frank Musgrove wrote in the *Sunday Times* that it was partly explained by the historical division between the north and south:

[12] P. M. Kendall, *Richard III* (1955), 46.
[13] See e.g. Horrox, *Richard III and the North*, and the essays therein.
[14] Charles Ross, *Richard III* (1981), 44.
[15] Jeremy Potter, *Good King Richard?* (1983), 46.

The conflict between north and south has its roots deep in medieval history: for five centuries England north of Pontefract was a militarised zone . . . Meanwhile the south grew fat . . . Briefly in the time of Richard of Gloucester (who later became King Richard III) Wensleydale was the centre of political power . . . The present miners' strike no less than the Pilgrimage of Grace in 1536 is an expression of a deep distrust on that [sic] part of the north for the south: a sense that they are an unregarded, marginal world which the south holds in contempt.[16]

Here too the traditional perception of the north has become caught up with the history of Richard III, with very obvious late-twentieth-century political overtones.

In fact the trend in recent historical scholarship has been to question the traditional perception of the north at the end of the Middle Ages. Taking their lead from A. G. Dickens, several contemporary historians have argued that the region cannot be regarded as 'belonging to the "backward", "immobile", and "reactionary" north of historical convention'.[17] B. W. Beckingsale demonstrated that 'feudalism, catholicism (after 1558) and a violent society were not the unique and unmistakable fingerprints of the North, but were rather the blurred and fading imprints of all provincial England in their period'.[18] John Le Patourel, questioning whether the north and its history have a meaningful identity, emphasized the point that the north was not an isolated frontier zone.[19] It is now doubted whether the north-east was as remote, backward, barbarous, or lawless as traditionally it has been painted; just as it may legitimately be questioned whether England really was divided into two nations, north and south; or whether Richard III's career should best be seen in the perspective of regional animosities.

This is a regional study. Conventionally the north-east is taken to be the old counties of the North Riding, Durham, and Northumberland. But, as Professor Dickens put it, it is advisable to 'avoid undue pedantry over boundaries'. Since successive great lords of the north-east were customarily wardens of the

[16] *Sunday Times*, 12 Aug. 1984.
[17] A. G. Dickens, *Lollards and Protestants in the Diocese of York, 1509–1558* (Oxford, 1959), 2–4.
[18] B. W. Beckingsale, 'The Character of the Tudor North', *NH* 4 (1969), 67.
[19] J. Le Patourel, 'Is Northern History a Subject', *NH* 12 (1976). See also R. B. Dobson, 'Cathedral Chapters and Cathedral Cities', *NH* 19 (1983), 15–17.

west march, it is impossible to exclude Cumbria from all
consideration.[20] Similarly the other Ridings of Yorkshire inevitably intrude. Thus the region is not to be defined as an aggregate
of counties. A regional history is broader in scope than a county
history, or even a collection of county histories. In recent years
the county or county community has become a favoured unit for
late-medieval studies. Whatever the merits of the county as an
entity in the century after the Reformation, it is not an appropriate unit for the study of northern England in the preceding
century. As we shall see, except in relation to royal administration, the north-eastern county was either engulfed by a wider
socio-political world or fragmented into narrower administrative units, neighbourhoods, and *pays*. Just as East Anglia had a
perceived regional identity at the beginning of the sixteenth
century transcending the counties of Norfolk and Suffolk,[21] so
also the north-east formed a region which overlaid its constituent counties in the late fifteenth century.

As a study of the north-east of England in the second half of
the fifteenth century this work explores the economic, social,
cultural, and political character of the region; examines the
relationship between the region and other parts of England; and
narrates its political history during the Wars of the Roses. In
particular it explores the relationship between the region and
Richard III, both as king and duke, and the impact that relationship had on contemporaries. But it is more than a study of
Richard III: it is a study of the region which he described as his
home,[22] and which has a history both before he came to the
north in 1471 and after he was deposed in 1485.

[20] A. G. Dickens, *Lollards and Protestants in the Diocese of York, 1509–1558*
(Oxford, 1959), 3. The west march is the subject of Dr Henry Summerson's
forthcoming study of medieval Carlisle.
[21] D. MacCulloch, *Suffolk and the Tudors* (Oxford, 1986), 7–13, 338.
[22] YCR i. 24.

PART I

ECONOMY, SOCIETY, AND GOVERNMENT

I

The North-East in the Fifteenth Century

ON 24 September 1485 Henry VII offered a pardon to all those of the north parts of his land who had of late done him great displeasure by being in the field in the company of his adversary, 'the enemy of nature'. The north parts were specified by him as including the counties of Nottingham, York, Northumberland, Cumberland and Westmorland, the city of York, the bishopric of Durham, and the town of Hull.[1] Henry no doubt excluded the duchy of Lancaster and the county of Chester because the knights, esquires, and gentlemen of those north-western shires had demonstrated their loyalty in the service of the Stanley brothers on the field of Bosworth. Presumably the enemy of nature himself, Richard III, had had a similar region in mind when two years earlier he appealed for help to the city of York. In a letter of 10 June 1483 he claimed that Queen Elizabeth Woodville was threatening 'the final distruction and disinheritance of you and all other the inheritors and men of honour, as well of the north parts as other countries that belongen us [are our dependants]'.[2] The north clearly formed a recognizable, if imprecisely defined, 'country' in fifteenth-century England.

Conventionally the river Trent separated these north parts from the south. Ecclesiastically it divided the provinces of York and Canterbury. Heraldically it divided the provinces of Norroy and Clarenceux Kings of Arms. And administratively it divided the royal forest and duchy of Lancaster into northern and southern parts; a division followed by lesser landlords such as the FitzHughs, who employed receivers and auditors for their estates *partes boreales* and *partes australes* respectively.[3] The north may thus be identified loosely as a province; but, as the

---

[1] *YCR* i. 125–6. [2] Ibid. 73–4.
[3] NYCRO, ZJX, 3/2/112. Essex RO, D/DDL M108, the account of William Catterick Receiver of William Lord FitzHugh 'in partibus borealis'.

late Professor Le Patourel pointed out, 'the North of England has always been a vague notion without rigid territorial limits and encompassing considerable internal diversity'.[4] It contains (and contained) several regions, of which one is the north-east.

What constituted the north-east in the fifteenth century presents a further problem of definition. Professor Everitt has noted that almost all our current regional terms are of recent origin. 'Expressions like ... the North East,' he reminds us, 'have no lengthy lineage.' Moreover, there are dangers in reading such terms back into the past. 'It is not simply that the generalizations they give rise to are often likely to prove spurious, but they usually impose the wrong kind of regional pattern upon the landscape of history.' His warning needs to be taken to heart by historians writing about the regions of England in the fifteenth century.[5] In contemporary usage the 'north-east' usually describes the pre-1974 counties of Northumberland and Durham and the county borough of Teesside: essentially eastern England north of the Tees. If it is a region that has a shared sense of its own identity, that identity was created by the experience of nineteenth-century industrialization. It does not follow that such an identity existed before 1800.

Yet in writing about the north-east in earlier centuries authors have tended to assume that the Tees always formed a regional boundary. Twenty years ago Graham Turner in his influential description of the north, *The North Country*, commented: 'Once over the Tees, you are aware of having crossed an important border line. The change of atmosphere is hard to describe but it is more marked than the sensation of entering either Scotland or Wales. . . . For centuries,' he continued, 'the North-east was largely cut off from the rest of the country both by geography and by its extraordinary history.'[6] Dr Smailes in his account of the historical geography of the north assured his reader that the four northern counties—i.e. Cumberland, Westmorland, Northumberland, and Durham—had a high degree of

[4] Le Patourel, 'Is Northern History a Subject?', pp. 6–8, 12.

[5] A. Everitt, 'Country, County and Town: Patterns of Regional Evolution in England', *TRHS* 5th ser., 29 (1979), 79–80. See also J. D. Marshall, 'Why Study Regions (2): Some Historical Considerations', *Journal of Regional and Local Studies* 6 (1) (Spring 1986), 2–4. I do not, however, share his confidence that a county was more naturally a region in pre-industrialized society than it is today.

[6] G. Turner, *The North Country* (1967), 299–300.

provincial consciousness, forming a transitional zone between England and Scotland.[7] The editor of the *Agrarian History of England and Wales* would seem to share this view, since in this massive work the same four counties are treated as one. Dr Brooks argued that it was a boundary, on the grounds that the Vale of York (unlike south Durham, presumably) was more socially akin to the midlands than to the wild dales of Northumberland. More recently Professor Dobson has added his own observation concerning the diversity of the north, that the 'river Tees may form a much more important internal frontier than either the Humber or Trent'.[8]

Now it is true that until the nineteenth century the Tees was the southern boundary of the major part of the county palatine of Durham: the land between Tyne and Tees was thus jurisdictionally and administratively set apart not only from Yorkshire but also from the rest of England. Indeed, as a result of the independence of the bishop's regality, the people of Durham are rarely to be found in the royal archives, and are thus less well known to us than their neighbours south of the Tees. They were not surveyed in 1086; they were not taxed in 1377. The historian hence finds different, intellectual justification for the adoption of the river as a boundary: the drying-up of comparative evidence.

But on the ground, in fifteenth-century England, the reality was different. The Tees was no barrier. Indeed on the contrary: its course, from dale to wide fertile valley, brought the inhabitants of both banks together— economically, socially, and culturally. It was the focus of two of Professor Everitt's *pays*; in its upper reaches the forest *pays* of Teesdale; in its lower the fielden *pays* of the Tees basin.[9] Landownership did not recognize the Tees as a boundary. From great lords such as Richard of Gloucester himself, who held both Barnard Castle and Middleham; through lesser peers such as Lord Greystoke (Coniscliffe and Henderskelfe); through gentry families such as the Salvins of Croxdale near Durham, who held twelve tenements in York, as well as various rents and tenements in five north Yorkshire

[7] A. E. Smailes, *North England* (1960), 4.
[8] F. W. Brooks, *The Council of the North*; Dobson, 'Cathedral Chapters', p. 17.
[9] Everitt, 'Country, County and Town', pp. 81–4.

villages; to humble yeomen such as Thomas Hill of Bishopthorpe, who in 1482 sold a burgage in Sadlergate, Durham to
William Smethurst of Bishopthorpe; *all* ranks of society possessed material interests in both Durham and Yorkshire.[10] It
followed, as we shall see below, that marriage and friendship,
service and clientage likewise showed scant regard for the
jurisdictional boundary that followed the course of the river. In
particular north-eastern lawyers, men such as Sir Robert Danby,
Richard Pigot, Miles Metcalfe, and Thomas Middleton were
equally at home in the service of lords and corporations both
north and south of the river.[11] Commerce flowed freely across
the Tees. Lady FitzHugh's steward purchased cattle for her
household at Ravensworth in Darlington; as did Richard
Neville, earl of Warwick's instaurer to stock his farm at Middleham in 1467–8. Thomas of Barnard Castle traded in wool at
Knaresborough; five men of Cowpen Bewley in south-east
Durham frequented Ripon market in Lent 1451, and on Sundays
too. Durham coal was transported by road to northern Yorkshire; and Yorkshire woollens were supplied to Durham
Cathedral Priory. Newcastle was frequently the staple port for
Richmondshire and Northallertonshire, as well as for Durham
and Northumberland wools.[12]

The ease with which inhabitants north and south of the Tees
moved within one society is revealed most graphically by two
contrasting but complementary kinds of evidence: the flight of
criminals to sanctuary in the cathedral of Durham, and the
migration of countrymen to crafts in the city of York. Of
thirty-seven persons granted sanctuary at Durham between
1464 and 1490, no fewer than twenty-three came over from
Yorkshire or further afield. Most came from northern Yorkshire: for them one presumes it was quicker to reach Palace

---

[10] For Gloucester and Greystoke, see below pp. 91–4; details of the Salvin
Estate are to be found in DurRO, D/sa/D 1408–18, 1571. For Thomas Hill see
Reports of the Deputy Keeper of the Public Records xliv (1883), 370.

[11] For legal practices see below, pp. 133–7.

[12] NYCRO, zjx 3/2/116; Durham, Church Commission, Bishopric Estates,
190316; *A History of Harrogate and Knaresborough*, ed. B. Jennings (Huddersfield, 1970), 89; *Depositions and other ecclesiastical proceedings from the
courts of Durham*, ed. J. Raine (SS, xxi; 1845), 32; Durh. 3/50/6; *Memorials of
the Abbey of St Mary of Fountains*, vol. ii, ed. J. R. Walbran (SS, lxvii; 1876),
89–90 and E. E. Power and M. M. Postan, *Studies in English Trade in the
Fifteenth Century* (1933), 43.

Green than Beverley. But a knot of eight homicides fled over the Pennines from the districts of Sedbergh, Dentdale, and Lonsdale.[13] Professor Palliser, in a recent analysis of the origins of the nearly thirty York men defamed as Scots between 1477 and 1513, found seventeen who were born and baptized in the four most northerly counties. Among them were John Colyns, who was born at Cockerton and baptized at St Cuthbert's Darlington, and John Halls, born and baptized in Bishop Auckland.[14] The River Tees was a boundary only so far as secular and clerical administration was concerned; it did not separate regions.

In using the expression 'the north-east' in the context of the fifteenth century we have to discard modern preconceptions not only about what the north-east is but also about what constitutes a region. We should heed Professor Everitt's warning, and remember that regions in the past were less homogenous and clearly defined than we might today expect. All regions were highly localized and fragmented, containing many overlapping 'countries' and extending beyond county borders. The north-east contained most of the eight *pays* identified by him—and probably one more; the unique border dales.[15] There were, however, economic, social, and political links which tended to pull these diverse countries together. The lure of York and the demand for its goods was felt as far north as the Scottish borders; the diocese of York stretched across to the Irish Sea in the archdeaconry of Richmond; the political weight of the two great magnates was felt through all the country north of York, west as well as east of the Pennines. Although the coast and the Scottish frontier fixed eastern and northern limits, the boundaries to the west, and especially the south, were indistinct. Furthermore, as Professor Everitt observed, regions are not static, but change.[16] In the nineteenth century the character of the region was shaped in shipyard, steelworks, and mine. In the fifteenth century,

[13] *Sanctuarium Dunelmense et Sanctuarium Beverlacense*, ed. J. Raine (SS, v; 1837), 1–16. See also J. C. Cox, *The Sanctuaries and Sanctuary Seekers of Medieval England* (1911), 107–19.

[14] D. M. Palliser, 'A Regional Capital as Magnet: Immigrants to York 1477–1566', *YAJ* 57 (1985), 111–12; for Colyns and Halls see *A Volume of English Miscellanies*, ed. J. Raine, SS, lxxxv (1890 for 1888), 35, 39.

[15] Everitt, 'Country, County and Town', pp. 81–4.

[16] Ibid. 81.

perhaps, it was shaped in castle, manor-house, and field. The captain of industry stamped his image on the nineteenth-century region; the feudal magnate stamped his on the fifteenth century. The wealth and power of an Armstrong or Bolckow was based on Tyneside and Teesside; the wealth and power of Neville and Percy lay in the lowlands of northern Yorkshire. The late-medieval centre of gravity thus lay not on the Tyne but further south. It was a different kind of society and a different kind of region, in which the Tees, far from being the southern boundary, lay near the centre.

It is neither desirable nor practicable to seek to define the north-east too closely or rigidly. In some respects, as for instance in relation to the borders, because of the involvement of the Nevilles as wardens of the west march it stretches to include Cumbria; in others, as for instance religious organization, it stretches south as well as west to embrace Nottinghamshire. In one important respect, moreover, the north-east as a region cannot really be separated from the north as a whole; the sense of being the hinterland of the Scottish border. Although the two kingdoms were frequently at war, England was not subject in the fifteenth century to frequent Scottish invasion; not since 1388 had the Scots penetrated south of the Tyne. But this restriction of Scottish armies to the border zone itself should not blind us to the fact that the men and women of Durham and Yorkshire could not be certain that the disasters of Edward II's reign were unrepeatable. As Dr Tuck has persuasively suggested in relation to the economic impact of the war in Northumberland, the fear of invasion was more compelling than the actuality: 'it is easier for the inhabitants to recover from the damage done by raiders than for them to come to believe that it will not happen again'.[17] This pervasive fear has left more tangible evidence in the form of the tower houses and peels built not just on the borders, but as far away as the Richmondshire and Craven districts of Yorkshire. These houses, mainly built between 1350 and 1500, were designed to resist a renewal of Scottish invasion, not local disorders. The fact that they never needed to, should not distract us from appreciating that tower houses, such as South Cowton, were still being built as late as the 1480s in

[17] J. A. Tuck, 'War and Society in the Medieval North', NH 21 (1985), 42.

the belief that full-scale Scottish invasion could happen again.[18]

The same anxiety concerning the Scots is occasionally expressed in justifications given for the privileges enjoyed by certain northern institutions. In 1447 a royal commission considering the complaints of Newcastle upon Tyne against its neighbour and rival North Shields found that 'the said town for all parts of the kingdom situate in the east marches over against Scotland and the people dwelling in the same is as a shield of defence and safe refuge against the invasions and frequent intrusions of the Scots'.[19] But only once in one hundred years had Newcastle been threatened. Newcastle's role in war was that of a forward headquarters and supply depot, not normally a front-line fortress.[20] Even more misleading, as has recently been stressed, is the myth that the palatinate of Durham derived its privileges from its role as a bulwark against the Scots.[21]

Nevertheless there was a clearly recognized and widely accepted obligation on the people of north-eastern England to contribute to the defence of the border. In his offer of a pardon to the north parts in September 1485 Henry VII drew attention to the fact that 'they of those parts be necessary and according to their duty must defend the land against the Scots'. The citizens of York for their part, in petitioning two weeks later for remission of their fee farm, pointed out that impoverishment of the region might have grave long-term consequences for the capacity of the north to defend the land.[22] This was no empty rhetoric. As is well known, the city of York and the Ainsty made substantial contributions in men and materials to Richard of Gloucester's campaigns in 1480–2.[23] The priory of Durham

---

[18] B. Harrison and B. Hutton, *Vernacular Houses in North Yorkshire and Cleveland* (Edinburgh, 1984), 19–20; P. Ryder and J. Birch, 'Hellifield Peel—A North Yorkshire Tower House', *YAJ* 55 (1983), 85–8; BL, Ad. Ch. 66451, in which deed, dated 12 October 1487, Cowton Castle is described as newly built.

[19] R. Welford, *A History of Newcastle and Gateshead in the Fourteenth and Fifteenth Centuries* (1884), 316.

[20] See below, p. 42.

[21] K. Emsley and C. Fraser, *The Courts of the County Palatine of Durham from the Earliest Times to 1971* (Durham, 1984) 93. The county palatine was first described as such by Edward II in 1311, nearly twenty years after Edward I recognized that Bishop Bek was count palatine, when he was providing Bishop Richard Kellawe with an excuse not to attend the Council of Vienne.

[22] *YCR* i. 135, 136.　　　[23] Ibid. 34–6, 39–42, 54, 57–64.

contributed men, as did, on earlier occasions, the town of Beverley.[24] In 1448–9 tenants of Mickleton, Lune, and Holwick, in the far north-west of Yorkshire, rode with their lord, Fitz-Hugh, to Scotland.[25] In the same year, on a more official level, Sir John Conyers as sheriff of Yorkshire led men of the county to assist both wardens. In a late war, 1455–6, Sir Thomas Harrington when sheriff set out 'on divers journeys with great puissance' to resist the Scots. And in the autumn of 1457, when war was threatened again, mandates were issued to the sheriffs of the border counties, Yorkshire, Nottingham, and Derbyshire to proclaim a general readiness for service in the marches.[26]

The obligation to assist in the defence of the border extended to the clergy. In December 1462 and again in July 1463 Archbishop William Booth was ordered, first by Edward IV and then by Warwick, to call out the clergy of his province to muster in defensible array at Newcastle and then at Durham, on both occasions because 'it was known for certain' that the Scots were planning to attack England. The archbishop did as he was bid: on 12 July 1463, the day after Warwick's letter was dated from Middleham, he himself wrote to his archdeacons giving the command. And it would seem some clergy did muster as required; for five weeks later the archdeacon of York was requested by his archbishop to give the names of such clergy of his district as had neglected the order.[27]

It is hard to tell whether the readiness of even the York clergy to serve against the Scots stemmed from a deep-seated antagonism and hatred of the old enemy. John Hardyng had nothing good to say of them. In 1463 he advised Edward IV:

[24] Durham, Dean and Chapter, Bursar's Account 1480/1, m6d; 1482/3, m5; HMC, *Report on MSS of Beverley* (1900), 107–8 (for 1436), 116–17 (for 1438), 133–4 (for 1449).

[25] Dur. RO, D/st/E3/1/4/21 Nov. 1448.

[26] PRO, E28/79/65, 159/238; *CPR, 1452–61*, 400, 405; Brooks, *Council of the North*, 6, cited the example of tenants of Edmund (*sic*) Mauleverer of Daletown in Hawnby who in 1482 agreed to serve the king with their own armour and arms when summoned by their lord. Brooks implied that this agreement was part of the terms of tenancies-at-will. The dating however suggests that it may alternatively have been specifically limited to service under Richard of Gloucester in his invasion of Scotland that year. I have unsuccessfully searched the Mauleverer–Brown archive at NYCRO and the papers at the YAS for Brooks' original source.

[27] *The Priory of Hexham* vol. i, ed. J. Raine, (SS, xliv; 1864), pp. cvii–cviii.

> And truste it well, as God is now in heven,
> Ye shall never fynde the Scottes unto you trew.

Hardyng, a Northumberland squire who had seen long service against the Scots under the banners of Percy and Umfraville, was virulently antagonistic towards his northern neighbours. His chronicle recalls all the great exploits of his lords against the old enemy, and he was convinced that:

> The Scottes will aye do you the harme they may,
> And so they have full ofte with odde and even,
> Afore that Christ was borne so of a maye,
> As yet they do at theyr power every daye.

His opinion was echoed by the author of Gregory's chronicle, who remarked that 'it is hard for to trust unto them for they be ever found full of guile and deceit'.[28] There is evidence to suggest that a large number of Scots migrated to England. A tax levied in 1440 on foreigners residing in England identified Scots living in fifteen places in Northumberland alone, including seventeen in Embleton. In times of war, or the threat of war, as the patent rolls show, it was often prudent for these immigrants to take out letters of denizenship. And if sixty or more surviving letters issued in 1479–82 are representative of the geographical distribution of settlement, there was a greater concentration in London and the home counties than in the north-east.[29] This might explain Gregory's xenophobia, but it leaves one uncertain as to whether Scots by travelling further south sought to avoid the hostility of north-easterners, or to benefit from greater economic opportunities offered by south-eastern England. One suspects the latter.

There is no doubt that Scots were excluded from business in the cities of Newcastle and York, where the statutes of the

[28] Hardyng, *Chronicle*, ed. H. Ellis pp. 410, 414; *The Historical Collections of a Citizen of London*, ed. J. Gairdner (Camden, NS, xvii; 1876), 224.

[29] *CDRS* iv. 297–8, 300–1. But see R. L. Storey's remarks concerning Scottish settlement in the northern counties in 'The North of England', in Chrimes, Ross, and Griffiths (eds.), *Fifteenth Century England, 1399–1509: Studies in Politics and Society* (Manchester, 1972), 131–2; and the 1440 tax on foreigners which identified Scots living in 15 places in Northumberland, including 17 in Embleton (E. Bateson, *A History of Northumberland, vol. ii: The Parish of Embleton*, ... [1895], 35).

guilds forbade their registration.[30] It is true that the dozen and a half cases recorded at York in the later decades of the fifteenth century in which freemen were defamed as Scots superficially suggest general hostility. But an alternative interpretation is possible. 'The children of iniquity' who in 1477 slandered John Colyns, born (as he proved) at Cockerton near Darlington of English parents, were, one suspects, seeking to run him out of business by exploiting the prohibition on aliens. This was made explicit in the case of the baker Andrew Lambe, who, one of his referees commented, was 'noised abroad by his neighbours and especially by his adversaries, to be a Scotsman born'.[31] Likewise the common clerk, John Harrington, who was forced to go to considerable lengths in 1486 to prove his English birth, was almost certainly facing his political enemies determined to profit from the recent change of regime. This is made clear in a letter from the fugitive Sir Robert Harrington, dated Cartmel 3 November 1486. 'Master John is my kinsman,' he threatened. 'Whosoever it is who vexes him, I shall put me in devoir to remember him.'[32] In some cases, especially when the victim was born near the border and probably possessed a strange and suspicious accent, genuine confusion no doubt existed. It would however be hasty to read from this collection of depositions prima-facie evidence of hatred of Scots as such. As aliens, Scots were neither subject to nor protected by English law.[33] Hence the rush for denizenship in times of international crisis. It was not necessarily the Scots individually who were distrusted, but the Scots as a nation at war who were feared.

The frontier was undoubtedly an important influence on north-eastern society. But one needs to be wary of exaggerating its significance. The whole of the north-east, let alone the north, was not itself a frontier zone. Professor R. L. Storey has sug-

---

[30] For example in Newcastle the statutes of the following craft guilds forbade those born in Scotland to become apprentices: Glovers, Smiths, Skinners, Saddlers, Fullers, and Dyers (Welford, *Newcastle and Gateshead*, pp. 297–8, 339, 374.)   [31] Raine, *English Miscellanies*, 35, 45–6; YCR i. 17–18.
[32] Ibid. 46–8 and YCR i. 175.
[33] Storey, 'North of England', pp. 131–2. From time to time they were clearly considered a security risk. In 1490, for instance, Henry VII ordered the expulsion of all Scots 'being suspect and not well disposed' who apply themselves to 'idleness and begging' from the counties of York, Cumberland, Northumberland, and Westmorland (CDRS iv. 318).

gested that a chain of castles running from Scarborough on the east coast to Castle Bolton in Wensleydale formed a defensive line which made Northumberland, Durham, and all but a small part of the North Riding a militarized zone prepared for defence in depth against Scottish invasion.[34] This line happens to delineate approximately the furthest extent of Scottish penetration in the early fourteenth century, but it had little concrete geopolitical significance for the later fifteenth century. F. W. Brooks suggested that if a Scottish force crossed the Tees a raid became an invasion.[35] This too seems to place such a distinction too far to the south. There can be little doubt that the Scottish attacks of 1329 and 1346 which were halted on the line of the Wear were considered by contemporaries to be major invasions: crossing the Tyne and leaving Northumberland was more likely to be construed as an invasion. The authority of the wardens of the marches did not extend south of the border counties. The wardens did not, as Dr Reid suggested, regularly hold a second commission as justices of the peace for the north parts. The granting of these exceptional powers to John of Lancaster and the earl of Westmorland in 1405 was made at the time of acute political crisis in northern England.[36] If subsequent wardens were justices of the peace in Yorkshire as well as the border counties it is because they were substantial landowners in the county. Their local influence and power stemmed from their private status, not from their official capacity. It is true that they were in 1468 specifically licensed to retain men throughout the north; but this concession in the Yorkist Statute of Liveries was designed to enable them, as they always had, to raise temporary reinforcements, 'at such time only as shall be necessary to levy people for the defence of the said marches'.[37] Indeed an Act of 1453 made it clear that the authority of the wardens was restricted to the counties of Westmorland, Cumberland, and Northumberland, and the city of Newcastle. A petition spelt out the abuses perpetrated by their officers in Yorkshire and elsewhere, who, 'for singular lucre or from sheer malice', had been accustomed to attach and indict people in the wardens' courts.

---

[34] Ibid. 130.   [35] Brooks, *Council of the North*, p. 6.
[36] Reid, *Council in the North*, pp. 35–6; Brooks, *Council of the North*, p. 6.
[37] *SR* ii. 428–9.

The Act reaffirmed that this right of enforcement of the truces only extended to the border counties.[38]

If there has tended to be a modern exaggeration of the north-east as a militarized frontier zone it is in part because contemporaries led the way. From London and the Thames valley it was perhaps understandable that, as the Venetian ambassador reported in 1496, York seemed to be a town on the borders of Scotland.[39] Richard III had less excuse for confusing historians. In 1484 he petitioned Pope Sixtus IV to pardon John Shirwood, the new bishop of Durham, the payment of first-fruits. In support of his request he painted a bleak and misleading picture of the county palatine. The temporalities, he explained, were all at the end of England which bordered with Scotland, and the bishop was responsible for defending those parts against the Scots. The cost of maintaining the defences of their towns and castles, which were in decay partly because of the ravages of war, was insupportable. The first-fruits, he claimed, were desperately needed to pay for urgent repairs;[40] yet (as the king well knew) only Norham lay adjacent to the borders: the main part of the bishopric lay further back, untouched by war for over a century. The king's hyperbole and sleight-of-hand did not apparently fool the pope, who refused to remit the first-fruits: it has, however, misled many a subsequent writer. If Durham was, in Sir Walter Scott's memorable words 'half house of God, half castle 'gainst the Scot', the halves were far apart; the house of God lay on the Wear, the castle lay on the Tweed, sixty miles to the north. The true frontier zone itself, the borders, covered only a relatively narrow band of territory. In this zone a unique clan-based and lawless society of cattle thieves and reivers had emerged in the wake of Anglo-Scottish war. But the borders were not characteristic of north-eastern society as a whole. Indeed they were largely restricted to the remote and upper

[38] Rot. Parl. v. 267.
[39] A Relation . . . of the Island of England, ed. L. A. Sneyd (Camden, os, xxxvii; 1847), 37, 41.
[40] Rymer, Foedera, xii. 224. The example cited of one castle in which it was claimed that it was always necessary to maintain 100 soldiers even in time of peace surely refers to Norham. In fact, in the terms of agreement drawn up between Bishop Dudley and Sir John Middleton in 1482 for its custody for two years the garrison was fixed at 30 in time of war, to be paid and equipped at the constable's expense (Durh. 3/55/8).

reaches of Tyne-, Redes-, and Coquetdales, where manorial organization had collapsed and royal authority vanished.[41] It was in this society that Aeneas Sylvius Piccolomini spent a fraught night among the natives in a country 'rude, uncultivated and unvisited by the winter sun'. Yet as Piccolomini also recorded with relief, he escaped from this world when he came down to Newcastle 'there for the first time . . . to see again a familiar world and a habitable country'.[42]

'A familiar world and a habitable country': that, for the most part, was what north-eastern England was to the more southerly visitor. It was neither closed nor isolated from the rest of England to the west or south.[43] There were three principal routes running to the west across the Pennines. The most northerly ran through the Haltwhistle gap linking Newcastle with Carlisle: it was along this route that Piccolomini travelled in 1436. The second was the road over Stainmore linking North Yorkshire and York with Cumberland and Carlisle. And the third and by no means the least important, which is clearly marked on the Gough map, was the old Roman road over Ribblehead, which linked Lonsdale to Wensleydale. This route warrants particular emphasis because Lonsdale (part in Westmorland and part in Lancashire) and Furness (as well as Copeland and Amounderness) were all part of the archdeaconry of Richmond. There were also important political connections forged between Lonsdale, Furness, and Copeland and the lords of Middleham in the fifteenth century.[44] The Nevilles of Latimer, as well as the lords of Middleham, were also extensive landowners in Cumberland and Westmorland. As their estate records show, their officials made regular journeys back and forth across the Pennines; even livestock was occasionally driven

[41] For the most recent discussion of border society see A. Goodman, 'The Anglo-Scottish Marches in the Fifteenth Century: A Frontier Society', in R. A. Mason, (ed.), *Scotland and England, 1286–1815* (Edinburgh, 1987), 18–33. See also below pp. 171–2.

[42] Gabel, *Commentaries of Pius II*, 35–6. My own reading of the text suggests that Piccolomini had passed beyond Carlisle when he stopped for the night. If I am correct, Dr Richmond is wrong to suggest that Piccolomini acquired that valued relic, St Penket's leg, at Bowness-on-Solway (C. Richmond, *The Penket Papers* (Gloucester, 1986), 15 ff.).

[43] Cf. J. Le Patourel's comment: 'If apart, the North was not isolated' ('Is Northern History a Subject?', p. 11).

[44] See below, p. 130.

over to supply Yorkshire tables.[45] But overshadowing these territorial links was the proximity of the west march. In the early fourteenth century Scottish raids into Yorkshire frequently descended or departed through the west marches and the dales.[46] Indeed Durham, Richmond, and Ripon were nearer to the west march than to the east. It is not surprising therefore that the warden of the west march throughout most of the fifteenth century was a magnate who drew his principal strength from northern Yorkshire.[47] Thus the history of the north-east, particularly its political history, cannot be written without reference to the north-western counties of the kingdom.

Similarly the north-east was not cut off from England south of Yorkshire. The principal landowners of the north-east also had material interests to the south; predominantly southern lords (Beauchamp and Lovell for example) held estates in the north (Barnard Castle and Bedale). Richard Neville, earl of Salisbury and his sons, albeit that they lived as great lords of the north, were buried in a family mausoleum at Bisham in Berkshire.[48] Many gentry likewise had divided interests. The Hoptons of Walberswick in Suffolk were also the Hoptons of Swillington, Yorks. In the reign of Edward IV, while the father John restricted his interests to East Anglia, his eldest son William cut a figure in Yorkshire, joining the household and council of the duke of Gloucester.[49] Sir Hugh Hastings of Fenwick, Yorks. was also the lord of Gresenhall, Norfolk, where the family's principal estates lay; notwithstanding which, he seems to have spent most of his career in Yorkshire, and his will was proved in York.[50] On a lesser scale, ecclesiastical corporations also possessed lands, rents, and churches in the north-east: for example, University College, Oxford (Newcastle) and Merton College (Stillington,

---

[45] Carlisle RO. D/Lec/28/22–9. The revenue of Bolton in Allerdale, Warcop, Morland, and Eversham was regularly delivered to the Latimer household at Snape in the 1450s. In 1447–8 cattle too were taken there. I am grateful to Dr Michael Hicks for generously making available to me his abstracts of these documents.

[46] I. Kershaw, 'A Note on the Scots in the West Riding 1318–19', NH 17 (1981), 231–9.

[47] See below, pp. 150–3.   [48] See below, p. 181.

[49] C. F. Richmond, John Hopton: A Suffolk Gentleman in the Fifteenth Century (Cambridge, 1981), 137–9.   [50] Test. Ebor. iv. 273–8.

Co. Durham and Embleton, Northumberland).[51] Durham Priory had its own hall at Oxford, at which its monks resided when studying at the university.[52] Some north-easterners who did not inherit subsequently acquired interests in the south. John, Lord Scrope of Bolton married, as his third wife, Anne Harling of East Harling, Norfolk (he was her third husband, too).[53] Halnath Mauleverer, a younger son of Mauleverer of Ingleby Arncliffe, married Joan Carminow, widow of Sir Thomas Carew, and through her acquired an interest in Cornwall, Devon, and Dorset which led him to be sheriff of Cornwall in 1470/1 and of Devon in 1479/80 and again in 1483/4.[54]

The servants of landowners who had interest both north and south of the Trent were accustomed to travelling to and fro. The auditors of the Beauchamp earls of Warwick regularly visited Barnard Castle. In July 1409 the receiver-general himself came north for a month to supervise repairs to the castle. William Sharpe, Fellow of University College, Oxford twice visited Newcastle in 1446 and 1447 to negotiate with Alice Bellasis the terms of her proposed benefaction to the college. The bursar of Merton College, Oxford travelled from Oxford to Embleton, north of Alnwick in August 1464 to survey war damage, supervise the collection of tithes, and no doubt conduct other business connected with the parish, which was appropriated to the college. The round trip took two months and cost £6. 7s. 3d. William Musgrave, as receiver for Archbishop Bourgchier, rode three times (May 1481, December 1481, and February 1482) in one accounting year from Westmorland to Knole, Kent to deliver revenue from the Neville of Latimer estates which were in the archbishop's custody. When Bishop Laurence Booth was Chancellor of England in 1473–5, his household in London was supplied by cattle driven up to town by men of the bishopric. The bailiff of Bishop Middleham was sent up to London in 1480 by Booth's successor, Bishop Dudley, to consult with the duke

[51] A. F. Butcher, 'Rent, Population and Economic Change in Late Medieval Newcastle', NH 14 (1978), 67–77; Bateson, Embleton, pp. 49–68.
[52] R. B. Dobson, Durham Priory, 1400–1450 (Cambridge, 1973), 349–59.
[53] Test. Ebor. iv. 94–6.
[54] W. E. Hampton, 'Further comment on Richard III by Charles Ross', The Ricardian vi 77 (1982), 46–7.

of Gloucester.[55] The *Plumpton Correspondence* and the York city records reveal a continuous stream of messengers travelling between London and Yorkshire, especially communicating with their agents at the royal courts—men like Godfrey Green, who looms large in the Plumptons' affairs.

Lawyers such as Green were constantly on the road. An eminent judge or serjeant like Sir Guy Fairfax, Sir Robert Danby, or Richard Pigot divided his time between clients in the north-east and the courts in London. One such judge fell in with Piccolomini on his journey from York to London in 1436.[56] Pigot had a town house in Clerkenwell, as well as property in Wensleydale. His harsh experience for twenty years or more of commuting between the two would appear to be reflected in a bequest of money to be spent 'in making of highways'.[57] Another group of people always on the road was pilgrims. The Pastons, and no doubt others, relied on passing pilgrims for much of their news. In September 1471, for instance, John Paston wrote to his mother concerning the current epidemic:

I can not hear by the pilgrims that pass the country, nor no other man that rideth or goeth any country that any borough town in England is free from that sickness.[58]

Such pilgrims would include those supported by devout will-makers such as Alice Neville, who in 1481 requested that a man be found to go to the shrine of St Thomas of Canterbury. William Ecopp, rector of Heslerton, made provision for visits to no less than fifteen shrines the length and breadth of Britain, including St Mary's, Walsingham and St Thomas's, Canterbury.[59] Pilgrims came north too, to visit St John of Bridlington, St William of York, and above all St Cuthbert of Durham. Margery Kempe was one visitor to York; but she did not travel as far as Durham. Perhaps the most famous of

[55] BL, Egerton Ch. 8772, m.5d; Butcher, 'Late Medieval Newcastle', p. 68; E. Bateson, 'Notes on a Journey from Oxford to Embleton in 1464', *Arch. Ael.* NS 16 (1894), 113–20; Alnwick, Syon MS X.II Box 2, 1; Durham, Church Commission, Bishopric Estates, 190109, 10; 189830, M.5.

[56] Gabel, *Commentaries of Pius II*, p. 36.

[57] *Test. Ebor.* iii. 285–6.   [58] *Paston Letters*, i. 440–1.

[59] M. G. A. Vale, *Piety, Charity and Literacy among the Yorkshire Gentry, 1370–1480*, Borthwick Paper 50 (York, 1976), 17; Welford, *Newcastle and Gateshead*, p. 364.

fifteenth-century pilgrims was Henry VI, who wrote enthusiastically in October 1448 that he had been 'right merry on our
pilgrimage' to both Durham and York.[60]

It was characteristic of Henry VI that he should have described his northern progress, which was intended by his
advisers to be a show of strength against the Scots, as a pilgrimage. Other royal cavalcades to the north-east, led by Edward IV
in 1462, by Richard III in 1484, and by Henry VII in 1487 and
1489, while also showing due reverence to the shrine of St
Cuthbert, were more hard-headedly political. In their trains
came household servants who may not otherwise have had
cause to visit the north-east. Such visits were frequently made at
times of open war with the Scots. Armies from the south, which
came to fight the Scots as well as to put down rebellion, provided another occaion on which southerners, like Sir John Paston
in 1463–4, could enjoy firsthand experience of the region.[61]

Equally, armies raised in the north took north-easterners
south: most notoriously in 1461, but also in 1455, 1469, and
1483. It was the huge, undisciplined force raised in Yorkshire,
Durham, and Northumberland that Margaret of Anjou led south
in 1461 which gave north-easterners such a fearful reputation in
the later decades of the fifteenth century.[62] This approaching
horde fired wild rumours and fed desperate propaganda, the
imprint of which was felt for decades to come.

The people in the north rob and steal and be appointed to pill all this
country, and give away men's goods and livelihoods in all the south
country.

So wrote Clement Paston to his brother John on 23 January.[63]
In London two weeks later a rattled Warwick and the Privy
Council sent out desperate letters seeking to rally support to
face this fearful army. 'The misruled and outrageous people in
the north parts of this realm', they claimed, are coming 'towards
these parts to the destruction thereof, of you and subversion of

[60] For St William see R. B. Dobson, 'The Later Middle Ages, 1215–1500', in
G. E. Aylmer and R. Cant (eds.), *A History of York Minster* (Oxford, 1977),
85–6; for St Cuthbert see Dobson, *Durham Priory*, pp. 29–30; *The Book of
Margery Kempe* (EETS os ccxii, 1940), 122; Welford, *Newcastle and Gateshead*,
p. 319.   [61] *Paston Letters*, i. 523.
[62] *St. Ingulph's Chronicles*, ed. H. T. Riley (Bohn's Library, 1854), 422–3.
[63] *Paston Letters*, i. 198.

all our land'.[64] And after the crisis was over, the battle of Towton won, and Edward IV seated on the throne, the poem known as 'The Rose of Rouen' celebrated the new king's triumph in similar tones.[65]

> The northern men made her bost, when thei had done that dede.
> We wol dwelle in the southe cuntry, and take all that we nede.
> These wifes and hur doghters, our purpose shal thei spede.
> Then seid the Rose of Rone: 'Nay that werk shal I forbede.'

The northern men were duly routed.

> The Rose wan the victorye, the feld and also the chace.
> Now may housband in the southe dwelle in his owne place
> His wife and eke his faire doghtre, and all the goode he has
> Such menys hath the Rose made, by vertu and by grace.

The hysteria whipped up in 1461 was to influence the attitude of southern gentry to Richard III, under whom they came to believe the northern men achieved for a brief while their ambition to 'dwell in the south country and take all that we need . . .'. Successive risings led or inspired by the earl of Warwick in 1469 and 1470, all focused on Richmondshire, helped stoke the fears. And after Bosworth, in 1486 and 1487, Richmondshire was again the centre of rebellions against Henry VII. Thus the second continuator of the *Crowland Chronicle*, writing in April 1486 when he had just heard of the outbreak of the latest uprising, fumed against 'the malignants responsible for an ungrateful, seditious movement in the North, whence all evil spreads'.[66] Henry VII willingly took up the theme in his proclamation against the Yorkshire rebels of 1489, whom he portrayed as intending to 'rob, despoil and destroy' all the south parts of the realm, and to bring its people into captivity.[67] And Polydore Vergil twenty-five years later echoed royal opinion in his

[64] C. L. Scofield, *The Life and Reign of Edward the Fourth* (1923), i, 135–6. Abbot Whetehamsted and the *English Chronicle* continuation of the *Brut* picked up the same attitude towards 'the pernicious northerners'. See A. Goodman, *The Wars of the Roses* (1981), 225.

[65] 'Verses on the Battle of Towton', *Archaeologia*, 29 (1842), 344–7.

[66] *Crowland Chronicle*, 191. 'Whence all evil spreads' is a biblical reference. Note Hardyng's similar view of Scotland: 'though scripture saith of north all evil is showed' (Hardyng, *Chronicle*, p. 420). The common source is *Jer.* 1:14: 'Then the Lord said unto me, Out of the north an evil shall break forth upon all the inhabitants of the land.'

[67] R. Steele, *Tudor and Stuart Proclamations*, i (Oxford, 1910), no. 19.

condemnation of the same 'folk of the north, savage and more eager than others for upheaval'.[68]

Thus a powerful sense of antagonism directed towards the north from the southern parts of the kingdom seems to have entered into English political vocabulary in the second half of the century. This phenomenon, deriving from the violent impact of north-eastern England on the affairs of the realm under the Yorkists, will be encountered elsewhere. It does not follow, however, that England was at the time a deeply divided society in which north and south looked upon each other in mutual hostility. A wealth of evidence exists to show how in many walks of life, in normal business and social relationships, neither were northerners unknown in the south, nor southerners unfamiliar with the north. England was not two nations.[69] There were, however, recognizable regional differences: northerners were conscious of being northerners, southerners of being southerners. A north-countryman in London might feel homesick, as seems to be suggested in a letter written by Thomas Betanson to Sir Robert Plumpton on 29 November 1486.[70]

If it please your mastership to hear of me, and where I abide, I serve in the sepulchre church without Newgate. There is a woman was born in Selby. I have ten marks and no charge, and the term times I have meat and drink of my lord Bryan, chief judge of the common pleas. Wherefore, if it would please your mastership to send me a letter how you and my ladies, with all your household, doth, for it were to me great comfort.

Betanson gave no indication that he was victimized as a savage from the north; but he was apparently reassured to find another person from Yorkshire in the metropolis, and to be taken under the wing of a third with local connections. To be a north-easterner in London was to this extent to be a stranger in an unfamiliar society.

[68] Vergil, Polydore, *The Anglica Historia of Polydore Vergil*, ed. D. Hay, Camden, 3rd ser., lxxiv (1950), 11.
[69] For examples of the recent tendency to exaggerate the 'ever-present threat' to the civilized south represented by a 'barbarous region inhabited by savage brutes' see Potter, *Good King Richard?*, p. 46 and D. Seward, *Richard III: England's Black Legend* (1983), 117. I owe these references to Keith Dockray, 'Richard III and the Yorkshire Gentry', in P. W. Hammond, ed. *Richard III: Loyalty, Lordship and Law* (Gloucester, 1986), 38–9.
[70] *Plumpton Correspondence*, 53.

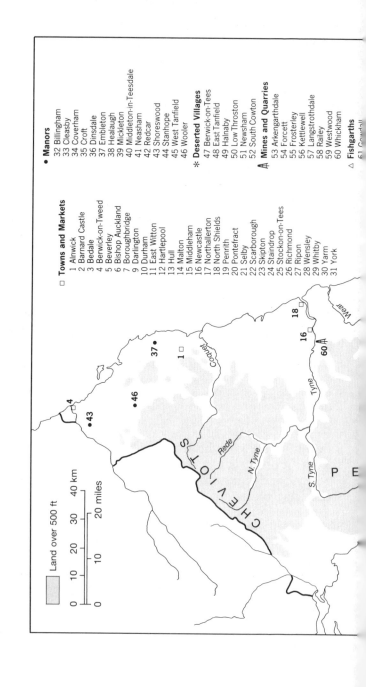

Towns and Markets

1 Alnwick
2 Barnard Castle
3 Bedale
4 Berwick-on-Tweed
5 Beverley
6 Bishop Auckland
7 Boroughbridge
9 Darlington
10 Durham
11 East Witton
12 Hartlepool
13 Hull
14 Malton
15 Middleham
16 Newcastle
17 Northallerton
18 North Shields
19 Penrith
20 Pontefract
21 Selby
22 Scarborough
23 Skipton
24 Staindrop
25 Stockton-on-Tees
26 Richmond
27 Ripon
28 Wensley
29 Whitby
30 Yarm
31 York

● **Manors**

32 Billingham
33 Cleasby
34 Coverham
35 Croft
36 Dinsdale
37 Embleton
38 Healaugh
39 Mickleton
40 Middleton-in-Teesdale
41 Neasham
42 Redcar
43 Shoreswood
44 Stanhope
45 West Tanfield
46 Wooler

✳ **Deserted Villages**

47 Berwick-on-Tees
48 East Tanfield
49 Halnaby
50 Low Throston
51 Newsham
52 South Cowton

⚒ **Mines and Quarries**

53 Arkengarthdale
54 Forcett
55 Frosterley
56 Kettlewell
57 Langstrothdale
58 Railey
59 Westwood
60 Whickham

△ **Fishgarths**

61 Cowdall

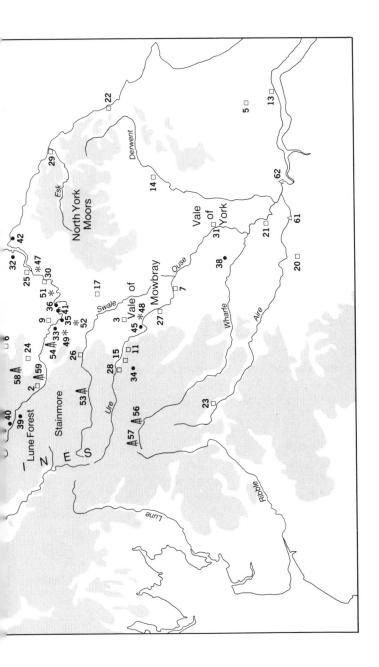

Map 1. PHYSICAL FEATURES AND THE ECONOMY

2

The Regional Economy
before 1450

NORTH-EASTERN England straddles that line between highland and lowland zones which has been said to have 'cleft England in twain'.[1] The dominating feature of the landscape is the contrast between the pastoral high Pennines and North York Moors on the one hand and the mixed arable and pasture lowlands of the coastal plain, the Vale of York, and the Tees basin on the other. Four hundred years ago William Camden observed the same contrasts in topography and land use. Northumberland, he commented, 'is mostly rough and barren'. The Pennine districts of Yorkshire and Durham 'with craggy rocks and vast mountains', 'always exposed to wind and rain', were 'wild, solitary and unsightly'. The Vale of York and the lower river valleys, however, were 'pleasant and fruitful'. County Durham may have been bleak to the west, but in the east parts and in the valleys of the Tees and Tyne 'the ground is made very fruitful by tillage'. Even in Richmondshire, he observed, although the sides of the mountains here and there yield pretty rank grass, the bottoms and valleys 'are not altogether unfruitful'.[2] Fifty years before Camden toured Britain, John Leland travelled north as far as the Tyne. On his journey he observed that the Vale of Mowbray was 'a meetly fertile valley between Blackmoor hills by east and Richmondshire hills by west'. North of the Tees, too, he passed by 'pure good corn' between Neasham and Darlington. There was more 'meetly good corn' to be found further up the Tees valley between Staindrop and Barnard Castle. But upper Weardale was 'not very fertile of corn, yet is there very fine grass in the dale itself'. While Teesdale above Eggleston, which he did not visit, was, he heard tell, but 'wild ground'.[3]

---

[1] *The Agrarian History of England and Wales*, vol. iv, ed. Joan Thirsk (Cambridge, 1967), 2.
[2] *Camden's Britannia, 1695* (Newton Abbot, 1971), 758–9, 761, 771, 847.

Closer inspection of the landscape, however, reveals a more complex kaleidoscope than a simple division between two sharply differentiated zones of highland and lowland. Although on the wild ground of the wet, peat-capped Pennines herds of freely roaming red deer shared summer grazing with domestic cattle, the dales which run deeply into them provided good grass on their slopes, and, on the sheltered, fertile floors, valuable arable land. Moreover the eastern flanks of the Pennines are gradually sloping. Five hundred years ago they were better wooded than today. Leland, for instance, noted that there was 'meetly good wood on each side of Tees about Barnard Castle'. These flanks formed an extensive transitional zone between highland and lowland. To the east in Yorkshire the North York Moors formed another bastion of high grassland. And although ringed by steep escarpments to the west and north, and sea cliffs to the east, the moors too sloped gently to the south, where the line of parishes running up from the Vale of Pickering en-compassed both good arable land and high pasture. Within the 'pleasant and fruitful' lowlands, too, there were sharp variations in fertility created by differences in soil, slope, and drainage. The deep rich loams of the Cleveland embayment, the alluvial gravels of the lower Tees valley and of the Wiske valley west of Northallerton, and the rich brown earths found between the Ure and Swale produced good arable land. The southern rim of the North York Moors (the district known as the Tabular Hills) and the northern periphery of the Vale of Pickering were likewise well suited to arable farming. On the other hand, the district of Tynemouth, lying on predominantly poor boulder clays, was marginal arable land. Within the predominantly fertile lower Tees valley there lies a band of heavy clays, which emerges at approximately 100 feet, and which is hard to cultivate. Leland was impressed by the good corn-growing country near North-allerton, yet he noticed 'a great peace of ground that I saw at hand between Northallerton and Smeaton bridge' which was 'low pasture and moors'. Indeed in the very south of our region the central Vale of Pickering formed a much more extensive area of undrained marshy land, unsuited to intensive arable farming.

---

[3] Leland, John, *The Itinerary of John Leland, in or about 1535–1543, Parts I to III*, ed. L. Toulmin Smith (1907), 67, 69, 71, 76, 77.

In truth north-eastern England was not so much cut in twain as a jigsaw of fertile and infertile, highland and lowland, supporting a variety of land uses from the intensively arable to the seasonal transhumance of moorland pasture.[4]

Farming in the Vale of York, Cleveland, the Tees basin and the coastal plain was, like that in lowland England in general, based on an open-field system of agriculture. The number of fields maintained by a village varied. Sometimes, as at Croft-on-Tees, there was just one large field; at other places, such as Billingham lower down the same valley, there were three.[5] These fields were subdivided into conventional furlongs and strips, held and worked by villagers, with demesne land reserved for the lord of the manor. On the estates of the priory of Durham some demesnes were separated units, but most demesne land, as elsewhere, was intermingled among the tenant holdings.[6] The customary rotations of crops were followed, the fields being communally ploughed and harvested. Farming practice was subject to by-laws passed by *plebiscitum* or *ex assensu*.[7] This system of open-field arable farming was carried up into the dales, at least as high as Lartington and Mickleton in Teesdale, Healaugh and Walburn in Swaledale, and Coverham, where

---

[4] Information in this paragraph is drawn from Smailes, *North England*, Ch. 4, *passim*; Brian Waites, *Moorland and Valeland Farming in North-East Yorkshire*, Borthwick Paper 32 (York, 1967); idem, 'Aspects of Medieval Arable Farming in the Vale of York and the Cleveland Plain', *Ryedale Historian*, ii (1966), 5–10; and R. D. Linacre, 'The Distribution of Lay Wealth in the North Riding during the early fourteenth century' (unpublished MA thesis, Teesside Polytechnic, 1981) 41–59. I would also like to record my thanks to Dr J. A. Tuck for allowing me to see an early draft of his contribution on the four most northerly counties to the forthcoming 3rd volume of the *Agrarian History of England and Wales*. For information concerning the soils of the Tees Valley I am indebted to Dr P. Weightman of Dinsdale Manor, Durham.

[5] A. J. Pollard, 'Richard Clervaux of Croft: a North Riding Squire during the Fifteenth Century', *YAJ* 50 (1978), 154; T. Lomas, 'Land and People in South-East Durham in the Later Middle Ages' (unpublished CNAA thesis, Teesside Polytechnic, 1976), 40–51; R. A. Lomas, 'Durham Cathedral Priory as a Landowner and a Landlord' (unpublished Durham University Ph.D. thesis, 1973), 119–20. I am grateful to Dr Lomas for permission to consult his thesis.

[6] Lomas, 'Durham Cathedral Priory', pp. 119–24.

[7] See e.g. those recorded in *Halmota Prioratus Dunelmensis, AD 1296–1384*, ed. W. H. Longstaffe and J. Booth (SS, lxxxii, 1889) and the formula used for recording a *plebiscitum* at Lartington in 1458 setting out penalties for allowing cattle to stray into the field 'in plena curia ex consensu et assensu omnium tenentium' (NYCRO, ZPS 1/12).

there appear to have been at least two fields.[8] Only rarely was vale land in severalty, as appears to have been the case in Dalton-on-Tees and Little Broughton in Cleveland; it was perhaps more common in the dales, as at Coverham, where in addition to their strips in the open fields, tenants held their own several plots.[9] The only parts of the north-east which can confidently be excepted from manorial organization were the border dales, Tynedale, Redesdale, and Coquetdale, where as a result of incessant local warfare a new clan-based society had emerged, quite unlike any other society found in England.[10] But the borders, which formed a world of their own, were a remote corner not only of England but also of the north-east.

In such upper-dale fields as were found at Mickleton barley and, especially, oats were the grains grown.[11] In central Durham too, in the valley of the Wear, oats and barley predominated. At Elvet Hall manor, on the outskirts of Durham City, where the cathedral priory maintained demesne production throughout the fifteenth century, as much as four-fifths of the land was sown with barley and oats—normally more barley than oats —while the remaining fragment produced wheat and rye. Oats were also the main crop of the coastal plateau of north-east Yorkshire north of Whitby, as well as of the abbey's own granges near the mouth of the Esk.[12] In the Tees basin, Cleveland, and the Vale of York, however, wheat was frequently the major crop. On the manors of Cleasby and Clowbeck in the central Tees valley, the tenants in the mid-fifteenth century produced wheat supplemented by malted maslin for delivery to the household of

[8] DurRO., D/St/1/3/15 Nov. 1457; 4/12 Nov. 1448 (Mickleton); NYCRO, zps/1/12 (Lartington); R. Fieldhouse and B. Jennings, *A History of Richmond and Swaledale* (Chichester, 1978), 41, 44 (Healaugh and Walburn); A. J. Pollard and M. Y. Ashcroft, 'Coverham: some fifteenth century documents', *NYCROJ*, 10, (1982), 31–2; PRO, sc6/1085/20 (Coverham).

[9] NYCRO, zhq/1 (Clervaux Cartulary), fo. 153; Pollard and Ashcroft, 'Coverham', p. 41; Raine, *Priory of Hexham*, i. p. 65.

[10] A. A. Cardew, 'A Study of Society in the Anglo-Scottish Borders 1455–1502' (unpublished St Andrews Ph.D., 1974), 83–8.

[11] See e.g. the assessment for distraint of the goods and chattels of Robert Colyar, who in Nov. 1446 possessed 3 qrs. of barley and 4 of oats; and the case 2 years later when Lord FitzHugh's horses broke into the field and destroyed the standing oats belonging to several tenants. (Dur. RO, D/St/1/4/21 Nov. 1446; 4/21 Nov. 1448).

[12] R. A. Lomas 'A Northern Farm at the end of the Middle Ages', *NH* 18 (1982), 30, 33, esp. Table 1; Waites, *Moorland and Valeland Farming*, 16.

Lord FitzHugh.[13] John Clervaux of Croft left an acre of standing wheat when he died in 1443.[14] Further downstream at the mouth of the river the Durham Priory villages of Billingham, Cowpen Bewley, Newton Bewley, and Wolviston were substantial producers of wheat and barley.[15] A bundle of inventories of husbandmen from the villages of Brompton, Kirby Sigston, Northallerton, and West Rounton reveal that at the end of the century wheat and barley were the principal crops of that district too.[16]

Husbandry in the Northallerton district, as everywhere in the vales and valleys of the north-east, was mixed. Beside their crops standing in the fields or safely gathered into their lathes, these countrymen kept horses, cattle, sheep, pigs, geese, and hens, although rarely (except for sheep) in more than single numbers. William Fox of Brompton's stock of thirteen oxen, five cows, ten horses, twenty sheep, two pigs, fifteen geese, and twenty hens, which he possessed when he died in September 1486, was the largest recorded in these inventories.[17] The presence of these animals is constantly revealed elsewhere in the presentments and by-laws of the manorial courts; in stinting common grazing; in regulating the folding of cattle, sheep, and horses on the fields after the harvest; and in controlling the strays that were forever threatening to destroy standing crops.[18] The sheer variety of the fruits of the land enjoyed by the north-eastern villager is revealed by an evaluation of the living of Dinsdale in the Tees valley in 1465. The rector's income was drawn not only from the glebe and great tithe of corn, but also from lesser tithes of milk, apples and pears, flax and hemp, doves, honey, and above all lambs and wool (at £1. 16s. the largest single item).[19]

The prominence of the Dinsdale tithes on lambs and wool reminds us that sheep-rearing was an important element of northern farming. In the vale and lower dales a characteristic

[13] See e.g. the deliveries section of the rent collector's account for 1439–40 (Essex RO D/DC, M108).   [14] NYCRO, ZHQ/I, fo. 143.

[15] T. Lomas, 'South East Durham: Late Fourteenth and Fifteenth Centuries' in P. D. A. Harvey (ed.), *The Peasant Land Market in Medieval England* (Oxford, 1984), 319–21.

[16] Durham, Dean and Chapter, Locellus VIII, 1–22.   [17] Ibid., No. 13.

[18] See e.g., detailed discussion by Lomas, 'Land and People', pp. 249–58 and the court rolls of Coverham (Pollard and Ashcroft, 'Coverham', *passim*).

[19] Surtees, *Durham*, iii. p. 239.

tenant flock seems to have been of twenty to thirty sheep. Three husbandmen in Allertonshire between 1486 and 1499 died in possession of twenty, twenty-two, and thirty-two sheep. Even John Stevenson, blacksmith of Northallerton, kept sixteen.[20] In Coverham manor court in the early fifteenth century tenants were frequently presented for pasturing sheep within the lord's closes, but the numbers involved were rarely above twenty.[21] Higher on the Pennines, however, flocks were larger. The tenants of Mickleton were regularly presented for grazing animals high on Mickle Fell in Lord FitzHugh's forest of Lune. Flocks of as many as forty or sixty sheep were frequently involved; once a flock of 200 was grazed illegally.[22] The largest flocks, however, were maintained by the lords themselves on their own sheep-ranges. Hexham Priory enjoyed the right to pasture 300 sheep on the commonland of Kimblesworth, just north of Durham City. The priory of Durham maintained a flock at Saltholme on the Tees estuary, where the salt-marshes produced a grass exceptionally good for the fleece.[23] In 1450–1 Lord FitzHugh was grazing over 2,250 sheep at his manor of Berwick-on-Tees.[24] The bishop of Durham from time to time kept sheep in his parks at Stockton and Auckland.[25] But large-scale seigneurial sheep-rearing was primarily an upland activity, both on the Pennines and the North York Moors. The grange system adopted by the Cistercian monasteries (Fountains, Jervaulx, Rievaulx, and Byland), as well as the Augustinian priory of Guisborough, had converted large stretches of wilderness into sheep-runs on the moors of Mashamshire, Nidderdale, and Craven and, to the east, the Hambledon and Cleveland Hills. They had brought wool production of a high quality and quantity to a peak in the thirteenth century. During the fourteenth century, however, this intensive, specialized wool production had declined, leading to a fall in both quality and quantity. In the

[20] Durham, Dean and Chapter, Locellus VIII, nos. 3, 9, 13, 19.

[21] Pollard and Ashcroft, 'Coverham', p. 39.

[22] See e.g. Dur. RO, D/St/E3/4/30 Nov. 1452. William Dent and Edward Rayne were both amerced for allowing 60 sheep to 'escape' into the forest. In November 1437 William Appleby was presented for grazing 200 sheep (ibid. 4/28 Nov. 1436).

[23] *The Priory of Hexham*, ii, p. 60; Dobson, *Durham Priory*, p. 277.

[24] NYCRO, ZJX 3/2/111.

[25] As e.g. in 1479–80, when over 800 sheep were kept in these 2 parks (Durham, Church Commission, Bishopric Estates, 190259).

fifteenth century less wool, and of a poorer quality, was being clipped by the monks, although flocks of 300 or so were still the characteristic size at some monastic granges.[26]

Latterly, however, a monastic grange was as likely to be stocked with cattle as with sheep.[27] Specialized stock-rearing first developed in the Pennines and North York Moors within the great royal and seigneurial forests in the thirteenth century, probably to supply the growing demand for draught animals created by agrarian expansion.[28] By the fifteenth century, however, the emphasis in cattle-rearing had shifted to dairying and raising store animals for human consumption. Cattle-rearing was concentrated in the large number of vaccaries, permanent cattle stations, in the upper dales, which exploited high moorland pasture during the summer months.[29] In the forest of Wensleydale there were twelve, in Coverdale six, in Arkengarthdale fourteen, and in Mickleton and the forest of Lune a further twelve.[30] An individual vaccary could support approximately 80 to 100 head of cattle. Henry, Lord FitzHugh's stock in the second decade of the century of 300 cattle of all ages in three vaccaries, among which there were three bulls and approximately ninety cows, suggests that the practice was to keep a bull with thirty cows and their offspring at each station.[31]

As with sheep, so cattle-rearing was a substantial tenant occupation in the upper dales. Most vaccaries were leased to tenants, who also took the agistments and herbage of the parks and other closes. The cattle, like the sheep, regularly 'escaped' into the restricted grazing of the forest. The appropriately named John Oxenherd, for instance, was presented at Mickleton

[26] Waites, *Moorland and Valeland Farming*, pp. 26–34; D. J. H. Michelmore, *The Fountains Abbey Lease Book* (YAS, RS, 140, 1981), pp. lviii–lx and *The Fountains Abbey Rental, 1495–6* (privately printed, Leeds, 1974), *passim*; and T. H. Lloyd, *The Movement of Wool Prices in Medieval England* (Econ. HR, Suppl. 6, 1973), 24–6.

[27] Michelmore, *Rental, passim*; R. A. Donkin, 'Cattle on the Estates of Medieval Cistercian Monasteries in England', *Econ. HR*, 2nd ser., 15 (1962–3), 37–40.

[28] See R. C. Shaw, *The Royal Forest of Lancaster* (Preston, 1956), 355.

[29] Ibid.; G. H. Tupling, *The Economic History of Rossendale* (Manchester, 1927), 17–27.

[30] PRO, SC6/1085/18,20; Dur. RO, D/St/E3/1/3/13 May 1432.

[31] NYCRO, JZX 3/2/62.

court in the autumn of 1452 for grazing eighty beasts in the forest. Parks too were converted into grazing for cattle.[32] The parks of Lord Latimer at Danby on Esk and Sennington were stocked with cattle as well as horses in 1452–3. But most parks were leased as herbage, as was the West Park at Thringarth in Lunedale, often to a syndicate of local herdsmen. In 1437–8 nearly all of the principal park at Barnard Castle was let in several farms. Stanhope Park, over the hill in Weardale, was developed in the same manner; here by 1476 there were no fewer than twenty farms.[33]

Large-scale cattle-rearing in the Pennines was based on commercial exploitation of seigneurially controlled forest. Seigneurial control of rivers also allowed the commercial development of fisheries. The rivers of Northumberland, Durham, and North Yorkshire are traditionally fine salmon and trout rivers. Fishgarths or yares were to be found all along these rivers from their mouths to their higher reaches. There was hardly a riverside manor that did not exploit its right to take fish. There were at least twelve yares on the Tyne, most below Newcastle. On the Tees, fishgarths are known to have existed at Ayresome, Stainsby, Berwick, and Newsham.[34] On the Ure there were garths at West Tanfield and Boroughbridge.[35] Lower down the Ouse illegal garths between Boroughbridge and York were a constant source of concern in the late fifteenth century to the authorities in both places, who wished to keep the river clear for navigation.[36] Economically sea-fishing was probably more important than river-fishing. The principal fishing ports were Scarborough, Hartlepool, and the new town of North Shields, where herring-houses for the drying and salting of fish were set up. An inquisition in January 1446, for instance, found that

[32] Dur. RO, D/St/E3/1/4/30 Nov. 1452.

[33] Alnwick, Syon MS X, I Box 26, Instaurer's account, 31–32 Henry VI (Danby and Sennington); Dur. RO, D/St/E3/1/3/13 May 1432, 4 Nov. 1434, 14 Jan. 1484 (Thringarth); PRO SC6/1303/13; J. L. Drury, 'Early Settlement in Stanhope Park, Weardale, c.1406–79', Arch.Ael. 4 (1976), 148–9.

[34] Lomas, 'Durham Cathedral Priory', 135; B. J. H. Harrison and G. Dixon, Guisborough before 1900 (Guisborough, 1981), 31; NYCRO, ZJX 3/2/111; PRO SC6/1303/13.

[35] NYCRO, ZJX 3/2/90; T. Lawson Tancred, Records of a Yorkshire Manor (1937), 146, 160–1.

[36] Lawson Tancred, Yorkshire Manor, pp. 87–8; YCR, i. 3–4, 19, 22–4, 29, 92–4, 98–100.

twenty cobles (the inshore fishing craft characteristic of the north-east coast) and seven larger craft fished out of North Shields, where there were fourteen staithes and associated herring-houses. Scarborough in the second and third decades of the century enjoyed a brief period of prosperity based on deep-sea fishing, but thereafter reverted exclusively to inshore fishing, like her neighbouring settlements up and down the coast.[37] Even fairly insubstantial settlements without the benefit of natural harbours, such as Redcar and Coatham, maintained fleets. At Redcar, for instance, Joan, countess of Kent held on her death the toll and profit of the aptly named cobleferme.[38]

The north-east was also rich in mineral resources. Iron was found in Weardale, where there was a bloomery in the fifteenth century; but the largest deposits lay in Eskdale in the North York Moors, where it had been exploited, especially by the canons of Guisborough priory, since the thirteenth century.[39] Lead was mined in the upper reaches of Weardale, Teesdale, Arkengarthdale, Wensleydale, Wharfedale, and Nidderdale. The Durham mines had first been exploited in the late twelfth century, but many mines had been abandoned in the early thirteenth century. Mining was re-established in the 1370s, and continued throughout the fifteenth century. Arkengarthdale mines were also revived in the fifteenth century, during which a series of pits was also worked at different sites in Wharfedale.[40] In the fourteenth century coal-mining in Northumberland and Durham was developed on a large scale, especially from pits near the banks of the Tyne, from which the coal could readily be shipped through Newcastle. There were more pits inland, especially in central and in south-east Durham near Bishop Auckland, which were worked throughout the fifteenth century[41]

[37] H. E. Craster, *A History of Northumberland, vol. viii: Tynemouth* (1907), 285; P. Heath, 'North Sea Fishing in the Fifteenth Century: the Scarborough Fleet', *NH* 3 (1968), 53–68.

[38] Harrison and Dixon, *Guisborough*, p. 31; *CIPM, Henry VII* i (1898), 251.

[39] Lomas, 'Northern Farm', 38; B. Waites, 'Medieval Iron Working in North-east Yorkshire', *Geography*, 49 (1964), 33–43; *VCH, Durham*, ii. 353–5.

[40] I. S. W. Blanchard, 'Lead Smelting in Medieval England and Wales', in D. W. Crossley (ed.), *Medieval Industry*, CBA Research Report, 40 (1981), 73, 80–3; Coles, 'Middleham', pp. 175–85.

[41] *VCH, Durham*, iii. pp. 322–5; J. U. Nef, *The Rise of the British Coal Industry*, i (1932), 8, 11; J. B. Blake, 'The Medieval Coal Trade of North-East England: Some Fourteenth Century Evidence', *NH* 2 (1967) 1–26.

(see Map 1). The rich mineral resources of the region were
known; but the scale of their exploitation was limited not only
by the state of technology but also by the size of the market.

There were other resources to be exploited. Limestone and
slate quarries were worked at Forcett in Richmondshire. Mill-
stone was taken from Arkengarthdale, and slate at Leyburn.
Marble was quarried in Durham, both at Westwood on the Tees
near Barnard Castle and at Frosterley in Weardale[42] (see Map 1).
There were saltings at the mouth of the Tees, centred on
Coatham and Cowpen,[43] and at the mouth of the Tyne at South
and North Shields. In terms of numbers employed, however,
manufacturing was more important than extractive industry in
the countryside. Practically every village had its corn mill;
many had blacksmith's shops. But the most important rural
manufacturing industry was clothing. The ulnage returns of
1394–7 reveal a flourishing cloth-manufacturing industry
in north-western Yorkshire, centred on the towns of Northallerton, Richmond, Bedale, Ripon, and Boroughbridge. In the
late fourteenth century north-western Yorkshire was a more
important clothing district than the West Riding.[44] Fulling
mills were to be found throughout the region; at the main towns
such as Richmond, Middleham, Barnard Castle, and Darlington,
and also in many smaller settlements such as Aysgarth, Crakehall, Constable Burton, Mickleton, East Witton, Thoralby, West
Tanfield, and Aycliffe.[45] Behind each fulling mill were count-
less weavers and spinners, most probably pursuing their trade as
a by-industry. In addition to woollen-cloth manufacturing,
there was a nascent linen-manufacturing industry in the Northallerton district by the end of the fifteenth century, as is revealed
by the inventories of local men who possessed stocks of flax,
linen sheets, heckles (combs), and other flax-working tools.[46]

[42] Coles, 'Middleham', pp. 199–205; PRO sc6/1303/13.
[43] Lomas, 'South East Durham', p. 322; Harrison and Dixon, *Guisborough*, p. 31.
[44] H. Heaton, *The Yorkshire Woollen and Worsted Industries*, 2nd edn. (Oxford, 1965), 68–71.
[45] Coles, 'Middleham', pp. 224–30; Fieldhouse and Jennings, *Richmond and Swaledale*, pp. 22–5; N. Sunderland, *Tudor Darlington*, i (Durham, 1974), 69–70; PRO sc6/1303/13; NYCRO, zfw 5/118; zjx 3/2/50, 97; Lomas, 'Durham Cathedral Priory', p. 132.
[46] Durham, Dean and Chapter, Locellus viii, Nos. 6, 17.

The finishing, including shearing and dyeing, and marketing of cloth was one of the several specialisms of the towns of the region. There were some fifty markets serving the north-east. Although some of these, such as East Witton and Staindrop, were no more than villages whose viability was always doubtful, at the other end of the scale Newcastle and York were decidedly more than mere market towns.[47] While in the county palatine the bishop was able strictly to control and limit the number of markets, there was in fact an overprovision of market towns in north Yorkshire. Richmondshire had eight weekly markets and twelve annual fairs in mid-fifteenth century. In lower Wensleydale, as a result of fierce competition between local lords, there were three markets within seven miles— Wensley, Middleham, and East Witton (see Map 1).[48] Middleham, a late starter which received its grant in 1389, emerged victorious because of the superior political influence of its lords. Indeed for a short while after 1450 it briefly threatened the supremacy of Richmond in the district, especially when in 1479 Richard of Gloucester secured for the town the right to hold two annual fairs. But Middleham was essentially an artificial phenomenon, the creation of its lords. Economically it could not sustain its privileged position, for the tolls of the markets were in steady decline between 1465 and 1487, when they fell from £1. 11s. 9d. to 15s. 1½d.[49]

Above the strictly local, and sometimes ephemeral, country markets stood the district market towns and ports, such as Richmond, Ripon, Northallerton, Yarm, Darlington, Malton, Whitby, and, above all, Scarborough (see Map 1). Richmond, an old-established borough lying at the meeting point of Pennine and vale, had developed as the point of exchange for the produce of the two. Grain from the vale was sold in the market to supply the predominantly pastoral districts of Lonsdale, Craven, Dentdale, and Sedbergh, as well as Swaledale itself. But it was also the centre at which dairy produce and wool from the dales was marketed. It became an important finishing centre of

---

[47] The figure is based on the valuations given in the *Agrarian History of England and Wales*, iv. 468.

[48] Coles, 'Middleham', pp. 230–2.

[49] Ibid. 232, 254–5; *CPR, 1476–83*, p. 154.

the local cloth industry, where fulling, shearing, and dyeing was undertaken.[50] Darlington was almost certainly busier than Richmond. Its Monday market and four fairs gave it a regional significance which Richmond lacked. Like Richmond it traded in wool and had its own fulling mill and dyeing works; but it was additionally the principal livestock market of the district, the November fair attracting customers from all over the north-east, including Alice, Lady FitzHugh, the priory of Durham, and even on occasion the monks of Holy Island. Associated with the cattle market were the butchers, skinners, tanners, and leatherworkers of the town. The importance of the leather industry is perhaps indicated by the fact that the saddlers' guild of York exempted Darlington from the fairs and markets at which it forbade its members to trade.[51]

Other towns in the region had failed to develop. Durham was no more than a conglomerate of three semi-urbanized villages clustered around the peninsula on which stood the cathedral and priory, dominated economically and socially, as well as physically, by the ecclesiastical corporations.[52] Hartlepool had been a port of some substance in the early fourteenth century, but by the fifteenth, largely as a result of the monopoly that Newcastle had secured in the export of northern wool, it had declined to little more than a fishing town, its natural harbour being of greater significance as a haven for storm-tossed ships than as a point of loading and unloading.[53]

The dominant towns of the region were Newcastle and York. Newcastle's wealth had a threefold foundation. From mid-fourteenth century it was the staple for the export of northern wool, which included, for all but a few years in the fifteenth

[50] On the basis of the 1377 Poll Tax Returns, Professor Dobson places Scarborough in the top tier of Yorkshire towns (alongside Hull, Beverley, and York), Whitby in the second tier, and the rest in the category of small market town. See R. B. Dobson, 'Yorkshire Towns in the Late Fourteenth Century', *Publications of the Thoresby Society*, 59, no. 1 (1983), 4–12 and Fieldhouse and Jennings, *Richmond and Swaledale*, pp. 20–5.

[51] Sunderland, *Tudor Darlington*, i. 43–5, 60–70; NYCRO, ZJX 3/2/116.

[52] Dobson, 'Cathedral Chapters', p. 32.

[53] *VCH, Durham* iii. pp. 276–7; Cuthbert Sharp, *History of Hartlepool* (Hartlepool, 1851), 156. For the early-fourteenth-century trade of Hartlepool see C. M. Fraser, 'The Pattern of Trade in North-East England, 1265–1350', *NH* 4 (1969), 44–60.

century, the wool of Richmondshire. In the fourteenth century its wealth was augmented by the export of coal from the pits lying either side of the Tyne. Moreover it also benefited from its role as a military base for operations against the Scots.[54] But Newcastle could not compare with York, which combined within its walls the roles of provincial ecclesiastical centre, county town, and regional entrepôt.[55] The foundation of York's commercial prosperity was its site on the Ouse, the principal artery of north-eastern trade. At the end of the fourteenth century the city jurors had declared that the river was a vital highway serving for the great increase of the kingdom and especially of York, Yorkshire and other counties and towns of the north parts.[56] This highway ran from the mouth of the Humber through to Boroughbridge. All goods passed to or through York, where they were either landed or transhipped on payment of toll. Its wealth was based on a triple axis, of internal trade and serving its own immediate hinterland; of industrial production, brass-founding, pewter work, glass-making, and above all cloth manufacturing; and of a flourishing export trade with the North-Sea and Baltic countries and even further afield. It was the supplier of luxury goods and specialist services for the whole of the north-east. As Professor Miller has evocatively written:

The markets of York were places where distant customers sought to buy fish of many kinds, brass fittings for hanging bells, wax, spices, wainscots, wooden chests, resin, altar bread and wine, oil, pewter and wooden vessels, boots, shoes, wine from Gascony, Greece and Spain, iron, cloth, furs, raisins, preserved ginger and Cypress sugar; places

[54] Power and Postan, English Trade, p. 43; Blake, 'Coal Trade', pp. 1–26; Fraser, 'Pattern of Trade', pp. 62–5; Welford, Newcastle and Gateshead, passim, and, for truces at Newcastle in 1451, 1459, 1465, 1466, and 1472, pp. 325–6, 339, 355, 363. For examples of Newcastle as a forward base against the Scots in 1481 and 1484 see YCR i. 40–1 and J. O. Halliwell, Letters of the Kings of England (1848), 156.

[55] For late-medieval York see E. Miller, 'Medieval York', in VCH, York, ed. P. M. Tillott (1961), 25–116; J. M. Bartlett, 'The Expansion and Decline of York in the Later Middle Ages', Econ. HR 2nd ser., 12 (1958), 17–33, esp. 25–6; D. M. Palliser, 'York under the Tudors: The Trading Life of the Northern Capital', in A. Everitt, (ed.), Perspectives in English Urban History (1973); and Dobson, 'Cathedral Chapters', passim.

[56] VCH, York, p. 97.

where a clockmaker could be found to mend a clock or a bookbinder a book.[57]

York, in short, was the capital of the region.

At the beginning of the fifteenth century the north-east was no backward, remote corner of England. Distant from Westminster it may have been, but it possessed rich and varied resources. It was not merely part of the highland zone, dependent principally on pastoral and industrial activity. As Professor Dobson pointed out in respect of the priory of Durham, 'the countryside . . . is one in which the plough is very much the king'.[58] The region might have seemed on the brink of a new era of prosperity in the late fourteenth century, when, led by York, there was a general expansion of its industrial and commercial activity. Lead-mining was revived, coal-mining around Newcastle was developed on a large scale for the first time, cloth manufacturing boomed in both town and country, and market towns flourished in many parts of the region. But this was a false dawn. Forces were already at work which were undermining the apparent turn-of-the-century prosperity.

Like the rest of Europe, north-eastern England passed through an extended economic crisis in the later Middle Ages. The major factors were climatic deterioration,[59] war damage, and, above all, population decline. These can be traced back to the early fourteenth century. They had struck an economy which in the preceding century had been expanding, particularly in north-eastern England.[60] A cyclical turn for the worse in the weather, perhaps coinciding with soil exhaustion, led to the Great Famine of 1314–21.[61] In addition to this the ravages of the Scots and the burden of wars to secure the northern border placed a

---

[57] Ibid. 99. Cf. the observation of Professor Dobson that York acted as a commercial entrepôt for Yorkshire ('Yorkshire Towns', pp. 14–15).

[58] Dobson, *Durham Priory*, p. 252.

[59] H. H. Lamb, *Climate, History and the Modern World* (1982), 168–72, 186–91.

[60] R. Newton, *The Northumberland Landscape* (1972), 89, 93; Waites, *Moorland and Valeland Farming*, pp. 4–5, 11–12; H. C. Darby, R. E. Glasscock, J. Sheaill and G. R. Veisey, 'The Changing Geographical Distribution of Wealth in England, 1086–1334–1525', *Journal of Historical Geography*, 5 (1979), 254; Linacre, 'Distribution of Lay Wealth', *passim*.

[61] I. Kershaw, 'The Great Famine and Agrarian Crisis in England, 1315–22', *PP* 59 (1973), 3–50.

further strain on the economy of the region.[62] It is not certain that population began to decline then.[63] But following the outbreak of plague, which reached the north-east in 1349 and returned periodically, but with particular virulence in 1379 and 1391,[64] population fell dramatically in the second half of the century. Economic contraction inevitably followed, and became all too apparent after 1400.

Early-fifteenth-century landlords were acutely aware of their worsening situation. The bursar of Durham Priory reported in 1420 that the income his office enjoyed from garbal tithes had been much reduced in Scotland and the borders because of the loss of English control and destruction by the Scots. In lands away from the border (primarily in the bishopric) the same income had fallen, he judged, because several places had been deserted as a result of frequent plagues, other lords had ceased cultivation of crops, and land had been converted to pasture.[65] Continuing plague was advanced as the principal reason for the dwindling population and the reduction of tillage in Hexham-shire in 1421. Eighteen years later an enquiry found that, where in Bamburgh there had once been 120 burgages, because of continual war there were then only ten.[66] In 1484, Richard III writing to Pope Sixtus IV on behalf of Bishop Shirwood blamed both the neglect of successive bishops and the ravages of war for the impoverishment of the diocese.[67] And in 1486 the bailiff of Alnwick gave 'war and pestilence long ago' as the cause of

[62] Kershaw, 'Scots in the West Riding', pp. 231–9; J. Scammell, 'Robert I and the North of England', *EHR* 73 (1958), 385–403; Linacre, 'Distribution of Lay Wealth', pp. 98–104, 108–13; J. R. Maddicott, *'The English Peasantry and the Demands of the Crown, 1294–1341'*, *PP* Suppl. 1(1975), passim. In the most recent discussion of the impact of war on northern society Dr Tuck has suggested that after 1332 even in the border areas there was some degree of recovery (Tuck, 'War and Society', pp. 40–1). See, however, the conclusion of R. A. Lomas that the decade 1318–28, when there were major border losses as a result of Scottish raids, was the turning point in the late-medieval financial history of Durham Priory (Lomas, 'Durham Cathedral Priory', p. 285).

[63] J. L. Bolton, *The Medieval English Economy, 1150–1500* (1980), 191–2.

[64] Jennings, *Harrogate and Knaresborough*, pp. 68–71; Lomas, 'South East Durham', pp. 259–60; C. I. Creighton, *A History of Epidemics in Britain*, i (Cambridge, 1894, 2nd edn., 1965), 218, 220.

[65] *Historiae Dunelmensis Scriptores Tres*, ed. J. Raine (SS, ix, 1839), p. ccl.

[66] *Rot. Parl.*, iv. 143; E. Bateson, *A History of Northumberland, vol. i: The Parish of Bamburgh* (1893), 132–3.

[67] Rymer, *Foedera*, xii. 224.

decays of rents in his barony.[68] War and pestilence: these were the reasons advanced by contemporaries for the continuing losses suffered by landlords.

In respect of war these testimonies are potentially misleading. The lasting effects of war were only felt in the far north of the region. The Conyers' properties in Wooler and the Forest of Cheviot in northern Northumberland were virtually worthless in 1490, because a great part of them was said to be ravaged by the Scots. Likewise, five years later the castle of Harbottle in Coquetdale and the manor of Otterburn in Redesdale were found to have been worth little to the deceased Sir Robert Tailboys because of the proximity of these estates to Scotland.[69] These assessments, made in time of peace, probably represent revenues long lost as a consequence of the breakdown of manorial control, as well as of permanent physical destruction.

In neighbouring but lowland Norhamshire and Islandshire, where the bishop of Durham was the principal landlord and the priory received the tithes, husbandry continued, and revenues were collected in all but years of open warfare. Norhamshire was, however, always the first to suffer when war broke out. In times of acute disruption it became extremely difficult to collect and deliver revenues. This is particularly apparent in 1463–4, a year in which, as a result of Lancastrian occupation, Norhamshire was totally out of English royal control. It was reported to the bursar of Durham that £20 and no more was received from tithes of Norhamshire and the rents of Shoreswood that year (normally worth £80–£100 per annum) 'propter guerram et invasiones Scottorum, et propter vastacionem factam per rebelles dominis regis Edwardi'.[70] An episcopal valor of the same year includes no entry for Norhamshire except a note to record that in peacetime it was worth £200 in rent.[71] Yet recovery from open war was relatively quick. Fields were sown and rents and tithes collected as soon as danger

---

[68] Tuck, 'War and Society', p. 33.

[69] *CIPM Henry VII*, (1898), 260, 414.

[70] *Foedarium Prioratus Dunelmensis*, ed. W. Greenwell, SS, lviii (1871), 98. For this reason the 1464 inventory represents an atypical year in the Priory's finances (see Dobson, *Durham Priory*, p. 271). Note too that an earlier, 1446–7, evaluation depended on the truce holding (Raine, *Scriptores Tres*, p. ccxc).

[71] Durham, Church Commission, Bishopric Estates, 189817.

passed. Thus tithal income had been restored to near its pre-war
level by 1466, and after the war of 1480–4, when once more
tithal income was disrupted, full recovery was made by 1488.[72]

The impact of open war was not restricted to the immediate
border area. It was felt, for instance, further away at Embleton,
where in May 1438 the auditor instructed that rents totalling
£44. 8s. 11d. should be remitted as partial compensation for
losses recently sustained at the hands of the Scots. In 1449 once
more tenants were barely able to pay half their rent.[73] As far
south as Alnwick, in 1449–50 some houses were derelict as
a result of damage inflicted by the Scots the previous year;
Chatton Park, normally farmed at £2. 13s. 4d., was worthless for
the same reason.[74]

Outside the more remote border dales direct loss as a result of
war was only sporadic. As Dr Tuck has observed, it may be that
generally in northern Northumberland the fear of invasion had a
more permanently depressing effect on rents and discouraged
the taking up of leases.[75] But it is only within a distance of
twenty or thirty miles of the border itself that war seems to have
had any significant economic impact in the fifteenth century.
South of Alnwick, where the Scots rarely penetrated after 1388,
it seems to have been of little consequence at all.

Away from the marches, where war with Scotland was no
longer directly experienced, pestilence rather than war was the
cause of impoverishment and falling population. What small
direct demographic evidence there is seems to point to a con-
tinuance of high death-rate and low replacement rates during
the fifteenth century. Neif lists drawn up for Billinghamshire by
the priory of Durham between 1386 and 1469, revealing that the
average size of household fluctuated between just under four
and just over five, suggest that birth-rates remained low.[76]

---

[72] Durham, Dean and Chapter, Norham Proctors' Accounts, 1461–6,
1482–9. The first places to suffer were Tweedmouth and Ord opposite Berwick.
No crops were sown there in 1461–2, 1483–4, 1484–5. Tithes gradually
recovered after 1484 from 20s. in 1485, to 23s. in 1486, reaching 60s. in 1488. In
1497–8, when war broke out again, Shoreswood, Cornhill, Tilmouth,
Tweedmouth, Morton, and Hornecliff were all waste per Scotos (ibid., 1497–8).
[73] Bateson, Embleton, p. 33.
[74] J. M. W. Bean, The Estates of the Percy Family, 1416–1537 (Oxford, 1958),
34.   [75] Tuck, 'War and Society', p. 42.
[76] Lomas, 'Durham Cathedral Priory', pp. 61–2.

Mortuary and churching offerings made in the parish of Scarborough between 1414 and 1442 suggest that deaths in years of pestilence or other epidemic more than offset a tendency in normal years for births to be slightly more numerous. Whereas births in the years for which evidence has survived fluctuated between 30 and 68, deaths ranged from 30 to a staggering 161 in 1438–9. These figures would suggest continuing population decline in Scarborough in the early fifteenth century, caused by periodic epidemic.[77]

The same characteristic of high mortality as a result of disease, especially in the 1430s (and between 1475 and 1486) is suggested by chronicle and other sources, and is confirmed by the incidence of will-making in the diocese of York. The citizens of Newcastle claimed that it had suffered the deaths of a substantial number of its inhabitants by pestilence in 1432.[78] Mortality in 1438–9, when Scarborough suffered, was generally very high. According to Gregory's chronicle, in 1438 there was 'great pestilence, and namely in the north country', which lasted until 1440. The *Brut* too noted the high mortality among common folk in 1438, 'throughout the realm and principally at York and in the north country'.[79] The probate records of the diocese reveal a larger than normal number of deaths in the last two quarters of the same year. In York itself the highest death-rate of the century occurred in this year, when at least eighteen merchants died. In the diocese as a whole, it has recently been suggested, mortality reached truly crisis proportions.[80] York

---

[77] Heath, 'North Sea Fishing', p. 65 and App. III.

[78] Welford, *Newcastle and Gateshead*, p. 294.

[79] Gairdner, *Historical Collections*, p. 181; R. S. Gottfried, *Epidemic Diseases in Fifteenth Century England* (Leicester, 1978), 39; J. F. D. Shrewsbury, *A History of Bubonic Plague in the British Isles* (Cambridge, 1971), 144; Creighton, *Epidemics*, p. 225. A parliamentary petition in 1439 referred to 'sickness called the Pestilence universally through this your realm more than hath been usual before this time'.

[80] R. Blenkarn, 'Mortality in the Diocese of York, 1430–1539' (unpublished Teesside Polytechnic MA thesis, 1983) 22, 27, 37; J. I. Kermode, 'Merchants, Overseas Trade and Urban Decline: York, Beverley and Hull, ca 1380–1500', *NH* 23 (1987), 60; P. J. P. Goldberg, 'Mortality and Economic Change in the Diocese of York, 1390–1514', *NH* 24 (1988), 45–6. In contrast to the north-east, Canterbury Cathedral Priory did not suffer an exceptionally high number of deaths in this year (see John Hatcher, 'Mortality in the Fifteenth Century: Some New Evidence', *Econ. HR* 2nd ser., 39, 1 (1986), 30.

wills show a return of mortality to crisis levels in the last
quarters of 1466, 1471, and 1479. The epidemic of 1479 seems to
have been as severe in the north-east as it was elsewhere.
However, the region escaped the 'flux', or dysentery, of the
summer of 1473, which in East Anglia proved to be as lethal as
any other epidemic. This epidemic coincided with an exceptionally hot summer. For once the cooler climate of the north-east
seems to have been a blessing for its inhabitants. But there was
no escaping 'the sweat' in 1485, when mortality as shown by
probate was again exceptionally high.[81] It was not until the last
decades of the century that the region seems to have enjoyed
lower than normal mortality.[82]

Thus there are few grounds for supposing that population in
the region began to grow much before the early sixteenth
century. Indeed a comparison of the subsidy returns of 1545 for a
group of Tees-valley villages in north Yorkshire with the poll-
tax returns of 1377 suggests that at the most population was
then only 10 per cent higher, and that in mid-fifteenth-century
it was probably lower than it had been on the eve of the Black
Death.[83] The historian should not perhaps seek for too early a
date for resumed population growth in the sixteenth-century
north-east.

Continued population decline, especially in the first half of
the fifteenth century, was matched by economic contraction. In
the first half of the century rents and other revenues from land
fell by approximately one-third. The net rent due from the
lordship of Barnard Castle fell from £362 to £279 between

[81] Blenkarn, 'Mortality', pp. 22–32; Gottfried, *Epidemic Diseases*, pp. 144–9;
Creighton, *Epidemics*, pp. 231–3. Plague in 1471 and the Sweating Sickness in
1485 caused a higher than usual number of deaths at Canterbury Priory
(Hatcher, 'Mortality', pp. 28, 30).

[82] Blenkarn, 'Mortality', pp. 21, 27; Goldberg, 'Mortality and Economic
Change', pp. 46–9. The lowest rates of mortality, as measured by will-making
(after allowance for the variation in probate rates) between 1430 and 1539, were
between 1490 and 1503. For changes in fertility rates after 1450 see Goldberg,
'Mortality and Economic Change', pp. 52–3.

[83] A. J. Pollard, 'Croft-on-Tees in the Later Middle Ages', *Teesside and
Cleveland Local History Bulletin*, 39 (1980), 18, 22. Also I. S. W. Blanchard,
'Population Change, Enclosure and the Early Tudor Economy', *Econ. HR*, 2nd
ser., 23 (1970), 441; but *contra* I. Kershaw, *Bolton Priory Rentals and Ministers'
Accounts, 1473–1539*, YAS, RS 132 (1970 for 1969), p. xv.

1390/1 and 1420/1.[84] The receipts of the receiver-general of the bishopric of Durham were reduced from £2,942 in 1416/17 to £1,761 in 1459/60. Garbal tithes paid to the priory of Durham fell from £404 in 1392 to £270 in 1446. Rents on the Percy estates in Northumberland too fell by one-third.[85] Yet the contraction of the regional economy in the first half of the fifteenth century was both geographically and chronologically uneven. An overall reduction of one-third in rents conceals the fact that in many places the second and third decades of the century witnessed a welcome respite from decline; and that where pastoral farming predominated the years 1410–30 actually saw short-lived recovery. But the decades of respite and recovery were brought to an abrupt end in the 1430s by a combination of high mortality and failed harvests which left the region devastated. Thus within the general downward trend lies a more complex cyclical pattern culminating in a severe agrarian crisis.

In the arable lowlands rents were held steady, and in one or two instances increased in the second and third decades. While garbal tithe income continued to slide, the rents of Durham Priory's own land stabilized. The income of one of its obedientiaries, the hostillar, was in 1410 as high as it had been in 1370.[86] Between 1416 and 1428 receipts from the bishop of Durham's estates in Darlington ward remained stable at £735–£740 p.a.[87] At Cleasby, across the Tees in North Yorks., the net rent due to Lord FitzHugh fluctuated between £41 and £43 between 1411 and 1432. During the same decades pastoral farming in the upper Pennine dales enjoyed a period of considerable prosperity. At Middleton-in-Teesdale rents rose from £39 to £43 between 1391 and 1421. On the south side of the dale, at Mickleton, they rose from £71 to £78 between 1389 and 1418. But by 1432 the Mickleton rents had leapt to £92.[88] Further south on Bowes

[84] Durham, Church Commission, Bishopric Estates, 189809, 189814; PRO, SC6/1303/11 and 12; Dobson, *Durham Priory*, p. 271; Bean, *Estates*, p. 35.

[85] Durham, Church Commission, Bishopric Estates, 189598; PRO, DL29/637/10357; Bean, *Estates*, p. 38.

[86] Lomas, 'Durham Cathedral Priory', pp. 150, 169. It is worth noting, however, that the income for the spot sales of the tithes of Heighington increased from £33. 16s. 8d. in 1391/2 to £48. 10s. 0d. in 1437/8.

[87] Durham, Church Commission, Bishopric Estates, 189809–190184.

[88] NYCRO, ZJX 3/2/50–85.

Moor and in Arkengarthdale gressums were being levied on the seven-year lease of vaccaries which were the equivalent of one year's rent.[89] And in upper Weardale to the north, Stanhope Park was converted to large-scale stock-raising in the same decades. For pastoral farming, especially stock-raising and dairy production, 1410 to 1430 were boom years.[90]

This period of respite in lowland arable husbandry and boom in upland pastoral farming was brought to an end by the high mortality and failed harvests of the 1430s. The impact of 'great pestilence' and the 'great dearth of corn' in the north noted by contemporary chroniclers was dramatic. Rents for the Darlington ward estates of the bishop of Durham fell from £667 in 1434/5 to £495 in 1438/9.[91] Rents in some FitzHugh lowland manors in northern Yorkshire, where there was a sudden surge of empty holdings after 1438 and a mounting burden of arrears, fell by as much as 50 per cent. The combined rents of Cleasby and Clowbeck were initially reduced by nearly 30 per cent. Although they recovered slightly by 1450, the manor still carried a 15 per cent decline directly attributable to the pestilence and dearth of 1438–40.[92] The priory of Durham, most of whose estates were in the bishopric, suffered a similar loss. The high level of wastes, decays, and disrepair revealed in a comprehensive survey and evaluation of the bursar's estate in 1446 is largely attributable to the same agrarian crisis. Prior Ebbchester described his house as being in a state of collapse in that year. It was, according to its modern historian, the most serious of all fifteenth-century challenges to the monastery's economy.[93]

---

[89] PRO SC6/1085/18.

[90] Dury, 'Early Settlement', p. 142. In Derbyshire too the 1420s represented a peak time for the Vernon of Haddon stock farm (S. M. Wright, *The Derbyshire Gentry in the Fifteenth Century* (Derbys. RS, 8, (1983), 19)) and in Tutbury forest there was increasing demand for pasture in the late fourteenth and early fifteenth centuries (J. R. Birrell, 'The Forest Economy of the Honour of Tutbury in the Fourteenth and Fifteenth centuries', *University of Birmingham Historical Journal*, 8 (1962)).

[91] Durham, Church Commission, Bishopric Estates, 188686, 189811.

[92] For this, the preceding, and the following paragraphs see A. J. Pollard, 'The North-Eastern Economy and the Agrarian Crisis of 1438–40', *NH* 25 (1989), 88–105.

[93] Dobson, *Durham Priory*, pp. 253, 266–7; Lomas, 'Durham Cathedral Priory', end pocket. The period 1430–42 was also a particularly difficult time for the manor of Elvet Hall (ibid. 196).

Similar declines in the net rents of the Percy manors of Healaugh and of some of the manors on the Middleham estate of the Nevilles were almost certainly created at the same time by the same cause.[94] Not even the pastoral economy of the uplands escaped. Vaccaries remained in hand and rents fell back at Mickleton, so that the annual sum due was reduced to £80 by 1440, at which level it remained for the rest of the decade.[95]

The ramifications of the agrarian crisis of 1438–40 were widespread. In attempts to entice tenants landlords offered rebates on rents and bore the cost of repairing tenements.[96] Both the priory of Durham and Lord FitzHugh reformed their methods of estate management in an effort to limit the damage done to their finances. At Durham the bursary was temporarily divided between three obedientiaries; Lord FitzHugh reverted to receiving a portion of his income in kind, delivered directly from some of his principal grain manors, such as Cleasby, to his household at Ravensworth.[97] Such a retreat towards self-sufficiency was bound to have a further effect on market towns suffering as a result of harvest failure. The commercial lives of Barnard Castle, Richmond, and Newcastle all suffered in the fifth decade of the century. It is surely no coincidence that the burgesses of Richmond appealed to the Crown in 1440 for a reduction in their fee farm, and that Newcastle appealed against the competition of North Shields in 1446. Both towns were suffering from local competition; but the timing of their appeals was almost certainly linked to a sudden worsening of their positions brought about by the general depression of agriculture in the region.[98] Moreover it was in this same decade that the city of York first found itself in serious economic difficulty. City rents fell dramatically after 1440, as did the recruitment of freemen to the principal manufacturing and commercial guilds.[99]

The crisis of 1438–40 was thus a major shock of the utmost

[94] Bean, *Estates*, p. 37; PRO sc6/1085/18, 20.
[95] Essex, RO, D/DC M108; Dur. RO, D/St/E3/1/1/1448–9.
[96] Pollard, 'Agrarian Crisis', pp. 95–7.
[97] Dobson, *Durham Priory*, pp. 253, 267; Pollard 'Agrarian Crisis', pp. 101–2.
[98] PRO, sc6/1303/13; *CPR, 1436–41*, 452, 509–10; Craster, *Tynemouth*, pp. 289–90; Welford, *Newcastle and Gateshead*, pp. 316–18.
[99] Bartlett, 'Expansion and Decline of York', p. 28.

importance for the later economic history of the north-east. Economic decline before 1450 was not steady and gradual: it was spasmodic. The second and third decades of the century formed a period of stability and respite from earlier decline, and, in one specialized sector of the agrarian economy, of short-lived boom. The impact of the crisis of the fourth decade was intensified by the relative prosperity of the preceding decades. A further downward twist in the spiral of rural recession of some 15 per cent plunged the region into deep depression in mid-century. As London chroniclers remarked, this was primarily a northern crisis. The effect was the greater because the midlands and southern England did not suffer as severely as the north in the 1430s.[100] There were to be profound consequences, not only for the internal structure of the north-eastern economy, but also for the balance of the whole English economy as it later came out of recession.

[100] C. C. Dyer, *Lords and Peasants in a Changing Society: the estates of the Bishopric of Worcester, 680–1540* (Cambridge, 1980), 188; Hatcher, *Plague*, 36–42; D. M. Palliser, 'Urban Decay Revisited', in J. A. F. Thomson, (ed.), *Towns and Townspeople in the Fifteenth Century* (Gloucester, 1988), 6.

3

Economic and Social Trends
after 1450

THE most complete evidence for the agrarian economy of the
north-east in the later fifteenth century lies in the archives of
the priory and bishopric of Durham. The net receipts of the
bursar of the priory rose slightly from an average of less than
£1,350 in the 1450s and 1460s to just over £1,400 in the 1470s.[1]
Evaluations made of the estates of the bishop of Durham in
1463/4 and 1477/8 show a more substantial improvement in the
revenues due from Durham and Yorkshire, which increased
from £2,940 to £3,427 p.a. In the bishopric alone the clear value
was calculated to be £2,305 in 1463/4 and £2,642 in 1477/8.[2]
The more detailed series of receiver-general's accounts for the
bishopric itself reveals, however, that actual receipts were consistently lower. These fell to an average of just under £1,900
during the decade 1459–69. The year 1459/60, when receipts
only totalled £1,761, was the worst for which documentation
has survived in the whole century, lower even than 1438/9. The
1470s, however, witnessed a revival of receipts to over £2,000
p.a., with £2,200 being received in 1476/7 and 1478/9.[3] It is to be

---

[1] R. B. Dobson, 'Richard Bell, Prior of Durham (1464–78) and Bishop of
Carlisle (1478–95)', *Transactions of the Cumberland and Westmorland Antiquarian and Archaeological Society*, 65 (1965), 202.

[2] Durham, Church Commission, Bishopric Estates, 189817, 189676. The
figures are those for clear value after wastes and decays, but before deduction of
fees, wages, and necessary expenses, and they exclude Hart, temporarily in the
bishop's hand by reason of forfeiture.

[3] Durham, Church Commission, Bishopric Estates, 189812–31 *passim*. The
discrepancy between the valors and the receiver-general's accounts would seem
to lie in the fact that actual receipts were often in arrears and did not normally
match the expected revenue of the particular year. The 1463/4 valor makes it
clear that in that year most of the current revenues were not received: in fact
only £1,100 was recorded as delivered, leaving a little over £1,300 in arrears
(including Hart), borne by the various bailiffs, coroners, and collectors. The
complex financial administration of the bishopric has yet to be disentangled;
but it would appear that in the later fifteenth century it operated substantially in
arrears.

noted, however, that this improvement, welcome as it no doubt was to Bishops Booth and Dudley, did not restore the revenues received from the bishopric to the levels enjoyed by their predecessor Thomas Langley before the crisis of 1438–40. This happy state of affairs was not reached until the first decade of the sixteenth century, when annual receipts for the bishopric itself once more touched £2,700, and were more in line with a valuation of £2,819 made in the final year of Henry VIII's reign.[4]

The modest improvement of the 1470s seems to have been the result of a series of better than normal harvests, the quality of which can be demonstrated from the garbal tithes collected in the parish of Billingham.[5] What precisely makes a good harvest depends on which side of the market stall one stands. For the producer a moderately abundant crop when prices are slightly higher than average gives the best return. For the consumer a bumper crop, causing prices to fall below average, is the best. Several harvests of the former kind occurred in the 1470s. The tithe of wheat in Billingham parish rose to an average of over 100 quarters a year, and prices of 6s. or over were fetched in five out of ten years. Barley tithes produced over 140 quarters a year, and again in five of the years the price reached 4 s. or more. The years 1471, 1472, and 1478 were good for both crops. But there was not one year in which returns for either wheat or barley were poor. The year 1478 was the best of all, yielding 146 quarters of wheat at 6s. and 155½ quarters of barley at 4s., and a total financial return to the priory, when oats, peas and beans, as well as the farm of Bellasis tithes are included, of £103. 1s. 6½d.

However, the improvement of the 1470s was not sustained. The harvest of 1481 was bad; 1482 was disastrous. In 1482 wheat rose to 13s. 4d.; barley to 8s. per quarter. The tithe fell to forty-five quarters and three bushels of wheat; fifty-seven and one of barley. Because of the high prices, the priory did not suffer financially. It was, nevertheless, the worst harvest failure since 1438. Yet the impact was surprisingly muted. The receipts of the bursar did fall once more below £1,400; but this was as much

---

[4] Durham, Church Commission, Bishopric Estates, 190217, 190317.
[5] The conclusions reached in this paragraph are based on an analysis of the garbal tithe returns for Billingham in the Bursar's Accounts for the decade 1470–9 (Durham, Dean and Chapter, Bursar's Accounts). It is to be noted that the accounts ran from Pentecost to Pentecost.

a consequence of the disruption by renewed war with Scotland to the yield of rents and tithes from Norhamshire as of a fall in revenue from lands in the bishopric. Indeed the first epidemic of sweating sickness in 1485–6 seems to have been a greater cause of disruption. The quantity of tithe grain collected in the parish of Billingham in 1486 was almost as low as in 1482. The spot sale of tithes in four other parishes where the priory did not rely on fixed farms was also more seriously affected than in 1482. The result was that the bursar's receipts, which had recovered to over £1,420 in 1484/5, fell again to under £1,380 in 1485/6.[6]

The evidence from Durham ecclesiastical estates suggests that sustained recovery and expansion of the agrarian economy, briefly promised in the 1470s, did not materialize. There were spells of greater prosperity in the 1470s and again in the 1490s;[7] but the conditions were generally not yet ripe for the losses suffered after 1438 to be regained. The meagre evidence provided by surviving documentation from other estates in the region would seem to confirm these conclusions. A view of account for Barnard Castle in 1488/9 suggests that the overall net rent due, at £304, was about 8 per cent higher than it had been in 1420/1. But only three manors showed a substantial increase: Barnard Castle itself had fallen, and the rents of Gainford and Piercebridge stood at the same level.[8] The rents of Cleasby and Clowbeck in 1497/8 stood at £1 less than the rents in 1450/1. The net rent of West Tanfield still stood at £40 in 1477/8.[9] The Percy lordship of Topcliffe, which in 1442/3 was evaluated at £88, was worth but £2 more in 1478/9.[10] Some rents in Craven, Malham, and Airedale from Bolton Abbey properties increased in the 1470s; but it is perhaps significant that an estimate in 1473 that a particular rent of 8s. 4d. could be demised for 15s. proved ill-founded, for the rent remained the

[6] Durham, Dean and Chapter, Bursar, 1480/1, 1481/2, 1482/3, 1486/7.

[7] No bishopric receiver-general's accounts survive for the 1480s. Three accounts for the mid-1490s, two damaged, indicate that gross receipts fluctuated between just over £2,000 and nearly £2,500 in the decade (Durham, Church Commission, Bishopric Estates, 189598, 190227, 190309). For evidence of Bishop Fox's concern to maximize his income see *The Letters of Richard Fox, 1486–1527*, ed. P. S. and H. M. Allen (Oxford, 1929), 26.

[8] PRO, DL29/637/10357.

[9] NYCRO, ZJX 3/2/110, 77, 120.

[10] Bean, *Estates*, p. 38.

same until 1539.[11] Neither in these properties, nor in the arable manors of the Middleham estate, are there any indications of substantial increases in rents before the end of the century.

The late fifteenth century offered little relief for landlords. A permanent contraction of land under the plough had occurred, which had a lasting effect on rents and income. Abandonment of arable also led to village contraction and desertion. As the bursar of Durham Priory noted in 1420, the abandonment of tillage and the desertion of settlements went hand in hand. The north-eastern lowlands contain a large number of deserted village sites, especially in the Vale of York and the Tees basin. In Northumberland 165 sites have been identified, in Durham at least 100, and in the North Riding 171.[12] Not all of these desertions can be attributed even to the later Middle Ages, let alone to the middle or late fifteenth century. Moreover, as is now well established, desertion was not a sudden, once-and-for-all migration: it was usually preceded by a long-drawn-out and agonizing contraction of the village and its economy. Such contraction was more characteristic of the region in the fifteenth century than out-and-out desertion.

Low Throston, near Hartlepool, seems to have been passing through such a period of contraction during the 1460s and 1470s, when many of its holdings were first in hand.[13] East Tanfield, as Professor Beresford has shown, suffered a sudden diminution in the number of its tenants between 1478 and 1484; but it was not finally abandoned until the following century.[14] Newsham-on-Tees provides perhaps the best documented example of one such shrinking village (Map 1). As the name implies, it was a relatively recent settlement, an outlier of the manor of Longnewton, sited on the band of heavy clays which

[11] Kershaw, *Bolton Priory Rentals*, p. xv. The evidence advanced above would suggest that the rising movement of rent between 1473 and 1538 discerned by Dr Kershaw was concentrated after 1500. Wright, *Derbyshire Gentry*, pp. 16–17, comes to the similar conclusion that recovery did not occur until the very end of the century.

[12] M. Beresford and J. G. Hurst, *Deserted Medieval Villages* (Cambridge, 1971), 35.

[13] D. Austin, 'Low Throston II: Excavations of a Deserted Medieval Hamlet, 1972', *Transactions of the Archaeological and Architectural Society of Durham and Northumberland*, NS, 4 (1978), 21.

[14] M. W. Beresford, 'The Lost Villages of Yorkshire, Part IV', *YAJ* 38 (1954), 282–3.

surfaces from place to place in that part of the river valley, and which is more suited to pastoral than to arable husbandry. In 1390/1 the rents from four free tenancies, seven bondholdings of twelve oxgangs each, cottages, a demesne of thirteen oxgangs, and the fishery below the village on the Tees, which had once been worth £17. 7s. 8d., produced £12. 13s. 4d. for the earl of Warwick. By 1420/1 it was let to farm for £10, suggesting that the process of desertion was well advanced. Yet it remained only a semi-deserted settlement; for even as late as 1608, besides the old mansion house, there were still three habitable farmsteads standing, and 36 of its 916 acres were under crops.[15]

A pattern of piecemeal and gradual desertion is to be found upstream in the parish of Croft on the other side of the river (see Map 1). In the fourteenth century there were six settlements in the parish: Stapleton, Croft, and Dalton on the river bank, Halnaby, Walmire, and Jolby away from the river. Halnaby and Walmire shrank considerably between 1301 and 1545. Halnaby, a sizeable settlement with twelve taxpayers in 1301, was Halnaby Grange in 1545, supporting five taxpayers. Walmire, only ever a small hamlet, had become two farms by the later date. The same evidence of tax returns suggests, however, that the riverside settlements suffered little contraction, and in the case of Dalton perhaps even grew. This pattern of local concentration of population into fewer and perhaps more favourably endowed settlements could perhaps have been the general experience.[16] Further south, for instance, some villages like Aldbrough St John and Carthorpe suffered large, long-lasting decays, while neighbours like West Tanfield, Wath, or Gilling were barely affected. West Tanfield seems to have maintained its prosperity at the expense of the satellite villages of Binsoe, East Tanfield, and Nosterfield, of which East Tanfield was ultimately deserted.[17]

[15] A. F. and P. M. Pallister, 'A Survey of the Deserted Medieval Village of Newsham', *Transactions of the Archaeological and Architectural Society of Durham and Northumberland* NS, 4, (1978), 7–21; PRO SC6/1303/11,12; DL29/637/10357. Nearby West Hartburn probably followed the same chronology of contraction and desertion (see L. Still and A. F. Pallister, 'The Excavation of One House Site in the Deserted Village of West Hartburn', *Arch. Ael.* 4th ser., 42 (1964), 187–206 and C. C. Dyer, 'Deserted Medieval Villages in the West Midlands', *Econ. HR*, 2nd ser., 35 (1982), 19–34).

[16] Pollard, 'Croft-on-Tees', pp. 18–22.

[17] Pollard, 'Agrarian Crisis', pp. 94–9; Beresford, 'Lost Villages', pp. 282–3.

The contraction and desertion of villages was accompanied by conversion to pasture. Berwick-on-Tees had become a pastoral 'grange' of the FitzHughs by the third decade of the fifteenth century.[18] South Cowton would seem to have been in an advanced stage of desertion when, in 1489, shortly after acquiring the manor from the lord of Middleham, Sir Richard Conyers evicted twenty inhabitants, pulled down the remaining four houses, enclosed the land, and converted 120 acres of arable to pasture (see Map 1).[19] The decline of the garbal tithes of Durham Priory provides another indication of change in land use. Woodham and Newhouse in Aycliffe parish both ceased to provide tithes in the 1420s. Ketton manor almost went the same way. It was not sown between 1456 and 1459, or again in 1465/6. But from 1466 the tithes were sold annually to a local farmer without a break.[20] There is other evidence that pastoral husbandry was becoming more important in the north-eastern lowlands. In south-east Northumberland almost all the arable land of the priory of Tynemouth was converted to pasture before the dissolution. At Billingham, where there had been tension created by the competing demands of animal and arable husbandry, stinting was intensified after 1470. In 1476 the villagers of Croft and Dalton agreed to partition Entercommon, the waste lying between their fields, so as to effect a more equitable use of rough pasture. Even on the higher ground pressure was increasing, for in 1458 the pasture of Lartington moor was limited to 200 beasts and allocated to just six users.[21]

In the circumstances it might have been expected that pastoral husbandry would compensate for the general sluggishness of arable farming in the later part of the century, especially where landlords held extensive estates on the higher ground to

---

[18] At farm to Christopher Boynton of nearby Acklam for much of the early century, in the later years of William, Lord FitzHugh's life Berwick was retained in hand for stock-rearing. NYCRO zjx/3/2/75,80,83,111; Essex RO D/DC/M108.

[19] I. S. Leadham, 'The Inquisition of 1517', TRHS, NS 6 (1892), 218–9 and below p. 203.

[20] Lomas, 'Durham Cathedral Priory', p. 153.

[21] Lomas, 'Land and People', pp. 252–4; NYCRO, zQH/1, fo. 153, zPS/1/12; I am grateful to Dr Tuck for permission to cite the evidence of Tynemouth from an early draft of his contribution, the forthcoming vol. 4 of the Agrarian History of England and Wales. See also Dyer, Lords and Peasants, pp. 323–31, for a general shift towards pastoral farming in the west midlands.

the west of the region. Some rents did indeed rise after 1460. In April 1465 the council of Richard Neville, earl of Warwick secured an agreement with the tenants of the vaccaries in Arkengarthdale that they would pay gressums totalling £35. 6s. 8d. for their next seven-year leases—an increase of £2 p.a. on the gressums levied in 1436.[22] Rents were rising too (if only marginally) on the granges and pastoral farms of Fountains Abbey between 1456/7 and the last decade of the century.[23] It seems however that really significant increases did not take place until the very end of the century and the early decades of the next. Mickleton rents show no surge before 1500 to match that of the 1420s. The net rent due from Middleton-in-Teesdale in 1488/9, at £41, like the rent of Mickleton, was on a par with the rent due in 1420/1. Substantial increases on the duchy of Lancaster Pennine estates, including the Middleham estate after 1485, were, as Dr Blanchard has pointed out, the result of the work of commissioners of improvement active in 1497 and 1505/6.[24] The evidence is scanty, but it would appear that in pastoral farming the substantial and sustained rise in profitability noticeable by 1530 did not take place until after 1500.

Nevertheless, the market for pastoral products was sufficiently buoyant to tempt lords from time to time to retain one or two parcels of land in hand and to experiment with stock-raising. Falling population and demand, as well as the rising cost of labour, had forced all lay magnates to abandon arable demesne production by the beginning of the fifteenth century. At least one religious house, Durham Priory, maintained an arable home farm throughout the century: Elvet Hall, hard by the monastery. But the operation at Elvet was exceptional, its

---

[22] PRO, sc6/1085/20. These increments coincide with the recovery from a mid-century slump in the pastoral economy of north-west Derbyshire (*The Duchy of Lancaster Estates in Derbyshire, 1485–1540*, ed. I. S. W. Blanchard, Derbys. Arch. Soc., RS (for 1969), p. 11.

[23] Michelmore, *Fountains Abbey Lease Book* pp. xxxviii–xxxix.

[24] Dur. RO D/St/34, 1 Richard III; DL29/637/10357; I. S. W. Blanchard, 'Population Change', pp. 433–4. Dr Blanchard has suggested that sustained recovery in north-west Derbyshire dating from 1475 was not reflected in rent increases until after 1495 because of administrative inefficiency (*Duchy of Lancaster Estates*, pp. 11–12). Either all north-west Yorkshire landowners were equally inefficient, or the sustained recovery itself was delayed in Derbyshire as well as Yorkshire.

purpose being the supply of the monastic household.[25] Ecclesiastical lords were more willing to exploit demesne, forest, and park as grazing land. Durham Priory maintained stock farms at Muggleswick, Beaurepaire, and Sacristonheugh, and a sheep farm at Le Holme at the mouth of the Tees.[26] Durham could not compete as a pastoralist with Fountains Abbey, which still retained substantial direct control over its numerous granges, especially in Craven and Nidderdale. Fountains in the fifteenth century was as much a cattle-rearing (especially dairy-producing) as a sheep-rearing establishment. Although many granges were in the hands of tenants rather than keepers, the tenants too operated according to criteria set down by the monks, and under their careful supervision.[27]

The bishops of Durham exploited their parks at Auckland, Evenwood, Bishop Middleham, Stockton, and Wolsingham for raising both sheep and cattle. The scale and character seems to have depended on the interests of individual bishops. Langley ran a stud for horses: in 1430/1 he had one stallion standing for twenty mares, who gave birth to thirty-nine foals.[28] Booth and Dudley, however, built up substantial herds of cattle and flocks of sheep. By the final years of his pontificate Booth had over a thousand cattle and a similar number of sheep in stock. The number of fleeces sold each year rose from 692 in 1469 to 900 in 1474. Dudley in his turn had 322 head of cattle and 828 sheep on his farms by 1480. Their operations were not entirely directed towards the market. The instaurer in charge needed to be funded by the receiver-general, and much of the produce was supplied to the bishop's household. In the summer quarter of 1459, for instance, fifty beasts were consumed at Stockton, Auckland, and Durham. In 1474 and 1475, when Booth's royal duties as Chancellor and councillor took him to Westminster, large numbers of stock were driven up to the capital. Forty steers were taken in April, and 120 sheep in July 1474. In the summer of

---

[25] Lomas, 'Northern Farm', pp. 26–53. Pittington continued to be held in hand until 1456. It would seem that the crisis of 1438–40, after which income dropped dramatically, finally decided its fate. (See Lomas, 'Durham Cathedral Priory', p. 124; idem, 'The Priory of Durham and its Demesnes in the Fourteenth and Fifteenth Centuries', Econ. HR 2nd ser., 31 (1978), 344, 352).

[26] Dobson, Durham Priory, p. 277.

[27] Michelmore, Fountains Abbey Lease Book, pp. xvi–xxxvii; l–lx.

[28] Durham, Church Commission, Bishopric Estates, 190307.

1475, when Booth served on the council ruling the kingdom during Edward IV's absence in France, no fewer than 247 oxen were driven up, at a cost in drovers' wages alone of £11. 13s. 1½d.[29]

In the early fifteenth century, especially between 1410 and 1430, when demand for dairy products and meat would appear to have been particularly buoyant, even lay lords were drawn into stock-raising. Henry, Lord FitzHugh took into hand at first two, and subsequently three of his vaccaries in Lunedale, in which he established a herd of three bulls and ninety cows. It took time to build up such a herd and to generate income. In 1417/18 the venture was still not in profit, for, with sales producing only £4. 6s. 6d. against costs of £7. 8s. 2d. and a foregone rent of £15. 10s., the loss on the year's trading was £8. 16s. 8d. In the following year, however, twenty-five steers were ready for market, and fetched £12. 12s. 3d. This and £2. 8s. from the sale of milk from forty-six cows put him into profit.[30] Unfortunately there is insufficient further evidence from which to judge the long-term profitability of the venture. It would seem, however, that, before his death in 1425, FitzHugh had felt sufficiently confident of the future to extend his operation to the lower valley at Berwick-on-Tees, whither cattle were being transferred in 1424.[31]

After his death, FitzHugh's widow quickly reverted to leasing all these lands. Nevertheless her son William re-established the stock farm at Berwick twenty years later. By Michaelmas 1450 he had a flock of nearly 1,600 sheep there; 686 lambs were born and 1,261 fleeces were shorn in 1451. In addition to the sheep, 6 bulls and 102 cows were kept at Berwick. Again the cost was high. Fees and wages alone came to £11. 7s. 6d. in this one year, and the rent foregone for the lease of the manor was £21. 13s. 4d. Against these costs, recorded sales only brought in £24. 8s. 7d.[32] Ultimately this enterprise too was wound up after its initiator's death in October 1452: the stock, by then run down to 746 sheep and 189 head of cattle, was sold for £108. 10s. by his executors.[33]

---

[29] Durham, Church Commission, 190108, 190109, 190110, 190256, 190257, 190259 (Instaurers' accounts, 1469–70, 1473–4, 1474–5, June–Sept. 1459, 1476–9, 1479–80).

[30] NYCRO, zjx 3/2/50, 62 (Instaurers' accounts, 1411–12 and 1418–19), Dur.RO d/St/e3/1/1/1417–18.   [31] NYCRO, zjx 3/2/75.

[32] Ibid. 3/2/111. The fleeces, sheepskins, and woolfells were delivered to the steward of the household at Ravensworth, who sold an unspecified number for £1. 8s. 11d. (ibid. 3/2/109).   [33] Ibid. 3/2/112.

Berwick was once more let to farm in 1453; the history of its pastoral farming suggests that its profitability was at best only marginal.

Later Lords FitzHugh do not seem to have imitated their predecessors. In 1467, however, Richard Neville, earl of Warwick, reviving his father's practice, took six parks and closes of his lordship of Middleham in hand in which to launch a stock farm. His instaurer's account for 1468/9 records the purchase of 324 head of cattle and over 1,800 sheep at a cost of £771. 16s. 7d., with funds transferred by the receivers of Sheriff Hutton, Middleham, and the Lovell lands in several instalments since 25 April 1467. By Michaelmas 1469 the enterprise had not been operational long enough to produce for sale any more than sixty-six stones of wool, the skins of a handful of dead sheep, and five oxen. Some other produce, including store cattle, was supplied to the households at Sheriff Hutton and Middleham and in London.[34] The enterprise needed time to prove itself, and this was denied to Warwick by his death in 1471. His successor, however, continued to maintain some stock, for the herbage of the parks of Sunscue, Caplebank, Woodhall, and Wanlass were still retained in hand by Richard of Gloucester in 1473/4 for the keeping of the store animals which provisioned his household. The instaurer delivered beasts worth nearly £75 to Pontefract, Middleham, and Barnard Castle in April and October 1474.[35]

Lay lords only sporadically committed themselves to stock-rearing, and, like the bishops of Durham and the priory, were concerned as much with household provision as profit. Like arable demesnes, vaccaries and the pasture of parks were normally leased. The farmers were both gentry and richer tenants. Christopher Boynton of Acklam took Berwick-on-Tees between 1425 and 1450.[36] Other prominent gentlemen took leases of vaccaries from the Middleham Estate. The vaccary of Sleight-

[34] Durham, Church Commission, Bishopric Estates, 190316. This is an undated account of the earl's instaurer Richard Darley which can be dated from internal evidence to 8–9 Edward IV. As part of his revenue Darley received the rents of the parks of Widdale, Sleddale, and Radale (£14 p.a.), in which, it was recorded, Richard, lately earl of Salisbury, had kept 700 head of cattle.

[35] PRO, DL29/648/10485. See Coles, 'Middleham', p. 245. The earl of Northumberland also kept cattle in Hulne Park at Alnwick and at Topcliffe (Bean, *Estates*, p. 14).

[36] Essex RO, D/DC/M108; NYCRO, ZJX 3/2/75, 83, 85.

holme within the manor of Bowes was taken by successive heads of the Burgh family of Brough Hall, Catterick between 1437 and 1474. In 1437/8 John Clervaux of Croft took Holgate in New Forest (Swaledale) and West Hope. His son and heir, Richard, took a part share in a neighbouring vaccary in Arkengarthdale. Roger Aske of Aske, Thomas Fulthorpe, William Frank, and Ralph FitzRandolph were other Richmondshire gentry who farmed Middleham vaccaries. John Stockdale, Richard, earl of Salisbury's attorney at the Exchequer, was a partner with William Burgh at Sleightholme, and later took Butterset in Wensleydale. Other servants and retainers of the lords of Middleham took leases of parks and whole manors. Sir John Conyers of Hornby was granted Skale Park, Kettlewell and the demesne of Rand, near Crakehall, rent-free by Richard Neville, earl of Warwick. He also farmed the sheep-walk of Crakehallcote for £2. 13s. 4d. in 1465/6. At the same time James Metcalfe of Nappa took a number of properties in Wensleydale, including Radale park. Richard Conyers, brother of Sir John and receiver of the lordship, was both reeve and farmer of outlying Moulton. And Richard Pigot, councillor to both Warwick and Gloucester, took a twenty-year lease in 1462 of the manor of Deighton, the capital messuage of South Cowton, a messuage and four bovates in Brompton, and one tenement in Great Smeaton for £24 p.a., being allowed a reduction of about £6 in lieu of fees.[37]

It is not easy to determine whether these well-born and well-connected farmers stocked and sowed their farms. Some, particularly lessees of whole manors, are likely to have sublet, as did Richard Pigot. On 28 July 1464 he contracted with Thomas Gales and Miles Bowes for them to take for sixteen years and with responsibility for maintenance the four 'fyre' houses, three of which had lathes, and one cottage, all occupied by sitting tenants, as well as all the garths in Deighton and one half of the moor at its south end. Pigot himself retained the chief place, the main meadow belonging to it, and the other half of the moor. It looks as if Pigot intended to maintain his own stock farm on the unlet land.[38] Other farmers are known to have maintained their own home farms. John Clervaux who died in

[37] PRO, SC6/1058/18,20; DL29/648/10485.   [38] NYCRO, ZFW, MIC 1160.

1443 left at least forty-five head of cattle (on his rented vaccaries?) and standing wheat at Croft. In 1478 Richard Clervaux,
his son, had land under the plough and kept cattle in an area
known as Stokemire. William Burgh too, farmer of Sleightholme, maintained a grange for his own use at Brough.[39]

Other gentlemen farmers are revealed by their wills. Two
busy servants of Richard Neville, earl of Salisbury also had time
to exploit their own lands. Thomas Witham of Cornburgh
remembered his 'instaurator', William Buttree, in his will of
1475. Robert Constable of Bossall left his working capital (eight
oxen, a plough, and a wain) to his son in 1454. Henry Eure of Old
Malton was left by his mother the same equipment of oxen,
plough, and wain in 1467: on his own death in 1476 he left to his
widow sixteen oxen, two ploughs, and two wains. Edmund
Thwaites of Lund (probate 1500) and Nicholas Conyers of
Stokesley (probate 1496) remembered their servants in husbandry: ploughmen, shepherds, cowherds, and swineherds.
Others left stock to their heirs. Alice, widow of John Sotehill of
Everingham (probate 1500) disposed of 220 ewes and 23 head of
cattle; Nicholas Robinson of Stokesley (probate 1450) bequeathed 120 ewes, 44 steers, milk cows and calves, and 10
horses.[40] It seems likely therefore that the well-born farmers of
vaccaries and parks took the leases because they intended to
work them.

One can be more confident that the less substantial men
(yeomen and richer husbandmen), who took the majority of
farms, worked them themselves. At Mickleton the vaccaries
were all taken throughout the century by local tenants; members of the families of Arrowsmith, Bales, Dent, Brownlees,

[39] Pollard, 'Richard Clervaux', pp. 156–7; idem, 'The Burghs of Brough Hall,
ca 1270–1574', *NYCROJ*, 6, (1978), 10.
[40] BI, Probate Register 5, fo. 170ᵛ: *Test. Ebor.*, ii. 175, 285; iii. 223, 266, 268;
iv. 129, 177, 186. In 1467–8 Thomas Witham sold 20 head of cattle and 200 sheep
to Thomas Lepton, receiver of Sheriff Hutton, for £5. 15s., which were driven to
Middleham to help stock Warwick's new farm there (Durham, Church Commission, Bishopric Estate, 190316). Gentlemen farmers were not uncommon in
15th-cent. England (see C. C. Dyer, 'A Small Landowner in the Fifteenth
Century', *Midland History*, 3 (1972), 1–14; idem, *Warwickshire Farming,
1349–c.1529*, Dugdale Society Occasional Paper 27 (Oxford, 1981), 18–22;
Wright, *Derbyshire Gentry*, pp. 19–20; C. Carpenter, 'The Fifteenth-Century
English Gentry and their Estates', in M. Jones, ed., *Gentry and Lesser Nobility in
Later Medieval Europe* (Gloucester, 1986), 47–9.

Longstaffe, Raine, and Withes. The herbage of the parks was frequently taken by a syndicate, as in 1432, when John and William Raine, John Edward, and John Arrowsmith took West Park at Thringarth for three years. Such tenants can be identified as local stockmen. In 1451, for instance, William Dent, who had taken the lease of Arnegilhouse eight years earlier, was presented at the manorial court for illegally pasturing thirty cattle, sixty lambs, and one mare in the forest of Lune.[41] On the Middleham estate, where gentlemen farmers were more frequent, lesser men occasionally took leases. The vaccary of Flenshope for example, which had been in the hands of Ralph FitzRandolph of Spennythorne, was taken in 1461 by a partnership of Thomas Robinson, Richard Hanley, and (the aptly named) John Yeoman.[42] On the priory of Durham estates, too, farmers of manors and tithes tended to be lesser men and officials of the priory itself. Although William Claxton (steward, 1465–96) took the farm of the tithes of Ferry for most of his period of office, and John Redman, bailiff of Auckland and of the family of Harewood, was lessee of the tithes of Chilton for a while, most farmers were of lesser gentry or yeoman status. In 1471/2, for instance, the farmers of the tithes of Aycliffe parish were as follows: Christopher Harrison and John Thomson at Aycliffe, James Bland at Brafferton, Thomas Popley at Preston, John Wright at Rickness, Thomas Robinson at Heworth, William Smith at Nunstainton, and Roger Cotesferth at Newton Ketton.[43] The Denom brothers, John and Thomas, descendants of a freed serf of Billingham, were established in the late fifteenth century at Cotesmore;[44] Thomas Strangways, a distant kinsman of Strangways of West Harlsey, and son of the one-time parker of Stanhope, was the lessee of Ketton and its tithes from 1432.[45]

[41] Dur. RO, D/St/E3/1/3/13 May 1432, 23 Nov. 1451.

[42] PRO, SC6/1085/20.

[43] Durham, Dean and Chapter, Bursar Account, 1471/2.

[44] The Denoms farmed Cotesmore, north of Darlington, from 1457/58 until 1481/2, when Richard Taylor replaced John Denom. A John Denom paid £40 for his manumission in 1386–7. A Richard Denom was collector of the Neville rent in Darlington when Ralph, 3rd earl of Westmorland died in 1497 (Durham, Dean and Chapter, Bursar Accounts 1457/8 to 1481/2 passim; Lomas, 'Durham Cathedral Priory', p. 62; WAM 6052).

[45] Durham, Dean and Chapter, Bursar Accounts 1456/7 to 1492/3. Lomas, 'Demesnes', pp. 347–8.

Yeomen farmers are to be found as lessees of arable demesnes. Leeming, a FitzHugh manor, was normally farmed to such men as Simon Milne and Thomas Robinson, who took the lease there for six years at £2. 13s. 4d. p.a. in 1437. In 1439/40 John Culling was farmer of West Applegarth in Swaledale.[46] A good example of a yeoman family is provided by the Hobsons of Cleasby. Henry Hobson was farmer of the demesne until the fourth decade of the fifteenth century, when he was succeeded, before 1439, by John, who in turn became joint tenant with John jun., who was still farmer in 1484. As part of their tenancy they were required to allow a room in the manor house to be used for the meetings of the twice-yearly manorial court (for which Lord FitzHugh bore the cost of house repairs). John jun. was bailiff of the court in the 1450s. Hobsons were still settled in the district in the early sixteenth century, as the subsidy returns of 1522 and 1545 show, but by then they had moved to Stapleton.[47]

The Hobsons were perhaps typical of the prosperous working farmers, yeomen, who dominated lowland villages late in the fifteenth century; men who held and worked sixty acres or more, and customarily served as local officials. In the neighbouring villages of Stapleton and Jolby, Robert Bellamy and Thomas Hipper held over ninety and sixty-four acres respectively. Bellamy, witnessing a deed in 1471, even gave himself the status of yeoman.[48] We might count in that number John Randson of Burntofts, Durham, whose possession of eighty acres was confirmed by Sir Robert Claxton of Horden in 1482;[49] and include the leading tenants of nearby Cowpen Bewley at the end of the century, Robert Clifton, Robert Sheraton, and William White, who paid rents of £3–£5 for conglomerate holdings containing up to four messuages, one or two cottages, bondland, saltings, and parcels of meadow totalling seventy-five acres and more. Sheraton and White, the most substantial tenants in their village in 1495, were jurors of the manorial court, and alternated

---

[46] Essex RO, D/DC/M108. A William Culling had been farmer of nearby Thorpe-under-Stone in 1424–5 (NYCRO ZJX 3/2/75).

[47] NYCRO, ZJX 3/2/3 passim; ZHQ/1, fo. 147; PRO E179/212/102, 181. The Hobsons had moved from Cleasby by 1508, when they no longer owed suit of court. They do not appear in the subsidy return of 1524 or 1544 under Cleasby.

[48] NYCRO, ZHQ/1, fos. 147, 158d. See Pollard, 'Richard Clervaux', pp. 50, 159.   [49] DRO, D/X/209/2,1.

as reeves in the last decade of the century.[50] Not even Sheraton or White, however, could compete with Randolph Dixson in Billingham two miles away. The total rent for his holdings in 1503, which included the capital messuage, was ten guineas, a ninth of the total expected rent from the village. A farmer on a large scale, in 1508 Dixson paid most of his rent in kind; nine quarters of wheat and twenty-five quarters of barley.[51]

Men like Dixson were the principal beneficiaries of lower rents and an abundance of vacant arable land. Was the fifteenth century therefore more generally a golden age for the north-eastern tenantry? Famine and grain shortage in 1438–9, recurring in 1481–2, as well as pestilence in the 1430s, returning in the late 1470s, should caution us against painting too rosy a picture of the standard of living of fifteenth-century husbandmen. The major crises were crises for all; the poorer, after all, stood to suffer more than the richer. But conditions, especially after 1440, were in some respects better for tenants than they had been in the fourteenth century, or were to be later in the sixteenth century. Settlement contracted, and, it has been suggested, concentrated on the better and more productive land.

One consequence of contraction was that landlords had difficulty in attracting tenants. Hence they adopted the practice of offering rewards, or rent rebates, to those willing to take up holdings that would otherwise have remained vacant, even for short periods. At Cleasby, this practice was followed throughout the 1440s. In 1441, for instance, Henry Richardson took a tenement normally farmed at £2. 19s. 4d. after securing a rebate of 6s. 8d. p.a. for three years. In 1444 he renewed the lease for a further three years with an increased rebate of 13s. p.a. Some properties could only be let after repairs had been completed at the landlord's expense. In 1439 a messuage and four bovates of land called Micklehouse, worth £2. 13s. 4d. p.a., were in hand for want of a tenant. Ten shillings were spent on repairs, but the

---

[50] Lomas, 'Land and People', pp. 157, 161–6, 179, 224, 229–30; App. pp. ix–x, xxi, xxvi, xxviii, lxix.
[51] P. W. Hall, 'Tenure and Tenants: Billingham 1495–1523' (unpublished CNAA MA thesis, Teesside Polytechnic, 1985), 45–7. Other Billingham tenants on the scale of the leading tenants of Cowpen Bewley were Robert Walsh, John Wearmouth, and William Jekill. Wearmouth and Jekill were prominent tenants throughout the 15th cent. (ibid. 47–53).

property was still untenanted. In 1442/3, William Swyndale would only take up a tenancy in Clowbeck after the lord had agreed an allowance of 13s. 4d. for the complete renovation of the property. Other tenements, such as Bakehouse Place, which for a number of years remained empty, could only be let after a permanent reduction of rent—in this case from 12s. 9d. to 8s.[52]

Short-term leases such as those found at Cleasby and Clowbeck in the middle decades of the century were the norm for the estates of Durham Priory. As has been convincingly shown, by 1430 leases for life on the priory estates had been completely replaced by leases mostly for three or six years. In mid-fifteenth-century there was a high turnover of tenants in certain arable manors. It was clearly in the interests of the tenants to restrict the length of their leases. Although it has been shown that these short tenancies were frequently renewed (indeed the land seems to have stayed in the same hands for longer on the priory estates after the development of short leases) such a practice gave tenants the important option of mobility.[53] Such mobility is revealed elsewhere in the changing names of tenants. The body of tenants at Coverham was almost completely changed in one generation between 1418/19 and 1442/4, at which later date there was practically nobody carrying the same family name as twenty-five years earlier.[54] There was a similar change in the tenants of Cleasby and Clowbeck. Of a dozen known tenants in 1453, only five were still tenants in 1472, and but three—Henry Richardson and the brothers John and William Hobson—in 1485. By 1508 there were none carrying the same family names as the tenants of 1453.[55] Likewise at Croft the names of none of the tenants listed in a deed of 1465 are to be found in the

---

[52] Essex RO, D/DL/M108; NYCRO, ZJX 3/2/98, 100, 102. In the 1440s schedules were attached to the Cleasby and Clowbeck rent collectors' accounts detailing these agreements. See also the contemporary schedule of repairs for Northallertonshire tenements of the bishop of Durham, Durh. 20/129/1. At Cleasby in December 1453, however, five tenants were presented to the manorial court for allowing their tenements to fall into disrepair. This may represent a reversal of policy by Henry, Lord FitzHugh, who succeeded his father in 1452. (ZJX 3/1/53).

[53] R. A. Lomas, 'Developments in Land Tenure on the Prior of Durham's Estate in the Later Middle Ages', NH 13 (1973), 37–40; idem, 'Demesnes', p. 348; T. Lomas, 'South-East Durham', pp. 311–14.

[54] Pollard and Ashcroft, 'Coverham', pp. 33–42.

[55] NYCRO, ZJX/3/1/53, 56, 63; Dur. RO, D/St/34, court rolls, Cleasby, 1485 and 1508.

Henrician subsidy returns of 1522 and 1545. Dr Kershaw has demonstrated a similar movement of population on the Craven, Malhamdale, and Airedale manors of Bolton Priory between 1473 and 1539.[56] In the fifteenth century many customary tenants do not seem to have developed, or sustained, a familial interest in their landholdings. Sons seem neither to have needed nor to have wished to wait for the deaths of their fathers before establishing their own households, so plentiful was the supply of vacant holdings in the region.

There were, however, exceptions to this general trend. In the predominantly pastoral villages upstream in Teesdale, fifteenth-century tenurial structure seems to have been more settled. Successive tenants with the same surnames—Raine, Dent, Longstaffe, Brownlees, Bales, Edward, Arrowsmith, and Oxenherd—are to be found taking leases of vaccaries, tenancies at will, and herbage, as well as being presented for trespasses in the forest and woods throughout the century. The terms of leases still tended to be short—but they tended to be kept within the family for succeeding generations. Since, during the first half of the century at least, when documentation is plentiful, most of these leases carried increments, it is to be assumed that there was competition.[57] Such competition implies a buoyant demand for their products and an incentive for dalesmen to stay put.

Circumstances in both vale and dale, albeit in different ways, seem to have favoured tenants. In vale the abundant supply of arable land forced down rents, and enabled them to retain a higher proportion of their output. In the later decades of the century the majority of the tenants of the priory of Durham in the parish of Billingham were selling surplus grain to the monastery. For several, it has been shown, income from sales to this market alone more than paid for the rent.[58] In so far as surpluses such as these led to a rise in the standard of living it is also to be expected that the demand for the products of the dalesman

[56] Pollard, 'Croft-on-Tees', pp. 27–38; Kershaw, *Bolton Priory Rentals*, pp. xvii–xviii.

[57] Dur. RO, D/St/3/1/3 and 4; cf. the farmers of Durham Priory manors, who similarly took a succession of short leases (Lomas, 'Demesnes', p. 348).

[58] Lomas, 'South-East Durham', pp. 317–26, esp. 320–1. But see the suggestion of R. A. Lomas that the 'sales' were fictitious and were a device to account for payments in kind (Lomas, 'Demesnes', p. 344).

—beef, lamb, cheese, and butter—was stimulated. It is not possible to comment on the circumstances of the landless, because our records do not concern them; but it would seem that, years of scarcity and pestilence apart, the second half of the fifteenth century was a time of greater comfort for the husbandmen and graziers of north-eastern England.

This conclusion would seem to be borne out by the evidence of a bundle of wills and inventories proved by the prior of Durham in four parishes in northern Yorkshire where he held peculiar jurisdiction. The inventories of thirteen villagers, including a smith, a butcher and at least three husbandmen from Northallerton, Brompton, Kirby Sigston, and West Rounton, who died between 1486 and 1498, provide a rare glimpse of the standard of living enjoyed by a generation of countrymen whose working lives spanned the second half of the century. Several had houses containing a hall, a kitchen, and a chamber, as well as a barn. The average evaluation of their movable goods was just under £7—the highest being £13. 4s. 4d. All those with full, detailed inventories owned some animals, including the smith, John Stevenson of Northallerton. William Fox, 'husbandman' of Brompton, had eighteen head of cattle, twenty sheep, and two pigs. Several, but not all, had grain in the barn or in the field, depending on the date of probate. Fox's grain was assessed as being worth £3. Six owned ploughs and wains—the sure sign of husbandry. Apart from the expected complement of trestles, benches, stools, cooking utensils, pots, and pans, two possessed hawlings (wall hangings), five owned one or more pieces of pewter (Fox, twenty), and four had mash vats for brewing. At least two of the group, one of whom was John Stevenson the smith, possessed linen sheets; and two died owing wages to servants. The only one of the twelve who would appear to have been no more than a cottager was Thomas Arkendale, whose goods were the lowest valued, at £1. 9s. 4d. He possessed neither plough nor wain, but did have two quarters of wheat and rye, four bushels of barley, a load of hay, an ox, a calf, and four sheep. In addition he owned a spinning-wheel—the only one to do so—as well as a collection of flax and wool-combs and seven pounds of wool.[59]

[59] Durham, Dean and Chapter, Locellus VIII/1, 3, 4, 6, 7, 8, 9, 13, 14, 17, 18, 19, 20.

The comparative prosperity of yeomen, husbandmen, and stockmen in the later fifteenth century could not however generate sufficient aggregate demand to compensate for the general sluggishness of the agrarian sector of the region's economy. It certainly was insufficient to stimulate the industrial and commercial sectors, which were at the same time passing through renewed and severe recession. While the second half of the fifteenth century was generally a period of respite and partial recovery in the countryside, in the towns it was one of deepening depression. The most obvious victim of late fifteenth century commercial and industrial slump was the city of York. In the later fourteenth century York had boomed. Partly because of the growth of its cloth manufacturing, partly because of a rise in disposable incomes locally, and partly because of an expansion of its overseas market, York had enjoyed unprecedented prosperity in the reign of Richard II. At the end of the fourteenth century York had been an independent international commercial centre.[60]

The tide had begun to turn in the early fifteenth century; but after 1440 serious depression set in. It is reasonable to suppose that York suffered first as a result of the general contraction of the agrarian economy; but the major causes of its decline were the failure of its cloth manufacturing, the loss of overseas trade, and, possibly, a shortage of trading capital. The new clothing towns of the West Riding—Bradford, Halifax, and Leeds— emerged as rivals of York in the 1460s; after 1475 they superseded the city as the major producers of woollens in Yorkshire.[61] At the same time the overseas trade of the city shrank. Between the end of the fourteenth century and the beginning of the sixteenth the value of annual imports and exports of York merchants through Hull, as measured by customs records, fell from £10,000 to £2,500. The total value of Hull's imports and exports fell by 58 per cent between 1404–9 and 1478–82.[62] The ports were cut down by a double-edged sword: not only was east-coast trade concentrating in London at the expense of other

---

[60] Bartlett, 'Expansion and Decline of York', pp. 25–7; Miller, 'Medieval York', pp. 84–5, 88–9.

[61] Heaton, *Woollen and Worsted Industries*, pp. 73–5.

[62] Bartlett, 'Expansion and Decline of York', p. 28; Miller, 'Medieval York', p. 105.

ports, but also the Hansards were ousting English merchants from the carrying trade to the Baltic.[63] The problems faced by York merchants were further exacerbated by the increasing difficulty they found in financing large-scale trading ventures, leaving them vulnerable to their more soundly backed London rivals.[64]

All the adverse trends facing York coalesced and came to a head in the 1470s. Between 1468 and 1474 English merchants fought and lost a war to recover access to the Baltic. Notwithstanding the terms of the Treaty of Utrecht, the English were excluded. One effect was to concentrate English overseas trading in one market—the Netherlands—where, by their proximity, London merchants enjoyed a massive advantage over their east-coast rivals. Londoners trading in the Netherlands were determined to secure the monopoly of the English-borne trade through a single, London-dominated company of merchant adventurers. Faced by the prospect of exclusion, York merchants turned desperately to the Crown for protection. They petitioned against the behaviour of John Pickering, the governor of the English merchant community in the Netherlands, who, they claimed, had discriminated against northerners. The establishment of two governors was requested, one specifically for the ports north of the Trent. Edward IV responded only with a royal proclamation exhorting fair play; and the Londoners were able to tighten their grip.[65]

The defeat of the York merchants in the 1470s may also have had a bearing on the demise of the city's cloth-manufacturing industry. Several reasons have been advanced for this: the high overheads created by an elaborate civic structure, and the lower labour costs of rural production in particular.[66] It has rarely been noted, however, that York City was not the only manufacturing centre to suffer in the face of West Riding competition. Ulnage returns for 1394–8 show that cloth production in north-west Yorkshire far outstripped the West Riding in the late fourteenth

[63] Bolton, *Medieval English Economy*, pp. 308–19.

[64] J. I. Kermode, 'Merchants, Overseas Trade and Urban Decline', pp. 62–71, esp. 70.

[65] Bolton, *Medieval English Economy*, pp. 309–19; Miller, 'Medieval York', pp. 103–6.

[66] D. M. Palliser, 'A Crisis in English Towns? The Case of York, 1460–1640', *NH* 14 (1978), 115–17.

century. The advantages of lower costs enjoyed over York by the West Riding were advantages also enjoyed by north-west Yorkshire. Yet by 1468 the West Riding produced more cloth than north Yorkshire, and by 1478 had surpassed York.[67] The decline and waste of fulling mills in the district confirms the evidence of ulnage payments. By 1478 the mills of Mickleton, Thoralby, Crakehall, and Aysgarth were closed. Darlington mill was to follow the same way in 1500; Middleham in 1507; and Barnard Castle mill, the rent reduced from £2. 0s. 0d. to 10s. in 1488/9, was apparently set on the same course.[68] Ripon in 1540 presented a sorry sight to John Leland, who remarked that

there hath been hard on the farther ripe of Skell a great number of tainters for woollen cloth wont to be made in the town of Ripon: but now idleness is sore increased in the town, and cloth making almost decayed.[69]

The one advantage which the West Riding enjoyed over the north-west was that it was not as far away from London. London merchants played a vital part in the development of West Riding clothing in the sixteenth century. It seems likely, although the evidence for this is scanty, that even in the later fifteenth century, in their competition with York merchants for control of English cloth exports, they were already buying in Halifax and Bradford, and thereby undercutting not only York but also the more northerly Yorkshire districts.[70] York's deepening

[67] Heaton, *Woollen and Worsted Industries*, pp. 70, 73–5.

[68] Essex RO, D/DL/M108; Coles, 'Middleham', p. 241; Sunderland, *Tudor Darlington*, i. 70.

[69] Leland, *Itinerary* p. 82. Ripon had been the wealthiest town in the West Riding in 1379 (Dobson, 'Yorkshire Towns', pp. 7 n. 15; 10 n. 21). At Leeds, on the other hand, a new fulling mill was built in 1455–6 and nine new tenters appeared along the river bank by 1466. *The Manor and Borough of Leeds, 1425–1662*, ed. J. W. Kirby, Publications of the Thoresby Society, lvii (Leeds, 1983 for 1981), p. lx.

[70] Heaton, *Woollen and Worsted Industries*, pp. 146–9; Kermode, 'Merchants, Overseas Trade and Urban Decline', pp. 70–1; Bartlett, 'Expansion and Decline of York', p. 38. York's obsession with clearing the Ouse waterway network from obstruction, especially fishgarths, should be seen in the context of this crisis, York's response, and the city's attempt to reassume its role as a collection and transit centre for Yorkshire. In 1477, in a petition to the Crown as duke of Lancaster to demolish Gowdallgarth on the Aire at Snaith (blocking the river route from Leeds to York) the city stressed that the garth 'so instrates the same river that all your lige people in the same [York] passyng and repassyng with thare shippes and botes ben gretely lettyd and stoppet'. *YCR* i. 230. See also Kermode, 'Merchants, Overseas Trade and Urban Decline', p. 72.

economic crisis in the 1470s and 1480s was, in part at least, the result of defeat at the hands of London in the competition for a share in the much reduced North Sea trade remaining in English hands. During the fifteenth century York, sadly, was reduced from a great international trading city to little more than a large provincial market town.

York was not the only north-eastern town to face serious economic decline in the fifteenth century. Newcastle, whose records unfortunately are largely missing, was once believed to have escaped. However, it has been shown recently that the value of the property held by University College, Oxford in the city fell steadily in the second half of the century, and the rents were exceptionally difficult to collect between 1466 and 1482. Moreover Newcastle faced a serious challenge from its new neighbour of North Shields, whose rights it was required to accept in 1463.[71] Scarborough too, which had briefly prospered as a deep-sea fishing port in the early fifteenth century, no longer sent fleets to Icelandic waters. It, like York, seems also to have suffered from the voracious appetite of Londoners: for by the end of the century deep-sea fishing was concentrated in the East Anglian ports, whose merchants had close financing and marketing ties with the capital.[72]

The only relieving feature to this picture of commercial and industrial decay seems to have been a revival in mining. Lead-mining during the fifteenth century was sporadic, probably, as Dr Blanchard has shown, because prices collapsed both locally and in London between 1406 and 1457. The Weardale mines of the bishop of Durham, for which the fullest evidence survives, although they were not commercially viable, continued to be exploited to meet household and episcopal needs.[73] Exports

[71] Butcher, 'Late Medieval Newcastle', pp. 67–77; Craster, *Tynemouth*, pp. 289–90; Welford, *Newcastle and Gateshead*, pp. 316–18, 347–8. In the 16th cent. conflict between the two flared again.

[72] Heath, 'North Sea Fishing', pp. 62–3, 66. Hull, to a lesser extent, and, on the opposite bank of the Humber, Grimsby, to a greater extent, also suffered in the later 15th cent. (R. J. Allison, 'Medieval Hull', in *VCH, East Riding, the City of Kingston upon Hull* (1969), ed. Allison, 28–9, 41, 55–6, 132–5; S. H. Rigby, 'Urban Decline in the Later Middle Ages', *Urban History Year Book* (1984), 47–53.

[73] I. S. W. Blanchard, 'Seigneurial Entrepreneurship and the Bishops of Durham and the Weardale Lead Industry, 1406–1529', *Business History*, 15 (1973), 97–111, esp. 100–1.

through Hull in the 1460s were low. However, a significant increase in the value of lead shipped in 1471/2 suggests that the overseas market had begun to revive.[74] Perhaps it was in anticipation of resurgent demand that nearly £50 was spent in 1465/6 on the repair and maintenance of the Kettlewell and Arkengarthdale mines of the lordship of Middleham. By 1489 Kettlewell was producing a return of almost £5, and was leased out by 1492 for £3. 13s. 4d. At the same time the Langstrothdale mines of the earl of Northumberland were let at £6. 13s. 4d. (Map 1).[75] Lead exports through Hull were buoyant during the 1490s: in 1492/3, 372 fothers worth £1,342 were handled. By the end of the decade the traffic in Yorkshire lead was so profitable that the merchants of York sought to secure a monopoly of its shipment down to Hull. Likewise, as Dr Blanchard has shown, there was a revival at the very end of the century of Weardale mining for export through Newcastle.[76]

Evidence from episcopal records suggests that coal production followed a parallel course to lead production in the century. By mid-fifteenth-century there had been a dramatic contraction in output, especially of the Tyneside pits. The Whikham mines, which had been let for £333. 6s. 8d. in 1356, were farmed for a mere £26. 13s. 4d. in 1438/9, when many smaller mines were in hand and waste for lack of tenants.[77] The most important mining district in mid-fifteenth-century seems, surprisingly, to have been the inland field of the Gaunless valley near Bishop Auckland (see Map 1). The mines here were usually leased to the Eure family for £112. 13s. 4d. p.a., or occasionally, when in hand, were worked directly by the bishop's own servants.[78] It seems remarkable, considering the exceptional cost of transporting coal by road, that these pits should be worth so much

[74] *The Customs Accounts of Hull, 1453–1490*, ed. W. R. Childs, YAJ, RS 144 (1986 for 1984), p. xxiv. I would also like to record my thanks to Jenny Kermode for advice on the Hull customs accounts.

[75] Coles, 'Middleham', pp. 177, 182–4; Bean, *Estates*, p. 15.

[76] Childs, *Customs Accounts*, p. xxiv; YCR ii. 142–4; Blanchard, 'Seigneural Entrepreneurship', pp. 109–10.

[77] VCH, *Durham*, ii. pp. 322–3; Blake, 'Coal Trade', pp. 1–26.

[78] VCH, *Durham*, ii. pp. 323–5, esp. 324–5 for a detailed analysis of the operation of the coal mines of Railey when in hand for the half-year June–December 1460, in which period sales of £41. 14s. 2d. were recorded and 38 wagon loads were delivered to the bishop's household.

more than the bishop's Tyneside pits. As Professor Dobson has suggested, the comparative abundance of timber and the high cost of overland transport gave no real opportunity for inland producers to engage in large-scale production.[79] Coal in the mid-fifteenth century was produced for a strictly limited market. This would explain the low farms of Tyneside pits and the limits imposed in both priory and episcopal leases on annual production. The 1450 lease (renewed in 1458) to William Eure of the Gaunless valley pits around Railey, for example, restricted him to just over 1,400 corfes or scopes a day. Some of the coal extracted was sold at pit-head and carried even as far as north Yorkshire, but most was consumed in the bishop's household at Auckland, to which Eure was, by the terms of his lease, to deliver as much coal as the bishop required at the artificially low rate of 4d. per chaldron. It would seem that the exploitation of coal, like that of lead, was undertaken in mid-fifteenth-century not to satisfy market demand, but to satisfy seigneurial consumption, and to preserve future supply.[80] This conservative (and conservationist) attitude surely explains why the episcopal pits nearest the bishop's principal residence, rather than those nearest convenient water transport, were the centres of mid-century production. In the last twenty-five years of the century, however, the market for coal, like that for lead, began to revive. The episcopal pits and licences to carry coal, which had been valued at £139. 11s. 4d. in 1463/4, were worth £247. 7s. 8d. in 1478/9 and generated revenue of £293. 18s. 0d. in 1495/6.[81] It was not, however, until well into the sixteenth century that the exports of coal from Newcastle reached and surpassed the levels achieved in the late fourteenth century.[82]

Although there are clear signs of revival in the lead and coal

[79] Dobson, *Durham Priory*, pp. 278–9. In the mid-15th cent. mining was restricted by the monks to within 10 miles of the priory.

[80] Durh 3/48/1, 50/6; *The Deputy Keeper's Report*, vol. xxv, 81 wrongly gives £12. 13s. 4d. (instead of £112. 13s. 4d.) as the rent in 1458. See also D. Wilcock, *The Durham Coalfield: Part One* (Durham, 1979), 14.

[81] Durham, Church Commission, Bishopric Estates, 189817, 189676, 189598. Although Tyneside pits were being redeveloped in 1495–6, commanding a rent of £198. 14s. 8d. p.a., the Railey complex was apparently still the major producer of coal. A detailed history of late-15th-cent. coal-mining in Durham is still to be undertaken.

[82] Nef, *British Coal Industry*, i. pp. 9–10.

industries of the region in the latter decades of the century, it is to be doubted that this was as yet on a sufficient scale to compensate for the generally stagnant state of the rest of the industrial economy. An important cause, it has been suggested, of the commercial and industrial difficulties faced in the region was the rise of London to dominate both the English section of North Sea trade and the international marketing of English cloth. Indeed London's triumph and late-fifteenth-century prosperity might explain the revival of the fortunes of the coal and lead trades. It was in the last decades of the fifteenth century that the early-modern role of the north-eastern economy as a supplier of London markets was established. But this structural change does not in itself explain the general inactivity of the local market in northern England in the middle to later fifteenth century. One reason for the low level of local demand was probably demographic. As we have seen, there is reason to believe that the population of the region continued to decline until mid-century, and there is little evidence of renewed growth before 1500. Another likely reason is monetary.

There is evidence to suggest that, in an age of general shortage of circulating bullion,[83] the north-east of England was particularly short of coinage. In the mid-fifteenth century agricultural rents were frequently paid in kind. At Cleasby and Clowbeck, from as early as the 1420s, the farmer of the demesne began to pay some of his rents in grain—a combination of wheat and malted maslin—to the steward of Lord FitzHugh's household. After the crisis of 1438–40, all the tenants adopted the same practice. In 1450/1, for instance, John Hobson quit his rent by delivering sixteen quarters of wheat and forty-seven quarters and six bushels of maslin, while the rent collector delivered almost the same quantities from the customary tenants. Only one man, John Baxter, settled his rent—the sum of 2s. 6d.—in cash.[84] At Danby in Eskdale a year later free tenants of Lord

---

[83] H. A. Miskimin, 'Monetary Movements and Market Structure: Forces for Contraction in Fourteenth and Fifteenth Century England', *Journal of Economic History*, 2nd ser., 24 (1964), 470–90; J. Day, *The Medieval Market Economy* (Oxford, 1987), 40–8, 59, 63, 94–7; see also the discussion in Lloyd, 'Wool Prices', pp. 21–2 and Hatcher, *Plague*, pp. 52–3.

[84] NYCRO, zjx 3/2/75, 110. The farmer of the demesne of West Tanfield also paid some rents in kind in the 1430s.

Latimer paid their rent in quantities of barley. Fountains Abbey rents too were paid in kind in the mid-fifteenth century.[85] Durham Priory tenants also paid in kind. The earliest concrete evidence comes from a bursar's rental of 1495, which reveals that one-third of the tenants in twenty townships, principally in the middle and south of the bishopric, paid rent to the value of almost £200 in 126 quarters of grain, 96 head of cattle, and various hens, geese, and pigs. This represented as much as two-fifths of the total rent paid.[86] At both these great ecclesiastical corporations, Fountains and Durham, agricultural wages were also paid in kind. At Elvet Hall *famuli* were paid metcorn, a dole of wheat and rye, from 1443 to 1514.[87] It may be that the resort to self-sufficiency on this scale, revealed in the household of Lord FitzHugh as well as in the priory at Durham, was the preference of conservative stewards. It may also be that tenants preferred to settle in kind. But the widespread acceptance by both estate officials and tenants of the practice could simply have resulted from necessity. Although it cannot be demonstrated, the most likely explanation for this mid-fifteenth-century retreat from a money economy is not cultural but practical. York merchants seem similarly to have suffered in mid-century from a shortage of investment capital and credit, particularly in the form of loans from the major ecclesiastical corporations.[88] All the evidence points to a conclusion that there was too little money circulating in the region, and that this may have been a contributory cause of continuing recession.

The fifteenth century after 1440 was a bleak era in the economic history of the north-east. In the agrarian sector the trough of recession seems to have been reached in the 1440s and 1450s. In the urban, industrial, and commercial sectors, the trough seems to have fallen in the 1470s and 1480s. There were relieving features—pastoral farming in the Pennines escaped

---

[85] Alnwick, Syon MS X. I, Box 1, 2b; *Memorials of Fountains Abbey*, ii. pp. 104–5; iii, ed. J. T. Fowler, SS, cxxx (1918), pp. 95–255 *passim*.

[86] Lomas, 'Durham Cathedral Priory', pp. 107–10.

[87] *Memorials of Fountains*, iii. pp. 119–21, 127–34, 198; Lomas, 'Northern Farm', pp. 34–5.

[88] Kermode, 'Merchants, Overseas Trade and Urban Decline', pp. 64–5.

the worst of depression, lead- and coal-mining revived in the last decades; but there is little evidence of sustained expansion before the end of the century. A low level of local demand and perhaps a shortage of circulating coinage conspired to depress the level of economic activity and hold back recovery, which, in the arable sector, was fleetingly glimpsed in the 1470s. This state of affairs was the worse for the fact that other parts of England, especially the home counties, the southern midlands, and the south-west, came out of recession earlier than the north-east, and began to enjoy the fruits of sustained economic resurgence from the 1470s.[89] Parts of southern England grew in wealth in the last decades of the century, while the north-east stood still. In no small part, as we have seen, this southern prosperity, especially in London and the home counties, was gained at the expense of the great northern city of York and its hinterland. These decades, it has been recently demonstrated, saw the beginning of a profound shift in the balance of urban wealth from the north and east to the south and west.[90] Studies of the relative distribution of taxable wealth have also suggested a similar shift of balance in the countryside between 1334 and the early sixteenth century.[91] In this context the plight of the north-east was even more grave; for during the second half of the fifteenth century the gap between prospering and expanding southern districts and a stagnant north-east widened. The north-east was experiencing relative as well as absolute decline. Moreover the region's role in the English economy was being

[89] For evidence of the resurgent economy of southern England in the last decades of the 15th cent. see e.g. Dyer, *Lords and Peasants*, 189–90, 288; R. H. Hilton, 'Medieval market towns and simple commodity production', *PP*, 109 (1985), 11; M. K. McIntosh, 'Local Change and Community Control in England, 1465–1500', *Huntingdon Library Quarterly*, 49 (1986), 220–5; and idem, *Autonomy and Community: The Royal Manor of Havering, 1200–1500* (Cambridge, 1986), 221–35; D. M. Palliser, 'Urban Decay Revisited', p. 17; and G. Rosser, 'London and Westminster: The Suburbs in the Urban Economy in the Later Middle Ages', in Thomson, ed., *Towns and Townspeople*, pp. 55–6.

[90] C. Pythian-Adams, 'Urban Decay in Late Medieval England', in J. Abrams and C. T. Wrigley (eds.), *Towns in Societies* (Cambridge, 1978), esp. 168–70.

[91] R. S. Schofield, 'The Geographical Distribution of Wealth in England 1334–1649', *Econ. HR* 2nd ser., 18 (1965), esp. 503–9; Darby et al., 'Changing Geographical Distribution of Wealth', pp. 257—61. It is to be noted however that the West Riding cloth-manufacturing district stood out in 1525 as a unique northern area of growth since 1334.

recast: what, at the beginning of the century, had been a thriving independent region was at its end in danger of becoming an impoverished dependent satellite of the metropolis. The poverty and backwardness of the north-east, as they appeared to some commentators of the early sixteenth century, were comparatively recent developments, the consequences of profound economic changes which took place during the fifteenth century.

4

Landed Society

THE possession of land was the key to social dominance and political power in fifteenth-century England. Nobility of blood and legal privilege may have enhanced local authority, but, as the senior branch of the Nevilles discovered, without the material resources secured by land, power was diminished and influence curtailed. An analysis of the political élite of any region of the realm needs to start therefore with the question of who held the land. What was the distribution in north-eastern England between clerical and lay, and, within the laity, between peerage and gentry? How important was clerical wealth? What was the balance between peerage and gentry landholdings? These are the questions which first need answering in an examination of the social and political structure of the region.

There is no fully satisfactory method by which the historian can calculate the distribution of landholding. Surviving estate records are far from comprehensive; and thus, although they are invaluable in illuminating economic trends, the management of family inheritance, and the character of estate administration, they are woefully inadequate for assessing the total pattern of landholding. The only remotely feasible approach lies through lordship and the distribution of manors. A manorial count is not in itself an entirely satisfactory method of calculating the distribution of landed wealth. The right to hold a manorial court was not, it must be stressed, identical with the possession of land. It was even possible for a lord of the manor to be virtually landless in the district over which he exercised jurisdiction as lord. Thus, after he had sold his holding in Croft to Richard Clervaux, Lord Scrope of Bolton, although retaining the lordship of the manor, ceased to have a territorial interest.[1] Similarly, at neighbouring Manfield, Lord FitzHugh, although he held the courts as of the barony of Ravensworth, was landless

[1] NYCRO, zQH 1, fos. 147–47d, 149, 152; Pollard, 'Richard Clervaux', p. 156.

there.[2] These, it is to be admitted, were exceptional cases. Normally possession of the manor brought with it possession of land, both demesne and customary tenements. Even so, lords rarely held all the land within the manor. At Croft, for instance, before Richard Clervaux systematically bought up all the land that he could, not only did Lord Scrope hold the chief messuage, nine messuages, 253 acres of customary land, and 173 acres of demesne; but also Ralph Rokeby of Mortham, Sir Thomas Markenfield, Roland Place of Halnaby, Thomas Frank of Kneeton, Thomas Shorte of Longnewton, and John Makadoo of Darlington each held a messuage with attached customary land.[3] In Brompton-on-Swale, to give another example, where the Abbey of St Agatha's Easby held the manor, land was additionally owned by the Scropes of Bolton, and the gentry families of Burgh, Conyers, Metcalfe, Swaldale, and Brian.[4] The court rolls of FitzHugh manors provide similar evidence of small holdings in the possession of freeholders: at Cleasby, for instance, in 1472, the Burghs, Conyers, Boyntons, and St Agatha's were free tenants.[5] The situation is revealed equally clearly when looked at from the point of view of family estates rather than townships. In 1440 Richard Clervaux of Croft inherited lands and tenements in a dozen different places, including a number of urban properties in York and as far away as Doncaster.[6] Later in the century, according to a valor of his estates, John Wandesford of Kirklington drew his income of nearly £200 per annum from rents in no less than twenty different places in Richmondshire and Allertonshire; of these he was lord of the manor of no more than five and a moiety.[7]

Moreover, land frequently changed hands. However unpropitious the economic circumstances might have been, there was a ready market for land in the later Middle Ages. Richard Clervaux of Croft expended a large sum of money consolidating

[2] NYCRO, zjx 3/1/2. For a Manfield court roll (14/4/1472) see 3/1/63. No rents from Manfield are recorded as paid to the lord's receiver in the 15th cent.

[3] Pollard, 'Richard Clervaux', pp. 154–7.

[4] NYCRO, zal 3/17.

[5] NYCRO, zjx 3/1/63.

[6] Pollard, 'Richard Clervaux', p. 154; A. H. Thompson, 'The Clervaux Chartulary', *Arch. Ael.* 3rd ser., 17 (1920), 2–44.

[7] H. B. McCall, *The Family of Wandesforde of Kirklington and Castlecomer* (1904), 319.

his estate in one place for no other reason apparently than to satisfy his pride and honour.[8] Others, the upwardly mobile, were buying to establish themselves in landed society; in 1460 Richard Pigot, then a rising lawyer, bought Little Burton Manor and all its appurtenances, once the property of William Routh, for £156. 13s. 4d. from a fellow lawyer, John Aiscough.[9] Perhaps more significant than major purchases and transfers of substantial estates was the almost constant traffic in small parcels of land which were employed as settlements on younger children or as endowments for chantries. For these purposes Christopher Conyers of Hornby, over a whole lifetime, purchased lands in at least seventeen places.[10] On a smaller scale the Burghs of Brough bought and disposed of lands in Leeming, Walburn, Eppleby, Hornby, and Richmond, which were used to support younger children and chantries;[11] and Henry Eure of Old Malton in 1476 granted to his wife Katharine 'all the lands by me purchased' in Malton, Scarborough, Stokesley, and Whitby.[12] The pattern of landholding was thus immensely complex and constantly changing. Land circulated among the landed élite. Nevertheless, since this was a general pattern common throughout the region, in a rough and ready way the process cancelled itself out; as a rule of thumb, it remained the case that the more manors held, the more land possessed.

Finally, for several reasons, as a measure of comparative wealth, a count of manors has an in-built bias against the clergy and towards the gentry. First, although it encompasses rectoral and prebendal manors, it can take no account of the spiritual income enjoyed by the clergy. As the records of both Durham Priory and York Minster show, the payments of tithes and

[8] Pollard, 'Richard Clervaux', pp. 156–7.

[9] NYCRO, zfw, Miscellaneous Deeds, MIC 1160.

[10] BL, Egerton MS 3402, fos. 96ᵛ–97; PRO, CP25(1)/281/16/43. In this fine levied on 10 February 1460, when his son and heir Sir John was under attainder, Christopher made contingent settlement of his estate should Sir John not secure a pardon. The details copied into BL, Egerton 3402 are not recorded in the foot of the fine deposited with the Court of Common Pleas. In the settlement, to cite one example, Christopher granted to his son Brian the manor of Pinchinthorpe, land in Kirkletham and Wardley, and all his purchased lands in Brompton, Appleby, Little 'Fourolds', Leeming, Kilburn, Newton Morkar, and Nether Sillington.

[11] NYCRO, zrl 1/40,42,43,45; A. J. Pollard, 'Burghs of Brough', p. 9.

[12] Test. Ebor. iii. 224.

other dues to incumbents or appropriators of parish churches represented a considerable diversion of landed income into clerical hands.[13] Secondly, because of the large numbers of grants of small parcels and rents made to religious houses in the twelfth and thirteenth centuries these bodies tended to have a disproportionate scattering of wealth in small holdings throughout the region, and in this way are net losers in a count of manors. Thirdly, the great landowners, lay peers and religious houses alike, tended to dominate the upland districts, where manors were larger and where forest existed over wide tracts of land: in terms of sheer acreage and related pastoral use a count of manors additionally understates the landed wealth of larger landowners, both clerical and lay. On the other hand, partly counterbalancing this, a manorial count can take no note of the submanorial gentry, who also held numerous smaller parcels of land.[14] As long as these reservations are borne in mind a count of manors is a helpful basis from which to start.

The North Riding, as the most comprehensively recorded district, has been taken as the basis of detailed analysis of the distribution of manors in 1475.[15] Of 662 manors in twelve wapentakes, the clergy held 26.7 per cent and the laity (excluding the Crown) 71.3 per cent. Of those 71.3 per cent in lay hands, 25.6 per cent were held by the peerage and 45.7 per cent by the gentry. Only in the five wapentakes of Richmondshire did the peerage approach the gentry in the number of manors held. The same pattern is duplicated within the county palatine of Durham. The gentry were numerically the most important section of the landed élite, even in this supposedly remote region.

[13] The most spectacular examples are those of the prebend of Masham and archdeaconry of Richmond, together worth approx. £300 to their holders in the late 15th cent. (Dobson, 'The Later Middle Ages', pp. 55–6).

[14] Some of these reservations were also expressed by J. P. Cooper in 1956, although his influential paper was more concerned with criticizing the use to which counts of manors were put (see 'The Counting of Manors', in G. E. Aylmer and J. S. Morrill (eds.), Land, Men and Beliefs (London, 1983), 1–16).

[15] The analysis is based on information in the 2 vols. of the VCH, North Riding. Though comprehensive the histories are not entirely reliable. Where identified, errors have been corrected. These are relatively minor. Such inaccuracies as there are do not significantly distort the general conclusions. Information of a less precise nature has been drawn for Durham from the Victoria County History, supplemented by the relevant volume of Surtees's and Hutchinson's histories (cf. Dyer, Warwickshire Farming, p. 3).

It is perhaps surprising that the church did not hold more manors. Even allowing for the undoubted underestimate that the above figure represents it is hard to square it with Dr Schofield's calculation that in 1513–15 almost two-thirds of the assessed taxable wealth of the North Riding was clerical.[16] Admittedly, the overall count for the North Riding conceals important internal variations. In particular, in the five more southerly wapentakes, nearer to York, the proportion of manors in ecclesiastical hands was 40 per cent. But this left the northern part of the Riding (Richmondshire, Northallertonshire, and Langbaurgh) below 20 per cent—a pattern continued north of the Tees, in the Durham wards of Stockton and Darlington. The number of clerically held manors was therefore exceptionally low in the central parts of the region, those furthermost from the principal religious seats.

The clerical presence in north-eastern England was, however, by no means negligible. Including hospitals, there were over 100 religious houses in the North Riding, Durham, Northumberland, and the City of York. In 1535 they enjoyed a net income from land in excess of £8,000. The metropolitan church of York and the palatine bishopric of Durham additionally enjoyed incomes of over £2,000 each. The wealthiest religious houses were the Benedictine abbeys of St Mary's York, Whitby, and the cathedral priory of Durham. Despite their fame, the Cistercian houses were not the major landholders in the region. More important were the orders of canons (seven Augustinian, five Premonstratensian, and two Gilbertine houses), whose lands were assessed at over £2,250 in 1535. All the religious houses in these counties supported over 450 monks, 200 friars, and 150 nuns at the Dissolution. Even including Fountains, a West Riding house with significant property in the North Riding, the 130 Cistercians were then outnumbered by 175 canons (see Map 2).[17]

---

[16] Schofield, 'Geographical Distribution of Wealth', p. 504. The discrepancy is almost certainly because lay wealth was significantly underassessed in 1513–15. See R. Fieldhouse, 'Social Structure from Tudor Lay Subsidies and Probate Inventories', *Local Population Studies*, 12 (1974), 9–24. I am grateful to Richard Hoyle for communicating his conclusions on local resistance to assessment and collection of subsidies in the early years of Henry VIII's reign.

[17] The above analysis is based on information drawn from D. Knowles and R. N. Hadcock, *Medieval Religious Houses in England and Wales* (1953), *passim*.

Comparisons are not easy; but it would appear that in 1535 only one-tenth of those in religious orders in England lived in the three furthermost north-eastern counties. The temporal significance of the clergy, especially within the county palatine of Durham, was undoubtedly greater than this survey of landed wealth and numbers suggests. The evidence leads one to suspect, however, that the high standing and respect enjoyed by the clergy on the eve of the Dissolution owed as much to the quality of their spiritual life as to the secular authority they wielded or the wealth they possessed.

The landed gentry, who held 45 per cent of the North Riding manors, formed the solid core of political society in north-eastern England, even in the fifteenth century. They included in their ranks at one extreme those who could only just sustain the image of idle gentility, and were only one rung above the yeomanry; and, at the other, very wealthy knights who were but a short step away from the peerage. Broadly speaking, the gentry can be divided into three categories: the mere gentlemen, the manorial squirearchy, and the knightly. It was soon to be the case in England, as Sir Thomas Smith observed, that 'whosoever can bear the port, charge and cost of being a gentleman shall be taken as gentleman'.[18] All that was necessary at the lowest level was to have a sufficient unearned income from land to allow one to live idly. At precisely what income this point lay is difficult to determine. By 1530 Garter King of Arms conceded that:

All those not vile born or rebels might be admitted to be ennobled to have arms having lands and possessions of free tenure to the yearly value of ten pounds sterling.[19]

By this date there had perhaps been a lowering of the threshold for the armigerous gentry. Although fifty years earlier a grant of arms may not have been so freely available, nevertheless at £10 per annum a man could adopt the style of gentleman with the ready acceptance of his neighbours. Indeed 10 marks may well have been sufficient, for this was the annual income most frequently set aside by armigerous gentlemen for the support of their younger sons.[20]

---

[18] Sir Thomas Smith, *De Republica Anglorum* (Menston, 1970), 27.
[19] Quoted by A. R. Wagner, *Heralds and Heraldry in the Middle Ages*, 2nd edn. (1973), 79.

At this distance of time, and given the paucity of evidence, it is impossible either to identify or to enumerate the submanorial gentry. They were more numerous and more fluctuating than the sources reveal. One such family was the Lockwoods, of whom one can identify at least seven male members in the middle decades of the century, but whose precise relationships, places of residence, and status are indeterminate. The will of a Thomas Lockwood of East Harlsey Grange was proved in 1436; that of John Lockwood of Little Broughton in 1452. This John was an attestor to the second parliamentary election of 1449; but he is to be distinguished from another John, who witnessed Clervaux and Brough deeds in 1467 and 1474. A Richard Lockwood was a feed retainer of Lord FitzHugh in 1436/7; a Henry a yeoman of the Crown in 1469; a William was pardoned in 1470; and another Thomas acted as an attorney for Roger Aske in 1474.[21] Another lesser family was that of Vincent of Great Smeaton, who were tenants of St Mary's Abbey, York. William Vincent in 1450 was sufficiently well-connected to be able to call upon both the earl of Salisbury and the earl of Northumberland to act as feoffees. William married Margaret, the sister of Richard Clervaux on whom the Clervaux property in Smeaton was settled. William and his son Roger both witnessed Clervaux deeds. Roger was still alive in 1486, aged eighty, when he gave evidence in a probate case concerning possession of lands in Great Smeaton.[22] To the Lockwoods and Vincents we can add prosperous townsmen like Robinson of Stokesley, Clerionet of Richmond, and Thomson of Bedale; and families of gentlemen in service like Sedgwick, Colville and Swaldale, Stockdale and Weltden; the latter two being families in the service of the Nevilles of Middleham.[23] In the county palatine several such families were established as lessees of the priory manors and

[20] See below, p. 105; see also D. A. L. Morgan, 'The Individual Style of the English Gentleman', in Jones, Gentry and Lesser Nobility, p. 16 for evidence that £10 was considered the appropriate sum in Yorkist England.

[21] BI, Probate Register, ii. fo. 282, iii. fo. 458ᵛ; NYCRO, zqh I, fo. 137: ZEL 1/78; zjx 3/2/91; CPR, 1467–79, 215; BL, Ad. Ch., 66716; PRO, c219/15/7/1, m.26.

[22] NYCRO, zqh I, fo. 148; Test. Ebor. iv. 11.

[23] A. J. Pollard, 'The Richmondshire Community of Gentry', in Charles Ross (ed.), Patronage, Pedigree and Power in Later Medieval England (Gloucester, 1979), 45. For Sedgwick in the service of the FitzHughs see below, pp. 124–5.

farmers of tithes. Prominent among them were the Denoms of Cotesmore and the Strangways of Ketton.[24] Strangways of Ketton were a junior branch of the Strangways of West Harlsey in Yorkshire. Many of the lesser gentry came from this background of cadet branches; others were Henry Tailboys of Hurworth, cousin of the lord of this manor, Tailboys of Kyme, and Thomas Clervaux of Croft, uncle of Richard. Better documented as one on, or just below, the borderline of gentility is John Harrington of Eastrington, near Howden, the common clerk of the city of York. A distant kinsman of the Harringtons of Hornby, Lancs. and Briereley, Yorks., John was described in 1486 by his mother's kinsman, Sir John Aske of Aughton, as being the son of a poor gentleman, 'though he never were taken here but for a yeoman'.[25]

The manorial gentry themselves are by their very definition more easily identifiable. In the North Riding alone there were approximately 130 such families in the second half of the century. They ranged from the insubstantial, who held but one manor (Holme of Hurlington, Lindley of Scutterskelfe, Sayer of Worsall, and Yearsley of Yearsley, for example) to the great county families with multiple holdings, of whom eighteen held four or more manors. The accepted social demarcation within this armigerous group lay between those who were merely squires and those who were knightly. Knightly families are here defined as those whose heads were eligible for knighthood, and thus subject to distraint if they declined the honour: that is to say those with net annual incomes from land of £40 or more.

The records of distraints of 1458, 1465, and 1503 for Yorkshire make it possible to calculate the number of knightly families in the North Riding. These reveal approximately thirty families eligible for knighthood, whose members, identified by royal commissioners, preferred to be fined for distraint.[26] If we add these to the fifteen or so known knights in the mid-fifteenth century and at the beginning of the sixteenth we have approximately forty-five knightly families. There are grounds for believing that this is an understatement; that one or two

[24] Durham, Dean and Chapter, Bursar's Accounts, *passim*.

[25] Pollard, 'Richard Clervaux', p. 160; *YCR*, i. 175; Horrox, 'Richard III and the East Riding', in *Richard III and the North*, p. 85.

[26] PRO, E370/2/22; 198/4/19; BL, Harley 6166, fo. 122.

families such as Percehay of Ryton escaped knighthood or distraint. But a figure of forty-five, or one-third of the identified manorial gentry, would not be wildly inaccurate for those whose
principal holdings and residence were in the North Riding.

It must be borne in mind that the knightly thus included some
families whose holdings were not very substantial: £40 clear
annual income was not a high threshold. In Richmondshire, for
instance, the following families, who possessed no more than
three manors each, were all knightly and had lands evaluated at
£40 or above in 1503: Aske of Aske (100 marks), Burgh of Brough
(£100), Catterick of Stanwick (£40), Clervaux of Croft (100
marks), Frank of Kneeton (£40), Place of Halnaby (£40), Rokeby
of Mortham (£40), and Wycliffe of Wycliffe (£40).[27] No head of
the Burgh family was prepared in the later fifteenth century to
take on the burden (or honour) of knighthood; rather, William
Burgh II, for instance, was prepared twice to pay a fine: £3 in
1458 and £2. 13s. 4d. in 1465.[28]

It was not the knightly families as such, but the more substantial of them (the greater knights), who possessed estates worth
more than £100 p.a., usually drawn from four or more manors,
who formed the county élite. There were a dozen and a half such
families in the North Riding alone.[29] Likewise County Durham

[27] BL, Harley 6166, fo. 122. This list of lords, knights, esquires, and gentlemen resident in the county of Yorkshire, many with an evaluation (all above
£40) noted, is probably a note of those distrained in 1500. A herald visiting
northern England a few years earlier also reported that the head of the Clervaux
family could spend 100 marks a year: *A Visitation of the North of England* ca
1490, ed. C. H. Hunter Blair, SS, cxliv, (1930) 104. The group accords with H. L.
Gray's lesser knights, ('Incomes from land in England in 1436', *EHR* 49 (1934),
623–4). In 1436 Conan Aske was taxed under Middlesex on land producing
income of £80 that year (Gray, 'Incomes', p. 638).

[28] PRO, E 370/2/22; 198/4/19.

[29] Families with 4 or more manors in the North Riding were: Bigod of
Settrington; Boynton of Acklam; Bulmer of Wilton; Conyers of Hornby; Conyers of Sockburn; Darrell of Sessay; De La River of Brandsby; Eure of Witton and
Old Malton; Gower of Stittenham; Hastings of Roxby; Lascelles of Sowerby;
Markenfield of Markenfield and Eryholme; Mauleverer of Ingleby Arncliffe;
Mountford of Hackforth; Norton of Norton Conyers; Percehay of Ryton; Pigot
of Clotherholme; Stapleton of Carlton; Strangways of West Harlsey; and Wan-
desford of Kirklington. It is to be noted that I use the terms 'gentry', 'county
gentry', and 'county élite' differently from C. Given-Wilson, 'The King and the
Gentry in Fourteenth-Century England', *TRHS* 5th ser., 37 (1987), 99–100. My
élite is more exclusive, but my county gentry more open than Dr Given-
Wilson's.

and Northumberland were dominated by similar, if smaller
élites: Bowes, Claxton, Conyers of Wynyard, Eure of Witton,
Fulthorpe, Hilton, and Tempest in Durham; Cartington,
Collingwood, Grey of Chillingham and Wark, Harbottle, Heron,
Manners, Middleton of Belsay, Ridley, and Swinburne in
Northumberland (Map 2). The interests of some of these leading
families crossed county boundaries. The Eures were influential
in both Durham and the North Riding. The Inglebies, Markenfields, and Mauleverers had important estates in both North and
West Ridings. The Constables of Halsham and Constables of
Flamborough, both seated in Holderness, also had holdings in
the North Riding. The Bigods of Settrington, East Riding, held
several manors in Cleveland. The Redmans held land in Westmorland, the West Riding, and the North Riding. The Tailboys
of Kyme, Lincolnshire had estates in both Durham and Northumberland. And a new family, Danby of Thorp Perrow, founded
by Robert, Chief Justice of Common Pleas, acquired land in the
West Riding and the county palatine to add to its North Riding
estate. Of all these families three stand out above the rest:
Conyers of Hornby, Eure of Witton, and Strangways of West
Harlsey, the first two of whom were to be promoted to the
peerage in the early sixteenth century. Conyers and Strangways,
holding sixteen and fifteen manors respectively in the North
Riding alone (twice as many as any other of the North Riding
gentry) were as wealthy as old-established lesser peers, Scrope of
Masham and Latimer of Snape. In c.1490 both were said to be
able to spend 1,000 marks annually.[30] The two families were
closely related, sharing by parallel marriages the succession of
two baronies. Sir John Conyers (c.1420–90) married Margery
Darcy, second daughter and heiress of Philip, Lord Darcy, in
right of whom he held Yarm; while Sir James Strangways
(1415–80) married Elizabeth, her elder sister. Their sons married
the joint heiresses of William Neville, Lord Fauconberg. John
Conyers (d. 1469) married Alice; Sir Richard Strangways
(d. 1488) married her elder sister Elizabeth. Thus their heirs,
William, Lord Conyers (d. 1525) and Sir James Strangways

---

[30] *Visitation of the North*, pp. 92, 106. In 1436 the Darcy lands, less dower,
were assessed as producing an income of £126, and the land of William Neville,
Lord Fauconberg, an income of £325 (Gray, 'Incomes', 617–18).

(d. 1521) each enjoyed the moieties of two baronies. Wealth and birth qualified both for peerages. It is thus puzzling that while William Conyers, the descendant of both younger heiresses, began to be styled Lord Conyers from 1505, the same dignity was not extended to James Strangways, the descendant of the elder heiresses.[31] Nevertheless both Conyers and Strangways, as residual legatees of Darcy and Fauconberg, were clearly on the threshold of the peerage in the later fifteenth century.

The peerage itself was well represented in the region: over a quarter held lands in Northumberland, Durham, and the North Riding. The dominant magnates were the Nevilles of Middleham and the Percy earls of Northumberland. In the early years of Henry VII, the Kingmaker's estates east of the Pennines (Middleham, Sheriff Hutton, and Barnard Castle), by then Crown lands, generated revenues of approximately £1,900 p.a. (Map 3).[32] After the restoration of Henry, fourth earl of Northumberland, in 1471 his north-eastern estates were worth a little over £2,000 (Map 4).[33] The Nevilles additionally drew approximately £350 p.a. from Penrith and associated Cumbrian estates;[34] the Percies approximately £500 p.a. from their Cumberland lands. Because of the overwhelming presence of the cadet line the senior Nevilles, earls of Westmorland, although landholders in both County Durham and the North Riding, were much reduced in status and wealth. Several English peers only enjoyed an absentee interest: the dukes of Suffolk (a handful of moieties in County Durham), the dukes of Norfolk (until 1476, Thirsk and Kirkby Malzeard), William, Lord Hastings (Slingsby, North Riding), and the Lords Lovell (a moiety of Bedale, North Riding; although Francis, Lord Lovell (d. 1487) developed a strong personal attachment to the region). The earls of Warwick at Barnard Castle had also held only an absentee interest until, in 1449, the title and lordship passed

[31] E. H. Powell and K. Wallis, *The House of Lords in the Later Middle Ages* (1968), 1505–6. The promotion of the Conyers may well have been a consequence of their greater political significance (see below Chs. 12–15 *passim*).

[32] This calculation is based on the surviving receivers' accounts for Middleham, Sheriff Hutton, and Barnard Castle for 1488–89 (PRO, DL29/637/10357; 649/10500; 650/10515).

[33] Calculated from Bean, *Estates*, pp. 46 (Table xvii), 81, and 111.

[34] Ibid. 46; M. Craster-Chambers, 'Penrith Castle and Richard Duke of Gloucester', *The Ricardian*, v, 86 (1984), 34.

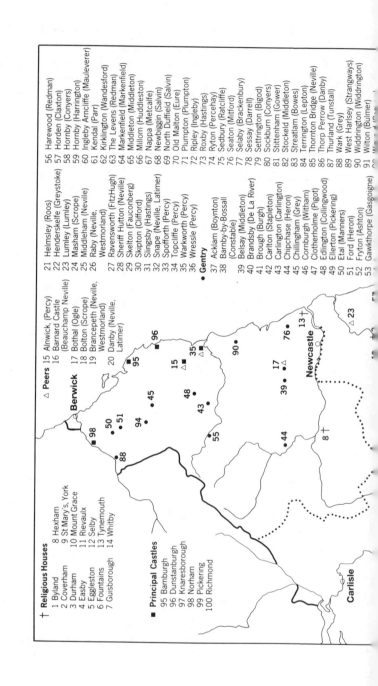

† Religious Houses

1 Byland
2 Coverham
3 Durham
4 Easby
5 Eggleston
6 Fountains
7 Guisborough
8 Hexham
9 St Mary's, York
10 Mount Grace
11 Rievaulx
12 Selby
13 Tynemouth
14 Whitby

△ Peers

15 Alnwick, (Percy)
16 Barnard Castle (Beauchamp Neville)
17 Bothal (Ogle)
18 Bolton (Scrope)
19 Brancepeth (Neville, Westmorland)
20 Danby (Neville, Latimer)
21 Helmsley (Roos)
22 Henderskelfe (Greystoke)
23 Lumley (Lumley)
24 Masham (Scrope)
25 Middleham (Neville)
26 Raby (Neville, Westmorland)
27 Ravensworth (FitzHugh)
28 Sheriff Hutton (Neville)
29 Skelton (Fauconberg)
30 Skipton (Clifford)
31 Slingsby (Hastings)
32 Snape (Neville, Latimer)
33 Spofforth (Percy)
34 Topcliffe (Percy)
35 Warkworth (Percy)
36 Wressle (Percy)

● Gentry

37 Acklam (Boynton)
38 Barnby-by-Bossall (Constable)
39 Belsay (Middleton)
40 Brandsby (De La River)
41 Brough (Burgh)
42 Carlton (Stapleton)
43 Carlington (Carlington)
44 Chipchase (Heron)
45 Chillingham (Grey)
46 Cornburgh (Witham)
47 Clotherholme (Pigot)
48 Edlington (Collingwood)
49 Ellerton (Pickering)
50 Etal (Manners)
51 Ford (Heron)
52 Fryton (Ashton)
53 Gawkthorpe (Gasgoigne)

56 Harewood (Redman)
57 Horden (Claxton)
58 Hornby (Conyers)
59 Hornby (Harrington)
60 Ingleby Arncliffe (Mauleverer)
61 Kendal (Parr)
62 Kirklington (Wandesford)
63 The Levens (Redman)
64 Markenfield (Markenfield)
65 Middleton (Middleton)
66 Millom (Huddleston)
67 Nappa (Metcalfe)
68 Newbiggin (Salvin)
69 North Duffield (Salvin)
70 Old Malton (Eure)
71 Plumpton (Plumpton)
72 Ripley (Ingleby)
73 Roxby (Hastings)
74 Ryton (Percehay)
75 Sedbury (Ratcliffe)
76 Seaton (Mitford)
77 Selaby (Brackenbury)
78 Sessay (Darrell)
79 Settrington (Bigod)
80 Sockburn (Conyers)
81 Stittenham (Gower)
82 Stockeld (Middleton)
83 Streatlam (Bowes)
84 Terrington (Lepton)
85 Thornton Bridge (Neville)
86 Thorp Perrow (Danby)
87 Thurland (Tunstall)
88 Wark (Grey)
89 West Harlsey (Strangways)
90 Widdington (Widdrington)
91 Wilton (Bulmer)

■ Principal Castles

95 Bamburgh
96 Dunstanburgh
97 Knaresborough
98 Norham
99 Pickering
100 Richmond

Berwick

Newcastle

Carlisle

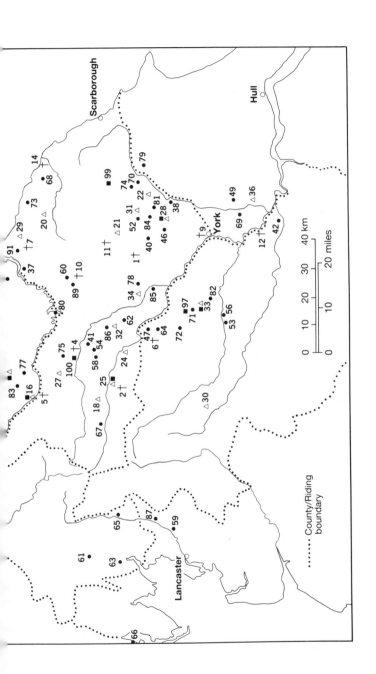

Map 2. RELIGIOUS HOUSES, SEATS OF PEERS AND GREATER GENTRY

County/Riding
boundary

0   10   20   30   40 km

0   10   20 miles

into the hands of Richard Neville, and was in 1461 united with the Middleham Neville patrimony.

There were six active, residential, lesser peers in the second half of the fifteenth century: Greystoke (Henderskelfe, North Riding and Conniscliffe, Co. Durham); FitzHugh of Ravensworth; Scrope of Masham; Scrope of Bolton; Ogle (created in 1461); and Lumley (restored in 1461) (Map 2). The first three of these families were assessed for income tax in 1436 on income from land together totalling £1,601.[35] There were other families, who were, for much of the later fifteenth century, and for different reasons, reduced in circumstance, and were of only limited importance. Roos of Helmsley were reduced to ineffectiveness, first, through a succession of dowagers, and secondly, after 1461, by attainder and minority.[36] Likewise the Cliffords of Skipton (and Hart in Co. Durham) were excluded by attainders and forfeiture between 1461 and 1485. The Neville lords of Latimer played only a minor role in north-eastern society because of the insanity of George (d. 1469) and the subsequent long minority of his grandson and heir Richard. One peerage, the barony of Fauconberg, fell into abeyance on the death of William Neville in 1463, although it was effectively replaced by the creation of the barony of Ogle.[37] One family, the Nevilles, stands out head and shoulders above all other peers. Until the demise of Richard Neville, earl of Warwick in 1471 there were at least four members of the family at the head of northern baronies, including his brother John as earl of Northumberland between 1461 and 1470.

The power and authority of certain peers was enhanced by the

---

[35] H. L. Gray, 'Incomes', p. 617. Greystoke was assessed at £650, Scrope at £457, and FitzHugh at £484. A receiver's account for William, Lord FitzHugh's northern estates in 1436/7 reveals that the expected revenue of his Yorkshire estates, excluding Ravensworth, stood then at £336 (NYCRO ZJX/3/2/91). None of these 3 peerages was burdened with dower in 1436 (see Ross and Pugh, 'The English Baronage and the Income Tax of 1436', BIHR 20 (1953), 26–8). William Neville, Lord Fauconberg was assessed at £325, Clifford at £250, and Latimer at £175 (Gray, 'Incomes', pp. 617–18). Dower of £75 had been arranged for Elizabeth Percy, widow of John, 7th Lord Clifford. She died in 1436 (Ross and Pugh, 'English Baronage', p. 26). No assessment of the landed income of Scrope of Bolton was made in 1436 because the wardship of the young Henry, Lord Scrope and the custody of his lands were in the possession of Richard Neville, earl of Salisbury, and the lands were exempt from taxation (Ross and Pugh, 'English Baronage', p. 12).

[36] Ross and Pugh, 'English Baronage', pp. 23–5.   [37] See n. 35, above.

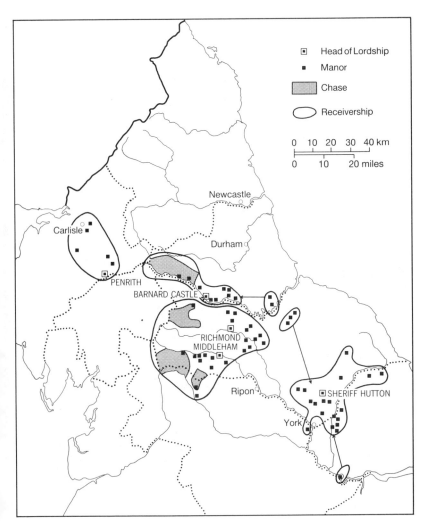

Legend

- ▣ Head of Lordship
- ■ Manor
- ▨ Chase
- ⬭ Receivership

0   10   20   30   40 km
0   10   20 miles

Newcastle

Carlisle

Durham

PENRITH

BARNARD CASTLE

RICHMOND
MIDDLEHAM

Ripon

SHERIFF HUTTON

York

Map 3. NEVILLE OF MIDDLEHAM ESTATES (INCLUDING HONOUR OF RICHMOND)

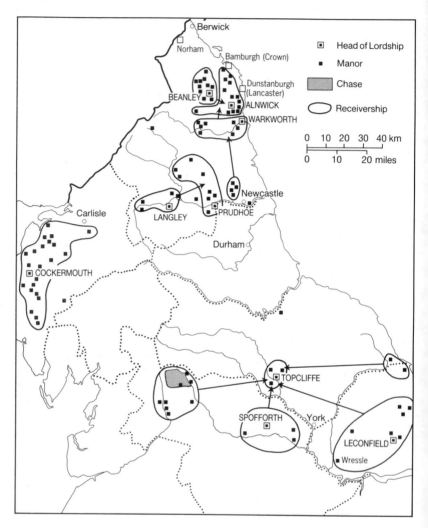

Map 4. PERCY ESTATES

possession of mesne lordship. Such mesne lordship, the relic of the original subinfeudation with knights' fees by the first Norman tenants in chief, gave a regular if insubstantial financial return even in the fifteenth century. The honour of Richmond in Richmondshire provides a well-documented example. Most of the principal freeholders of Richmondshire held their land by knight's fee as of the honour of Richmond. An undated, late-fourteenth-century list shows a total of just over sixty knights' fees belonging to the honour. All the inheritors of the fees owed castleguard at Richmond, usually for two months in the year. The actual physical duty had long since been commuted, but the annual payment for wards was still made. Thus the Clervaux of Croft paid 3s. 4d. p.a. for one knight's fee in Great (East) Cowton, as did the Markenfields for a half fee in Eryholme. The Nevilles of Middleham held six fees, for which they paid £2 per annum in lieu of service at the castle in June and July. In total, castleguard at Richmond, although in itself an anachronism, raised over £20 per annum for the earl or the grantee of the honour, who for much of the later fifteenth century was the lord of Middleham.[38] Within the honour of Richmond, however, subinfeudation had taken place. By the fifteenth century there were three lesser fees held by the Nevilles of Middleham, the Scropes of Bolton, and the FitzHughs (this one known as the Marmion Fee) for East Tanfield.

The tenants of these fees paid free rent, fines for suit of court, and a part of the castleguard. Thus the Middleham fee in the reign of Henry IV produced a total of £12. 8s. 10d. from forty-three subtenants, of which £2 was delivered to the bailiff of the Wapentake (Hang West) as the earl of Westmorland's contribution toward castleguard for his six knights. The Marmion Fee rendered £8. 14s. 8d., and the Scrope of Bolton fee just under £2. A careful check was maintained by the mesne lords on these rents, and each employed a feodary to collect them.[39] The

---

[38] Roger Gale, *Registrum Honoris de Richmond* (1722), 33–5.

[39] Ibid. 78–80, 81–2, 87. Several feodary's accounts of the Marmion Fee have survived in the Jervaulx archive deposited at the North Yorks. Record Office. See e.g. ZJX 3/2/40, 76, 89, 96, 99, 114, 115. The feodary also collected the perquisites of the old baronial court which still met 17 times a year at the village of Thornborough near Tanfield to deal with suits concerning the free tenants of the barony. The records of this court have survived in great number (see ZJX 3/1/70–116).

impact on the subtenants can be illustrated in the case of the township of Croft, which was part of the Scrope fee. In c.1440 John Clervaux paid 2s. 11d. in the free rent for his lands there, his brother Thomas 1s. and a barbed arrow, his son Richard 2½d., and three lesser tenants a penny, a halfpenny, and a pound of cinnamon respectively.[40] The fines and wards ran at a few pence each. In material terms these payments meant little. But it would seem that they retained symbolic significance. In 1465 John, Lord Scrope of Bolton was prepared to sell all his customary lands in Croft to Richard Clervaux; but he insisted on retaining the free rents, fines, and castleguard for all the land held by knight-service, as well as the lordship of the manor.[41] Thus the annual rendering of this rent continued to provide a ritual renewal and reminder of the feudal subservience of tenant to lord.

More tangible and substantial than the delivery of a rose at midsummer or a barbed arrow on St Ellen's day was the feudal right to relief and wardship which was exercised by mesne lords over their tenants. In 1465 Lord Scrope conceded this right in Croft. But Scrope, like FitzHugh, continued to exercise the right elsewhere. For instance, in 1417/18 Henry FitzHugh received £33. 6s. 8d. from William Danby for the marriage of John Laton, one of his wards, and £14. 6s. 8d. from William Appleton for Marmaduke Exelby.[42] The right of wardship of his subtenants was clearly of significant financial value to FitzHugh. Henry, third earl of Northumberland in the 1420s enjoyed the wardship of young William Plumpton, who held Plumpton of his barony of Spofforth. And one should not forget that it was over just such an issue as the wardship of the heiress of Sir John Hastings of Fenwick that his descendant fell foul of Henry VII in 1505.[43]

[40] Gale, Registrum, pp. 81–2.   [41] Pollard, 'Richard Clervaux', p. 156.
[42] NYCRO, zjx 3/2/60.
[43] Plumpton Correspondence, l; M. M. Condon, 'Ruling Élites in the Reign of Henry VII', in Ross, Patronage, Pedigree and Power, 119. See also M. E. James, 'The First Earl of Cumberland and the Decline of Northern Feudalism', NH 1 (1966), 48–51 and K. B. McFarlane, The Nobility of Later Medieval England (Oxford, 1973), 215–16 for the persistence of mesne lordship and its continuing profitability on the Clifford and Percy estates in the early 16th cent. McFarlane's brief comment on the importance of feudal lordship was directed to its financial implications; its social significance was perhaps greater. Note also the quickening royal interest in feudal dues apparent from the last years of Edward IV (Somerville, Duchy of Lancaster, i. 243–5).

Certain lords enjoyed further legal privileges which set them apart from and above their fellow peers and gentry. All lords of manors, by definition, enjoyed the right to manorial jurisdiction. Some additionally held the assizes of bread and ale, gallows, and infangetheof. But in north-eastern England there were more substantial liberties held by some of the king's greater subjects (Map 5). The earls of Richmond possessed return of writ in Richmondshire, as did the Lords Fauconberg in Langbaurgh. The sheriff of Yorkshire had no access to these districts, where the lord's steward or bailiff carried out his functions. By the later fifteenth century the hereditary bailiwick of Langbaurgh had in fact been transferred to the Middleham Nevilles, so that these lords exercised shrieval authority right across the far north of Yorkshire from the Pennines to the coast.[44] Others also enjoyed substantial franchises; the archbishop of York in Hexham and Ripon; the prior of Tynemouth in Tynemouth; and the lords of Kyme, the Tailboys, in Redesdale.[45] The greatest liberty of all was that of the bishops of Durham, which extended to enclaves beyond the land between the Tyne and Tees in Norham, Islandshire, and Bedlington to the north and the manor of Crayke to the south. Although mesne lord of Northallertonshire and a substantial landowner, by the fifteenth century the bishop had however lost the privilege of return of writ there. In the bishopric itself, the bishop was a great baron as well as prelate. In terms of landed wealth, jurisdictional privilege, and the men he commanded he was potentially a regional magnate in his own right. But, because of his peculiar elective position, his office being in practice filled by the king, and because of the influence exerted even within the palatinate by the Nevilles, no bishop in the later fifteenth century was able to realize his independent power.[46]

These extensive privileges enjoyed by certain northern noblemen (lay and clerical) not only set them above and apart from

---

[44] M. Clanchy, 'The Franchise of Return of Writ', *TRHS* 5th ser., 17 (1967), 60; *VCH, NR* i. 12, 17; ii. 218; *CPR 1467–77*, 483.

[45] For descriptions of the liberties of Hexhamshire and Tynemouth see A. B. Hinds, *A History of Northumberland, vol. iii: Hexhamshire*, pt. i (Newcastle, 1896), 23–30; and Craster, *Tynemouth*, pp. 207–16.

[46] K. Emsley, 'The Yorkshire Enclaves of the Bishop of Durham', *YAJ* 57 (1975), 106–7; and below, pp. 123–4; 145–7.

gentry, but also gave them quasi-regal authority. They represented a significant diminution of direct royal authority in the region. Moreover, as a landowner, until 1483 the Crown was conspicuously badly endowed. The only substantial Crown lands north of the Ouse were the duchy of Lancaster's honour of Pickering (including Easingwold and Huby) and barony of Embleton (Dunstanburgh), and the royal barony of Bamburgh (Map 5). This, apart from a small parcel of ancient demesne at Deighton in the North Riding (let to farm to the Nevilles of Middleham), was the extent of the royal estate in the region, until the accession of Richard III (swiftly followed by Henry VII) brought in the Neville of Middleham patrimony and the earldom of Richmond.[47] Although the Crown, through the duchy of Lancaster, had a strong presence in the West Riding, further north it was, until 1483, singularly weak. This territorial weakness, as well as the independent strength of the magnates, especially the Middleham Nevilles, was of profound significance for the balance of local power before 1483.

A central tenet of landed society was that the patrimony, the core of an inheritance, descending from father to son by primogeniture, should remain intact. Marriage contracts of eldest sons commonly contained a clause guaranteeing that the groom would ultimately inherit the patrimony. Thus, in 1427 Ellen Pickering secured for her daughter the undertaking from William Burgh I that 'the said William the father grants, promises and accords that after his mother's decease, his wife's and his own the said William the son or his heirs aforesaid shall inherit immediately lands and tenements to the value of 100 marks yearly'.[48] The lion's share customarily passed to the eldest son. Passions were aroused when exceptionally a father sought to break custom, particularly, as in the famous case of Ralph, first earl of Westmorland, in favour of the eldest son by the second marriage. Fortunately for the stability of north-eastern society few lesser men sought to emulate the earl.

[47] Tynedale was held by the Crown from 1415 to 1474, when it was granted by Edward IV to his cousin Isabel and her husband, Henry Bourgchier, earl of Essex. In 1484 it reverted to the Crown (M. H. Dodds, *A History of Northumberland, vol. xv: Parish of Simonsburn, etc.* (1940), 284–5).

[48] NYCRO, ZRL/1/24.

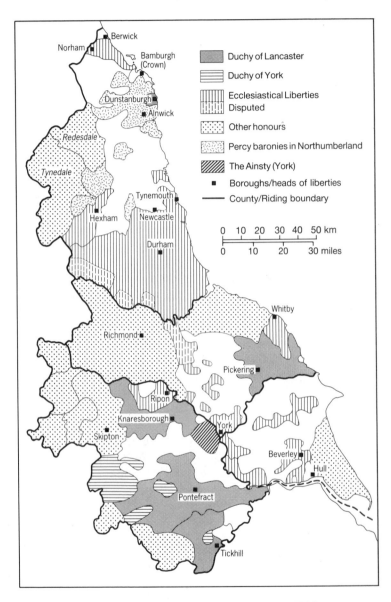

Legend:

- Duchy of Lancaster
- Duchy of York
- Ecclesiastical Liberties
- Disputed
- Other honours
- Percy baronies in Northumberland
- The Ainsty (York)
- ■ Boroughs/heads of liberties
- — County/Riding boundary

0   10   20   30   40   50 km
0   10   20   30 miles

Labels on map:
Berwick, Norham, Bamburgh (Crown), Dunstanburgh, Alnwick, Redesdale, Tynedale, Tynemouth, Hexham, Newcastle, Durham, Whitby, Richmond, Pickering, Ripon, Knaresborough, York, Skipton, Beverley, Hull, Pontefract, Tickhill

Map 5. BARONIES, HONOURS AND PALATINE LIBERTIES
(based on R. R. Reid, *King's Council in the North*, end map).

A system of primogeniture put pressure on the heads of families to make special provision for their younger sons. It is well established that some were placed in the professions or trades. Many examples can be cited. Most prominent families sponsored at least one of their sons in an ecclesiastical career. They normally aspired to no more than a comfortable country living, more often than not on the presentation of their own kinsman. Such modest careers were enjoyed by George Mountford, George Wandesford, and Thomas Danby, third son of Robert Danby, Chief Justice of Common Pleas.[49] Christopher Conyers, younger son of Christopher of Hornby and younger brother of Sir John, came somewhat late in life to his vocation. He progressed from acolyte, through subdeacon and deacon to priest in rapid succession within seven months in 1455–6; a progress culminating in his presentation to the rectory of Rudby in Cleveland by his brother, who had only recently acquired the advowson in right of his wife. Christopher enjoyed a rectoral manor in Rudby, and was content to play the role of ecclesiastical squire until his death in 1483.[50] Master William Eure, son of Sir William, on the other hand, rose to be precentor of York. Equally ambitious was George Strangways, son of Sir James, who was admitted MA at Oxford in 1468, was rector of Bulmer 1468–84, and held the cure of the family free chapel at Whorlton castle (1475–1503). He was collated to the prebend of Osmotherley in the North Riding, and ended his days as Rector of Lincoln College, Oxford.[51]

George FitzHugh, a younger son of Henry, Lord FitzHugh, 'pushed forward with that scandalous haste which marked the rise of so many members of noble families' (James Raine), rose to be Master of Pembroke College, Cambridge at eighteen and Dean of Lincoln at twenty-one (in 1483). But there his career

[49] BL, Ad. Ch. 66416; *Test. Ebor.* iii. 285–6; *Yorks. Deed.* iii, 74; *Test. Ebor.* iv. 117. For the most recent discussion of careers open to younger sons see Morgan, 'English Gentleman'. I have found little evidence of north-eastern younger sons making a career out of the profession of arms. For the question of chivalry generally see below, Ch. 6.

[50] *Test. Ebor.* iii. 287–93. Rudby was valued at £42 p.a. for the clerical subsidy of 1428, and was the richest living in the North Riding (*Feudal Aids*, vi. *Yorkshire* (HMSO, 1906), 343–52, esp. 346).

[51] A. B. Emden, *A Biographical Register of the University of Oxford to AD 1500*, iii. (Oxford, 1959), 1796.

stopped, either because he had reached the limit of his ability or because he lost his patron. He died twenty years after the death of Richard III without having enjoyed further preferment.[52] More spectacularly successful careers were enjoyed by Robert Stillington, a younger son of Stillington of Nether Acaster, who was Bishop of Bath and Wells 1465–91, and by Richard Redman, the younger son of Sir Richard of Levens, Westmorland and Harewood. A Premonstratensian canon, Redman became abbot of his house, Shap, before being promoted to St Asaph in 1468, holding the abbacy *in commendam*. He was a tireless vicar-general of his order in England, and rose under Henry VII first to Exeter (1496) and finally to Ely (1501).[53] But not even Redman's career could compare with the meteoric careers of the younger Nevilles, Robert, bishop of Durham (d. 1457) and George, archbishop of York (d. 1476).

The most profitable alternative to an ecclesiastical career was a legal career. Robert Danby, CJCP (d. 1474) was the younger son of Thomas Danby of Yafforth, North Riding. His own second son, Richard, followed in the law. Others to take the same route were Thomas Conyers, brother of Christopher the clerk; Miles Metcalfe, younger son of James of Nappa; Richard Pigot, serjeant-at-law; and Thomas Middleton of Stockeld.[54] Another career opportunity lay in secular administration: Edward Plumpton, brother of Sir Robert, became secretary to Lord Strange; Robert Constable, a younger son of Marmaduke Constable of Flamborough, became one of the chief financial officers in the north of Richard Neville, earl of Salisbury.[55] If a profession were not followed, a son could be put to trade. George Burgh, a younger son of William II of Brough (d. 1465), made his way in London, his grandson Roger eventually inheriting the family estates in 1546.[56] Edward Gower, younger brother of Thomas of Stittenham, seems to have begun his career as a

---

[52] *Test. Ebor.* iv. 245; Emden, *A Biographical Register of the University of Cambridge to AD 1500* (Cambridge, 1963), 231. It is to be presumed that several young gentlemen of their generation destined for the church owed their name 'George' to their godfather, George Neville, archbishop of York.

[53] For Redman see E. A. Gasquet, *Collectanea Anglo-Premonstratensia*, Camden, 3rd ser., vol. vi, pt. i (1904), pp. xix–xx.

[54] For fuller discussions of the careers of these men see below, pp. 133–7.

[55] *Plumpton Correspondence*, p. 44, and below, pp. 137–9.

[56] A. J. Pollard, 'Burghs of Brough', pp. 19–20.

stockfishmonger in Hull, although later he seems to have risen through archiepiscopal to royal service as an usher of Richard III's chamber.[57] Younger sons of Crathorne and Salvin set themselves up in trade in York. Brian Conyers, younger son of Christopher of Hornby, exceptionally seems to have combined possession of the manor of Pinchinthorpe, purchased and granted to him by his father, with a career in the city of York which saw him take on the burden of being a city chamberlain in 1475/6.[58]

It would appear, however, that most younger sons, like Brian Conyers, relied first and foremost upon the settlements that their fathers were prepared to make for them; or if they were lucky, the windfall of marriage to an heiress. Only the very wealthiest families, such as the Eures, Strangways, or Conyers, could afford to establish younger sons independently in the ranks of the manorial gentry. Henry Eure, second son of Sir William of Witton, succeeded to his father's property in Old Malton. James Strangways, second son of Sir James, was established by his father at Sneaton near Whitby.[59] However the most thorough and generous towards his younger sons was Christopher Conyers of Hornby. The scale of his largess is revealed in a settlement made in February 1460, whereby he added to his gift to his second son Thomas of the manor of Stakesby, near Whitby, his purchased lands in East Hawkswell, West Hawkswell, and Hunton; granted to another son Robert the manor of Hutton Wiske and lands to the value of £10; granted to Richard his lands in South Cowton, Melsonby, and Hutton; to George his manor of Thornton-on-the-Moor; to Brian, his eldest son by his second wife, the manor of Pinchinthorpe and purchased lands in eight other places; and to Nicholas, his second son by his second marriage, his manor of Holtby (which ultimately passed to a third brother, Henry).[60] Christopher was perhaps able to be so generous to his younger sons because his oldest son

[57] Horrox, 'Richard III and the East Riding', p. 83.
[58] BL, Egerton Ch. 3402, fo. 96ᵛ; York City Chamberlains' Accounts Rolls, 1396–1500, ed. R. B. Dobson, SS, cxcii (1980), 151. For discussion of urban gentry in general and men like Conyers in particular see R. E. Horrox, 'The Urban Gentry in the Fifteenth Century', in Thomson, Towns and Townspeople, pp. 22–44, esp. 27.
[59] Test. Ebor. iii. 223–4; J. S. Roskell, 'Sir James Strangeways of West Harlsey and Whorlton', YAJ 34 (1958), 481.   [60] BL, Egerton Ch. 3402, fos. 96–7.

and heir, Sir John, had already married the joint heiress of Philip, Lord Darcy, and was by 1460 an extremely wealthy man in his own right.

The younger Conyers sons were very much the exception. Most younger sons found themselves trying to sustain the style of gentleman on a small life interest. William Neville of Thornton Bridge (d. 1469) willed his younger sons Geoffrey and Ralph 10 marks yearly out of Kirby-on-the-Moor. Their elder brother in his turn (1484) made a life settlement out of Cundall for his younger son, Thomas. Sir John Constable of Halsham (d. 1472), a more substantial man than either of the Nevilles, was no more generous to his younger sons Ralph and William, who were to have similar life estates of 10 marks per annum in Thrintoft and Dodington. Edmund Mauleverer of Ingleby Arncliffe willed only 6 marks each to his younger sons, adding a condition that if any be preferred in marriage or benefice to the value of £20 yearly the life interest would revert to his eldest son and heir.[61] These younger sons, without professional careers or heiresses to rescue them, seem to have sunk without trace into the lower ranks of society. What happened, for instance, to Henry, William, and Christopher Mountford, who are all portrayed in full armour in their family brass memorial at St Mary's Hornby?[62] And whither did Thomas, John, Richard, James, Edward, and Brian Burgh, all sons of William Burgh II of Brough, disappear? Thomas was granted by his father £40 'to find him at court in London'; John, Richard, and James each received cash legacies of 40 marks under the terms of their father's will; Edward and Brian, still children, were to be kept at school until they were eighteen. None later seems to have made any impact on the world.[63] These boys, and many like them, victims of the English

---

[61] *Test. Ebor.* iii. 263–4; iv. 279 n; W. Brown, *Ingleby Arncliffe and its owners* (Leeds, 1901), 104. But Sir Hugh Hastings of Fenwick 10 years later set aside 20 marks each in Norfolk and Yorkshire for his 3 younger sons (*Test. Ebor.* iv. 275–6). Cf. Wright, *Derbyshire Gentry*, p. 48 and Carpenter, 'Gentry and their Estates', p. 52 for a similar level of endowment in Derbyshire and Warwickshire.

[62] E. C. Holman, *The Church of St. Mary the Virgin, Hornby, North Yorkshire* (Bedale, 1978). A deed of 1474 reveals that George—not Henry, as given by Flower and followed by Holman—was the son in holy orders (BL, Ad. Ch. 66416).

[63] NYCRO, ZRL/1/53. For the plight of younger sons in general see Morgan, 'English Gentleman', p. 21.

custom of impartible inheritance, seem already to have embarked on a downward social journey.

One hope for a younger son was to marry an heiress. But for this to happen his father had to be prepared to put up the appropriate jointure. Moreover, since there were never enough heiresses to satisfy demand, inevitably the wealthiest families were in the best position to secure those available. Thus Sir James Strangways arranged the marriage of Anne, sole daughter of Robert Conyers of Ormesby, to his second son James, independently established by him at Sneaton. Robert Danby, CJCP secured Anne, heiress of Sir John Langton of Farnley, for his eldest son Sir James.[64] But again it was the Conyers family, with large broods to satisfy and the resources at hand to do so, who were most successful. Their own fortunes were in fact founded on such a marriage, for John Conyers, father of Christopher, was a younger son of Robert Conyers of Sockburn, who in the reign of Richard II had married Margaret, heiress of Anthony St Quintin of Hornby.[65] Christopher married one son, Roger, to Sybil Langton, the heiress of Wynyard in Co. Durham, and another, William, to Elizabeth Cleasby, heiress of Marske in Richmondshire. In the next generation Richard, second son of Sir John, was married to Elizabeth Claxton, joint heiress of Sir Robert Claxton of Horden, Co. Durham.[66] This was not, however, a one-way traffic: Sir Richard, brother of Sir John, died in 1503, leaving three daughters; and the lion's share of his lands passed with the eldest, Margery, into the hands of Ralph Bowes of Streatlam, Co. Durham.[67]

It was clearly a matter of major concern to gentle families that the right marriages were made by their children; and much time, money, and energy were expended on arranging them. Most important to the makers of a marriage contract were the financial terms agreed. The father or guardian of the groom provided a jointure to support his daughter-in-law, held jointly in survivorship with her new husband, which would enhance or

---

[64] Roskell, 'Strangeways', p. 481; J. Fisher, *History and Antiquities of Masham and Mashamshire* (1865), 252–3.

[65] BL, Egerton 3402, fos. 92^v–93. He, too, was a lawyer, who prospered in the service of John of Gaunt (Somerville, *Duchy of Lancaster*, i. 481–2).

[66] For their marriages see Pollard, 'Richmondshire Gentry', p. 58.

[67] *VCH, North Riding*, i. 75.

supersede the dower should the groom predecease his bride. The father or guardian of the bride paid a high price for the jointure, in the form of the portion she took with her. The cost of a marriage portion ran at approximately eight to ten times the annual income of the agreed jointure. Thus Robert Tempest put up £40 for the marriage of his daughter Jane to John Trollope in 1478, which secured a jointure of 8 marks. On a more modest scale Robert Sedgwick found a portion of £20 for his daughter when she married Roger Marley, whose father made an enfeoffment of £2 on her behalf. Richard Clervaux seems to have secured a good bargain in 1475, when the portion cost only 80 marks, to be paid over seven years, in exchange for a jointure of £10 p.a. for his daughter Jane. But this was because her husband, Christopher, was but the younger brother of Roger Aske, then the head of the family, who demanded, as the price for his support, that a third of the jointure should be paid to him for the rest of his life. At the other extreme, earlier in the century, Ellen Pickering agreed to provide a down payment of £100 on the day of the wedding, followed by an instalment of 50 marks a year later, for a jointure of £10 p.a. for her daughter on the occasion of her marriage to William Burgh, son and heir of William Burgh.[68]

The proper provision for unmarried daughters was evidently a matter of concern to will-makers. Leading gentry made very substantial allowances. In 1472 Sir John Constable of Halsham left a total of 1,200 marks to be divided between four daughters, Janet, the eldest, being allocated 500. Sir Hugh Hastings of Fenwick arranged for £1,000 to provide for the marriage of his four daughters in 1482. More modestly, Edmund Mauleverer willed in 1488 that 80 marks be set aside for each of his three daughters, adding a life interest in his purchased lands in Ingleby Arncliffe for the elder, Beatrice. William Neville of Thornton Bridge provided £40 for each of his daughters in 1469; but William Conyers of Thormanby could only set aside 20 marks for his daughter Margaret.[69] Patrons sometimes helped out.

[68] Dur. RO, D/St/2, 147, 157, 175; NYCRO, ZRL/1/24; Glamis MS, NRA (S), 885, Box 13. Sir William Plumpton, who spent £376. 13s. 4d. on the marriages of 3 of his 6 daughters, paid approximately 10:1 (*Plumpton Correspondence*, lxxxii–lxxxxv). Rates in Derbyshire seem to have fluctuated more than in north-east England (Wright, *Derbyshire Gentry*, pp. 42–6 and App. 4a).

[69] *Test. Ebor.* iii. 263n., 278; iv. 110, 274, 278; Brown, *Ingleby Arncliffe*, pp. 104–5.

Joan, countess of Westmorland provided £20 for Alice, the daughter of Isabel Whixley, one of her servants; and Henry, earl of Northumberland, in his will dated 10 May 1485, set aside 100 marks for his niece Elizabeth Gascoigne.[70]

Parents seem to have shown greater concern for the well-being of daughters than of younger sons. Perhaps sons were considered to be more able to look after their own interests. Be that as it may, provision for daughters was a major drain on resources, and clearly left little for younger sons. The concern of parents to see that their daughters were properly married and well-provided should caution us against too ready condemnation of the fifteenth-century landed élite as heartless marriage brokers. We should not forget, moreover, that most of the evidence comes from legal documents. A contract of marriage or a last will by its very nature and purpose is concerned with the material side of marriage: neither is the customary place for expression of affection or love.[71]

When fifteenth-century match-makers spoke of lovers they were more likely to refer to the parents than to the betrothed; as did Sir James Strangways of West Harlsey, when he wrote to an unidentified correspondent, 'his good master', seeking his help in the matter of a papal dispensation for the marriage of Thomas Surtees of Dinsdale and Elizabeth Conyers of Sockburn. 'It is so', he wrote, 'that two of my friends and nigh of my blood would marry their children together: and the children be siblings at the third and fourth degree; and the fathers of the children love right well together and they be right nigh neighbours.'[72] Strangways's intervention on behalf of his friends draws our attention to the manner in which intermarriage linked the landed into a close-knit social network, bound together not only by neighbourhood but also by blood. Although eldest sons tended to be married

---

[70] *Scriptores Tres*, p. cclx; *Wills and Inventories*, p. 100.

[71] For recent discussion of medieval marriage see: K. Dockray, 'Why did Fifteenth-Century English Gentry marry? The Plumptons and Stonors Reconsidered', in Jones, *Gentry and Lesser Nobility*; C. F. Richmond, 'The Pastons Revisited: Marriage and the Family in Fifteenth-Century England', *BIHR* 58 (1985), 25–36; and A. McFarlane, *Marriage and Love in England* (Oxford, 1986), 181–3, 196–7.

[72] *Test. Ebor.* iii. 292 n. The impediment to the projected marriage was that the couple were both descended from daughters of Henry, Lord FitzHugh (d. 1425).

into a higher social status or into families residing further away, the marriages of younger children frequently cemented local alliances. Sir James Strangways himself married Elizabeth Darcy, joint heiress of Philip, Lord Darcy; and his eldest son Richard married Elizabeth Neville, joint heiress of William Neville, Lord Fauconberg. Sir James's daughters, however, married sons of Aske, Clervaux, Ingleby, and Mauleverer.[73] Clervaux and Aske may have been seated further to the west in Richmondshire; but Ingleby and Mauleverer had landed interests very near to Strangways at West Harlsey. Three generations of Clervaux heirs married daughters of Lumley, Co. Durham, Vavasour of Haslewood, in the West Riding, and Hussey of Sleaford, Lincs.; but Richard Clervaux's younger children married, in addition to Strangways, children of Aske, FitzHenry, Laton, and Conyers of Wynyard.[74] Once again the proliferous Conyers family provides one of the best examples of these tendencies. As we have already seen, Sir John Conyers married Margery, the other Darcy heiress, making him Strangways's brother-in-law. His own eldest son married Joan, the other Neville of Fauconberg heiress, and his grandson and heir William married first Mary, daughter of John, Lord Scrope, and secondly Ann, daughter of Ralph, third earl of Westmorland. Sir John had twenty-four brothers and sisters. Four younger brothers married daughters of Wycliffe, Frank, Cleasby, and Langton of Wynyard. Sisters married sons of Aske (two of them), Burgh, Lascelles, FitzHugh, Pickering, Pudsay (two again), Nelson, and Wycliffe. For some of Sir John's own eleven younger children marriage alliances were concluded with Askew, Claxton (of Horden, Co. Durham), Markenfield, Mountford, Place, and FitzWilliam of Sprotbrough in the West Riding.[75] Most of these were Richmondshire families; and those that were not were from nearby districts.

It would be merely repetitious to catalogue further examples of gentle intermarriage. The fact is that in the later fifteenth century gentry families tended to form marital alliances within their own localities. An analysis of Plumpton family marriages,

---

[73] *Visitation of the North*, pp. 106–7; Roskell, 'Strangeways', pp. 480–1.
[74] Pollard, 'Richard Clervaux', pp. 160–1.
[75] Pollard, 'Richmondshire Gentry', pp. 47–8.

for instance, shows in the neighbourhood of Knaresborough a
different social network to that in which the Conyers were tied
further north.[76] These networks were not altogether mutually
exclusive; rather the gentry seem to have been linked to one
another by a series of interlocking networks of kin and
friendship groups. These links were not restricted to their own
social status. Although peers tended to marry their eldest sons
to the daughters of fellow peers, their younger children married
into the senior ranks of the gentry, as well as the peerage. Thus
successive generations of FitzHugh married the daughters of
fellow northern peers. FitzHugh girls married both peers and
gentry: three sisters of Henry (d. 1474) married peers, three
married gentry; two of his daughters married peers, two
gentry.[77] Other examples of prominent gentry marrying daughters of local lords can be cited. Sir James Strangways II married
Alice, daughter of Thomas, Lord Scrope of Masham; Christopher Danby, son of Sir James, married her sister Margery; Ralph
Eure (d. 1461) married Eleanor Greystoke and Thomas Salvin of
Newbiggin married Maud Greystoke, who later also married Sir
Edmund Hastings of Roxby.[78] Widows such as Maud Greystoke
had greater freedom, and sometimes married men of less exalted
station. Thus Eleanor, widowed daughter of John, Lord Scrope of
Masham, married William Claxton, a younger son of Thomas
Claxton of Old Park, Durham; and Agnes, daughter of Henry,
fourth Lord Scrope of Bolton, chose, after the death of Sir
Christopher Boynton,[79] Richard Ratcliffe as her second husband. There was no rigid line between peers and gentry when it
came to marriage. Hence it could be proudly proclaimed of
Richard Clervaux of Croft in his epitaph that, as a result of a
common Neville ancestor, 'he was of the blood of both Edward
IV and Richard III in the third degree'.[80] A lesser Yorkshire
knight was in fact the second cousin of Yorkist kings.

    Besides kinship, the landed were brought together as a group,

---

[76] *Plumpton Correspondence*, p. lxxix.
[77] *CP* v., interleaves 432–3; vi. 197–8; J. W. Clay, *The Extinct and Dormant
Peerage of the Northern Counties of England* (1913), 75–98.
[78] *Test. Ebor.* iii. 273; *CP* vi. 197–8; xi. 569–70; Clay, *Peerage*, pp. 204,
109–200.
[79] *Plumpton Correspondence*, p. xl.
[80] Pollard, 'Richard Clervaux', pp. 168–9.

not always amicably, by their common interest in the protection of the titles to their estates. Because of the development
of legal forms such as the use and the last will, which enabled
greater flexibility in the settlement of lands, which provided a
means of setting aside income for the payment of debts, and
which formed a device for avoiding the incidents of feudalism,
the landed constantly called upon their friends and neighbours
as feoffees, executors, witnesses, and, when things went wrong,
arbitrators to help arrange their affairs. Here was a second
important network; a network of mutual co-operation in the
management of property. Out of innumerable examples of enfeoffments to use three may be cited. On 4 April 1463 John
Wandesford of Kirklington arranged for his property, which had
been enfeoffed in the hands of William Burgh, Sir James Strangways, Christopher Conyers of Hornby, and Randolph Pigot of
Clotherholme, to be transferred to a younger group of Thomas
Mountford, John Pigot, and Richard Pigot.[81] On 20 March 1469
Sir John and Lady Conyers enfeoffed their principal properties at
Hornby, Yarm, Whorlton, and elsewhere in the hands of Sir
Christopher Conyers of Sockburn, Sir John Pickering of Oswald-
kirk, Thomas Tunstall, William Tunstall (Lady Conyers' half-
brothers), Richard Conyers of Cowton (Sir John's brother), Miles
Metcalfe, Cuthbert Lightfoot, John Shirwynd, clerk (vicar of
Hornby), and Richard Greyson.[82] And on 1 December 1474
Roger Aske similarly placed his estates in the hands of the
following feoffees: Richard, Lord FitzHugh, Richard Strangways
(son of Sir James), Richard Pigot, James Strangways (son of
Richard), James Strangways of Sneaton, William Conyers of
Marske, Thomas Mountford of Hackforth, Thomas Mountford
(the last's son and heir), George Strangways, clerk, and George
Mountford, clerk.[83] Several general characteristics of enfeoffment are revealed in these three examples. One is the desire of
feoffors to maintain continuity, either by periodic renewal (as in
the case of Wandesford) or by employing representatives of

[81] McCall, *Wandesforde*, p. 198.
[82] *CIPM, Henry VII*, i. 278; H. T. McCall, *Richmondshire Churches* (1910), 59.
[83] BL, Ad. Ch. 66416. The most spectacular, if late, example is the group of 22 local gentlemen who became trustees of a jointure made in 1510 on behalf of the infant Elizabeth Aske (Dur. RO, B/BO/F17).

different generations of the same family (as in the case of Aske). A second is the importance of having legal representation. Richard Pigot, serjeant-at-law, is found on two of the three, Miles Metcalfe on the third. And finally one may note the trust placed in the clergy. Cuthbert Lightfoot, who was made a feoffee of Sir John Conyers in 1469, was probably a household chaplain at the time. He was subsequently presented by his master to Hutton Rudby, following the death of Christopher Conyers, in 1483. The lawyers are particularly significant: a man such as Richard Pigot was much in demand in northern England under Edward IV, not only as a feoffee, but also as legal counsel.[84]

It is perhaps more surprising to find men of similar rank also fully employed as witnesses to a whole variety of deeds concerning property, including enfeoffments. But at a time when titles were often uncertain (and frequently disputed), and when there was no system of registration, the evidence of witnesses could be critical. In a probate case at York in 1486, for instance, several men, including Roger Vincent, gave evidence concerning a disputed legacy in the Thwaites family, testifying that they were present at Great Smeaton when a grant of land was made to Henry Thwaites.[85] Some indication of the care that needed to be taken is revealed by the endorsement to a power of attorney issued by Robert and George Conyers (jun.) of Danby Wiske and John Fox, clerk, to deliver seisin of estates in South Cowton and elsewhere to Sir Richard Conyers in October 1487. In the endorsement, now only partially legible, it was noted that the possession had been delivered for all the lands in a close called Longwawde, and that four named and many other persons had been witnesses at the possession-taking.[86] Witnessing of deeds and all acts concerned with the conveyance of property was therefore of vital concern.[87] If the transaction was of major

---

[84] See below pp. 135–7.   [85] *Test. Ebor.* iii. 11.   [86] BL, Ad. Ch. 66451.
[87] The same concern is revealed by the steps taken to preserve title-deeds. John Lepton of Terrington, for instance, instructed that all the evidences of his land in Cleveland were to be put in the custody of his brother Master Ralph Lepton, and that all the rest were to be securely kept in a chest at Kirkham Abbey (*Test. Ebor.* iv. 129–30). Local monasteries offered a like service to modern banks as a depository for title-deeds. In 1510 the rival claimants to the Burgh inheritance agreed that the family deeds should be deposited in sealed chests at Durham, Jervaulx, or St Agatha's Easby (Pollard, 'Burghs of Brough', p. 19).

significance, the witnesses needed to be of high social standing. On 11 January 1465 for instance, Sir James Strangways, Sir Christopher Conyers of Sockburn, Christopher Boynton, and Thomas Surtees of Dinsdale, neighbours and friends, travelled to Croft to witness the final sealing of deeds and exchange of contracts which completed a complex exchange of property between Richard Clervaux and John, Lord Scrope of Bolton in Croft, Stapleton, and Cleasby. Even for the seemingly less important taking of a hundred-year lease by William Burgh III of the mills of Richmond from Mount Grace Priory Sir James Strangways jun., Sir John Conyers, Thomas Mountford, Richard Clervaux, and Roger Aske all gathered together at Brough Hall on 12 June 1482.[88] The extent of the circle of friends that could be called upon is revealed by the nineteen relatives, friends, and neighbours (all of whom were resident within twelve miles of Croft) who were witnesses to the numerous deeds executed by Richard Clervaux between 1440 and 1473, some of them as frequently as six times.[89] The variety of assistance that an individual could provide is indicated by the example of William Burgh III of Brough Hall, head of his family 1465–92, who is recorded as feoffee for William Clarke of Richmond in 1466, as a witness to deeds in 1476, 1482, and 1486, and as an executor to Robert Pynkney, vicar of Kirby Fleetham, in 1490.[90]

William Burgh III also acted as an arbitrator in three disputes in the year 1477/8.[91] However much the landed sought to avoid legal entanglement over their property, disputes inevitably arose, some of them time-consuming, costly, and potentially violent. Indeed the existence of conflicts over land, rents, and other rights seems to loom in the record as large as the routine day-to-day conveyancing. Sometimes these resulted from deliberate fraud. Jane, a daughter and joint-heiress of Sir Miles Stapleton of Ingham, found herself cheated by her second husband Sir John Huddleston of Millom because she could not read Latin. She had inherited from her father his share of the manors

---

[88] Pollard, 'Richmondshire Gentry', pp. 49–50.

[89] Pollard, 'Richard Clervaux', pp. 161–2.

[90] Dur. RO, D/St/2/143; BL, Ad.Ch. 66451; McCall, *Wandesforde*, p. 99; *Yorks. Deeds* iii. 74; *Test. Ebor.* iv. 43.

[91] McCall, *Wandesforde*, p. 327; NYCRO, ZQH, 1, fos. 155–6; A. H. Thompson, 'The Register of the Archdeacons of Richmond, 1422–77, Part 2', *YAJ* 32 (1936), 127–8; and Pollard, 'Burghs of Brough', p. 12.

of Cotherstone and Hunderthwaite in Teesdale. Sir John tricked Jane into signing the conveyance of a rent charge of £10 annually from Cotherstone to their son John, his wife, and the heirs of their bodies, at the expense of her eldest son and heir by her first husband, Christopher Harcourt. At the end of his life Sir John is reputed to have shown great remorse for his act. In her will, proved in 1519, Jane insisted that 'whereas my son John Huddleston had a feoffment within my lordship of Cotherstone as gift of my husband, that feoffment was made without my consent and I never did agree thereunto'. Her will was that the rent charge be restored to the heirs of Harcourt.[92] But the terms of the will were not executed, and the Huddlestons retained possession.

More commonly, conflict arose out of neither deliberate deceit nor malice, but from defective titles. How easily this could occur is shown by the failure of Richard Pigot, serjeant-at-law, of all people, to secure sound titles to his purchased lands. After his death in 1483 his widow was challenged by Robert Wyvill of Ripon, his nephew or cousin, for possession not only of his Yorkshire estates, but also of lands in Essex, Hertfordshire, and Whitechapel which he had devised to her for life. It is not that Pigot did not take the care one would have expected. He had bought lands in Little Burton, Wensleydale from John Aiscough in 1460. As part of the conveyance he specified that Aiscough should also hand over the title-deeds. Moreover in the following year he received a deed of gift from Richard Pigot senior (an uncle) for the same manor which had lately been the property of William Routh. On the same day he paid £10 to his uncle for a special deed of warranty in which he 'grants and appoints by this writing upon his truth and worship and as that he be a true gentleman and by the faith that he owes unto God that he shall not vex nor trouble' Richard the younger in respect of Little Burton. Notwithstanding these precautions, in 1484, a year after his death, his widow was constrained on bond of £1,000 to seek the arbitration of her husband's erstwhile legal colleagues Sir Guy Fairfax, Sir John Catesby, William Danvers, and Roland

---

[92] *North Country Wills* i. 96–7; H. S. Colper, 'Millom Castle and the Huddlestons', *Cumberland and Westmorland Antiquarian and Arch. Soc. Trans.*, NS, 24 (1924), p. 210; J. A. H. Moran, *The Growth of English Schooling, 1340–1548* (Princeton, 1985), 153.

Ludworth over the possession of Little Burton and his other acquisitions.[93] The outcome we do not know; but ultimately, as Pigot's own young son died without issue, Little Burton passed to the Wyvills without dispute.

It is not clear to what extent the nine or so separate suits in which Sir William Plumpton was involved between 1464 and 1477 (and which kept his solicitor Godfrey Green occupied) were unavoidable, or were the result of his own cantankerous zeal for litigation. The dispute with the minister and canons of St Robert of Knaresborough (over fishing rights and the mill dam at Plumpton) seems to have been the result of imperfect or conflicting titles; the obscure case concerning 'Ailmer wife', on the other hand, seems to have been more malicious. In the winter of 1476/7 Godfrey Green reported to Plumpton that the judges in the case understood that 'these men be not guilty, and is but only your maintenance . . .'. Furthermore, he wrote, 'Guy Fairfax said openly at the bar, that he knew so, verily they were not guilty.' 'I seeing this, took Mr Pigott and Mr Collow', Green concluded.[94] Whether right was on his side or not, all these suits were time-consuming and costly—a point that Green, and later Robert Plumpton, his own illegitimate son, were at pains to remind their master. 'It hath cost you money this term,' Green wrote concerning the question of the rights over the mill dam in 1469; 'Mr Middleton had great labour therewith [and] you may reward him yourself as it pleases you.' 'I send your mastership the bill of expenses and costs that I have made since I came hither and please you to see it and send money the next term,' wrote Plumpton on 1 April 1476.[95] In 1475 Green was duped by a supersedeas-monger, a fact which he embarrassingly admitted, explaining that 'I may not arrest him nor strive with him for the money, nor for the deceit, because the matter is not worshipful.'[96] Most of the cases dragged on for many years, as rival attorneys employed the customary delaying tactics available to them. 'As for all your other suits', Green commented ironically in 1475, 'they have the speed the law will give them.'[97] It is no wonder then that even Plumpton was prepared

[93] NYCRO, ZFW, MIC 1160.
[94] *Plumpton Correspondence*, pp. 9, 12, 22–3, 35.
[95] Ibid. 23, 37.   [96] Ibid. 30.   [97] Ibid.

to go to arbitration, although such a recourse was not instantly successful. By June 1464 Plumpton and the minister of St Robert had agreed to stand by the award of Sir John Mauleverer, but nothing came of this. It was not until 1471, when the parties came to terms through new arbitrators, that their long-standing dispute was settled.[98]

It is in the light of the cost and frustration suffered by Plumpton in his litigation that we should view the more abundant evidence of the settlement of disputes between other north-easterners by arbitration. Although no doubt quicker and cheaper, the putting of a dispute to the award of a panel of arbitrators representing both parties did not automatically guarantee an immediate settlement. Elizabeth Bulmer discovered this to her cost when she agreed to go to the arbitration of Sir Robert Claxton and Sir William Bowes (probably in the early 1460s) to settle a dispute with Lord Greystoke over some rents in Bulmer. From a letter subsequently written by Elizabeth to Claxton it would appear that an agreement was reached by the arbitrators at Durham, and the terms were then dispatched in sealed letters, delivered by Bowes to Elizabeth's brother Ralph at Yarm, and then taken on by his hand to Greystoke's son John. Greystoke however refused to implement the terms: 'so that me thinks', she wrote, 'his agreement but futile and his letters deceive me withal'. Moreover she had heard that Greystoke was once more attempting to raise the rents ('John his son has charged the tenants to make ready in all haste the remnant of the farm.'). She thus begged Claxton 'to ride and speak with Sir William for he is at coming home' to persuade him to write again, but this time to show the content to Claxton before the letter was sealed. And so her appeal to her 'most special and trusty cousin' ended.[99] Whether it was successful we do not know; but it is evident that attempts at arbitration did not necessarily run smoothly.

Arbitration, as an informal, extra-legal approach, could never be as secure as a legal verdict. Its advantages, however, in speed, cost, and, perhaps most of all, in repairing good relationships between the parties, assured that it was frequently preferred to

[98] Ibid. 22.
[99] BL, Add. MS 40746, fo. 6.

an all-out battle at law.[100] The putting of differences to a panel
of friends and neighbours was therefore another important
aspect of mutual assistance within landed society. A sense of
the importance of the role of friends and neighbours in settling a
dispute is revealed in the reconciliation of a long-running conflict over the claim of Thomas Fitton of Cawarden, Cheshire to a
rent of £5 in Croft and East Cowton. The Fittons had been lords
of East Cowton until they sold the manor to the Clervaux in the
early fourteenth century. Sir James Strangways and (for Fitton)
John Needham, justice of common pleas, were called in to
arbitrate, and in an indentured agreement made at Harlsey
castle on 15 June 1463 Clervaux bought out Fitton's claim for
£53. 13s. 8d., to be paid in four instalments ending on 24 June
1465. Strangways himself, and Roger Vincent and Thomas
Tailboys, both Clervaux's brothers-in-law, agreed to act as
Clervaux's guarantors. Three days earlier, at Croft on 12 June,
Fitton had formally quit his claim to the rent in the presence
of Strangways, Sir John Conyers, Thomas Mountford, John
Catterick of Stanwick, and John Killinghall of Middleton-St-
George, Durham.[101] The arbitrations in which William Burgh
III of Brough Hall was involved show the same concern of friends
and neighbours. On 7 August 1477, with Roger Aske, Thomas
Frank, Alan Fulthorpe, and Thomas Mountford, all Richmond-
shire squires, he gave judgement on behalf of the archdeacon of
Richmond in favour of Francis, Lord Lovell over the right of
advowson in the parish of Bedale.[102] In the following spring, on
10 March 1478, he arbitrated with Thomas Mountford, Richard

[100] For recent discussion of arbitration in late-medieval society see: I.
Rowney, 'Arbitration in Gentry Disputes in the Later Middle Ages', *History*, 67
(1982), 367–76; E. Powell, 'Arbitration and the Law in England in the Later
Middle Ages', *TRHS* 5th ser. 13 (1983), 49–67; M. A. Hicks, 'Restraint,
Mediation and Private Justice: George, Duke of Clarence as "good lord"', *J.
Legal History*, 4 (1983), 56–71; C. Carpenter, 'Law, Justice and Landowners in
Late Medieval England', *Law and History Review*, 1 (1983), 205–37; C. Rawclif-
fe, 'The Great Lord as Peacekeeper; Arbitration by English Noblemen and their
Councils in the Late Middle Ages', in J. A. Guy and H. G. Beale (eds.), *Law and
Social Change in British History*, RHS Study in History 40 (1984); and S. J.
Payling, 'Law and Arbitration in Nottinghamshire', in Joel Rosenthal and Colin
Richmond (eds.), *People, Politics and Community in the Later Middle Ages*
(Gloucester, 1987), 140–60.
[101] NYCRO, zQH I, fos. 158^{r–v}, 148, 146^v.
[102] Thompson, 'Archdeaconry of Richmond', pp. 127–8.

Pigot, and Sir Guy Fairfax in a quarrel between the abbot of St Mary's, York and the abbot of St Agatha's, Easby over the boundary between properties in Hudswell.[103]

Frequently lawyers were brought in to expedite arbitration. The Fitton–Clervaux issue was settled by two men with legal training. Pigot and Fairfax were two of the leading common lawyers of northern England. Not surprisingly lawyers were involved in the first attempt in 1480 to settle the dispute over the Plumpton inheritance between the heirs general and Robert Plumpton. As well as several prominent knights and esquires, among whom were William Gascoigne, Robert Constable, and Hugh Hastings, the matter was entrusted to the lawyers Thomas Middleton and Miles Metcalfe. The death of Sir William Plumpton in October 1480 brought this process prematurely to an end. When the matter was taken up again, on 21 May 1482, a new team of arbitrators was agreed, with serjeant John Vavasour replacing Middleton, but now led by Richard, duke of Gloucester and Henry Percy, earl of Northumberland. An award was made only after Gloucester became king.[104]

Ultimately an appeal to the local magnate seems to have been the resort of many gentlemen seeking to resolve their differences amicably. The services of Richard, duke of Gloucester were much in demand in this respect. In the spring of 1478, Richard Clervaux and his neighbour Roland Place of Halnaby took their quarrel over several issues to the duke. On 20 March they agreed to accept his arbitration, and bound themselves over in £100 each to keep the peace until such time as Gloucester should deliver his award. This was duly done at Middleham on 12 April, when Gloucester, 'tendering the peace and weal of the country where the said parties do inhabit and also gladly willing good concord, rest and friendly unity to be had from henceforth between the said parties' declared his decision. No doubt the duke's council put together the detailed terms concerning the prevention of future conflict over straying cattle, a recent exchange of lands, seating arrangements in the parish church, retaining of servants, and hunting rights. The implementation of the award, its supervision, and the resolution of any future

---

[103] McCall, *Wandesforde*, p. 327.
[104] *Plumpton Correspondence*, pp. lxxxi, lxxxix–xcvi.

problems was entrusted to a group of local dignitaries who may conceivably have advised on the award in the first place. These were Thomas Mountford, William Burgh, Thomas Frank, and William Pudsay, lately rector of Croft. These men were indeed called upon two years later to resolve a new dispute about the possession and maintenance of a dike. Apart from this, good concord, rest, and friendly unity seems to have been secured.[105] On other occasions, such as in a case between Thomas Ashton and Robert Hesketh in 1481, Gloucester seems to have delegated the decision to his legal counsel—Richard Pigot, Miles Metcalfe, and Thomas Ash.[106]

It was clearly as much in the interest of the magnates themselves as of the parties that the 'peace and weal of the country' was maintained, particularly if their own retainers and servants quarrelled. The earl of Northumberland was anxious to stifle and resolve any such disputes within his own affinity. In the early 1480s he wrote to Sir Robert Plumpton concerning a dispute between John Pullen of Knaresborough and George Tankard of Boroughbridge which had already been put to arbitration. 'I am informed,' wrote the earl, 'that the said parties be now at traverse in that behalf, contrary to such directions as were taken. I, willing the pacifying and reformation hereof by the advice of you and other of my counsel, desire and pray you Cousin, at your coming to me at York upon Thursday next coming, to cause the said George and the other persons to come with you.'[107] Presumably Pullen and Tankard had their heads knocked together for the last time. There was undoubtedly an underlying concern shared by gentry and lords alike to defuse and settle among themselves as many of their quarrels as they could. It was in their own self-interest so to do. In the settlement of property, as in marriage, landed society in north-eastern England revealed a strong sense of self-preservation.

[105] NYCRO, ZQH 1, fos. 155–156ᵛ; A. J. Pollard, 'Richard Clervaux', pp. 162–3.   [106] Yorks. Deeds, iii. 143–4.

[107] Plumpton Correspondence, p. 45. Cf. also Northumberland's concern to 'peacify' the grudge between Plumpton and Sir William Beckwith (pp. 72–3), and his letter instructing Plumpton to settle the quarrel between Thomas Saxston and Richard Ampleforth at Spofforth, telling him that since he 'had the rule there' he should use his discretion in settling such disputes, and make sure that the parties did not trouble the earl himself.

Two broad conclusions may be drawn about landed society in north-eastern England. The first is that in the distribution of land between laity and clergy, and lords and gentry, and in the practices relating to marriage, the management of inheritance, and the settlement of property the north-east was like the rest of England. The region's landed élite was part of one single, English, aristocracy. The second conclusion is that no qualitative difference can be drawn between lords and gentry. Recently historians have tended to emphasize the independent role and significance of the gentry. In so far as it is undoubtedly wrong to see the gentry of late-medieval England as merely subservient to the lords, this is a welcome development. But it goes too far to see them as a separate social group. Lords and gentry were all part of the same class: in chivalric and continental terms, gentry were but lesser nobility. Lords were the richer, the legally more privileged, and the more powerful; but they were still *primi inter pares*, not a caste apart. In so far as there was a community, or, more precisely, localized communities of landed society, these were communities of landed society which included *all* the landed, lords as well as gentlemen, all bound together by blood and common material interests. Yet it was a society led by its lords. This leadership is observable most directly in service, retaining, and local government; but it is also apparent, by example, in religion and chivalry.

5

Service: Good Lordship and Retaining

SERVICE to lords and to the Crown was a central feature of all gentlemen's lives; any discussion of it is bound to focus on retaining and bastard feudalism. This is not only the best documented, but also historiographically the most prominent feature. It is almost certainly the case, however, that the formal indenture of retainer and grant of an annuity were untypical and unrepresentative of the links between man and servant in fifteenth-century society. Informal ties and obligations resulting from myriad small services rendered by well-wishers in return for favours granted by good lords or masters were more characteristic of the relationship.

> Right worshipful and my especial good master, I recommend me unto your mastership, thanking your mastership heartily of your kindly and hearty mastership showed unto me, underserved of my part as yet. I beseech almighty *Jesu* that I might do that thing that might be pleasure to your mastership; you shall have my service. I have many things to thank your mastership for . . .[1]

So begins an undated letter written by John Morre to Sir Robert Plumpton: a letter which continues either to thank Plumpton for favours done, or to beg for favours to be done, on behalf of two of his friends—Richard Ampleforth and John Myming. The words 'master' or 'mastership' are used no fewer than twenty-one times in this nakedly fawning appeal. Such sycophancy was the common currency of a society whose wheels were oiled by the constant exchange of small favours. A quick glance through the *Plumpton Correspondence* reveals Sir Robert, and his father before him, being approached by all manner of people for assistance in all manner of matters, declaring themselves their true servants or good lords. Sir Robert himself behaved in the same cringing way towards Henry, earl of Northumberland. Henry

---

[1] *Plumpton Correspondence*, p. 77.

Hudson wrote to Robert from Greenwich in November 1486, reassuring him that: 'my lord faireth well and recommends him unto you, with hearty thanks of your good and fast love, which he intendeth to content your mind for'.[2] Plumpton was in fact a feed retainer of the earl. But we should place our understanding of the more precisely defined, legally and financially bound relationship between lord and retainer in the context of the wider world of well-wishers, good servants, and true lovers, who were constantly seeking the benefits of good mastership or good lordship at all levels of society. Formal retaining was but the tip of the iceberg.

By the law of the land, enshrined in the statute of 1468, retaining for life for service outside the household and other than legal counsel was restricted to the lords. And even the lords could only retain men of the rank of esquire or above, and then only on a life contract.[3] Such retaining, in peace as in war, was a restricted privilege. An alternative, favoured by the earls of Northumberland, was to pay annuities; but in practice, perhaps because the cost was similar and retaining was in fact no more certain to secure undivided and loyal service, there was no difference between the two.[4] It could be thought that, since the payment could be stopped at any time, an annuity paid during pleasure gave a lord more control than a contract for life. In fact, as evidence of the financial administration of both Richard, earl of Salisbury and his brother Robert, bishop of Durham shows, it was just as easy to stop the payment of a fee when a retainer failed to honour his contract.[5] In effect annuities and life retainers were interchangeable.

Retaining of armigerous gentry or knights on a large scale was

[2] Ibid. 52.

[3] McFarlane, *Nobility*, pp. 106–7; W. H. Dunham, *Lord Hastings' Indentured Retainers, 1461–1483*, Trans. of the Connecticut Academy of Arts and Sciences, 39 (1955), 67–89; J. P. Cooper, 'Retainers in Tudor England', in *Land, Men and Beliefs*, pp. 78–82.

[4] Bean, *Estates*, pp. 95–6. In this respect it is perhaps revealing that the receiver of Middleham listed the payment of fees to indentured retainers under the heading 'Annuitates' (PRO, DL 29/648/10485).

[5] As happened in c.1458 when the earl declined to pay the fee due to Sir Richard Hammerton, and in 1453–4 when the bishop cancelled by his privy seal payment of no fewer than 7 fees. A. J. Pollard, 'The Northern Retainers of Richard Neville, earl of Salisbury', *NH* 11 (1976), 61–2; Durham, Church Commission, Bishopric Estates, 189812. See also McFarlane, *Nobility*, pp. 105–6.

not generally widespread during the fifteenth century. Notwithstanding the attention paid to retaining by historians, the evidence of the income tax of 1436 shows that most lords were
sparing in the numbers of fees and annuities they paid to men
not in their household and administrative service or of their
legal counsel.[6] The most quoted of late-fifteenth-century retaining lords, William, Lord Hastings, was to a large extent acting as
the king's deputy as steward of the duchy of Lancaster at
Tutbury, when Edward IV needed to secure his control of the
kingdom.[7] In the north-east, in the second half of the century,
only the two leading magnates, the earls of Northumberland
and the Middleham Nevilles, retained on an equivalent scale. In
their cases this stemmed partly from their responsibilities as
wardens of the east and west marches (retaining was first and
foremost for service in war) and partly from their political
rivalry.

It might be expected that the bishops of Durham would have
vied with the earls. But only Bishop Neville (d. 1457) retained on
any significant scale. He shamelessly did so for the benefit of his
family. Booth (1457–76) had little desire to act as a temporal
power at all. He pointedly declined to use the resources of the
bishopric to retain knights and esquires for the cause of Lancaster at the start of his pontificate. Only when the Nevilles briefly
secured control of the temporalities (1462–4) was the bishopric
once again placed at the disposal of a local lay power. Dudley
(1476–83), on the other hand, reverted to earlier practice and
willingly retained men who were in the service of the duke of
Gloucester, though on a more modest scale than Neville. Shirwood (1483–93), as an absentee for most of his pontificate, was
for that reason unable to play an independent political role; and
Fox (1493–1502), as Henry VII's right-hand man, administered
the palatinate in the king's interest. Different causes led to the

---

[6] Ibid. 104; T. B. Pugh, 'The Magnates, Knights and Gentry', in Chrimes *et al.*,
Fifteenth-Century England, p. 103. See also Carole Rawcliffe, *The Staffords,
Earls of Stafford and Dukes of Buckingham, 1394–1521* (Cambridge, 1978),
72–7.
[7] I. Rowney, 'Resources and Retaining in Yorkist England: William, Lord
Hastings and the Honour of Tutbury', in A. J. Pollard (ed.), *Property and Politics:
Essays in Later Medieval English History* (Gloucester, 1984), 139–55; C.
Carpenter, 'The Duke of Clarence and the Midlands: A Study in the Interplay of
Local and National Politics', *Midland History*, 11 (1986), pp. 34–6, 41.

same effect: successive bishops did not seek to use the income of their temporalities, or their authority as a great baron, to create an independent affinity with which they might have challenged the lay magnates.[8]

The evidence for other lords is admittedly skimpy, but it would appear that they neither had the resources (the Percies and Middleham Nevilles were at least four times as wealthy) nor the political ambition to match the magnates. The lesser lay peers, Dacre, FitzHugh, Greystoke, and the Scropes, were content to follow the magnates, and indeed were often retained by them. Thus Salisbury retained both Thomas, Lord Dacre and Ralph, Lord Greystoke.[9] Henry, Lord FitzHugh (d. 1475) was retained by Richard Neville, earl of Warwick for one year at least in 1466 as his deputy warden of the west march, with an annual fee of £1,000; and Lords FitzHugh, Greystoke, Scrope of Bolton, and Scrope of Masham all entered Gloucester's service.[10]

In the first half of the century both Lord Henry and Lord William FitzHugh had eschewed large-scale retaining for other than household, estate, or legal service. Richard Burgh and Thomas Sedgwick were responsible for paying the retainers and servants of William, Lord FitzHugh after his death on 22 October 1452. In their account, presented to the dead baron's feoffees two and a half years later, they answered for £85. 19s. 7d., spent on the fees and rewards of thirty-nine people until Lady Day 1453. These thirty-nine included three chaplains and men with occupational surnames, such as Wardrope, Kitchen, Butre, and Faucondre. Only a handful, William Tailboys, Conan Lascelles, John Lasenby, and Sir James Strangways, drawn from the local

[8] This paragraph is based on an analysis of the evidence contained in the Durham Receiver-General accounts 1453–c.1497 (Durham, Church Commission, Bishopric Estates, 189812–31, 189598, 190217, 190288, 190309) and the record of grants made under the episcopal seal (Durh. 3/44,48,54,58, and 60). In 1453/4 Neville paid £223 to 22 annuitants and retainers. Of this sum £136. 6s. 8d. was paid to his brother Richard, earl of Salisbury and 2 of the earl's sons, John and Thomas. A further annuity of £60 had been granted to his brother William, Lord Fauconberg in 1441; but this was not paid in 1453/4, perhaps because Fauconberg was still at that time in prison in France. See also A. J. Pollard, 'St. Cuthbert and the Hog: Richard III and the County Palatine of Durham, 1471–85', in R. A. Griffiths and J. W. Sherborne (eds.), Kings and Nobles in the Later Middle Ages (Gloucester, 1986), 114–17.

[9] Northants RO, FitzWilliam MS 2049, 2052.

[10] W. Dugdale, The Baronage of England, i (1675), 405; Ross, Richard III, p. 49.

gentry and receiving substantial fees of £3 or more, would appear to have been indentured retainers. Of these Strangways was the best rewarded, taking his £6. 13s. 4d. p.a. in full until the closing of the books on 8 April 1455.[11]

Receivers' accounts for the FitzHugh northern estates suggest a similar state of affairs both earlier in William's life and during the life of his father Henry. In the late 1430s, William paid fees of £50 to £60 per annum from a regular rent charge of £300–£340 to a similar number, of whom the most generously rewarded were the receiver himself, William Catterick, William Aiscough, serjeant-at-law, and Thomas Middleton, esquire, all with fees of £3. 6s. 8d. Others who were still feed at the end of his life (John Catterick, William Tailboys, Richard Burgh, and John Lasenby) were then in receipt of fees of £2 or £2. 13s. 4d.[12] The situation was no different even under that great Lancastrian, Henry, Lord FitzHugh, who in 1413/14 paid fees totalling £67. 3s. 0d. to 55 people, of whom the most generously individually rewarded were his receiver and steward.[13] The financial records of the Lords FitzHugh in the first half of the century reveal no great commitment to, or burden of fees for, retaining beyond household, administrative, and legal needs.

Compare these figures with what is known of the scale of retaining undertaken by the earls of Northumberland and the lords of Middleham. If the schedule of costs for his funeral can be relied upon to indicate the size of his retained affinity, Henry, fourth earl of Northumberland was at the time of his death retaining eighty-four lords, knights, and esquires beyond his immediate household and legal needs.[14] The total burden of the fees and annuities he paid was £1,708. 14s. 7d.; 42.26 per cent of

[11] NYCRO, zjx 3/2/112.
[12] Ibid. 91, 93. Aiscough, Burgh, John Catterick, and Richard Sedgwick represented FitzHugh before Archbishop John Kemp on 24 Nov. 1434 in securing a dispensation for the marriage of their lord's daughter Elizabeth to Ralph, son and heir of Lord Greystoke (*Test. Ebor.* ii. 286).
[13] NYCRO, zjx 3/2/51.
[14] E. B. De Fonblanque, *Annals of the House of Percy*, i (1887), 550; compare this with the 86 lords, knights, esquires, and gentlemen identified by Dr Hicks who are known to have been retained by or served Northumberland at some time between 1470 and 1489 and who were alive in 1489 (M. A. Hicks, 'The Career of Henry Percy, 4th earl of Northumberland, with Special Reference to his Retinue' (unpublished University of Southampton MA thesis, 1971), Table III, pp. 87–99).

all his rents and farms. Eight years earlier, at least twenty-one knights served the earl in his Scottish campaigns.[15] The Nevilles and Richard of Gloucester retained on a comparable scale. In January 1458 John Bottoner wrote to Sir John Fastolf giving details of the retinues which were brought up to London for the great reconciliation or 'Loveday' organized by Henry VI. Richard Neville, earl of Salisbury, he reported, entered the city with 400 horse in his company and eighty knights and esquires. His comment is cryptic, but it appears to mean that Salisbury had eighty retainers accompanying him, and that the total number, including his own personal riding household, numbered 400. This was an impressive display.[16] At this time Salisbury was paying extraordinary fees of retainer to at least twenty men from the revenues of his lordship of Middleham alone; Warwick and Gloucester feed approximately twenty-four in 1465/6 and 1473/4 from this same lordship. The burden of all fees and annuities (household included) paid by Warwick and Gloucester from Middleham was just over £250 to forty-seven people in 1465/6, and £308 to sixty or more in 1473/4, from an expected income of approximately £1,000 p.a.[17]

Comprehensive documentation is lacking for both the Percies and the Nevilles in the second half of the fifteenth century, making it impossible to identify all their northern retainers. From the evidence that does survive, however, it is possible to see that much retaining was concentrated in the districts where each magnate held land. Mesne lordship and office ensured that in some districts family traditions of 'belonging' to one or other magnate persisted. The barony of Spofforth, hard by the duchy of Lancaster's honour of Knaresborough in which the earls of Northumberland frequently held the office of steward, is one such example, fortunately better documented than most because of the *Plumpton Correspondence*. In the 1480s Henry, fourth earl retained from this district not only Sir

[15] Bean, *Estates*, pp. 129–30. In 1471–2 the earl's receiver of Prudhoe and Langley paid 6 fees, including those of the steward and constable of Prudhoe, totalling £46, on the total current charge of £400 (*Percy Bailiff's Rolls of the Fifteenth Century*, ed. J. C. Hodgson, SS, cxxxiv (1921), 91–3); Hicks, 'Fourth Earl of Northumberland', pp. 103–7.   [16] *Paston Letters*, i. 532.
[17] Pollard, 'Northern Retainers', pp. 64–6; PRO sc6/1085/20; DL29/648/10485.

Robert Plumpton, but also Sir William Beckwith of Clint, Sir William Gascoigne of Gawkthorpe, Sir Piers Middleton of Stockeld, Sir Randolph Pigot of Clotherholme, John Roucliffe of Cowthorpe, and Sir Christopher Ward of Givendale. Most of these men were knighted by him during the 1481 campaign on the eastern marches, and, joined by Sir William Ingleby of Ripley, they were in the company of thirty-three knights of his feedmen who welcomed Henry VII to Yorkshire at Robin Hood's stone in April 1486.[18] They formed a tightly knit and closely related group, some being mesne tenants, some deputies and sub-officers of the honour. Gascoigne was even the earl's son-in-law.[19] It is not surprising that service to the earls in the district stretched over several generations: at least three generations of Plumpton, receiving by custom an annuity of £10,[20] and several members of the Gascoigne and Middleton families served the Percies in the fifteenth century. Similar but less well-documented relationships existed in Craven, in the neighbourhood of Leconfield and Wressle in the East Riding, in the honour of Cockermouth in Cumberland, and in Northumberland itself.

The *Plumpton Correspondence* also affords a rare glimpse of how one of these retainers was employed. Sir Robert Plumpton succeeded his father in 1480, but, unlike him, seems rapidly to have gained the complete trust of the earl. It is apparent that he not only succeeded his father as steward of Spofforth ('you have the rule there under me')[21] and bailiff of the borough of Knaresborough; but that also after Sir William Gascoigne's death in 1487, he became the earl's deputy as steward of Knaresborough ('the lordship of Knaresborough, where at you have rule')[22] and constable of the castle, posts in Northumberland's service which he enjoyed until Northumberland's death in 1489. As a feed retainer Plumpton was called, often at short notice, on at least five occasions during the decade to fight the Scots or put down insurrection (the last being the occasion of Northumberland's death).[23] He seems also to have been expected to accompany his lord at the half-yearly march days on the border, for in November 1486 or 1487 he was specifically

---

[18] *Plumpton Correspondence*, pp. xcvi, 53.
[19] Ibid. 34.   [20] Ibid., *passim*.   [21] Ibid. 76.
[22] Ibid. 81.   [23] Ibid. 40, 42, 55, 61, 73, 74.

excused attendance by the earl.[24] He was summoned to council with the earl and instructed to aid the earl's servants, arrest malefactors, protect his parks, and pacify quarrels between his tenants and servants. Such latter responsibility was specifically delegated to Plumpton in an undated letter from Warkworth:

I pray you to show you of semblable disposition, if any matter of variance hereafter happen within your said rule [the stewardship of Spofforth]; so that the parties sue not me, if you by your discreet wisdom can reform it.[25]

Plumpton would seem to have earned his annuity.

Further to the north, the lords of Middleham too enjoyed the affiliation and service of many of the principal families of Richmondshire. As in the neighbourhood of Knaresborough, the Neville possession of a landed estate was enhanced by mesne lordship, and for much of the later fifteenth century, control of the honour of Richmond. Members of eight local families were retained by Salisbury, of five by Warwick, and of six by Gloucester. Franks, Wycliffes, Rokebies, and Burghs served two of the three.[26] Particularly significant were the roles of the Conyers of Hornby and Metcalfes of Nappa in their service. The head of the Conyers family, (Christopher until c.1463, and Sir John thereafter) was by tradition steward of Middleham and other lordships in Richmondshire (that is to say those parts of the honour of Richmond held by Salisbury, Warwick, and Gloucester), as well as bailiff of the four wapentakes. Before he succeeded his father as head of the family and steward, Sir John Conyers was retained by Salisbury with a fee of £8. 6s. 8d. By 1465/6 Conyers, now steward, was joined as retainer by his brothers William and Richard. In 1473/4 Gloucester was paying fees to three more members of the family—Sir John's grandson and heir John, his younger son Richard of Ulshaw, and his brother Roger. Moreover, two of Sir John's brothers-in-law, William Burgh of Brough and Roland Pudsay; his son-in-law, Sir

[24] Plumpton Correspondence, 56–7.
[25] Ibid. 73–6, esp. 76.
[26] NYCRO, ZQH 1, fly leaf; PRO sc6/1085/20; DL29/648/10485. For fuller discussion of these 3 lists of Middleham retainers see Pollard, 'Northern Retainers', passim; idem, 'Richmondshire Gentry', pp. 37–59; and idem, The Middleham Connection: Richard III and Richmondshire, 1471–85 (Middleham, 1983), passim.

Thomas Markenfield; and his wife's half-brother Thomas Tunstall[27] were also retained. Like Conyers, the head of the Metcalfe family was also retained throughout this period: Thomas followed his father James after 1467. Miles Metcalfe, Thomas's brother, was retained by both Warwick and Gloucester as attorney general. But several other members of the family (seven by Warwick, eight by Gloucester) were retained mainly as foresters and parkers.[28] In the Conyers and Metcalfes we have two service families whose fortunes were closely tied to those of the lords of Middleham.

Where formal retainers led, their friends and neighbours in Richmondshire followed in seeking and gaining the fruits of good lordship. Towards the end of his life, shortly after Richard III's accession to the throne, Thomas Wandesford of East Lutton, a younger son of John Wandesford of Kirklington, was granted an annuity of £3 for his sustenance in his old age, in recognition of his service done for the king's father.[29] Richard Clervaux of Croft, though never formally retained by either Warwick or Gloucester, appealed to both for assistance. In January 1463 Warwick successfully pressed Clervaux's suit with the king at Middleham to be excused public service on account of his being 'vexed with such infirmity and disease' that he 'be not of any power to labour without great jeopardy'. Fifteen years later he appealed to Richard of Gloucester to arbitrate in his dispute with his neighbour Roland Place. Clervaux perhaps moved closer to the duke during these years; for in September 1483, in gratitude for recent unspecified services, Richard and his son Marmaduke were granted jointly by the new king the offices of steward and receiver of the lordship of Manfield during the minority of John FitzHenry (Clervaux's grandson), as well as the revenue of the whole lordship without account. A year later, as king's servant, he received a tun of wine from the customs of Hull.[30]

Less is known, because of the loss of comparable records, of those associated with the lordships of Sheriff Hutton and

---

[27] Pollard, 'Northern Retainers', pp. 54–5, 58–9; idem, *Middleham Connection*, pp. 4–16.
[28] Ibid.
[29] *Harleian MS 433*, ii. 29.
[30] Pollard, 'Richard Clervaux', pp. 163–6.

Barnard Castle. A recent examination of the neighbourhood of
Sheriff Hutton, however, has shown that the Withams of Corn-
borough, Gowers of Stittenham, Leptons of Terrington, Hard-
gills of Lilling, and Constables of Barnby-by-Bossall were all
active in the service of the lords there, several over succeeding
generations. Barnard Castle, unfortunately, remains all but a
closed book.[31] The Nevilles too, like the Percies, exerted influence beyond the north-east, especially in the west march.[32]
More surprising, perhaps, is the extension of this influence into
Lonsdale, which lay over the Pennines from Wensleydale. The
Nevilles had no land in this district, which is divided by the
Lancashire–Westmorland border. It was, however, part of the
archdeaconry of Richmond. Here successive lords of Middle-
ham retained members of the families of Harrington of Hornby,
Middleton of Middleton, and Redman of the Levens.[33] A Cum-
brian family particularly worthy of note is the Huddlestons of
Millom. Sir John (d. 1494), steward of Penrith, married his eld-
est son Richard to Margaret, illegitimate daughter of Richard
Neville, earl of Warwick, to whom the earl granted rents in
Coverdale worth £6. 11s. 3½d. p.a. His third son, William,
married Isabel, daughter of John Neville, Marquess Montagu. Sir
John himself married as his second wife, Jane Stapleton, widow
of Christopher Harcourt, in right of whom he held a moiety of
Cotherstone and Hunderthwaite in Teesdale. Like Sir John
Conyers, the steward of Middleham, he easily transferred his
service to Richard of Gloucester, for whom he was one of his

[31] Horrox, 'Richard III and the East Riding', p. 84. Richard Ratcliffe is before
1483 the only known officer or retainer of Barnard Castle, of which he was
constable by 1476 (see Pollard, 'St. Cuthbert and the Hog', pp. 122–3).

[32] See R. L. Storey, The End of the House of Lancaster (1966), 105–23; Ross,
Richard III, pp. 53–5; M. A. Hicks, 'Richard, Duke of Gloucester and the North',
in Horrox, Richard III and the North, pp. 20, 53–4; and Cardew, 'Anglo-Scottish
Borders', pp. 169–74.

[33] NYCRO zqh/1, fly leaf; PRO sc6/1085/20; DL 29/648/10485. For these
families, see Michael K. Jones, 'Richard III and the Stanleys' in Richard III and
the North, pp. 37–41 and Pollard, 'Northern Retainers', p. 57 (Harringtons); W.
H. Chippindale, 'The Tunstalls of Thurland Castle', Trans. of the Cumberland
and Westmorland Antiquarian and Arch. Soc., NS 28 (1928), pp. 296–300; W.
Greenwood, 'The Redmans', ibid. 3 (1903), 297–300; T. D. Whitaker, An History
of Richmondshire, ii (1823), 280, 303; and Joseph Nicholson and Richard Burn,
The History and Antiquities of Westmorland and Cumberland, i (1777), 253–4
(Middleton).

feoffees of Middleham by 1477, and reputedly sheriff of Cumberland for life after 1483.[34] In Craven, too, Warwick and Gloucester retained Thomas Talbot of Bashall.[35] Most remarkable of all was the toehold that the Nevilles maintained in the honour of Knaresborough through lesser gentry families— the Pullens of Scotton, the Percies of Scotton, the Birnands of Knaresborough, and the Knaresboroughs of Knaresborough, in addition to the Redmans, who were lords of nearby Harewood. Ralph Pullen was retained by Salisbury; his son John was rewarded by Warwick after 1461, and became cellarer of Richard III's household. Robert Percy acted on Salisbury's behalf in 1459–61, and later became comptroller of Richard III's household. Members of the Birnand family, too, were active supporters of Salisbury, and later Ralph and Robert were esquires of Richard III's household.[36] Not surprisingly the interest of the lords of Middleham within the honour of Knaresborough was one of the sources of conflict between the Percies and the Nevilles.[37] This was not the only area of friction between the two great magnate affinities, east or west of the Pennines. But the evidence suggests that, for the most part, clearly understood zones of influence existed in the north-east, and that within these, as long as they remained undisturbed by rivals, magnate affinities enjoyed a large degree of continuity and stability, built around established traditions of local family service.

It is not to be denied that some men served more than one master. In the 1440s, Richard Clervaux of Croft was retained both by Robert Neville, bishop of Durham, who granted him an annuity of £5 in 1445, and by Ralph Neville, earl of Westmorland, who granted him an annuity of £6. 13s. 4d. in 1448. The two Nevilles were representatives of rival branches of the

---

[34] See Colper, 'Millom Castle and the Huddlestons', pp. 201, 207–8 and W. E. Hampton, *Memorials of the Wars of the Roses* (Gloucester, 1979), 35–7. Like the families of Richmondshire, these families west of the Pennines were closely linked by marriage.

[35] PRO, SC6/1085/20; C. E. Arnold, 'A Political Study of the West Riding of Yorkshire, 1436–1509' (unpublished Manchester University Ph.D. thesis, 1984), 54, 166–7; App. II, p. 86.

[36] NYCRO, ZQH I, flyleaf; W. Wheater, *Knaresburgh and its Rulers* (Leeds, 1907), 187–90; Arnold, 'West Riding', pp. 162–3 and App., 34–5, 50, 61, 75–6. In 'Northern Retainers' I wrongly transcribed Polan as Polard.

[37] See below, pp. 270–1.

family. Clervaux perhaps attracted such attention because he was at the time a young and rising esquire of the body to Henry VI, and appeared to have a glittering future. In the event ill health cut short his career as a courtier. Locally, nevertheless, he maintained his loyalty to the house of Lancaster and to the earls of Westmorland until 1461. His later service to Richard III may well have owed something to his continuing association with the earl of Westmorland, whose family had become reconciled to the king while he was still duke of Gloucester in 1476.[38]

Sir James Strangways of West Harlsey, Clervaux's friend and neighbour, has been presented as a classic example of one who had multiple commitments. In his covenant with the earl of Salisbury dated 7 October 1447 he contracted to 'be belast and witholden with the earl for life against all folks saving Katherine duchess of Norfolk, Robert Bishop of Durham and his kin and allies . . . at and within the third degree of marriage'.[39] The first two were Salisbury's sister and brother; and the third group may not merely have provided the commodious escape route that McFarlane suggested. We have already witnessed how seriously Strangways took his responsibilities to his kith and kin.[40] He could not foresee in 1447 that he would within twelve years be on the opposite side to his wife's kinsmen, the Eures of Witton and Malton. But this does not seem to have stopped him taking the part of the earl of Salisbury and his son (whose retainer he subsequently became) in 1459–61.[41]

Arguably just as significant as his extended family were the people Strangways did *not* name in 1447. He was already receiving a fee from Archbishop John Kemp of York as steward of Ripon, and was soon to receive a fee from William, Lord Fitz-Hugh, if he was not already doing so.[42] No doubt he placed his service to Salisbury before these men. In fact Strangways was well established in the service of the earl of Salisbury, as well as

---

[38] Pollard, 'Richard Clervaux', pp. 163–5. Cf. Sir Roger Conyers of Wynyard, retained by Richard of Gloucester on 3 Sept. 1473 when he was already the retainer of the earl of Westmorland. In his contract with Gloucester it was agreed that he would receive 10 marks during the earl's life, increasing to £10 after his death. (PRO, DL 29/648/10485).

[39] Northants RO, FitzWilliam MS 2051; K. B. McFarlane, 'The Wars of the Roses', *Proceedings of the British Academy*, 50 (1964), 108–9.

[40] See above, p. 108.   [41] Roskell, 'Strangeways', pp. 468–73.

[42] Arnold, 'West Riding', p. 27; NYCRO, zjx 3/2/112.

of other members of his family, before 1447, for he had served Salisbury's mother before her death in 1440, and was one of the feoffees entrusted to see that her joint-enfeoffment of Middleham, Sheriff Hutton, and Penrith did indeed pass safely into Salisbury's hands.[43] Moreover, his son and grandson continued the family tradition in their service to Richard of Gloucester after 1471. James, the younger, was knighted by the duke in 1481; and in 1484 he was granted an annuity of £16. 13s. 4d. from Middleham and the revenues of the manor of Deighton by Richard as King.[44] Sir James Strangways the elder may have received fees from many quarters, perhaps an indication of his high standing; but he and his family nevertheless sustained over several decades and three generations a primary attachment to the Nevilles of Middleham and their successor. He may well have had access to a commodious escape route; but Strangways seems never to have taken it.

Significantly, Strangways had legal training; and lawyers in general enjoyed a special status. Retained for their counsel, successful lawyers (especially those who rose to serjeant or judge) were much in demand, and were able to build up flourishing practices in which they could count among their clients several lords, gentlemen, and corporations. Nevertheless Yorkshire lawyers, like Strangways, tended to owe a primary attachment to one particular patron. Robert Danby of Thorp Perrow, whose career was launched under the auspices of Robert FitzHugh, bishop of London (d. 1435), married as his first wife Katherine, daughter of Ralph FitzRandolph of Spennithorne, a retainer of Richard Neville, earl of Salisbury. He was himself a councillor and executor of the earl. Probably with the help of Salisbury's patronage he became a justice of common pleas in 1452, and was made Chief Justice in 1462, no doubt on the recommendation of the earl of Warwick. Dismissed by Edward IV in 1471 for his continued support of Warwick and the Readeption of Henry VI, he was retained in the last year of his

---

[43] Roskell, 'Strangeways', p. 461. On 19 May 1459 he was appointed executor to Salisbury's will. He represented Yorkshire in the Yorkist Parliaments of 1460 and 1461 (Speaker), and was rumoured to have died at the battle of Wakefield, after which Salisbury himself was killed (*Paston Letters*, iii. 249, *Test. Ebor.* ii. 246).

[44] W. A. Shaw, *The Knights of England* (1906), ii. 20; *CPR, 1476–85*, 435.

life by the earl's political heir, Richard of Gloucester.[45] A feoffee and executor from time to time for other members of the Neville family and their servants, his career suggests a particularly strong attachment to them: an attachment which was continued after his death by his sons Sir James and Richard (another lawyer), in the service of Duke Richard.[46]

Miles Metcalfe, younger son of James of Nappa, was another whose career owed much to Warwick and then Gloucester, whose attorney general, councillor, and deputy as chief steward of the duchy of Lancaster in the north he became.[47] His favoured position put his services much in demand, leading to his being retained as counsel by the city of York, by whom he was appointed recorder in 1477; by the priory of Durham, from 1479; by the bishopric of Durham, from 1467; and by the county palatine of Lancaster, of which he became a justice in 1483.[48] Neighbouring gentry also sought his services: he was nominated an executor by Thomas Witham of Cornburgh in 1475 and William Neville of Thornton Bridge in 1481; he was a feoffee of Christopher Boynton of Acklam before 1482; and he was a witness to one of the instruments settling Brackenthwaite and lands in Little Ribston on his fellow lawyer, Thomas Middleton, in 1468.[49] Metcalfe fell from favour after his master's death in 1485, and died within a few months.[50] Thomas Middleton, younger son of William Middleton of Stockeld, a candidate to succeed Metcalfe as Recorder of York in 1486, was however part of the circle of Henry Percy, fourth earl of Northumberland. Thomas married Joan Plumpton, daughter of Sir William, in 1469, and is to be found engaged from time to time in the business of his in-laws and neighbours. He became a feoffee and

---

[45] *North Country Wills*, i. 43; *Test. Ebor.* ii. 245–6; NYCRO zQH/1; PRO DL29/648/10485; Fisher, *Masham*, pp. 249–51; T. Horsfall, *The Manor of Snape and Well* (Leeds, 1912), 78; E. W. Ives, *The Common Lawyers of Prereformation England: Thomas Kebell, a case study* (Cambridge, 1983), 223.

[46] Pollard, 'St. Cuthbert and the Hog', pp. 121–2.

[47] PRO sc6/1085/20; Ross, *Richard III*, p. 51; K. R. Dockray, 'The Political Legacy of Richard III in Northern England', in Griffiths and Sherborne, *Kings and Nobles*, p. 215; *Yorks. Deeds*, iii. 143.

[48] Dobson, *York Chamberlains' Accounts*, 136, 151; Wedgwood, *Biographies*, p. 588; Durham, Dean and Chapter, Bursar's account, 1479/80; Durham, Church Commission, Bishopric Estates, 189820.

[49] *Test. Ebor.*, iii. 263, 268; *Yorks. Deeds* iii. 74.

[50] Dockray, 'Political Legacy', pp. 215–16.

steward of the earl in the 1470s.[51] He too was retained as counsel
by the city of York from 1470; by the bishopric of Durham from
1467, becoming steward from 1476 to 1484, when he was
replaced by Richard Danby; and by the priory from 1478. An
executor and feoffee of Sir Hugh Hastings of Fenwick, he also
acted as feoffee to Sir Brian Stapleton of Carlton and Thomas
Darrell of Sessay.[52] He is not to be confused with Thomas
Middleton of Middleton in Lonsdale, one-time chief forester of
Wensleydale under Warwick and a councillor of Richard of
Gloucester, who died in 1481.[53]

The most independent of these busy and, no doubt, 'right wise
and discreet learned men in Yorkshire'[54] seems to have been
Richard Pigot, serjeant-at-law. The son, elder or younger is not
clear, of John Pigot of Ripon (himself the second son of Randolph
Pigot of Clotherholme, and a lawyer), Pigot became serjeant in
1467. He married Joan, daughter and sole heiress of William
Romanby of Romanby near Northallerton.[55] He was retained as
legal counsel by Bishop Laurence Booth in 1461, and became
second justice of Durham in 1466 and a justice of assize and gaol
delivery in the bishopric from 1476. From 1462 he was retained
by the priory of Durham, and from 1470 by the city of York. In
1480 he was appointed steward of Northallerton by Bishop
William Dudley of Durham.[56] He was retained as counsel by the
earl of Warwick by 1465, with a fee of £4: a retainer continued

---

[51] *Plumpton Correspondence*, pp. lxxxii, 13, 17, 19, 23, 49, 73, 98; Petworth
House Archives, MAC D/9/8/2; *CIPM, Henry VII*, i. 202.

[52] Dobson, *York Chamberlains' Accounts*, pp. 136, 151, 168, 184; Durham,
Church Commission, Bishopric Estates: 189820, 30; Durham, Dean and Chapter, Bursar's account, 1478/9; *Test. Ebor*. iii. 273–8; *CIPM, Henry VII*, i. 77; iii.
no. 138.

[53] This Thomas was a feoffee of Middleham (PRO, CP 25 (1) 281/164/32;
165/23; W. Atthill, *Documents of the Collegiate Church of Middleham*, Camden OS, xxxviii (1847), 84–5). In 1477 with Gloucester, styled 'of Lonsdale', he
became a feoffee of Richard Musgrave of Hartley, Westmorland (*CIPM, Henry
VII*, i. 291). See also Pollard, 'St. Cuthbert and the Hog', p. 121.

[54] The words are those of Halnath Mauleverer to Sir Robert Plumpton
(*Plumpton Correspondence*, p. 48).

[55] In his will Pigot's father left 'omnes libros de lege terrae' to his other son
John (*Test. Ebor*. i. 416). Richard's wife is wrongly identified as a daughter of Sir
Richard Welles, Lord Willoughby in *North Country Wills*, i. 73.

[56] Durham, Church Commission, Bishopric Estates, 189818, 19; Durh. 3/49/
14, 15, 19; Durham, Dean and Chapter, Bursar's account 1462/3; Dobson, *York
Chamberlains' Accounts*, pp. 136, 151, 168.

after 1471 by Richard of Gloucester, whose councillor he was. His reward from Warwick included the farm of the manor of Deighton, North Yorks. for twenty years at £24 p.a., and the chief messuage and demesne of South Cowton at £2. 13s. 4d. from 1462.[57] From 1461 he was under-steward of Knaresborough, perhaps on Warwick's recommendation; from 1476 he was retained as counsel by the duchy; and from 1480 until his death three years later he was second justice at Lancaster itself.[58] He was feoffee for Laurence Booth, as archbishop of York, Henry Stafford, duke of Buckingham, and many of his friends and neighbours, including Sir William Plumpton (1464), Randolph Pigot (his cousin, 1466), Roger Aske (1474), Sir Robert Danby (1474), the earl of Northumberland (1475), Christopher Ward of Givendale (1479), and Sir Brian Stapleton (temp. Edward IV). In 1475 he was nominated as an executor by Thomas Witham.[59]

Most significantly—and this is perhaps the explanation of the high demand for his services—he was one of the executors nominated for Edward IV's will in 1475, and an executor of William, Lord Hastings in 1483. As serjeant-at-law and a justice of Lancaster he was first and foremost the king's servant.[60] His closeness to Hastings, however, is confirmed by the fact that he was one of Hastings's feoffees in 1475, that he made Hastings a supervisor of his own will (proved, after Hastings's own death, at Lambeth on 21 June 1483), and that his widow subsequently married Hastings's brother, Richard Lord Willoughby and Wells.[61] Pigot was perhaps fortunate in the moment of his death, for he thereby escaped having to choose between his loyalties at court, to the new king and Hastings, and his attachment in the country to the duke of Gloucester. In the latter

[57] PRO, SC6/1085/20; DL 29/648/10485. See esp. Warrants for Issue and Pigot's account as farmer of Deighton.

[58] Somerville, Duchy of Lancaster, i, 452, 473, 524.

[59] CPR, 1476–85, 232, 255, 257, 283; Plumpton Correspondence, p. lxxii; Test. Ebor. iii. 158, 265; BL, Ad. Ch. 66416; Durh. 3/166/14; CIPM, Henry VII, i. 77, 542; Yorks. Deeds, iii. 74.

[60] S. Bentley, Excerpta Historica (1831), 378–9; North Country Wills, i. 71.

[61] CPR, 1467–77, 516–17; Test. Ebor. iii. 285–6; North Country Wills, i. 73–5. For a brief note on Pigot see also Ives, Common Lawyers, p. 473. For his connections with East Anglia, where he was a circuit judge from 1467, see ibid. 299 and 410.

years of his life, however, his position of trust in the service of the king, his brother, and his chamberlain no doubt was the principal reason for the respect in which he was evidently held.

Unlike lawyers, the other gentlemen-bureaucrats, that is accountants and estate administrators, tended to be more exclusively attached to particular lords.[62] Early in the fifteenth century Henry, Lord FitzHugh enjoyed the services of John Burgh of Brough and, after his death in 1412, of his son William as his steward. Father and son were both rewarded with fees of £4. 13s. 4d. Although William campaigned with his lord under Henry V in Normandy, his expertise was soon needed again in England, for by 1420 he was once more his lord's councillor, and 'governor of his land in Yorkshire'. Burgh retained this trusted position until FitzHugh's death in 1425.[63] He seems to have been replaced by the new lord, William; but his younger brother Richard continued the family tradition, serving as *domicellus* in William's household until his death in 1452, and holding, at different times, the posts of steward of his household and receiver.[64] Later heads of his family, William II (d. 1465) and William III (d. 1492) served the lords of Middleham, though not, it would appear, in an administrative capacity.[65]

Richard Neville, earl of Salisbury seems to have placed a special trust in two administrators—Thomas Witham of Cornburgh and Robert Constable of Barnby-by-Bossall. Both began their careers as servants of Joan, countess of Westmorland, of whose will they were executors; Witham was a beneficiary and executor of Salisbury's will.[66] Witham, steward of Sheriff Hutton and of the Latimer lordship of Danby in Salisbury's custody, gained the post of Chancellor of the Exchequer through Salisbury's influence in 1454, and was restored to that office for life

---

[62] For the rise of the gentleman-bureaucrat in general see R. L. Storey, 'Gentlemen-bureaucrats', in C. H. Clough (ed.), *Professions, Vocations and Culture in Late Medieval England* (Liverpool, 1982), 9–129; R. A. Griffiths, 'Public and Private Bureaucracies in England and Wales in the Fifteenth Century', *TRHS* 5th Ser., 30 (1980), 109–38; and Morgan, 'English Gentleman', pp. 25–6.

[63] NYCRO, ZJX 3/2/45, 51, 60; A. E. Goodman, 'Responses to Requests in Yorkshire for Military Service under Henry V', *NH* 17 (1981), 240–52, esp. 249. See above, p. 125.

[64] NYCRO, ZJX 3/2/87, 91, 93, 109, 112.

[65] Pollard, 'The Burghs of Brough', pp. 13–17.   [66] *Scriptores Tres*, p. cclx.

in 1456. After Salisbury's death he continued to serve both Warwick and Gloucester until his own death in 1480.[67] Robert Constable, a younger son of Marmaduke Constable of Flamborough, died in 1454. Before his death he was receiver-general and chancellor of the bishopric of Durham under Bishop Robert Neville. He probably also held high financial office from the earl of Salisbury in his northern estates.[68] Both Witham and Constable remembered their early patrons in their wills. Witham bequeathed £20 to pay for prayers to be said for the souls of Ralph, first earl of Westmorland and Joan his wife, and Richard, earl of Salisbury and Alice his wife. Constable bequeathed to his 'most noble lord the Earl of Salisbury a gilted cup called a fate covered' and to his 'Lady Salisbury a ring of gold with the more [larger] diamond'.[69]

North of the Tees William Claxton, a younger son of Thomas Claxton of Old Park, County Durham, served the priory of Durham and the earls of Westmorland for many years. Lay steward of the priory from 1467 until his death in 1496, he was also constable of the Neville castle of Brancepeth, a post to which he had succeeded his father and to which he was succeeded by his son Ralph. Found a fee by Bishop Dudley in 1478, he followed the earl into the service of Richard III.[70] Last but not least of this quartet of gentlemen-bureaucrats is Thomas Metcalfe of Nappa, who served Richard Neville, earl of Warwick as receiver of the Lovell lordships in Yorkshire during the minority of Francis, Lord Lovell, before becoming auditor and supervisor of the lordship of Middleham under Richard of Gloucester. In 1476, probably through the duke's patronage, he became an auditor of the bishopric of Durham. Richard III so valued his expertise that on 7 July 1483 he made him his chancellor of the

---

[67] *Test. Ebor.* iii. 264–8; Alnwick, Syon MS X, I, Box 1, 2b, account of the bailiff of Thornton. Witham was appointed steward of the Yorkshire estates of George, Lord Latimer in 1449–50. He was also a feoffee of Lord Latimer's estates (*Harleian MS 433*, ii. 138).

[68] *Test. Ebor.* ii. 174–7; Alnwick, Syon MS X, I Box 1, 2b, especially memoranda and receipts to Constable, 'Receiver General unto my Brother Latimer of his livelihood in my governance', dated between 12 June 1452 and 6 Jan. 1454.

[69] *Test. Ebor.* iii. 265; ii. 175.

[70] Surtees, *Durham*, iii. 289; Hampton, *Memorials*, pp. 50–1; Westminster Abbey Muniments, 6052; Pollard, 'St. Cuthbert and the Hog', pp. 119, 121. See also Dobson, *Durham Priory*, pp. 125–9.

duchy of Lancaster.[71] Henry VII dismissed him from this post, but despite Metcalfe's doubtful loyalty continued to employ him as overseer and surveyor of the castle and lordship of Middleham and all his other estates in Richmondshire. Metcalfe, fully reconciled to the new regime by 1490 (by which date he had become king's servant), died in 1504, to be succeeded in this post by his son James.[72] Leland wrote of Thomas that he 'was in those quarters a great officer, steward, surveyor or receiver of Richmond lands, whereby he waxed rich and able to build and purchase'.[73]

A common feature of these careers is the long, loyal, and profitable service rendered. But such loyalty was rarely taken to the point of risking patrimony and place. When a cause was believed to be irretrievably lost the necessity of transferring service to another lord was accepted. Thus a Conyers or a Metcalfe moved with the times, from Warwick to Gloucester to Henry VII. The path was eased by the fact that each was the mesne lord of Middleham or Richmond, to whom loyalty was properly due. On occasion fine judgement needed to be exercised in deciding when a cause was lost, or when it was politic to lie low; but it would be wrong to assume that all were turncoats and mere time-servers by choice.[74]

The problems created when retainers misread the signs, and were subsequently suspected of being insufficiently loyal, are revealed in Sir William Plumpton's well-documented troubles with the fourth earl of Northumberland in the 1470s. He seems to have come too readily to terms with Warwick after the battle of Towton for the liking of the earl; a battle in which both Plumpton's eldest son and heir and Northumberland's father had fallen. Plumpton, to be sure, had some difficulty persuading Edward IV that he could be trusted. A bond of £2,000 had to be put up to secure his protection. When this could not be found he surrendered himself to the Tower until pardoned by the new

[71] Durham, Church Commission, Bishopric Estates, 190316; PRO, DL 29/648/10485; Coles, 'Middleham', pp. 83–5, 308, 310; Pollard, 'St. Cuthbert and the Hog', p. 117; Somerville, *Duchy of Lancaster*, i. 298; *Harleian MS 433*, i. 126; ii. 28.   [72] Dockray, 'Political Legacy', p. 219; see also below p. 375.   [73] Leland, *Itinerary*, iv. 86.

[74] For recent emphasis on loyalty and faithfulness see R. M. Warnicke, 'Lord Morley's Statements about Richard III', *Albion*, 15 (1983), 176; and I. Arthurson, 'A Question of Loyalty', *The Ricardian*, vii, 97 (1987), 401–13.

king on 5 February 1462. Even then he was restricted from returning to Yorkshire, and faced further charges of treason, from which he was acquitted in January 1464. But thereafter he was restored to his offices in Knaresborough, now under the rule of the earl of Warwick; and by means of the marriages of his daughters he sought alliances with two of Warwick's servants—Guy Roucliffe and Henry Sotehill. Letters in the *Plumpton Correspondence* suggest that he was well regarded by both Warwick and his brother Montagu.[75]

After Northumberland's restoration in 1470, and the deaths of Warwick and Montagu in 1471, Plumpton was removed from his local offices. The place of deputy steward of Knaresborough was given by the earl to William Gascoigne, who had been more steadfast in his loyalty to the house of Percy.[76] Plumpton, who resented the loss of office and the reduction in his status, bore a grudge against Gascoigne. As early as 27 October 1471 he and Gascoigne agreed to keep the peace and accept the earl's arbitration—with no lasting effect, as the comment of Godfrey Green in November 1475 shows: 'as soon as he [Northumberland] comes into the country he shall see such a direction betwixt his brother Gascoigne and you as shall be to your heart's ease and worship'.[77] In 1475 Plumpton was bombarding Green at court with letters to the effect that Green should labour Sir John Pilkington, Richard of Gloucester, or the king himself to persuade Northumberland to restore him. Green reported back that it was thought by Plumpton's friends at court that such an approach would 'rather hurt in that behalf than avail; for certain it is, as long as my lord of Northumberland's patent thereof stands good, as long will he have no deputy but such as shall please him, and can him thank for the gift thereof'. Moreover Plumpton had asked Green to inform the lords of the court of Gascoigne's misgovernance. Green refused, pointing out that this would be taken as inspired by malice rather than truth, and also as a disworship to Northumberland.

Finally, Green referred to another matter which rankled

---

[75] *Plumpton Correspondence*, pp. lxvii–lxxi, 16, 25.
[76] Ibid. lxxv–lxxvi. It may be that Plumpton was held responsible for the fact that 'the manor place [Spofforth] was sore defaced' by the Neville brothers (Leland, *Itinerary*, p. 88).   [77] *Plumpton Correspondence*, pp. 32, 33.

Plumpton. He had been removed from the commission of the peace after 1471. Knowing that Northumberland would not lobby on his behalf, he instructed Green to lobby Hastings. Green received a stiff rebuke for his pains. Hastings accused Plumpton and Green of seeking to make a 'jealousy betwixt' Northumberland and him, in that Northumberland should labour for his own men. 'Sir,' Green added memorably, 'I took that for a watch word for meddling betwixt Lords.'[78] The whole letter, while being intensely revealing about the ways of the court and lobbying for patronage, also demonstrates the extent to which the lords and courtiers of Yorkist England perceived the world as being divided between clearly defined affinities. Plumpton was Northumberland's man. If he had a grudge and was dissatisfied with his treatment at the hands of his lord, that was a matter for him and his lord to resolve. No doubt the king reminded Northumberland of the need to keep his own retinue in order. Certainly the earl did as he promised Green, and patched up an agreement between Gascoigne and Plumpton which was cemented within two years by a marriage alliance between the families.[79]

The rift between Gascoigne and Plumpton was, if not the most serious, certainly the best documented conflict to occur within either of the two great magnate affinities of the north-east in the later fifteenth century.[80] There were others of a lesser nature which the magnates were quick to stifle. Gloucester, as his willing intervention in the Clervaux–Place quarrel shows, was anxious to prevent any kind of disturbance between the gentry within Richmondshire; Northumberland took it upon himself to pacify similar disputes within the honour of Knaresborough.[81]

The continuity, unity, solidarity, and durability of these two affinities, which withstood some substantial shocks and up-heavals between 1455 and 1485, appear to mark them out in contrast to the world of bastard feudalism characterized by K. B. McFarlane. McFarlane, especially in his later writings on the

[78] Ibid.   [79] Ibid. lxxix–lxxx.
[80] The contemporary quarrel between Pilkington and Saville which was the subject of a commission of oyer and terminer should correctly be seen as a dispute within the king's own household (see Arnold, 'West Riding', pp. 189–92).   [81] See above, pp. 118–19.

subject, emphasized the instability and fickleness of relationships between lord and retainer. The gentry, he wrote,
'turned their coats as often and with the same chequered success
as their betters. As many were wise or greedy enough to have
more coats than one to turn, they may have been more dexter-
ous than the lords at changing them to suit the demands of
survival.'[82] It is no part of this argument to suggest that the
north-eastern gentry did not put a high premium on survival.
But it does appear that they were more successful than some at
balancing loyalty with self-interest. Certainly neither is it true
that in north-eastern England 'the giving and receiving of fees
had by the middle years of the century become so indiscriminate
that their effectiveness may be doubted',[83] nor was it the case in
this region that by mid-century most stewardships were sine-
cures held by courtiers.[84] A Conyers at Middleham, though he
had a working deputy, a Plumpton at Spofforth, and a Witham at
Sheriff Hutton and Danby were men exercising the authority of
their offices on behalf of their lords. It may be that in more
southerly counties courtiers attracted stewardships of outlying
manors belonging to the magnates: this was not the case in the
north. The north-east was different. The proximity of the border
may be one explanation. Another may be that in the midland
counties (from which much of the evidence of ineffective retaining comes) the power of individual lords after 1440 was shifting
and unstable.[85] In the north-east, however, despite the swings in

[82] McFarlane, 'Wars of the Roses', p. 106.   [83] Ibid. 109.
[84] Ibid. 110. Christopher and John Conyers, for instance, as joint bailiffs of the
Wapentakes of Richmondshire presided over the twice-yearly courts between
October 1443 and October 1445 (PRO, E199/51/1,2,3).
[85] Before 1439, it would seem, the Beauchamp earls of Warwick had enjoyed a
hegemony over the west midlands. This collapsed after the death of Richard, the
5th earl. A struggle for supremacy ultimately ensued between the successor
lords, especially Richard Neville, earl of Warwick and Humphrey Stafford, duke
of Buckingham, leaving local politics particularly volatile. Warwick's victory in
1461 temporarily brought stability back to the region; but after his fall in 1471
there was renewed uncertainty, as Clarence sought to impose his authority. As
Dr Carpenter has commented, in 'a region where the firmness of old allegiances
was slackening' the gentry discovered 'that safety lay in acquiring a number of
alternative lords' ('The Duke of Clarence and the Midlands', pp. 26–8, 42). See
also Carpenter, 'Law, Justice and Landowners', pp. 219–25; and I. Rowney,
'Government and Patronage in the Fifteenth Century in Staffordshire, 1439–
59', *Midland History*, 8 (1983), 49–66, who comes to identical conclusions
about the uncertainties of local politics in mid-century.

fortune, the Percies and Middleham lords enjoyed a degree of commitment and continuity, at least until 1485, which their fellow magnates further to the south might have envied. As will become apparent in respect of government, administration, and politics, the strength and durability of these two great affinities helped make them, and one of them in particular, exceedingly powerful forces in the later fifteenth century.

6

Local Government and Administration

INSTITUTIONALLY England was one of the more centralized of late-medieval European kingdoms. Even a region as distant from the 'capital' as the north-east was subject to royal control through scores of local officials—sheriffs, coroners, escheators, justices of the peace and their assistants—answerable to the offices of state at Westminster. In theory local government was the king's. In practice, since royal officers in the localities were men of local roots and standing, and not the king's paid agents, local government and administration was dominated by local landed élites. In the north-east, the resulting propensity for local government to fall under the sway of mighty subjects was intensified by the distance from Westminster, by the complex and fragmented structure of government in the region, and by the need to make special provision for the defence of the border. The structure of local government itself, as well as its staffing, tended further to enhance the power of the magnates at the expense of the Crown.

Although north-eastern England is conventionally considered to have comprised three counties, strictly speaking there were but two—Yorkshire and Northumberland. Both were unusual. Yorkshire, by far the largest county in England (approximately the size of the four south-western counties together), was like other counties in that it was a royal shrievalty, possessed a county court, and sent two representatives to the king's parliament. It was unlike other counties in that it was divided into three Ridings, each with its own commission of the peace. Even within the Ridings there existed extensive liberties which excluded the king's officers and justices, most notably the archbishop's liberty of Ripon, which had its own commission of the peace, the bishop of Durham's tiny liberty of Crayke, and the Ainsty, which in mid-fifteenth century was attached to the city of York. Moreover, many honours and baronies within the county enjoyed the franchise of return of writ. Of these, in addition to the duchy of Lancaster lordships of Pickering, Knaresborough, Pontefract, and Tickhill (reunited with the Crown in 1399), and the honour of Wakefield (reunited in 1461), the honours of Richmond, Langbaurgh, and Whitby Strand were particularly significant, since they removed much of the North Riding from direct royal control. In these honours where the sheriff was excluded royal justice at the lowest level was administered by baronial stewards and the bailiffs of wapentakes and bailiwicks which belonged by heredity to their lords. Thus, although the sheriff of Yorkshire would seem at first to have been responsible for an impossibly large fief, in reality nearly two-thirds of the county lay outside his jurisdiction.[1]

Northumberland was an even more truncated county than Yorkshire. Included within its boundaries were the liberties of Tynemouth, held by the priory of Tynemouth; Hexham, held by the archbishop of York (whose bailiff acted as sheriff); Redesdale (Tailboys), and Tynedale (Crown, except 1474–84); and all the liberties of the bishop of Durham (Norhamshire, Islandshire, and Bedlington). Furthermore, the land between Tyne and Tees, commonly called 'the Bishopric' (the later County Durham), was technically a liberty within the county of Northumberland. This was made explicit in the *Quo Warranto* proceedings of 1297, although it was strenuously denied by Bishop Langley in his defence of his liberties against his subjects in 1433.[2] Thus, according to royal perception, Northumberland contained the most important private liberty in all the kingdom, the county palatine of Durham.

The precise privileges and boundaries of this mosaic of liberties had in the fifteenth century only recently been determined, or were still uncertain. Only two hundred years earlier had the Crown tackled the independence of the baronial honours of the north. The situation in Durham was in effect a compromise: for, although the bishops had successfully held on to their franchises north of the Tees, south of the river in Northallerton and Howden they had been reduced to little more than manorial lords, without possession even of the right of

---

[1] Reid, *Council in the North*, pp. 7–13; Clanchy, 'Return of Writ', p. 60.
[2] *Placita de Quo Warranto* (HMSO, 1818), 604; R. L. Storey, *Thomas Langley and the Bishopric of Durham, 1406–1437* (1961), 130.

return of writ. In November 1448, Bishop Robert Neville secured a new grant of the liberties from Henry VI, and subsequently issued commissions of the peace and gaol delivery for both Northallerton and Howden; but nothing came of this attempt to reassert palatine authority in Yorkshire.[3] North of the Tees, by the early fourteenth century the bishops had secured recognition of their regalian authority and their right to hold their own courts of law, to maintain their own chancery and exchequer, and subsequently to issue their own commissions of the peace. North Durham (Norham and Holy Island) had its own commission of the peace; but all the lands of the palatinate between Tyne and Tees, as well as north of Tyne, were administered from Palace Green in Durham. The bishop appointed his own sheriff; but whereas the king had had to concede annual reappointments, in the palatinate the bishop had succeeded in retaining the right to appoint during pleasure. The office of sheriff of North Durham, along with that of escheator and steward, was usually held by the constable of Norham castle. There was a single court of assizes, combining the functions of King's Bench and Common Pleas under two justices, who were usually prominent royal justices with local connections. A lay council including all the officers of the palatinate—sheriff, justices, temporal chancellor, receiver-general, auditors, and lay steward—was responsible for day-to-day administration. The lay steward customarily presided over this council, as well as over halmotes.[4] There is a suspicion, however, that under Bishops Booth and Dudley (1457–83) the chancellor came to play a more central and dominant role.[5] Durham, uniquely, was administered directly and locally by its bishop, exercising regalian authority.

In practice bishops of Durham enjoyed less independent power than in law their privileges promised. The law and policy executed in the palatinate was invariably the king's; the bishop was usually a loyal servant of the Crown, and when it deemed it necessary the Crown did not hesitate to intervene. In 1462–4

[3] Emsley, 'Yorkshire Enclaves', pp. 103–8; Durh. 3/44/2,3,4.

[4] G. T. Lapsley, *The County Palatine of Durham: a study in Constitutional History* (Harvard, Mass., 1900), esp. Chapters 2–5; K. Emsley and C. M. Fraser, *The Courts of the County Palatine of Durham from the Earliest Times to 1971* (Durham, 1984), 25–32, 46–8, 72–6; Storey, *Langley*, pp. 57–104.

[5] See below p. 162.

Edward IV removed the temporalities from Bishop Booth and instituted his own administration. And in more subtle ways the king interfered at will. In 1467, Edward IV, on appeal from the prior and convent, ordered the bishop not to trouble his neighbours while his council enquired into a dispute between the two. Ten years later the king himself took over the bishop's responsibility for surveying and supervising the repair of episcopal castles.[6] However, as a result of its *de jure* independence the palatinate was neither taxed by the Crown nor represented in the king's parliament. It is probable that the inhabitants paid taxes to the bishop, and that a local representative assembly met from time to time; but if so, no record of its activities has survived.[7]

While the principle and practice of government within the palatinate changed little during the fifteenth century, the question of what precisely constituted its boundaries was still a live issue. As Professor Storey put it, 'the acid test' of palatine privilege lay in the right to forfeiture. Although this was breached during the pontificate of Bishop Skirlaw in 1400–5, Langley secured confirmation of the right to take forfeitures, and subsequently exercised such rights in 1415.[8] Thereafter there was no dispute over the principle. However, there was dispute over what precisely constituted land falling within the palatinate. Confiscation of property from Scots who 'rebelled' against Edward I created confusion. The baronies of Barnard Castle and Hart, confiscated from Baliol and Bruce respectively, were granted to Beauchamp and Clifford by the Crown. Anthony Bek and succesive bishops claimed that the Crown held no right of forfeiture in these estates, since by virtue of their franchise that right lay with them. In the case of Hart the bishop was successful. In 1461 it was he who confiscated and occupied the lordship, until it was restored to Henry, Lord Clifford in 1485.[9] But in Barnard Castle the bishop was ultimately defeated.

The dispute over Barnard Castle began in 1293, when Edward I seized the lordship as forfeiture from John Baliol. Bishop Bek

---

[6] Storey, 'North of England', p. 141; Pollard, 'St. Cuthbert and the Hog', p. 117. In 1482 Edward IV's knight of the body, Sir John Middleton of Belsay, was made constable of Norham 'at the contemplation, desire and request of the king' (Durh. 3/55/8).   [7] Storey, *Langley*, p. 55.   [8] Ibid. 53.
[9] As is clear from the Receivers'-General Accounts (Durham, Church Commission, Bishopric Estates, 189816–31, *passim*.)

took forcible possession the following year. But in 1302–3 and again 1306–7 the king, as a result of his wider dispute with Bek, reoccupied the lordship; and finally, on 2 February 1307, he granted it to Guy Beauchamp, earl of Warwick. During Edward II's reign there followed a long legal wrangle between Beauchamp, the Crown, and successive bishops. When in 1315 Guy Beauchamp died the custody of the lands and wardship of his two-year-old heir were seized by the Crown. It was not until the first parliament of Edward III's reign, a month after Edward II's death, that Bishop Beaumont secured a grant of restoration, and the constable of the castle was ordered to hand the lordship back. Yet five years later Beaumont petitioned the Crown, complaining that the order had not been executed. In 1333, however, Beaumont was succeeded by Richard Bury, Edward III's confidant, who seems to have conceded the right of Thomas Beauchamp, now of age, to enter the lordship as tenant in chief of the king.[10]

For the next century the issue lay dormant. No attempt was made in 1397 by Bishop Skirlaw to recover the lordship on the death of the disgraced Thomas, earl of Warwick, whose *inquisition post mortem* on his lands north of the Tees was held by the king.[11] Only on the death of Richard Beauchamp in 1439 was the ancient episcopal claim revived. In the summer of that year, in defiance of a royal grant of the lordship to the use of the dowager Countess Isabel during the minority of Henry Beauchamp the heir, Bishop Robert Neville 'with a great multitude, in manner of riot and war' took possession. Just before Christmas a commission was set up, headed by the bishop's brother, Richard Neville, earl of Salisbury, to enquire into the matter; and a month later, in response to their petition, the king ordered the restoration of the lordship to the earl's feoffees, who included Salisbury. The bishop's attempted forcible recovery of Barnard Castle had failed. It is to be noted, however, that the Crown and Warwick's feoffees were careful to assert that the lordship lay in Northumberland, not in the liberty of Durham.[12] Indeed twenty-two years later Robert Rhodes, one-time steward of the priory

---

[10] C. M. Fraser, *History of Antony Bec* (Oxford, 1957), 203–5, 208; *Records of Antony Bec*, ed. C. M. Fraser, SS, clxii (1953 for 1947), 39, 86, 92–3, 125, 209–12; *Northern Petitions*, ed. C. M. Fraser, SS, cxciv (1982 for 1981), 225–6, 245, 248, 255–6.   [11] *CIM*, vi. No. 339, pp. 346–7.

[12] *CPR 1436–41*, p. 405.

of Durham, admitted on behalf of Bishop Laurence Booth that he had wrongly given evidence at an *inquisition post mortem* on Richard Beauchamp to the effect that Barnard Castle lay in the county of Northumberland, to the harm of 'the liberty and title of the church of St Cuthbert'.[13]

Bishop Booth followed Neville in pursuing the claim to the lordship, initially with more success. In 1459, following the rebellion of Richard Neville, earl of Warwick, it was confiscated by Booth with the connivance of the government of Henry VI, even though correctly the title lay with Neville's countess. Despite Booth's pleas, Edward IV restored the earl of Warwick in 1461. Nevertheless nine years later, when Warwick (now in rebellion against Edward IV) fled the kingdom, Booth was once more granted the lordship. The letters patent, enrolled at Durham, recited that it had been wrongly taken by Edward I, and that the restitution of 1327 was valid. Yet once more Booth lost control: between 1471 and 1474, in circumstances which remain obscure, the lordship was surrendered by the bishop to the king's brother, Richard of Gloucester, who became king himself in 1483. On his death in 1485 Barnard Castle was retained in royal hands by Henry VII. The final loss of the lordship to the bishopric is confirmed by its absence from the land reported to be held by the late King Richard in the palatinate in an *inquisition post mortem* held in 1485. By this date, it is clear, the question was resolved in favour of the Crown. Barnard Castle was not at that date part of the liberty of the bishop of Durham.[14]

[13] *Memoirs of Ambrose Barnes*, ed. W. D. Longstaff, SS, l (1867 for 1866) 95; Pollard, 'St. Cuthbert and the Hog', pp. 109–11. In the 1448 inquisition on the death of Henry, duke of Warwick, Barnard Castle was said to be in Northumberland: *CIPM*, iv (1828), 227. In the light of these inquisitions, the inclusion of Durham as part of Northumberland in the terms of reference of the commission to enquire into infringements of royal rights in the north in 1433 was not as anachronistic as R. L. Storey suggested (*Langley*, pp. 119–20, 130–1).

[14] Pollard, 'St. Cuthbert and the Hog', pp. 110–11 and 126 n. 54. The courts of Durham did, however, hear cases concerning men of Barnard Castle from time to time during the 15th cent. At the Lent sessions of the Justices of Assize in 1456, for instance, John Tiptoft, earl of Worcester (as attorney for the earl of Warwick, then installed as captain of Calais?) sued 18 tenants of Piercebridge, Langton, Denton, Longnewton, Headlam, and Barnard Castle itself for detinue of rents totalling £124 (Durh. 3/227/8d); and on 30 Jan. 1472 Stephen and Richard Colpottys of Middleton in Teesdale were presented to the Justices of the Peace for feloniously killing Robert Nattress of Stanhope in Weardale in the preceding July (Durh. 3/10/1/1/4).

Durham's special status was said from 1311 to derive from its role as a bulwark against the Scots. In Sir Walter Scott's famous line, it was 'half house of God, half castle 'gainst the Scot'. The military role, and its use as a justification for the bishop's franchise, only developed during the wars of Scottish independence,[15] and was largely founded on the possession of North Durham, and especially of the castle of Norham, which was the principal fortress on the English bank of the Tweed. Norham, not Durham itself, was the castle. Its importance in the defence of the north-eastern frontier is easily overlooked. Berwick, with which the defence is associated, was part of the ancient kingdom of Scotland; and its possession was disputed throughout the later Middle Ages. Captured by Edward I in 1296, lost in 1318, and retaken by Edward III in 1333, Berwick remained in English hands (apart from a brief interval in 1355) until surrendered by Margaret of Anjou in 1461. Thereafter for twenty-one years, until its recovery by Richard of Gloucester, it was reunited with Scotland. Between 1461 and 1482 Norham was once again the principal bulwark against the Scot. The bishop of Durham thus had an important role to play in defence of the border, in partnership with the warden of the east march.[16]

The warden, as his office evolved in the reign of Richard II and was fixed from 1389, was a retained military commander, the castellan of the royal castle of Berwick, in receipt of fixed annual payments from which troops were to be found to defend the border. During the fifteenth century the size of the garrison at Berwick was not normally specified; but in its last decade Henry VII maintained 150 men there in time of truce. During most of the century the warden was paid £2,500 in time of peace, and £5,000 in time of war.[17] The constableship of Norham followed this model. When Roger Heron was appointed to office in April 1476 he was to serve under the same terms as Sir Robert Ogle in 1436; receiving the revenues of Norhamshire in peace-time (valued at £194 in 1478/9) and a further £200 from the

[15] Emsley and Fraser, *Courts of Durham*, pp. 92–3.

[16] The role of the bishop of Durham in the wardens' commissions of 1357–84 is largely explained by the strategic role of Norham. (See R. L. Storey, 'The Wardens of the Marches of England towards Scotland, 1377–1489', *EHR* 72 (1957), 594–5, 609–11.

[17] Storey, 'Wardens', pp. 600–1, 604; PRO DL 29/651/10528.

exchequer of Durham during war. An indenture of March 1482, at a time of war, between Bishop Dudley and Sir John Middleton of Belsay reveals that the constable was expected to retain at least thirty able-bodied men for the garrison.[18] Norham was a petty wardenry. In addition to Norham, until 1460, Roxburgh lay in English hands: for his garrison the keeper was paid £1,000 in peacetime and £2,000 in time of war.[19]

During Henry VI's reign the wardens and keepers found great difficulty in securing their payments: in the second half of 1436 there was even a short period in which both marches were left without a warden. In 1434 the earl of Northumberland resigned after seventeen years in office, in exasperation at the government's inability to pay him. After a series of stop-gap appointments his son and heir, Henry, Lord Poynings was persuaded to take it on. But his payments soon fell into arrears. By 14 May 1455 he was owed £6,400; by 20 November 1459, nearly £17,000. Likewise the keeper of Roxburgh since 1443, William Neville, Lord Fauconberg, claimed £3,500 in unpaid wages in 1449, and his debt had increased to over £4,000 in 1451.[20] The castles too fell into serious disrepair. In 1451 Berwick was in such a state of dilapidation that £466. 13s. 8d. was set aside for repairs over four years.[21] Norham was a cause for almost as much concern. When William Dudley became bishop in 1476 a royal commissioner was sent down to survey the castle, and a programme of repair was set in motion. Not much appears to have been achieved; for Richard III claimed in 1484 that all the castles and property of the bishop, and especially Norham, were ruinous and beyond the resources of the palatinate to restore. It was not until the episcopacy of Richard Fox in the 1490s that any substantial progress appears to have been made.[22]

In the circumstances it would seem surprising that men would be willing to take on the responsibility of the wardenships and the safe-keeping of the castles. In fact the Crown found no difficulty in finding wardens after 1440, because of the

[18] Durh. 3/49/15; Durham, Church Commission, Bishopric Estates, 189676; Storey, *Langley*, 145.   [19] R. A. Griffiths, *The Reign of Henry VI* (1981), 405.
[20] Storey, 'Wardens', pp. 604–5, 606 n. 1; Griffiths, *Henry VI*, pp. 405–6.
[21] CPR, 1446–52, 505.
[22] Durham, Church Commission, Bishopric Estates, 189830; Rymer, *Foedera*, xii. 224; Allen, *Letters of Richard Fox*, p. 17.

opportunities the offices offered to build up political and military power, and the scope they still offered for profit. Thus in the west march the Nevilles and in the east march the Percies were anxious to secure appointments for as long a term of years as possible, even at reduced rates of pay and with a doubtful prospect of full settlement. In the west march the earl of Salisbury secured a grant in survivorship with his son and heir, the future earl of Warwick, for twenty years in 1446, extended in 1454 until 1474, and renewed by Warwick alone for a further twenty years in 1462. This process reached its logical end after Warwick's death in the creation of an hereditary wardenship for Richard of Gloucester in 1483. In the east march the Percies were never able to achieve such security of tenure. Henry, Lord Poynings, third earl of Northumberland 1455–61, stretched his term of appointments from an initial four years to ten years in 1457. John Neville, Lord Montagu was granted only a six-year term in 1463. After his restoration in 1470 Henry Percy, fourth earl of Northumberland enjoyed tenure of office for five and then seven years, until the reign of Richard III, after which it was reduced to annual contracts.[23] For one year, 1481–2, Northumberland in partnership with his retainer Roger Heron served as constable of Norham. But normally the constable was drawn from the Northumbrian gentry: Sir Robert Ogle, later Lord Ogle, from 1436, apparently until his death in 1469. And afterwards, for shorter terms of office, Roger Heron, Sir John Middleton of Belsay, and, for seven years from 22 May 1485, Sir Thomas Grey of Chillingham.[24]

The government of Northumberland itself was dominated by the warden of the east march. The warden's commission extended beyond the defence of the border in time of war to the supervision and conservation of the truce in time of peace. His jurisdiction extended throughout Northumberland north of the Tyne and into Newcastle. By the early sixteenth century march days were held every twenty days to deal with breaches, and special diets were convened to deal with any backlog of cases. The royal deputy on the borders, the warden enjoyed a unique position as supervisor of the administration of justice in the

[23] Storey, 'Wardens', pp. 605–8, 614–15.
[24] Durh. 3/49/15; 55/7,8; 56/2.

county. It is to be noted, however, that this supervisory role did not extend south of the Tyne—a restriction clearly established by Act of Parliament in 1453.[25]

Thus the need to provide for the security of the border, as well as the existence of extensive liberties, severely limited the direct exercise of royal authority in the region. The circumstances seem also to have hindered the development of clearly defined county communities, even in Yorkshire. The county court which met at York castle, and at which the county's members of parliament were elected, was dominated by the principal tenants in chief of the Crown. Until 1429 the county's representatives were nominated by a handful of tenants in chief or their attorneys, who in 1427 were said to hold power for the community of the county. The practice of election by forty-shilling freeholders and the community as a whole was a novelty in the later fifteenth century. Indeed the tenants of the great honours, which had their own courts, were still exempt from suit at the county court.[26] To a considerable degree the old feudal honours continued to act as an alternative focus to the county, a circumstance reflected, as we have seen, in the patterns of marriage, friendship, and service. Landed society tended to identify itself with the 'counties' within the county, such as Cleveland, Richmondshire, Craven, or, further to the south, Hallamshire, each dominated by a great lord. The centrifugal tendency was reinforced by the existence of three commissions of the peace, one for each Riding. Perhaps the Corpus Christi Guild at York was beginning to play the role of county club for the gentry; but Yorkshire was too large and administratively too fragmented for it yet to have generated a fully-fledged community of the shire.[27]

In Durham, not strictly speaking a county, there may have

[25] Storey, *Langley*, pp. 136–9; Cardew, 'Anglo-Scottish Borders', pp. 292–319; *Rot. Parl.* v. 267.

[26] *The Parliamentary Representation of the County of York, 1258–1832*, ed. A. Gooder, ii., YAS, RS xci (1935), 3–6. Curiously, certain prominent tenants in chief and heads of honours, notably FitzHugh, Scrope of Bolton, and Furnival, were never represented in early 15th cent. elections for which evidence has survived (ibid., App. c, Table 1).

[27] Cf. Suffolk, where early Tudor dominance by local nobles effectively stifled the development of a county community (MacCulloch, *Suffolk*, pp. 165–7, 338).

been a stronger sense of community, focused on local identification with St Cuthbert. Bishops tended to defend their privileges
in the name of the liberties of St Cuthbert. The group of leading
subjects of the bishopric who challenged episcopal privileges in
the fourth decade of the fifteenth century did so in the name of
King John's charter to the 'Haliwerk' of St Cuthbert.[28] Piccolomini, although he appears to have confused Bede with Cuthbert,
observed that the tomb of the saint was revered by inhabitants of
the region.[29] Indeed the greatest honour that could be bestowed
was to be accepted as a member of the fraternity of St Cuthbert
in the cathedral. On a secular level, too, the administrative
offices and courts clustered around Palace Green, as well as the
regular meetings of the free court of the palatinate there, gave a
cohesion to the community of St Cuthbert. Although there were
no elections of Member of Parliament, gatherings, such as that
of five knights, fifty-one esquires, and eighteen others in the
cathedral on 23 September 1434 to swear not to maintain
lawbreakers, suggest a sense of the body of the county
palatine.[30]

The oath of 1434 was sworn before the bishop, exercising his
regalian authority. Elsewhere, too, in the absence of a strong
royal presence, the magnates dominated local government.
Apart from 1464 to 1470, when Percy was replaced by Neville, in
the person of Lord Montagu, as its earl, Northumberland was
largely the fief of the Percies. Only after the death of Henry
Percy, the fourth earl, in 1489 was the grip of a single magnate
loosened. The power of these earls, who were also wardens of
the east march, was further enhanced by Edward IV's grants of
the shrievalty for life to John Neville in 1466 and to Henry Percy
in 1474. In Richmondshire, where the lords of Middleham
controlled the office of bailiff of the four wapentakes, shrieval
authority was similarly held in the interest of the Nevilles and
their successor, Richard of Gloucester, by the Conyers of
Hornby.[31] It is not surprising that the local officers of the Crown

---

[28] Storey, *Langley*, pp. 125–6.

[29] Gabel, *Commentaries of Pius II*, p. 36.

[30] *The Register of Thomas Langley, Bishop of Durham, 1406–37*, ed. R. L.
Storey, iv., SS, cxx (1961), 142–3; Storey, *Langley*, p. 55.

[31] C. H. Hunter-Blair, 'The Sheriffs of Northumberland', *Arch. Ael.* 4th ser., 20
(1942), 18–19.

(sheriffs, escheators, justices of the peace), as well as the elected Members of Parliament, tended to have close connections with the magnates. Nevertheless, it must not be overlooked that representatives of prominent local families filled these posts not only by virtue of their baronial connections, but also as a consequence of their own independent local standing. In considering parliamentary representation and the personnel of local government it is not to be assumed that every knight of the shire, sheriff, or justice of the peace was a political nominee. Care needs to be taken to distinguish, where possible, between the operation of patronage or political influence, and the expression of custom, social obligation, or personal inclination.

This is apparent in the case of parliamentary representation. In an analysis of the representation of four northern counties to Parliament between 1450 and 1470, Miss Jalland concluded that local magnates—Richard, duke of York, the Nevilles, and the Percies—exercised considerable influence over elections.[32] Such a conclusion, based on consideration of the connections of the MPs, is not to be challenged. It is not, however, the whole story. In Northumberland, for instance, for which the returns of only nine of twenty-one elections from 1449 to 1497 have survived, the MPs elected in November 1449, 1450, and 1453 were with one exception stalwart Percy men: they were Sir William Bertram (twice), Robert Mitford, John Ogle (twice), and Sir Gerard Widdrington. Widdrington, married to Elizabeth Boynton, daughter of Christopher Boynton of Sadbury, Yorks., later served the Nevilles and Edward IV in Northumberland; but this association may not necessarily have existed when the parliament was elected in March 1453. After 1460 the Percy influence was disrupted and diminished. In 1460 and 1461 men upon whom the Yorkists could rely were returned. In 1472 one member, Sir John Middleton of Belsay, was a man with long-standing Yorkist and Neville associations, although his colleague, John Cartington, had an impeccable Percy pedigree. In 1478 two Percy men, one (Ralph Hotham) brought in from Yorkshire, were returned. But in the 1490s, during the minority of the fifth earl, royal influence over elections seems to have

---

[32] P. Jalland, 'The Influence of the Aristocracy on Shire Elections in the North of England, 1450–70', *Speculum*, 47 (1972), 483–507.

been paramount. In particular the election in 1491 of Sir William Tyler, Henry VII's knight of the body and captain of Berwick, clearly suggests pressure from above.[33]

There can be no doubt that the elections in Northumberland were subject to magnate or royal influence. But for the most part the men elected were also drawn from the county's leading families, who had a tradition not only of serving Percy, but also of sitting in Parliament. William Bertram, Robert Mitford, and John Cartington were the sons and grandsons of MPs; John Ogle the son and brother; and Gerard Widdrington the grandson of an MP. There was a parliamentary élite in the county, albeit closely associated with the Percies. The grip of this élite was loosened only when the power of the Percies was removed.[34] Thus in 1460 and 1461 lesser men, such as Thomas Weltden and Robert Folbery, represented the county; and in 1491 the king's servant Sir William Tyler was returned.

The same pattern is apparent in Yorkshire, for which the returns for only eleven of the twenty-one elections have survived. Representation was drawn from the highest knightly ranks throughout the county. MPs were both members of the charmed circle of rich gentry and closely associated with local magnates or with the Crown. Only three men from the North Riding were returned in those elections for which evidence has survived: Sir James Strangways (February 1449, 1460, and 1461, when he was Speaker), Sir William Eure (February 1449), and Sir Thomas Mountford (1461).[35]

Magnate influence on these elections is apparent; but what actually happened at the county court on election day is impossible to tell. According to the surviving indentures of Yorkshire elections between 1442 and 1478 attendance fluctuated between a maximum of 451 and a minimum of 24, although on all but three occasions the number was less than 100. Attenders were of all ranks, but in general there was rarely a high turn-out

[33] P. Jalland, 'The Influence of the Aristocracy on Shire Elections in the North of England, 1450–70', *Speculum*, 47 (1972), 493–5; C. H. Hunter-Blair, 'Members of Parliament for Northumberland, 1399–1558', *Arch. Ael.* 4th ser., 12 (1935), 109–21.

[34] Wedgwood, *Biographies*, pp. 71, 161, 597, 645, 947.

[35] Jalland, 'Shire Elections', pp. 487–95. Sir John Conyers is not known to have been an MP; it is highly likely that either he or a member of his family was elected to one of the many parliaments for which no returns have survived.

of armigerous gentry. Senior county figures were poor attenders. Of North Riding grandees, although Sir James Strangways was elected three times and was returning officer once (1453), he was recorded as present as an elector on only two other occasions (the first election of 1449, and 1455). Sir John Conyers, returning officer twice in 1449, and Sir William Eure, elected in 1449, never attested. As far as other senior North Riding gentry were concerned, attendance was occasional at best: John Norton twice, Sir Thomas Mountford twice, William Burgh twice, John Wandesford three times, and John Wycliffe three times. Attendance seems to have been a personal rather than a political decision. Thomas Gower of Stittenham was present at every election for which record has survived from 1449 to 1478; Thomas Witham at most. These two were both key Neville men. On the other hand Robert Constable of Bossall attended only once (in 1449), and members of the Conyers family but occasionally.[36]

Politically the elections for which returns have survived were either 'neutral' or 'Yorkist'. That of November 1449, for instance, attended by forty-nine knights and esquires, among them prominent retainers of both Neville and Percy, elected 'a balanced ticket' of Sir James Pickering and Sir William Normanville.[37] The surviving returns of 1455–78, however, were all for 'Yorkist' parliaments. On 23 June 1455, shortly after the first battle of St Albans, under the guidance of the duke of York's retainer Sir John Saville as sheriff, fifty-four men, many clearly identifiable as followers of either York or Neville, met to elect Sir James Pickering and Thomas Harrington. A similar band of fifty-eight gathered on 28 July 1460 to elect Sir James Strangways and Sir Thomas Mountford, both the earl of Salisbury's retainers.[38] The most impressive turn-out of North Riding gentry occurred on 16 January 1478, when Sir John Pilkington and Sir Robert Constable were elected to the parliament called for no other purpose than to condemn George, duke of Clarence. At least 100 knights and esquires, many with close

[36] Gooder, *Parliamentary Representation*, 238; PRO, C219 15/2/1/23, 4/1/24, 6/1/26, 7/1/26; 16/1/1/24, 2/1/29, 3/1/15, 6/1/6; 17/1/1/33, 2/1/27; 3/1/33.
[37] PRO, C219 15/7/1/26; Gooder, *Parliamentary Representation*, p. 238.
[38] PRO, C219 16/3/1/15, 6/1/6; Gooder, *Parliamentary Representation*, p. 238.

associations with the royal household or the duke of Gloucester and the earl of Northumberland, attested their election. Thirty came from North Riding families, including three members of the Conyers family, Thomas Metcalfe of Nappa, Thomas Mountford, Thomas Tunstall, and Thomas Witham, all councillors of the duke. Of all the elections this seems to be the one most obviously subject to pressure from above.[39]

Borough representation in the north-east was restricted to four places. The three principal towns tended to return their own burgesses or servants. There was an increase in the numbers of gentry and lawyers who represented the boroughs; but in the case of the flourishing towns this was not so much an invasion resulting from urban weakness as a deliberate exploitation of influential support. Thus Miles Metcalfe, who represented York in 1478 and 1483, came from a prominent gentry family, and was a trusted servant of the duke of Gloucester. Yet he was a lawyer, retained as counsel by the city from 1470, and was its recorder from 1477 to 1486. As Recorder of York Metcalfe was a true representative of the city. Similarly Richard Weltden, MP for Newcastle in 1450–1 and 1467–8, was a lawyer resident in the city; and Robert Folbery, MP in 1472–5, another lawyer, was both collector of customs and subsidy and the city's Recorder. These men may not have been in trade; but they were eminently qualified to represent their constituencies, and can hardly be classified as representatives of an invading gentry.[40] Only in the fourth borough, Scarborough, where over a third of the men who represented the town between 1439 and 1509 were non-resident and had no obvious link with it, can one perhaps detect a willingness to seek or accept outside representation. Men such as Henry Eure of Malton (February 1449), Sir Thomas Gower of Stittenham (1464 and 1484), Ralph Hotham, a younger son of Hotham of Scorburgh (1472), and Edmund Thwaites of Lund (1478, 1483, 1484) were outsiders, and owed their election to local magnate influence (Neville in the case of Gower; Percy

---

[39] PRO, C219 17/3/1/33; Gooder, *Parliamentary Representation*, p. 238.
[40] P. Jalland, 'The Revolution in Northern Borough Representation in mid-fifteenth-century England', *NH* 11 (1976), 27–51; R. E. Horrox, 'Urban Patronage and Patrons in the Fifteenth Century', in R. A. Griffiths (ed.), *Patronage, the Crown and the Provinces* (Gloucester, 1981), 158–60; Wedgwood, *Biographies*, pp. 343, 931.

in the case of Hotham and Thwaites).[41] Scarborough seems to have provided the one opportunity for men not from the very top rank of the gentry to have found a seat in Parliament, provided they had the backing of one of the local magnates.

In Yorkshire the sheriff, like the Members of Parliament, was always drawn from the top rank of substantial knightly families. Some men served several times. Thus Sir Edmund Hastings of Roxby was sheriff four times (1464/5, 1470/1, 1476/7, and 1483/4); Sir John Conyers three times (1448/9, 1467/8, and 1474/5); and Sir James Strangways, three times (1445/6, 1452/3, and 1468/9). Two of Hastings's shrievalties would seem to have been particularly politically sensitive: in 1470/1, during the Readeption, and in 1483/4, during the first year of Richard III's reign. But he was also a man of local standing and experience. This is also particularly true of Conyers and Strangways. While they were both prominent retainers of the Nevilles, they were also the most substantial of the North Riding gentry. They were pricked as sheriff when there was no great political significance. Clearly at times of acute political tension and uncertainty reliable men were pricked by the government: thus in November 1455 the Neville retainer Sir Thomas Harrington was chosen; in March 1461 the Yorkist servant Sir John Saville stepped into the office; in 1471 Edward IV put Sir Ralph Ashton in for two years; and Richard III called upon his retainer Sir Thomas Markenfield in 1484.[42]

In Northumberland such political considerations, especially after 1460, were more prominent. In the latter years of Henry VI the sheriff was usually drawn from the ranks of those senior gentry who were also clients of the Percies—Herons of Ford or Manners of Etal. From November 1460 a series of Yorkist appointments was made, beginning with Sir John Middleton of Belsay, a Neville retainer. For three years of civil war in the county (1461–4) Sir George Lumley, son of Lord Lumley, was sheriff; and he was succeeded by another Durham man, Sir William Bowes, in 1465. Lumley is the only known deputy

---

[41] P. Jalland, 'Borough Representation', pp. 40–3; Wedgwood, *Biographies*, pp. 472, 854–5.
[42] Arnold, 'West Riding', pp. 276–7. I am grateful to Dr Arnold for allowing me to draw upon her appendices covering the whole of Yorkshire for the above paragraph.

of John Neville, who became sheriff for life in 1466. For three years after 1471 the office was held by John Widdrington of Chipchase, who, besides being a servant of the earl of Northumberland, was also retained by Richard, duke of Gloucester. Widdrington continued to serve as Northumberland's undersheriff after 1474; subsequent deputies of the earl, thereafter sheriff for life, came from the same group of families (Greys, Harbottles, Manners, Lilburnes, and Thorntons) who had traditionally supplied the sheriff.[43]

Durham, as in so much else, was exceptional. Not only was the sheriff by custom appointed during pleasure; but he tended also until the last quarter of the century to be a man of lesser standing than in other counties, the bishop's servant, answerable directly to him. Such was Geoffrey Middleton, appointed during pleasure by Bishop Neville in 1441, and granted, uniquely, the office for life in 1445. He was removed by Bishop Booth at the end of 1461, but restored a year later, after the temporalities of the bishopric were seized by the Crown. Middleton died in or before 1465, to be succeeded by Booth's earlier appointee John Atherton. William Claxton of Old Park served as sheriff for three years, to be followed by Henry Radcliffe in 1469, Atherton again in 1472, and Robert Tempest, appointed by Bishop Dudley, in 1476. He was succeeded by Sir Ralph Bowes in 1482, who served four bishops in twenty years.[44]

In Durham the office of steward carried more weight than that of sheriff. It has been claimed that the Nevilles (one or other branch of the family) held a monopoly of the office throughout the second half of the century.[45] In fact this was far from the case. There seem to have been alternative approaches to the appointment of a steward. One was to call upon a leading layman of the palatinate, exploiting his standing and connections to buttress the bishop's authority: the other was to appoint a trusted servant of the bishop, or a trained lawyer, who would

[43] Hunter-Blair, 'The Sheriffs of Northumberland', pp. 18–19, 67–71; Hicks, 'Fourth Earl of Northumberland', pp. 82–3.

[44] Hutchinson, *Durham*, i. 416, 442, 448, 456 as amended by reference to Durham, Church Commission, Bishopric Estates, 189822–30.

[45] M. Weiss, '"A Power in the North?"', The Percies in the Fifteenth Century', *Historical Journal*, 19 (1976), 504; M. E. James, *Family, Lineage and Civil Society: A Study of Society, Politics and Mentality in the Durham Region, 1500–1640* (Oxford, 1974), 43 n. 3, 44.

be more amenable to the bishop's will. Sir Ralph Eure, steward
1391–1422, was of the former type; but he was succeeded in
1422 by Thomas Holden, a life-long servant of the bishop.
Bishop Neville returned to earlier practice by appointing Robert
Eure, Sir Ralph's younger son, as his first steward.[46] On 12 April
1441 Neville replaced him by his brother, William, Lord
Fauconberg, for life; on the same day, but by separate commission, he was made during pleasure 'governor and ruler of all and
every single man and tenant' of the palatinate 'for the time of
war as well as of peace', for which he was granted a fee of £60 in
addition to the £40 per annum as steward.[47] It is clear that
Fauconberg was not expected to exercise these functions in
person: at the time he was serving in Normandy, and had been
since 1436. In September 1441, therefore, the function of presid-
ing over the halmote courts was put into commission; and
sometime before March 1442 Fauconberg appointed his
nephew, Sir Thomas Neville, son of the earl of Salisbury, his
deputy. Fauconberg was back in England by October 1443, when
he presided over the courts, as he did again in 1447; but thereafter Sir Thomas presided until the end of his uncle's pontificate
ten years later.[48] Whether in the person of uncle or nephew, it is
clear that between 1441 and 1457 the stewardship was firmly in
the hands of the Middleham Nevilles.

One of Bishop Booth's first acts was to remove Fauconberg
from his offices as steward (and one assumes 'governor'), and to
replace him provocatively by Sir Thomas Neville of Brancepeth,
the younger brother of the earl of Westmorland. Under Sir
Thomas, too, the holding of courts was put into commission;
but he retained the stewardship until Booth was removed from
the temporalities at the end of 1462. At that point John Neville,
Lord Montagu was put in, and held the post until 1466.[49] Thus
for twenty-five years in mid-century the rival branches of the
Neville family did indeed share the stewardship. At first a
reflection of the aggrandizement of the Middleham branch,
latterly the pattern mirrored the conflict between the two
branches as supporters of Lancaster and York.

---

[46] Storey, *Langley*, pp. 101–3.   [47] Durh. 3/42/14.
[48] Durh. 3/42/14; 15/108–15, 122ff.; A. J. Pollard, *John Talbot and the War in France, 1427–53*, RHS Study in History, 35 (1983), 33, 41–53.
[49] Durh. 3/48/2, 5, 12.

Bishop Booth, however, when he was able in December 1466 to dispense with the services of Lord Montagu (by then earl of Northumberland), began a new practice of appointing trained lawyers, who were paid a fee of only £20 instead of the earlier £40 per annum which successive Neville stewards had received. The first was Thomas Morslaw (1466–73). Although he was succeeded briefly by Henry Radcliffe (not a lawyer), from 1476 Thomas Middleton of Stockeld, Yorks., who had been retained as counsel by Booth since 1467, was steward.[50] Just before he was translated to York, Booth apparently reverted to earlier practice by making Ralph, Lord Neville, nephew and heir to the earl of Westmorland, his steward with a fee of £40. But in reality this appointment was a sinecure, for Middleton was to continue in post as sub-steward, paid his fee of £20 p.a. by Neville, while Thomas Farehare, Middleton's deputy, was retained as 'clerk to the Halmotes', with his fee of £3. 6s. 3d. p.a. also secured. Five months later, after Booth's translation, Middleton was restored by Bishop Dudley, and Neville compensated with a straight annuity of £20.[51]

Middleton remained steward until 1484, when, for political reasons, he was replaced by Richard Danby, (also *legis peritus*), the younger son of Sir Robert Danby, one-time Chief Justice of Common Pleas, and also chief justice of Durham for many years. Danby remained steward, jointly with Percival Lambton in the 1490s, until 1507.[52] During the last quarter of the century the stewardship became more narrowly defined as a legal office, and its downgrading was reflected in the halving of the customary fee. At the same time, it would appear, the office of chancellor, usually held jointly with that of receiver-general, seems under the imprint of a series of able clerical administrators (Henry Gillow, John Kelyng, and Ralph Booth) to have become the pivot of palatine government.

The stewardship of the county palatine was a unique post. The steward and the other senior officials (including the justices of assize) were invariably justices of the peace and of gaol

---

[50] Hutchinson, *Durham*, i. 442.

[51] Durh. 3/49/15; Durham, Church Commission, Bishopric Estates, 189830. For Middleton, see above pp. 134–5.

[52] Durh. 3/18/5; Hutchinson, *Durham*, i. pp. 456, 467, 469. See also below, p. 356.

delivery in the bishopric. The strong official presence probably explains why the commissions were reissued only twelve times between 1448 and 1500. The bench was small too, only rising to over a dozen under Bishop Neville, who regularly packed it with five of his kinsmen (the earl of Salisbury, Lords Fauconberg, Latimer, and Abergavenny, and Sir Thomas Neville). After 1457 there was usually a representative of the Nevilles of Raby on the commission—the earl of Westmorland or a brother or nephew. Gentry participation was slight: usually no more than three at a time, drawn from the leading families of Claxton, Conyers of Sockburn, Conyers of Wynyard, Eure, and Hilton. Rarely did the bench have an explicit political colour: the most obvious political nomination being that of Richard Neville, earl of Warwick in 1463, when briefly the temporalities were in royal hands.[53]

Like that of Durham, Northumberland's bench was small and was infrequently renewed (fourteen times between 1455 and 1500). There were normally a dozen or fewer justices: only in the commission issued in December 1455 was this number significantly exceeded, so as to accommodate an attempted political balance (York and Salisbury as well as Northumberland and Westmorland were included). Between 1455 and 1471 there was a degree of political instability. Before 1461 the earl of Northumberland and representatives of his client gentry were prominent; but between 1461 and 1471, when the Percies were in disgrace, the bench was dominated by the Nevilles and their allies (Greystoke, Lumley, and Ogle). Normality and continuity returned following the restoration of Henry Percy, fourth earl of Northumberland, in 1470, who, along with the dukes of Clarence and Gloucester, was joined by John Cartington, Robert Manners, John Lilburne, John Swinburne, and John Widdrington. Although the commission was reissued four times between May 1483 and September 1485, its composition changed little. Only after the death of the earl in 1489 was the pattern re-established in 1471 broken. Then, under the nominal headship of Arthur, Prince of Wales, Thomas Howard, earl of Surrey introduced several of his own and the prince's household, only John Cartington from that group which had sat for the previous

[53] Durh. 3/43/6; 44/21; 48/1, 6, 12, 15; 49/5; 54/2,3; 58/1; 60/2,5; 63/2.

fifteen years continuing to serve as a justice under the new regime.[54]

The North Riding differed from Durham and Northumberland in that the bench was rarely less than a dozen-and-a-half strong; and in that no fewer than thirty-four commissions were issued between 1455 and 1500.[55] It was perhaps more typical of commissions of the peace in the kingdom as a whole, and its composition is worth analysing in greater depth. It seems to have been customary for all the peers with local interests to be justices, unless they were politically untrustworthy. Thus before 1460 there were as many as twelve peers serving as justices, including Humphrey, duke of Buckingham. While in March 1460, after Ludford, the duke of York and the Neville lords were removed, lesser peers connected with the Nevilles, such as Greystoke and FitzHugh, retained their places. After 1461, because of the reduction in number of adult and politically reliable peers, the number on the bench fell to six. But it seems to have been a general principle that all eligible and not outrightly hostile peers were included. In addition to the peers the archbishop of York and bishop of Durham were regularly included; and from 1464 to 1472 John Shirwood, archdeacon of Richmond as well. Arguably more significant for the working of the bench was the presence of men with legal training. The northern circuit judges, serjeants-at-law or full justices, were on the bench as a matter of course. These included men of local birth, Sir Robert Danby (d. 1474) and Richard Pigot (d. 1484); but also men from outside the county, Peter Ardern, William Jenney, Thomas Littleton, and John Needham earlier in the period, and Roger Townsend, John Fisher, and Thomas Kebell after 1483. The circuit judges were supported by other local lawyers: Nicholas Girlington until his death in 1464, Henry Eure (1468–77), Thomas Asper (1464–93), Miles Metcalfe

[54] CPR, 1452–61, 673; 1461–7, 569; 1467–77, 624; 1477–85, 568; 1485–94, 495–6; 1494–1504, 652–3.

[55] This and the following 3 paragraphs are based on an analysis of the commissions printed in the Calendars of Patent Rolls, viz: 1452–61, 682–3; 1461–7, 576; 1467–77, 637; 1477–85, 579; 1485–94, 506–7; 1494–1509, 667–8. For the composition of the West Riding bench and a similar development of royal household involvement see C. Arnold, 'The Commission of the Peace for the West Riding of Yorkshire, 1437–1509', in Pollard, Property and Politics, pp. 116–33.

(1470–85), and Richard Danby (1480–1507). There were usually six of these lawyers on the bench at any one time.

In the light of the substantial peerage, clerical, and legal presence, the contribution of the gentry to the bench (frequently emphasized in recent historical writing) is less significant. There were rarely more than half a dozen of the gentry serving as justices of the peace at any one time, and these were not necessarily the most substantial. While the heads of the families of Conyers, Eure, and Strangways normally sat, many substantial knightly families were never represented. No Boynton, Darrell, De La River, Percehay, Stapleton, or Lascelles was a justice in the North Riding in the second half of the fifteenth century. Some members of lesser families sat: John Catterick (March–June 1460); William Burgh, father and son (1461 to 1470); William and John Colville (on several occasions from 1460 to 1483); and (after 1485) Robert Wyvyll. In total only 30 of the 130 armigerous gentry families were represented on the bench in this fifty-year period.

The political affiliations of the gentry on the commission of the peace were nevertheless significant. Sir John Conyers, attainted in 1459, was removed in March 1460, to be restored in May 1461. He thereafter served without a break until removed by Henry VII in 1485. Sir James Strangways, not attainted in 1459, survived the subsequent purge, although he stepped down briefly between June and August 1460. On the other hand he was removed during the Readeption, in November 1470. Restored in 1472, he died in 1480. Sir Thomas Mountford, the earl of Salisbury's retainer, became a justice in February 1459, was removed in March 1460, was restored by the victorious Yorkists in August 1460, but dropped out on the accession of Edward IV. However, a fourth Neville retainer, Thomas Witham, served without a break through all these vicissitudes until his death in 1480. It is not easy to explain the differences in the careers as justices of the peace of these four men. They may or may not reflect different degrees of commitment to their masters' causes. However, they do illustrate the fact that most of the North Riding gentry who sat on the bench had strong Neville connections, just as their counterparts in Northumberland had strong Percy connections.

These connections were maintained after 1471 by Richard of

Gloucester. He brought in new men such as Sir James Danby, Thomas Metcalfe, and Sir Richard Ratcliffe. But he was clearly not the sole arbiter of the bench: three knights of the body, Sir Ralph Ashton, Sir Edmund Hastings of Roxby, and Sir John Pickering of Oswaldkirk, all of whom were subsequently to serve Richard III after 1483, were magistrates after 1471. It is a measure of Richard III's hold on the North Riding, however, that the most sweeping changes in the composition of the bench occurred in September 1485. The size was halved to nine, only the archbishop of York, Lords Greystoke and FitzHugh, and Richard Danby remaining. Brought in were Sir William Eure, Sir Ralph Bulmer, Sir John Norton, and Robert Wyvyll, the last three of whom had not served previously on any of the Yorkist benches. A year later the earl of Northumberland and Serjeant Townsend were restored, and the earl of Shrewsbury, Sir Ralph Bigod, and Serjeant John Fisher added. Other than Richard Danby, there was no room for anyone associated with the old Neville–Gloucester affinity. Although, after 1489, the new heads of the Conyers and Strangways families, as well as a chastened Thomas Metcalfe, were allowed to take their traditional places, Henry VII took one stage further Edward IV's precedent of bringing in his own household men, prominent among whom, in the company of the earl of Surrey, were the outsiders Sir John Cheyney and Sir Richard Cholmley, as well as Sir Henry Wentworth and Sir Thomas Wortley from further south in the county.

Gentry involvement was not substantially greater in commission of array and other *ad hoc* commission. A handful who were not justices of the peace served as commissioners of array in the North Riding. In May 1461 four of the twelve commissioners were not or had not been justices. Similarly five of the eighteen on two commissions of array in 1484 were not on the bench. But in 1472 and again in 1480 commissioners of array were all justices of the peace, with the exception of William Parr of Kendal (an outsider) in 1480. Furthermore, with the possible exception of Richard III's servant Geoffrey Frank, all commissioners of array were either lords or of the more substantial knightly rank. In Durham, where the commission of the peace was dominated by palatine officials, the commissioners of array, for obvious reasons, tended to be more clearly a body of the lords and senior gentry of the bishopric. Thus in 1480 ten of the sixteen commissioners were not on the bench. Two of these men, Richard Hansard and John Hutton, may, in the light of their later careers, have had particular military expertise.[56]

Ad hoc commissions tended, as one would expect, to be dominated by interested parties. Thus the commission of 1475 to enquire into the waterways of Yorkshire contained representatives of the local gentry of the Vale of York, several citizens of York, and a clutch of lawyers. A twenty-one-man commission to look into disturbances in Knaresborough in February 1483 was headed by the duke of Gloucester and the earl of Northumberland (as duchy of Lancaster officials), and comprised local landowners, local officers, and five lawyers. Bishop Dudley's commission of 1478 to survey all his possessions was in effect an extended council, upon which lawyers and financial officers were strongly represented. Only commissions of enquiry into wrecks seem to have been dominated by the local gentry. In March 1477 the actions of Thomas, Lord Lumley in looting a Hanseatic merchantman on the North Riding coast were examined by ten commissioners, four of whom were gentry not also justices of the peace. Half that number, three being local gentry, enquired into a Dutch wreck near Hartlepool.[57] In general, however, gentry participation in *ad hoc* commissions, as on the bench itself, was limited and secondary to the role of local lords and lawyers; only a small proportion of the gentry were ever nominated to commissions, and those that were tended to come from the more substantial families.

Who actually carried out the work of the commissions is rarely known. Very little evidence of commissioners at work has survived. The only surviving record of proceedings is that of presentments to eleven sessions of the peace and gaol delivery in Durham between 4 November 1471 and 30 January 1473. In this instance, the justices sat monthly between November 1471 and February 1472, and then (if the record is complete) in the following April, October, and January (twice). Sessions of gaol delivery were held on the same days as sessions of the peace. The

---

[56] *CPR, 1461–7*, 576; *1467–77*, 349; *1476–85*, 213, 401, 492; Durh. 3/54/11. For Hansard and Hutton see below, pp. 347–8, 349, 351.

[57] *CPR, 1467–77*, 572; *1476–85*, 49, 345; Durh. 3/54/1, 13.

bench sat in Durham, except for one session in Chester-le-Street and one in Bishop Auckland. Ralph, Lord Neville presided on five occasions (4 November 1471, 13 January 1472, 10 February 1472, and 20 January and 30 January 1473). On every other occasion the chair was taken by Henry Gillow, the chancellor. Only three or four justices were ever named as present, the most frequent attender being the steward, Thomas Morslaw (nine times).[58]

Of the proceedings of the justices of the peace in the north-east we have no evidence, except for the work of the Durham bench in 1471-3. In this fifteenth-month period 103 cases were heard. Fifty concerned theft, predominantly of livestock, and 46 involved assault; 5 presentments were for keeping greyhounds illegally, and 2 for regrating. There were 21 of bodily harm and 10 of homicide, 2 of which were presented as premeditated murder. Thirteen of the assaults involved the offence of lying-in-wait, *vi et armis*, to cause bodily harm, and 5 were forcible entries: riot under the statutes of 1380 and 1381.[59] One particularly unfortunate victim was Robert Batmanson of Langley. On 18 April 1471 a gang of five men lay in wait on him in Sadlergate in Durham. He was struck in the chest by an axe, on the back of the head by a bill, in the back by an axe, and in the face and on the left side of the head by other weapons. He died from his wounds; and his assailants were presented for his murder—two days later.[60]

What level of lawlessness and disorder these figures indicate is hard to determine. The proportion of offences presented under the title of lying-in-wait (13 out of 103 in fifteen months) is high compared with 6 out of 184 in Staffordshire in 1409-14, and 2 out of 48 in Leicestershire in 1410-14.[61] This could mean a more violent and disorderly society; or alternatively it could mean a higher rate of detection and presentation. It is noticeable that half the offences were presented within three months of

[58] Durh. 3/19/1/1. It is to be noted that these were not quarter sessions. They may have been interim sessions to receive indictments which only sat for one day (see B. Putnam, *Proceedings before the Justices of the Peace in the Fourteenth and Fifteenth Centuries* (1938), p. xcvi).

[59] Durh. 3/19/1/1. J. G. Bellamy, *Criminal Law and Society in Later Medieval and Tudor England* (Gloucester, 1984), 59-64.

[60] Durh. 3/19/1/1, 2d.

[61] Putnam, *Justices of the Peace*, pp. 91-103, 295-303.

their alleged commission, 31 within a month, and several, like Batmanson's murder, within a matter of days. Frequent, at times monthly, sessions no doubt helped speed up the hearing of some cases. Nevertheless, approximately a third of the cases were not heard for over a year; one, a case of horse-stealing, was not presented until fourteen years after the offence.

Relatively few offenders of gentle status were presented to the bench (12 out of 223). The prior of Tynemouth was presented for taking timber worth £200 from the bishop's park at Wolsingham.[62] Four chaplains were brought before the bench for illegally keeping greyhounds.[63] But the great majority were presented as yeomen, labourers, or craftsmen. The largest single group was of yeomen (117). Riot, assault, forcible entry, and homicide in Durham in the late 1460s and early 1470s were, according to this evidence, largely offences committed by ordinary men and women on other ordinary men and women.[64] This is not to say that there were no cases of gentry lawlessness. On 30 January 1473 Alexander Madyson of Unthank in Weardale, gentleman, was presented as having, with other malefactors arrayed as for war with force and arms, assaulted Thomas Killinghall and taken him against his will to the house of Sir Thomas Doket in Lunedale (Lonsdale), outside the liberty of the Bishop, and there held him against his will.[65] At an unspecified date in the same decade Thomas Fishburn made a forcible entry on Gerard Salvin in his house at Croxdale: an assault which led Salvin to appeal to the duke of Gloucester for redress.[66]

Salvin's case may or may not have come before the justices of the peace. Disputes over titles, and other matters concerning property which were likely to give rise to violence, were usually dealt with in Durham by the justices of assize, sitting at Palace Green. Records of pleas before the justices have survived from 17 December 1455 and Lent 1456, and for the period September 1484 to Lent 1493. Cases heard before the justices included: forcible entry into the free warren of the Conyers of Sockburn at Bishopton, and the taking of their game there; disputes over rights of pasture at Harsleyhope between the prior of Durham

---

[62] Durh. 3/19/1/1,4.   [63] Ibid. 1,3.
[64] Cf. Bellamy, *Criminal Law and Society*, p. 83.   [65] Durh. 3/19/1/1/4.
[66] Surtees, *Durham*, iv. pt. 2, pp. 114–15; Pollard, 'St. Cuthbert and the Hog', p. 120.

and local inhabitants; innumerable claims for detinue of rent;
and a claim in 1487 by Sir John Conyers of Hornby that Sir Ralph
Bowes, John Redman, and William Dycon and Joanna his wife
had unjustly disseised him of a croft and garden in North
Auckland.[67] Cases took a long time to be determined, and many
were merely delayed to the following session, months later.
Thus Katherine Surtees, whose claim against John Killinghall
for unpaid rent for a fishgarth was being heard for the fourth
time in Lent 1491, was put off yet again to the session due to be
held in August.[68] One dispute which was eventually settled
concerned a claim by Richard Clervaux of Croft against Roger
Conyers of Wynyard for settlement of an estate on his daughter
Isabel. Clervaux had been unfortunate, or careless, in failing to
secure agreement over a jointure before the early death of his
son-in-law William Conyers. In November 1484 Clervaux
reached an agreement with Conyers senior for compensation of
£100 or a life interest in Redmarshall for his widowed daughter;
but thirteen months later he took Conyers to court at Durham
for failure to honour his agreement. Conyers successfully
prevaricated; and it was not until Lent 1489 that a compromise
was reached by which he agreed to pay 30 marks to Clervaux and
settle six messuages, twelve bovates of land, and some gardens
in Redmarshall on Isabel, a fine being then levied in the court.[69]

From the evidence of the proceedings of the courts it is not
possible to determine whether Durham was more lawless in the
later fifteenth century than it had been earlier in the century;
the level of pardons recorded in the chancery rolls suggests that
conditions were little changed.[70] Much depended on the personal relationships between the more powerful. Thus the disputes between the two branches of the Neville family, and in
Yorkshire between the Nevilles and the Percies, were the major
causes of the disorder which disrupted the region between 1450
and 1471 and largely determined its political history. After 1471
the hegemony of Richard III and the more assertive rule of Henry
VII may well have seen a more general improvement.[71] There
was, however, one part of the region which was endemically

---

[67] Durh. 3/227/3d, 13; 228/13d, 16.
[68] Ibid. 228/7d.   [69] Ibid. 228/12,17,18.   [70] Storey, *Langley*, pp.
111–16.   [71] See below, Chapters 13, 14, and 15 *passim*.

lawless, and which even the early Tudors had difficulty in repressing—the borders.

By the end of the fifteenth century the scale of disorder in the liberties of Tynedale and Redesdale was a matter of serious concern to the Crown. Bishop Fox of Durham issued a monition threatening wholesale excommunication if the inhabitants did not mend their ways; and in 1498 they were accused of glorifying crime, and regarding theft as a work of art.[72] The problem was old, stemming from the collapse of authority and manorial organization which followed in the wake of the Scottish Wars of Independence. Whether it was any worse at the very end of the fifteenth century, or rather was less tolerated by a regime seeking to reassert authority throughout the realm, is hard to determine. In 1414 a petition was presented to Parliament to curtail the archbishop of York's liberty in Hexhamshire; this emphasized the disorder and lawlessness of brigands the length and breadth of the border, especially in Tynedale and Hexhamshire.[73] It is hard to believe that conditions had improved by mid-century. In 1461 the prior of Durham, seeking repayment of a loan made to Queen Margaret, included the depredations of thieves from Tynedale among his many sufferings. Sir Humphrey Neville, bailiff of Hexham and unrepentant Lancastrian, fled after the battle of Hexham into Derwentdale, where he lived like a brigand on the land for five years.[74] In fact war with Scotland and the complete collapse of royal control in the far north between 1460 and 1464 probably led to a worsening of the situation. Renewal of war with Scotland in 1480–4 and again in 1496–7, on which occasions the borderers became licensed privateers for the Crown, did nothing to diminish the problem. What could happen in time of war is illuminated by events in 1522 and 1524. In 1522 it was reported to Thomas Wolsey (as archbishop of York) that every market day up to a hundred thieves descended on Hexham from Tynedale and helped themselves. In April 1524 'highland' thieves, to the supposed number of four hundred, accompanied by Scottish borderers, went on the rampage within eight miles of

---

[72] *The Register of Richard Fox, Lord Bishop of Durham, 1494–1501*, ed. M. P. Howden, SS, xlvii (1932), 80–4.   [73] Hinds, *Hexhamshire, vol. i:* 40.
[74] Raine, *Priory of Hexham*, i. pp. cv–cvii.

Newcastle, leaving Hexhamshire, Weardale, and other parts of the bishopric 'adjoining to the highlands in danger utterly to be destroyed'.[75]

Certainly the endemic disorder of the border dales represented a threat as far south as the bishopric in the fifteenth century. Conditions were not much changed in 1561, when Bishop James Pilkington wrote to William Cecil about his brother Leonard's benefice of Middleton-in-Teesdale, which 'lies so near the thieves, having not a hedge between him and Tynedale, that none dare lie there almost, and in winter especially'.[76] Cattle on the high pastures were at great risk. And not just on the high ground. On 7 October 1470, men from Tynedale stole ten beasts from John Essh, esquire, at Essh; and a month later others took six head of cattle from William White, chaplain of Hayrom-next-Durham. It was a gang of Tynedale men, too, who on 15 November 1469 assaulted Ralph Eure at Witton in Weardale, stole £20 in cash and two of his horses worth £4, and took him against his will to Lynnelford in Hexhamshire.[77] These thieves may have been taking advantage of the disturbed state of the kingdom at the time; but the cases well illustrate the extent to which Durham as well as Northumberland was vulnerable to border lawlessness.

Border lawlessness was one of the problems to which that energetic royal servant Richard Fox turned his attention during his brief pontificate. Fox was one of several members of the royal household who were sent down to the region after 1489 to assert the power of the Crown. Henry VII, taking advantage of his extended royal estate in the region and of the temporary eclipse of the earls of Northumberland, sought during the last decade of the century to recover some of the authority which had been surrendered by previous kings. Thus, while in mid-century it would be true to say that local government and administration were effectively in the hands of local magnates, by the end of the century significant changes were taking place, not only on the borders, but also elsewhere in the north-east, which were eventually to bring the region more firmly under direct royal control.[78]

[75] Hinds, *Hexhamshire, vol. i:* pp. 47, 49.
[76] H. C. Surtees, *A History of the Parish of Middleton in Teesdale* (Newcastle, 1925), 11.
[77] Durh. 3/19/1/1/3,4.   [78] See below, Chapter 15 *passim*.

7

Lay Piety: Religious Practice and Belief

BISHOP FOX threatened excommunication of the borderers if they did not mend their ways. Presumably he had reason to believe that even they were sufficiently devout to take heed of such a threat. There can be little doubt that most of the inhabitants of the rest of the region would have taken it very seriously indeed. As the home of Mount Grace Priory, one of the leading centres of the school of English mysticism, the region could perhaps claim to be a particular focal point of Christian devotion. Before endeavouring to characterize the quality of north-eastern piety, however, it is worth making some more general observations about the subject. It should be stressed at the outset that the mystical yearning for closeness to God (and sometimes the distinctly hysterical pursuit of such intimacy) emphasized in the works of Richard Rolle, Walter Hilton, Richard Methley, and Margery Kempe, was but an extreme manifestation of religious fervour, and was by no means shared by all. It was possible, for lay and clergy alike, to have a cooler, more rational approach to religion, even in the fifteenth century. Moreover, although 'personalization', 'privatization', and 'internalization' of worship were undoubtedly features of fifteenth-century religious practice,[1] they did not replace older, more communal, public and external manifestations of belief. The vicarious mediation of the Church remained the main route to salvation, alongside which lay the meditative and devotional road.[2] Personal devotion, in other words, was a supplement to, not a substitute for, external religious observation. When von Poppelau, the imperial ambassador, finally caught up with the

---

[1] The words are those of Colin Richmond, 'Religion and the Fifteenth-Century Gentleman', in R. B. Dobson (ed.), *The Church, Politics and Patronage in the Fifteenth Century* (Gloucester, 1984), 193–203.
[2] See Dobson, 'The Later Middle Ages', p. 108 and J. Bossy, *Christianity in the West, 1400–1700* (Oxford, 1985), 64–72.

royal entourage in York in 1484 it was the quality of a regular divine service in the Minster, not the personal devotion of the king, which impressed him.[3]

Indeed, it may be that modern emphasis on some elements of the personal nature of religious practice is partly the result of a distortion created by the sources, especially the last wills, which become comparatively abundant in the fifteenth century. The great series of probate registers kept by the courts of York in particular have provided, and continue to provide, a wealth of invaluable personal evidence about northern men and women; but they also contain hidden traps for the unwary. Central to the manifestation of late medieval piety is the concern, some might say obsession, with the redemption of the soul and the relief of its passage through purgatory. This looms large in wills, whether it is in the form of bequests for obits, trentals, distributions of alms, or the support of a fully-fledged perpetual chantry. In all these the object is the same: the purchase of paradise.[4] But wills might deceive us into laying too great an emphasis on the concern for the fate of the soul. Although all were certain of death, none knew the hour. Wills therefore were usually composed when the hour was expected, or its striking considered a distinct possibility.[5] Thoughts about the afterlife and provision to alleviate some of the soul's pains on its journey were therefore likely to be at the forefront of the will-maker's mind. Secondly, wills were usually written by, and almostly certainly with the advice of, a priest or priests. A priest would be failing in his duty if he did not make sure that his charge made proper provision for his soul; and no doubt he gave

[3] D. Mancini, *The Usurpation of Richard III*, ed. C. A. J. Armstrong, 2nd edn., (Oxford, 1969), 137. My reading of von Poppelau's statement is that he was referring to divine service celebrated at York, where he joined Richard III's household, and not later, as is usually supposed, in the chapel at Middleham. For the king's movements see R. Edwards, *The Itinerary of King Richard III, 1483–1485* (Upminster, 1983), 18–19.

[4] Cf. Joel T. Rosenthal, *The Purchase of Paradise: Gift Giving and the Aristocracy, 1307–1485* (1972), *passim*. For a recent and perceptive discussion of the doctrine see Clive Burgess, 'A Fond Thing Vainly Invented' in S. M. Wright (ed.), *Parish, Church and People: Local Studies in Lay Religion, 1350–1750* (1988), 56–84.

[5] For example, the wills of Sir Hugh Hastings of Fenwick and Sir John Constable of Halsham made in June and July 1482, when the testators were 'proposing to go in voyage into Scotland' (*Test. Ebor.* iii. 273–9).

his professional advice as to the efficacy of various steps that could be taken. Thus the will, by its very nature, emphasizes the purchase of paradise. Given the widespread acceptance of the doctrine of purgatory, there was much to commend an obsession with it when making a will. Indeed the cynic might go so far as to suggest that the excessively lavish provision for prayers and good works after death is just as likely to betoken a misspent life as a life devoted to Holy Church. If the prospect of death concentrates the mind wonderfully, it could as well concentrate it on those things left undone and those things that ought not to have been done.[6] The last will is, therefore, more ambivalent than it is sometimes recognized to be. It is not easy to distinguish between the newly repentant and the lifelong devout, between the voice of the testator and the voice of his or her gossip, and between the merely conventional and the distinctly personal.

A second, specific, difficulty facing the historian of north-eastern England is that the evidence is largely restricted to Yorkshire: relatively few fifteenth-century wills survive for the people of Durham and Northumberland. Our conclusions on the faith of the north-eastern laity are therefore drawn largely from the evidence of those resident in the diocese of York, or those whose wills for other reasons were proved in its courts. Wills however can be supplemented by other documents—legal instruments concerning religious foundations, licences to alienate land in mortmain, and the certificates and surveys of the chantry commissioners in mid-sixteenth century. It is on the basis of this evidence that an attempt is made to assess the character of north-eastern lay piety.

On the face of it, it seems implausible to suggest that the laity took their lead from the great lords. The clergy, after all, were the acknowledged spiritual leaders. Yet the example set by the richest and most powerful of the laity, and the seal of approval they set on various religious practices, were highly significant. Their mediation, their setting of fashion as it were, was as important as the exhortation, example, and inspiration of the clergy itself. This is particularly apparent in practices directed

---

[6] Cf. Sir Thomas Markenfield (pr. 20 Jan. 1497) requesting that prayers be said for 'all the souls whom I have injured, wronged and trespassed to' (*Test. Ebor.* iv. 126).

less towards personal piety than towards the public display of social standing and prestige; 'worship' in the contemporary secular sense of the word, rather than in its religious meaning. The clearest examples of the maintenance of a good show for secular purposes seemed to occur at funerals, especially the funerals of nobles. Richard Neville, earl of Salisbury ordained in May 1458 that 100 marks should be spent on his funeral, and that it should be conducted with the customary chivalric pomp 'prout moris est pro dominis status mei oblando'. An account of this funeral, a reinterment at Bisham on 15 February 1463, shows that his wishes were fully honoured by his son, Warwick the Kingmaker, when under the direction of the king's officers of arms the elaborate ritual of disposing of his achievements was enacted. To commemorate the occasion the Salisbury Roll of Arms was commissioned.[7] Henry, the fourth earl of Northumberland's executors in 1489 also incurred expenditure on the appropriate chivalric display, for two officers of arms came down from London (at a cost to the executors of £20) to make sure things were done properly. But this was but a small item of expenditure in a funeral that cost over £1,000, most spent on the livery of 20 gentlewomen, 24 lords and knights, 60 squires and gentlemen, and 200 yeomen; the livery of 160 poor folk and torch-bearers; and the distribution of 13,340 doles to poor folk at 2d. each. Such extravagance, especially in ensuring a good turn-out from retainers, may well have owed something to a need to compensate for the distinctly disworshipful nature of the earl's death.[8] Gentry funerals were usually far more modest. Edmund Thwaites of Lund, one of those who as a retainer of the earl presumably attended his funeral in 1489, was content eleven years later to provide the white gowns and candles

---

[7] *Test. Ebor.* ii. 240–1; A. Payne, 'The Salisbury Roll of Arms, 1463', in D. Williams (ed.), *England in the Fifteenth Century* (Woodbridge, 1987), 187–93. For what was customary see also Salisbury's grandfather's will of 1386. John, Lord Neville willed 'quod cista corporis mei cooperiatur cum panno laneo de russeto et j cruce rubea, et quod bararii circa corpus meum die sepulturae meae ordinentur de eadem setta; et quod j equus sit arraiatus pro guerra cum j homine armato de armis meis, cooperto de russeto, cum scochons de armis meis, et j alius equus de eadam setta cum j homine desuper pro banerio meo absque pluribus equis' (*Wills and Inventories*, 41).

[8] De Fonblanque, *Annals of the House of Percy*, 550–1; and see below, pp. 380–1.

for thirteen bedesmen. Some men left the arrangements to the discretion of their executors. Thus Sir James Danby left instructions in 1497 that

all manner of expenses as well as alms to poor folks, rewards to priests, clerks and scholars, in money and also in meat and drinks, as well to men of worship, friends and poor people be done after the discretion of my executors.[9]

Presumably discretion led them to a scale of expenditure more on the level of Edmund Thwaites than of the earl of Northumberland.

Memorial stones, brasses, and effigies were a more frequent and more durable form of social display than lavish funerals, popular with gentry as well as the nobility. Testators occasionally commissioned such memorials; more frequently they or their sons made independent arrangements. Northern Yorkshire is particularly noted for its fine fifteenth-century alabaster effigies, originally mounted on great tables. In some churches, for instance St Mary's South Cowton, only the effigies remain (of Sir Richard Conyers and his two wives); in others, such as St Peter's Croft, the inscribed table stands alone. The most complete collection is to be found at the recently restored All Saints Harewood, where the tombs of successive heads of the Gascoigne and Redman families are to be seen. Perhaps the finest is that of Sir Edward Redman and his wife Elizabeth Huddleston (c.1510), in which is depicted under one foot, as it rests on a lion's back, a bedesman praying for his soul.[10]

[9] *Test. Ebor.* iv. 175–7, 122. Sir Alexander Neville of Thornton Bridge (pr. 25 June 1457) requested that £20 be spent on meat, drink, wax torches, and such things necessary (*Test. Ebor.* ii. 208). See also Vale, *Piety*, pp. 11–12. My debt to Dr Vale's work will be apparent. His paper, arising out of an occasional lecture, was understandably limited in scope. It is based on a relatively small sample of the wills of the greater gentry only; it did not encompass other sources; and it did not extend beyond 1480. Where my conclusions differ from Dr Vale's it is largely because, without being as systematic, I have drawn on a socially wider sample, made use of other sources, and extended the period. My remarks, though, tend to amplify most aspects of his study, rather than to supersede his conclusions.

[10] See P. E. Routh, *Medieval Effigial Alabaster Tombs in Yorkshire* (Ipswich, 1976) 42–69. Wills occasionally contain instructions for the erection of such effigies. Dr Vale gives in detail the instructions left in December 1467 by John Langton of Farnley (*Piety*, p. 10). Thomas Witham (pr. 1481) wished to be buried 'sub marmorie . . . per me disposito' (*Test. Ebor.* iii. 264). In 1487 Robert Saltmarsh of Cotingworth (ER) instructed his executors 'to buy a stone of marble or alabaster to lie upon me and my brother Edward' (BI, Probate Register, v. fo. 427).

Effigies, brasses, and memorial stones are the most visible and tangible surviving evidence of the way in which many parish churches, or substantial sections of them, 'began to resemble', as Dr Vale observed, 'private mausoleums for the most prominent local families'.[11] In this, the gentry was, as in so much else, only aping the local nobility. Many peers, who were patrons of religious houses, were by family tradition buried in their churches. Thus the FitzHughs were buried at Jervaulx, the Scropes of Bolton at St Agatha's Easby, and the Fauconbergs at Guisborough. These monasteries were in effect the old-established collegiate chantries of these families. Some peers in the fifteenth century converted parish churches into new collegiate foundations for the same purpose. Thus Richard, Lord Scrope of Bolton converted Wensley parish church in 1403; Ralph Neville, first earl of Westmorland transformed St Mary's Staindrop; and later Richard, duke of Gloucester turned St Alkelda's Middleham into a similar body. Before he died Gloucester, then king, embarked on an even more ambitious project to convert York Minster into his royal mausoleum.[12] The more humble and less well-endowed gentry, however, had to be satisfied with their parish church, whether or not they enjoyed advowson.

Several gentry are known to have contributed to the rebuilding of their parish churches. Sir Richard Conyers undertook repairs at St Mary's South Cowton, where he founded a perpetual chantry.[13] Roland Place and Richard Clervaux appear to have commissioned the construction of the porch of St Peter's Croft.[14] Earlier in the century (1410–12) Sir John Conyers the elder put up the whole of the south aisle of St Mary's Hornby, at a cost of £34. 6s. 8d.[15] The most complete example of a parochial mausoleum is that of St Anne's Catterick, created by the neighbouring Burgh family. The church was totally rebuilt in 1412–15 by William Burgh I and his mother Katherine, in memory, it would seem, of his father John, who died in 1412. According to the contract made in 1412 with Richard of Crakehall, the master

---

[11] Vale, *Piety*, p. 9.

[12] *Test. Ebor.* i. 272n.; *Wills and Inventories*, 73; and below, p. 345.

[13] BL, Egerton 3402, fo. 97.   [14] Pollard, 'Richard Clervaux', p. 163.

[15] Holman, *St. Mary's, Hornby*, pp. 9–10, 23. The date 28 Jan., 11 Henry IV is wrongly given as 1409 instead of 1410 in this otherwise excellent church guide.

mason who had just completed the south aisle at Hornby, the existing church was to be pulled down, and the new structure put up on a nearby site. The Burghs decided on the plan and provided the materials, but Crakehall hired the labour. For his services Crakehall was paid £106. 13s. 4d. The contract makes it clear that this was for the first stage of a building encompassing choir, nave, and two aisles: for bonding stones were to be left for the future building of a vestry and tower. Later generations did indeed complete the project. And at the end of the century chantry chapels were added as extensions to the north and south aisles. Under the floors of these chapels the bodies of four successive William Burghs and their wives were buried, and memorial brasses were laid down.[16] Although architecturally conservative in style, St Anne's is, as a result, one of the most uniform of surviving North Riding churches of the fifteenth century.

It was not only in death but also in life that the local family exhibited a proprietorial interest in the parish church. Private and privileged seating was important. Sir Alexander Neville of Thornton Bridge (proved 1457) wished to be buried in St Mary Oldwalk, York, 'before the stall where I sit at mass'. Robert Constable of Barnby-by-Bossall, brother of Sir John of Flamborough, also wished to be buried in the choir 'afore the place where my seat is'.[17] Roland Place and Richard Clervaux quarrelled over the seating arrangements in Croft parish church, where perhaps they competed for precedence. In the end they had to be content with occupying the seats on either side of the chancel where customarily their families sat.[18] Dr Richmond has suggested that the private pews in East Anglia 'are a manifestation of the interiorization of religion'.[19] This may be so, but equally there was a dimension of external display involved.

---

[16] NYCRO, zRL/1/20, 42, 43. See also L. F. Salzman, *Building in England down to 1540* (Oxford, 1954), 487–90 and Pollard, 'The Burghs of Brough', pp. 17–18. Cf. Brian Roucliffe who rebuilt the parish church of Cowthorpe (WR) which was reconsecrated in 1458 (*Plumpton Correspondence*, p. 8 n.).

[17] *Test. Ebor.* ii. 175, 207.

[18] NYCRO, zQH 1, fos. 155–6. Pollard, 'Richard Clervaux', p. 162. It is to be noted that in 3 of these cases the gentry were accustomed to sit in choir or chancel, separated by the rood screen from the general body of parishioners, but close to the miracle being performed by the priest.

[19] Richmond, 'Religion', p. 199.

It may have been considered that the nearer the altar one sat in
life, or lay in death, the nearer one was to God; but equally
powerful was the desire to be seen to be in the best-placed
position.

   Closely related to the need to sustain social standing was the
dynastic emphasis in religion. It was not just the status of the
individual, but also the standing of his whole lineage which
needed to be demonstrated. Thus tombs and churches, as well as
houses, were liberally decorated with coats of arms carved in
stone and stained in glass. The remnants of Conyers arms are
still to be seen displayed at Hutton Rudby. All Saints Hurworth,
despite nineteenth-century restoration, preserves on its tower
the arms of Tailboys, Ingleby, and Neville, the three principal
families associated with the parish in the fifteenth century. St
Mary's South Cowton displays the arms of many families, but
particularly those of Conyers, in several places, and the arms
of Christopher Conyers senior in glass, now set in the east
window. But perhaps the most powerful bond of lineage was
that provided through inherited patronage of a religious house.
As Dom David Knowles put it, 'in the deathless community and
the founder's descendants [existed] a body and persons with
undying relationships and obligations to one another'. The
founder's descendants could claim not just a resting place, but
also hospitality, privilege of fraternity, nominations to places,
and corrodies in return for their continuing alms.[20] Such a
relationship is well documented between the Scropes of Bolton
and St Agatha's Easby. Richard, first Lord Scrope of Bolton (d.
1403), who had inherited the patronage of the abbey, not only
wished to be buried at St Agatha's, but also made provision for
the addition of no fewer than twelve canonries. The surviving
wills of three of his four fifteenth-century descendants reveal
that they too wanted to be buried there, even Richard the third
Lord (d. 1420), who made his will at Rouen. John the fifth Lord
(d. 1498) left his executors a choice between St Agatha's and the
Blackfriars at Thetford, depending on where he died; but he
bequeathed some of his books to the abbey.[21] What reciprocal
benefits the Scropes received is not as fully documented.

[20] D. Knowles, *The Religious Orders in England*, ii (Cambridge, 1955), 286.
[21] *Test. Ebor.* i. 272–3, 328; iii. 38; iv. 1, 95.

Richard Neville, earl of Salisbury was exceptional in adopting
his countess's lineage and the patronage of Bisham Priory in
Berkshire.[22] His own family ties were perhaps denied him: his
grandfather had been closely associated with Durham Cathedral, and his father had developed a new college at Staindrop. In
the late 1450s his half-brother, the second earl of Westmorland,
held the family's Durham estates.[23] But there were probably
also political considerations involved in associating himself
with the Montagu shrine at Bisham, which lay close to Windsor
Castle. Richard of Gloucester also took up his wife's inheritance
in his patronage of Coverham Abbey, a Neville foundation near
Middleham. In 1472 and 1473 he donated £40 towards the repair
of the impoverished abbey's church. In 1476 he purchased for
100 marks the advowson of Seaham parish church in County
Durham, worth some £15 p.a., which he granted to the canons.
In 1483 he donated a further £20.[24] It is perhaps not surprising
that after 1485 Gloucester's generosity should be forgotten,
even by his one-time close associate Bishop Richard Redman,
who, as visitor of the Premonstratensians in England, praised
Abbot John Askew for his building repairs, and even likened him
to a new founder.[25] One suspects that the credit for reviving this
somnolent house lay rather with Gloucester: in the 1490s,
however, such things were better not mentioned.

Lineal connections with local religious houses extended into
the gentry. Sir Thomas Markenfield desired to be buried 'before
the altar of Saint Andrew in the monastery of Saint Wilfrid in
Ripon among the burial of my ancestors', but he also left a
bequest of 10s. to the prioress and convent of Arden 'where I am
founder'.[26] Better documented is the association of local families with the priory of Mount Grace. It has recently been shown
that John de Ingleby rather than Thomas Holland, duke of
Surrey was the prime mover in its foundation in 1398. It was

[22] Ibid. ii. 240.
[23] *Wills and Inventories*, 38, 69. Salisbury did, however, as an afterthought,
make provision for an obit to be sung in perpetuity for him at Staindrop College
(*Test. Ebor.* ii. 246).
[24] PRO, DL 29/648/10485; Dur.RO, D/130/D22; Durham, Dean and Chapter,
Reg. Parv. iv. fos. 174ᵛ–175; *Harleian MS 433*, ii. 20. A century earlier John, Lord
Neville left a bequest of 100 marks for the repair and support of the church of
Coverham (*Wills and Inventories*, 38).
[25] Gasquet, *Collectanea*, i. 140–6.   [26] *Test. Ebor.* iv. 124–5.

Ingleby's manor of Bordelby that was set aside for the conventual buildings; it was to be called 'the House of Mount Grace of Ingleby'; the Inglebies had a prominent place in the roll-call of prayers; and in the fifteenth century John's descendants were to hold the advowson of the priory. During the course of the century, however, another more wealthy local family—the Strangways of West Harlsey—began to take a pronounced interest. From 1456, when Sir James and his wife Elizabeth presented the advowson of Beighton in Derbyshire to the convent, the house developed a very close relationship with its parochial neighbours. Successive heads of the Strangways family were buried in the Lady Chapel above the charterhouse (burial of lay persons within the precinct being forbidden); a string of bequests was made by members of the family, including Sir James's daughter Joan; and finally, at the Dissolution his great-grandson, Sir James, purchased the site. Founded by one landed family of the parish in which it stood, in the end Mount Grace was quite literally taken over by another.[27]

The religion of the fifteenth-century nobility and gentry of the north-east was therefore as much a matter of custom, honour, and 'worship' as other, secular, aspects of their lives. But religion was not entirely a matter of convention and public show. It was also a family, household, or private matter. While they patronized their parish churches and local religious houses, the landed élite also maintained and worshipped in their own private chapels. As Dr Mertes has pointed out, one would be hard pressed to find a gentle or noble establishment devoid of a chapel of sorts, or without the service of at least one chaplain.[28] The evidence from ecclesiastical licences, bequests, and deeds leaves no doubt that gentry as well as lords valued their household chapels. Licences for marriages to take place or masses to be held in private chapels can be cited for the castle at Middleham, the manor houses of Leconfield and Wressle (Percy), and

---

[27] C. B. Rowntree, 'Studies in Carthusian History in Later Medieval England' (unpublished University of York D.Phil. thesis, 1981), 114 ff., 331–5, 337–8; E. M. Thompson, *The Carthusian Order in England* (1930), 229–37. Much of what I have argued in the above paragraphs agrees in substance with Dr Carpenter's comments in 'The Religion of the Gentry in Fifteenth-Century England', in Williams, *England in the Fifteenth Century*, pp. 68–71.

[28] K. Mertes, *The English Noble Household, 1250–1600* (Oxford, 1988), 140–6.

the gentry manors of Thorp Perrow (Danby) and Sedbury (Boynton).[29] Bequests made by testators of chapel furnishings and books confirm their importance. Christopher Conyers, rectoral squire of Hutton Rudby, bequeathed 'omnia linthiamina pertinentia meo altari existentia in domo mea propria'. In 1488 Edmund Mauleverer willed the ornaments of his chapel ('all the stuff that belongs to my chapel, chalice, mass book, porteous, psalter, pyx') to his son and heir; and Joan Boynton, née Strangways, widow of Christopher Boynton of Sedbury, bequeathed her 'mass book, chalice and vestment' to Yarm Priory.[30] Additionally we know that even the gentry were accustomed to maintain two or more chaplains in their households. Sir Thomas Markenfield remembered two chaplains, Richard Clarkson and Robert Whixley, in his will; Joan, Lady Hastings, née Romanby left £2 each to her chaplains William and Oliver.[31] Sir John Conyers had at least three in his service: Cuthbert Lightfoot, who succeeded Christopher Conyers as rector of Hutton Rudby in 1483, John Shirwynd, and Robert Pynkney, vicar of Kirkby Fleetham, chaplain of Brompton-on-Swale, and, at the time of his death in 1490, the chantry priest at Hornby.[32] From the frequency of their appearance as witnesses and attorneys it can also be seen that Richard Clervaux of Croft employed at least two chaplains at any one time.[33] This reminds us that household chaplains had other, administrative and secretarial, functions; but nevertheless the numbers retained in household service suggest that their religious duties were considered important.

In addition to chapels many of the nobles and gentry seem to have set aside an oratory to which members of the family could withdraw to pray and contemplate in private, often with the assistance of their lavishly illustrated primers or books of hours.

[29] A. H. Thompson, 'The Register of the Archdeacons of Richmond, 1422–77', Part 1, YAJ 30 (1931), 116, 117, 118, 131; Part 2, YAJ 32 (1936), 119; Test. Ebor. iii. 345, 348, 349.

[30] Test. Ebor. iv. 14, 287; v. 39; Brown, Ingleby Arncliffe. Cf. Thomas Witham, who left his vestment and other altar furnishings to be divided between his 2 chantry chapels (Test. Ebor. iii. 268).

[31] Ibid. iv. 125, 197; North Country Wills, i. 74.

[32] CIPM, Henry VII, 1, 278; Thompson, 'Archdeacons of Richmond', i. 110, 111, 122; Test. Ebor. iv. 41–3.

[33] Pollard, 'Richard Clervaux', 158–9.

Here, in such closets, we come closer to that inner, personalized and privatized faith. Yorkshire men and women frequently received licences from their bishop, or, in Richmondshire, their archdeacon, even to hear mass in these oratories. Such licences, usually for a term of no more than three years, seem to have been granted in times of sickness or mourning. It is impossible to tell whether more generally gentlemen and gentlewomen celebrated mass in private without licence; but the relative frequency with which licences were sought suggests that the practice was exceptional. There is a strong presumption that the licence granted to William Burgh II to employ a chaplain to celebrate mass daily for two years in his oratory at Brough Hall on 30 September 1465 arose from his failing health, for he died on the last day of the same year. Likewise Burgh's neighbour Conan Aske, granted the same privilege in May 1465, was soon to be succeeded by his son Roger. Richard Clervaux, given the right for one year in March 1454, by his own later admission was dogged by ill health (although he lived until 1490). Others were perhaps in mourning. Joan Boynton was granted the privilege to hear mass in her oratory at Sedbury for two years in 1455 shortly after the death of her husband. She remained a widow until her death in 1488–9. But licences were reissued in April 1464 for anywhere in the diocese of York, and in March 1474 for three years at her house in Yarm, where she was living at her death.[34]

But normally oratories were for private prayer, not the celebration of mass. Associated with this private prayer are the books of hours, psalters, and breviaries that so many will-makers possessed, which played an important part in the education of well brought up young men and women. 'Your daughter and mine', wrote Brian Roucliffe to Sir William Plumpton in December 1463 about Margaret Plumpton, 'with humble recommendations desires your blessing, and speaks prettily [skilfully] in french and has nearly learned her psalter.'[35] Elizabeth De La River, widow of Thomas of Brandsby, disposed of a primer and her 'boke of rules' in 1494. John, Lord Scrope of Bolton, with more resources at his disposal, possessed two bibles, 'my little bible' and 'my bible imprinted', a 'portose', a 'great primer', and

---

[34] Thompson, 'Archdeacons of Richmond', i. 110, 115, 132; ii. 112. *Test. Ebor.* iv. 13 n.   [35] *Plumpton Correspondence*, p. 8.

a mass book.[36] Only rarely can one observe the actual use made
of these books. One such glimpse is allowed us by Robert
Constable of Barnby-by-Bossall. In an unusually direct and
personal will, Constable bequeathed to his son Robert 'my
Portative which I say upon my self' and to his friend and
executor Thomas Witham 'my diurnal that I bear in my sleeve
daily'.[37] Robert Constable was one at least who, we can be
confident, sought to enjoy a more personal relationship with
God, and was perhaps one of that group who in the fifteenth century had developed a more sophisticated knowledge of liturgy.[38]

There were no doubt others who, like Constable, were particularly devout. Perhaps we can count his fellow servant of
Richard Neville, earl of Salisbury, Thomas Witham, in their
numbers. Witham, who was given Constable's diurnal, himself
made provision for two perpetual chantries in his will drawn up
in March 1475, and instructed his executors to conduct his
funeral 'absque custubus excessivis tunc vel postea pro pompa
munda'.[39] Ten years or more before he made his will, Witham
paid for the building of a chapel of ease at Cornburgh, one mile
from the parish church of Sheriff Hutton, so as to maintain
divine service in the community of the hamlet.[40] By their deeds,
or intended deeds, as well as their words, some men and women
are thus known. Another was William Burgh III. In 1474 he
conveyed property to the value of 26s. 8d. to the Franciscans of
Richmond for masses to be celebrated on every Wednesday and
Saturday in the chapel of St Anne on Catterick Bridge. Near the
end of his life, in November 1491, and in association with his
neighbour Richard Swaldale, he founded a perpetual chantry in
the parish church of Catterick dedicated to St James, endowed
with rents from Catterick and Tunstall to the yearly value of
£2. 14s. In this chapel, created out of the east end of the north
aisle of the church, memorial brasses were laid to his grandfather and father.[41]

Among northern women who may have followed the example
of Cecily Neville, duchess of York, we may note Joan Boynton
(probate 1489), who, we have seen, was rarely without a licence

[36] *Test. Ebor.* iv. 96.   [37] Ibid. ii. 175–6.
[38] Cf. Vale, *Piety*, p. 15.   [39] *Test. Ebor.* iii. 264.   [40] *CPR, 1461–67*, 447.
[41] Pollard, 'Burghs of Brough', p. 18; NYCRO, ZRL 1/38, 42.

to hear mass in her own oratory, and who, among other bequests to the priory at Yarm, instructed her executors to have made an image of the annunciation ('the salutation of our Lady and St Gabriel') for the high altar.[42] Joan, Lady Hastings, seems also to have fitted the Cecily Neville mould; she specified that all the four orders of friars should sing *Placebo* and *Dirige* and a requiem mass. Residing in London at the time she made her will, she left 15s. to the anchoresses at Bishopgate and Westminster, and lesser sums to the hermits there. Although she was generous to the friaries both in London and Yorkshire, her greatest munificence was to the Carthusian and Bridgetin houses in both regions: £2 to Sheen; £3. 6s. 8d. to Syon; £3. 6s. 8d. to London; and above all £6. 13s. 4d. to Mount Grace.[43]

Finally one cannot leave the question of individual piety without considering Cecily Neville's son: Richard III himself. Although perhaps it is open to dispute whether we should consider him *genuinely* devout,[44] there can be no doubt that Richard III, both as duke and king, publicly and privately demonstrated that he was himself convinced of his own piety. We have already noted his patronage of Coverham Abbey and his collegiate foundations. Something of the inner man is surely shown by his own collection of books and by the statutes of Middleham College. It is known that Gloucester possessed a copy of the *Visions of Matilda* (his mother had a particular devotion to St Matilda), a collection of Old Testament stories, an English New Testament, and a book of hours. In the book of hours is transcribed the prayer in which Richard, as king, invoked Our Lord to protect him from the hatred of his enemies and free him from false accusation, tribulation, grief, and

---

[42] Above, p. 184; *Test. Ebor.* iv. 14. For Duchess Cecily see C. A. J. Armstrong, 'The Piety of Cecily, Duchess of York', in D. Woodruff (ed.), *For Hilaire Belloc* (1942).

[43] *North Country Wills*, i. 73–4. By way of contrast see the will of Maud FitzHugh, widow of Sir William Eure (pr. 30 May 1467), which, apart from a cursory preamble and provision for the customary prayers and masses, is taken up with the distribution of her movable goods to her family and servants (*Test. Ebor.* ii. 285).

[44] See C. F. Richmond's comment concerning 'Richard III, also recently described, somewhat unnervingly, as "a genuinely pious and religious man" —which is like calling Joseph Stalin a genuinely devout Marxist' ('Religion', p. 201).

anguish.[45] Its insertion specifically in the name of 'thy servant King Richard' implies that it was adopted (and adapted) by him and was incanted by him (or on his behalf) at a time when he was under great personal stress. Whether or not it reveals a mind in an advanced state of schizophrenic paranoia is not here at issue:[46] it does surely reveal, however, a devotional inclination.

In the same prayer there is also expressed the sentiment that the supplicant was made from nothing, and, apparently, the confident knowledge that he has already been redeemed by Christ's most wonderful love and mercy from eternal damnation. The same sense of personal worthlessness, without the confidence in redemption, is revealed in the preamble to the statutes of Middleham College (1478), in which Richard, as duke, refers to himself as 'a simple creature, nakedly born into this wretched world destitute of possessions and inheritances'.[47] Moreover, Gloucester, it is supposed, possessed a copy of a Wyclif translation of the New Testament.[48] But before we cast Gloucester in the role of closet Lollard, we should remember the long tradition of such personal abasement by the great, stretching back beyond Wyclif and the wider possession of Wyclif bibles in the later fifteenth century.[49] Furthermore, the detailed provisions of the statutes reveal a very knowledgeable but decidedly conformist grasp of liturgy. It would be wrong to assume that Gloucester drew up the statutes himself; they were undoubtedly the result of long deliberation with his gossips and ecclesiastical councillors (including no doubt the first dean,

[45] Lambeth Palace, MS 474, fos. 181–3. For a transcript see P. Tudor Craig, *Richard III*, 2nd edn. (National Portrait Gallery, London, 1977) 26–7, and for recent comment, establishing that the prayer did not also, as has been generally assumed, begin with an appeal to St Julian, see A. F. Sutton and L. Visser Fuchs, 'Richard III and St Julian: A New Myth', *The Ricardian*, viii, no. 106 (1989), 265–70; J. T. Rosenthal, 'Aristocratic Cultural Patronage and Book Bequests', *BJRL* 44, 2 (1982), 533, 544; Ross, *Richard III*, pp. 128–9.

[46] J. R. Lander, *Government and Community: England 1450–1509* (1980), 329–30.

[47] 'The Statutes . . . for the College of Middleham', ed. J. Raine, *Archaeological Journal*, 14 (1857), 160. It is perhaps worth noting that Margery Kempe also habitually called herself a 'creature'.

[48] Tudor Craig, *Richard III*, p. 29; P. W. Hammond, 'Richard III's Books: III. English New Testament', *The Ricardian*, vii. no. 98 (1987), 479–85.

[49] Points emphasized by Vale, *Piety*, pp. 2–3 and Hammond, 'New Testament', p. 483.

William Beverley). But they seem to bear the imprint of his own views. If nowhere else this is indicated by the clause reserving to the duke the sole power to revise and adjudicate on disputed interpretation of the statutes, as well as in the adoption of the Use of Salisbury. One can perhaps also detect the founder's own mind in his injunction that all the chaplains are to be priests able in 'litteral cunning, good disposition and in worldly policies' and that none 'haunt tavern or other unhonest place or person at any time'. Moreover, there is a strong presumption that the duke was fully conversant with the liturgical details spelt out, not only for the daily round of divine service, but also for the annual obits eventually to be celebrated for him and his duchess. In Richard we surely can observe a personal, knowledgeable, and sincere piety.[50]

The religious attitudes of north-easterners in the fifteenth century thus encompassed both the socially conventional and the individually devout. To distinguish with certainty between the two in any one case is perhaps harder than some recent writers have been willing to concede. Moreover, in much of what we know about the particular character of the faith of the nobility and gentry of the north-east there is little to set them apart from their fellows in other parts of England. In so far as they followed new fashions and trends, with an emphasis on the personal and the private (in such matters as pilgrimages and the collection of relics, as well as in others more fully discussed above), one could not argue that northerners were more pious or more religious than other English people.[51] There were, however, certain manifestations of piety which had a distinctive regional character. Some are simply northern variations on common themes; but others suggest a distinctive quality, in which one

[50] Raine, 'Middleham Statutes', pp. 160–70 passim, esp. 162, 164–5, 166, 169. A. F. Sutton, 'A Curious Searcher for Our Weal Public', in Hammond, Loyalty, Lordship and Law, pp. 64–9; R. B. Dobson, 'Richard III and the Church of York', in Griffiths and Sherborne, Kings and Nobles, pp. 140–1. For a more sceptical view of Richard III's puritanical streak see Ross, Richard III, pp. 136–8.
[51] For comparative regional studies see: C. F. Richmond, 'Religion', passim; P. Fleming, 'Charity, Faith and the Gentry of Kent, 1422–1529' in Pollard, Property and Politics, pp. 36–53; C. Carpenter, 'Gentry and their estates', pp. 52–4; N. Saul, 'The Religious Sympathies of the Gentry in Gloucestershire, 1200–1500', Bristol and Gloucestershire Arch. Soc. Trans., 98 (1980), 99–112; and the remarks of N. P. Tanner, 'The Reformation and Regionalism', in Thomson, Towns and Townspeople, pp. 141–4.

may discern a significant divergence from more southerly parts of the realm.

North-easterners had their own particular guilds and fraternities, to which it was both socially desirable and personally satisfying to belong. Membership of guilds and fraternities, like much else in late medieval religion, was at bottom another means to the end of remission of sins. But membership of the Corpus Christi Guild of York was perhaps early seen as less a means towards salvation than a socially desirable end in itself. Many Yorkshire nobles and gentry became members. It surely was not only devotion to the cult of the Body of Christ, or participation in the Corpus Christi procession, or the contribution to the guild almshouse, or even the solemn mass and prayer of the dead celebrated on the morrow of Corpus Christi, which attracted them. Founded in 1408, and incorporated in 1458 with the support of Bishop George Neville, the guild, which seems to have begun as the parish fraternity of Holy Trinity Micklegate, had become by the end of the century something akin to a county club, with membership ranging from the high ranks of the nobility (Richard of Gloucester and his duchess became members in 1477) to the lesser gentry (John Vincent of Smeaton, 1453; John Lockwood, 1449).[52] The following representatives of Richmondshire families joined the guild: John Wandesford (1441–2); Thomas Rokeby (1445); Joan Catterick (1451); Richard Clervaux (1455); William Burgh (1457); Roger Aske (1467); Thomas Frank (1471); Sir Robert Danby and James Danby (1473); Thomas Tunstall of Hornby (1473); Thomas Metcalfe (1490). In all representatives of some fifty-five noble and gentry families with land and other connections in the county of York were at times members of the guild between 1440 and 1490.[53]

[52] *The Register of the Guild of Corpus Christi in the City of York*, ed. R. H. Scaife, SS lvii (1872), pp. v–vi, 47, 52, 101, 285–6. See also H. F. Westlake, *The Parish Gilds of Medieval England* (1919), 53–8 and P. Tudor Craig, 'Richard III's Triumphal Entry into York, August 29th, 1483', in Horrox, *Richard III and the North*, pp. 110–13. For a recent discussion of guilds, in which the social as well as spiritual advantages are stressed, see G. Rosser, 'Communities of Parish and Guild in the Late Middle Ages', in Wright, *Parish, Church and People*, pp. 29–55.

[53] Scaife, *Register*, 40, 44, 49, 59, 61, 66, 81, 88, 130. The Register is not entirely accurate in respect of Christian names. As well as Anne, Duchess of Gloucester being given as Elizabeth, Roger Aske is styled Richard; Richard Clervaux is given the name and title of his father (Sir John), who died in 1442; and Sir Robert Danby is listed as Sir Thomas.

Two general points perhaps need to be made. Although there was a large contingent of county members, they were outnumbered by citizen and clerical members: the clerical including two archbishops—William Booth and George Neville. Secondly, some prominent noble and gentry families are notable by their absence. No representative of the Percy family seems to have belonged. And although the Scropes of Bolton and Masham and Greystokes joined, no FitzHugh became a member. Likewise many members of the Strangways family were members, but few of the Conyers (Christopher, rector of Rudby, Conan, Thomas, and Brian only), and noticeably not Sir John. Neither Sir William nor Sir Robert Plumpton joined before 1490; but their neighbours—Pullen of Scotton, Middleton of Stockeld, Gascoigne of Gawkthorpe, and Ward of Givendale—were well represented. There were other prominent absentees— Constable of Flamborough, Redman, Pilkington, and Saville. On the other hand some families were represented by several members, male and female, over several generations. This is true of the Askes of Aske, the Wandesfords of Kirklington, the Clervaux, the Nevilles of Thornton Bridge, and the Gascoignes.[54] One explanation for this pattern might have been that membership was related to possession of property in York, especially in the increasingly fashionable suburb of Bishophill. Certainly the Clervaux held property in the city, as did the Thwaites of Lund and the Nevilles of Thornton Bridge.[55] However, the earls of Northumberland had a town house, which it is known that they used in the fifteenth century;[56] yet none of the earls is known to have joined the guild. It may be, therefore, that it was simply family custom for some to join. Nevertheless, it seems plausible that for those nobles and gentry who did join the Corpus Christi Guild, membership represented as much a social act as an act of personal piety.

Membership of other north-eastern fraternities was probably more distinctly religious and considerably more restricted than

[54] Ibid. 38–130, *passim*. A large number of county gentry joined between 1469 and 1473.

[55] Pollard, 'Richard Clervaux'. I am grateful to Dr Sarah Rees-Jones for information concerning the Thwaites and Nevilles.

[56] *Plumpton Correspondence*, p. 45.

the Corpus Christi Guild. This would seem to have been the case with the leading religious houses, especially Mount Grace and Durham. The Carthusian order originally forbade the granting of letters of fraternity, whereby in consideration for services rendered the monks offered up prayers for the soul of the lay brother (or sister). There were few north-easterners who persuaded the prior and convent of Mount Grace to accept them. Two exceptions were Elizabeth Swinburne and her daughter, who by dint of donations to individual monks persuaded the house to admit them.[57] The monks of Durham were more amenable, especially to the power of money. Once admitted, a brother or sister was entitled to be addressed as such, and to participate in all vigils, masses, prayers, and other works of piety performed by the monks for the welfare of his or her soul. In particular, it would seem, membership of the fraternity was prized because it gave access to the choir during divine service. Agnes Rhodes, widow of Robert, one-time lay steward of the priory, was admitted late in her life, in recognition of her well-known deeds and her precious presents conferred upon the house. John Robinson, merchant of Newcastle, and Joan his wife, were admitted after they had granted a messuage in Pilgrim Street to the convent.[58] Admission to the fraternity of St Cuthbert was therefore limited to the most prominent or the more generous of the laity. Richard, duke of Gloucester and his duchess Anne were welcomed in 1474. They seem to have availed themselves frequently of this privilege, for they were almost annual visitors to the convent and the shrine of St Cuthbert for the next decade.[59]

St Cuthbert was the north-east's special saint. Parish churches and chantry chapels were dedicated in his name; children were baptized in his honour. The shrine of the saint in Durham Cathedral was an important stop on the itinerary of pilgrims, who included in the fifteenth century eminent persons such as the future Pope Pius II and Henry VI. The saint was regularly invoked, and his banner unfurled, to bless campaigns

[57] Rowntree, 'Studies in Carthusian History', pp. 336, 373–8.
[58] Welford, *Newcastle and Gateshead*, pp. 356, 408.
[59] Pollard, 'St. Cuthbert and the Hog', pp. 117–18.

against the Scots. The importance of St Cuthbert needs little reiteration.[60]

But there were other saints of northern provenance—St Wilfrid, St William of York, John of Beverley, and John of Bridlington. Curiously none of these features more than occasionally in wills. Another, however, who seems to have enjoyed a special veneration in the later fifteenth century, was St Ninian. St Ninian of Whithorn, Galloway came to symbolize the claims of the metropolitan of York for jurisdiction over south-west Scotland, which were revived from time to time during the later Middle Ages.[61] His cult's English centre was at York Minster, where there was a chapel dedicated to him. It was perhaps because of their traditional role as wardens of the east march that the earls of Northumberland demonstrated a particular attachment to this chapel, where the third earl wished in 1461 to be buried in the same manner as his ancestors, and where support was given by them for three perpetual chantries.[62]

Richard of Gloucester, warden of the west march, was not slow to adopt the Scottish saint. He was to be honoured in Richard's foundation at Queens' College, Cambridge in 1477, and in both of his projected colleges at Middleham and Barnard Castle.[63] In the statutes for Middleham (1478) it was ordained

[60] For St Cuthbert's unique vogue as a northern saint see Dobson, *Durham Priory*, pp. 29–32.

[61] See R. Brentano, *York Metropolitan Jurisdiction and Papal Judges Delegate, 1278–96* (Berkeley, 1959), 94–108; G. Donaldson, 'The Bishops and Priors of Whithorn', *Transactions of the Dumfriesshire and Galloway Natural History and Antiquarian Society*, 3rd ser., 27 (1950), 133–4; and Dobson, 'Richard III and the Church of York', 153 n. 84. In 1464 the canons of York produced a notarial instrument reiterating these claims, a copy of which was preserved in *Harleian MS 433*, iii. 76–98.

[62] *The Fabric Rolls of York Minster*, ed. J. Raine, SS xxv (1859 for 1858) p. 305 n.; De Fonblanque, *Annals of the House of Percy*, i. 547. It is often assumed that the earliest known data for this altar come from 1483 (e.g. D. M. Palliser, 'Richard III and York', in Horrox, *Richard III and the North*, p. 61, citing E. A. Gee, 'The Topography of Altars, Chantries and Shrines in York Minster', *Antiquaries Journal*, 64 (1984), 347–8) because of its appearance in York Minster Library M 2(2)c under the heading 'Chantries founded in 1483'. In fact, Henry 3rd earl of Northumberland's will makes it clear that the altar was already well established in 1461, and had a particular association with his family. I have not been able to consult the original will. I am grateful to Professor Dobson for sharing his thoughts on St Ninian with me.

[63] W. G. Searle, *History of Queens' College Cambridge* (Cambridge 1867), i. 89; W. Dugdale, *Monasticon Anglicanon*, Vol. iii. Part Two (1673), 203–4.

that Richard Cutler, the third of the six priests, should occupy the second stall on the left side, to be called St Ninian's stall. Moreover Gloucester instructed that the anthem of St Ninian Confessor should be said daily after matins; that after evensong nightly a memory of St Ninian (as well as of St George), with their versicles and collects, should be sung; and that the days of both saints be served as principal feasts.[64] St Ninian moved with St George to Richard's planned college in York Minster, for, besides God and Our Lady, the new college was also to be dedicated to these same two saints.[65]

Where the magnates and especially the king led, others followed. Lights were burnt before images of the saint in the parish churches of Kellow, Co. Durham, and Stokesley, North Yorks., and at the friary of Tickhill by bequest of John Trollope of Thornley (1476), Nicholas Conyers (1496), and Sir Hugh Hastings of Fenwick (1482).[66] Children were named in his honour by Thomas Markenfield and John Pullen. Pilgrimages to Whithorn were sponsored by William Ecopp, rector of Heslerton, who made provision in 1472 for pilgrims to visit various British shrines in which St Ninian was included; and by Margaret Aske, widow of Richard Aske of Aughton, who willed six years earlier that 'a man shall be appointed to go on pilgrimage to St Ninian's in Scotland at my expense, and offer there for my soul a gold ring with a diamond set in it'.[67] Margery Salvin, the daughter of Sir Robert Danby of Thorp Perrow, was even the proud possessor of one of the saint's bones, which she left to the Greyfriars, York in 1496.[68]

The cult of St Ninian seems to have been a peculiarly northern phenomenon of the later fifteenth century. But the cults of saints in general, pilgrimages, and relics were commonplace. In other ways too north-easterners were similar to English men

---

[64] Raine, 'Middleham Statutes', pp. 161, 165, 169. The collect was also added to his book of hours (Sutton, 'Curious Searcher', p. 65).

[65] Dobson, 'Richard III and the Church of York', p. 146; *Harleian MS 433*, i. 201. [66] *Wills and Inventories*, i. 98; *Test. Ebor.* iii. 276; iv. 128.

[67] BI, Probate Register, iv. fo. 69ᵛ; *Test. Ebor.* iii. 200–1.

[68] *Test. Ebor.* iv. 116. This evidence is also cited by Professor Palliser in his discussion of the cult of St Ninian ('Richard III and York', p. 61). The bone may well be the same relic, St Ninian's arm, which was recovered by the monks of Douai, it was said in 1627, from certain English Catholics (see H. Chadwick, 'The Arm of St Ninian', *Transactions of the Dumfriesshire and Galloway Natural History and Antiquarian Society*, 3rd ser., 23 (1946), 30–5.

and women from more southerly shires. Because of the late
spiritual flourishing of Mount Grace Priory, exemplified in the
writings of Richard Methley and John Norton, and the associated resurgence of bequests to the priory after 1470, it is tempt-
ing to see evidence of a specific northern phenomenon here.[69]
But the Carthusian order enjoyed a general late-fifteenth-
century revival, and renewed support for it and its sister order is
to be observed in other parts of England where there were
houses, especially in Kent and London. Likewise the friars
retained and indeed intensified their popularity in both Yorkshire and Kent.[70] In one respect, however, towards the end of the
fifteenth century northerners seem to have diverged from south-
easterners: this is in their continuing commitment to the provision of prayers for the dead, and, perhaps, a concomitant
intensification of their belief in purgatory.

It has been demonstrated that in rural Yorkshire there was a
revival of perpetual chantry foundations after 1450 (especially
after 1480), quickening in the early sixteenth century.[71] Typical
of the new foundations in north Yorkshire were the chantry in
the parish church of South Cowton, endowed by Sir Richard
Conyers in 1493 with lands worth £5. 11s. 8d.; the two chantries
founded by Thomas Witham in Sheriff Hutton and in the chapel
a mile away at Cornburgh; and the chantries founded by two
successive William Burghs in the parish church of St Anne
Catterick in 1491 and 1505, with endowments of £2. 14s. and £3.
18s. 4d.[72] The certainty of the reality of purgatory which such
northern foundations suggest is further indicated by grants of
enhancement to already existing chantries which occurred
during the same period. Thus Christopher Conyers, rector of
Hutton Rudby, and Robert Pynkney, vicar of Kirkby Fleetham,

[69] James Hogg, 'Mount Grace Charterhouse and Late Medieval English
Spirituality', *Collectanea Cartusiensia*, iii (1980), 1–43; Rowntree, 'Studies in
Carthusian History', ch. 6 *passim*.

[70] Rowntree, 'Studies in Carthusian History', pp. 363–6, 387–402; L. M.
Goldthorpe, 'The Franciscans and Dominicans in Yorkshire', *YAJ* 32 (1936),
264–320, 365–428; Fleming, 'Charity', pp. 48–9.

[71] A. Kreider, *English Chantries: the Road to Dissolution* (Cambridge, Mass.,
1979), 87, Table 3.7, correcting J. T. Rosenthal, 'The Yorkshire Chantry Certificates of 1546: an analysis', *NH* 9 (1974), 26–47.

[72] *Yorkshire Chantry Surveys*, ed. W. Page, SS xli (1894), 43, 93–5, 113–14.
For the foundation deeds and endowments of the Catterick Chantries see
NYCRO, ZRL 1/42, 43, 45.

seem effectively to have refounded the chantry of St Cuthbert at Hornby. In his will proved in May 1490 Pynkney made several bequests for the 'repair and upholding' of the chantry, which he claimed to have founded with Conyers, including provision for his half of the cost of making the 'closet of timber'.[73] Nicholas Conyers of Stokesley in 1496 made provision for prayers to be sung perpetually for him in the Lady Chantry in the parish church which had been founded several decades earlier.[74] Joan, Lady Hastings, who ordered her executors to sell all her manor of Romanby and other lands to provide six priests to sing perpetually at a salary of 30s. each for her soul and the souls of her deceased husbands, wished that three of them serve at the London Greyfriars, one at Clerkenwell Friary, one at Mount Grace, and the last 'at the chantry founded by my father in the parish church of Northallerton'.[75] Others who did not found or support existing perpetual chantries made provision for prayers to be said for many years after their deaths. Thus Joan Boynton requested masses to be sung in Yarm parish church for twelve and a half years after her death in 1488–9; and Randolph Pigot of Clotherholme before his death in 1467 made provision for a priest to pray for his soul in two locations for twenty-four years (four before the altar at St Wilfrid at Ripon, and twenty in the family chantry at Clotherholme).[76]

[73] *Test. Ebor.* iv. 41–3. The exact history of the chantries in Hornby parish church is not known. Pynkney's refoundation was of a chantry originally established in 1332. Architectural evidence and a reference in an early will of William, Lord Conyers suggest that he established and dedicated to Our Lady a chantry served by two priests, as ordained by his grandfather Sir John (d. 1490), which was sited at the east end of the south aisle. The chapel still stands, fenced by a late-15th-cent. wooden parclose screen, with its original ornamental decoration. The chantry dedicated to St Cuthbert probably stood at the east end of the north aisle. Neither chantry was listed in the principal surveys of the Chantry Commissioners, although reference was made to the qualifications of their chaplains. Page, *Yorks. Chantry Surveys*, p. 498; Holman, *St. Mary's, Hornby*, pp. 14–15; H. B. McCall, *Richmondshire Churches* (1910), 55–6.

[74] *Test. Ebor.* iv. 128.

[75] *North Country Wills*, i. 74. The Northallerton chantry, separate from the chantry founded by Richard More and Sir James Strangways in 1539, did not apparently survive until the Dissolution (Page, *Yorks. Chantry Surveys*, i. 123).

[76] *Test. Ebor.* iv. 14; iii. 158. The evidence cited here and above tends to confirm Dr Carpenter's observation that chantries founded by the gentry were more individualistic than the great family establishments of the peerage. There are exceptions. It is to be noted that some gentry founders both honoured their ancestors and set up their own individual foundation (Carpenter, 'Gentry and their Estates', pp. 54–5).

These last examples of prayers being said for over ten years are exceptional. Normally one to two years seem to have sufficed.[77] However, the continuing popularity of chantries, perpetual and temporary, allied with the ubiquity of household chapels and oratories, stimulated after 1460 a revival in demand for priests to serve as stipendiary chaplains, a growth in ordinations, and an increase in basic educational provision.[78] It seems highly likely that in the diocese of York the belief in purgatory remained strong, and was perhaps becoming more intense, in the century before the Reformation. Costly and legally risky, provision of perpetual chantries remained only the work of a minority. Nevertheless such provision was more common in the diocese of York than in the dioceses of Norwich or Canterbury. Dr Kreider has demonstrated that although a similar enthusiasm for perpetual chantries was maintained in the north-west and west of England, in the south-east and the midlands it was missing. In both Essex and Kent the number of new foundations was declining in the century before the Reformation. In the North and West Ridings of Yorkshire there were 1.5 intercessory institutions per parish in 1546, ten times the number in Suffolk. 'In comparison with the intensity of the Yorkshireman's trust in the efficacy of endowed masses for the dead', he concluded, 'the piety of the inhabitants of Suffolk appears to have been cooler, more anti-institutional, and more modern.'[79] Similar conclusions have been reached for the gentry of Kent. Here too a significant minority have been discovered turning to

[77] For example Maud Eure, 1467, founding masses for a twelvemonth (*Test. Ebor.* ii. 285).

[78] J. A. H. Moran, 'Clerical Recruitment in the Diocese of York, 1340–1530', *JEH* 34 (1983), 47–9 and idem, *English Schooling*, pp. 125–36, in which it is suggested that increase in provision of fixed-term obits, trentals, and other masses for the dead was as significant as the rise in perpetual chantry foundations in creating a demand for stipendiary chaplains.

[79] Kreider, *English Chantries*, pp. 18, 90–2; cf. C. Haigh, *Reformation and Resistance in Tudor Lancashire* (1975), 71, and Richmond, 'Religion', p. 195 on the 'casual attitude towards Purgatory' displayed by the Pastons. See, on the other hand, the persistence of traditional forms of piety within the city of Norwich (Tanner, 'Reformation and Regionalism', pp. 133, 135). It is on the question of perpetual chantries that Dr Vale's limited sources and restricted period prove most deceptive, for, basing his conclusion only on wills proved in and before 1480, he commented that the establishment of perpetual chantries was comparatively rare among the Yorkshire gentry (Vale, *Piety*, p. 23).

a more directly philanthropic approach to charity, which, it has been suggested, reveals a turning away from an imagined purgatory towards the actual suffering that lay all around.[80] Philanthropic concern can be found in Yorkshire; but indiscriminate alms-giving rather than specific bequests remained the general rule well into the sixteenth century.[81]

Considerable caution has to be exercised in interpreting the comparative evidence of different parts of the realm. The differences that appear concern minorities only. But perhaps it is just the differences between these minorities in respect to the question of purgatory that reveal what was to be a future divergence between south-eastern and north-eastern England. There is no need to doubt the strength of lay piety in both regions on the eve of the Reformation. But the south-east was to be more quickly receptive to Protestantism, while parts of the north were to remain more stubbornly loyal to Catholicism. Rejection of the doctrine of purgatory was a key element in the one; enthusiastic endorsement of it a feature of the other. In 1535 Richard Layton observed that the people in the north 'are more superstitious than virtuous, long accustomed to fantasies and ceremonies' and alienated from 'true' religion.[82] In so far as the doctrine of purgatory still had a hold on the imagination of many members of even the highest ranks of north-eastern society, he was undoubtedly accurate in his diagnosis. The roots of later recusancy and doctrinal conflict in the north-east can perhaps be traced back to the later fifteenth century.[83]

[80] Fleming, 'Charity', pp. 45–6, 53. See also Bossy, *Christianity in the West*, p. 168 for the changing meaning of the word 'charity'.

[81] But see Vale, *Piety*, p. 27: 'The general and vaguely worded gifts to the poor have given way by about 1450 to very detailed provisions.' A wider sample of wills than that taken by Vale would almost certainly reveal a less dramatic change. See for instance the will of Edmund Mauleverer, first drafted in 1488, in which he both requested that 20s. be distributed in alms to the poor on the day of his funeral and provided for 2 beds at the almshouse at Bramham for the elderly homeless and sick of good repute. (Brown, *Ingleby Arncliffe*, pp. 104, 105–6; *Test. Ebor.* iv. 39–40).

[82] *Letters and Papers, Hen. VIII*, viii. 375.

[83] As Dr Carpenter has pointed out, generalizations about the significance of trends based on the imperfect evidence available are suspect. I agree that many changes were changes in fashion rather than in purpose. But it seems to me that there was indeed a fundamental divergence between north-east and south-east which was more profound than mere fashionable trend ('The Religion of the Gentry', pp. 57–8, 67).

8

Gentility: The Chase and Chivalry

WHEN in 1460 Richard Pigot senior of Ripon gave a warranty to his nephew for Little Burton and other lands he swore, as well as by the faith he owed unto God, 'not to vex nor trouble him upon his truth and worship as a true gentleman'. His word as a gentleman was as important as his oath as a Christian.[1] But what was meant by 'gentleman'? It is well established that the fifteenth century witnessed in England the development of the concept and style of a gentleman.[2] As we have seen, a line was drawn at approximately £10 clear income a year from land between those who were taken to be gentle and those who were not.[3] But *true* gentility did not reside in material wealth alone. It derived ultimately from personal qualities: lineage, courtliness, generosity, and honour. But getting beneath the skin to the true feeling of the north-eastern gentleman towards chivalry is as hard as getting to the heart of his religious conviction. A code of honour, martial at heart, was no doubt instilled at an early age (or acquired by the new arrival), and subscribed to; but in the absence of direct personal testimony we can do little more than assume this. We have largely to rely on the evidence of gentility in action, of its visible show and demonstration to the world, especially in the skills of hunting and in expertise in arms.

The chase and chivalry were practical pursuits deemed to be the occupation of a proper gentleman.[4] They were set out for contemporaries in the Book of Hawking, Hunting, and Blasing of Arms known as the *Boke of St Albans* (1486). The *Boke* was a compilation of several manuscript pieces, bringing together the principal works of instruction and guidance to behaviour for the would-be gentleman. In these pages it is made clear that it was through knowledge and practice of the chase, as well as of

<hr/>

[1] NYCRO, ZFW, MIC 1160.
[2] Morgan, 'English Gentleman', pp. 15–20.
[3] See above, p. 86.
[4] M. H. Keen, *Chivalry* (Newhaven, Conn., 1984), 249–50; *The Master of Game*, ed. W. A. and F. Baillie-Grohman (1909), esp. p. 8—'an hunter is not idle'.

chivalry, that 'gentlemen shall be known from ungentlemen'.[5] Modern discussion of late-medieval gentility has tended to concentrate on the question of chivalry alone.[6] But the chase was almost as important, and should not be overlooked. As Edward, duke of York stated in the prologue to his *Master of Game*, quoting Gaston de Foix:

he never saw a man that loved the work and pleasure of hounds and hawks that had not many good qualities in him, for that comes to him of great nobleness and gentleness of heart of whatever estate the man may be . . .[7]

The gentility of fifteenth-century north-easterners is thus to be sought in the chase as well as chivalry.

However, a difficulty faces the historian seeking to determine whether late-medieval lords and gentry followed the precepts of the *Master of Game*: relatively little evidence exists either of the possession of the principal advice books or of participation in hunting itself. Richard, duke of Gloucester owned a copy of the *Tristram*, the treatise used as a source for the *Boke of St Albans*; but few other such works are known to have been in circulation in the region.[8] There is slightly more evidence of actual participation. Lord FitzHugh held a great hunt at West Tanfield for five days in 1426–7. It is clear from the findings of a special enquiry held at Pickering in September 1495 that during the preceding five years local lords and gentry, the earl of Surrey, Lord Latimer, Ralph Bigod, William Eure, John Hotham, and Ralph Salvin among them, had been accustomed to hunt in the forest, from which they had taken at least thirty-eight harts and hinds. William Eure of Ayton, for instance, was prosecuted for hunting a great hart from Rawcliffe to Scarwell, a distance of approximately ten miles as the crow flies, and there killing him on 20 June 1494. In the summer of 1500 Thomas Darcy, captain

---

[5] E. F. Jacob, 'The Book of St. Albans', in *Essays in Later Medieval History* (Manchester, 1968), 196, 199, 209.

[6] See Keen, *Chivalry*; Morgan, 'English Gentleman'; J. P. Cooper, 'Ideas of Gentility in Early Modern England', in *Land, Men and Beliefs*, pp. 46–8; and M. E. James, 'English Politics and the Concept of Honour', *PP* Suppl. 3 (1978), reissued in *Society, Politics and Culture* (Cambridge, 1986), pp. 310–32.

[7] Baillie-Grohman, *The Master of Game*, p. 13.

[8] J. T. Rosenthal, 'Aristocratic Cultural Patronage', p. 533. In 1420 Maud, widow of Sir William Bowes, disposed of a *Tristram* in her last will (Surtees, *Durham*, i. 5).

of Berwick, in the course of a leisurely journey north from London to resume his post, met a party of fellow Yorkshire gentlemen (including Sir John Hastings of Fenwick) who, so he wrote, 'held me company, and so I tarried in hunting with them a fortnight'. Fifteen years later Sir John Bulmer was out hawking near Guisborough, and had just rewarded his bird for taking a magpie, when he nearly came to blows with his neighbour Christopher Conyers of Pinchinthorpe.[9] No one quite matched the legendary Sir Thomas Wortley, who used to spend weeks at a time 'hunting and making other worthy pastimes' in his forest of Wharncliffe.[10]

But these are rare glimpses of the north-eastern gentleman in pursuit of game. Indirect evidence, however, is more plentiful, if paradoxical. On the one hand there is much to show that the lords and gentry of the region highly valued the possession of hunting rights as property; that they were much concerned to preserve the game itself; and that they would go to great lengths to create new deer reserves. On the other hand, throughout the later Middle Ages, forests and parks were progressively given over to animal husbandry, which inevitably reduced the stocks of deer and limited the scale of hunting. Moreover, a deer park was both a hunting ground and a food resource: it is not ultimately possible to determine whether a park was stocked with deer primarily for sport, or to maintain a ready supply of venison culled from the herd by the parkers. In the absence of specific evidence of the organization of hunting in parks it can only be assumed that their owners hunted in them as well as using them as larders.

Nature made the north-east good hunting country. The greater part of the Pennine chain, from Peak to Cheviot, and the eastern part of the North York Moors, still then the habitat of roaming herds of wild red deer, was reserved and divided into seigneurially controlled forests or chases. At the foot of each forest, as at Stanhope in Weardale, Middleton-in-Teesdale, or Bainbridge in Wensleydale sat the forest court and headquarters of forest administration. The special forest law of vert and

[9] NYCRO, zjx 3/2/80; *The Honor and Forest of Pickering*, i, ed. R. B. Turton, North Riding Record Ser., NS I, (1894), 166; Allen, *Letters of Richard Fox*, p. 20; *Yorkshire Star Chamber Proceedings*, ed. W. Brown, YAS, RS, 41 (1909 for 1908), 69.   [10] J. Hunter, *South Yorkshire*, ii (1831), 311.

venison carefully controlled the farming activities of tenants within its jurisdiction, and jealously guarded the game itself.[11] The red deer, however, were already in decline in the fifteenth century. Although in the late sixteenth century Camden reported that in the remote high Pennines of Richmondshire there was still 'safe living in this tract for goats, deer and stags which for their great bulk and branchy heads are very remarkable and extraordinary,'[12] their numbers were by this time already much reduced. The deer in the Forest of Pickering had declined to no more than a hundred in 1499, before Sir Richard Cholmley as chief forester by rigorous management restored their numbers to three hundred in four years.[13]

The main cause of the decline in red deer, which had probably been in progress since the thirteenth century, is not hard to find. It lay in the development of pastoral farming, especially cattle-rearing, in the same high moorland. Cattle, unlike sheep, do not destroy the deer's grazing. They need, however, to be carefully controlled. In some parts they were restricted to lawns, special enclosures into and out of which deer could leap, but from which cattle could not stray;[14] everywhere attempts were made to restrict their numbers. But, inevitably perhaps, the widespread development of vaccaries and summer grazing had the effect of curtailing the deer. Moreover, the illegal pasturing of animals by tenants, impossible it seems to stamp out, remorselessly undermined all attempts to preserve the vert. Court records reveal either an unending stream of presentments, or a recognition of the inevitable by accepting piecemeal leases and settlement. In the FitzHugh forest of Lune, as we have seen, presentments were regularly made of tenants grazing

[11] For forest courts see Tupling, *Rossendale*, pp. 6–15; J. L. Drury, 'Durham Palatinate Forest Law and Administration, specially in Weardale up to 1440', *Arch. Ael.* 5th ser., 6 (1978), 87–105; Turton, *Forest of Pickering*, i, ii (1899); and L. M. Cantor, 'Forests, Chases, Parks and Warrens', in idem (ed.), *The English Medieval Landscape* (1982), 56–73, esp. 70–3 and Fig. 3.5. Cantor not only overlooks the Pennine chases and misplaces Weardale in his map, he also underestimates the extent to which forest law was administered in the northern chases.

[12] Camden, *Britannia*, 759. See also Leland's remarks that 'The king hath a forest of red deer in the moor land at Middleton' and that 'there are many red deer in the mountains of Weardale' (*Itinerary*, pp. 76, 71).

[13] Turton, *Forest of Pickering*, i. 198–9.

[14] See Shaw, *Forest of Lancaster*, p. 358.

cattle or sheep in large numbers throughout the fifteenth century. In Weardale, the bishop's forest administrators were leasing grazing on the high moor on an ever-increasing scale from the early fourteenth century. By 1400 much of the Forest of Knaresborough had already been let out, and piecemeal enclosure by forest settlers occurred throughout the century.[15] Indeed it is to be wondered how much the red deer were still hunted. The last time a bishop of Durham or his servants is known to have hunted in Weardale was in the mid-fourteenth century.[16] By the fifteenth century profit seems to have been as important as pleasure as far as much of the high forest was concerned.

The alternative to open forest hunting of red deer was the hunting of fallow deer in specially created parks. Deer parks seem to have developed to supplement the forest from the early thirteenth century, either as a convenience or as a response to the early signs of decline in red-deer stocks; and, it must be said, as a larder from which venison could be taken when needed.[17] Parks were established in most of the forests; sometimes adjacent to the principal dwelling house. In Knaresborough Forest, parks were made at Haverah, Beckwith, and Hay, in Pickering at Blandsby Park. Bishop Bek (1283–1311) created Stanhope Park in Weardale. The lords of Barnard Castle, who owned Teesdale Forest, created Bredpark immediately next to the castle.[18] In the early or middle years of the fifteenth century, a Neville de-

[15] See above, pp. 64–5; Drury, 'Early Settlement', pp. 141–2 and idem, 'Forest Law', pp. 97, 102; Jennings, *Harrogate and Knaresborough*, pp. 46–9, 72–3. In 1453 the lawns of Danby Forest on the North York Moors were leased for £4. (Alnwick, Syon MS X I, Box 1 2b). Cf. also Tupling, *Rossendale*, pp. 33–8 and Birrell, 'Honour of Tutbury', pp. 116–25.

[16] NYCRO, zjx 3/2/73; Drury, 'Forest Law', p. 95. Most references to venison in the 15th cent. are to bucks and does, i.e. to fallow not to red deer. In the 1480s the earl of Northumberland ordered a buck to be sent to the mayor of York (*Plumpton Correspondence*, p. 86). In 1512 his son's household consumed 29 does in winter and 20 bucks in summer (T. Percy, *The Northumberland Household Book* (1777), 112).

[17] L. M. Cantor and J. Hattersley, 'The Medieval Parks of England', *Geography*, 64 (1979), 73, 79. In this survey the authors do not relate the development of parks to the parallel development of cattle-rearing in forests. Cf. the 100–200 deer taken from Framlingham Park in 1508–13 and 1515–19 by culling as well as hunting (MacCulloch, *Suffolk*, p. 56).

[18] Jennings, *Harrogate and Knaresborough*, p. 46; Drury, 'Forest Law', p. 93; *CIM*, vi. 200–1.

molished the settlement of East Lilling and incorporated its land into an enlarged Sheriff Hutton park. The Lords of Middleham possessed nine in Wensleydale and its tributaries. In the mid-1460s Richard, earl of Warwick even created a new park at Cotescue. In the following decade Richard, duke of Gloucester enlarged both this and the older-established Sunscue Park.[19]

No self-respecting gentleman could be without his park. There seems to have been a fashion for making new hunting grounds after 1470, a fashion that might have been set by Edward IV. Sir Robert Danby is reputed to have met his death in his new park at Thorp Perrow when he was shot by his parker in 1474. His heir, Sir James, also had a park at Farnley in Wharfedale, and remembered its keeper in his will.[20] Sir William Plumpton received a licence to create a park at Plumpton in 1474. An attempt was made to stock this park with red as well as fallow deer, for later the earl of Northumberland wrote to Sir Robert from Spittle-in-the Street, Lincolnshire, not only asking if he could have a couple of his running dogs (of which he was 'destitute') but also begging the loan of his 'tame hart, for my deer are dead.'[21] Sometimes the creation of a new park, next to or surrounding the house, necessitated the destruction or moving of the village, so important was it to the Lord of the Manor. Sir William Gascoigne received licence to empark 2,600 acres at Gawkthorpe in 1476, the result of which was the disappearance of the old village.[22] Early in the next century William, Lord Conyers, the grandson and heir of Sir John, pulled down the old village of Hornby, converted the arable to pasture, and enclosed the land into a park adjacent to his castle. At Brandsby, 'some squire' (a De La River) pulled down the village and constructed a large park in about 1500. Likewise the villages of Thornton Bridge and Stittenham were removed by the Nevilles and Gowers respectively, and parks took their places by 1517.[23] In some cases it was not so much sheep as deer that ate up men.

[19] Beresford, 'Lost Villages', p. 284; Coles, 'Middleham', pp. 242–6.

[20] Fisher, *Masham*, pp. 249–51; *Test. Ebor.* iv. 122; T. Horsfall, *The Manor of Snape and Well* (Leeds, 1912), 79; Birrell, 'Honour of Tutbury', p. 121.

[21] *Plumpton Correspondence*, p. lxxxvi.   [22] *CPR, 1476–85*, 203.

[23] Beresford, 'Lost Villages', pp. iv, 295, 297, 300, 306. In *YAJ* 37, 4 (1951), 485 Beresford appears to concentrate only on enclosure for sheep-runs as a cause for these acts, whereas the evidence produced in 1954 clearly shows that several villages were pulled down to make way for parks.

Before and during the fifteenth century, however, many of these parks too were being used for pastoral farming, either by piecemeal sales of agistment and herbage, or by full leasing. The West Park of Thringarth in Teesdale, part of the FitzHugh Lordship of Mickleton, was equipped with a 'New Grange' which needed repairs in the first decade of the century. In 1388/9 a 'new close' in Coltpark nearby was let out to farm. Bredpark, Barnard Castle was almost entirely in the hands of tenants by 1437/8.[24] A good example of the process whereby even parks were converted to animal husbandry is provided by Stanhope in Weardale. Stanhope was initially reserved exclusively for deer, apart from a few cattle kept by the keeper. In 1419, however, the grazing of the whole park was leased to the master forester, Robert Strangways. After his death (c.1442) his successor Lord Lumley began piecemeal letting, and in 1458 formally let out six farms. By 1476 the number of farms had increased to twenty, and permanent settlement had begun. Ultimately, in the last decade of the century, so much of the park had been given over to cattle that the area reserved for deer was substantially reduced, and concentrated in the New Park enclosed within the pale of the old.[25]

By the second half of the fifteenth century, therefore, the land reserved for deer, either in forest or park, was much reduced. Yet even reduced in number, the deer and the hunting of them were still highly valued. Richard of Gloucester kept deer in some of his parks at Middleham, for the dean and canons of his new college were given two bucks and a doe each year from West Park and Sunscue.[26] A careful check was still kept on the deer in Stanhope and Haverah Parks by the officials of the bishopric and duchy of Lancaster.[27] The fourth earl of Northumberland, the *Plumpton Correspondence* shows, was anxious to preserve his game in Spofforth and Topcliffe Parks. Robert Plumpton was

[24] Dur. RO, D/St/E3/1/1/1405–6; NYCRO, ZJX 3/2/9; PRO, SC6/1030/13.

[25] Drury, 'Stanhope Park', *passim*. See also Tupling, *Rossendale*, p. 33 for a similar development at Musbury Park in Rossendale Forest by 1480. For the economic exploitation of parks in general see Cantor and Hattersley, 'Medieval Parks', pp. 80–1. See also Birrell, 'Honour of Tutbury', pp. 14–34.

[26] W. Atthill, *Documents of the Collegiate Church of Middleham*, Camden, OS, xxxviii (1847), 86–7.

[27] Drury, 'Stanhope Park', p. 146; *Plumpton Correspondence*, p. liii n. There were 200 head of deer in Stanhope in 1456 and 160 at Haverah in 1439.

once ordered to view the deer at Spofforth to take steps to see
that cattle and horses did not stray into the spring. On another
occasion he was ordered to take bonds from two servants of his
brother-in-law, Thomas Middleton, who had been caught
poaching. Richard Green once had to apologize to Sir Robert for
missing an engagement because he had been ordered at short
notice by the earl to join Ralph Neville of Thornton Bridge in a
survey of the woods, park, and game at Topcliffe. 'There are
complaints,' he wrote, 'made of the keepers of the game,
wherein my lord is sore displeased withal.'[28] The earl's careful
conservation of his game seems to have borne fruit, for in 1512
his son had over five and a half thousand deer in his twenty-one
forests and parks in Northumberland, Cumberland, and
Yorkshire.[29]

The fullest evidence of the continuing popularity of hunting
comes from the Forest of Pickering during the reign of Henry
VII. Under Sir Edmund Hastings of Roxby, chief forester for
Richard III and Henry VII until his death in 1489, and his
successor Brian Sandford, there was so much overhunting that
the red deer was in danger of extinction. In 1489, and again in
1494, a moratorium on all hunting without special royal war-
rant was imposed for three years.[30] The prohibitions fell on deaf
ears. With Sandford's apparent connivance Lionel Percehay of
Ryton took seventy-nine fallow deer from Blandsby Park, and
Sir Roger Hastings of Roxby took twenty red deer from the open
forest in the five years 1490–4. The claim made by them that
they had a right as tenants to this game was disallowed by a
forest court in September 1495.[31] Overhunting of the game was
finally brought to a halt by Sir Richard Cholmley after 1499.
Cholmley too was later accused by an embittered Roger
Hastings of destroying the game. Cholmley's reply, upheld by a
special court of enquiry under the archbishop of York, was that
he had given permission to certain lords and gentry bordering

[28] *Plumpton Correspondence*, pp. 75, 79, 86.
[29] Percy, *Northumberland Household Book*, p. 112. See also the record of
gifts of bucks and does from the earl of Northumberland to the mayor and
aldermen of York (e.g. *YCR* i. 79; ii. 28–9).
[30] Turton, *Forest of Pickering*, pp. 123, 126.
[31] Ibid. 141–54. Cf. the presentation of Thomas Beckwith and associates for
hunting in Haverah Park in Knaresborough in March 1460 (Wheater,
Knaresburgh, p. 187).

the forest to take a limited number so that they would be 'loving and favourable' to the King's game. It would seem that the neighbours were now allowed an occasional day's sport so as to curb excessive poaching. Such a policy, as well as a more rigorous enforcement of forest law, enabled Cholmley rapidly to replenish stocks both in the open forest and in Blandsby Park, which by 1503 held over five hundred head of fallow deer.[32] Comment on the number of parks and substantial stocks of deer by Italian visitors to England in the early sixteenth century would seem to have been accurate as far as Yorkshire was concerned.[33]

In addition to a park, or as an alternative if he were not so fortunate or ruthless, a gentleman might enjoy the privilege, like the De La Rivers of Brandsby for instance, of free warren. Free warren was the right to take all lesser game within the bounds of the manor—especially hare, fox, badger, otter, pheasant, and partridge. Could Sir James Danby's appointment as master of the king's harriers in 1484 have been more than a sinecure and an acknowledgement of Danby's expertise in this kind of hunting?[34] Sir Robert Plumpton received a licence of warreny with his licence to empark in 1474, which immediately led to trouble with the duchy of Lancaster officials because of the disturbance he caused to the king's deer and the tenant's rights of common by his hunting of fox and hare.[35] Richard Clervaux of Croft was granted free warreny in 1478. The assertion of his new privilege seems to have been one of the major issues in his quarrel with his neighbour Roland Place, which rapidly flared thereafter. In the terms of arbitration which both parties accepted it was agreed that neither should hunt, hawk, or fish the other's game; and that if any hounds should chase game on to the other's ground, the hunter was not to follow but to call

---

[32] Ibid. ii. 207–11; see above, p. 201.

[33] Polydore Vergil, *Anglica Historia* (Basle, 1546), ed. D. Hay, Camden, 3rd ser., 74 (1950), 196; Sneyd, *Relation*, p. 39. It is not clear what grounds, other than size and absence of surviving archaeological evidence of retaining banks, Cantor and Hattersley have ('Medieval Parks', pp. 74, 79) for arguing that these late-medieval parks were 'ornamental' and 'conceived from the beginning as amenity parks rather than hunting parks.' Indeed one wonders what 'amenity' other than stocking and hunting game would have been devised by the late-15th-cent. gentleman.

[34] *CPR, 1476–85*, 438.   [35] Arnold, 'West Riding', pp. 9–10.

them back, while the one whose land had been trespassed was merely to 'rebuke' the hounds, and do no other hurt.[36] For these men, too, hunting would seem to have been an important part of life.

Despite the temptation to convert hunting grounds to stock-raising, the lords and gentry of the north-east seem in the closing decades of the fifteenth century to have retained, if on a reduced scale, their enthusiasm for the idle pastime which was to be the subject of caustic criticism from humanists. Many were happy to live up to Poggio's gibe that to be noble meant to live in the country and to waste time in the open on hawking and hunting.[37] 'I swear by God's body,' thundered Richard Pace's reactionary gentleman at the dinner table, 'I'd rather that my son should hang than study letters. For it becomes the sons of gentlemen to blow the horn nicely, to hunt skilfully, and elegantly carry and train a hawk.'[38] Plumpton, Place, or Clervaux, had he been present, might well have taken his part. To keep hawks and hounds and to be knowledgeable about them were attributes of their gentility which men such as these still valued at the end of the fifteenth century.

Fifteenth- and early-sixteenth-century commentators saw hunting more specifically as a prelude to and training for war; the very imitation of battle. 'For if he had need to go to war,' wrote the Master of Game of one not skilled in the chase, 'he would not know what war is, for he would not be accustomed to travail.'[39] John Hardyng, that stalwart Northumberland squire, wrote in mid-century of the education of gentle boys:

> At fourtene yere they shalle to fielde I sure
> At hunte the dere; and catch an hardynesse.

---

[36] NYCRO, zQH I, fos. 155–6.

[37] Keen, *Chivalry*, p. 154; J. H. Hexter, 'The Education of the Aristocracy during the Renaissance', in *Reappraisals in History* (1961), p. 46.

[38] *Early English Meals and Manners*, ed. F. J. Furnivall, EETS xxxii, (1814), p. xiii.

[39] Baillie-Grohman, *The Master of Game*, 13; N. Orme, *From Childhood to Chivalry* (1984), 191–8, esp. 196. Note too how Edward IV, calling himself 'the Master of the Game', replied to a mock received from Louis XI in 1475 in the form of a hunter's boast, claiming that he and his lords would 'hunt thorugh parts of France and there will I blow my own horn and release my hounds' (C. F. Richmond, '1485 and all that', in Hammond, *Lordship, Loyalty and Law*, p. 206).

For dere to hunte and slea, and se them blede,
An hardyment gyffithe to his corage,
And also in his wytte he takyth hede,
Ymagynynge to take thouym at a-vauntage.
At sextene yere, to werray and to wage,
To juste and ryde, and castels to assayle.[40]

Undoubtedly hunting was secondary; gentility was supposed, above all, to be demonstrated through the actual profession of arms. The highest secular ideals of gentle society were chivalric. A coat of arms itself, as fifteenth-century grants expounded, was a badge of virtue. Men who spent their days in deeds of arms and other virtuous works were rewarded and their lineage honoured by blazon, helm, and crest; the insignia of true gentility. As the literature of heraldry makes clear, armorial bearings were regarded as more than mere tokens of superior rank; they were held to demonstrate the possession of true worth and virtue.[41] That armorial bearings were proudly borne by the lords and gentry of the north-east is readily apparent: they were, in some cases quite literally, plastered everywhere. Houses, castles, and churches were liberally decorated in stone, glass, and tapestry with the blazons of their owners and patrons. In the late fifteenth century too began the practice of heraldic visitation, whereby the old-established gentry families could have their coats of arms and lineage recorded to impress their neighbours, and the parvenus could pay to have their ancestry and arms discovered.[42]

Wills reveal that it was common for men of gentle status to own both war-horse and armour. In 1449 Sir John Neville, son and heir of Ralph, earl of Westmorland, bequeathed a 'courser called Lyard Nevill' (a dappled grey horse) as his corpse-present. In 1475 Thomas Witham willed his best horse and his best set of armour to the church of Sheriff Hutton as mortuary (he clearly

[40] Hardyng, *Chronicle*, i.
[41] Keen, *Chivalry*, p. 44; Morgan, 'English Gentleman', pp. 17–18; A. R. Wagner, *Heralds and Heraldry in the Middle Ages*, 2nd edn. (Oxford, 1973), 56–120; Jacob, 'Book of St Albans', pp. 203–9.
[42] Morgan, 'English Gentleman', pp. 18–19; A. R. Wagner, *Heralds of England: a history of the Office and College of Arms* (1967), 205, 191–8, esp. 196. For an early visitation of the north see *A Visitation of the North of England ca 1490*, ed. C. H. Hunter Blair, SS, cxliv (1930).

owned more than one suit of armour). A year later John Trollope of Thornley, Co. Durham willed all his arms, except that set aside for mortuary, to be divided equally between his sons Thomas and Andrew. Edmund Mauleverer willed in 1488 'my best horse and harness that belongs thereto, with my harness for my body . . . to be my corpse present'. In 1494 John Lepton left to his son Thomas '1 pair of briganders and all other jacks and sallets, except 1 pair of splints and a sallet that I give to my son Wivell'. Even Christopher Conyers, clerk, rector of Hutton Rudby, left 'meam tunicam defensibilem' to be disposed by his executors.[43] Arms and armour seems to have been owned in profusion.

Nowhere is the public demonstration of chivalric virtue more vividly revealed than in sepulchral monuments. An alabaster effigy or memorial brass should have shown, according to one heraldic treatise, how a noble had lived and used his life in the profession of arms. Precise rules existed as to the manner in which by fine detail and minute variation the figure should declare to the *cognoscenti* the exact degree of prowess achieved in life.[44] The lords and gentry of the north-east, as we have seen, were by custom honoured by such memorials, depicting them in full armour. But it hardly appears that the makers of these effigies, skilled craftsmen that they were, paid much attention to the fine points of chivalric symbolism. By the second half of the fifteenth century the form is stereotyped. A fashionable outward show seems to be more important than the demonstration of actual achievement.[45] The question thus arises as to whether these men, proud bearers of blazon, helm, and crest, were truly dedicated to the profession of arms.

---

[43] *Wills and Inventories*, i. 98; *Test. Ebor.* iii. 264, 288; iv. 13; *Testamenta Vetusta*, ed. N. H. Nicolas, i (1826), 265. Witham is a fine example of the gentleman serving-man who was primarily a civilian administrator, yet was also equipped to offer military service: 'armes and gentilnes' seem in his case to have mixed happily with 'custom of lande'. See above pp. 137–8 and Morgan, 'English Gentleman', pp. 24–6. For the ritual of chivalric burial see the account of the funeral of Richard, earl of Salisbury in 1463 printed in *A Collection of Ordinances and Regulations for the Government of the Royal Household* (Society of Antiquaries, London, 1970), 131–3 and Payne, 'Salisbury Roll', pp. 187–8.

[44] Keen, *Chivalry*, p. 169.

[45] For detailed description of the effigies in 24 Yorkshire churches see Routh, *Alabaster Tombs*, *passim*.

The question is important because it has indeed been doubted whether the later-fifteenth-century gentry retained any deep attachment to the spirit of chivalry. The criticism of those such as Worcester and Caxton, who called for a return to the discipline and practice of arms as a necessary step towards social and moral reform, has recently been dismissed as the sour opinion of a dwindling band of ultra-conservatives.[46] By implication, too, the views of heralds on the importance of coats of arms might be disparaged as the expression of a vested interest. By the mid-fifteenth century, it has been suggested, the knights and squires of England were no longer genuinely committed to an ethic to which they gave no more than lip-service. Such doubts would seem to be supported by the record of excuses and failures even to acknowledge Henry V's exhortation to the Yorkshire gentry to serve him in France in 1420. Of 143 gentlemen approached by Sir Robert Waterton and Sir John St Quintin on the king's behalf, 47, one-third, did not even respond. From the answers of those who did, it was discovered that 2 were already committed to serve, 5 now agreed, 3 were serving against Scotland, and a further 8 had served, and were discharged. Brothers or sons of 8 other gentlemen had or were serving, and 9 expressed a willingness to find a substitute, individually or collectively. Only 22 per cent had or were prepared to serve in person, or had or were willing to support a member of their family in France.[47] Even at the height of his fame and success in France Henry V does not seem to have been able to excite the chivalric enthusiasm of an overwhelming majority of Yorkshiremen. How much success is his lack-lustre son likely to have been able to achieve?[48]

The implications of this survey of 1420 are inescapable; but there are certain caveats one must enter. There were some genuine excuses given to the king's commissioners. Several drew attention to family commitments; others were genuinely

---

[46] Lander, *Government and Community*, pp. 160–1.

[47] A. E. Goodman, 'Responses to Requests in Yorkshire for Military Service under Henry V', *NH* 17 (1981), 24–52.

[48] Sir Robert Plumpton seems to have been one man the commissioners failed to contact. He had served in Normandy under Lord FitzHugh, came home in the summer of 1419, and set out again to France in October 1420, where he reputedly died in December 1421 (*Plumpton Correspondence*, pp. xlv–xlix). Cf. the complaint in 1437 by the king's council that 'the gentlemen of his land be out of array' (Morgan, 'English Gentleman', p. 122).

sick. But most of all many drew attention to the financial strain imposed by such service in the king's cause. The hope of ultimate gain does not seem to have outweighed the certainty of initial heavy cost. Secondly, only 18 of the 143 approached came from the North Riding. Over half were from the East Riding. The possibility exists that the gentry of the North Riding, and more especially of the counties north of the Tees, were more martial than their more southerly neighbours. In 1416, for instance, Sir William Claxton of Horden and Sir William Bulmer of Wilton, intending to go to the war in France, agreed with Sir Thomas Surtees that their wives would lodge in his house at Dinsdale for one year with their waiting maids and pages, at a charge of ten marks each.[49] It might be particularly relevant that Henry V was looking for men to serve him in France. The response to a call to arms for a full-scale invasion of Scotland might well have been more positive. Indeed, John Hardyng later remembered that at the end of Henry V's reign Sir Robert Umfraville maintained a two-year harassment of the east march of Scotland with no other help except from the bishopric and Northumberland.[50]

Even so, there still remained some who served in France. In Henry V's day the chivalric lead in northern Yorkshire came from two peers; Henry, Lord FitzHugh of Ravensworth and Richard, Lord Scrope of Bolton, who both fought at Agincourt and participated in the conquest of Normandy.[51] Among the men who had served with FitzHugh was Sir Halnath Mauleverer, who in 1420 was already preparing to return to his lord in Normandy, having recently come back to England 'right sick and hurt from your service'.[52] William Burgh of Brough explained in 1420 that he had leave of the king to come home to be with my Lord FitzHugh 'to be of his counsel with my lady his wife and governor of his land'. Nevertheless, he expressed his willingness to return if he were sent for. The seriousness with which he meant this might be indicated by his grant on 12 July 1419 of the livery of one robe and two bushels of wheat annually for life to William de Hesilton of Tunstall on condition that he held himself ready to go or ride with Burgh wherever he pleased. In 1427, when Burgh contracted with Ellen Pickering for the

[49] Surtees, *Durham*, iii. 231 and n.   [50] Hardyng, *Chronicle*, p. 382.
[51] For FitzHugh see A. C. Reeves, *Lancastrian Englishmen* (Washington, DC, 1981), 65–138; for Scrope, *CP*, xi. 542.   [52] Goodman, 'Responses', p. 245.

marriage of his son and heir William with her daughter, he entered a reservation to the fulfilment of his obligations in the event of his being taken prisoner by the king's enemies.[53] Perhaps even then he was contemplating a return to France.

There are several other north-easterners who are known later to have served Henry VI in France. Sir William Bowes, who first went to Normandy with Henry V, is reported to have fought in France for more than twenty years, and to have built his castle at Streatlam on the profits.[54] Sir William Plumpton served as a young man in France. John Markenfield referred in his will drawn up in 1431 to his 'coming again from the parts of France'. Sir Edmund Darrell of Sessay and Richard Ferriby both made wills in September 1436, the one at Fécamp and the other at Rouen, suggesting that they had but recently sailed to France in the company of either Richard, duke of York or Richard Neville, earl of Salisbury.[55] Sir John Salvin of Newbiggin served for many years after 1436 in France.[56] The mantle of Henry, Lord Fitz-Hugh as the leader of north-eastern chivalry seems however to have fallen in Henry VI's reign on the shoulders of William Neville, Lord Fauconberg, 'little Fauconberg, a knight of great reverence'.[57] He first went to France in 1436 with his brother the earl of Salisbury. But while Salisbury returned home the following year, Fauconberg stayed in Normandy serving as a field commander until the truce of Tours, and was back in France again in 1448.[58] How many north-easterners served with him it is hard to know.

Only a few north-easterners have been identified as serving in France during the fifteenth century; there may indeed have only ever been a minority who did so. The profession of arms was always more likely to have been exercised against the Scots.

[53] Goodman, 'Responses', p. 249; NYCRO, ZRL 1/22, 24.

[54] Surtees, *Durham*, iv. 107.

[55] *Test. Ebor.* iv. 124 n.; Vale, *Piety*, p. 4.

[56] A. E. Curry, 'Military Organisation in Lancastrian Normandy, 1422–1450' (unpublished CNAA Ph.D. thesis, Teesside Polytechnic, 1985), App. vii. p. cxxvii.

[57] *An English Chronicle of the reigns of Richard II, Henry IV, Henry V and Henry VI*, ed. J. S. Davies, Camden, os lxiv (1856), 93.

[58] Pollard, *John Talbot*, pp. 49–53, 57–9, 71; Curry, 'Military Organisation', pp. 306, 311. It has not been possible to tell how many north-easterners accompanied the duke of Gloucester and the earl of Northumberland to France in 1475.

There was open warfare with Scotland on at least nine separate occasions during the fifteenth century, and more frequently in the later two thirds. Major conflict took place in 1436–8, 1448–9, 1455–6, 1460–4, 1480–4, and 1496–7. Richard Neville, earl of Salisbury, who twice served in France (1431–2 and 1436–7), was primarily engaged as warden of the west march for most of his life. Even his brother William divided his time between northern France and the Anglo-Scottish border, for in the mid-1440s and much of the 1450s he was actively serving as captain of the strategically placed Roxburgh.[59] William, Lord FitzHugh called out his Teesdale tenants to fight in Scotland in 1449; Sir John Conyers and Sir Thomas Harrington both led Yorkshire armies north to the border during their shrievalties (1448/9, 1455/6).[60] Ralph, Lord Greystoke even went to the trouble on 10 July 1448 to insert a clause into his indenture of retainer with Richard, earl of Salisbury that he would be 'always ready to ride and go to with and for the same Earl aswell in time of peace and of war unto all places and coasts *except the parts of France*' [my italics]. The point could hardly be made more clearly than to him war meant war with Scotland.[61] Greystoke may well have agreed with John Hardyng, a man of undoubted military experience and chivalric enthusiasm, who wrote the amended version of his verse chronicle early in the reign of Edward IV to encourage the new king to attempt the conquest of Scotland:

> I had it lever then Fraunce or Normandy,
> And all your rightes that are beyonde the sea.

It was a shame in everyone's eyes, claimed Hardyng, that Scotland should continue to defy England. Within three years, he optimistically stated, Scotland could be conquered and subdued. If that were done no one in the world would be able to resist the king. He even set out a detailed plan as to how the conquest could be achieved.[62]

It was not Edward IV but his brother Richard of Gloucester,

---

[59] *CP* x. 396; v. 282–3; *DNB* xii. 279, 304–5; R. A. Griffiths, *The Reign of Henry VI* (1981), 404–7, 734–5.   [60] See above, p. 16.

[61] Northants RO, Fitzwilliam MS 2052. I am grateful to Dr Michael K. Jones for making this and other transcripts of these documents available to me.

[62] Hardyng, *Chronicle*, pp. 412, 414, 420, 422–9.

the future Richard III, who came nearer to carrying out Hardyng's scheme. Gloucester himself ranks with Henry, Lord FitzHugh and William, Lord Fauconberg as an exemplar of northern chivalry. He gained his first substantial experience at the age of eighteen in the campaign of 1471 in which Edward IV recovered the throne. As warden of the west march he was apparently eager for war with Scotland in 1474, at a time when his brother was even more anxious to remain at peace with his northern neighbour.[63] Reputedly frustrated by the abandonment of the French campaign in 1475, Gloucester finally satisfied his desire for war against Scotland in 1480–3. When reappointed lieutenant-general for the war in 1482 his commission specifically noted that he was 'proved in the arts of war'. Once king he was unwilling to abandon his martial ambitions. In February 1484 he was calling up troops for a planned invasion of Scotland.[64] Richard's own chivalric zeal is revealed by his commissioning of a copy of Vegetius' *de re militari*, and by the conscientious exercise of his duties as Constable of England; and is demonstrated by his enthusiasm for St George in his collegiate foundations; by his patronage of the College of Arms; and by his gifts to Allhallows, Barking by the Tower, a church identified since the reign of Edward I with military causes.[65] His commitment was recognized by his contemporaries. William Worcester's *Book of Noblesse* was revised and presented to Richard, whose 'most courageous, princely disposition' was praised by the author in his preface.[66] William Caxton seems similarly to have believed that such flattery of Richard III would secure sales of his edition of Ramon Lull's *The Book of the Order of Chivalry*. In his epilogue complaining of the decay of chivalric usage, Caxton appealed to the king to institute a programme of training jousts, and dedicated the edition to·him in the hope that the king would command its reading by all young lords, knights, and gentlemen of England; 'and herein he

---

[63] N. Macdougall, *James III: a Political Study* (Edinburgh, 1982), 113, and see below, pp. 232–3.   [64] Halliwell, *Letters*, pp. 156–7.

[65] A. F. Sutton and L. Visser-Fuchs, 'Richard III's Books: IV. Vegetius' *De Re Militari*', *Ricardian*, vii. no. 99 (1987), 541–52; Sutton, 'Curious Searcher', pp. 70–2; Raine, *Middleham Statutes*, pp. 160–70; Wagner, *Heralds of England*, pp. 123 ff.; R. E. Horrox, 'Richard III and Allhallows Barking by the Tower', *The Ricardian*, vi. no. 77 (1982), 38–40.   [66] Tudor Craig, *Richard III*, p. 71.

shall do a noble and virtuous deed'.[67] Conservative critics of contemporary moral standards in the 1480s looked to Richard III for a chivalric revival. Their appeals were not misplaced.

In 1481 and 1482 Gloucester seems to have been able to inspire the lords, knights, and gentlemen of northern England to turn out in strength for his campaigns against the Scots. During these campaigns five peers (FitzHugh, Greystoke, Lovell, Lumley, and Scrope of Masham) and over fifty esquires and knights of Yorkshire, Durham, and Northumberland were dubbed bachelor or promoted banneret by Gloucester or the earl of Northumberland. Ten who were dubbed bachelor in 1481 were promoted banneret in 1482. In total nearly sixty men from the three north-eastern counties were knighted.[68] By any standard this was an impressive show of military zeal, if not even, in the number of knightings, of chivalric excess.

Many of these north-eastern lords, knights, and esquires were also, no doubt reluctantly and unhappily, veterans of the civil wars which since 1453, and especially between 1453 and 1464, had not just divided England, but, more harmfully for them, torn apart north-eastern society itself. From the skirmish at Heworth in 1453 until the final suppression of the Northumberland castles in 1464 north-easterners turned their swords on each other. After 1469, north-eastern society was more united; but the involvement in civil war did not cease altogether. Many were called upon again to don their brigandine, jack, and sallet in 1469, 1470, 1483, 1485, and 1487; but now their enemies tended to be from other parts of the realm.

Our evidence suggests that in 1484 north-easterners could confidently answer Caxton's question:

how many knights be there now in England that have the use and the exercise of a knight, that is to wit that he knoweth his horse, [and] his horse him; that is to say, he being ready at a point to have all things that belongs to a knight, an horse that is according and broken after his hand, his armour and harness meet and fitting and so forth.[69]

[67] *The Prologues and Epilogues of William Caxton*, ed. W. J. B. Crotch, EETS, os clxxvi (1928), 83.

[68] W. A. Shaw, *The Knights of England*, ii (1906), 17–21; M. A. Hicks, 'Dynastic Change and Northern Society: the Career of the Fourth Earl of Northumberland, 1470–89', *NH* 14 (1978), 103–7.

[69] Crotch, *Prologues and Epilogues*, p. 83.

There is but little evidence to show whether they could have completed his course of chivalric reading or whether they would have been interested in his programme of jousts and tournaments. Many no doubt were sufficiently experienced in the real thing to have had little need for practice in the tiltyard. One cannot determine whether they looked upon war as an unavoidable, costly, and dangerous necessity, or perceived the profession of arms as the very purpose of life. One suspects, however, that the war-hardened veterans among them took for granted as a part of day-to-day existence the code of chivalry admired by heralds and narrative poets, and believed by some civilian critics to be wanting.

PART 2

WAR AND POLITICS

9

Anglo-Scottish Relations,
1448–1485

A STATE of war existed between England and Scotland throughout the fifteenth century. Open war broke out on no fewer than
six occasions between 1448 and 1496, and was waged for a total
of eleven years in the half-century. When there was no open
warfare a fragile truce was sustained, which needed frequent
renewal and constant monitoring. Breaches of the truce were
dealt with at special march days and diets. The wardens of the
marches on both sides of the border needed to be vigilant that
cross-border cattle-thieving and other incidents did not develop
into major conflict. The chronic insecurity of the border and the
instability of truces was an ever-present backdrop to life in the
north-east: the whole of its society was drawn in when truces
collapsed and open war was renewed. Not only was the success
of kings and their deputies in defending the border itself vital to
north-easterners, but also they tended to consider frontier security, in all but the most intensive periods of civic strife, as
important as dynastic loyalty. Civil war and Scottish war became entangled at the beginning of Edward IV's reign. Modern
historians have tended to see the foreign entanglement as
secondary. But it is arguable that north-easterners in the early
1460s saw Scottish intervention as the greater threat to life and
property. The Lancastrian rebels lost support because they
joined forces with the Scots. Conversely, twenty years later
Richard of Gloucester enhanced his reputation by his success on
the border. Thus the significance of Anglo-Scottish relations for
the domestic politics of Yorkist England, especially northern
politics, is not to be underestimated.

The Treaty of Edinburgh of 1474 made an attempt to reach a
more lasting and secure amity; but this, like the more promising
peace of 1502 between Henry VII and James IV, foundered.
Neither treaty resolved the fundamental problems that lay at
the root of the hostility between the two realms: the English

claim to overlordship; the control of the debatable lands in the
west march; and the possession of Berwick. The English claim
to overlordship and the intransigence of all English kings over
the issue tends to be overlooked; but it was the main stumbling-
block to the formulation of a permanent peace. In negotiations
at Durham in September 1449, the English ambassadors insisted
that a public statement should be issued that the truce agreed
then should not prejudice the king's right to sovereignty and the
homage of Scotland. In 1457 Henry VI's overlordship was reiterated by York in an exchange of hostile letters with James II; and
in 1462 Edward IV's pact with the earl of Douglas included a
recognition of English overlordship.[1] Edward revived his claims
at the end of his reign. In a letter of 20 May 1481 to Pope Sixtus
IV justifying his planned invasion of Scotland he declared that,
his enemies having shown ill faith and disregard of honour as
well as having struck the first blow, he could no longer 'abstain
from asserting our primeval right'; and urged the Holy Father to
persuade James III to acknowledge his indubitable right of
sovereignty. A year later, in the treaty of Fotheringhay, Edward
insisted on Alexander, duke of Albany's recognition of his
supremacy as part of the price of supporting his bid to take the
throne.[2] Undoubtedly there was a measure of diplomatic
huffing behind Edward IV's pursuit of his overlordship in these
years: he hardly expected any king of Scotland actually to
recognize it. To a large extent, by reasserting his 'primeval
right', Edward was establishing a legal point that he was about to
wage a 'just war'. Nevertheless, the very fact that Edward IV
revived the claim as a means of advancing his aims in 1480
reveals what a valuable card it was. No English ruler seriously
contemplated surrendering it: only the Union of the Crowns
made it irrelevant. While it existed the two kingdoms could
never make peace; and from time to time it could be exploited to
exacerbate relationships and to justify war.

Friction between the kingdoms was sustained by border disputes. In the west march the question of the debatable land was
a continuing irritant. The first surviving record of this as a cause

[1] *CDRS*, iv. 246; *Rot. Scot.* ii. 375–482.
[2] *Calendar of State Papers, Venice*, ed. R. Brown (1864), 142–3; Rymer,
Foedera, xii. 156–7.

of tension is in 1449; from 1474 it was given more edge by the emergence of conflict over the fishing rights on the lower Esk.[3] But in the later fifteenth century the possession of Berwick, and until 1460 the English occupation of Roxburgh, were the principal focal points of conflict. Berwick had changed hands several times between 1296 and 1356, but thereafter remained in English possession for over a century. The loss of Berwick was not easily accepted by Scottish kings. After 1452, having ruthlessly disposed of the Douglases, James II turned his attention to the recovery of his southernmost town, which he besieged in 1455 and threatened once more in 1457. His objective was achieved a few months after his death, when the town and castle were ceded and handed over by Margaret of Anjou in 1461 as the price for Scottish support in her war to save the English throne for Henry VI. For James III of Scotland the retention of Berwick, secured for him during his minority, and its recovery after 1482, became an obsession not shared by all his subjects.[4] For England, control of Berwick was of vital strategic importance. The town and its castle guarded the crossing of the Tweed on the main east-coast route between the two kingdoms. Berwick in Scottish hands presented a constant threat to the peace of the far north-east; Berwick in English hands, Northumberland was more secure and Scotland itself threatened. It was, in the words of a parliamentary declaration of 1461, 'the key of the east marches of England'. No wonder that two or three years after its surrender John Hardyng scathingly wrote that Margaret and her advisers 'might well be accunted them for sots as fools that were then of no governail'.[5] For north-easteners the possession of Berwick was of more immediate and tangible concern than English overlordship.

Throughout the latter years of Henry VI there was a state of high tension on the borders, characterized by periods of open warfare interrupted by brief and fragile truces. After 1448 the balance of power tilted decisively towards Scotland. The war of 1448–9 was an embarrassing failure for English arms. Its genesis lay in the revival of the 'auld alliance' during the minority of

[3] W. M. McKenzie, 'The Debateable Land', *Scottish Historical Review*, 30–31 (1951–2), 111–13.
[4] Macdougall, *James III*, pp. 149–50.
[5] *Rot. Parl.* v. 478; Hardyng, *Chronicle*, p. 406.

James II, which was sealed by a series of marriage treaties binding Scotland with Brittany, Burgundy, and France. Tit-for-tat border raiding erupted in the summer of 1448, which prompted Henry VI to set off to visit the far north in what his advisers intended to be a show of strength. The Scots raided Northumberland shortly before Henry reached Durham (27 September); and a retaliatory raid was mounted by the English, which ended in disaster on the river Sark on 23 October, where the English force was engaged and several notable prisoners were taken. A futile attempt led by the earl of Salisbury to avenge this defeat ended ignominiously a month later. In the aftermath of these failures the Scots ravaged northern Cumberland and set fire to the suburbs of Carlisle. Not surprisingly the English were willing to restore the truce, negotiations for which were under way by May 1449. A series of short-term agreements paved the way for a full conference at Durham in September 1449, reconvened in November; this agreed a renewal of the truce ratified by James II in June 1450.[6] Little had been achieved in the war other than the humiliation of English arms.

The English position was made more precarious by the general neglect, dilapidation, and undermanning of the principal border fortresses. But the Scots were not able to press home their advantage, because they themselves faced financial problems of their own, and because in the early 1450s they were diverted by their own internal conflicts. Thus the uneasy truce was maintained. In April 1451 commissioners were appointed to enquire into the conduct of conservators of the truce; later in the year representatives of both kingdoms met at Newcastle and agreed that proclamation should be made to preserve the truce, especially in the neighbourhoods of Berwick and Roxburgh and in the debatable lands, while the truce itself should be extended for three years to 1454. Two years later, in May 1453, further negotiations led to an extension to May 1457.[7]

But by May 1455 James II, having dealt decisively if ruthlessly with the Douglases, and taking advantage of England's dissensions, felt confident enough to return to the offensive.

[6] Griffiths, *Henry VI*, pp. 409–10; *CDRS* iv. 245–8.
[7] *CDRS* iv. 250–2, 255–6.

Hearing news of the first battle of St Albans, the Scottish king opportunistically diverted an army that was to have attacked the Douglas castle of Threave near Castle Douglas, and in late June assaulted Berwick. He was repulsed; but the king had shown his hand.[8] The young James, a man who clearly saw himself in a chivalric light, was eager for war against the English. In November 1455 he wrote to Charles VII of France that the time was ripe for the two kingdoms to combine against England; France to recover Calais and he to recover Berwick.[9] Charles VII was reluctant to join the headstrong youth, who on 10 May 1456 took the provocative and bombastic step of formally renouncing the truce. James tried once more to persuade Charles VII to join him against the common enemy, and endeavoured to suborn Richard of York, Henry VI's lieutenant in the north of England.[10] Neither was to be tempted; and York in his dismissive reply to James on Henry VI's behalf pointedly refused to acknowledge James as king of Scotland. The war of words ultimately spilled over into deeds in July and August. James briefly threatened Roxburgh, and launched at least two raids into Northumberland, which York, even though he came north as far as Durham, was powerless to prevent.[11] To meet what York described as the daily forays of the Scots, late in August reinforcements were hurriedly raised in Yorkshire, and no doubt elsewhere. But the danger had passed.[12] James II had had his taste of military adventure, and was once more ready to renew the truce: he had had, as one Scottish chronicler put it, 'mickle mair [much greater] travail and charges of war' than he expected.[13]

The truce, reconfirmed in June 1457, was extended in December to 1463. But the situation remained tense and unsettled, and James II volatile. The English took steps to reinforce and

[8] Ibid. 263–4.
[9] A. I. Dunlop, *The Life and Times of James Kennedy, Bishop of St. Andrews* (Oxford, 1950), 163–4.   [10] Ibid. 166–7.
[11] Ibid. 168–9; see also J. Raine, *History and Antiquities of North Durham* (1852), pp. iv–v for the letter of Sir Ralph Grey from Roxburgh to Bishop Neville on 3 July reporting a raid launched that day and a rumour that James II was planning to lay siege to him.
[12] *The Official Correspondence of Thomas Bekynton*, ed. G. Williams, ii. (1872), 142–4; HMC, *Report on MSS of Beverley* (1900), 138; Dunlop, *James Kennedy*, p. 168–9.
[13] Dunlop, *James Kennedy*, p. 170.

strengthen the border; and in July 1458, and again in the following year, special commissions were established and meetings
arranged to deal with infractions. Developments in England
strengthened James II's hand. By the summer of 1459 Margaret
of Anjou was fully in control of English affairs, and determined
once and for all to deal with her enemies. Secret and highly
suspect negotiations took place between the Scottish and English courts, which suggest that the queen was seeking to secure
the Scottish king's help against York and his friends. At the
same time James was careful to keep open his lines of communication with York, who was apparently also bidding for his
support.[14] The opportunity for which James had no doubt been
waiting came in the summer of 1460, following the battle of
Northampton. As soon as he heard the news he laid siege once
more to the isolated and neglected English garrison in Roxburgh. Although he himself was killed when one of his guns
exploded, a week after his death the castle, which had been in
English hands since the reign of Richard II, was retaken.[15] A few
days later Wark was seized and razed to the ground. The road to
Berwick lay open. But the Scots were saved the necessity of
mounting a costly siege by the surrender of the town and castle
to them on 25 April 1461 by Margaret of Anjou, then desperate
in the aftermath of Towton, and willing to pay almost any price
for Scottish help.[16] Thus, posthumously, did the belligerent
James II ultimately succeed in recovering his kingdom's lost
possessions on its south-east border.

Edward IV inherited an unhopeful situation. The north-east
frontier was less secure than it had been at any time since the
mid-fourteenth century. The new king's prospects of reversing
recent events were diminished by continued civil war in the far
north, and the refuge given by Scotland to his rivals. During the
first three years of his reign, in which he rarely held full control
of Northumberland, Edward IV's ambitions were restricted to
ensuring that matters did not deteriorate further. By fevered
diplomacy, punctuated by outright war, the king managed to

[14] CDRS iv. 261, 263–4; Dunlop, James Kennedy, pp. 201–5.
[15] R. Nicholson, Scotland: the Later Middle Ages (Edinburgh, 1974), 395;
Dunlop, James Kennedy, pp. 207–10.
[16] Cardew, 'Anglo-Scottish Borders', p. 208; Scofield, Edward the Fourth, i.
176; Dunlop, James Kennedy, p. 221.

hold on; to detach the Scots from a Lancastrian alliance; and ultimately to suppress Lancastrian resistance in the far north. By 1464 the position was stabilized; but the initiative still lay firmly with the Scots.

In the very first months of Edward's reign, with the backing of Lancastrian exiles, the Scots threatened to take even greater advantage of England's misfortunes. After Towton the new king travelled as far north as Newcastle: a Scottish attack on Norham was feared, which in the event did not materialize. But, with Northumberland in Lancastrian hands, the river Tyne became for a few weeks the effective front line, left in the general command of Lord Fauconberg, who became captain of Newcastle. Fauconberg was nevertheless powerless to prevent a raid into County Durham two months later, which penetrated as far as Brancepeth; while on the other side of the Pennines it was left to Lord Montagu to beat off an attempt against Carlisle.[17] By the autumn of 1461, however, having secured Alnwick and Dunstanburgh, Edward IV was sufficiently in control to open negotiations with the Scots; and in October Robert, Lord Ogle, the captain of Norham, was able to conclude a year's truce.[18] English diplomacy also sought to take advantage of the continued hostility of the exiled earl of Douglas and certain dissident Highland lords to the government of the infant James III. Thus in February 1462 Edward IV reached agreement with Douglas, Ross, and Buchan to raise the Highlands, while he himself threatened to return north to 'resist the maliciousness of his outward enemies'. The pressure so created, as well perhaps as the willingness of the Regent, Mary of Guelders, to play off York against Lancaster in the pursuit of Scottish aims, led to a meeting between the Regent and Warwick at Dumfries in April, followed by formal negotiations and renewal of the truce at Carlisle in June. After Edward had been a year on the throne the far north seemed to be secure from both Scottish and Lancastrian threats.[19]

[17] C. D. Ross, *Edward IV* (1974), 46; Scofield, *Edward the Fourth*, i. 175–7, 186.   [18] Ibid. 214.

[19] Ibid. 246–9; Dunlop, *James Kennedy*, pp. 226–9; Ross, *Edward IV*, pp. 49–50. By the end of July Naworth had been seized from Lord Dacre, who had succeeded in holding out till then, and Alnwick, briefly reoccupied by Sir William Tailboys, had been retaken.

But Margaret of Anjou, who in April 1462 had slipped over to France, had in the mean time concluded a treaty with Louis XI for help in mounting a new invasion, in return for secretly ceding Calais. Although in the event only minimal French support was forthcoming, in October Margaret landed at Bamburgh, and Alnwick and Dunstanburgh once more declared for her. Taking advantage of this change of circumstance, Mary of Guelders threw her backing behind the Lancastrians yet again. To the Yorkist court the situation looked grave. Warwick returned north with a substantial army, and during December 1462 and early January 1463 mounted a determined and powerful investment of all three castles, co-ordinated from his base at Warkworth.[20] The general English expectation was that the Scots would intervene to relieve the sieges. John Paston who was in Warwick's army wrote home on 11 December:

Please it you to wit that as this day we had tidings here that the Scots will come into England within seven days after the writing of this letter for to rescue these three castles.[21]

They were still expected on 28 December, when Edward IV wrote to Chancellor Neville that the invasion was anticipated daily. Three days later reinforcements were summoned to muster on Town Moor, Newcastle, to resist it. In the event the Scots did too little too late, and only in sufficient strength to rescue the garrison of Alnwick just before the castle surrendered.[22] Thus, despite Franco-Scottish opposition, Edward IV was able to recover control of the far north.

However, in the spring of 1463 Sir Ralph Percy and Sir Ralph Grey betrayed Edward, thus reviving Scottish and Lancastrian hopes; Percy, who had been retained at Bamburgh and Dunstanburgh, declared for Henry VI, and Grey seized Alnwick on his behalf.[23] Scottish support was still forthcoming. But now the price was assistance in a combined assault on Norham, the last remaining fortress on the Tweed. From the Scottish point of view this was a more significant and feasible objective than the defence of Lancastrian positions in Northumberland, which

[20] Ross, *Edward IV*, pp. 50–1; Scofield, *Edward the Fourth*, i. 262–5.
[21] *Paston Letters*, i. 523.
[22] Ross, *Edward IV*, pp. 50–1; Scofield, *Edward the Fourth*, i. 266–7.
[23] See below, pp. 298–9.

would remain in English hands whoever was victorious. The capture of Norham would consolidate the recovery of Berwick, and secure completely the south-eastern border. The investment of Norham by a large Scottish army headed by both queens impressed contemporaries rather more than it has recent historians. On 5 July Edward IV, recognizing the seriousness of the threat, sought money from the Exchequer to pay for the defence of the realm. Ten days later, from Northampton, on his way to the north parts, he reported the attack to Convocation, and was voted the desired tenth. At the same time the Common Council of the City of London stumped up 500 marks towards the victualling of his army going to Scotland. On 11 July, the earl of Warwick, nearer the scene at Middleham, wrote to the archbishop of York asking him to call out his clergy to resist the Scots. The siege, however, lasted only eighteen days. Lord Ogle and his garrison were relieved by the earl with his hurriedly raised northern levies; the earl, according to an account given in a letter by Lord Hastings, followed this up with a raid into Scotland, the biggest launched for many a year. Norham was saved by Warwick's prompt and decisive action.[24]

Yet the position in the far north was still grave. Lancastrian rebels were in possession of the Northumberland castles; they were still backed by Scotland. Accordingly, Edward IV renewed his call for men to be at Newcastle on 13 September 'towards our voyage against our enemies of Scotland'; although by that date he in fact had only reached York, in whose county he stayed for the following four months.[25] It is impossible to tell how serious was Edward's intention to attack Scotland in the autumn of 1463. His subjects later 'grouched sore' that the subsidies voted to pay for the projected campaign were not so spent.[26] An army and navy were gathered; but neither went into action. There were several reasons for this. One was that, even with a parliamentary grant, Edward did not have the resources to sustain a campaign. But circumstances were changing too. In October an English embassy to France secured a truce with Louis XI by which the French king agreed to withdraw all support from both

[24] Ross, *Edward IV*, pp. 53–5; Scofield, *Edward the Fourth*, i. 290–2; Dunlop, *James Kennedy*, pp. 236–7; Macdougall, *James III*, p. 60.

[25] Ross, *Edward IV*, p. 54; Scofield, *Edward the Fourth*, i. 292–3, 309.

[26] Warkworth, *Chronicle*, p. 3.

Scotland and Lancastrians. And at approximately the same time the earl of Douglas, who had been successfully harassing the west marches of Scotland on behalf of Edward, was defeated, and many of his lieutenants, including his brother, were captured and executed.[27] Thus, while the military situation looked less hopeful, the prospect for a renewal of the truce brightened now that Scotland stood alone.

Accordingly, on 5 December, letters of safe conduct were issued to a Scottish embassy, which travelled to York and on 4 December concluded a temporary truce, and agreed to meet again at Newcastle early in March. This meeting was not in fact held, but postponed to 20 April at York. It was while marching north to Norham to meet and escort the Scottish ambassadors south that Lord Montagu beat off an attack by the Lancastrians at Hedgeley Moor (25 April). After some delay, and after the crushing defeat of the Lancastrians at Hexham on 15 May, a more permanent truce was finally agreed at York on 1 June, ratified by Edward IV two days later; this was to last fifteen years. With many of its leaders dead, and abandoned by the Scots, the Lancastrian resistance in Northumberland crumbled for the third and last time. By the final week of July all the Northumberland castles were back under royal control.[28]

The time taken by Edward IV to secure control of the far north at the beginning of his reign has troubled his historians. While it is no longer accepted that he was irresponsibly more concerned with enjoying the fruits of office, his judgement in so frequently pardoning known Lancastrian sympathizers and allowing them to remain in positions of trust in the far north which they promptly abused, is still questioned.[29] That the king made matters worse cannot be denied. But the king's action becomes more explicable if it is understood that he and his advisers were as concerned about the threat from Scotland as about the threat from continuing Lancastrian resistance. With Berwick in Scottish hands and only Norham in English possession on the Tweed, the north-east lay open to Scottish attack. Bamburgh and Dunstanburgh are close to the Scottish border, and a long

---

[27] Scofield, *Edward the Fourth*, i. 309.

[28] Warkworth, *Chronicle*, pp. 37–9; Ross, *Edward IV*, p. 61; Scofield, *Edward the Fourth*, i. 336–7.

[29] Ross, *Edward IV*, pp. 51–2, 62.

way even from Newcastle. The king, and no doubt Warwick and Montagu too, were unwilling to use cannon against strategically vital castles now on the front line. It was not until after the treaty of York that he was prepared 'to suffer any great gun laid unto the wall, and be shot and prejudice the wall' of Bamburgh, which 'marches so nigh his ancient enemies of Scotland'.[30]

It was equally desirable to win over the leaders of Northumberland society to garrison them. The king needed them to defend their country more than he feared their potential treachery. Moreover, it should be borne in mind that there was a reasonable chance that erstwhile north-country rebels and enemies, men such as Sir Ralph Percy and Sir Humphrey Neville, would be prepared to forget old enmities in the face of the Scottish threat—as Scottish rebels tended to do in the face of English invasion.[31] What Edward IV took time to grasp was that Percy and Neville put their loyalty to the house of Lancaster (and their hatred of the Nevilles of Middleham) before their distrust and fear of the Scots. Only when they had betrayed him twice, and he had secured a lasting truce with the Scots, was he willing, no doubt with Montagu's encouragement, to deal decisively and ruthlessly with the traitors.[32]

While Edward IV was himself a frequent visitor to the northeast (April 1461; November 1462 to January 1463; September 1463 to January 1464; May to July 1464), and called Parliament to meet twice in York (February 1463 and February 1464), the diplomatic and military burden fell largely on the shoulders of the Neville brothers. It was a burden they bore with distinction. Although it should not be overlooked that they were pursuing their own self-interest, and prosecuting with vigour their own feud against members of the Percy and senior Neville families, as wardens of the marches they were also defending the north against the Scots. In this they proved to be notably more successful than their father. Montagu's prompt action saved

---

[30] Warkworth, *Chronicle*, pp. 37–8.
[31] A. Grant, *Independence and Nationhood: Scotland, 1306–1469* (1984), 199.
[32] See below, p. 298. For a reassessment of Edward IV's policy towards the rebels which approaches the topic from a difficult angle, but reaches similar conclusions, see M. A. Hicks, 'Edward IV, the Duke of Somerset and Lancastrian Loyalism in the North', *NH* 20 (1984), 23–37.

Carlisle in May 1461; Warwick with Montagu recovered the Northumberland castles in the winter of 1462–3, in the face of a Scottish threat of intervention. Warwick rescued Norham in July 1463. Thereafter it was Warwick and Montagu, with their retainers, who held the line of the Tyne, while Scots and Lancastrians enjoyed undisputed possession of virtually the whole of Northumberland. Warwick in particular was tireless, constantly on the move from one part of the kingdom to another, prompt to rush north when a new crisis broke. From the point of view of the inhabitants of Durham and Yorkshire the years following the cession of Berwick had been perilous. The potential had existed for a repetition of the Scottish raids and the devastation of Edward II's reign. This did not happen partly because the Scots lacked resources and effective leadership, and partly because Edward IV and the Nevilles recognized the danger, and effectively contained the threat north of the Tyne. Not only Edward IV but also the people of north-eastern England south of the Tyne had cause to be grateful to the Neville brothers in 1461–4.

Even though the immediate threat to the north had been relieved by the end of 1464, with Berwick in Scottish hands the long-term security of the eastern border was fragile. The only defensible castle on the Tweed was Norham: and Norham belonged to the bishop of Durham, not the king. Its constable was an episcopal appointee. To maintain his garrison, thirty-strong in time of war in 1482, he received the bishop's income from North Durham (valued at £194 p.a. in 1478/9) during peacetime, supplemented by £200 from the exchequer at Durham during war.[33] Between 1461 and the recovery of Berwick in August 1482 the king understandably took an interest in the castle. At the height of the crisis of the 1460s, between December 1462 and April 1464, it was in the king's hands as a result of the confiscation of the bishop's temporalities: a desire to be absolutely sure of Norham may itself have been one of the reasons for seizing the temporalities.[34] From 1476, after the arrival of William Dudley as bishop, Edward IV took an over-

[33] Durh. 3/49/15; 55/8; R. L. Storey, *Thomas Langley and the Bishopric of Durham, 1406–1437*, 145.
[34] See below, pp. 294–8.

sight of its maintenance. In September 1477 a royal commission was appointed, headed by Alexander Lee, king's almoner and ambassador to Scotland, and Sir Richard Tunstall, knight of the body, to survey and supervise the repair of all the castles and manors of the palatinate. This commission, given full backing by the bishop, carried out its work over the following six months, Lee spending almost all the month of September at Norham.[35] Three years later, in the spring of 1480, when war between England and Scotland was renewed, Edward IV despatched forty-six guns and other munitions to Norham from the royal arsenal at Nottingham.[36] And in March 1482, Sir John Middleton of Belsay was appointed constable for two years by the bishop 'at the contemplation, desire and request of the king'.[37] Norham was clearly too important to be left entirely to the bishop.

From 1464 for a decade or more it was in the interest of both kingdoms to maintain peace. The Scots were content to rest on their laurels: the English were in no position to resume fighting. Further negotiation at Newcastle from 4 December to 12 December 1464 led to an extension of the truce to 31 October 1519. The readiness with which thereafter Scottish notables were issued with safe conducts to pass through England suggests the development of a new amity.[38] Moreover, the English civil wars of 1469–71 passed by without major Scottish intervention; in part because coincidentally in these years James III was preoccupied with the establishment of his own personal control of his kingdom.[39] Once Edward IV recovered his throne, the two kings were of one mind to develop closer ties between their realms: Edward so as to secure his rear before launching his projected invasion of France, James so as to secure Berwick. After three years' negotiation, in which Bishop Booth of Durham seems to have played a prominent role, the Treaty of Edinburgh was sealed in October 1474; this settled a marriage between the eighteen-month-old heir to the Scottish throne and

[35] Durham, Church Commission, 189830, m.4.
[36] Scofield, *Edward the Fourth*, ii. 279; J. H. Ramsay, *Lancaster and York*, ii. (Oxford, 1892), 437.
[37] Durh. 3/55/8.
[38] *CDRS* iv. 270–80.
[39] Macdougall, *James III*, p. 88.

the four-year-old princess Cecily of York, as well as a confirmation of the truce to 1519. The high hopes of the two kings were expressed in the preamble of the treaty:

> this noble Isle called Great Britain cannot be kept and maintained better in wealth and prosperity than such things to be practised and concluded between the kings of both realms of England and Scotland whereby they and their subjects might be assured to live in peace, love and tenderness.[40]

But the new-found friendship between the two realms was only skin-deep. Tensions existed beneath the surface, which erupted into open war once again five years later. Persuading borderers who were accustomed to a state of war and mutual hostility to live in love and tenderness was almost impossible. The magnitude of the problem is revealed by the efforts made in the early 1470s to conserve the truce more rigorously. On 28 September 1473 a meeting of the conservators at Alnwick decided to hold more frequent march days, and established a series of six special diets to be held at different points along the border before 3 December, at which all complaints and breaches since May 1472 should be settled; and at the same time agreed that all illegally taken men and ships should be returned.[41] Two issues which prompted this fresh effort to make a reality out of the truce were recent conflicts between the men of Tynedale and Redesdale and those of Liddesdale, which had led to a heated correspondence between James III and the earl of Northumberland, and the looting of the Scottish ship 'Le Salvator', which had been wrecked off Bamburgh earlier in the year. The question of 'Le Salvator' was specifically dealt with at Alnwick, where Richard, duke of Gloucester, as Admiral of England, was charged through his lieutenant based at Norham to negotiate with the lieutenant of his counterpart, Alexander, duke of Albany at Berwick.[42] But nothing came of these negotiations. In July 1474 the matter was taken out of the duke of Gloucester's

---

[40] Rymer, *Foedera*, xi. 820ff.; *CDRS* iv. 289; *Rot. Scot.* ii. 446. For Booth's employment as ambassador and negotiator see ibid. 470, 430–1, 433–4, 437, 443–4, 445–6.

[41] *CDRS* ii. 285–6.

[42] Rymer, *Foedera*, xi. 788–91; *CDRS* iv. 285–6; Macdougall, *James III*, p. 116.

hands and added to the charge of the ambassadors treating for renewal of the truce with James III. It was settled by them on 25 October as a prelude to the sealing of the Treaty of Edinburgh itself.[43]

The treaty also specified that both kings would cease to give assistance to each other's rebels and traitors. For Edward IV this meant no longer supporting the earl of Douglas, who received a pension of £200 p.a.; or Robert, Lord Boyd, whose pension was 200 marks. For James III this required his abandoning the cause of John de Vere, earl of Oxford. But the agreement was to no avail; for as early as July 1475 James III and the earl of Northumberland were writing to each other objecting to the 'resetting' of Boyd in Alnwick, and the continued harbouring of Oxford in Scotland. Moreover on 1 February 1476 Edward IV formally renewed his annuity to Boyd for seven years from Michaelmas following.[44] Other breaches of the truce continued, notwithstanding the treaty, and almost immediately complaints were made to Edward IV that march days and diets for resolving disputes were not being held.[45]

But the efforts of both kings to establish a more lasting peace between their realms were ultimately undermined by their greater subjects, who on both sides of the border were opposed to it. On the Scottish side the king's brother Albany led the opposition; and he was rumoured as early as July 1475 to be planning to make trouble. On the English side Edward IV's brother, Richard of Gloucester, was equally intransigent. In April 1474 a general alert had been called in the Scottish marches, and Albany had mustered a force at Lauder to resist an anticipated raid by the English duke.[46] In the event no such raid took place; but Edward IV soon found his brother to be a truculent and unwilling executant of the terms of the Treaty of Edinburgh.

The royal instructions to Alexander Lee, king's chaplain and almoner, and ambassador to Scotland, for his embassy in March 1475, reveal Gloucester's attitude.[47] Lee was to apologize to

[43] *CDRS* iv. 288.
[44] Ibid. 291, 293, 408–10.
[45] Ibid. 291; Ellis, *Original Letters*, ser. 1, i. 17.
[46] Macdougall, *James III*, p. 113.
[47] BL, Cotton MS, Vespasian c.xvi, fos. 121^v–126.

James III for the failure of the king's commissioners to appear on 6 March at a diet to resolve the issue of possession of a fishlock on the Esk in the Debatable Lands. He was to explain that this was because the English commissioners had been attending Parliament. He was also ordered to make restitution for two acts of piracy against Scottish ships. If the king of Scotland complained that failure so far to make restitution was because the English had failed to hold march days, he was to offer such excuses as the wardens of the marches, Gloucester and Northumberland, gave him, but to assure him that the wardens had been ordered hastily to hold them. Lee was commanded 'to take his way' by the two lords, and not only to show them the instructions 'concerning the sea' but also to reprimand them for not holding meetings set and agreed at Edinburgh, of which agreement they both had copies. Moreover, he was to tell them both to hold march days every fifteen days according to the terms of the treaty. Having given these instructions to the wardens, Lee was to assure the king of Scotland that the king had made arrangements for keeping the peace on the borders after his departure to France and,

hath so ordained and disposed for the rule of the marches in his absence that he trusteth there shall be of his part no cause of trouble nor breach given to the hurt or derogation of the truce. And in this point [he] shall advertise my said lords of Gloucester and Northumberland in his going by them that they, according the king's pleasure for his honour and surety, proved in this case as it appertaineth.[48]

Gloucester himself was further ordered to hold an admiralty court at Alnwick on 8 May at which complaints by the English against the Scots would be heard, and to assure the Admiral of Scotland that a similar session would be fixed for a later date at which Scottish complaints against the English could be heard. Lee was to inform Gloucester that the king 'trusts his brother of Gloucester will set a speedy sad and just direction therein for the peace and rest of his subjects'. And as a postscript Edward added a comment concerning piracy against two Scottish ships, of which one was robbed by the *Mayflower*: 'the king will that my lord of Gloucester be spoken with in that part considering that

<hr />

[48]   BL, Cotton MS, c.xvi, fos. 125ᵛ–126.

the said ship was his at that time'.[49] Thus were the ducal knuckles severely rapped. Not only had he been dilatory in carrying out his duties as warden and Admiral, but also he himself had been personally guilty of a breach of the truce. With the king's brother himself, the Admiral and one of the wardens, so clearly reluctant to enforce the truce, there was little chance of the pious hopes of the Treaty of Edinburgh being realized.

For the two kings, however, there remained the prospect of the marriage of their children. To keep the hopes of peace alive it was essential that, under the terms of the treaty, the annual instalments of Princess Cecily's dower be paid. The first three payments were to be of 2,000 marks; thereafter they were to be of 1,000 marks, to be delivered to St Giles, Edinburgh every Candlemas. The king's agent and ambassador in this vital and hazardous task was Alexander Lee. Every year between 1475 and 1479 he travelled north to Norham, where elaborate and precise arrangements were made for his passage into Scotland. It was laid down that the English mission should arrive at the castle on 30 January, and that a Scottish escort should come up from Berwick on the opposite bank of the Tweed on the following morning. The English party, of no more than forty persons, would not cross until sealed letters of credence from the king of Scotland were produced by the escort and handed over to the lieutenant or constable of the castle. Only then, protected by safe conducts, would Lee and his party enter Scotland.[50] Clearly no risks were to be taken in an unsettled border region with the ambassador's valuable cargo. For the first two years, 1475 and 1476, the instalments were delivered promptly on time. In 1477 Lee was delayed until April; in 1478 until after 31 March, when a second escort was appointed by James III; and in 1479 until March. 1479 was the last payment. In all 8,000 marks of a contracted 20,000 were paid before the final rupture of the truce.[51]

There was no single reason for the collapse of the truce in 1479–80. Edward IV, having come to terms with Louis XI, no longer had a pressing need for an undisturbed northern frontier. Louis XI, for his part, seems to have been encouraging James III

---

[49] Ibid.   [50] *CDRS* iv. 410–11.
[51] Ibid. 290–7.

to be more aggressive.[52] It was, however, not the kings, but their subjects, especially their brothers, who on either side of the border incited the breaches of the truce which led ultimately to the outbreak of war. Both Richard of Gloucester and Alexander of Albany were, as we have seen, reluctant accepters of the Treaty of Edinburgh. Albany in particular seems to have taken the initiative in 1479, perhaps in response to Louis XI's secret blandishments—for he fled to France in May 1479, and at the trial subsequently held in his absence he was accused of deliberately violating the treaty.[53] Conditions on the border deteriorated rapidly during the autumn of that year, when major breaches of the truce appear to have been committed by Scottish borderers, allies perhaps of the duke of Albany, whom James III was unable to control.[54] Edward IV held James responsible; and when Alexander Lee travelled to Scotland early in 1480 on his annual embassy he brought not a further instalment of the dowry, but a demand for reparations. Threatening retaliation if his demands were not met, Edward insisted that his terms for the maintenance of the truce were the handing over of James's son and heir, as a pledge that the marriage would take place, and the restoration of Berwick to England.[55] These demands were rejected outright and both sides made active preparation for full-scale war. On 12 May Gloucester was appointed the king's lieutenant-general to command the northern counties, an office immediately extended by Bishop Dudley to include his palatinate; on 20 June royal commissions of array were issued for the defence of Yorkshire, Cumberland, and Northumberland, followed on 4 July by an episcopal commission for Durham, in which the defence of the marches following the breaches of the truce by the Scots was specified.[56] At this stage the English seem still to have been on the defensive. Fighting does not seem to have broken out until the autumn.

It is difficult, because of the inadequacy of the evidence, to unravel the precise chronology of raid and counter-raid in 1480 and 1481. Three incompletely dated letters, two from the earl of Northumberland and one from Richard of Gloucester, present a

---

[52] Ross, *Edward IV*, p. 278.   [53] Macdougall, *James III*, pp. 128–9.
[54] Ibid. 143.   [55] *CDRS* iv. 412–15.
[56] *Rot. Scot.* ii. 458; *CPR, 1476–85*, 205, 213–14; Durh. 3/54/4.

particular problem. Northumberland wrote two letters on 7 September to Robert Plumpton and the mayor of York calling upon them to send men to a rendezvous on Monday next to resist the Scots, who *are* entered into Northumberland. On 8 September Gloucester wrote to York that he and Northumberland had intelligence that the Scots '*intend* this Saturday night' (my italics) to enter in three hosts into all three marches, and calling for men to join him at Durham on the following Thursday.[57] P. M. Kendall suggested that all three belonged to 1481, and not 1480, to which they were allocated by their editors, Stapleton and Raine, because they are linked with minutes of the York council on 8 and 9 September 1481 making preparation for 'this voyage against the Scots' and delaying departure from Monday until Tuesday.[58] However, it is puzzling that both Gloucester and Northumberland called independently at the same time on the city of York; and even more so that Northumberland in the earlier letter reported that the Scots were already in Northumberland, while Gloucester a day later knew only that they were about to descend on Saturday night. It seems more probable therefore that the letters from Gloucester and Northumberland date from different years. Thus Gloucester might have written on Friday 8 September 1480 about an attack he had just heard was to be launched the following night, and Northumberland on Friday 7 September 1481 to both Plumpton and the city about a raid already under way. If this is so, the council minutes of 8 and 9 September 1481 would be a response to a request from Northumberland alone; and Gloucester's intelligence about concerted raids along the length of the border, and his mustering of troops at Durham on Thursday 14 September, may well relate to a raid reported by a Scottish chronicle by the earl of Angus on Bamburgh in September 1480.[59] But whatever the correct allocation of these letters, it is clear from other evidence that in August 1480 York was already on the alert, and had on the last day of the month been warned by the duke of his own intention to attack the Scots. And indeed

[57] *YCR* i. 34–5; *Plumpton Correspondence*, p. 40.
[58] P. M. Kendall, *Richard III* (1955), 457.
[59] Macdougall, *James III*, pp. 144–5. In her forthcoming edition of the *York House Books*, Dr Attreed accepts Kendall's dating. I am grateful to her for the opportunity to look at her draft text and for discussing the problem with me.

incursions into Scotland, presumably by Gloucester's levies, were reported by the Milanese ambassador in France on 29 October.[60]

Over the winter Edward IV determined to mount a major offensive. Between February and April 1481 considerable time and expense was devoted to arranging the recruitment, equipping, victualling, and transporting of an army the king declared it his intention to lead in person, and a navy under the command of Lord Howard, which was to support him. At least £18,000 was committed; and to find the money the remnant of a subsidy outstanding from 1475 was collected, a tenth was voted by the Convocation of Canterbury, and a benevolence was demanded.[61] On 20 May 1481 Edward wrote to the Pope justifying his projected action in self-righteous terms, and asserting his sovereignty.[62] But nothing came of all this fevered activity and bluster apart from the harassment of the Scottish coast by Lord Howard in late May and early August.[63] It was left to Gloucester and Northumberland, with northern levies rather than the royal army, to make an attempt on Berwick. This siege, like so much of the action in this year, remains a shadowy affair. The lords were before Berwick on 22 August, when they knighted many of their captains. But Northumberland was apparently back in Yorkshire by 7 September, hurriedly raising fresh troops to march north as soon as possible to face the Scots who had entered his march; perhaps the same borderers who, according to one Scottish source, took much loot and many prisoners back with them. According to the same source Berwick was besieged throughout the winter, and 'great troubles and invasions was [sic] between the two realms all that year'.[64]

The English war effort was revitalized in 1482 by the successful suborning of Alexander, duke of Albany, James III's dissident

[60] YCR i. 34; *Calendar of State Papers, Milan*, ed. A. B. Hinds, i. (1902), 244. See also R. Benson and H. Hatcher, *Old and New Sarum* (Salisbury, 1843), 199 for a royal statement confirming the raid. The priory of Durham provided a contingent of its tenants to serve under Gloucester against the Scots on an unspecified occasion between Pentecost 1480 and Pentecost 1481. This could well have been it. (Durham, Dean and Chapter, Bursar's Account, 1480/1).

[61] Ross, *Edward IV*, pp. 279–81.

[62] *Calendar of State Papers, Venice*, i. 142–3.

[63] Macdougall, *James III*, pp. 145–8; Ross, *Edward IV*, p. 282.

[64] W. C. Metcalfe, *A Book of Knights Banneret, Knights of the Bath and Knights Bachelor* (1855), 5–6; YCR i. 34; J. Lesley, *History of Scotland* (Bannatyne Club, Edinburgh, 1830), 45.

brother, who landed in England in April. An agreement reached between Edward IV and Albany, formalized at Fotheringhay on 11 June, set down that Edward would recognize Albany as lawful king of Scotland and assist him to take the throne in exchange for homage, the return of Berwick, and the cession of a significant stretch of land in south-west Scotland to Edward.[65] For the second year running a powerful army was raised, but at Fotheringhay Edward decided to delegate its command to Gloucester, who had already in May inaugurated the campaigning season by a successful raid into south-west Scotland as far as Dumfries.[66] He was once again appointed lieutenant-general. The army under his leadership marched immediately north, reaching York on 18 June, and by mid-July arrived before Berwick. Faced by such overwhelming might the town immediately surrendered, although the castle stood out. Leaving a small force to invest the castle the main army marched on to Edinburgh unopposed, for James III had faced a mutiny when mustering his troops at Lauder, and had been taken prisoner. The way was open for Albany to be installed as king. However, at the eleventh hour Albany switched allegiance. He came to an agreement with his brother and the Scottish lords which left the government of the kingdom in his hands. There was no alternative for the English but to withdraw, which they did, leaving the city of Edinburgh itself unmolested. Returning to Berwick by mid-August, the whole army succeeded in reducing the castle. And thus after twenty-one years Berwick came once more under English control.[67]

But the war did not end in 1482 with this success. In November writs were issued to summon Parliament to vote taxes for 'the hasty defence of the realm'.[68] During the session early in 1483 Edward IV rewarded his victorious brother handsomely with the creation of a palatinate in Cumberland and all the lands in south-west Scotland (Liddesdale, Eskdale, Ewesdale, Annandale, and even Clydesdale) ceded to him by Albany in the Treaty of Fotheringhay. In the preamble to the Act it was declared that

[65] Rymer, *Foedera*, xii. 156–7.

[66] BL, Cotton MS, Julius B xii, fo. 305; *YCR* i. 54–5; Alison Hanham, *The Cely Letters, 1472–1488* (Oxford, 1975), 164.

[67] Ross, *Edward IV*, pp. 288–90; Scofield, *Edward the Fourth*, ii. 344–8; Macdougall, *James III*, pp. 152–5, 168–70.   [68] Ross, *Edward IV*, p. 290 n. 3.

it was Gloucester's intention to continue the war in the next campaigning season, presumably to make good his claim to these lands.[69] Prospects for the new season were enhanced by a rapid deterioration in relationships between James III and Albany which led to a second defection and flight, but not before the duke had surrendered Dunbar to the English in April 1483.[70] Edward IV's death intervened before any advantage could be taken; and the dramatic events of the summer in London, whereby Gloucester himself became king, effectively put paid to any English campaign. But, while he entertained negotiations for a truce at the end of 1483,[71] the new king remained, once he had suppressed rebellion against him in the autumn, as enthusiastic as ever for continuing the war. On 18 February Richard III declared his determination 'to address us in person with host royal' towards Scotland, and called for a muster of troops at Newcastle by the end of May.[72] He himself travelled north at the end of April for the summer, spending part of the time at Scarborough fitting out a fleet to victual and replenish Dunbar against Scottish attempts at blockade.[73]

But, no doubt because of shortage of money, the threatened major invasion never materialized. Instead, the king yet again exploited Albany, whom he sent into south-west Scotland. But on 22 July Albany was decisively defeated at Lochmaben, and fled for the last time to France.[74] Even before the defeat at Lochmaben Richard III had taken up James III's repeated proposals for a truce; and negotiations now rapidly followed. In September Scottish ambassadors arrived at Nottingham; and on the twentieth of the month a three-year truce was agreed.[75] The truce held for the rest of Richard's reign. Thus ended a five-year war: a war which had effectively wrested the initiative in Anglo-Scottish relations back to England, which now held both Berwick and Dunbar.

[69] *Rot. Parl.* vi. 204.
[70] Ross, *Edward IV*, p. 293; Macdougall, *James III*, pp. 180–88.
[71] *Rot. Scot.* ii. 461.
[72] J. O. Halliwell, *Letters of the Kings of England* (1848), 156–7.
[73] Edwards, *Itinerary*, pp. 18–22; Macdougall, *James III*, pp. 209–10.
[74] Ross, *Richard III*, p. 193; Macdougall, *James III*, pp. 210–13.
[75] Ross, *Richard III*, p. 193; Macdougall, *James III*, pp. 213–14. For a more specific, if brief, discussion of relations between the 2 monarchs, see Norman Macdougall, 'Richard III and James III', in Hammond, *Richard III, Loyalty, Lordship and Law*, pp. 166–7.

Although the later stages of the war of 1480–4 were desultory and inconclusive, it was without doubt the most sustained and costly period of Anglo-Scottish warfare since the early part of the century. Professor Ross, who was puzzled by the extent to which the king became entangled in a war which diverted his attention from more important continental foreign affairs, may perhaps have underestimated its significance and overlooked its political context.[76] In particular, the jaundiced view of the Crowland Chronicler, who wrote later that Edward was ultimately disappointed by the achievement of a campaign in 1482 which cost so much money, has distorted perceptions. The Crowland Chronicler, writing in 1486 with little sympathy for Richard III or understanding of northern England, commented disparagingly on the *chevauchée* to Edinburgh and the taking of Berwick—a trifle which he felt was not worth the cost of its recovery, and which he remembered consumed 10,000 marks a year for its safe keeping.[77] On this he is misleading. While it is true that until the Truce of Nottingham in 1484 the annual wages of the garrison of 600 came to over £6,000 per annum, during the first ten years of Henry VII's reign the annual cost during time of truce was only a little over £2,000.[78] And it was a matter of opinion as to whether the recovery of Berwick was an insignificant military achievement. Certainly, it was a major, if not *the* major, objective of the war. From his original ultimatum in 1480 the question of Berwick was emphasized in all Edward IV's pronouncements. As Dr Macdougall has recently shown, the English army in 1482 was only contracted for a short campaign, the focal point of which was likely to be the siege of Berwick.[79] Edward's first reactions to its recovery were exultant. Writing to Pope Sixtus IV on 25 August 1482 he stated

The chief advantage of the whole expedition is the reconquest of the town and castle of Berwick, which one and twenty years ago before our

[76] Ross, *Edward IV*, p. 294.   [77] *Crowland Chronicle*, p. 149.
[78] R. E. Horrox, 'Financial Memoranda of the Reign of Edward V', in *Camden Miscellany*, xxix, Camden, 4th ser., xxxiv (1987), 215–16. In the autumn of 1482 agreement was reached to pay Northumberland £5,220 a year as captain, and considerable expenditure was incurred in victualling the place (Scofield, *Edward the Fourth*, ii. 349 n. 4).
[79] Macdougall, *James III*, pp. 154–4. But see however Dr Macdougall's refutation of the idea that the recapture of Berwick was the main purpose of the campaign, in 'Richard III and James III', p. 161.

coronation went over to the Scots; but previously it was in the uninter-
rupted possession of our forefathers, whose just title having descended
to us, we were bound to recover what was ours.[80]

But it was not just a matter of honour and regal pride. Berwick,
as Edward well knew, was the gateway to north-eastern England; and as long as it remained in Scottish hands his northern
subjects were threatened and the security of his realm at risk.
For this reason, in the summer of 1483, £1,000 was allocated by
the hard-pressed government for the repair of the walls of the
town and castle, which had been breached in the siege of 1482.[81]

Edward IV surely understood the strategic value of Berwick;
but his brother Richard of Gloucester was even more keenly
aware of its importance. Insufficient attention has been paid to
Gloucester's probable role in shaping the direction of the war, or
in influencing the king's decision to make a major commitment
to it. Above all else this was Gloucester's war. As we have seen,
as early as 1474 and 1475 the young duke revealed his lack of
enthusiasm for the policy of *détente*. The collapse of the truce in
1479 was a vindication of his belligerent attitude; and his
pressure may well explain the rapid change in his brother's
attitude in 1479–80. As lieutenant-general for the war in
1480–1 and 1482–3 he no doubt helped to determine strategy, as
well as taking command of troops in the field. His was probably
an influential voice at the Westminster council meeting of
November 1480, at which Edward IV resolved to mount a major
invasion of Scotland in the following season. He was clearly a
prominent figure in the negotiations which led to the Treaty of
Fotheringhay in June 1482. And he was lavishly rewarded in
1483. Indeed it can be argued that Edward IV's failure—twice
—to lead his army in person stemmed from the fact that he was
only reluctantly persuaded to give his backing to a major campaign; his reluctance may also explain his reported anger when
he later realized that the Scottish entanglement had undermined his continental policy. But, whatever reservations he
may have had, Edward IV had little choice but to give his brother

---

[80] *Calendar of State Papers, Venice*, i. 146.
[81] Horrox, 'Financial Memoranda', p. 225. Macdougall, 'Richard III and James
III', pp. 161–2, suggests that Berwick was only of importance to the English as
well as the Scots as a matter of prestige.

his head; for after the destruction of Clarence in 1478 he could little afford to alienate him. It is plausible therefore that the explanation for Edward IV's misjudged and irresolute foreign policy in his last four years lies in the influence of Richard of Gloucester, who had for long wished to mount a war against Scotland, and whose pressure after 1478 was, for internal political reasons, irresistible.[82]

From the point of view of northern England, Gloucester's achievement in the field was anything but trivial. He was not able to prevent all Scottish raids into England. But, as his letter of 8 September 1480 shows, he had established an effective system of intelligence, was alert to threats of attack, and was prompt in raising troops to meet such threats. No Scottish force penetrated more than twenty miles into England during the war. On the other hand, the war was carried most effectively to Scotland. The preamble to the Act of Parliament of January 1483 offered fulsome praise of the duke, who:

> by his manifold and diligent labours and devoirs, hath subdued great part of the west borders of Scotland, adjoining to England and by the space of thirty miles and more, thereby at this time not inhabited with Scots, and hath got and achieved diverse parcels thereof to be under the obedience of our said sovereign Lord, not only to the great rest and ease of the inhabitants of the said west marches, but also to the great surety and ease of the north parts of England.[83]

The report of George Cely in July/August 1482 that forty-four towns and villages in Scotland, as well as Dumfries, had been burnt may well refer to this same action. Alternatively it might refer to the march on Edinburgh in July, for Cely also commented cryptically that the king had sent Albany into Scotland, and within a month the devastation had been caused.[84] Raids on this scale, with such a level of destruction, had not been seen for decades. Indeed, from the point of view of northerners, neither was the march on Edinburgh a failure, nor the decision of Gloucester quickly to return to England 'strange'.[85] Whether

---

[82] But see Ross, *Edward IV*, pp. 289–90.
[83] *Rot. Parl.* vi. 204.   [84] Hanham, *Cely Letters*, p. 164.
[85] Ross, *Edward IV*, p. 287. Macdougall, on the contrary, points to the impossibility of the situation facing Gloucester on his arrival in Edinburgh, and finds it difficult to see what more he could have done ('Richard III and James III', pp. 164–5).

James III or Albany was king, or whether Edward IV secured the return of the dowry payments, was of no concern to the bowmen and billmen who accompanied Gloucester and Northumberland. What did impress them was the opportunity for looting along the way, even though they were to be denied in Edinburgh itself. To the Crowland chronicler the campaign may have been a useless squandering of resources, but to the men of the north, to whom border raids were more important than royal ambitions, it was a raid on a grand scale. Even thirty years later Lord Dacre, who at the time was a boy, remembered a great raid of the duke and Northumberland into Teviotdale, which he promised Henry VIII he would attempt to emulate.[86] To cap it all there was the recovery of Berwick, which would henceforth make it far more difficult for the Scots to enter at will into coastal Northumberland. The inhabitants of the north parts would heartily have applauded Edward IV's appraisal of his brother that 'his success was so proven that he alone would suffice to chastise the whole kingdom of Scotland'.[87]

From the perspective of north-eastern England, therefore, the Anglo-Scottish war of 1480–4 was of major significance. Since 1448 the balance of advantage had tilted Scotland's way. The loss of Roxburgh and Berwick in quick succession in 1460–1 had left northern England dangerously vulnerable to major Scottish invasion. Fortunately between 1461 and 1464 the Scots had not been able to take as much advantage as they might. In the 1460s and 1470s a policy of peace and *rapprochement* had suited the ends of both James III, who was anxious to retain the advantage he had inherited, and Edward IV, who was content to hold the line while he followed a more adventurous policy in France. The war of 1480–4 put an end to this, and reversed the trend of 1448–61. Edward IV had been persuaded reluctantly to change his policy towards Scotland, although he put the best face possible on the achievements of his brother. But this was Richard of Gloucester's war and Richard of Gloucester's victory. He strengthened the security of the border, and brought back a sense of pride to northern English society by his exploits against the old enemy. Thereafter England once again held the initiative in Anglo-Scottish relations.

[86] *Letters and Papers, Henry VIII*, ed. D. S. Brewer, i. Part 2 (HMSO, 1920), 1054.   [87] *Calendar of State Papers, Venice*, i. 145.

10

Neville against Percy, 1450–1455

THE political history of northern England in the 1450s and early 1460s is dominated by the great feud between the Nevilles of Middleham and the Percies, which at times threw central Yorkshire into turmoil. The private war between the dominant families was described by one annalist as the beginning of the greatest sorrows in England—the start of the Wars of the Roses. And indeed it is plausible to suggest that what happened in Yorkshire in 1453 and 1454 led directly to the first battle of St Albans, Ludford, and all-out civil war. Not only were the subsequent battles, reaching a climax once more in Yorkshire at Towton, a continuation of the feud between Neville and Percy; but also, since the royal dukes of York and Somerset were dragged in as partisans, the struggle between Neville and Percy became inseparable from the struggle between York and Beaufort. The part played by the northern feud in the last years of the house of Lancaster has been clearly established and fully explored;[1] its place in the history of the north-east is central. But, perhaps because the conflict between Neville and Percy has never been considered in its regional context, its genesis has been misunderstood. Most accounts assume that the two families were long-standing enemies in 1450, that they were equally matched, and that their rivalry came to a climax in 1453–4. Closer scrutiny suggests, however, that, far from this being so, enmity only flared up after 1450; that collectively the Nevilles outstripped the Percies in wealth, power, and favour; and that events in Yorkshire in the early 1450s were but the prelude to a developing, deadly feud that was not settled until 1471.

It was by no means inevitable that Neville and Percy should have been at each other's throats in the middle of the fifteenth century. It is not the case, as has been recently suggested, that

---

[1] R. A. Griffiths, 'Local Rivalries and National Politics: the Percies, the Nevilles and the Duke of Exeter, 1452–55', *Speculum*, 43 (1968), 589–632; R. L. Storey, *The End of the House of Lancaster*, 24–32, 142–9.

for three-quarters of a century before 1450 the two families 'had
made mutual hostility a way of life'.[2] On the contrary, the
treason and disgrace of the first earl of Northumberland in 1405
had left Ralph Neville supreme and unrivalled for over a decade.
And after the restoration of the second earl in 1416 the two
families had co-operated in defending the north against the
Scots and sustaining the minority government of Henry VI.
Circumstances before 1440 had perhaps led both families to be
preoccupied with their own internal affairs. The Percies were
concerned with re-establishing themselves in their estates and
areas of traditional local influence;[3] the Nevilles of Middleham
in making good Earl Ralph's settlement in their favour.

Earl Ralph, who died in 1425, had settled the greater part of his
landed estate on his second countess, Joan Beaufort, and the
heirs of her body, at the expense of his grandson and heir, Ralph
the second earl. While the great Yorkshire lordships of Middleham and Sheriff Hutton, as well as Raby in Durham and Penrith
in Cumberland, were granted to Joan, the second earl was left to
enjoy only the lordship of Brancepeth in Durham and a handful
of other manors. Not surprisingly the earl, when he came of age
in 1429, contested his disinheritance, the two parties coming to
blows at least once in the late 1430s. The death of the dowager
countess in 1440 may have paved the way for Westmorland's
surrender to her powerful and influential son, Richard, earl of
Salisbury, in August 1443. By the terms of an agreement between the two earls, Salisbury was confirmed in possession of
Middleham, Sheriff Hutton, and Penrith, while Westmorland
recovered Raby, and, as was his due, his stepmother's dower
there and elsewhere. The accord of 1443 nevertheless left
Salisbury, as the head of the Middleham Nevilles, the undisputed successor to his father as the leading magnate of the
north.[4]

While Salisbury until 1443 was preoccupied by his conflict
with the earl of Westmorland, the earl of Northumberland's

[2] Griffiths, *Henry VI*, p. 629. Cf. the comment of Charles Ross, 'The Yorkshire Baronage 1399–1435' (unpublished Oxford D.Phil. thesis, 1951), 456: 'Not
until the troubled years of the middle century . . . were their energies directed
into less lawful and more dangerous activity.'   [3] Bean, *Estates*, pp. 69–77.
[4] Ross, 'Baronage', pp. 52–8, followed by E. F. Jacob, *The Fifteenth Century*
(Oxford, 1961), 322–3 and Storey, *House of Lancaster*, pp. 113–14.

attention was directed to a quarrel with Archbishop Kemp of York. Kemp's determination to extend and exercise his secular rights and prerogatives led him into conflict with the tenants of the duchy of Lancaster at Knaresborough over the levying of tolls at Ripon market. Northumberland was drawn into the dispute, and fighting broke out at Thornton Bridge on 5 May 1441 between the archbishop's and the earl's men, in which lives were lost. It was not until 1443 that a settlement by arbitration, which effectively found Northumberland and the men of Knaresborough at fault, was imposed. This was not the end of trouble between Kemp and the Percies, for further fighting broke out between the archbishop's men of Beverley and Percy followers at Stamford Bridge in 1447.[5] During the 1440s the archbishop, not Salisbury, was the earl's principal rival in Yorkshire.

Throughout the 1440s there was no overt sign of conflict between Salisbury and Northumberland or their followers. Indeed, the two families seem to have worked closely and amicably together in the defence of the borders during the war of 1448–9.[6] On 6 May 1450 it was still possible for both earls to act together as feoffees of William Vincent of Great Smeaton in the North Riding.[7] And during the autumn of that year both Salisbury and Northumberland appear, with others, to have given their backing to York in his first attempt to oust the duke of Somerset from court.[8] Moreover, the parliamentary elections of 1449–53 suggest that Neville and Percy were still on speaking terms. In the first election of 1449 on 2 January, during the war with Scotland, two of the three leading gentry of Yorkshire, Sir William Eure and Sir James Strangways, were returned at an election conducted by the third, Sir John Conyers. A Neville

---

[5] Griffiths, *Henry VI*, pp. 577–9. Northumberland's retainer, Sir William Plumpton, was joint steward of Knaresborough.

[6] Storey, *House of Lancaster*, 124. It will be apparent from the rest of this paragraph that I do not share Professor Storey's assumption that Sir Thomas Percy, Lord Egremont had laid down an open challenge to the Nevilles in the west march in 1449. The earliest unambiguous evidence of conflict in Cumberland dates, as in Yorkshire, from 1453 (ibid. 126).

[7] NYCRO, ZQH 1, fo. 148.

[8] Griffiths, *Henry VI*, pp. 707–8. Neville and Percy support for York is perhaps reflected in the election of 2 of the duke's men, Sir John Saville and Sir John Melton, as the county's MPs on 8 Sept. 1450 (PRO, C219/16/1/1/24).

interest appears pre-eminent then.[9] But later in the year, on 23 September, Conyers presided over an election which seems to have produced a balanced ticket. Those elected were Sir James Pickering, a Neville associate, and Sir William Normanville, a follower of the earl of Northumberland. The list of attestors was headed by none other than Sir Thomas Percy, shortly to be created Lord Egremont, and destined to be in direct conflict with Conyers and Pickering in 1453, followed by such eminent Neville servants as Sir James Strangways, Sir Ralph Fitz-Randolph, Sir Ralph Greystoke, Sir Thomas Mountford, and Christopher Conyers, and equally prominent Percy retainers, such as Sir William Plumpton, Sir William Rither, Sir John Tempest, Sir Ralph Pudsay, and John Hotham. Several of these men were to be indicted four years later as Percy adherents.[10] Equally noteworthy is the election return of 21 January 1453. Once more the sheriff was Salisbury's man: Sir James Strangways. But both the MPs elected were Northumberland's associates, Sir Brian Stapleton and Sir William Gascoigne; while the attestors again included both Neville and Percy associates, such as Sir James Pickering and Walter Calverly. Pickering's presence at York Castle on this day, lending his support to the election of Sir William Gascoigne, gives particular food for thought, since six months later he was one of those organizing and leading Neville gangs against Percy retainers. Another attestor, Laurence Catterall, was himself the victim of a Percy assault at Gargrave in September.[11] The evidence of these Yorkshire election returns seems to contradict the idea that the outbreak of violence between Neville and Percy was the culmination of a long build-up of mutual antagonism and conflict between the two families. Rather it suggests an unexpected and rapid deterioration in relationships in 1453.

Any explanation of the sudden outbreak of violence between

[9] PRO, c219/15/6/1/26.
[10] PRO, c219/15/7/1/26. Although a larger than usual number of attestors were entered by the sheriff, this seems not to have been a contested election: no names are repeated, and the order of the leading knights and esquires alternates Percy and Neville supporters (cf. S. J. Payling, 'The Widening Franchise: Parliamentary Elections in Lancastrian Nottinghamshire', in Williams, *England in the Fifteenth Century*, pp. 175–85).
[11] PRO, c219/16/2/1/29. For the indictments of 1454 see Griffiths, 'Local Rivalries', pp. 596, 602, and Storey, *House of Lancaster*, p. 131.

Neville and Percy in the mid-fifteenth century has to take account of the disparity in wealth and power between the two sides. Without any shadow of doubt by 1453 the Nevilles were the stronger; and their strength was still growing. Salisbury's advantage derived from the fact that he was the son of Joan Beaufort, and a kinsman of the king. Because of his birth his father had directed most of his estates to him. Throughout the 1430s and 1440s Salisbury was in receipt of a stream of favours and rewards from the court, especially while his uncle, Cardinal Beaufort, was alive. Salisbury's standing as a councillor and his connections at court had undoubtedly been decisive in securing victory over his kinsman the earl of Westmorland. It had brought him other material rewards. He was made chief justice of the king's forests north of the Trent. In 1444, shortly after the final confirmation of his possession of Middleham, he had been granted two-thirds of the honour of Richmond in North Yorkshire, which included not only Richmond Castle, but also eight manors in the district. The remainder was in the hands of Jacquetta, dowager duchess of Bedford. In 1449 this grant, with the reversion of the duchess's dower, was converted to tail male. Thus the prospect was created of ultimately uniting the lordships of Middleham and Richmond into one hereditary estate.[12] Further to the south in Yorkshire the earl had held the stewardship of the duchy of Lancaster lordship of Pontefract since 1425. To this he added the stewardship of Tickhill in 1432 and of Blackburn in 1437, and the master forestership of Bowland in the same year. In August 1445, in a regrant of the stewardship of Pontefract to himself and his sons Sir Richard and Thomas for lives, the reversion of the stewardships of Knaresborough and Pickering was included.[13] At that time Knaresborough was in the hands of John Feriby and Sir William Plumpton for lives. In the event, Plumpton outlived the earl. Pickering was in the hands of Lord Cromwell, and so it remained

[12] *CPR*, *1441–6*, 96, 108, 191, 429, 458; *1446–52*, 281, 544. Before he was granted Richmond, Salisbury held the office of steward and chief forester, for which he received a fee of £10 (PRO, E199/50/32).

[13] Somerville, *Duchy of Lancaster*, i. 506–7, 513–14, 524, 528, 533. Salisbury surrendered Tickhill to his deputy Ralph Babthorpe in 1443. Neville influence in the duchy lands in Yorkshire stretched back to 1397, when John of Gaunt settled 500 marks yearly on his daughter Joan as her marriage portion. She received this income until her death in 1440 (see Ross, 'Baronage', 38–9).

until his death in 1456. Although no confirmation has survived, it seems likely that Salisbury then succeeded to the office.[14] But the most significant extension of his power and authority took place in the west march.

Salisbury had first held the wardenship of the west march in 1420, in succession to his half-brother John, Lord Neville, when he was only twenty. He had relinquished the office in 1435; but in 1439 he secured the reversion of the office after the expiry of Bishop Lumley of Carlisle's seven-year term. Salisbury accepted a reduction in salary for a guarantee of a ten-year term. In December 1443 he succeeded once more to the office. Three years later the grant was revised in Salisbury's favour, to extend the term to twenty years from 1453, and to associate his son, the future earl of Warwick, with him in survivorship. Significantly Salisbury was able to use his privileged position to secure prompt payment of his salary and wages in cash, an arrangement which in the England of Henry VI was exceptional.[15] Thus, uniquely among the wardens of the marches in the fifteenth century, Salisbury did not find his wages falling substantially into arrears. Moreover, secure of regular payment, the earl seems to have been able to make a comfortable profit out of his office, despite the reduced annual salary. Perhaps, as Professor Storey has suggested, the financial aspect was a secondary consideration.[16] Salisbury's main objective may have been to convert the wardenship into a hereditary office, on the basis of which he could extend his power west of the Pennines on a more permanent basis.[17]

Salisbury's personal pre-eminence was enhanced by the promotion of his brothers. George had succeeded by marriage to the barony of Latimer, with estates at Snape and Well in Richmondshire, Danby in Eskdale, and others in Cumberland. Lord Latimer served early in his life as his brother's deputy warden; but in the 1440s he became insane, and all his lands

---

[14] In November 1459 it was stated in the Act of his attainder that 'he and his had in rule' all the king's castles and offices north of the Trent save Knaresborough. This is not entirely accurate, but implies possession of Pickering (Rot. Parl. v. 346).

[15] Griffiths, Henry VI, p. 404; Storey, House of Lancaster, pp. 115–17.

[16] Ibid.

[17] Ibid. This objective was finally achieved by Richard of Gloucester in 1483.

were placed in Salisbury's custody in 1451.[18] Thereafter the Latimer resources were used to support the earl's household at Carlisle and elsewhere.[19] Equally significant for Salisbury was the position of his brother William as Lord Fauconberg, whose estates were concentrated in Cleveland in north-east Yorkshire. Fauconberg was a professional soldier. He had served with distinction in France between 1436 and 1443, and had returned to England shortly before the Truce of Tours to take up the appointment of captain of Roxburgh, thus extending Neville influence in the marches east of the Pennines.[20] Sometime during his lifetime (he died in 1463) he granted his rights in the wapentake of Langbaurgh, which included return of writ, to his brother Salisbury, whose officers subsequently fulfilled the role of bailiff.[21]

The most important of Salisbury's brothers in the north was Robert, bishop of Durham from 1438. Robert put the secular resources of his palatinate at Salisbury's disposal. Salisbury was granted an annuity of £100 on 10 June 1439; Latimer had already been appointed chamberlain for life, with a fee of £40 p.a., in the preceding December; and an annuity of 40 marks was granted to another brother, Edward, Lord Abergavenny, on the same day.[22] More was to follow. On 12 April 1441 Fauconberg was appointed lay steward for life, with a fee of £40 p.a., and, additionally and without precedent, 'governor and ruler of all our tenants and men in time of peace and war' during pleasure.[23] Fauconberg for one exercised his duties as steward in person from time to time, for he presided over the halmote courts both in October 1443 and in October 1447. When he was absent his deputy, his nephew Sir Thomas Neville, frequently stood in for him; and in 1448, on Fauconberg's return to France, Sir Thomas succeeded him as full steward.[24] All four brothers of the bishop were commissioned as justices of the peace in the bishopric until the end of the pontificate in 1457.[25] Bishop Neville's first chief

[18] *CP* vii. 479.
[19] Carlisle RO, D/Lec/28/25,26,27; Alnwick Castle, Syon MS, X.I, Box 1, 26.
[20] Fauconberg did not share his brother's preferential treatment at the Exchequer (Griffiths, *Henry VI*, pp. 405–6).
[21] *VCH, North Riding*, ii. 28.
[22] Durham, Church Commission, Bishopric Estates, 189811; Durh. 3/42/6.
[23] Durh. 3/42/14.
[24] Ibid. 3/15/108–15, 116, 122–8, 182–6, 216.   [25] Ibid. 3/44/16, 21.

justice was Salisbury's retainer Sir James Strangways: he was ultimately followed in this post by another, Robert Danby, who rose from attorney general in 1438.[26] In 1453–4 Salisbury's son Sir Thomas, the steward, was awarded an additional £20 from the revenues of the diocese; and an annuity of £13. 6s. 8d. was granted to his brother, Sir John, on 24 January 1454.[27]

Bishop Neville pursued his own ambitions. In 1439 he seems to have overreached himself in seizing and occupying Barnard Castle after the death of Richard Beauchamp, earl of Warwick. He had, however, miscalculated badly; for his brother the earl of Salisbury was the new earl's father-in-law, and clearly would not tolerate such a loss of his daughter's prospects. Neville was quickly expelled, partly at the instigation of his brother, to whom he had only recently granted an annuity of £100, and who perhaps he had foolishly thought would give him his backing.[28] Robert later received some compensation for his failure in Barnard Castle, when in November 1448 his palatine powers were extended by Henry VI to Northallerton and Howdenshire. While in the event he and his successors were not able to sustain this enhancement of their privileges, in 1448 it appeared to represent a significant extension of Neville authority in Yorkshire.[29] The commission of the peace for Northallerton issued by Bishop Neville in April 1449 was led by servants and associates of his brother the earl, prominent among them being Sir James Strangways and Robert Danby.[30]

However, the Nevilles were soon to lay their hands on Barnard Castle by other means. The young Henry of Warwick, by then made Duke, died on 11 June 1446, leaving a two-year-old daughter Anne as his only child and heiress. She was the granddaughter of the earl of Salisbury. It is not surprising, therefore, that Salisbury was granted the custody of Barnard Castle during her minority. But Anne herself died on 3 January 1449; her heir was her aunt Anne, the sister of Henry and the wife of Sir Richard Neville, Salisbury's eldest son and heir. In the summer of the same year the twenty-year-old Richard was admitted to the title and estates of the earldom of Warwick, and

[26] Durham, Church Commission, Bishopric Estates, 189811, 12.
[27] Durh. 3/44/22.
[28] See above, pp. 148–9.
[29] Durh. 3/44/2.   [30] Ibid. 4.

thus inherited the lordship of Barnard Castle.[31] Yet another major addition was thus made to the territorial power of the Nevilles in north-eastern England. By 1450 the earl of Salisbury, his brothers William, George, and Robert, and his son Richard between them controlled a block of land between the Pennines and the east coast running fifty miles northwards from Wensleydale to the Tyne. With further lands and lordships, in Howden and Sheriff Hutton to the south in Yorkshire, at Penrith in Cumberland, and to the north of the Tyne in Bedlington and North Durham, and the authority of the wardenship of the west march, the captaincy of Roxburgh, and the stewardship of Pontefract, the Nevilles of Middleham were well on the way to having the north of England in their pockets. There was but one overmighty magnate family in north-eastern England at the beginning of the sixth decade of the fifteenth century: the Nevilles of Middleham. It was a restrained understatement to comment, as the Act of Attainder against Salisbury in 1459 did, referring to the king, that 'you showed your grace and bounteous grants in right ample wise'.[32]

With such territorial and official power Salisbury and his family had no difficulty in creating an extensive network of retainers and dependants. Several of the lesser peers of the region were drawn in. Sir Thomas Dacre, later Lord Dacre of Gilsland, had been retained since 1436; Sir Ralph Greystoke, Lord Greystoke was retained in 1448, his fee to be found from Barnard Castle, where he had been retained by Richard Beauchamp, earl of Warwick.[33] FitzHugh and Scrope of Bolton, both active in the Neville cause in 1453, followed suit.[34] In Cumberland, where both Dacre and Greystoke held land, as Professor Storey has demonstrated, Salisbury had for many years been challenging Percy dominance based on

[31] *CP* xii. Part 2, 384–5.
[32] *Rot. Parl.* v. 346. Ross, 'Baronage', p. 453 suggested tentatively that Salisbury's influence grew at the expense of the lesser baronage: in truth it grew at the expense of all the baronage.
[33] Northants RO, Fitzwilliam MS 2049, 52. I am grateful to Dr Michael K. Jones for making his transcripts of these documents available to me. The Greystokes, who held land at Coniscliffe downstream from Barnard Castle, enjoyed a well-established family tradition of office-holding in the lordship (see PRO, sc 6/1303/12).
[34] Griffiths, 'Local Rivalries', p. 605.

Cockermouth: Sir Henry Threlkeld had been retained in 1431, and Sir Walter Strickland in 1448.[35] In Westmorland and Furness too his influence was extended. It was at this time that such prominent families as the Musgraves of Hartley, the Parrs of Kendal, the Huddlestons of Millom, the Redmans of the Levens, the Middletons of Middleton, and the Harringtons of Hornby came into the Neville orbit. In South Yorkshire too, based on Pontefract, Salisbury recruited William Scargill of Lead, and Thomas Wombwell. Wombwell was his deputy steward at Pontefract until his death in 1452, when he was succeeded by Sir John Neville.[36] It is not surprising that the earl's men also found favour with Archbishop Kemp of York. Sir James Strangways became his steward of Ripon, and Robert Danby one of the justices of the peace.[37]

In the face of this remorseless aggrandizement and ever-increasing might the Percies were gradually being pushed to one side. Still struggling to rehabilitate themselves after the attainder and disgrace of Henry IV's reign, still not in full control of all the estates lost then, and enjoying no such preferential treatment at the court and the Exchequer, it was as much as they could do to hold on to their traditional influence in Northumberland and the east march, the East Riding, and the Wharfedale and Craven districts of Yorkshire. The prospect facing them after 1450 was of steadily eroded power and permanent subordination to the Nevilles of Middleham. This was undoubtedly the fundamental reason for their ultimate resort to violence. But there were other factors which exacerbated matters. Economic circumstances in the north-east in the 1440s made both earls and their supporters more anxious to maintain, if not increase, their lands, and to secure office. A reduction in landed income of some 10 to 15 per cent after the agrarian crisis of 1438–40 gave an immediate and pressing material incentive to both sides, but especially to the Percies, who were otherwise so disadvantaged.[38] Percy sensibilities were also no doubt offended by Salisbury's misconduct of the war of 1448–9. They

[35] Storey, *House of Lancaster*, pp. 117–23.
[36] Arnold, 'West Riding of Yorkshire', pp. 124–6.
[37] BI, Register John Kemp, fo. 172; Griffiths, *Henry VI*, pp. 582, 602.
[38] Pollard, 'Agrarian Crisis', esp. pp. 104–5.

could legitimately lay the blame for the capture and ransoming of Lord Poynings on Salisbury's shoulders.[39] Undoubtedly, too, the emergence as an active member of his family of Sir Thomas Percy, Lord Egremont, a wild and belligerent young man, heightened tensions. Indeed the rashness and impatience of the younger generation on both sides, Salisbury's three sons as well as Northumberland's, seem to have hastened the outbreak of violence. But, as we have seen, certainly until the end of 1450 there is no indication of conflict between the two families or of any unwillingness on the part of the two earls to co-operate. What turned an uneasy *modus vivendi* into bitter antagonism was the marriage between Sir Thomas Neville and Maud Stanhope, niece of Ralph, Lord Cromwell, and Cromwell's willingness to settle Wressle on the young couple.

Until the death of Maud's first husband, Lord Willoughby, in July 1452, there was no predicting this development. But soon after Maud became a widow Cromwell and Salisbury came to terms for a marriage. For Cromwell this alliance offered the prospect of further protection for the inheritance of one of his two heiresses. He may have been impressed by the manner in which Salisbury had acted to protect the Beauchamp inheritance in Barnard Castle twelve years earlier. For Salisbury the match offered another opportunity to extend his family's power, mainly south of Yorkshire, and to provide a fitting estate for his second son. Wressle was one of three or four Percy manors forfeited in 1405 (the others were in Lincolnshire and Essex) which were still unrecovered. They had been granted to Cromwell for life in 1438, and in fee simple two years later.[40] Settlement on Sir Thomas Neville added insult to injury. Wressle had been, and was ultimately to become again, a favoured residence of the family. It was not a particularly rich manor (yielding but £31 in 1435/6); but the castle, which impressed Leland ('one of the most proper beyond Trent'),[41] was new, substantial, and strategically close to York. Moreover, in Neville hands it represented an intrusion into the East Riding, where Percy authority was as yet unchallenged. Even more to the point, it may already

---

[39] See above, p. 222.
[40] Griffiths, *Henry VI*, pp. 582–3; Bean, *Estates*, pp. 74–5.
[41] Ibid. 38; Leland, *Itinerary*, Part I, p. 53.

have been earmarked, once recovered, for Lord Egremont.[42] Until 1453 Neville aggrandizement had taken place at the expense of others: this was the first time that Neville was to gain directly at the expense of Percy. It touched directly on the future prospects of the younger generation in both families, and in the first instance precipitated them, rather than their fathers, into open conflict.

When Northumberland and his family first heard of what was planned is not known: apparently not until after the elections to Parliament of January 1453, and possibly not even before 1 May, when a royal licence for the marriage was issued.[43] Disorder broke out shortly afterwards. Lord Egremont was recruiting men and distributing the Percy livery from 12 May at the latest. The king, knowing something was afoot, sent repeated summonses to Egremont, first to appear at court, and ultimately to prepare for service abroad in the defence of Gascony.[44] All these Egremont ignored. Sir John Neville thereupon decided to take matters into his own hands, and raided the Percy lordship of Topcliffe, where he hoped to seize Egremont. Violence flared up in several places in Yorkshire and elsewhere. Sir John Salvin forcibly expelled Margaret Clervaux, widow of Sir John, from her manor at Sandholme on 12 July; Sir Richard Percy attacked the duchy of Lancaster manors of Halton and Swinden on 24 July. There were other riots and assaults, as others took advantage of the sudden collapse of law and order to settle old scores. The government was impotent. A series of commissions of oyer and terminer were issued, first under the earls of Salisbury and Northumberland, who it was forlornly hoped would be able to call their sons and retainers to order, and then under Sir William Lucy: reprimands were issued, but no effective steps were taken to bring Yorkshire back under control.

Then in August the earl of Salisbury, his countess, and Sir Thomas and his new bride, travelling north from Tattershall where the wedding had been celebrated, were intercepted at Heworth, just outside York, by a large force led by Egremont and

---

[42] On 10 June 1458 Egremont received a royal grant of the estate for life (CPR, 1452–61, 428).   [43] CPR, 1452–61, 64.
[44] PPC vi. 140–1. The following discussion draws heavily upon Griffiths, 'Local Rivalries', to which I am much indebted.

Sir Richard Percy, who, it was later alleged, intended to kill them. The Nevilles were probably too strong for the Percy brothers to press home their attack, and they continued un-molested to Sheriff Hutton. But both sides continued to commit breaches of the peace: Sir Richard Percy attacked and seized Laurence Caterall, a servant of the earl of Salisbury, at Gargrave church on 6 August 1453, and carried him off to imprisonment in Cockermouth castle. Sir John Neville sacked what may have been Egremont's house at Catton, north of Topcliffe.

With Henry VI now in a state of mental collapse, the govern-ment was completely paralysed, and could resort only to ex-hortation. Letters in his name issued on 8 October revealed that matters were coming to a head. The 'king' told Salisbury and Northumberland that he had heard that they had made the 'greatest assembly of liegemen, and thereto had appointed time and place, that ever was made within this land at any time that man can think', and warned them of the consequences if they went ahead. The earl of Westmorland and the bishops of Durham and York were thanked for the pains they had been taking and were still taking to try to pacify the quarrel, and urged to continue with their efforts.[45] But nevertheless on 20 October the forces of both sides converged on Topcliffe, both at full strength, the earls for the first time joining their sons. Salisbury took his stand at Sand Hutton four miles to the north, accompanied by Warwick, Sir Thomas, Sir John, Lord FitzHugh, and Lord Scrope of Bolton. Lord Poynings, Northumberland's son and heir, joined his father, his younger brothers, and Lord Clifford. But battle was avoided. The 'discreet mediation' of the archbishop of York and his fellow arbitrators seems to have persuaded both sides to back off and to suspend hostilities for the winter months.[46]

By 1454 the conflict had become significantly widened to draw in the conflicting parties at court, and had been made more complex by their intervention. The involvement of the dukes of York and Exeter, especially the duke of York on behalf of the

[45] PPC vi. 158–9, 160–1. Salisbury was at Middleham on 6 Oct.; Sir John at Sheriff Hutton on 11 Oct. (Alnwick Castle, Syon MS, X.I, Box 1, 26).

[46] Ibid. 178. A letter to Northumberland on 10 May 1454 refers to the discreet mediation which prevented further trouble. See also Griffiths, 'Local Rivalries', p. 610 and Storey, House of Lancaster, pp. 131–2.

Nevilles, was to have far-reaching and fateful consequences. There is uncertainty as to when Richard of York and the Nevilles first became allies, but it would appear that they began to act in concert during the autumn and winter of 1453–4, as the different groups of courtiers manœuvred for power in the aftermath of Henry VI's mental collapse. By January 1454 it was apparent that York and Neville had come together, and that the duke of Exeter had thrown his weight behind the Percies. The York–Neville alliance was cemented by the nomination of York as Protector on 27 March, and Salisbury as Chancellor on 12 April.[47]

In some respects this alliance between York and the Nevilles was surprising. After all, York had been the excluded political leader while Salisbury and his family had enjoyed high political favour. Salisbury, as a Beaufort, might have been expected to maintain close ties with the duke of Somerset while York made common cause with the Percies. On the other hand York and Salisbury had a long-established association. Not only was York married to Salisbury's youngest sister, Cecily; but he had also been brought up in the household of Joan Beaufort from the age of twelve until he reached his majority in 1432. In 1430 he had accompanied Henry VI and his brother-in-law Salisbury to France. And when he returned to France as lieutenant-general for a year at the age of 25 in 1436 he took both Salisbury and Fauconberg with him as captains.[48] In his youth he had been close to the Nevilles of Middleham: he may even have looked upon Salisbury as his mentor. Salisbury too had already revealed that he was not particularly close to York's rival Edmond Beaufort, duke of Somerset. In the autumn of 1450 he had supported York, although his support had not stretched to backing York's armed demonstration at Dartford in February 1452, when Salisbury had publicly stood by the court. But Salisbury may already have come to fear that his star was on the wane. The creation of Edmund Tudor as earl of Richmond on 23 November 1452 was at his expense, for the king endowed the

[47] Griffiths, 'Local Rivalries', pp. 605–10; P. A. Johnson, *Duke Richard of York, 1411–1460* (Oxford, 1988), 140–5.
[48] Griffiths, *Henry VI*, pp. 666–9.

new earl with the honour of Richmond, the Yorkshire estates of which had previously been granted to him in tail male.[49]

What finally determined the issue in the winter of 1453–4 were short-term and immediate considerations. The earl of Warwick had become embroiled in a violent feud of his own with the duke of Somerset in Glamorgan, and was probably pressing for an alliance with York. In October the Nevilles seem to have backed York in his demand for recognition as the king's principal councillor against the duke of Somerset and the queen. At the same time, and possibly in response, the Percies found a backer in Henry Holland, duke of Exeter, with whom they shared an antagonism towards Lord Cromwell, and who himself had ambitions of his own.[50] It was essential for the Nevilles in 1453–4 to maintain their position of favour at court. They could not afford to lose this advantage to the Percies. Thus they backed York. In the short term the decision paid off; and during the summer of 1454 they continued to hold the whip hand.

As soon as York became Protector he began to take steps to impose the authority of the government on the north; now by implication the authority of the Nevilles as well as of the Protector. By the middle of May Egremont and the duke of Exeter had raised a force in Yorkshire with which to resist. Exeter appears to have had ambitions in the duchy of Lancaster; and it seems that he was hoping to use the rebellion to displace York and have himself installed as Protector. Duke Richard acted swiftly, and arrived in York itself on 19 May. For a time he appears to have been powerless to do much against the rebels, who, based on Spofforth, overran the neighbourhood. But Duke Richard was able to gather strength; and, early in June, Egremont and Exeter broke camp and their troops dispersed. In the middle of the month judicial proceedings were opened against Egremont and Exeter by a commission headed by York and containing most of the nobles of the north other than those favourable to the Percies. Northumberland, Egremont, and

[49] Ibid. 699. It is to be doubted, however, that Salisbury surrendered possession.

[50] Ibid. 719–25. The dispute between Cromwell and Exeter, and the manner in which it quickly became bound up with conflict between Neville and Percy is discussed in S. J. Payling, 'The Ampthill Dispute: A Study in Aristocratic Lawlessness and the Breakdown of Lancastrian Government', *EHR* 104, (1989) 881–907.

Exeter were indicted; but the last session was held on 3 August,
and no judgements were reached. Indeed on 23 July Northumberland received a stay until the following spring. In the
mean time Egremont and Exeter were still at large. Exeter fled to
sanctuary in Westminster, where he was seized on 23 July and
sent north to be imprisoned at Pontefract in the custody of the
earl of Salisbury. Egremont continued to cause disturbances in
Cumberland, Westmorland, and Lancashire. Yorkshire remained tense throughout the summer. Salisbury, taking the
Great Seal with him, toured his estates in August and September, visiting Middleham, Sheriff Hutton, and his son's lordship
of Barnard Castle. At the same time Northumberland and his
son fortified Spofforth. Finally late in October Egremont and his
brother Sir Richard Percy and a band of men were intercepted
and engaged by Sir Thomas and Sir John Neville near Stamford
Bridge. In the ensuing skirmish one of the Percy men, Sir John
Salvin of Duffield, was killed, and the Percy brothers were
captured. Egremont was taken first to Middleham, then York.
He was indicted and condemned for trespass, and required to pay
damages of over £11,000 or face incarceration as a debtor—the
intention. The two brothers were taken south and committed to
Newgate. The victory at Stamford Bridge finally brought the
disorder of two summers to an end in a Neville victory.[51]

Because of the graphic detail given in the surviving indictments, and the tendency of proclamations and royal orders to
dwell on the 'great slaughters [and] murders of our people' and
the 'great trouble and vexation of our subjects'[52] it is easy to
exaggerate the scale and significance of the Yorkshire disturbances of 1453 and 1454. There were in fact few deaths. The only
casualty of note was Sir John Salvin at Stamford Bridge. Until
Stamford Bridge, the chief participants, the Neville and Percy
sons, while frequently threatening and confronting each other,
held back from actual combat. As significant as the brush at
Heworth and the skirmish at Stamford was the battle that did

---

[51] Griffiths, 'Local Rivalries', pp. 612–24; Storey, *House of Lancaster*, pp.
142–9. But see the recent suggestion that York sought an accommodation with
the earl of Northumberland (Johnson, *Richard of York*, p. 144).
[52] *PPC* vi. 154; Griffiths, 'Local Rivalries', p. 626. It was a later Neville
accusation that their assassination was intended at Heworth on 24 Aug. (ibid.
597–8, 618).

not take place when the two sides confronted each other north of Topcliffe in October 1453. On this occasion the presence of both the earls of Salisbury and Northumberland may have acted as a restraining influence.[53] Indeed, until Exeter threw in his lot with the Percies and raised open rebellion against the Protector, the government seems to have believed that it was still possible for the earls to restrain their boisterous and unruly sons, especially Egremont and Sir John Neville, whose quarrel in its early stages this primarily was. Undoubtedly widespread disorder and lawlessness erupted in Yorkshire in 1453 and 1454: riots occurred in the countryside and in the city of York; houses were ransacked; individuals were assaulted and beaten. The dramatic collapse of order certainly occurred because of the 'great discord'[54] that suddenly arose between Neville and Percy, and the inability of the Crown to impose its authority.

But it is likely that several of the reported disorders were not directly related to the quarrel itself. Others took advantage of the situation to settle their own scores. Thus the attack by Sir John Salvin of North Duffield on Margaret Clervaux at Sandholme near Howden on 12 July 1453 appears to have arisen out of an independent dispute between branches of the Salvin family. Likewise the robbery of the vicar of Aughton by the same Sir John in September does not seem to have been directed against the Nevilles.[55] And similarly the ransacking of Sir John Salvin of Newbiggin's house at Egton by Sir Thomas Neville of Brancepeth on 26 March 1454 was probably a completely unconnected affair. (This was not the same Sir John Salvin (of Duffield) who had committed so many acts of violence in 1453, and was killed at Stamford Bridge later in the year.) There seems no reason to suppose that Sir Thomas had 'indulged in an unusual display of cousinly affection towards Salisbury and his sons'.[56] There was a general collapse of law and order in Yorkshire in 1453 and 1454, the consequences of which were also to play

[53] Ibid. 603–4.
[54] Cartularium Abbathiae de Whitby, ii, ed. J. C. Atkinson, SS, lxxii (1879), 694–5.
[55] PRO, KB 9/149/12, 23; Griffiths, 'Local Rivalries', pp. 602–3; Storey, House of Lancaster, pp. 129, 131.
[56] Arnold, 'West Riding', App. V, pp. 89–93; Griffiths, 'Local Rivalries', p. 610.

havoc with Crown finances in the country.[57] The situation perhaps reveals how dependent on the continuing harmony between Neville and Percy the maintenance of law and order in the north-east had become; but it does not follow that even at the end of 1454 the quarrel between the two families had reached the point where reconciliation was impossible.

The events of 1453 and 1454 were but the beginning and first stages in the feud between Neville and Percy. The Percies, stung by the attempt to settle one of their ancient properties on a member of the Neville family, resorted to violence in an effort to arrest the crumbling of their local authority in Yorkshire. The attempt was a dismal failure. The commission of oyer and terminer which sat at York in June 1454 roundly condemned them; the capture of Egremont and Sir Richard Percy at Stamford Bridge in October left them at their enemy's mercy. Clearly the earl of Northumberland was unlikely to accept as final the defeats of 1454; but as yet no Neville or Percy blood had been shed. That stage was not reached until the battle of St Albans on 22 May 1455, which was the culmination of two years of escalating conflict.

Whatever significance the first battle of St Albans may have as the beginning of the Wars of the Roses, from the point of view of northern politics it was but the end of the first round of the quarrel between Neville and Percy. The battle took place as a direct consequence of Henry VI's recovery of his senses at the end of 1454, which led to Richard of York's stepping down as Protector, and to the release of the dukes of Somerset and Exeter from custody and their return to favour at court. Inevitably in the circumstances royal favour was extended to the Percies. On 7 March 1455 Salisbury resigned the Great Seal; then or shortly thereafter he, York, and Warwick precipitately withdrew from court. Summoned to a meeting of a Great Council at Leicester which they believed would lead to their own condemnation, they resorted to arms to remove Somerset and his allies once more. The speed with which York and the Nevilles raised troops in the north and marched to intercept their rivals took the court by surprise. The king had barely left London before he was confronted by a Yorkist force. On 22 May, after the failure of

[57] Griffiths, 'Local Rivalries', p. 626.

attempts to negotiate the surrender of Somerset, the Yorkists launched an attack on the town of St Albans, in which the king and his household were resting. The attack was initially staved off by Lord Clifford's determined defence of the town's perimeter. But Warwick forced an entry, and soon the main part of the Yorkist army was engaging the king's men in the marketplace. The king himself took shelter in a tanner's cottage, but was 'rescued' and taken to the abbey. Somerset and the earl of Northumberland were cut down and killed.[58]

Whether the death of Northumberland was intended at St Albans is a moot point. Most accounts assume this. Storey confidently concluded that the character of the battle was murder, a settling of scores by the Nevilles against Northumberland and his ally Clifford, and, less certainly, by York against Somerset.[59] Yet two sources commented that his death was unintentional: Gascoigne, and John Hardyng, who wrote:

> Therle then of Northumberland was there,
> Of sodein chaunce drawen forth with the kyng,
> And slain unknowne by any manne there were.

One should beware of taking either author at face value. Gascoigne's whole account is sympathetic to the Yorkists. And Hardyng, writing in the early 1460s, was endeavouring in this, the second version of his history, to persuade Edward IV to recruit all England in a campaign against the Scots. In this circumstance he is likely to have wanted to gloss over the roles of the earls of Salisbury and Warwick in causing Northumberland's death.[60] It is hardly plausible that the earl was at court by chance. He had a strong vested interest in supporting Somerset and in seeking to reverse the decisions of 1454.

There is no doubt that the Nevilles and the men raised by them in the north were prominent in the force of some 3,000

---

[58] C. A. J. Armstrong, 'Politics and the Battle of St Albans, 1455', *BIHR* 33 (1960), 8–46.

[59] Storey, *House of Lancaster*, p. 162.

[60] Hardyng, *Chronicle*, pp. 402, 409–14. See also A. Gransden, *Historical Writing in England*: ii c. *1307 to the Early Sixteenth Century* (1982), 277; A. J. G. Edwards, 'The Manuscripts and Texts of the Second Version of John Hardyng's Chronicle', in Williams, *England in the Fifteenth Century*, p. 76.

that carried the day. Abbot Whetehamstede in his register made much of the role of the northerners in securing the victory and in looting the town afterwards.[61] Another account specifically states that Sir Robert Ogle and 600 men of the Scottish marches led the assault on the market-place. Ogle, who may already have been receiving a fee of £20 from Salisbury, was constable of Norham, a servant of Bishop Neville of Durham; and it is to be assumed that he had raised his men in that official capacity.[62] But, as Armstrong showed, the situation in the king's party was complicated by the presence also at court of at least two men whose ties were with York and the Nevilles. One was William Neville, Lord Fauconberg.[63] Fauconberg seems to have returned to England from captivity in France in July 1453, and to have stood aside from the family's conflict in Yorkshire. He remained at court in the spring of 1455 after his brother and nephew withdrew, and, it would seem, had been a valuable contact for York and his friends there, who had already presented their case to the king. Understandably Fauconberg, caught in an embarrassing situation on 22 May 1455, did not personally oppose his brother and nephew: he may even have acted as a fifth column.[64] A deliberate decision by the Nevilles to single out Northumberland and kill him cannot therefore be ruled out. Among the dead were men from families associated with him: Sir John Stapleton, Averley Mauleverer, Ralph Babthorpe, and William Curwen. After the battle a younger son, Sir Ralph Percy, was one of those initially held publicly responsible for what happened; and another, William, bishop of Carlisle, who had been with him, was despoiled and humiliated.[65] There is no doubt that after the event it appeared that, while York had sought out Somerset, Salisbury's purpose had been to deal with

[61] Armstrong, 'St Albans', pp. 27, 42.

[62] Pollard, 'Northern Retainers', p. 68.

[63] Armstrong, 'St Albans', p. 21. The other was Lord Berners, brother of Viscount Bourgchier.

[64] Fauconberg was still *persona grata* at court in 1459. He became Warwick's *de facto* lieutenant of Calais in 1455, but did not declare his hand until after the rout of Ludford (Griffiths, *Henry VI*, pp. 754, 808, 839).

[65] Armstrong, 'St Albans', pp. 48, 57, 71; Griffiths, 'Local Rivalries', p. 629. Babthorpe, Constable of Dunstanburgh, had apparently been expelled by Salisbury from the stewardship of Tickhill in 1453-4 (Somerville, *Duchy of Lancaster*, i. 525, 538).

Northumberland. Intentional or not, the consequences of Northumberland's death were momentous: a deadly blood feud had been set in motion, from which there would be no turning back.

11

Feud and Civil War, 1455–1461

WHAT had begun in 1453 as an attempt to alter the balance of power in Yorkshire by force became after St Albans a feud which was to be inextricably bound up with the developing politics of the whole realm, and was not to burn itself out until after many more deaths and a change of dynasty. From that day in May 1455 the fortunes of Neville were inseparable from those of York. At first the family benefited from the fruits of victory. Salisbury succeeded to the chief stewardship of the duchy of Lancaster north of the Trent, the chief stewardship of Lancashire, and probably the stewardship of Pickering after the death of Lord Cromwell in 1456. He and Warwick had their grant of the wardenship of the west march reviewed on more favourable terms. Thus their hold on the north was tightened. Warwick became captain of Calais; Fauconberg received a half share of the constableship of Windsor Castle (with Lord Berners); and the bishopric of Exeter was secured for young George Neville. Sir Thomas Lumley, presumably therefore present at the battle, was appointed constable of Scarborough Castle in the place of Ralph Babthorpe, who had fallen.[1] But in the longer run it proved impossible for the Yorkist lords to hold on to the power they had won by force. During 1456 they found themselves gradually losing control. In the autumn the court moved to the midlands, and a number of changes in senior office, probably initiated by the queen, brought a new court faction into power. From the end of 1456, as Professor Griffiths has suggested, 'the court determined to strip them of almost all public authority in the realm, starve them of lucrative royal patronage, and neutralise the local influence of their tenantry and retainers in the shires'.[2] It is what happened in the shires, especially Yorkshire, that was critical to the Nevilles.

---

[1] CPR, 1452–61, 242, 245, 248; Somerville, *Duchy of Lancaster*, i. 421, 493, 533–4.
[2] Griffiths, *Henry VI*, p. 798.

The Neville supremacy in the north seems to have remained unchallenged until March 1457, when Henry Percy, the new earl of Northumberland, was belatedly granted livery of his lands without relief, and entered his inheritance. Northumberland had been fully occupied in defending the east march and Berwick from his father's death until the renewal of the truce in the preceding autumn. On 28 February he had been reappointed warden for a further ten years; and on 12 March his brother Sir Ralph Percy was made constable of the duchy of Lancaster castle of Dunstanburgh in Northumberland. For the next two years Northumberland received preferential treatment at the Exchequer in paying his wages and settling his debts; Salisbury received nothing.[3] A more direct challenge was offered when on 11 March 1457 Humphrey Neville, brother of the earl of Westmorland, was granted the stewardship of Richmondshire and the constableship of Richmond Castle during the minority of Henry Tudor, earl of Richmond, who had been born on 28 January three months after the death of his father Edmund.[4] It seems unlikely that Neville was able to enter these offices, which were then in the hands of Christopher Conyers of Hornby, Salisbury's nominee. Indeed two and a half years later the Chancery seemed to have forgotten the abortive grant of 1457 when it issued letters granting the same stewardship to Henry, Lord FitzHugh, taking it to be in royal hands by the rebellion of the earl of Salisbury.[5]

A more effective threat to Neville dominance came with the death of Robert Neville, bishop of Durham on 8 July 1457. His successor, provided on 22 August, was Laurence Booth, Queen Margaret's Chancellor since 1451, and keeper of the Privy Seal since September 1456.[6] Booth's arrival at Durham inevitably led to loss of influence in the bishopric. Most of the annuities granted by Neville to his kinsmen were cancelled. Sir Thomas Neville of Middleham, Salisbury's second son, was replaced as steward by his kinsman and namesake Sir Thomas of Brancepeth. But the changes were not so sweeping as to remove all

---

[3] *CPR, 1452–61*, 356; Storey, 'Wardens', p. 614; Griffiths, *Henry VI*, pp. 799, 812–13, 845.
[4] *CPR, 1452–61*, 335.   [5] Ibid. 536.
[6] Griffiths, *Henry VI*, p. 773; *Handbook of British Chronology*, ed. E. B. Fryde, D. E. Greenway, *et al.*, 3rd edn. (1986), 242.

traces of the preceding regime. A new chancellor and receiver-
general, Henry Preston, esquire, was appointed to succeed John
Lound. But Preston had held the offices before in 1452–6, and he
had been constable of the castle for life since 1438, an office he
was to hold throughout Booth's pontificate. Likewise, the sheriff, Geoffrey Middleton, appointed for life by Bishop Neville in
1445, remained in office for the time being. Robert Danby, chief
justice since 1454, was retained. Furthermore Salisbury, his
brother Fauconberg, his retainer Sir Thomas Lumley, and John
Lound were all reappointed as justices of the peace in December
1457. And finally Salisbury himself continued to enjoy his grant
of Stanhope Park, which he occupied in lieu of an annuity.[7]
Until his attainder two years later Salisbury and his associates
continued to enjoy favour with the new bishop. Whatever the
hopes of the government might have been in promoting Booth to
the see, in the event his arrival only diminished, but did not
remove Neville of Middleham's influence from the bishopric.[8]

Thus in 1457 the Nevilles were able to maintain their position and to limit their loss of influence in the north-east. Booth's
conciliatory approach in Durham may have reflected the king's
new initiative to 'eradicate the roots of rancour' between the
lords involved at St Albans by means of arbitration. In November the king presided over a Great Council at Westminster, at
which he first attempted to persuade the new duke of Somerset,
the earl of Northumberland, and the new Lord Clifford to patch
up their differences with York, Salisbury, and Warwick.
Whether it was because Salisbury was an unwilling participant
constrained to attend, or because he feared for his safety,
Viscount Beaumont escorted him from Doncaster up to
Westminster.[9] The first attempts at reconciliation failed. But
the lords reconvened again in January, this time all in strength.
For several weeks tensions ran high as the Yorkists lodged in the
City and the Lancastrian lords camped to the west, between the
City and Westminster. Eventually, after protracted negotiation

---

[7] Durham, Church Commission, Bishopric Estates, 189812, 14; Durh. 3/43/
16; 48/1.

[8] The appointment of Booth as bishop was not as serious a blow to the
Yorkists as R. L. Storey concluded (see *House of Lancaster*, p. 183).

[9] *CPR, 1452–61*, 428; Griffiths, *Henry VI*, p. 805.

conducted in the presence of the king himself, an agreement was reached and an arbitration award announced on 24 March in which the Yorkists agreed to pay compensation to the sons of those who fell at St Albans, and the Nevilles to forgo the fines for damages imposed on Egremont in 1454.[10] Egremont, who had dramatically escaped from Newgate in November 1456, was bound over to keep the peace for ten years, a bond being given to Salisbury on 15 June. At the same time as Egremont put up his bond he received from the king a grant of Wressle for life.[11] This too would seem to reflect a compromise reached between the two parties, for a lease from the king indicated that the property belonged neither to Percy nor to Neville, but to the Crown, still in royal possession following the forfeiture of 1416. Finally, on 23 June Egremont received a licence to leave the realm on the pilgrimage he had promised to make.[12] No doubt he had been persuaded to make this pilgrimage, which was yet another means of attempting to remove him from the scene; an expedition to France in 1453 and imprisonment in 1454–6 having both signally failed to curb him. The award of 24 March was solemnly and ritually celebrated by a 'love-day' at St Paul's on the following day. Celebrations of this new-found peace and amity were continued with a round of jousts, feasting, and other entertainments until May.[13]

But the peace of 1458 was shallow and short-lived. By November both sides were beginning to prepare for a final confrontation. Ministerial changes made at a Great Council at Westminster demonstrated that Queen Margaret was tightening her grip on the running of the kingdom. An attempt to arrest or even assassinate the earl of Warwick on 9 November, from which he escaped to Calais, perhaps confirmed that a new and uncompromising stand was being taken at court.[14] The Yorkist lords on their part were also resolving to take steps to protect themselves. According to a document among the Hornby Castle papers seen by T. D. Whitaker, in November 1458 the earl of Salisbury summoned a meeting of his council at Middleham,

[10] Ibid. 805–6.
[11] Ibid.; Storey, *House of Lancaster*, p. 149.
[12] *CPR, 1452–61*, 428.
[13] Griffiths, *Henry VI*, pp. 806–7.
[14] Ibid. 789, 807; Davies, *An English Chronicle*, p. 78.

including among its numbers Sir Thomas Harrington, at which it was agreed that they would 'take full part with the full noble prince, the Duke of York'. On returning to Hornby, Harrington 'remembering himself of the great war and troubles likely to fall' took steps to protect his inheritance should 'the said wars to go against' him.[15] This document would seem to present conclusive evidence that the Yorkist lords were preparing once more to resort to force long before the summer of 1459, and even before the attempts on the earl of Warwick on 9 November. Both sides, independently, were set on a course of conflict.

In north-eastern England Salisbury had for some time been intent on increasing the number of his retainers and penetrating areas where the Percies traditionally dominated. A fragment of the receiver of Middleham's account roll for c.1457–9 shows that in the years immediately preceding the outbreak of civil war Salisbury had attracted men to his service in Northumberland, Durham, the honour of Knaresborough, and Craven, where one would have expected Percy or Neville of Raby to have dominated. Sir Robert Ogle of Bothal, Northumberland was captain of Norham, and a long-standing servant of the bishop of Durham: his neighbour Sir John Middleham of Belsay was apparently a new recruit to Neville service. Together they provided the nucleus of a small group able to challenge the monopoly of the Percies in the county. In Durham, Salisbury recruited Sir Thomas Lumley and William Pudsay of Selaby. Pudsay was perhaps as significant a catch as the more substantial Lumley, who, like Ogle, was to be promoted to the peerage after 1461. Pudsay lived close to Raby, and his attachment to the Nevilles of Middleham became a constant reminder to the earl of Westmorland of his local powerlessness. Perhaps more surprising is the fact that at the same time in the 1450s Salisbury retained Sir Richard Hamerton of Helifield, one of the leading gentry of Craven, where the Percies and Cliffords dominated. Hamerton's sister Jane was married to a Metcalfe of Nappa, and many of her husband's kinsmen were retained by Salisbury and later his son. This might explain his brief attachment to the earl. But Hamerton was more closely connected with families of impeccable Percy provenance, and this would no doubt explain the cancellation of his fee at the end of the decade.[16]

Salisbury's intervention in the honour of Knaresborough, not far south of Middleham, was more successful than his attempt to secure a foothold in Craven. From their lordship of Spofforth the Percies commanded the district. But Salisbury entertained ambitions of challenging Percy dominance. In 1445 he secured a grant of the reversion of the stewardship of Knaresborough after the death of the incumbent Sir William Plumpton. Plumpton was a retainer of the earl of Northumberland, and steward of Spofforth and other Yorkshire estates. Pending the reversion of the duchy of Lancaster office, Salisbury set about securing the service of local gentry. Richard Roos of Ingmanthorpe, near Spofforth itself, was retained for a fee of £13. 6s. 8d.; Ralph Pullen of Scotton for a fee of £1. 6s. 8d.[17] By the late 1450s Salisbury had secured the support of other local figures. In July 1459 Richard Louther (feodary under the earl of Warwick from December 1461) and three members of the Birnand family of Knaresborough itself (John, George, and William) on Salisbury's instruction disrupted a meeting at which Sir William Plumpton read a royal proclamation. The Birnands, joined by Robert Percy of Scotton, William Wakefield of Ouseburn and two of his sons, Ralph Pullen, James Wilstrop of Ouseburn, and several other local men were later indicted for mustering with the earl's forces at Boroughbridge on 18 September *en route* for Blore Heath. Pullen led some of these men to Knaresborough, which he occupied on behalf of the earl on 26 September.[18] It would seem that by the time he rose in arms in September 1459 Salisbury had already won over a considerable body of support in the honour.

According to the parliamentary indictment of the Yorkist lords two months later, Salisbury set off from Middleham with 5,000 men, among whom his principal captains were his sons Thomas and John, Sir Thomas Harrington, Sir John Conyers, Sir

[16] For the whole of the above paragraph see Pollard, 'Northern Retainers', *passim*.

[17] Ibid. 58, 68. I incorrectly rendered Pollan as Pollard in the original transcription of the document.

[18] Lawson Tancred, *Yorkshire Manor*, p. 67; Wheater, *Knaresburgh*, pp. 158–9.

Thomas Parr, William Stanley, and Thomas Mering of Tong, Shropshire.[19] The last two may have joined the force later; certainly Stanley seems to have done so only on the eve of the battle at Blore Heath. We should probably also add William Bowes of Streatlam, Co. Durham to their number, for he was pardoned by the king in Parliament 'for rearing war against his highness at Ludford'.[20] Salisbury's army was marching to meet York and the earl of Warwick at Worcester. It was intercepted by a Lancastrian force at Blore Heath. The battle which took place on 23 September was a bloody affair. The northern army won; but on the following day, part of the force was ambushed, and Sir Thomas and Sir John Neville and Sir Thomas Harrington were taken prisoner. It was a battered and reduced force which finally joined York and Warwick. Outnumbered by the gathering royal forces the Yorkist lords retreated to Ludlow, where they drew up before the town at Ludford to face their enemies on 12 October. But the desertion of part of the Calais garrison under Andrew Trollope decided the issue. During the night the lords broke camp and fled, making their separate ways to Ireland and Calais, and leaving their men to submit to the king.[21] Six weeks later at a parliament called to Coventry the lords and their principal captains, including Sir Thomas and John Neville, Harrington, Conyers, Parr, Sir James Pickering, and Alice, countess of Salisbury, were condemned for treason and attainted, and their lands forfeited.[22] The resort to force had ended in disaster, and the likely destruction of Neville power in the north. The earl of Northumberland and his family and friends were poised to reap the benefit.

Yet the personal advantage gained by the Percies in the region proved to be strictly limited. Northumberland himself became justice of the forests north of the Trent in succession to Salisbury and constable of Scarborough in succession to Sir Thomas Lumley, and received an annuity of 100 marks from Wakefield. His brother Egremont was granted the office of constable of Conisbrough, but the wardenship of the west march was placed

[19] *Rot. Parl.* v. 348. The precise date might have been 2 Sept., on which day Sir John Conyers was deemed to have become a traitor.　　　[20] *Ibid.* 368.
[21] Gairdner, *Historical Collections*, pp. 204–5; Davies, *An English Chronicle*, p. 80; Griffiths, *Henry VI*, pp. 819–23.
[22] *Rot. Parl.* v. 348–50; Griffiths, *Henry VI*, pp. 823–5.

in the hands of Lord Clifford; the chief stewardship of the duchy of Lancaster in the north went to Viscount Beaumont; and the stewardship of Pontefract to the earl of Shrewsbury. Other royal offices previously held by Neville, the chamberlainship of the receipt of the Exchequer and the stewardship of Kendal, were passed to Sir Richard Tunstall, the king's Chamberlain.[23] Northumberland's principal benefit was financial. Salisbury's estates were retained in royal hands, and their management passed into the control of the chamber of the royal household. New officers were appointed: John, Lord Neville, brother of the earl of Westmorland, as constable and steward of Sheriff Hutton; Lord FitzHugh as steward of Middleham and Richmond.[24] Richard Clervaux of Croft became under-steward; Ralph Eure, son and heir of Sir William of Witton, was appointed receiver-general. Of these only Eure could be considered a Percy servant. Several small cash annuities and lesser offices were distributed to other loyalists. William Branklow of the royal household became parker of 'the Great Park' of Middleham; Humphrey Neville, brother of Lord Neville, became parker of Caplebank in Middleham; Lord Neville himself received 100 marks from Worton and Wensleydale, part of the same lordship; and Thomas, Lord Scrope of Masham received £40 from several of its manors.[25] But the greater part of the revenues of these lordships was earmarked to contribute towards the settlement of all Northumberland's outstanding arrears of wages for the captaincy of Berwick and the wardenship of the east march, totalling nearly £17,000. On the first day of the meeting of the Coventry parliament Northumberland was granted £208 annually from Middleham; £237 from Sheriff Hutton; and just over £300, nearly all the annual revenue, from Penrith. No

[23] CPR, 1452–61, 533–41, 538, 544, 594–5; Somerville, Duchy of Lancaster, i. 421, 514; Storey, 'Wardens', p. 164.

[24] CPR, 1452–61, 528, 536, 540, 543. There seems to have been some confusion over these grants. At first Lord Neville was granted the offices in Middleham and Sheriff Hutton (19 December) and Lord FitzHugh those in Richmond (22 December). But on 29 Jan. a new patent created FitzHugh steward of all the lordships within Richmondshire, a formula which conventionally included Middleham. The grant of an annuity of 100 marks to Lord Neville charged to the forest of Wensleydale on 18 March may have been in compensation for lost office.

[25] Ibid. 539–40, 546, 551–3.

doubt the appointment of Ralph Eure as receiver-general was intended to facilitate actual payments, orders for which were not issued until the following March. Perhaps not even this arrangement was working satisfactorily, for on 3 June the grants were converted to a lease for twelve years from Easter, at a farm yet to be agreed.[26] Northumberland was to be satisfied in his demands for payment as warden; but he was not to be given the same overmighty power in the region that Salisbury had enjoyed.

Deliberate policy not to repeat the mistake of putting too much power into the hands of one man may have been one reason why Northumberland was not able to take extensive advantage from the Yorkist failure in 1459. Another possible reason is that other lords stood in his way. Lord Clifford, as we have seen, not Northumberland, took over from Salisbury and Warwick in the west march. Bishop Booth of Durham completed the expulsion of Neville influence from his diocese. After his attainder Salisbury lost his annuity, and he and his brother Fauconberg were removed from the bench. Perhaps more significantly, Booth stepped in and confiscated the lordship of Barnard Castle from the earl of Warwick. He did so, moreover, *before* the meeting of Parliament at Coventry which attainted the earl. On 17 November 1459 he issued letters to his officers, Henry Gillow, Geoffrey Middleton, and Robert Weardale authorizing them to hold the manorial courts at Barnard Castle, Gainford, Middleton-in-Teesdale, and Longnewton. It was the bishop, not the king, who exercised the right of forfeiture. He thus, probably with royal connivance, secured what Robert Neville had attempted in 1439: the recovery of the lordship for the palatinate. Other appointments followed. Booth's own receiver, John Ireland, was put in, and on 2 January John, Lord Neville was appointed constable and master forester of Teesdale, with the customary fees of 20 marks. The restoration of the Nevilles of Raby in the bishopric was completed by Neville's appointment to the bench on 6 March.[27]

In the North Riding the chief beneficiary of Salisbury's fall was Henry, Lord FitzHugh, who became the royal steward of

---

[26] CCR, 1454–61, 411–14; CFR, 1452–61, 274.
[27] Durh. 3/48/5,6,7.

Middleham and Richmond. FitzHugh's willingness to serve the
victorious court is on the face of it surprising, since he was
apparently a committed follower of the earl against Northumberland. Salisbury's son-in-law, he had succeeded to his
estates in 1452, and had supported the Nevilles in 1453–4.[28] But
his first grant of the stewardships on 22 December 1459 was
specifically for his good service against the rebels.[29] He had
taken the oath of allegiance to the Crown demanded of the lords
in Parliament on 11 December; his presence at Coventry clearly
implies that he concurred in the attainders of the Neville earls
and their principal lieutenants. The one concession he seems to
have secured was a pardon for his brother-in-law, William
Bowes, who was originally included in the number of those to be
attainted for making war against the king. He solemnly swore to
be henceforth ready at all times to serve the king and resist any
acts against him. On 20 December and 28 April 1460 he served
as a commissioner of array in the North Riding.[30]

Yet later FitzHugh, and Lord Greystoke, who had also taken
the parliamentary oath at Coventry, came under suspicion.
According to the pseudo-Worcester, at the council of war held
by Queen Margaret at York in January 1461, 'they suffered much
trouble, and they swore an oath to be loyal to the queen and her
son': in effect they were obliged to renew the Coventry oath.[31]
Only one chronicle recorded their presence at Wakefield;
perhaps they had held back.[32] They did march south with the
queen to St Albans, but neither is identified by any source as
having fought there or at Towton six weeks later. Both avoided
attainder by Edward IV. It may be guessed therefore that they
deserted Queen Margaret some time during these weeks.
Perhaps their desertion is recorded, but garbled, in Gregory's
comment that on the eve of the battle 'the most part of Northern
men fled away'.[33] It is even conceivable that Greystoke was
playing a double game, with Neville encouragement. Salisbury's retainer, he was immediately employed by Edward IV in

[28] Griffiths, 'Local Rivalries', p. 605.   [29] *CPR, 1452–61, 536.*
[30] *Rot. Parl.* v. 351–2, 368; *CPR, 1452–61, 559, 603.*
[31] *The Wars of the English in France*, ed. J. Stevenson, ii. 2, RS, 22 (1864), 775.
[32] 'John Benet's Chronicle', ed. G. L. and M. A. Harriss, in *Camden Miscellany*, xxiv, Camden, 4th ser., ix (1972), 228.
[33] Gairdner, *Historical Collections*, p. 212.

the north after he came to the throne, was retained on the commission of peace, and served with Warwick and Montagu in northern campaigns in the early years of the new reign.[34] FitzHugh, on the other hand, was not at first trusted. He had to work his way back into favour. He was not, for instance, recalled to the commission of the peace in the North Riding until November 1465.[35] Only grudgingly was he welcomed by a Yorkist (and Neville) establishment to which he had been judged insufficiently loyal during the years of crisis.

Salisbury appears to have raised rebellion against Henry VI in 1459 without taking the precaution of settling his lands in the hands of feoffees. One or two of his principal lieutenants, who were attainted alongside him, had been more careful. There is unequivocal testimony that Sir Thomas Harrington, having decided to take up arms on his lord's behalf, took deliberate steps to protect his inheritance. He,

remembering himself of the great wars and troubles likely to fall among such mighty princes not having [knowledge] how God would dispose them, . . . made a feoffment to William Booth, late archbishop of York, John, the earl of Shrewsbury, John, late lord Clifford and divers other to the intent that for the same lords were mighty and in consort with the contrary party [they] should by fair means, if God fortuned the field the said wars to go against that party that the said Sir Thomas was upon, and if law happened to proceed as well against him as other and he be attainted, should save his lands unforfeited.[36]

In the event his worst fears were realized; but it is to be assumed that his lands were protected under the proviso of the Act of Attainder that explicitly excluded such enfeoffments from the penalty of the law. Harrington deliberately enfeoffed his land in the hands of those he anticipated would be on the opposite side. Perhaps Sir John Conyers took similar steps in enfeoffing those lands which he held in right of his wife in the hands of men drawn from both sides: John, Lord Neville and Sir Richard Tunstall, who were 'in consort with the opposite party'; Robert Danby and Richard Pigot, lawyers, closely associated with his

---

own party; and Lord FitzHugh himself. On 19 December 1459 the right of these feoffees was recognized, and the lands granted to them on condition that the issue and profits were delivered to Lady Margery Conyers.[37] The concern of the Conyers family not to jeopardize its inheritance as a result of Sir John's acts is made apparent both by the promptness with which Christopher, Sir John's father, secured a general pardon on the same day; and by the complex resettlement he made of his own lands by final concord in February 1460, against the event of his dying while his son was still attainted.[38]

The precautions taken by these two attainted men, Harrington and Conyers, leaves one to wonder, therefore, whether Salisbury, if he did not make similar enfeoffments of his lands, did not nevertheless instruct certain of his servants (including Greystoke) to co-operate with the regime in the event of his defeat in 1459. This is one plausible explanation of the government's leniency towards his councillor Thomas Witham, who secured a pardon on 3 December 1459 and was retained on the bench for the North Riding.[39] Many others of Salisbury's retainers and associates received pardons over the following months: Sir John Huddleston, Ralph Rokeby, John Acklam, Sir John Middleton; William Burgh the elder and his son; Richard Scrope, son of Lord Scrope of Bolton; Richard Conyers, brother of Sir John; James Harrington, son of Sir Thomas; Thomas Lepton of Terrington, Sir Thomas Mountford of Hackforth, and William Pudsay of Selaby.[40] There is no knowing how many of these fought at Blore Heath and marched to Ludford, but escaped attainder. Sir James Strangways, who acted openly for the Yorkist lords immediately after their victory at Northampton, fought at (and survived) Wakefield, and was the Speaker in Edward IV's first parliament, did not need to secure a royal pardon at all.[41] Sir Thomas Mountford, of whose loyalty the court clearly became suspicious, was at first put on the commission of array alongside Lord FitzHugh in December

[37] *CPR, 1452–61*, 537–8.
[38] Ibid.; PRO, CP 25(1) 281/16/43 and BL, Egerton MS 3402, fo. 96d, in which the purpose of the settlement is made explicit.
[39] *CPR, 1452–61*, 540, 576. He was one of Christopher Conyers's plaintiffs in the fine of February 1460.
[40] Ibid. 527, 545, 549, 568, 577, 581, 591–2.
[41] *Paston Letters*, i. 540; Wedgwood, *Biographies*, p. 820.

1459. But after he took out a pardon on 11 February he was dropped from the commission of the peace in March, and not trusted to be a commissioner of array again in April.[42]

It is clear, however, that the core of the Neville affinity, while under suspicion, remained intact, and was not destroyed in the aftermath of Ludford. Indeed, by the summer of 1460 Neville retainers were beginning once more to disturb Yorkshire. On 30 May Northumberland, Roos, Sir Ralph Percy, and a number of Percy retainers were granted a commission of oyer and terminer to deal with treasons, insurrections, and felonies in the county. Four days later orders were issued to Northumberland and others to arrest Sir John Middleton, the probable instigator, and to bring him before the king and council.[43] This rising may well have been deliberately timed to keep Northumberland and his allies in the north while the Yorkist lords landed at Sandwich.

The evidence all suggests that, notwithstanding the scale of the defeat suffered by the Nevilles in 1459, the attainders, and the redistribution of lands and offices, the court was not able to break Neville power in the north-east. One reason why the Neville affinity remained intact and ready to fight another day may have been that the earl had deliberately not committed all his strength in 1459. Moreover, after Ludford his interests may have been covertly protected and sustained by men such as Greystoke, Witham, Christopher Conyers, and Sir James Strangways. Another reason may have been that the court was neither sufficiently aware of the strength of the Nevilles in the north, nor sufficiently determined to impose its authority immediately. Far from being over-ruthless in the proscription of their enemies, as is generally assumed, the adherents of Queen Margaret were arguably not ruthless enough in seeking to eradicate the nest of Neville followers in the north-east. And time was not on their side.

Salisbury, Warwick, and the earl of March landed at Sandwich on 26 June 1460. They entered London on 2 July. Leaving Salisbury to blockade the Tower, Warwick, March, and Fauconberg set out two days later to face the royal army at Northampton on 10 July. Thanks to the timely desertion of Lord Grey of Ruthin the day was theirs. Among the dead was Thomas

---

[42] *CPR, 1452–61*, 559, 603, 682–3.   [43] Ibid. 609.

Percy, Lord Egremont. They returned to London in triumph, the king in their company and the royal government in their hands. Salisbury imposed himself as the king's Chamberlain in place of Sir Richard Tunstall; Laurence Booth was removed from the office of Privy Seal; George Neville, bishop of Exeter became the new Chancellor. Writs were sent out for a new parliament to meet at Westminster on 7 October, the principal purpose of which was to annul the Acts of the Coventry parliament and to reverse the attainders.[44]

Equally pressing needs were to crush in the field the remaining Lancastrians, who were gathering in the north, and to recover actual possession of forfeited estates. Neither was easily achieved. Although in the first flush of victory the Yorkist lords were able to secure the election of Sir James Strangways and Sir Thomas Mountford as MPs for Yorkshire on 30 July,[45] control of the county was not fully recovered. Even before the election, on 28 July, Sir Thomas Neville, Sir John Neville, and Sir Thomas Harrington were appointed to arrest disturbers of the peace.[46] As the lack of authority of the new government in the north-east became more apparent a series of increasingly desperate commissions and orders were issued. On 24 August a second and more powerful commission, headed by the Yorkist lords and composed entirely of their retainers, was charged with the responsibility of arresting fifteen men, several from Percy manors, who were said to be uttering falsehoods to arouse discord among the magnates of the realm. On the same day Northumberland and his servants were ordered to surrender Pontefract and Wressle to Salisbury. On 26 August, the gravity of the situation having sunk in, a new commission was issued to arrest all oppressors, plunderers, and slayers of the king's people in Yorkshire.[47] None of these royal commands was effective. The lords remained in London awaiting York's return from Ireland and the meeting of Parliament called for 7 October; their Yorkshire retainers were powerless in the face of the entrenched

---

[44] Griffiths, *Henry VI*, pp. 859–63; Ross, *Edward IV*, pp. 26–7.

[45] PRO, c219/16/6/1/6.   [46] *CPR, 1452–61*, 607.

[47] Ibid. 608, 610. Wressle had escheated to the Crown on the death of Lord Egremont. It would appear that after the battle of Northampton Henry VI had been persuaded to grant it to Salisbury or his son Sir Thomas, but that Northumberland had taken it into his own hands.

military strength of Northumberland and his allies in the north.

A renewed effort to assert authority in Yorkshire was made once Parliament had met and the attainders were reversed. On 8 October mandates were issued to Lord Clifford to expel evil-doers from Penrith and return the lordship to Salisbury. Similarly Northumberland was ordered yet again to do the same with Pontefract and Wressle.[48] Since Clifford and Northumberland were almost certainly themselves the principal 'evil-doers' it is unlikely that any more note was taken of these orders. Indeed six days later a commission which included hostile peers such as Scrope of Masham, Dacre, and Neville, as well as retainers such as Lumley, Sir John Conyers, and John Harrington was ordered to take further action, the use of force if necessary, to recover all three.[49] An undated petition to Parliament concerning these vain efforts has survived, in which it is recited that the earl of Northumberland had persistently refused to surrender Wressle and at least one another castle to Salisbury, and had been responsible for the murder of the unfortunate messenger and bearer of one of the letters. Northumberland was ordered to appear before Chancery by the following 20 January, but it is highly unlikely that he would have done so.[50] In fact the reported retort of the earl and Clifford, joined by Dacre and Neville, was to indulge in an orgy of looting of Yorkshire estates belonging to York and Salisbury.[51]

Salisbury probably enjoyed greater success in securing possession of Middleham and Sheriff Hutton. On 8 October, on the same day that Clifford was ordered to expel evil-doers from Penrith, the inhabitants and tenants of Middleham were ordered henceforth to pay to the earl all those rents which by Act of the Coventry parliament and subsequent grants they had been commanded to pay elsewhere.[52] It would seem that the local

---

[48] CPR, 1452–61, 649.   [49] Ibid. 651.

[50] PRO, Chancery, Parliament and Council Proceedings, 32/8. Professor Griffiths ('Local Rivalries', p. 626) tentatively allocated this document to 1456. But it is clear from the wording of the letter sent under the Great Seal that it refers to the order of 8 Oct. 1460. I am grateful to Margaret Condon for her advice on this matter.

[51] Stevenson, Wars of the English, ii. 2, 774.

[52] CPR, 1452–61, 647. No such order was issued for Sheriff Hutton, where perhaps Thomas Witham was fully in control.

administration as well as tenants needed assurance that they would not be committing an offence in recognizing the restoration of the earl; although it is to be wondered whether Salisbury was actually able to raise any revenues, or even to protect his estates from looting by his enemies. By the time Parliament went down early in December Yorkshire was in anarchy, and in a state of disorder on a scale far exceeding the troubles of 1453 and 1454.

In these circumstances it is no wonder that York and Salisbury marched north as soon as possible in an attempt to recover control. But it would appear that the Lancastrian lords had brought together an unprecedentedly large army in the late autumn of 1460, whose size, and the speed with which it was raised, apparently took the Yorkist lords in London by surprise. Queen Margaret herself had fled from Northampton to Wales, and eventually made her way to Scotland in December, and thence to York in January 1461.[53] The earls of Northumberland and Westmorland (or at least the latter's agent acting in his name) had already raised the far north on her behalf. On 15 and 16 November the north gate of Palace Green at Durham was reinforced as a precaution, while their men, arrayed for war, passed through the city on their journey towards 'Pomfret' and other parts of the county of York. At the same time the duke of Somerset, who had been attempting to recover Calais, returned to England, landed in Dorset, and with the earl of Devon marched north with a contingent of men.[54] Ultimately all gathered at Hull, where they prepared to launch their counter-attack. This huge army, reported to be 15,000 strong, was drawn with varying degrees of willingness largely from the ranks of retainers and tenants of the lords themselves.[55]

On 8 December a commission of oyer and terminer was issued under York, Salisbury, and Warwick, still including Westmorland and Lord Neville, touching all treasons, insurrections, and rebellions in the midlands as well as the northern counties. A day later York and Salisbury set out for the north, backed by a

---

[53] Gairdner, *Historical Collections*, p. 210; Stevenson, *Wars of the English*, ii. 2, 775.

[54] Durham, Church Commission, Bishopric Estates, 189815.

[55] Stevenson, *Wars of the English*, ii. 2, 774; Davies, *An English Chronicle*, pp. 106–7.

further commission issued on 10 December giving them
responsibility for restoring order and royal authority.[56] They
reached York's castle of Sandal shortly before Christmas,
accompanied by York's son the earl of Rutland, Sir Thomas
Neville, and Sir Thomas Harrington. It would seem that even at
this eleventh hour they had underestimated the strength of the
enemy. On 30 December, either out foraging, or, as seems
equally likely, seeking to retreat from their over-extended and
exposed position, their army was intercepted and defeated outside Wakefield. York, Rutland, Sir Thomas Neville, and Harrington were killed; Salisbury was taken alive, brought to Pontefract, and then seized and murdered by the local commons,
who 'loved him not'.[57]

The way was now open for the victorious Lancastrians to
march on London. Their huge and poorly disciplined force
poured south, creating panic as it advanced. There is little doubt
that those communities through which the army passed were
pillaged. It is likely too that religious houses and churches were
robbed. One frightened chronicler recorded that they left a
thirty-mile-wide swathe of destruction in their wake.[58] Before
them the rumour ran that they were 'appointed to pill . . . in all
the south country'; that Queen Margaret herself had given leave
for them to sack London, Coventry, Bristol, and Salisbury and
the neighbouring shires in payment for their service. The hysteria, stoked by the earl of Warwick in Westminster, who drew
upon the same fears to rally support for his cause,[59] ultimately
forced the queen to hold back. For although she achieved a
second resounding victory over Warwick outside St Albans on
12 February, and recovered control of the person of the king, she
hesitated before moving into London, which lay within her

[56] CPR, 1452–61, 652–3. The author of the English Chronicle, p. 106,
claimed that Neville 'under a false colour' secured a commission to raise a force
to put down the rebellion; which force he promptly put to the service of the
Lancastrian lords.
   [57] Griffiths, Henry VI, p. 820; Ross, Edward IV, p. 30; Davies, An English
Chronicle, p. 107. The manner of Salisbury's death is a telling indictment of his
regime as steward of Pontefract.
   [58] Davies, English Chronicle, p. 107; Riley, St. Ingulph's Chronicles, pp. 422
–3.
   [59] Paston Letters, i. 541; Davies, An English Chronicle, p. 109; Scofield,
Edward the Fourth, i. 135–6.

grasp. Instead she retreated north, surrendering the initiative to Edward, the new duke of York. Entering the city in triumph with the earl of Warwick on 26 February, Edward assumed the crown six days later, and prepared in all haste to pursue the queen's army northwards.[60] All was set for the final, bloody climax of six months of civil war on the field of Towton.

On 11 March the advance guard, under the command of Lord Fauconberg, set out on foot. By 27 and 28 March the whole army had reached Pontefract. The Lancastrians sought to hold the line of the River Aire; but on 28 March a crossing was forced at Castleford, and the Lancastrian defences were turned. This vanguard was driven north, and in the fighting Lords Clifford and Neville were killed. The initial success was achieved by Lord Fauconberg, the most experienced soldier on either side, who led the Yorkist attack on the main Lancastrian army on the following day. With a strong wind behind blowing flurries of snow into their enemies' faces, the direct frontal assault of the Yorkists gained the first advantage. But the battle was long and savage. Only at the end of the day, when the duke of Norfolk came up with fresh troops to reinforce the Yorkist army, did the Lancastrians break and flee. The death-toll was huge. The earl of Northumberland and Lord Dacre fell on the field; the earls of Devon and Wiltshire were later captured and executed. No fewer than forty-two knights were said to have been slain after the battle. Henry VI, Queen Margaret, and the Prince of Wales, who had awaited the outcome at York, escaped to Scotland; other survivors, Exeter, Somerset, and Roos among them, made their escape to join them.[61]

The battle of Towton resolved two issues. It established Edward IV on the throne and it restored the Nevilles to complete control in Yorkshire. Towton was not only the climax of the dynastic struggle between Lancaster and York, it was also the denouement of the feud between Neville and Percy. For eighteen months after Ludford the Percies had enjoyed their one period of ascendancy, and at Wakefield had avenged the deaths of the second earl of Northumberland and Egremont on Salisbury and Sir Thomas Neville. At Towton all that had been reversed, and Warwick had avenged himself on the third earl for

---

[60] Ross, *Edward IV*, pp. 32–4.   [61] Ibid. 36–8.

the deaths of his father and brother. Now the Percies were routed; the challenge to Neville dominance in ruins. Moreover, in the final battle the Nevilles of Raby had been dealt another blow, and the power of other local lords, Clifford and Roos, who had allied themselves with Percy, had been broken. Neville control of the north-east was not quite complete: the bishop of Durham, Laurence Booth, was yet to be subdued. But the earl of Warwick had the monopoly of power in the region within his grasp. The Nevilles of Middleham stood on the threshold of being the unchallenged lords of north-eastern England.

12

The Neville Ascendancy, 1461–1471

IT took three years for the Yorkists to secure the whole of north-eastern England after their resounding victory at Towton.[1] Henry VI, in flight from York, was for a brief while besieged by Sir Robert Ogle, Sir John Conyers, and others in Carham Castle, Northumberland. He was able, however, to escape to Scotland.[2] While Edward IV remained in York for three weeks, celebrating Easter there, Lords Fauconberg and Greystoke were sent to Beverley to secure the support of the townspeople. The king meanwhile moved north to Durham, where he arrived on 22 April and received Laurence Booth, the bishop, into his service, conferring on him the honour of being his confessor. By 1 May Edward IV reached Newcastle, where the earl of Wiltshire, John Morton, Sir William Plumpton, and other fugitives from Towton who had fled to Cockermouth in Cumberland were brought before him.[3] Wiltshire was promptly executed. Beyond Newcastle Edward did not venture: but he left Fauconberg in command of the castle and Sir George Lumley at Tynemouth to support Sir Robert Ogle and others who were endeavouring to subdue Northumberland.[4] He returned to Durham; to Middleham to stay with Warwick (5–7 May); and then to York again, before setting off for Westminster and his coronation.[5] The Nevilles remained behind, for there were

---

[1] Full accounts of the northern campaigns of 1461–4 already exist in print in Ross, *Edward IV*, pp. 46–63, and Scofield, *Edward the Fourth*, i. 244–9, 261–6, 292–3, 309–14, 328–31. See also Ch. 9 above, in which the Scottish dimension is emphasized.

[2] *Paston Letters*, ii. 233; Scofield, *Edward the Fourth*, i. 166–7.

[3] Ibid. 174–5.

[4] Ibid. 177. On 2 May the king commanded Ogle to take possession of Harbottle and Redesdale, belonging to Sir William Tailboys, and Ford and other properties of John Heron, and to crush all resistance in Northumberland (*CPR*, 1461–7, 29).

[5] Scofield, *Edward the Fourth*, i. 177–8. For the grants made to Warwick at Middleham on 5 and 7 May see *CPR*, 1461–7, 45, 95.

further disturbances even in the North Riding, which Warwick and his retainers were commissioned to suppress on 13 May.[6] Early in June a joint Lancastrian and Scottish force attacked Carlisle, but were beaten off by Lord Montagu. Later in the same month Sir Thomas Neville of Brancepeth led a raid into Durham, which the bishop's levies resisted.[7] Only slow and incomplete progress was made north of the Tyne. Alnwick and Dunstanburgh were taken by the end of September; but it is to be doubted whether the new regime could be sure of much of the Northumberland countryside. Bamburgh was still in Lancastrian hands late in 1461; Alnwick was retaken by Sir William Tailboys, and was not recovered until July following, when Sir Ralph Grey was put in as captain.[8] But by the time Parliament assembled on 4 November the north appeared to be sufficiently secure for Warwick, Fauconberg, and Montagu to attend.

By this time Edward IV had already begun to reward his friends and punish his enemies. Warwick was understandably the most generously rewarded. To him was entrusted the keeping of the east as well as the west march. While staying with him at Middleham on 7 May the king appointed him Great Chamberlain, constable of Dover, Warden of the Cinque Ports, steward of the royal lordship of Feckenham, Worcestershire, and master of the royal mews. By 14 December 1461 he was acting as Admiral.[9] But apart from the extension of authority to the east march (revoked in favour of his brother Montagu two years later) sufficient reward in northern England was the confirmation, also issued at Middleham on 5 May, of all offices for life which his father had held jointly with him, and for twenty years all farms and custodies held similarly. In particular this encompassed the chief stewardship of the duchy of Lancaster in both the north and the south, chief steward of the duchy honours in Lancashire, and the stewardships of Pontefract, Knaresborough, and Pickering.[10]

---

[6] *CPR, 1461–7*, 30.   [7] *Rot. Parl.* v. 478.

[8] Scofield, *Edward the Fourth*, i. 204; Stevenson, *Wars of the English*, ii. pt. 1, p. 204. William Tunstall, brother of Sir Richard, held Bamburgh for Henry VI. Alnwick was probably taken by Tailboys on 30 Nov. Sir William Bowes was later paid for its custody from 17 Sept. to 30 Nov. 1461 (*CPR, 1461–7, 79*).

[9] *CPR, 1461–7*, 45. Salisbury had been Chamberlain since Jan. 1460.

[10] Ibid. 95. He was also given the custody of George Neville, Lord Latimer by separate grant on the same day (ibid. 71). See also above, p. 251.

In the spring of 1462 he was granted in fee simple the Percy lordship of Topcliffe in the North Riding and all Percy estates in Craven, as well as the Clifford possessions in Westmorland (Brough, Brougham, and Appleby).[11] Three years later, on 11 April 1465, the fee simple was converted to tail male, and he was additionally granted Cockermouth, a third part of the barony of Egremont, and the hereditary shrievalty of Westmorland. The grants in Cumberland and Westmorland, including the custody of the temporalities of the see of Carlisle (12 December 1463 to 5 June 1464), were no doubt intended to help defray the costs of the wardenship of the west march.[12] The grants of Percy estates in the North Riding and Craven, which yielded a net income to him of £212 in 1467/8,[13] enhanced his authority in northern Yorkshire.

William Neville, Lord Fauconberg's services were also quickly recognized by Edward IV. He was created earl of Kent, made steward of the royal household, and on 1 August 1462 granted fifty-six west-country manors, largely from the Courtenay inheritance, on the intention that he should establish the king's authority there. But he died a year later, before he could do so.[14] The third Neville, John, Warwick's brother, had to earn his rewards. He had been created Lord Montagu in February 1461, and was initally granted the royal mines in Devon or Cornwall for his services at Towton, and for life the issues of subsidy and ulnage of cloth at Hull, and nine forfeited manors of the Beaumont family.[15] These relatively insubstantial grants were all he received until, on 1 June 1463, to face renewed emergency in Northumberland, he was made warden of the east march in succession to Warwick. Only after he had decisively defeated the Lancastrian rebels in the county at Hedgeley Moor and Hexham (March and May 1464) was he more generously rewarded. He was created earl of Northumberland on 27 May, granted all the estates of the Percies in the county of Northumberland on 1 August following, and subsequently appointed sheriff of the county for life on 26 July 1466. The only

[11] Ibid. 189.
[12] Ibid. 292, 332.
[13] Durham, Church Commission, Bishopric Estates, 18908.
[14] Ross, *Edward IV*, p. 72; CPR, 1461–7, 73.
[15] *CPR, 1461–7*, 19, 130, 195.

other Percy possession he received after the death of his uncle Fauconberg was Wressle, which had once been intended for his elder brother Sir Thomas.[16]

The Percy estates were in fact divided three ways. The third share, the remaining Yorkshire properties in the East and West Riding, were settled on the king's younger brother, George, duke of Clarence. These, principally Healaugh, Seamer, and Spofforth, were first granted to him in 1462. He also received a grant of the reversion of Leconfield, Catton, and other places which were held in dower by Eleanor, the countess of Northumberland.[17] Clarence did not do homage for his land until July 1466,[18] and it is possible that until then the earl of Warwick or his servants looked after his Yorkshire interests. Such an arrangement might lie behind Leland's inaccurate report concerning Spofforth that

the manor place was sore defaced in the time of the Civil War betwixt Henry VI and Edward IV by the Earl of Warwick, and Marquis Montagu his brother, to whom, as I remember, the Percy's lands were given.[19]

In law too, Clarence held the lordship of Richmond in north Yorkshire and the reversion of the dower in it held by Jacquetta, duchess of Bedford. But the Middleham estate records of 1465–6 make it clear that Warwick, like his father before him, retained actual possession.[20]

Only a few Neville retainers and servants received significant grants from Edward IV. Sir Robert Ogle, created Lord Ogle, was appointed steward of the Percy estates in Northumberland, and granted in tail male in January 1462 the Tailboys lordships of Redesdale and Harbottle. He was also granted several Percy estates at the same time, which were later transferred to Lord Montagu.[21] Sir Thomas Lumley was likewise raised to the

---

[16] *CPR, 1461–7*, 341, 426, 525.

[17] Ibid. 198, 212–13.

[18] M. A. Hicks, *False, Fleeting, Perjur'd Clarence: George, Duke of Clarence, 1449–78* (Gloucester, 1980), 26.

[19] Leland, *Itinerary*, pp. 87–8.

[20] *CPR, 1461–7*, 212–13; PRO, SC6/1085/20. The grant to Clarence superseded a grant made a month earlier to his younger brother Richard. The earl of Warwick's council met to agree leases of Arkengarth vaccaries at Richmond Castle on 22 Apr. 1466.

[21] *CPR, 1461–7*, 113–14, 466.

peerage; but his only other royal reward, notwithstanding his long and costly service as sheriff of Northumberland from 1461 to 1463, was restoration to the constableship of Scarborough.[22] On the whole the king was not called upon, or did not choose, to shower many gifts on Warwick's men. Thomas Witham was confirmed as Chancellor of the Exchequer; Henry Sotehill, one of Warwick's principal legal counsellors, was made Attorney-General.[23] Otherwise they benefited mainly from grants of custody of the lands and heirs of attainted Lancastrians, or from the grants of offices on their estates. Thus Sir Thomas Parr received the custody of the Hotham lands; John, Lord Scrope of Bolton, received the custody of the Bigod lands and the wardship of the young heir Ralph.[24] Sir Robert Constable was appointed steward of Spofforth and other Yorkshire properties of the Percies on 8 August 1461; William Harrington received herbage worth £12 p.a. from a moor belonging to Lord Clifford; Richard Musgrave, son of Sir Richard of Hartley, was made constable, master forester, and bailiff of the Clifford lordships of Pendragon, Kirkby Stephen, and Brough on 1 February 1462; and Sir John Conyers was promoted steward of Topcliffe three weeks later. But these latter were clearly related to the subsequent grant of the same places to Warwick, and might be taken more as his appointments than the Crown's.[25] Royal office of a minor kind, such as the grant of a riding forestership at Galtres to Thomas Gower of Stittenham, and clerk of the works of Clarendon to his brother Edward, were few and far between.[26] Only Sir John Huddleston of Millom, Cumberland and Hunderthwaite in Teesdale, whose son was to marry Warwick's illegitimate daughter in 1465, amassed a number of rewards. Between 15 November and 23 December 1461 he received offices and lands in four separate royal grants, said to be worth £113. 3s. 4d. per annum.[27]

Yet it is clear that several of Warwick's other retainers gave unstinting service during the early 1460s. Sir William Bowes, knighted early in the new reign, with a hundred men garrisoned

[22] Ibid. 44, 84, 332.   [23] Ibid. 6.   [24] Ibid. 27, 228.

[25] Ibid. 39, 116, 118, 143. In Jan. 1464 Sir John Conyers was replaced as steward of Topcliffe by John Burgh, Warwick's appointee (PRO, SC6/1085/20).

[26] CPR, 1461–7, 53, 151.

[27] Ibid. 62, 87, 151, 154.

Alnwick at his own cost from 13 September to 30 November 1461, for which he was later compensated by the crown. He died in office as sheriff of Northumberland in the summer of 1466.[28] Sir James Strangways and Sir John Conyers served under Warwick in Northumberland in December 1462 and sat on many Yorkist commissions, but their royal reward was negligible.[29] William Burgh of Brough, whose son was married to one of Sir John Conyers' sisters, threw himself into service in the Yorkist cause immediately after Towton. He was a commissioner appointed on 13 May 1461 to deal with lingering opposition in the North Riding; fifteen days later he joined the commission of the peace; and on 13 November he became a commissioner of array to resist the Scots. On 10 February 1462 he was appointed constable of Prudhoe, a Percy castle on the Tyne then still in royal hands.[30] When a year later Prudhoe was granted to George, duke of Clarence, Burgh's appointment was renewed. In his contract with the duke it was agreed:

The same William is to keep the said castle at his proper charge, and costs, at his own peril to the use of the said Duke, unless that such casualty falls by infortune of war that it shall pass his right and power so to do; for the which in such case it is to be kept at the costs and charges of the said Duke.[31]

To help defray his costs he was granted the lease of all the demesne of the lordship for a farm of £6. 13s. 4d.[32] Burgh apparently held Prudhoe secure for the house of York. But by late 1463 practically all Northumberland north of the Tyne had fallen back into Lancastrian hands, and Prudhoe was on the front line. On 8 December Burgh entered into a local truce with the Lancastrian leaders, and was issued a letter of protection and safeguard in the name of Henry VI, in which the king ordered that no one should 'vex, trouble nor hurt' William and his servants; while William himself undertook for the next six months to 'do nothing nor procure to be done that shall be hurt

[28] *CPR, 1461–7*, 79, 525, 536.
[29] *Three Fifteenth Century Chronicles*, ed. J. Gairdner, Camden, NS xxviii (1880), 157. Other Warwick retainers serving in December 1462 included Robert Conyers, Sir William Harrington, Sir John Huddleston, and Sir Thomas Mountford.
[30] *CPR, 1461–6*, 30, 66, 143, 576.
[31] NYCRO, ZRL 1/27.   [32] Ibid. 1/28.

or prejudicial unto us'.[33] This appears to have been accepted as a service well done. Certainly Prudhoe was thereby preserved as a base for Lord Montagu on the eve of the battle of Hexham in the following May. And a year later, in May 1465, when Prudhoe had passed to Montagu, now earl of Northumberland, William Burgh the younger, Burgh's eldest son and heir, was appointed to 'be of counsel of the letting of my land and tenancies' within the lordship, and granted the profits of the orchard.[34]

The case of William Burgh, for which by chance documentation is fuller, suggests that Warwick and Montagu themselves were expected to find the major part of rewards for their retainers from their own resources. This they no doubt did. In Knaresborough, for instance, Warwick quickly rewarded Robert Percy, John Pullen, Richard Louther, and William Wakefield with office and farms.[35] While in the short term this represented a saving for the young king, in the longer term the effect was to strengthen the house of Neville at the expense of the house of York. The king himself did promote some of his own men in Yorkshire, notably John Pilkington, esquire of the body, who was granted three Yorkshire manors forfeited from Lords Roos and Clifford and a clutch of reversions in February 1462, and two years later the master forestership of Sowerby. He became a JP in the West Riding in 1464. Other royal servants to benefit were Ralph Ashton of Fryton and Edmund Hastings of Roxby, granted the Neville manor of Gilling in December 1461.[36] Yet the king's men in Yorkshire, especially northern Yorkshire, remained relatively few in number—a circumstance which was to have important consequences at the end of the decade.

Edward IV's judgement was as questionable in the treatment of his enemies as in the rewarding of his friends. The Act of Attainder passed in November 1461 meticulously identified those responsible for separate acts of treason, from the killing of the heir to the throne (Richard of York) at Wakefield on 30 December 1460 to the Lancastrian raid on Durham in June 1461. All the great Lancastrian nobles, living and dead, were included: Exeter, Somerset, Northumberland, Devon, Pembroke, Roos,

[33] Ibid. 1/30.
[34] Ibid. 1/32. For further discussion see Pollard, 'Burghs of Brough', p. 15.
[35] Arnold, 'West Riding', p. 163.
[36] CPR, 1461–7, 86, 113, 141, 269, 344, 577.

Clifford, Beaumont, Neville, and Dacre. FitzHugh and Greystoke escaped: FitzHugh saved perhaps only by his close blood
and territorial relationship with Warwick. Prominent gentry,
especially Percy retainers, were caught in the net too. Of Percy
retainers the following Yorkshiremen were attainted for their
involvement in one or more acts of treason: Sir Ralph Bigod,
Sir Philip Wentworth, Sir Robert Babthorpe, Sir William
Gascoigne, Sir Richard Tempest, Sir John Hotham, Roger Ward,
and Sir Thomas Everingham. Sir William Tailboys and Sir
Thomas Neville, brother of Lord Neville, and his son Humphrey
were attainted too. Fewer Northumberland men suffered: the
most prominent being John Heron of Ford. Finally an example
was made of selected lesser men, most of them casualties, who
had taken part in the battle. Thus an unprecedented 130 or more
people were punished.[37]

But Edward's apparent severity was tempered by a willingness
to lift the penalties of attainder and forfeiture on any prepared to
come to terms with him. Indeed, in his early years this policy
was occasionally taken to dangerous lengths. His magnanimity
towards the duke of Somerset, pardoned and restored amid great
publicity in 1463, ended in disaster in December of that year,
when the duke turned traitor again.[38] As remarkable was Edward's wooing of the recalcitrant Humphrey Neville. Pardoned
in February 1462, Neville was nevertheless kept in prison, from
which he escaped. In June 1463 he was received back into the
king's grace again, and restored to almost all his lands. But
before the end of the year he once more joined the Lancastrians
in Northumberland. In 1464, on the surrender of Bamburgh to
Lord Montagu, his life was spared; but a year later he was
attainted. Still at large, he continued to stir up rebellion until he
was finally taken and executed in 1469.[39]

---

[37] *Rot. Parl.* v. 476–83; J. R. Lander, 'Attainder and Forfeiture, 1453 to 1509',
in *Crown and Nobility, 1450–1509* (1976), pp. 133, 307; Stevenson, *Wars of the
English*, ii. 2, 778–9.
[38] Hicks, 'Lancastrian Loyalism', pp. 23–37; Lander, 'Attainder and Forfeiture', pp. 134–5.
[39] Lander, 'Attainder and Forfeiture', p. 134 n. 33. Between 6 May and 3 Dec.
1461 he had succeeded his uncle, Lord Neville, as bailiff of Hexham (Hinds,
'Hexhamshire', i. 45).

Perhaps, however, one should not judge Edward's policy on the grounds of its notorious failures, Somerset, Neville, and Sir Ralph Percy,[40] who were the leading, active members of their houses in 1461–4, and nourished a deep hatred of the king and the Nevilles of Middleham. In other cases the king's mixture of severity and leniency was more effective. Sir William Gascoigne the elder, father of the attainted Sir William, was pardoned in July 1461; Sir Ralph Pudsay was granted a royal annuity of £20 on 20 December; Sir Richard Tempest of Bracewell, pardoned on 29 July 1465, was retained for life by Warwick on 8 January following, with a fee of £10 p.a. paid from Topcliffe.[41] Others, not attainted, were held under bonds for good behaviour. On 13 May Sir William Eure of Witton, Co. Durham and Malton, and his sons Robert, Henry, and William, George Darrell of Sessay, and Sir William Plumpton all agreed to pay £2,000 each before Whitsun coming as recognizances for their future good behaviour. Sir Ralph Eure, Sir William's eldest son, and William Plumpton, Plumpton's eldest son, were both killed at Towton. These bonds were the price paid to escape attainder. The Eures were released on 12 August, Darrell on 28 August 1462.[42] Plumpton, who had been unable to raise the sum required, surrendered himself as a prisoner to the Tower. Pardoned on 5 February 1462, he was released from his bond on 2 September. Nevertheless, he was constrained to remain in London, and found himself again accused of treason, of which he was acquitted, on 29 January 1464. Only then was he able to return to a normal life. He made his peace with Warwick, serving as a deputy at Knaresborough and apparently keeping, under Clarence, his office at Spofforth. Further to protect himself he arranged, on 11 February 1464, the marriage of his daughter Elizabeth (who at that time was taken to be one of his joint heiresses), to John Sotehill, son and heir of Henry Sotehill, Warwick's councillor. Even then Plumpton's problems were not at an end. Between 1465 and 1467 he faced a suit in Chancery brought by Robert Percy of Scotton, who accused him

---

[40] See above, p. 229.

[41] CPR, 1461–7, 24, 67, 455; Durham, Church Commission, Bishopric Estates, 189808. Tempest was, however, no longer receiving his fee in 1467/8.

[42] CPR, 1461–7, 39, 177.

of ransacking his home and having sought to have him executed after the rout of Ludford in 1459.[43]

In dealing with Percy adherents in Yorkshire Edward IV and Warwick were helped by the fact that many had been killed during or immediately after Towton, several leaving sons under age. Thus the number of potential enemies had been reduced, while the custody of the heirs, such as of Bigod and Hotham, could be placed in trusted hands such as those of Lord Scrope and Sir Thomas Parr.[44] By one means or another the Percy affinity in Yorkshire was suppressed: a success which stands in marked contrast to the failure of Henry VI and Northumberland to destroy the Neville affinity in 1459–61. The principal beneficiary, however, once again was Warwick, whose dominance over Yorkshire was further enhanced.

Warwick found it more difficult to dominate Durham and Northumberland. In Durham all depended on the bishop, Laurence Booth. Booth, keeper of the Privy Seal 1456–60, had been a committed Lancastrian. But at the end of April 1461 he submitted to Edward IV, was received into his grace, and became his confessor. In the following eighteen months he served the new king loyally, and was rewarded by him. Troops raised by him defeated Sir Thomas Neville, who raided the bishopric in June 1461. He participated in negotiations with Queen Mary of Scotland which culminated in the agreement of a truce in July 1462. On 20 February 1462 he was granted, jointly with the earl of Kent, the custody of Wressle; and four days later the alien priory and manor of Tooting Bec, with the advowson of Streatham, Surrey.[45] Yet on 7 December of that year Edward, then at Durham, suddenly seized the temporalities of the diocese into his own hands, and removed Booth to house arrest at Pembroke College, Cambridge. On 28 December the temporalities were committed to Sir John Fogge, treasurer of the household, Sir John Scott, controller of the household, and Thomas Colt, one of the chamberlains of the Exchequer—all three of whom were presumably in the king's entourage at Durham at the time.[46]

---

[43] *Plumpton Correspondence*, pp. lxvi–lxxii; Arnold, 'West Riding', pp. 144, 149.   [44] See above, p. 289.

[45] *CPR, 1461–7*, 73, 113, 115; Scofield, *Edward the Fourth*, i. 244, 248.

[46] Hutchinson, *Durham*, pp. 425–6; Storey, 'North of England', p. 141.

The received explanation for the sequestration of Durham is that Booth had thrown in his hand with Queen Margaret, who, at the end of October, had recovered the Northumberland castles of Bamburgh, Dunstanburgh, and Alnwick. Indeed, some numismatic evidence, the issue of coinage by Booth in the name of Henry VI, which might date from 1462, would possibly confirm this.[47] Edward IV had responded immediately to the Lancastrian–Scottish invasion, raised a large army, and marched north. He arrived in Durham towards the end of November. Here he succumbed to an attack of measles; but his army was sent forward to join Warwick, who had already set about the recovery of the castles. It was in these circumstances that Booth was removed. Edward IV's concern probably centred not on the main part of the bishopric between Tyne and Tees, but on Norham and Islandshire, which lay between Scotland and the castles captured by the Lancastrians. Indeed, in November a party of French soldiers, shipwrecked on the Farnes, had taken shelter in the priory on Lindisfarne, in which they had been attacked and overwhelmed by the earl of Warwick's men. According to some accounts men were killed actually in the church. By early December news had reached the king at Durham that the Scots were planning to intervene in force.[48] It was imperative that Norham remain securely in loyal hands. Thus, if the bishop's loyalty was in any way doubted, military necessity might have appeared to demand the assumption of direct control of the bishop's lands adjoining Scotland and Berwick.

It is probably wrong to assume, however, that the initiative for the sequestration was the king's. It is more likely that Booth was the victim of Neville vindictiveness and ambition. Relationships between Bishop Booth and the earl of Warwick were far from cordial. In November 1459 the bishop had successfully claimed and exercised his right of forfeiture of war within the liberty of Durham by seizing the lordship of Barnard Castle, which he had occupied and exploited until April 1461. At the end of that month both Booth and Warwick appeared before

[47] I am grateful to Mr David Walker of Matlock for drawing this information to my attention and for giving me the benefit of his expertise. It is possible that the coins were issued not in 1462, but during the Readeption.

[48] See above, p. 226 and Scofield, *Edward the Fourth*, i. 265.

Edward IV at Durham to press their cases for possession of the lordship. Booth was able to produce no less a person than Robert Rhodes, lay steward of the priory, who testified that the right of forfeiture lay with the bishop, and that therefore the lordship lay with the liberty of Durham. He even confirmed that he had wrongly testified in 1439 before an inquisition *post mortem* that the lordship lay in the county of Northumberland, in other words outside the county palatine, to the harm and hurt of 'the liberty and title of the church of St Cuthbert'. Edward IV in the event ruled that forfeiture lay with himself as king, and restored Warwick to his estate.[49]

That the title to Barnard Castle was of vital concern to Booth is amply demonstrated by Edward's reversal of his decision of 1461 nine years later. On 2 June 1470, after Warwick had fled the kingdom, Booth petitioned the king for the restoration of Barnard Castle, reiterating his case that the lordship had been wrongly forfeited by Edward I, a wrong in fact recognized in the first parliament of Edward III, but never rectified. In 1470, Edward IV, seeking to secure Booth's support against Warwick, conceded his request, and granted that 'ye occupy, have and enjoy the said manor and castle with all the appurtenances according to your rights and title'.[50] The sequestration of Booth's temporalities in December 1462 should be seen in the context of the quarrel between bishop and earl over possession of Barnard Castle.

Warwick was not the only Neville with whom Booth was in conflict. His brother George, bishop of Exeter had taken up the cause of Durham Priory in its dispute with Booth concerning its right to archidiaconal jurisdiction over its appropriated churches in the diocese, and the bishop's insistence on his feudal prerogatives over the priory's lands. These issues caused friction between bishop and prior throughout the 1460s. John Lound, who had been a senior servant of Bishop Robert Neville, lost favour under Booth. In 1461 Prior Burnby wrote to George Neville on his behalf, complaining that Booth had become a

[49] Pollard, 'St Cuthbert and the Hog', p. 110, and above, pp. 148–9. In compensation the king confirmed the bishop's right of forfeiture to Hart, which Booth had taken into his hands in 1461. See the memorandum dated after 1483 printed in Hutchinson, *Durham*, i. 435.

[50] Durh. 3/49/4; Lapsley, *County Palatine of Durham*, pp. 46–7 n. 3.

'heavy lord' to him. Immediately after Booth was restored in 1464 he instituted a visitation of the priory, which alarmed the monks. Later George Neville, archbishop of York after 1465, took up the priory's causes against Booth.[51] Booth was a stubborn defender of the liberties of his see. He relentlessly pursued all his rights great or small, with little regard to political niceties. He may have been 'a polished courtier who could hide hostility under a fair mask';[52] but the key to his career as bishop of Durham lay not in loyalty to a particular dynasty, but in his obsessive pursuit of the rights and prerogatives of the church of St Cuthbert. He thereby created powerful enemies; in particular in the early 1460s a formidable alliance of Neville and priory.

The disposition of offices during the fifteen months when the temporalities were in royal hands reveals that the Nevilles were the principal beneficiaries. Indeed, one of the guardians, Thomas Colt, originally from Carlisle, was a councillor of the earl of Warwick, as well as a royal servant. John Lound was restored as temporal chancellor, Geoffrey Middleton as sheriff: both Neville appointments before 1457. John Neville, Lord Montagu, became steward: an office which he exercised in person from time to time. He and Warwick joined the commission of the peace.[53] While a proportion of the revenues of the bishop's lands were transferred to the royal coffers,[54] the exercise of power in the bishopric passed into the hands of the Nevilles.

Booth was released from house arrest on 15 April 1464: on 17 April the temporalities of his diocese were restored to him.[55] The restoration occurred ten days after Edward IV appointed commissioners to treat for peace with the Scots, and ten days before Montagu, going to meet the Scottish negotiators, defeated Sir Ralph Percy and a Lancastrian force at Hedgeley Moor.[56] It would appear that it was the imminent development

---

[51] R. B. Dobson, 'Richard Bell', pp. 205–7; Storey, 'North of England', pp. 140–1.   [52] Ibid.

[53] Durh. 3/48/11–15; 3/16/115; 141; Wedgwood, *Biographies*, p. 209. But Sir John Pilkington, knight of the body, became steward of Howden (Durh. 3/48/12).

[54] Scofield, *Edward the Fourth*, i. 260. At least £600 was delivered to the king in 15 months.

[55] Durh. 3/48/15; *CPR, 1461–7*, 374–5; Hutchinson, *Durham*, i. 427.

[56] See above, p. 228.

of peace with Scotland, and not the continued presence of
Lancastrian rebels in Northumberland, which weighed more
heavily with the king. The Scottish threat having subsided, he
judged it appropriate to make amends to the bishop. Booth, on
his part, at first trod warily. He put in his own temporal
chancellor and sheriff, but continued to retain John Neville,
soon to be promoted earl of Northumberland, as his lay steward
until 1467.[57] Normality returned to the county palatine in
1464; but the Nevilles of Middleham still overshadowed its
administration.

Northumberland proved the most difficult county for the
Yorkists to subdue in the early 1460s. Twice it was brought
under control (autumn 1461, January 1463); twice it was retaken
by the Lancastrians (October 1462 and spring 1463). For over a
year between May 1463 and July 1464 the county was in enemy
hands, during which it proved virtually impossible for landlords
south of the Tyne to collect their revenues. And for residents the
devastation of war and the impact of troops living off the land
severely reduced income.[58] Most of the Northumberland gentry
were attached to the Percies, who had a safe refuge and support
in Scotland. It is not surprising that Edward IV sought to win
over Sir Ralph Percy, who could command the loyalty of his
family's retainers. But there also existed a handful of prominent
gentry on whom he could rely. Foremost was Sir Robert Ogle,
now Lord Ogle, a Neville retainer, as was his brother-in-law,
Sir John Middleton of Belsay. Ogle's son-in-law Sir John
Widdrington, his brother Gerard, and Ogle's nephew, Sir Robert
Manners of Etal were others who rallied to Edward. So did Roger
Thornton of Ludwith, brother-in-law of Sir John Middleton,
who had his own quarrel with the earl of Northumberland over
possession of Newham in the county.[59]

Another on whom Edward thought he could rely was Sir
Ralph Grey of Heaton, first cousin of Lord Ogle, who had
established family connections with the houses of York and
Neville. His grandfather, Sir Thomas, had joined Edward IV's
grandfather, the earl of Cambridge (from whom he had bought

[57] Hutchinson, *Durham*, i. 442.   [58] See above, pp. 45 and 226–8.
[59] Hunter-Blair, 'The Sheriffs of Northumberland', pp. 63, 67–70; Wedgwood,
Biographies, pp. 571, 591, 645; Bean, *Estates*, pp. 78–9.

Wark) in the disastrous Southampton plot against Henry V in 1415. His grandmother was Alice Neville, a daughter of Ralph Neville, first earl of Westmorland; and his grandfather as a consequence was a retainer of the earl. His mother was Elizabeth, daughter of Henry FitzHugh. When he succeeded his father in 1443 family tradition and blood ties led him into a natural association with the Nevilles. This was sustained by his appointment on 1 March 1452 as joint keeper of Roxburgh for twelve years with William Neville, Lord Fauconberg, who was then a prisoner in France. He seems to have carried out his duties assiduously until Roxburgh fell to the Scots in the summer of 1460. It is sometimes stated that Grey fought against Edward IV at Towton; but the evidence, based on the false report that he was killed, is questionable. On the contrary, immediately he became king (and before the battle) Edward proclaimed a special protection of Grey's estates and tenants. Later, in 1461, Grey was one of those entrusted to recover Alnwick, of which he subsequently became captain until its loss in October 1462.[60] Grey's treachery in 1463 was not a reflection of deep-rooted Lancastrian loyalty: it was the result of pique at Edward IV's failure to reappoint him captain after its recovery, in which he assisted, earlier in the year. Sir John Astley was entrusted with its custody, according to the pseudo-Worcester, at Grey's great displeasure. Grey's first treasonable act was to seize it back for himself in May 1463.[61] At his trial in 1464 he was reminded that the king had placed a special trust in him, which he had betrayed. His offence was the worse for the fact that he was taken to be one of the king's own men. But in the end he was saved one last disgrace, that of wearing his coat of arms reversed to his execution, 'for thy noble grandfather, the which suffered trouble for the King's most noble predecessors'.[62] It is not at all 'difficult', as Wedgwood put it, 'to explain Edward IV's tenderness towards Sir Ralph Grey':[63] until his treachery in 1463 he

[60] T. B. Pugh, 'The Southampton Plot of 1415', in Griffiths and Sherborne, *Kings and Nobles*, pp. 78–9; Wedgwood, *Biographies*, pp. 397–8; Scofield, *Edward the Fourth*, i. 156–7.   [61] Stevenson, *Wars of the English*, ii. 1, 781.
[62] Warkworth, *Chronicle*, pp. 37–8.
[63] Wedgwood, *Biographies*, p. 398. Twentieth-century historians have tended to assume that Grey was a Lancastrian at heart. See Scofield, *Edward the Fourth*, i. 157; Ross, *Edward IV*, pp. 53, 61; and Hicks, 'Lancastrian Loyalism', p. 32.

was a man of Yorkist and Neville pedigree, trusted all the more because the king had relatively few men on whom he thought he could rely in Northumberland.

Only in 1464, and after a truce had been agreed with the Scots, was Northumberland finally reduced. It was immediately placed under the rule of John Neville, who was created earl of Northumberland, made sheriff for life in 1466, and endowed with all the Percy estates in the county. Thus Northumberland too passed securely into Neville control. After 1464 the Nevilles were pre-eminent in all three north-eastern counties. The high-water mark of the Neville tide was reached with the promotion of George to the diocese of York in March 1465. Not only the spiritual authority, but also the temporal power in Ripon, Beverley, Hexham, and elsewhere was added to the Neville empire. The 'gargantuan banquet' held to celebrate George's enthronement at York on 22 September 1465 was in effect a gathering of the Neville affinity to celebrate their assumption of complete power in northern England.[64] As Warkworth wrote later concerning the disgrace of George Neville in 1473, 'he and his brothers had the rule of the land, and had gathered great riches many years'.[65] Either because of his own inexperience, indifference, or generosity Edward IV had allowed Warwick to consolidate too much power. Perhaps, as the sequestration of Durham suggests, Edward found himself unavoidably conceding to demands made by his mighty northern subject, to whom he owed so much. But one cannot escape the conclusion that he played a weak hand badly. It was particularly foolish to allow Warwick to be the main source of reward and fount of patronage for those who had served them both. Once Edward was more secure on his throne he was to find it all the more difficult to assert his authority over the kingmaker. The seeds of future conflict had been sown.

The breach that subsequently developed between Edward IV and Warwick after 1465 was succinctly summarized in the following words by Warkworth:

and after that [Edward's revelation of his marriage in September 1464] rose great dissension ever more and more between the king and him, for that and other, etc. And then the king put out of the chancellorship the

[64] Dobson, 'Richard III and the Church of York', p. 133.
[65] Warkworth, *Chronicle*, pp. 25–6.

Bishop of Exeter, brother to the Earl of Warwick ... After that [June 1467] the Earl of Warwick took to him in fee many knights, squires, and gentlemen as he might, to be strong; and king Edward did that he might to feeble the Earl's power. And yet they were accorded diverse times: but they never loved together after.[66]

As a brief statement Warkworth's comment can hardly be bettered. It may be, as modern historians judge, that the secret marriage to Elizabeth itself did not poison the relationship between the two men. Much more might lie in the 'other, etc.'—particularly a developing difference of view over the direction of foreign policy.[67] But fundamentally the two drifted apart because Edward could not reign for ever under the shadow of the mighty earl and his brothers, while Warwick could not accept any eclipse of his power and authority. A collision was almost inevitable. But, as Warkworth noted, they patched up their differences several times. The first public rift occurred in the winter of 1467–8, when Warwick was implicated in Lancastrian intrigue and had to clear his name. Much of that winter Warwick spent withdrawn on his northern estates. Yet he was reconciled with the king in the spring of 1468, and was apparently once more in favour, and still considered to be of influence at court. However, by the spring of 1469 the earl was secretly plotting to use force to oust his rivals at court, and finally declared his hand in open rebellion in July.[68]

Warkworth clearly believed that Warwick and the king were never truly reconciled after the autumn of 1467. It was then, according to him, that the earl began to enlarge his retinue. Since it was then too that he withdrew north, it would seem highly probable that Warwick concentrated on recruiting new retainers in the Neville heartland. Unfortunately it is not possible, through want of relevant documentation, to discover whether this was so. It can be seen, however, that Warwick did not cease to expand his personal following in the north throughout the 1460s. On 20 November 1461 he retained Thomas Clapham of Beamsley in the West Riding for life, with a fee of £6. 13s. 4d. p.a., charged to Middleham; two months later he

---

[66] Ibid. 3–4.
[67] See, for instance, Ross, *Edward IV*, p. 104, drawing on the comment of the Crowland Continuator (*Crowland Chronicle*, p. 115).
[68] Ross, *Edward IV*, pp. 114–25.

retained Sir Richard Redman of Harewood, near Knaresborough,
and the Levens for life, with a fee of £10 p.a. charged to the same
lordship; and in October 1466 he retained William Clerionet of
Richmond and Catherine his wife, with a fee of 10 marks paid
from Middleham.[69] In 1465–6 he retained the two men principally responsible for the capture of Henry VI near Clitheroe in
July 1465. Sir Thomas Talbot of Bashall was retained with a fee
of £10 from Middleham on 17 October, and Sir Richard Tempest
of Bracewell with a similar fee charged to Topcliffe on 6 January
1466. Both men had been rewarded by Edward IV; and they were
now recruited into Warwick's affinity.[70] The key to this
development may lie with Sir James Harrington, the third man
involved in the capture of Henry VI, who might have persuaded
Tempest and Talbot to betray the man they were sheltering.
Harrington, of Hornby in Lonsdale, was the eldest surviving son
of Sir Thomas Harrington, who had died at Wakefield, and was
himself one of Warwick's principal retainers, receiving a fee of
£13. 6s. 8d. from Middleham.[71]

Another significant recruit to Warwick's service was William
Tunstall, younger brother of Sir Richard Tunstall of Thurland,
Henry VI's Chamberlain, who had avoided capture in 1465 and
escaped to Harlech. William had fought in Northumberland for
Henry VI, but by 1464 was in receipt of an annuity of £20 from
Edward IV. On 10 June 1465 he was granted a fee of £20 by
Warwick, charged to Knaresborough.[72] The Tunstalls had close
links with the men close to Warwick. William's mother was
Eleanor FitzHugh, sister of Henry, Lord FitzHugh. Her first
husband had been Philip, Lord Darcy, and her daughters by this
marriage (and thus the half-sisters of the Tunstalls) were Lady
Margery Conyers and Lady Elizabeth Strangways. In March
1469 both William Tunstall and his younger brother Thomas
became feoffees of Sir John Conyers in his Yorkshire lands.[73]
Thus the route was clearly marked for the absorption of the

[69] PRO, SC6/1085/20; Lancashire RO, DDMa 228/7d. Catherine Clerionet
was the daughter of Richard Clervaux of Croft.
[70] PRO, SC6/1085/20; Durham, Church Commission, Bishopric Estates,
189808; Warkworth, Chronicle, p. 41; Scofield, Edward the Fourth, i. 381; B. P.
Wolffe, Henry VI (1981), 337.   [71] PRO, SC6 1085/20.
[72] Wedgwood, Biographies, pp. 482, 484; Scofield, Edward the Fourth, i. 261,
264; Arnold, 'West Riding', p. 164.   [73] CIPM, Henry VII, i. 278.

Tunstalls, including Sir Richard himself after his submission in 1468, into Warwick's affinity.

Perhaps most important in terms of the consolidation of Warwick's northern power was his reconciliation with his own brother-in-law, Lord FitzHugh. FitzHugh was with the earl and the thirteen-year-old duke of Gloucester at Warwick in the summer of 1465. At approximately this time he was granted the manor of Worton in Wensleydale for life by the earl; and on 18 November he was restored to the bench in the North Riding.[74] Most importantly of all, at Michaelmas 1466 he was retained by Warwick as his deputy warden of the west march, with a salary of 1,000 marks p.a. When a year later FitzHugh received a licence to go on pilgrimage to Jerusalem one of his companions was his nephew Thomas Tunstall.[75] The full significance of FitzHugh's return to the Neville fold was to be revealed in August 1470, when he raised Richmondshire on Warwick's behalf.

The events of 1469–71 clearly demonstrate that by then Warwick enjoyed the backing of a large and committed following in the north; a following upon which he came to depend in his struggle for supremacy against Edward IV. The earl was not without support elsewhere. He was able to call on the Calais garrison; he had established a following in the midlands based on the Beauchamp estates; and he enjoyed, at least initially, a general popular appeal. But in the last resort Warwick's strength was northern, and was rooted deeply in the old-established Neville affinity drawn from northern Yorkshire and the west march. The north-east was thus drawn into the struggle between earl and king from its very beginning.

When precisely Warwick determined to raise rebellion against Edward IV is not known. And it is not clear whether initially he planned to hitch his rebellion to popular unrest. Discontent in Yorkshire, focusing on the payment of 'peter-corn', an ancient rent of a thrave of wheat and other first-fruits paid by all the northern counties to the hospital of St Leonard's York, came to a head in 1468 when Sir Hugh Hastings of Fenwick and others from the West Riding had refused to pay,

[74] Hicks, *Clarence*, p. 26; PRO, SC6/1085/20; *CPR, 1461–7*, 576.
[75] Dugdale, *Baronage*, i. 405.

and prevented its collection. The hospital had petitioned the king in Chancery, and received judgement in its favour. Far from being a movement prompted by Warwick, as Polydore Vergil suggested, it is more likely to have been linked to growing opposition to the Nevilles, and a desire for the restoration of Henry Percy as earl of Northumberland. This became explicit in May 1469 in the brief rising in the East Riding led by one who called himself Robin of Holderness, in which the abolition of petercorn and the restoration of Percy were both demanded. This rising was promptly suppressed by John Neville, earl of Northumberland, and its leader was executed.[76]

There was, however, more widespread dissatisfaction in the north. Briefly, it seems a separate movement under the leadership of one Robin of Redesdale had flared up in April 1469. It was to this strand of popular discontent that Warwick was to hitch his wagon in the summer.[77] His plot was well laid. In June the third and most substantial rising in the north began. This time it was co-ordinated by Warwick's retainers. It is not certain which of Warwick's men took up the name Robin of Redesdale; but it was probably a member of the Conyers family, and possibly, as Warkworth stated, William of Marske.[78] The significant point is

[76] K. R. Dockray, 'The Yorkshire Rebellion of 1469', The Ricardian, vi, 83 (1983), 249–52; Ross, Edward IV, pp. 126–7; Scofield, Edward the Fourth, i. 490–1. Warwick himself conducted an enquiry which concluded in favour of the hospital.

[77] See Ross, Edward IV, pp. 431–40 for the chronology of the Yorkshire rebellions. Richard Hoyle has pointed out to me that there is evidence of possible resistance to taxation in 15th cent. Yorkshire which might be connected with the initial popular rising linked with the name of Robin of Redesdale.

[78] Warkworth, Chronicle, p. 6. Warkworth confidently identified him as Sir William Conyers. However, there was no member of the family at the time enjoying both the title and the name. There was a William Conyers esquire of Marske, a younger brother of Sir John and also a retainer of the earl. Warkworth, who was not reliable about Christian names, appears not to have believed that 'Robin' was either Sir John himself or his eldest son and heir, also John (but not knighted), both of whom have been advanced as candidates (W. Archbald in DNB, xvi. 1319; Ross, Edward IV, p. 128; Dockray, 'Yorkshire Rebellion', p. 254; and Scofield, Edward the Fourth, i. 488 [John]), for later in his account he states that 'James [sic] Conyers, son and heir to Sir John Conyers, knight' was killed. There is neither repetition of a mistaken identity nor confirmatory comment here, as one might have expected, that one or the other was 'Robin'. Indeed it is inherently unlikely that the head of the family, Sir John, would have taken such a risk. In 1459 the then head, his father Christopher, had carefully

not who precisely played the part of Robin of Redesdale, but the fact that 'a great insurrection in Yorkshire of divers knights, squires and commoners' was raised by Warwick's men in the north under the colour of yet another popular rising. It clearly was a rebellion of Warwick's northern retinue. Included in the casualties at Edgecote on 26 July were Sir Henry Neville, son and heir of Lord Latimer, John Conyers, and a member of the Mauleverer family.[79] The purpose of the rising was to draw Edward IV's attention away from the earl himself, who was to slip over to Calais early in July with his brother the archbishop of York and George, duke of Clarence to celebrate the marriage of his daughter Isabel to the duke. Edward IV was on pilgrimage to Walsingham when he heard of the rising. By 18 June he had decided to march to the north himself to deal with it. He reached Grantham on 7 July, and Newark a day or two later. By this time, however, he heard rumour of what Warwick, Clarence, and the archbishop of York were up to. Indeed on 28 June Warwick had declared his hand by announcing the forthcoming marriage, and had crossed to Calais on 4 July, where the ceremony was performed on 11 July. Immediately Warwick issued a proclamation condemning the king's evil ministers, and calling the people of Kent to arms. The king, who had withdrawn to Nottingham, found himself caught between Warwick's two forces, and was awaiting reinforcements from Wales. The issue was finally decided on 26 July, when the northern army, which had bypassed the king, met and defeated the Welsh army under the earl of Pembroke at Edgecote. A few days later, Edward, seeking to return to London, was intercepted and taken prisoner by the archbishop of York at Olney in Buckinghamshire.[80]

For a brief while power lay in Warwick's hands. Edward IV was escorted first to Coventry, then Warwick, and finally, in

---

remained uninvolved; Sir John is likely to have followed his late father's example in 1469. Warkworth, therefore, may in this case have been correct about the Christian name, but wrong about the title. It is to be noted that as yet no one has advanced the case for *Robert*, Lord Ogle, who was possessor of *Redesdale*, and died, possibly of wounds sustained at Edgecote, in 1469. For my earlier suggestion concerning William Conyers see 'Richmondshire Gentry', pp. 39–41.

[79] Warkworth, *Chronicle*, pp. 6–7; Dockray, 'Yorkshire Rebellion', pp. 254–5.

[80] Ross, *Edward IV*, pp. 128–33; Scofield, *Edward the Fourth*, i. 491–7.

mid-August, to Middleham. It was his third and least auspicious
visit as king to the earl's Wensleydale castle. A parliament was
to be called at York for 22 September; but it was cancelled at the
beginning of the month because of the 'great troubles' which
were afflicting the kingdom. One of these was a renewed Lancastrian rising led by the incorrigible Sir Humphrey Neville in
the far north. Faced by this threat to his own position in the north,
and having as yet no desire to depose the king, Warwick had no
choice but to allow Edward IV his freedom of action, so that
he could effectively give royal authority to steps to crush
Humphrey Neville. This was done. The king was a free agent
soon after 10 September; Sir Humphrey Neville and his brother
Charles were taken and executed at York on 29 September. Early
in October Edward IV returned to Westminster in state.[81]

The next eighteen months from September 1469 to March
1471 saw a series of bewildering changes of fortune for both king
and earl. The story of Warwick's second rising in March 1470,
his defeat and flight to France, his return in September, the
Readeption of Henry VI, and finally Edward IV's recovery of his
throne in the spring of 1471 has been told elsewhere.[82] From the
point of view of the north-east, however, the extent to which the
region, and especially the Neville affinity, was involved in the
unfolding events is of more immediate significance. Having
played such a major part in the defeat of Edward IV in July 1469,
it is hardly surprising that Warwick's northerners continued to
play an important role in his machinations thereafter.

Although a reconciliation had been effected between Warwick and his king in October 1469, the two distrusted each
other. On 27 October Edward began the process of restoring
Henry Percy to the earldom of Northumberland, when the
young Henry was released from the Tower on surety of good
behaviour. His full restoration was clearly envisaged; and the
process began as early as November whereby John Neville could
be compensated for his imminent loss. His son and heir George
was created duke of Bedford, and betrothed to the king's eldest
daughter Elizabeth, whom the king declared his heir. In February 1470 Neville was granted lands in Devon that were in the

[81] Ross, *Edward IV*, pp. 134–5; Scofield, *Edward the Fourth*, i. 501–3.
[82] Ross, *Edward IV*, pp. 135–77; Scofield, *Edward the Fourth*, i. 503–95.

king's hands following the death of the earl of Devon without
issue. These estates, worth approximately £600 p.a., were intended to make good the loss of the Percy lands in the county of
Northumberland that he had enjoyed since 1464, which were
restored to Henry Percy on 1 March. Edward IV's intention was
clear: to divide John Neville, who had been loyal during the
summer of 1469, from his brothers. Indeed, while plans were
laid to compensate John for the loss of his share of the Percy
estates, no such preparations were made to benefit Warwick and
Clarence in Cumberland and Yorkshire. Moreover, on 14 January 1470 Sir Humphrey Dacre, male heir to the barony of Dacre,
was granted the forest of Inglewood, in a move foreshadowing
his restoration. It was probably becoming all too apparent to
Warwick that Edward was now intent on curtailing his power in
the north. Clarence too found himself excluded.[83] It is not
surprising, therefore, that from the beginning of 1470 the earl
and the duke were plotting a new rebellion.

In the spring of 1470 Warwick and Clarence exploited the
grievance of Richard, Lord Welles and Willoughby against Sir
Thomas Burgh of Gainsborough, Edward IV's right-hand man in
Lincolnshire. Welles had married Margery, a daughter of Sir
James Strangways, in 1468, and thus had a ready-made link with
Warwick.[84] By February he had been suborned, and with his son
Sir Robert Welles raised the commons. This time Edward acted
promptly. He met and defeated Sir Robert Welles at Losecoat
Field on 12 March, and in the course and aftermath of the battle
the extent of the involvement of both earl and duke as 'partners
and chief provokers of all their treasons', with the aim of placing
Clarence on the throne, became apparent. The plans laid by the
two were revealed. They had hoped to trap Edward between
troops raised by them in the midlands, Welles's Lincolnshire
men, and a force raised in the north.[85]

In the event Warwick's northern retinue did not become fully
involved. This is not because they refused to mobilize: rather
they were isolated by Edward IV's prompt action. There is little
reason to doubt the *Chronicle of the Lincolnshire Rebellion*'s
statement that Warwick hoped 'out of Yorkshire to [have]

[83] Bean, *Estates*, p. 109; Hicks, *Clarence*, pp. 58–63.
[84] *CP* xii. Part 2, 667.
[85] Hicks, *Clarence*, pp. 65–70; Ross, *Edward IV*, pp. 137–43.

assembled so great a puissaunce that they might have been able to have fought with the king's highness in plain field'.[86] But immediately after the victory at Losecoat Field, having discovered this, the king

understanding that the commotion in moving people in Richmondshire by the stirring of the lord Scrope and others, sent by the said duke and earl there for that cause with many letters, his highness sent into Northumberland and Westmorland to array certain fellowship to have followed upon them if they had come forward and to Marquis Montagu, with his fellowship to have countered them in their faces; they [Scrope, etc.] understanding and having tidings also of the king's victory, and, as divers gentlemen of that fellowship said, thinking, by the manner of the said earl of Warwick's writing sent thither in his own name only to array the people, that their stirring should be against the king, and fearing his speedy coming unto their parts with his host, left their gathering and sat still.[87]

The comment concerning Warwick's orders in his own name only would seem deliberately to reflect the king's concern to demonstrate in this official account that his subjects obeyed him and only him. For on 16 March he ordered the sheriff to proclaim that the men of Yorkshire should only array in response to orders under a royal seal; and two weeks later, in the proclamation finally condemning Warwick and Clarence, he reiterated that the two had, after Losecoat

sent into Yorkshire unto divers persons charging them to make proclamation in their own names without making mention of his highness, that all men under pain of death should come to them and assist them in resisting the king.[88]

The king's purpose in all these official statements is clear: to establish that the earl and the duke had acted treasonably. One wonders, however, whether it made much difference to Warwick's men that the earl alone was calling them out: it had made no difference before, and was to make no difference subsequently. More significant is the fact that for once Edward successfully anticipated Warwick, and gave a specific counter-

[86] 'The Chronicle of the Rebellion in Lincolnshire, 1470', ed. J. G. Nichols, in Camden Miscellany, i, Camden, os xxxix (1847), 5.
[87] Ibid. 12.
[88] CCR, 1468–76, 135–6, 137–8.

order, which was backed by the knowledge of his speedy coming with a large and growing array. Common sense, not the lack of a royal commission, made the people of Richmondshire sit still.[89]

Edward reinforced his orders by a promise that he would abide by his pardon lately proclaimed in Yorkshire—after Robin of Redesdale's rebellion—for all offences committed before 11 October last, and indeed extend it to 25 December.[90] Shortly after he arrived at York on 21 March, Warwick's lieutenants came in to him and submitted:

> there came to the king the Lord Scrope, Sir John Conyers, Young Hillyard of Holderness and others which had laboured, specially provoked and stirred the people in their parts to have made commotion against the king, wherein they freely submitted them to the king's grace and mercy.[91]

The submission of Scrope and Conyers marked the end of Warwick's hopes for support from the north. He and Clarence, who had advanced as far as Chesterfield and Manchester, now turned and withdrew to the west country. On 9 April they took ship at Dartmouth for France.[92]

Having so comprehensively defeated Warwick, Edward was in a position to tackle his power base in the north. However, his room for manœuvre was limited by the submission of Scrope and Conyers at York. The possessions of only a handful of northern men were seized by him for their part in this rebellion. Those singled out were Richard Scrope, a brother of Lord Scrope of Bolton; Robert Strangways, a son of Sir James of West Harlsey; John Conyers, the grandson of Sir John; and three members of the Otter family, household servants of the earl.[93] Their particular offence is unknown. The earl's own estates were, with one exception, for the time being left alone. The exception was Barnard Castle, which the king restored to Bishop Booth of Durham on 2 June.[94] The custody of the person and estates of the infant Richard Neville, grandson of George Neville, Lord

---

[89] But see Hicks, *Clarence*, pp. 69–70 for the alternative view.
[90] *CCR, 1468–76*, 137–8.
[91] Nichols, 'Rebellion in Lincolnshire', p. 17.
[92] Hicks, *Clarence*, pp. 71–4.
[93] *CPR, 1467–77*, 218. The order wrongly states that John Conyers was the son of Sir John.
[94] Durh. 3/49/4.

Latimer, who died at the end of 1469, was taken into the king's
hands. Between March and May 1470 Edward appointed his own
men to senior office in the Latimer estates, including Sir
Edmund Hastings of Roxby as master forester of Danby, and
Nicholas Leventhorpe as receiver. On 19 May he granted
the custody of Richard Neville to his great-uncle, Thomas
Bourgchier, archbishop of Canterbury, with a sum of £100
drawn from the estates to pay for his upkeep.[95] By these means
he sought to remove at least one other source of local influence
which the Nevilles of Middleham had enjoyed since George
Neville had been declared insane in the early 1450s. In practice,
as a pardon issued to Lord FitzHugh in August was to show, the
grant to Archbishop Bourgchier was abortive, for young Richard
Neville was illegally held by Lord FitzHugh on Warwick's
behalf.[96] During the summer of 1470 Edward IV proved quite
unable significantly to curtail Warwick's power in the north. As
long as his officers and council retained possession of his
estates, and his affinity in northern Yorkshire remained substantially intact, the earl, even in exile, remained a potent threat
to the king.

Edward IV's only resort was to take a stage further the restoration of Henry Percy. On 25 March, before he left York, he
re-created him earl of Northumberland, and at the same time
promoted John Neville to the title of Marquess Montagu. Three
months later Henry Percy, who now held both the title and the
estates of his forebears in Northumberland, was appointed
warden of the east march in place of Neville.[97] Neville had been
recompensed with a higher title, lands to the same value in the
west country, and a marriage into the royal family. The king
could only hope that this was accepted as sufficient reward for
his loyalty over the previous months. Edward was walking a
tightrope until he could finally dispose of Warwick.

The earl, for his part, having made his peace with Margaret of
Anjou at Angers by the end of July 1470, was determined to
return to England as soon as possible. To pave the way for an
unopposed landing in southern England he called on his north-

---

[95] CPR, 1467–77, 205–7, 209. In 1471 the full custody of lands and wardship
was granted to the archbishop (ibid. 295–6).
[96] Ibid. 215.   [97] Bean, Estates, p. 109; Storey, 'Wardens', p. 615.

ern retainers to rise yet again. At the very same time as the
Treaty of Angers was being formalized, the earl's brother-in-
law, Henry, Lord FitzHugh, called out the men of Richmondshire, and, over the Pennines, Richard Salkeld of Corby, Warwick's constable at Carlisle, led a parallel rising of Cumbrians.
On 5 August Sir John Paston reported from London: 'There be
many folks up in the north so that Percy is not able to resist
them: and so the king hath sent for his freedmen to come to him,
for he will go to put them down.'[98] Edward reacted quickly. He
reached Ripon on 14 August, and the rebellion melted away on
his approach. On 10 September nearly 200 men received pardons. Edward stayed north for a month after the suppression of
the rebellion; he was still there when on 13 September Warwick
landed in the west country. Within three weeks he found
himself abandoned, even by Marquess Montagu, and fled the
kingdom.[99] Fortune had turned full circle.

The northern rising of July to August 1470 was as serious
as that of Robin of Redesdale. In Yorkshire it was in effect
that 'commotion . . . in Richmondshire' which Warwick had
planned to take place in March. From the list of those who were
pardoned it is possible to see that at least twenty men from some
of the most substantial gentry families of Richmondshire and
Cleveland were implicated. Several were retainers of the earl or
relations of retainers; many had connections with Sir John
Conyers of Hornby. Although FitzHugh was the titular head of
this rising, as Lord Scrope had been of the abortive attempt in
March, one suspects that once more the focal point and organizing genius had been Sir John Conyers, Warwick's steward at
Middleham.[100] Edward IV, who was alert to the danger these
men presented, rightly took this rising seriously. He probably
deduced that the rising, planned to coincide with a landing by
Warwick in Yorkshire, had taken place prematurely. Thus he
stayed on to intercept the earl on his arrival. In fact, whether
intended or not, FitzHugh's rising proved to be a diversion
which left the king stranded when the earl landed in the west

[98] *Paston Letters*, i. 431; A. J. Pollard, 'Lord FitzHugh's Rising in 1470', *BIHR*
52 (1979), 170.
[99] Ross, *Edward IV*, pp. 150–4; Hicks, *Clarence*, pp. 82–5.
[100] Ibid. 172–3.

country. No other rising in these years, not even that of Robin of
Redesdale, reveals as clearly the central role of the northern
Neville affinity, especially that part based on Middleham and
Sheriff Hutton, in the exercise of the earl of Warwick's military
power.

By the same token the failure of the northern retainers to turn
out in strength for Warwick in the spring of 1471 was a major
reason for his ultimate defeat. There was no major contingent of
Richmondshire men at Barnet: certain northerners were there
and escaped with the earl of Oxford, but it was not a force on the
scale of that raised in 1469 by Robin of Redesdale.[101] Even more
crucially, no force of Richmondshire men intercepted Edward
IV after he landed at Ravenspur on 14 March with a company of
barely 2,000 men. The author of the official account of Edward's
recovery of his throne, *The Arrivall*, fully appreciated the
significance of this, and devoted a long passage to its explanation.[102] Warwick relied on Montagu, who was at Pontefract, to
stop him. This he failed to do. The author of *The Arrivall*
thought that Montagu might privately have wished Edward
well; but in any case he commented 'he could not have gathered,
nor made, a fellowship of number sufficient to have openly
resisted him'. This is the nub. Montagu was marooned. Edward
had landed in Percy country, and in his progress from Ravenspur
to Hull, to York, and then to Wakefield, he purposefully kept
close to districts dominated by the Percies. It was in these ten
days that his restoration of Henry Percy bore fruit. Northumberland had found himself removed from the wardenship of the east
march, and Montagu restored, in October 1470. In January or
February 1471 Edward IV had sent Nicholas Leventhorpe with a
message to him from Flanders, and had no doubt received
assurances of support. According to Warkworth, after he landed
at Ravenspur, Edward displayed a letter from the earl pledging
support, and claimed that he came by his advice.[103] *The Arrivall*
confirmed that the earl 'loved the king truly and perfectly, as the
king thereof had certain knowledge, and would, as of himself
and all his power have served him truly'. Yet Northumberland

---

[101] *Historie of the Arrivall of King Edward IV*, ed. J. Bruce, Camden os, 1
(1838), 20.
[102] Ibid. 6–7, upon which pages the following discussion is based.
[103] Warkworth, *Chronicle*, p. 11; Somerville, *Duchy of Lancaster*, i. 256 n. 2.

was unable to persuade his client gentry in the East and West Ridings to take the king's part. Men like Sir Richard Tempest or Sir William Gascoigne, who had lost fathers, sons, or kinsmen ten years earlier at Towton, could not be persuaded now to fight for the man who had been responsible for their deaths. Yet nevertheless, 'they would not strive with any low or noble man other than the said earl, or at least by his commandment'. Thus, since he did not command them either to assist or to resist Edward, the king was able to pass.

Montagu for his part was unable to call them to arms, for since the earl sat still, the local gentry would not follow him 'neither for his love, which they bare him none, nor for any commandment of higher authority'. He was in no position to command the support of the gentry of these southern parts of Yorkshire. Apart from the manor of Wressle, restored to him again during the Readeption, he had held no Percy estates in Yorkshire. Indeed one can be sure that his possession of Wressle reminded many local men all too clearly of his role in the feuds between his family and the Percies, in which they or their kinsmen had been on the opposite side. He had himself been personally responsible for one or two deaths over the years. As recently as 1469 he had, with his customary ruthlessness, suppressed pro-Percy rebellion in the district. It is hardly surprising that the leaders of local society bore him no love. They had not done so since 1453.

But above all what happened in southern Yorkshire effectively prevented the men of Richmondshire and further north from coming to Montagu's aid. The earl of Northumberland's inaction, his sitting still, caused: 'every man *in all those north parts* to sit still also, and suffer the king to pass as he did not withstanding many were right evil disposed of themselves against the king' [my italics]. Who else could the author be referring to other than the men of northern Yorkshire, who had so consistently supported Warwick in his quarrel with Edward IV over the previous two years? It was not Montagu who held these men back, but Northumberland. His service to Edward IV lay not only in allowing him to pass through his own country in the East and West Riding, but also in preventing men from further north coming south to join the Neville cause. Rightly *The Arrivall* remarked that this was 'a notable good service and

politiquely done by the earl'.[104] The significance and effectiveness of Northumberland's action became apparent six weeks
later, early in May, when at length the men of Richmondshire
rose in arms, but too late to help their lord. This last, forlorn
rising quickly collapsed when the rebels heard that the Lancastrians had been defeated at Tewkesbury, and that Edward was
preparing to march against them, and because now they no
longer had 'any of Warwick's, or Neville's, blood whom unto
they might have rested, as they had done before'. The leaders
quickly submitted to the earl of Northumberland, through
whom they secured pardons.[105] Thus did the last throes of the
Neville–Percy feud help decide the issue for Edward IV in 1471.

To a significant extent the north-east was the arbiter of
English politics in 1469–71. When Warwick was able effectively
to deploy his north Yorkshire affinity he was successful; when
not he failed. The north-east was neither the only part of
England from which Warwick and Clarence drew support, nor
the only region to be caught up in renewed civil war; but it was
on the military strength drawn from the north that Warwick
stood and ultimately fell. It was a source of strength which the
inexperienced Edward had unwisely allowed, perhaps even encouraged, Warwick to consolidate in the uncertain early years of
his reign. It was a source of strength which he found he was
subsequently powerless to curtail during the years of crisis. No
one was brought to trial for treason; no one suffered for the
support they gave to the earl. Pardons were issued early in 1470,
confirmed in March, and issued again in September for all
offences. The men of Richmondshire, co-ordinated it would
seem by Sir John Conyers and others of Warwick's council based
at Middleham, rebelled with impunity against their king no
fewer than four times in two years. Even after his recovery of the
throne in May 1471 Edward IV did nothing to punish erstwhile
offenders. The opportunity then arose for the king, secure on the

---

[104] I disagree with Michael Weiss's analysis ('A Power in the North?', pp.
505–7). Weiss neither pays specific enough attention to the precise district in
which these events took place nor gives sufficient weight to the evidence of
Montagu's local unpopularity in south Yorkshire. Thus I cannot accept that 'it
was possible for John Neville to have kept the men of Yorkshire, many of whom
were long-standing Neville supporters, in check' (p. 507).

[105] Bruce, *Arrivall*, pp. 31–2.

throne, and with Warwick and Montagu killed in rebellion against him, to attaint the Nevilles, forfeit their estates, and break up their affinity. In fact, far from taking these elementary precautions to prevent a repetition of the troubles caused him, Edward IV took the entirely different course of entrusting these same lands, and thus the same powerful affinity, to his brother Richard of Gloucester, with fateful consequences for his dynasty and for the kingdom.

13

The Hegemony of Richard of Gloucester, 1471–1483

THE history of north-eastern England after the fall of the King-maker at Barnet in April 1471 is dominated by the career of Richard of Gloucester. After his establishment in Warwick's place in 1471, control of the region passed quickly and relatively smoothly into his hands. By the end of the decade Gloucester had established a personal hegemony in northern England that eclipsed even the might of Richard Neville at the height of his power. With such backing it was but a small step for Gloucester himself to take the throne in 1483. These momentous developments were not inevitable. In the first instance it was a deliberate decision of Edward IV to grant to his youngest brother the Neville of Middleham estates and the northern offices previously enjoyed by the earl of Warwick. On his part, Richard of Gloucester exploited to the full his brother's dependence on him to build up an unassailable power in the region, choosing to concentrate his landed estates in the northern counties. He needed first to resist the challenge of potential rivals—his brother the duke of Clarence; Henry Percy, earl of Northumberland; and Laurence Booth, bishop of Durham. Having achieved unquestioned supremacy over his peers in the region, he proceeded to secure the support of the greater part of the political élite in country, town, and cloister, both by the generosity and quality of his good lordship and by the effectiveness of his political leadership. By his own ability Richard of Gloucester reunited north-eastern society and created a following of awesome proportions personally committed to him. The only brake on his ambition was the fact that he was a younger son without his own inheritance, depending, because of the nature of his title to his estates in the north (the foundation of the whole edifice), on the continued favour of his brother the king or whoever should succeed to royal authority.

When the eighteen-year-old duke of Gloucester came north in

the summer of 1471 to enter the Neville of Middleham estates he was not unfamiliar with the north-east nor unknown to its leading families. Between the late spring of 1465 and the beginning of 1469, between the ages of twelve and sixteen, he had been brought up in the household of Richard, earl of Warwick.[1] Some of his time was no doubt spent at Middleham or Sheriff Hutton. He was present at the enthronement banquet of Archbishop George Neville in September 1465, as was his future duchess, Anne Neville, then a child of ten. During 1468, with his guardian, he was received with the customary gifts by the city of York.[2] But early in 1469 he was recalled to court by his brother the king, and thus received his political and military baptism at Edward IV's side against his erstwhile mentor.[3] At eighteen he was already a young man of some experience, who had won his spurs in two bitter and hard-fought battles. A return north was not inappropriate, for he knew from his adolescence men like Sir John Conyers and Sir James Strangways, leading councillors of the earl of Warwick, whom it was essential to reconcile to the Yorkist regime.

On 14 July Duke Richard was granted the lordships of Middleham, Penrith, and Sheriff Hutton, almost certainly as forfeiture in anticipation of a future Act of Attainder against the earl of Warwick.[4] But Parliament did not assemble until October 1472; and in the intervening time intensive competition for possession of the Warwick inheritance led to the shelving of any such Act, and the need to devise other means by which the estates could be divided between Gloucester and Clarence. Gloucester was concerned to turn his title in Middleham, Penrith, and Sheriff Hutton into something more secure than mere royal gift. He was also ambitious to make good the claim possessed by his predecessor to the reversion of the earldom of Richmond in Richmondshire (eight manors as well as the castle of Richmond and the fee-farm of the town), and to succeed him as the lord of

---

[1] For the years before 1465 see Ross, *Richard III*, pp. 3–7; Hicks, *Clarence*, p. 26 and A. F. Sutton, 'The Lord Richard, Duke of Gloucester', *The Ricardian*, viii, no. 100 (1988), 20–6.

[2] J. Leland, *Collectanea*, ed. T. Hearne (1774), vol. vi. 2–14; Dobson, *York Chamberlain's Accounts*, p. 126.

[3] Ross, *Richard III*, p. 14.

[4] *CPR*, 1467–77, 260, 266.

Barnard Castle north of the Tees. These ambitions led him into conflict with his brother George and the bishop of Durham.

Conflict with the duke of Clarence came to a head in February 1472, over Gloucester's desire to marry Anne Neville, Warwick's younger daughter. Anne had been held in virtual house arrest by Clarence since the death of her husband, Edward, Prince of Wales, at Tewkesbury in May 1471.[5] As a joint-heiress to the kingmaker she threatened Duke George's possession of the greater part of the Warwick inheritance through the right of his duchess Isabel. Even after Edward IV had granted the old Neville estates in the north to Gloucester, Anne (and any second husband she found) could claim to have as good a right as Isabel to the rest of the inheritance, which the king had granted to Clarence. In February 1472 Gloucester rescued Anne, and proposed to marry her. Clarence objected vociferously, but conceded that Gloucester 'may well have my lady his sister-in-law, but they shall part no livelihood'. At first Clarence had his way. Gloucester and Anne were married after Easter. Clarence was created earl of Warwick and Salisbury on 25 March, and in the same month received a royal promise of the possession of all the Warwick estates save those already granted to Gloucester.[6]

Precisely which estates Clarence feared to lose to his brother at this stage is not clear. But in northern England there were two claims that Clarence was pursuing which brought him into direct conflict with Gloucester. One was over Richmond. As part of that abundant flow of royal largess enjoyed by him before 1450 Richard Neville, earl of Salisbury had a grant, in its final form in tail male, of two-thirds of the lordship of Richmond, with the reversion of the other third, held by Jacquetta, duchess of Bedford. This, however, had been superseded by a grant of 1452, which transferred the whole honour of Richmond to Edmund Tudor as his patrimony as the newly created earl. Notwithstanding this grant, and after Edmund's death, Salisbury seems to have retained possession; possession which passed on his death to his son Warwick.[7] Edward IV added to the confusion by granting Richmond to Clarence in 1462. After

---

[5] Hicks, *Clarence*, pp. 114–15; Ross, *Richard III*, p. 28.
[6] Hicks, *Clarence*, pp. 115–16; Ross, *Richard III*, pp. 28–9; *CPR, 1467–77*, 330.   [7] See above, p. 249.

Warwick's own death in 1471 confusion was further confounded: Gloucester was granted all the tail male lands of the earl, which included his claim through Salisbury to the lordship of Richmond; Clarence received a renewal of his grant of 1462. By virtue of this grant Clarence was licensed on 5 August 1472 to enter freely all the estates of the earldom of Richmond which had been held by Jacquetta, duchess of Bedford until her recent death.[8] Thus the king at this point recognized Clarence as the possessor of the whole of the lordship of Richmond in Richmondshire itself, two-thirds of which he had a year earlier granted to Gloucester. Yet it is abundantly clear from the Middleham receiver's account of 1473/4 that by Michaelmas 1473 Gloucester was in occupation, appointing officers and receiving the revenue from its constituent members, as had Warwick before him in 1465/6. The form of words used to describe the office-holders who received their fees from the receiver is instructive, for in the account the receiver himself, steward, and auditor are entered twice: once as officers of all the aforesaid lordships within Richmondshire (i.e. Middleham and two-thirds of Richmond); and secondly, with supplementary fees, as officers of the one-third part of the same lordships (i.e. the reversionary interest which had fallen in with the death of the duchess of Bedford in 1472).[9] Whatever else might have been the outcome in the other estates of the earldom of Richmond, in Richmondshire Gloucester, notwithstanding royal letters to the contrary, had taken possession. In the compromise finally reached between the brothers in 1474–5 Clarence was allowed the castle and fee farm; but the constituent manors which produced most of the revenue were kept by Duke Richard.[10] Here then in Richmondshire was one focal point of conflict between the brothers, ultimately resolved in favour of Gloucester.

The second issue of fraternal conflict lay over Barnard Castle. The dispute over Barnard Castle was complicated by the intervention of the bishop of Durham, who had been granted the

---

[8] *CPR, 1461–7*, 212–13; *CPR, 1467–77*, 342–3.   [9] PRO, SC6/1085/20.
[10] BL, Cotton MS, Julius B xii, fos. 135^v–137; *CPR, 1467–77*, 483. While Clarence received Richmond Castle itself, Gloucester took the income from castleward, other rents, and the services of free tenants belonging to it, i.e. the mesne lordship.

lordship by Edward IV in 1470, and who had probably taken possession. Durham's case, as we have seen, rested on the pretended right to forfeiture, and had its origins in the early fourteenth century. But by his grant to Clarence of *all* the lands to which the heirs general of Warwick had hereditary expectation, which included all the estates of the dowager countess of Warwick, Edward IV gave him a claim to Barnard Castle.[11] It was possibly the fear that Gloucester would challenge him over this claim in the name of Anne Neville which led him in February 1472 to insist that he and his duchess would part with no livelihood. In strict law, however, neither Clarence nor Gloucester, nor even their duchesses, had a right to Barnard Castle. This right lay with Anne the dowager countess, who as the sole heiress of Beauchamp had been dispossessed by the king in 1470. An Act of Attainder against her late husband would not have removed her right to all the Beauchamp and Despenser lands of the Warwick inheritance.[12] As Clarence and Gloucester (and her daughters) squabbled over her property, she, poor woman, lay in sanctuary in Beaulieu Abbey, prevented from leaving by the soldiers detailed by the king to protect her, from which she wrote a string of pitiful letters pleading her just cause.[13]

Characteristically, Gloucester broke the deadlock by his own decisive action. At the end of May 1473, apparently with the king's assent, the countess of Warwick was escorted northwards from Beaulieu Abbey by Sir James Tyrell to join the duke's household in the north. It was rumoured that the king had restored her to her inheritance, and that she had granted it all to Duke Richard, of which it was aptly said 'folks greatly marvel'.[14] It probably never was the intention of the countess to grant all her inheritance to Gloucester, or of the king to countenance such a step. Rather, as the removal to the north indicates, the new development involved the concession of Barnard Castle to Gloucester, perhaps with the agreement of Bishop Booth, but almost certainly against the wishes of Clar-

---

[11] *CPR, 1467–77*, 330.
[12] M. A. Hicks, 'Descent, Partition and Extinction: The Warwick Inheritance', *BIHR* 52 (1979), 120.
[13] BL, Cotton MS, Julius B xii, fo. 314[r-v].
[14] *Paston Letters*, i. 464; HMC, *11th Report*, App. vii.

ence, with whom a new round of conflict was inaugurated.[15] In the autumn of 1473 both dukes were reported to be arming themselves, and the king to be acting as a stifler between them. The threat to the peace and stability of the regime probably prompted the king to find a settlement of the legal confusion by Act of Parliament, while at the same time imposing his authority on Clarence by threatening resumption.[16]

The legal confusion was largely of Edward IV's own making. He had made contradictory grants involving both the earldom of Richmond and lordship of Barnard Castle; he had illegally seized and distributed the Beauchamp and Despenser sections of the Warwick inheritance; and, by failing to attaint Warwick, had expelled his male heir, the young George Neville, duke of Bedford, who should have succeeded under tail male to the Neville estates in the north. It was imperative that this mess was cleared up, not only to give some semblance of legality to the proceedings but also to resolve the conflict between his brothers. By July 1474 Clarence and Gloucester had agreed to a partition. Consequently two Acts of Parliament were passed in 1474 and 1475, which in effect disinherited both the countess of Warwick, treating her as if she were dead and passing her estates to her daughters as heirs general, and the male heirs of Richard Neville. At the same time the acts formalized the agreed partition, in which Gloucester took the northern half and Clarence the southern. Some anomalies remained: Clarence retained Richmond Castle, the fee farm of the town, and a share of Cottingham; Gloucester kept estates in Wales and the home counties. But in effect the inheritance was ultimately divided geographically.[17]

---

[15] Pollard, 'St Cuthbert and the Hog', p. 111. In the light of Gloucester's treatment of another dowager countess, Elizabeth, countess of Oxford, 6 months earlier, one might wonder whether the Countess Anne's conveyance of Barnard Castle was entirely voluntary. Rous later alleged that she was held in custody by the duke. It is intriguing to note, too, that according to 2 deponents in 1495 the duke's servants threatened the Countess Elizabeth that she would be sent to Middleham ('the north country') 'there to be kept' unless she agreed (M. A. Hicks, 'The Last Days of Elizabeth, Countess of Oxford', *EHR* 103 (1988), 76–95, esp. 91, 95; Rous, 'Historia de Regibus Anglie', in A. Hanham, *Richard III and his Early Historians, 1483–1535* (Oxford, 1975), p. 121).
[16] *Paston Letters*, i. 468; Hicks, *Clarence*, pp. 122–6; idem, 'Warwick Inheritance', pp. 122–3; Ross, *Richard III*, pp. 30–1.
[17] *Rot. Parl.* vi. 100–1, 124–5; Hicks, 'Warwick Inheritance', pp. 122–3.

The terms by which his share was settled on Duke Richard were, however, less than satisfactory. By the Act of 1474 Gloucester and his duchess acquired Barnard Castle in her right as an eventual heir general. This was relatively straightforward, and, the claims of the Countess Anne excepted, secure. Possession was taken in or before October 1474.[18] The act of 1475 dealt with the much trickier problem of the paternal inheritance of the earl of Warwick (Middleham, Penrith, and Sheriff Hutton), which had been settled in tail male. Rather than attaint the earl and his male heir, his brother John, Marquess Montagu, who had died alongside him, the king (at the request, he said, of his brothers) would break the entail and debar John's son George, duke of Bedford, and vest his part of the inheritance in the duke and duchess jointly in tail male 'as long as there be any heir male begotten of the body of the said Marquess' living. It was further enacted that should George die without a male heir himself, Gloucester's title would revert to a term of life only. In those circumstances the reversionary interest of the original tail male would revive, the beneficiary being Richard Neville, Lord Latimer, then a child of six. The original entail was suspended under tightly controlled conditions, which allowed the duke and duchess of Gloucester to inherit her father's estates only if the direct line of the true male heir was sustained and perpetuated.[19] While giving Gloucester greater short-term security than a mere grant during pleasure or for life, the extraordinary limitation placed on him by the Act did nothing to secure his longer-term, dynastic interest. The king was prepared at the time to offer no more; no doubt it was accepted because the duke hoped that the opportunity would occur in the future to amend it to his advantage. In short the Act of 1475 could only have been seen as a temporary measure.

For the time being, however, Gloucester could be satisfied. He had successfully added Barnard Castle to his northern estate, had secured a stronger title, and could claim through his marriage to Anne Neville to be the successor to the earl of Warwick. He did not draw only on the estates his father-in-law had held;

[18] Pollard, 'St Cuthbert and the Hog', pp. 111.
[19] *Rot. Parl.* vi. 100–1; M. A. Hicks, *Richard III as Duke of Gloucester: A Study in Character*, Borthwick Paper 70 (1986), 26–7.

he succeeded him in his major northern offices too. He was first created warden of the west march for three years on 18 August 1470; the post was resumed in the summer of 1471, and the term of the office was extended for another ten years in 1480. This was followed by the stewardship of the duchy of Lancaster in the north, and several lesser offices, including the constableship of Bewcastle and the master forestership of Bowland. To support him in the wardenship he received, in June 1472 for an annual farm of £46. 17s. 8d., the custody of almost all the royal rights in Cumberland, followed in 1475 with the shrievalty of Cumberland for life and all the issues for an annual farm of £100. Although he had to pay for these additions to his authority and power in Cumberland, he no doubt hoped to profit from them, as well as thereby to consolidate his hold on the west march.[20]

With land and office came men. Gloucester wasted no time in recruiting the prominent retainers of the earl of Warwick into his service, even before he married Warwick's daughter Anne. Sir John Conyers was confirmed in his post of steward of Middleham, and his fee was increased from £13. 6s. 8d. to £20 per annum, while he also continued to serve as constable of the castle, with a fee of £6. 13s. 4d. Conyers, who had been Warwick's deputy in the lordship and one of his principal lieutenants in the north-east, was thus in a position to ensure the rapid establishment of Gloucester's authority in Richmondshire. During the autumn and winter of 1471–2 a significant number of his relations, as well as former servants of Warwick, were retained by the duke. In the space of six months Sir John's grandson and heir John, his son Richard, his brother Richard, his brothers-in-law William Burgh (an old Warwick servant) and Roland Pudsay, his son-in-law Sir Thomas Markenfield, and his wife's half-brother Thomas Tunstall all joined the Middleham payroll. Tunstall, who was granted a larger fee (£33. 6s. 8d.) than Sir John, was a particularly important recruit; for he, with his brother Sir Richard of Thurland Castle, near Tunstall, Lancashire, had been a prominent supporter of the Readeption of Henry VI. Members of the other family which traditionally served the lords of Middleham—the Metcalfes of Nappa—were

[20] CFR, 1471–85, No. 116; CPR, 1407–77, 485, 556; Storey, 'Wardens', pp. 607–8; Somerville, Duchy of Lancaster, i. 471, 507, 508.

also quickly retained. Thomas and Brian, sons of James, the founder of the family, were recruited in the autumn of 1471. The Metcalfes were of relatively modest means, and specialized in estate and forest management. Under Warwick no fewer than nine of them had been retained, the majority as reeves, parkers, and foresters. In time Gloucester was to find similar employment for an even larger number. It was also important for Gloucester to secure the best legal counsel that was available. Hence he retained Sir Robert Danby, seated at Thorp Perrow, Chief Justice of Common Pleas since 1462, who was no doubt engaged in the matter of the title to the estate, while he continued to retain the services of Richard Pigot, who was his tenant at South Cowton and Deighton, and received a fee of £4 p.a. A last recruit in 1471 was Robert Clifford, youngest son of the Thomas, Lord Clifford killed at the first battle of St Albans in 1455, and an uncle of the attainted Henry, the 'shepherd' lord, who had taken to the Cumbrian fells rather than submit to Edward IV.[21] By bringing these men into his service, many of them old followers of Warwick, most of local stature, one or two old enemies of his family, the duke was able quickly to establish his position in Middleham and Richmondshire.

Duke Richard's retaining extended beyond Middleham. Unfortunately, since the equivalent documentation is lacking, we are far less well-informed about the beneficiaries. At Sheriff Hutton he quickly secured the service of five one-time Neville servants: Thomas Gower, Thomas Witham, John Lepton, John Hardgill, and Robert Constable of Barnby-by-Bossall.[22] The office of constable of Barnard Castle, and probably that of master forester too, was in the hands of Richard Ratcliffe by 1476 or earlier.[23] Robert Brackenbury of Denton near Gainford was probably another Barnard Castle retainer. As chief steward of the duchy of Lancaster the duke had further offices at his disposal: most notably he appointed Miles Metcalfe, brother of

[21] PRO, DL 29/648/10485. For Conyers and Tunstall see above, p. 302. William Tunstall, a third brother, was also in Gloucester's service by this time (see Hicks, 'Countess of Oxford', p. 90 and also Pollard, *Middleham Connection*, p. 5. For the legend that Cuthbert Tunstall, later bishop of Durham, was the illegitimate son of this Thomas Tunstall and one of Sir John Conyers's daughters, see C. Sturge, *Cuthbert Tunstall* (1938), 3–6.

[22] Horrox, 'Richard III and the East Riding', p. 83.

[23] NYCRO, ZQH 1, fo. 167ᵛ; Skaife, *Register*, 98.

Thomas, who had been Warwick's attorney general, his deputy. And the appointment of Sir James Harrington of Hornby, Lancashire and Brierley, Yorks. as steward of Pontefract, as well as as deputy forester of Bowland, almost certainly owed much to Gloucester's influence.[24]

Gloucester's rapid consolidation of power on both sides of the Pennines quickly created tension with other magnates. In northern Lancashire he ran into conflict with Lord Stanley. The genesis of this dispute lay in Edward IV's grant of the honours of Clitheroe and Halton as well as the foresterships of Amounderness, Bowland, and Blackburn, to his brother in 1469. Lord Stanley was the loser, and the king's action seems to have quickly led to 'variance' between them—even perhaps an armed confrontation on the banks of the Ribble near Preston. In 1471 Gloucester retained most of his duchy of Lancaster possessions and offices in Lancashire. Matters were complicated, however, by dispute over the possession of Hornby castle in Lonsdale between Sir James Harrington, second and eldest surviving son of Sir Thomas Harrington, who died at Wakefield, and Edward, the second son of Lord Stanley, who had married Anne Harrington, one of the granddaughters of Sir Thomas Harrington and joint heiress of his eldest son Sir John, who had also been killed in 1460. Dispute centred on whether Hornby was held in tail male, in which case Sir James was the heir, or in fee simple, in which case Anne was an heiress. Harrington had taken the law into his own hands and occupied Hornby, and kept Anne in his custody. The Harringtons found a powerful backer in Richard of Gloucester. As Dr Jones has shown, in March 1470 Gloucester was in residence at Hornby at about the time that it was besieged by the Stanleys. In 1473 Gloucester headed a commission appointed by the king, with instruction to take possession of the castle and deliver it to Lord Stanley, which significantly failed to carry out its task. Gloucester had good cause to support Sir James. His father and brother had died fighting for Gloucester's father, and had been leading retainers of the earl of Salisbury. Moreover his reputation as a good lord was at stake. The

[24] Somerville, *Duchy of Lancaster*, i. 426, 508, 514. For a fuller discussion of Gloucester's hold on the duchy in the north see R. E. Horrox, *Richard III: A Study of Service* (Cambridge, 1989), 42–8.

Nevilles of Middleham had established themselves as the dominant lords of Lonsdale and Furness. Not only the Harringtons, but also the Middletons of Middleton, the Redmans of the Levens, and the Huddlestons of Millom had become closely tied to the Nevilles' fortunes. Gloucester himself had retained younger members of the Tunstalls of Thurland, also in Lonsdale. It was imperative that Duke Richard should be seen, during this first test of his lordship, to be standing firm for his man, a man with established Neville connections in what was a border district of his newly established zone of influence. The dispute over Hornby thus had wider than local implications in the early 1470s. It was not until the eve of the king's departure to France in 1475 that a compromise which satisfied the honour of all parties was reached by the king's council. Harrington was awarded Farleton in Lancashire and Brierley in the West Riding, while Edward Stanley was granted Hornby itself. Sir James made Brierley his principal residence, and Yorkshire became thereafter his home county. Gloucester had passed his test.[25]

At the same time, and closer to home, tensions were developing between Duke Richard and Henry Percy, earl of Northumberland. By becoming heir to Neville, Gloucester became heir to the feud with Percy. Moreover Henry Percy could well have resented Gloucester's intrusion in the region just when he might have hoped to profit substantially from Warwick's fall. Northumberland had indeed made some slight gain. He had secured for himself the stewardship of Knaresborough, which Warwick had held. In May 1472, however, Gloucester was granted the office of chief justice of the royal forests north of the Trent, which the earl had previously held.[26] Conflict seems to have focused on possession of these offices. For Gloucester, acquisition of the stewardship of Knaresborough would have significantly extended his direct influence south of Richmondshire. The retaining of John Redman, a younger son of Sir Richard of Harewood and the Levens, on 20 March 1473, and Richard Knaresborough a month later may well have been linked with such ambitions.[27] Matters had reached such a state

[25] For the above paragraph I have drawn on Michael K. Jones, 'Richard III and the Stanleys', in Horrox, *Richard III and the North*, pp. 35–40.
[26] Somerville, *Duchy of Lancaster*, i. 524; *CPR, 1467–77*, 338.
[27] PRO, DL 29/648/10485.

that both duke and earl were called before the king and his council at Nottingham in May, where a settlement was reached in which the duke promised 'that he shall not ask, challenge nor claim any offices or fee that the said earl hath of the king's grant' and that 'he shall not accept nor retain into his service any servant or servants that was . . . with the said earl retained of fee'. A year later the duke formally retained the earl, and the agreement of May 1473 was affirmed.[28]

In 1473–4 Duke Richard was also in conflict with the bishop of Durham and his brother George over Barnard Castle, Richmond, and Cottingham. Over the winter of 1473 he and Clarence nearly came to blows. In November Sir John Paston reported home that Clarence was gathering strength to deal with his brother; and in February 1474 the Milanese ambassador remarked that Gloucester was 'constantly preparing for war' with Clarence.[29] It might be that the retaining on 3 July 1473 of William Clerionet, one of the leading townsmen of Richmond, who had also been in Warwick's service, and in September following of three Durham men—Sir Roger Conyers of Wynyard, Thomas Blakeston his neighbour, and Lionel Claxton of Horden—was connected with these 'constant preparations' for war.[30] These conflicts too were eventually resolved by the settlement of Barnard Castle on Gloucester, and the formal division of the Warwick inheritance by Acts of Parliament in 1474–5.

It is apparent, however, that Gloucester's arrival in northeastern England in July 1471 was initially a cause of major dislocation, which threatened to perpetuate local divisions and rivalries. The king and his council had their work cut out containing his youngest brother's ambition, and smoothing the

[28] Hicks, 'Fourth Earl of Northumberland', pp. 83–4. It is possible that, as part of the agreement, Northumberland was restored to the office of chief justice of forests, for he held it in 1482–3, and after Bosworth it was one of the offices granted to him by Edward IV, for which he was exempted in the first Tudor Act of Resumption (*Harleian MS 433*, iii. 208; Campbell, *Materials*, ii. 54; *CPR, 1485–94*, 138).

[29] *Paston Letters*, i. 468; *Calendar of State Papers Milan*, ed. A. B. Hinds, i (1902), 178.

[30] PRO, DL 29/648/10485. But note also the threat to Hartlepool by a Lancastrian band under Thomas Clifford in the autumn of 1473, and the commission of array issued to the duke on 10 Sept. (Durham, Church Commission, Bishopric Estates, 189826; *CPR 1467–77*, 408).

ruffled feathers of others. But by 1475, when the king led an
apparently united kingdom to war against France, the balance of
power in post-Neville north-eastern England had been settled:
Gloucester was dominant. Clarence, Northumberland, Stanley,
and the bishop of Durham had come to accept the new lord of
Middleham as Warwick the Kingmaker's successor. The way
was then open for Gloucester to complete the establishment of a
hegemony which not even his predecessor achieved.

Having secured his dominance, and having squeezed as many
concessions as he could from his brother the king, Duke Richard
then turned his attention to winning the confidence of those
around him. After their early rivalry the duke and the earl of
Northumberland, bound as lord and retainer by the agreement
of July 1474, settled into an amicable partnership. Northumberland was supreme in his comital county, where he was not only
warden of the east march, but also, after 1474, sheriff for life.
The earl was also pre-eminent in the East Riding, although the
duke's presence was felt in the north-west of the Riding from the
lordship of Sheriff Hutton.[31] In the West Riding king, duke, and
earl shared influence, although Gloucester emerged as the
dominant force. In addition to the duchy of Lancaster, the duchy
of York lordship at Wakefield was an important source of local
royal authority. Particularly important servants of the house of
York were Sir Richard FitzWilliam of Sprotbrough and Wad-
worth near Doncaster (constable of Tickhill and Conisbrough)
and Sir John Pilkington of Sowerby and Sir John Saville of
Thornhill (steward of Wakefield and constable of Sandal respectively). These men, all three knights of the body, and from
well-established Yorkist families, were first and foremost
answerable to the king himself. But they inevitably developed
close links with his brother; especially Pilkington, who became
Gloucester's councillor and retainer. All three died between
1479 and 1482, and their heirs became even more closely
associated with Duke Richard. Lesser men from the southern
parts of the Riding were also drawn into Gloucester's service,
notably John Everingham of Birkin, John Dawney of Cowick,

[31] Hicks, 'Fourth Earl of Northumberland', pp. 84–5; Hunter-Blair, 'The
Sheriffs of Northumberland', p. 19; Horrox, 'Richard III and the East Riding',
passim.

and William Hopton of Swillington.[32] Thus the duke, as the resident representative of the royal family, cast his net southwards into an area where the Nevilles had never been strong.

It is not surprising that the lesser northern peerage, especially those with landed interests in the North Riding, quickly attached themselves to Duke Richard: Greystoke, FitzHugh, Scrope of Bolton, and Lumley all became councillors or retainers.[33] The arrangement through which the young Thomas, Lord Scrope of Masham entered the duke's circle is particularly worthy of note. On 14 January 1476, after the death of the fifth Lord Scrope, Elizabeth his widow agreed with Gloucester that her sixteen-year-old son should henceforth 'be beleft, withheld and retained with the said duke and wholly be at his rule and guiding' and that all her servants and tenants 'shall be hereafter at all times belonging to the said duke and to him give their faithful attendance'. In exchange the duke merely promised 'to be good and loving lord to all of them' and to 'support, succour and assist at all times'. Thus a significant northern barony seems to have been put at the duke's disposal. Thomas, who one supposes joined Gloucester's household at this time, entered his father's lands in 1480 (when the agreement of 1476 presumably came to an end), and was subsequently a devoted follower of his lord.[34]

Among the Scrope of Masham estates was Winston on the north bank of the Tees between Whorlton and Gainford, both members of the lordship of Barnard Castle, from the churchyard of which Raby Castle is in full view. There is no doubt that Gloucester was anxious to extend his influence in the county palatine. At first he was blocked by Bishop Booth, who took the young Ralph, Lord Neville under his wing. But after Booth's translation to York in the later summer of 1476 the way was open. The new bishop, William Dudley, had been dean of the Chapel Royal, and was one of the king's most trusted clerical servants. He quickly revealed himself to be a self-effacing

---

[32] Arnold, 'West Riding', pp. 59–60 and App. 3, pp. 61–3; Dockray, 'Richard III and the Yorkshire Gentry', pp. 41–2, 51–2; Richmond, *John Hopton*, pp. 137–9; Wedgwood, *Biographies*, pp. 684–5, 743; Horrox, *Richard III*, pp. 59–60.

[33] Ross, *Richard III*, pp. 48–9.

[34] L. C. Attreed, 'An Indenture between Richard, Duke of Gloucester and the Scrope Family of Masham and Upsall', *Speculum*, 58 (1983), 1018–25.

and pliant figurehead, prepared in effect to hand over the secular leadership of his palatinate to the duke of Gloucester. Gloucester was appointed for the first time to the leading commissions; he was granted the forest of Weardale and Stanhope Park, worth £100 p.a., and created lieutenant for the war against Scotland in 1480; he placed prominent servants on the episcopal council, and secured annuities for several others. In Dudley's wake, Ralph, Lord Neville, the heir to the simple-minded earl of Westmorland, also entered Duke Richard's service. At Easter 1477 he quit his claim to Middleham, Sheriff Hutton, and Penrith. Sometime between July of that year and January 1479 the earl himself vested Raby and a group of south-east Durham manors in his infant great-nephew (Lord Neville's son) and a panel of feoffees, the majority of whom were Gloucester's councillors. Subsequently, in circumstances which remain obscure, Gloucester as king was able to take possession of the lordship, appoint his own officers, and collect the revenues. Even as early as 1478 the duke was to be found residing at the castle. Both bishop and Neville of Raby had come under the duke's sway. In March 1477 Prior Bell of Durham Cathedral Priory had written to Bishop Dudley, advising him to cherish the Nevilles and their servants, remarking that should they stand as one he would be able to rule and lead all those that inhabited the bishopric. He was wrong: it was Richard of Gloucester who had the *de facto* rule.[35]

Gloucester's expanding power extended beyond lay society. His relationship with Laurence Booth, bishop of Durham and then archbishop of York, was ambivalent. While at Durham, Booth had good cause to resent Gloucester, who had snatched Barnard Castle from him; and he excluded him from the palatinate. Nevertheless he had been willing to collude with the duke in his designs on the countess of Oxford's estates in 1473; these did not touch his own episcopal interest.[36] The most likely key to Booth's behaviour is his obsession with the rights and

---

[35] For the above paragraph see Pollard, 'St Cuthbert and the Hog', pp. 115–19. For the earl of Westmorland see William Worcester, *Itineraries*, ed. J. H. Harvey (Oxford, 1969), 345 in which he is described as 'innocens homo'.

[36] Pollard, 'St Cuthbert and the Hog', pp. 114–15. Hicks, 'Countess of Oxford', pp. 77–8.

privileges of his see (demonstrated in other matters besides the possession of Barnard Castle), which led him to be intransigent where Durham was concerned, but more amenable over other matters when Chancellor.[37] Certainly after his move to York relationships with Gloucester were more cordial, the duke becoming his steward of Ripon almost immediately.[38] His own successor, Thomas Rotherham, however, was no friend of the duke. But perhaps the personal relationships between Gloucester and successive archbishops of York were of less importance than his carefully cultivated connection with the principal residentiary canons, Dean Robert Booth, Treasurer Thomas Portington, and Archdeacon William Poteman. Poteman was, as Professor Dobson has shown, the key figure in maintaining continuity between the later, non-resident years of Archbishop Neville (1471–5) and the pontificates of Booth and Rotherham. As early as 1474 Poteman was discussing the *ecclesiastical* affairs of York with Duke Richard at Middleham. Thereafter, he and his fellow residentiaries developed an even closer relationship with the duke, which came to a climax in 1483. As Professor Dobson has concluded, 'these three residentiary canons showed themselves responsive and amenable to the desires of Richard of Gloucester long before the duke's accession to the throne made those desires absolutely irresistible'.[39]

Gloucester's ecclesiastical patronage and influence was not restricted to the two dioceses of the region: it extended to some of the religious houses. Where, as at Coverham, he inherited the position of patron, his role was unexceptional.[40] In 1480, having secured from St Albans Abbey the right of presentation to its priory at Tynemouth, he became involved in a long dispute over the position of Nicholas Boston, his appointee, as prior, which was not settled until after he became king.[41] But of all the north-eastern religious houses the Cathedral Priory at Durham was the nearest to Gloucester's heart. In 1474 he and his duchess were admitted to the fraternity of the priory, a privilege granted

---

[37] See above, pp. 295–7.

[38] BI, Register Neville and Booth, fo. 290ᵛ.

[39] Dobson, 'Richard III and the Church of York', pp. 130–8. As Professor Dobson noted, Gloucester was even in this respect the heir to Neville.

[40] See above, p. 181.

[41] Craster, *Tynemouth*, pp. 104–6.

to those who by their acts, usually donations, had demonstrated their affection for St Cuthbert. Inevitably Gloucester was drawn in as a patron, and he and his duchess sought to benefit from the ecclesiastical patronage offered by the priory. In 1478 Gloucester ill-advisedly supported Prior Bell in his attempt to hold the priory *in commendam* on becoming Bishop of Carlisle. This led to a cooling of relationship with his successor Robert Ebbchester. But by 1479 Gloucester had recovered his position as *dominus specialissimus* by coming forward as the priory's champion in its long struggle to recover Coldingham. In 1482 his troops were inspired during the recovery of Berwick by the presence of the banner of St Cuthbert itself, brought out to bless the campaign.[42]

Finally Gloucester happily adopted the role of patron and special lord of the boroughs of north-eastern England, above all of the city of York. Gloucester's relationship with York has been thoroughly studied, and need not be reiterated in detail.[43] The principal documentation, the corporation minutes, is sufficient only from 1476, so it may be that the duke was already a well-established patron of the city before a visit in 1475 with his duchess. But it was not until 1477 that they joined the Corpus Christi Guild, and only in the second half of the decade did he begin to influence appointments to senior administrative posts (Miles Metcalfe as Recorder in 1477; Nicholas Lancaster in 1476 and John Harrington in 1484, both as common clerk; and probably John Brackenbury as macebearer in 1480). And on the aldermanic bench he attracted a significant and loyal following led by Thomas Wrangwysh, twice mayor and twice MP. From 1476 he was intervening in the internal affairs of the city, being called upon in 1482 to settle a dispute over the mayoral election; and, as has so often been remarked, he frequently summoned military support from the corporation.[44] In 1483 and thereafter York consistently gave its backing to a king who, the official minute of the morrow of Bosworth famously recorded, 'was

---

[42] Dobson, 'Richard Bell', pp. 205–6, 209–11; Pollard, 'St Cuthbert and the Hog', pp. 117–18.

[43] See esp. L. C. Attreed, 'The King's Interest: York's Fee Farm and the Central Government, 1482–92', *NH* 17 (1981), 24–43; Miller, 'Medieval York', pp. 60–6; Palliser, 'Richard III and York', pp. 51–81.

[44] Palliser, 'Richard III and York', pp. 55–6, 62–6.

piteously slain and murdered, to the great heaviness of this city'.[45]

York looked to Gloucester to act on its behalf; to provide the 'good and benevolent lordship that he at all times have had unto this city', as it was put in March 1482.[46] York was not alone. All the north-east came to look to the mighty duke for his benevolent lordship. And on balance he did not fail it. To begin with the city itself. As we have seen, York had suffered severely since mid-century. While the city still remained the northern metropolis and entrepôt, it was passing through a period of prolonged economic decline. The corporation tended to blame this recent ill-fortune on two things: unfair competition from London in the battle for a share of North Sea trade, and the obstruction of the waterways in Yorkshire which were the arteries of York's internal trade. On both these issues the duke acted vigorously on the city's behalf. Concern to compete on equal terms with London merchants in the Low Countries became uppermost after 1470, when York merchants found themselves virtually excluded from the Baltic. Gloucester was one of those whose support was enlisted in seeking to persuade the king to approve the establishment of a separate northern organization in the Low Countries, under its own governor. The king, however, was unmoved, being prepared to go only so far as to issue a proclamation urging fair treatment.[47]

Richard of Gloucester himself was more fully engaged on the citizens' behalf in the matter of fishgarths which obstructed the inland waterways. In 1475 York secured an Act of Parliament which made it illegal for the local inhabitants to maintain fishgarths across the Ouse, the Aire, and their tributaries. The commission established by the Act, in effect the mayor and other representatives of the city, faced hostility in its attempt at enforcement. The citizens therefore appealed to Duke Richard, as well as to other lords, to use his authority on their behalf. He was himself quick to ensure that his own tenants complied with the law. And he was willing too that the commissioners should cite his own letter to the bailiff and tenants of Hook, which

[45] *YCR* i. 118–19.
[46] Ibid. 52.
[47] Miller, 'Medieval York', pp. 103–4.

instructed them to destroy their garths, in their letter of
22 March 1476 to the bishop of Durham asking him to deal
similarly in Howden on the opposite bank of the Ouse.[48] But the
commissioners found the duchy of Lancaster tenants of
Gowdall on the Aire, near Snaith, obdurate in their refusal to
comply with the law. The city council, which sought the advice
of John Vavasour on how best to proceed, appealed directly to
the king in October 1477, claiming that the garth 'so instrates
the river that all your liege people in the same passing and
repassing with their ships and boats been greatly letted and
stopped'. They enlisted the support at court of Duke Richard,
who on 15 November wrote from London that he had moved the
king's grace, and would deal with the problem at his next
homecoming.[49] It was no doubt in connection with this same
issue that a deputation led by two aldermen rode to Middleham
in March 1478 to confer with Gloucester over the matter of
fishgarths, which led to an inspection of the rivers in the
following month in which representatives of both the duke and
the earl of Northumberland participated.[50] These steps seem to
have dealt satisfactorily with the problem for the time being.
But in 1482 there was a riot at Snaith over the breaking up of a
(reconstructed?) fishgarth, and on 19 May 1484 the city was
appealing once more to Richard, now king (and duke of Lancaster), about the continuation of a fishgarth at Gowdall, 'which, if
it should stand should be example to all other to set up
fishgarths'. King and council seem to have responded promptly,
for Sir Robert Dymock was ordered to pull down a garth set up at
Barlow on Ouse, and a full list of illegal garths was compiled,
presumably with a view to further action.[51]

   In representing the city's cause at court, and throwing his
considerable weight behind the enforcement of the Act of 1475
in Yorkshire, Richard of Gloucester demonstrated his benevolent lordship in the most effective possible way. Similarly he
took up the cause of the remission of the fee-farm, which by
1482 the citizens had decided was necessary so that trade free of
tolls could be offered in their struggling markets. In September

---

[48] YCR i. 4.   [49] Ibid. 24, 29.
[50] Dobson, York Chamberlains' Accounts, pp. 163–4.
[51] YCR i. 64, 92–4, 98–100.

1483, now king, he was able himself to take the step of offering a substantial reduction.[52] Gloucester's patronage of the city of York had implications which reached wider than the city itself, for York's economic plight was a reflection of that of the region as a whole. Support for the economy of York was support for the well-being of the north-east in general. While some sectional interests were adversely affected—most notably the tenants of riverside settlements who wished to take fish from the rivers—the country people could only hope to gain from moves designed, however forlornly, to halt the slide in York's prosperity.

Besides taking an active interest in the economy of his adopted region, Richard of Gloucester was also concerned to improve the administration of local justice. Documentation is not substantial; but it is clear from two or three cases that, where his own immediate self-interest was not concerned (an important proviso), the duke wished to see that the law was administered impartially and that the weak were not overborne by the strong. His appearance at York in March 1476 with a powerful retinue to enforce law and order may have had as much to do with the anxiety of the king about the restlessness of the realm after the ignominious withdrawal from France the previous year as with the duke's own inclination.[53] But his action in April 1482, when he sent his councillor Sir Ralph Ashton to the city to deliver his treasurer's servant, Thomas Redhead, for trial and punishment for an offence committed against a citizen, is particularly revealing.[54] One might have expected that in the circumstances as described, a fracas between the duke's servant and a citizen, the duke would have maintained his servant's quarrel, and would have done his utmost to prevent justice being done. No doubt because the case concerned the city of York there was an element of political calculation in such a magnanimous act. But even so the action was also a public declaration of a desire to see justice done impartially to all. The same attitude is revealed in the duke's letter of 12 August 1480

---

[52] Ibid. 65–6, 71–2, 82; Attreed, 'York's Fee Farm', pp. 29–31 and *passim* for the subsequent administrative confusion in implementing the concession. It is to be noted that from 1482 Gloucester was 'keeper' of the farm, retaining £50 p.a. to contribute to his salary as warden of the west marches.

[53] YCR i. 2–3.   [54] Ibid. 53–4.

to Sir Robert Claxton of Horden, a substantial, senior, and much respected leading light of Durham society, on behalf of John Randson, an insignificant husbandman. Randson had complained to Gloucester that Claxton was preventing him from working his land. The duke, moved by his 'piteous complaint', took Randson's part and 'advised' Claxton to appear before his learned counsel at Durham, where, he assured him, justice would be done. 'And so demean you,' threatened the duke, 'that we have no cause to provide his lawful remedy in this behalf.' It did not matter that Claxton's illegitimate son was one of the duke's retainers, or that his daughter was married to another. In this case the duke had already determined that right lay on Randson's side, and that he personally would settle the issue in the husbandman's favour. There can be no clearer evidence that the duke's council had already begun to act as a court of poor requests in the north, bypassing if necessary the usual channels.[55]

The duke's council willingly acted as a court of arbitration in all manner of disputes. Randson and others knew that it offered effective remedy. A few years earlier Gerard Salvin of Croxdale had appealed to the duke to intervene on his behalf against his neighbour Thomas Fishburn, whom he accused of assaulting him in his manor house. Salvin, 'a poor gentleman' not attached to any lord, declared that he loved 'no one so well as you under God and the king', offered himself as a feed retainer, and, the purpose of his petition, besought Gloucester to take his part against Fishburn.[56] The outcome is not known. More conventional was the appeal of Richard Clervaux and Roland Place to the duke to settle their differences, which led to an arbitration published on 12 April 1478. The duke declared that his award was made 'tendering the peace and weal of the country where the said parties do inhabit and also gladly willing good concord, rest and friendly unity to be had from henceforth between' them.[57] The phraseology is conventional, but it nevertheless

[55] Library of Congress, Washington, DC, Thatcher Collection 1004; Pollard, 'St Cuthbert and the Hog', pp. 120, 128, nn. 89, 90. I am grateful to Mr Geoffrey Wheeler for giving me a photocopy of this document.

[56] Surtees, *Durham*, iv. Part 2, pp. 114–15; Pollard, 'St. Cuthbert and the Hog', p. 120.

[57] NYCRO, zqh 1, fos. 155–6 and above, p. 118.

sums up the duke's wider purpose in offering his services as a
lawgiver and arbitrator. Good concord, rest, and friendly unity
were the hallmarks of his hegemony over the north after 1474.

One must be careful not to exaggerate the degree of harmony
in north-eastern England under Gloucester's rule after 1474. In
1478, for instance, a violent quarrel blew up between two of the
king's right-hand men, Sir John Pilkington and Sir John Saville,
which threatened to undermine the stability of the regime. A
powerful commission of oyer and terminer met under Gloucester's presidency at Pontefract Castle on 21–5 September to
attempt to calm things down.[58] But it was probably Pilkington's
death early in 1479 which fortuitously brought it to an end.
There were lesser disturbances and popular upheavals, especially in 1481–2, when the combined impact of harvest failure
and the burden of war led to unrest.[59] And there were other
resentments. Gloucester's hegemony depended in part on the
exclusion of attainted and exiled Lancastrians, especially Lord
Clifford, Lord Roos, and, it must not be overlooked, Henry
Tudor, earl of Richmond, whose titular estate Gloucester himself occupied. And within northern society there were divisions.
These are most clearly revealed in York, where, Professor
Palliser has recently suggested, Richard of Gloucester may only
have enjoyed the committed support of a dominant faction, the
most prominent member of which was Thomas Wrangwysh;
and where there seems to have been an undercurrent of some
popular hostility to the duke, which, if its precise strength
cannot be gauged, nevertheless made the corporation nervous
about 'seditious words . . . of my lord of Gloucester'.[60]

However, Richard of Gloucester's service to the north-east
was immense. Perhaps the greatest benefit he bestowed was to
bring to an end the era of bitter and violent internal conflict
which had torn the region apart since 1453. Whereas Warwick
the Kingmaker's dominance after 1461 had represented the
victory of one faction, Gloucester's position was founded on the
healing of old wounds. Yet if the administration of justice
improved and the level of local disorder declined after 1474 it

---

[58] PRO, KB9/349; Arnold, 'West Riding', pp. 189–92.
[59] Scofield, *Edward the Fourth*, ii. 333–4.
[60] Palliser, 'Richard III and York', pp. 56, 62–9.

may have been due less to the duke's own desire for the law to be upheld than to the fact that his very dominance removed the chief cause of recent disorder—aristocratic feuding. The duke, as the king's brother and a man personally untainted by two decades of animosity, was able to stand above old divisions, and restore a unity not experienced for several years. The seal was put on this restoration of northern unity by Gloucester's presenting himself as the champion against the common foe—the Scots. His victories in 1482 finally established his unchallenged mastery of the whole of the north.[61]

By 1483 Richard of Gloucester had gathered to himself an awesome power. The climax of this process came with the creation of a ducal palatinate in Cumbria and the substantial slice of south-west Scotland ceded to Edward IV by the duke of Albany.[62] It was the first such apanage created since the county of Lancaster in the fourteenth century. The king's generous recognition of Gloucester's achievements against the Scots demonstrates beyond any doubt that the duke was high in his brother's favour. Gossip circulating in London in the early summer of the same year (picked up by Dominic Mancini) that in 1478 Gloucester had withdrawn from court to his estates, and there deliberately fostered the reputation of a worthy man so as to build up his power, is entirely without foundation.[63] It is true that, especially after he came down from London in March 1478 following the trial and execution of the duke of Clarence (his 'next homecoming', as he put it to the corporation of York in November 1477),[64] he was resident mainly in Yorkshire and County Durham. But he maintained a regular contact at court. This is demonstrated by his witnessing of royal charters, which, if they do not prove that he was actually present at each and every occasion, reveal that he was *persona grata*.[65] As Dr Horrox has pointed out, being high in the king's favour was one of the

---

[61] See above, pp. 235–40.
[62] *Rot. Parl.* vi. 204–5.
[63] Mancini, *Usurpation*, pp. 62–5.
[64] *YCR* i. 24.
[65] PRO, C53/197. There is no evidence to show that Gloucester was not with the king at Woburn and Westminster on 4 and 8 July 1479 or at Westminster in April–May 1481.

very advantages he enjoyed in attracting northern men and institutions to him.[66]

The question is also raised as to whether the king actively promoted his brother's power in the north as part of a policy of delegating regional authority to him, or whether Gloucester took power for himself, leaving the king no choice but to acquiesce.[67] The two are not mutually exclusive. There is no doubt that Edward IV began the process in 1471. It is apparent, as Dr Hicks has established, that after 1475 Gloucester deliberately concentrated his landed estate in the north, being prepared to pay for royal grants or to exchange more southerly properties for those in Yorkshire (Scarborough, Skipton, and Helmsley, for example). Gloucester consolidated his power in the north, and concentrated on building up his influence in the region at the expense of that elsewhere.[68] To this extent he took power for himself. At the same time, however, he enjoyed his position only by licence and authority of the king.

As we have seen, Duke Richard had been obliged by Edward IV to accept a title to his principal northern estates that was less than satisfactory. In 1475 he no doubt hoped that within a short while he would be able to renegotiate the terms. Such an opportunity might have appeared to present itself with the fall of the duke of Clarence in 1477–8. Gloucester gave at least tacit

---

[66] Horrox, *Richard III and the North*, p. 2; idem, *Richard III*, p. 61; idem, 'The English Court', *Ricardian*, viii, no. 101 (1988), 77–8.

[67] Horrox, *Richard III and the North*, pp. 1–4; idem, *Richard III*, pp. 88, 128–30; D. A. L. Morgan, 'The King's Affinity in the Polity of Yorkist England', *TRHS* 5th ser., 23 (1973), 17–18; Ross, *Richard III*, pp. 24, 26; M. A. Hicks, 'Richard, Duke of Gloucester and the North', pp. 13–16; idem, *Richard III as Duke of Gloucester: A Study in Character*, Borthwick Paper 70 (York, 1986), 15–17. Dr Horrox is surely correct to emphasize that in the short term Gloucester's power in the north enhanced Edward IV's authority. As a senior member of the royal household and the king's brother he represented the court in the country. But, as the events of 1483 were tragically to prove, in the longer term his power was turned against Edward IV's heir. This development was neither inevitable nor predictable. Nevertheless it happened; and it could not have happened had Gloucester not been able, under royal licence, to consolidate such power from 1471.

[68] Hicks, *Richard III as Duke of Gloucester*, pp. 17–18. As Dr Hicks observes, 'his holdings in the south were increasingly peripheral to his main concerns' (p. 18). It is to be noted, however, that the duke retained interests elsewhere, especially in East Anglia. For a discussion of his more fragmented following in the rest of England see Horrox, *Richard III*, pp. 72–85.

support to the king. But his reward was meagre: a slight readjustment that completed his hold on Richmondshire.[69] It might have been that he had hoped for a major revision of his title. But, if so, this was not forthcoming. At about this time, however, he began belatedly to take steps to insure against the future, and against the eventuality of the Neville reversionary interest in Middleham, Sheriff Hutton, and Penrith being realized. He secured a quitclaim from Ralph, Lord Neville to make sure that confusion was not confounded by the revival of an even older claim.[70] He did his best to neutralize the claims of Richard, Lord Latimer. Latimer was in the custody of Thomas Bourgchier, archbishop of Canterbury, and thus beyond his reach. But he obtained quitclaims from other members of the family: Latimer's aunt Katherine Dudley (née Neville) in 1477,[71] and his grandmother Elizabeth, Lady Latimer, in 1480. The agreement of 20 March 1480 with Lady Latimer, yet another widow, reveals Gloucester's hopes. He agreed that should he 'at any time hereafter' obtain the custody of Richard Neville and his estates he would continue to pay the annuity of 300 marks which she received from Cardinal Bourgchier in lieu of dower, and even do so if the archbishop cancelled payment because she carried out 'the desire and pleasure of the said duke'. The contingency arrangement would seem to imply that Lady Elizabeth had given her support to plans of the duke to secure the custody of her grandson.[72] In the event Lady Elizabeth died in 1481, and her dower and other estates reverted to the crown. That part which lay in Yorkshire, the lordship of Snape and Well, was granted on lease to Gloucester in 1482.[73] But the custody of young Lord Latimer still lay out of the duke's grasp.

More important even than Lord Latimer was the position of George Neville, duke of Bedford, who in 1478 was still in the

---

[69] Hicks, *Clarence*, pp. 150–1; Ross, *Richard III*, pp. 32–4. In Richmond Gloucester now received the castle and fee farm, to complete his holding of the entire honour.

[70] PRO, CP25(1)/281/164/32.

[71] Ibid., 165/23; BL, Cotton MS, Julius B xii, fos. 241ᵛ–243ᵛ; *CCR, 1476–85*, 189.

[72] Burghley House, Unsorted Deeds. I am grateful to Dr Michael K. Jones for giving me a transcript of this document. See also the discussion in Hicks, *Richard III as Duke of Gloucester*, pp. 28–9.

[73] *CFR, 1471–85*, 238–9.

care of his mother. By an act of 1478 George was stripped of his duchy. By 1480, if not earlier, Gloucester had secured his custody. But Duke Richard was not able to arrange a marriage, let alone to induce young George to produce the heir upon whom the duke's own hereditary title to the estates depended. This was still the situation when George died in May 1483, a month after Edward IV's death. At that moment Gloucester's title reverted to a mere life interest, and Lord Latimer became his heir.[74]

In May 1483 Richard of Gloucester found himself in a dangerously vulnerable position. His nephew, who had just become king, was a minor. He had secured his role as Protector, but his place was by no means assured, not least because of the violent means by which he had secured it. He could not be confident in the new political situation of his ability to adjust the settlement of 1474–5 in his favour. For all the immense power he had acquired in the north, indeed deliberately concentrated in the north, its foundation was dangerously unsound. The future of all that he had striven to achieve stood in doubt because of his insecure title to his estates. Paradoxically, while Gloucester's achievement in the north outshone that of even the earls of Salisbury and Warwick, at bottom it was less stable. In the early summer of 1483 the deaths of Edward IV and George Neville in quick succession left Gloucester exposed and at risk. This was the political and personal context in which he took the fateful step of seizing the throne for himself.

[74] *Rot. Parl.* vi. 173; *CPR, 1476–85,* 192; Hicks, *Richard III as Duke of Gloucester,* pp. 26–8, 29–30.

14

The Reign of Richard III, 1483–1485

THERE can be little doubt that the north provided the platform from which Richard III launched his bid for the throne in 1483. But there is no reason to believe that he created his northern hegemony for that purpose. Until Edward IV's death in April 1483 Richard of Gloucester's ambition was concentrated on creating a patrimony in the north—an ambition which culminated in the grant of the Cumbrian palatinate just two months before the king's death threw his kingdom's and brother's future into jeopardy. In the developing political crisis of the early summer of 1483 Duke Richard's aims appeared to contemporaries to be limited to securing the role of Protector for himself: an aim achieved dramatically and high-handedly at Stony Stratford on 30 April. In the few weeks that he allowed the minority of Edward V to run Gloucester made very few changes to the personnel of government. His close associate Francis, Viscount Lovell became butler, and some of his principal servants, such as Miles Metcalfe, John Kendal, and William Tunstall, were promoted and rewarded.[1] Apart from a handful of grants to his own men it was very much business as before.

Nevertheless the north-east and north-easterners were drawn into events from the beginning. Earl Rivers, Richard, Lord Grey, and Thomas Vaughan were sent north for safe custody at the beginning of May;[2] and the first step in Gloucester's bid for the throne was a summons for military help from the north-east. On 10 June letters were despatched from London and carried by Sir Richard Ratcliffe to the city of York, Lord Neville, and no doubt others. Citing the supposed plot of the Queen and her family 'to

---

[1] R. E. Horrox, 'The extent and use of Crown Patronage under Richard III' (unpublished Ph.D. thesis, Cambridge, 1975), 30; *Richard III*, pp. 103–6.
[2] Rivers was held at Sheriff Hutton in the charge of Sir Thomas Gower; Grey was at Middleham (*Harleian MS 433*, ii. 25).

murder and utterly destroy us . . . and also the final destruction and disinheritance of you and all other the inheritors and men of honour, as well of the north parts as other countries, that belongen us [are our dependants]', the duke urged his followers to come up to London in as great a strength as they could array.[3] The earl of Northumberland gathered a force at Pontefract, where on 25 June, one assumes under the duke's instruction, Rivers was summarily executed.[4] The army did not arrive in London until the beginning of July.[5] They found that their lord was already king, and about to celebrate his coronation.

It took longer to gather this army than was initially and optimistically hoped.[6] Nevertheless, even if all had gone to plan, it would still have arrived too late to influence the dramatic events of 13–26 June by which Richard became king. The usurpation was completed without military intervention, earlier and by means other than at first intended—probably because Lord Hastings and those removed on 13 June discovered what was afoot.[7] The army of the north, therefore, rusty sallets and all, was in the event deployed only to police the ceremony. Several north-easterners, probably some of the leaders of that army, are known to have attended the coronation. The earl of Northumberland was prominent, with Lords FitzHugh, Scrope of Bolton, Scrope of Masham, and Lumley. Among Gloucester's own retainers present were Sir John Conyers, Sir James Strangways, Sir Robert Harrington, Sir Robert Middleton, Sir John Middleton, Sir Ralph Ashton, Sir Richard Huddleston, and Sir

---

[3] *YCR* i. 74–5.

[4] Ross, *Richard III*, pp. 87–8.

[5] The army camped in Moor Fields. One observer described it as 4,000 strong 'in their best jacks and rusty sallets, with a few in white harness, nor burnished to the sale' (R. Fabyan, *New Chronicles of England and of France*, ed. H. Ellis (1811), 669).

[6] At first it was intended to muster at Pontefract on 18 June; but the York contingent of 200 men did not set out until 21 June at the earliest (*YCR* i. 74–5).

[7] For a review of the debate over the date of Hastings's death see Ross, *Richard III*, p. 84n. 62, and for the most recent comment Charles T. Wood, 'Richard III, William, Lord Hastings and Friday the Thirteenth', in Griffiths and Sherborne, *Kings and Nobles*, pp. 155–61. What precisely was going on in June 1483 will never be known. On balance I find Dr Horrox's reconstruction ('Patronage', pp. 34–8; *Richard III*, pp. 115–16), which I have followed here, more plausible than Professor Wood's ('Friday the Thirteenth', pp. 158–60) suggested cocktail of confusion, distrust, and fear.

James Danby.[8] Among the women attending the queen were the dowager Lady FitzHugh, Lady FitzHugh, Lady Scrope of Masham, Margaret Huddleston (her illegitimate half-sister), Elizabeth Mauleverer, Joyce Percy (wife of Sir Robert of Scotton, the controller of the household), and Grace Pullen (née Mauleverer, whose husband was serjeant of the kitchen).[9]

But the coronation was by no means exclusively a northern affair. The peerage as a whole attended in strength, and several prominent members of the late king's household, who later rebelled against Richard III, were present. Their number included John Cheyney, Sir Thomas Berkeley of Beverstone, Sir Giles Daubeney, Sir John Lewkenore, Sir John Guildford, Sir John Seyntlowe, and Sir Nicholas Latimer.[10] At the beginning of his reign, as he had during the Protectorate, Richard III did his utmost to retain the loyalty of those household men of his brother whose roots were southern. For this reason he made great show of a public reconciliation with Sir John Fogge on the eve of his coronation.[11] For this reason too, as well as because of the limited scale of patronage at his disposal, rewards granted to members of his ducal affinity were still modest and insignificant in comparison with the generosity shown to those whose support it was imperative for him to win. His own men took over key posts at the head of his household and the centre of administration: Viscount Lovell succeeded Hastings as Chamberlain, Sir Robert Percy became controller, and James Metcalfe was made coroner of the Marshalsea. Robert Brackenbury was appointed constable of the Tower; and, on the day after the coronation, Thomas Metcalfe became chancellor of the duchy of Lancaster.[12] Equally important were the immaterial rewards: Sir John Conyers and Sir Richard Ratcliffe were elected

[8] *The Coronation of Richard III*, ed. A. F. Sutton and P. W. Hammond (Gloucester, 1983), 271–3, from BL, Add. MS 6113. This roll-call is clearly incomplete. It neither includes Sir Richard Ratcliffe, who is said in another document to have helped bear the canopy, nor names Sir Edmund Hastings, who was given a length of green velvet by the king expressly for his coronation robe (ibid. 221, 173). Lord Neville might possibly have been on duty in command of the army.

[9] Ibid. 167–71.

[10] Ibid. 271–3.

[11] Ross, *Richard III*, p. 112; Sutton and Hammond, *Coronation*, p. 25.

[12] Horrox, 'Patronage', pp. 39–45; CPR, 1476–85, 363–4.

to the vacant stalls of the Garter created by the deaths of Hastings and Rivers.[13] But north-easterners did not at first overrun the new administration.

Rather, Richard III's gratitude to the north-east for its support was demonstrated by his return in triumph at the end of August. The climax of the visit was the investiture of the Prince of Wales in the archbishop's palace on 8 September. The whole visit was carefully stage-managed to create the maximum effect. The king was anxious that his entourage should be impressed by a demonstration of his popularity in the city. John Kendal wrote to the corporation from Nottingham on 23 August hinting that should they put on a good show the king would accede to their request for a reduction in the fee-farm; for, he pointed out, 'there come many southern lords and men of worship with them which will mark greatly your receiving their graces'. The king timed his arrival for the Feast of the Decollation of St John the Baptist on 29 August, a feast associated with the cult of Corpus Christi, and he followed the same processional route from Micklegate Bar to the Minster, where a solemn thanksgiving was held. The investiture, too, was preceded by celebration of mass. It is likely that the gowns, doublets, cloths, banners, standards and 13,000 'cushions of fustian with boars' sent for on 31 August were to be used on that occasion.[14] Everything seems to have lived up to the king's expectations, for at a formal ceremony in the chapter house of the Minster on 17 September the city's fee-farm was reduced.[15] Finally, while at York the king laid the plans for the establishment of a chantry of 100 priests, with the likely intention of transforming the Minster into his mausoleum.[16] In so far as it is possible to enter the king's mind, the triumphal celebrations at York suggest that he intended to continue to regard the north-east as his own special country.

However, celebration was brought abruptly to an end by the outbreak of widespread rebellion across the southern counties of England in early October. While John Howard, duke of

<hr />

[13] Shaw, *Knights*, i. 17.

[14] *YCR* i. 78; *Harleian MS 433*, ii. 42; *The Fabric Rolls of York Minster*, ed. James Raine, SS, xxv (1859), 210–12; Tudor-Craig, 'Richard III's Triumphal Entry', pp. 111–13; Dobson, 'Richard III and the Church of York', pp. 130–1.

[15] Attreed, 'York's Fee Farm', p. 30.

[16] Dobson, 'Richard III and the Church of York', pp. 145–7.

Norfolk was sent to suppress the eastern sector, the central and western risings were crushed by an army mustered by the king himself at Leicester on 21 October. The city of York was called upon again, and sent 300 men. Sir Ralph Ashton was made Vice-Constable on 24 October; and an army which included Lord Scrope of Bolton, Lord Neville, and many other northerners, who were subsequently rewarded for their good service against the rebels, marched south.[17] On 2 November the duke of Buckingham was brought before the king at Salisbury and executed. About a week later the king's host arrived at Exeter. The risings were easily put down; many rebels who had been unable to combine their forces or co-ordinate their actions fled to join the earl of Richmond in exile.[18] Nevertheless, the revelation of such widespread dissidence from Kent to Cornwall, and the emergence of Henry Tudor as a major contender for the throne, with substantial support in southern England, created a serious threat to Richard's hold on power. To help secure the southern counties in the aftermath of the rebellion the king turned to loyal members of his ducal affinity, who were now posted in the more sensitive parts of the kingdom. Thus was initiated the infamous plantation of the south by his northern adherents: 'whom he planted in every part of his dominions, to the shame and sorrow of all the southern people who murmured ceaselessly and longed more each day for the return of their old lords in place of the tyranny of the present ones'.[19]

Richard III's settlement of the south after the autumn of 1483 has been described as 'nothing less than a veritable invasion of northerners'.[20] And it is true that a significant number of men from northern England, many of whom had been closely connected with him as duke of Gloucester, were granted forfeited estates, given military commands, and put into positions of

<hr/>

[17] *YCR* i. 83–6; *CPR, 1476–85*, 368, 370–1, 380, 383, 415, 427.

[18] Ross, *Richard III*, pp. 104–18. Holinshed, citing information received from John Hooker of Exeter, tells of a plot hatched in Devon *after* the king's departure from Exeter in mid-Nov., which was dealt with by Lord Scrope at a session of oyer and terminer at Torrington. At this time, according to Hooker, over 500 of the accused escaped. (R. Holinshed, *Chronicles of England, Scotland and Ireland*, iii (1808), 421). The Crowland Chronicler places this rising *before* the king's arrival (*Crowland Chronicle*, p. 165). For an important new interpretation of the rebellion, see Horrox, *Richard III*, pp. 149–77.

[19] *Crowland Chronicle*, p. 171.   [20] Ross, *Richard III*, p. 119.

administrative responsibility. The process began before an Act of Attainder in Parliament in January 1484 legitimized the forfeiture of the estates of 103 rebels. In strict law widow's rights, joint enfeoffments, or enfeoffments to use protected substantial parts of an estate even against forfeiture. These rights were not necessarily respected by the king's agents, who did not wait for inquiries to be completed before acting. Thus some widows and feoffees were stripped of lands which in law should have remained inviolate.

The beneficiaries of the sequestration included a significant number of northern men who were granted estates, normally for an annual rent to the Crown of $7\frac{1}{2}$ per cent of the assessed annual income. Sir Robert Brackenbury was granted land in Kent worth £400 p.a.; Sir Marmaduke Constable of Flamborough, the Stafford honour of Tonbridge and manors of Penshurst, Brasted, Hadlow, and Yalding; Sir Ralph Ashton lands in the same county worth £116 p.a. In Hampshire Sir John Saville of Thornhill, Yorks., John Hutton of Hunwick, Co. Durham, John Nesfield, Robert Carr, and William Mirfield received similar grants of land. But it was in the south-western counties of Cornwall, Devon, Somerset, Dorset and Wiltshire, where forfeited estates were most numerous, that the plantation was most thorough. In total some three dozen northerners, including the earl of Northumberland and Lords Stanley, Bolton, FitzHugh, and Neville, received lands valued at approximately £3,000 p.a., for which most of them had to pay only nominal reserved rents. The most spectacularly rewarded was Sir Richard Ratcliffe, who on 6 September 1484 was granted estates, principally in Devon, Dorset, and Somerset, and drawn mainly from the patrimony of the earls of Devon, to the value of 1,000 marks, or £666. 13s. 4d. p.a. In one step he rose into the greater landowning class, and was poised to fill the vacuum left in west-country politics by the flight of the head of the Courtenay family.[21]

As important as the settlement of confiscated estates on these

---

[21] *Harleian MS 433*, iii. 140–55; Ross, *Richard III*, pp. 120–1; A. J. Pollard, 'The Tyranny of Richard III', *Journal of Medieval History*, 3 (1977), 153–62. It will be seen from what follows that I have modified my interpretation of the 'plantation' since this article was published. See also the much fuller discussion by Dr Horrox, *Richard III*, pp. 180–205, which my discussion supplements.

northern retainers was the appointment of some of them to strategic military command: John, Lord Scrope of Bolton became constable of Exeter castle; Sir Thomas Everingham, constable of Barnstaple; Sir Thomas Mauleverer, keeper of Plympton castle; John Hutton, constable of Southampton and Christchurch castles; Richard Hansard, of Odiham; William Mirfield, of Porchester; Sir John Saville, captain of the Isle of Wight; and Sir Ralph Ashton, lieutenant of the elderly earl of Arundel as constable of Dover.[22] Moreover, others were quickly employed as the king's sheriffs in the more unstable counties: Edward Redman in Somerset and Dorset in 1483/4; Halnath Mauleverer in Devon in the same year, followed by his nephew Sir Thomas in 1484. In November 1484, when anxiety was growing over a possible invasion by Henry Tudor, no fewer than six of the ten sheriffs pricked for fifteen southern counties were from the king's northern affinity. The commissions of the peace were similarly strengthened by the king's men from northern counties: Lord Scrope and Sir Thomas Mauleverer in Devon; Scrope and Halnath Mauleverer in Cornwall; FitzHugh in Dorset; FitzHugh, Scrope, and Sir Thomas Markenfield in Somerset; and Lovell, John Musgrave, and Edward Redman in Wiltshire.[23] These same men served on other commissions, including commissions of array in their adopted counties.[24]

It is significant, too, that many of these incomers, land grantees as well as office-holders and commissioners, were expected to reside in their new counties. A Signet letter of 22 January 1484 to the inhabitants of Tonbridge, Penshurst, and other places granted to Sir Marmaduke Constable made this plain:

we . . . have deputed and ordained him to make his abode amongst you and to have the rule within our honour and lordships aforesaid. We therefore will and straightly charge you nor any of you in no wise presume to take clothing or be retained with any manner of person or persons whatsoever he or they be, but that you be ready to attend wholly upon our said knight at all times that you by him shall be commanded to do us service.[25]

---

[22] CPR, 1476–85, 410, 412, 425, 429, 480, 531.
[23] Ibid. 556, 558–9, 571, 577.   [24] Ibid. 397–9, 425, 488–91, 517, 519–20.
[25] Harleian MS 433, ii. 81.

In this part of Kent Constable, as a knight of the body, was expected to act directly as the King's deputy. It is perhaps particularly worthy of note that the king hereby anticipated Henry VII's legislation and policy in seeking to restrict retaining to his own licensed servants. A requirement to reside and a proscription on alternative retaining make it abundantly clear that the king did indeed intend that Constable and his like were 'to have the rule' of the district where they were granted estates and offices.

It is not easy to demonstrate, however, that such men actually did take up residence.[26] There is reason to believe that Lord Scrope of Bolton and Edward Redman did; and so did Sir Christopher Ward of Givendale near Ripon, who was granted land in Sussex, served on the commission of array of that county, was listed as one of those of the county on whom the king could rely, and received a general pardon on 9 May 1485 as of Tratton, Co. Sussex. John Hutton, constable of Christchurch, steward of Christchurch and Ringwood, and possessor of forfeited lands in Hampshire, seems to have been resident from June 1484 at the latest. He became a commissioner of the peace, a commissioner of array, and commissioner to raise loans in the county. Moreover several other men who came, as he did, from Durham were appointed to office in the New Forest, the administration of which they appear to have assumed. Settlement in this case involved not only the appointee, but also his own servants and followers.[27] The king could be displeased if one of his men refused to take up residence and carry out the duties expected of him. In November 1484 Sir John Saville was refused leave to exercise his office of captain of the Isle of Wight by deputy. The king removed him from his posts as steward and constable of Wakefield, and required him to enter into a humiliating bond in which he had to pledge his future 'good and true behaviour' as captain.[28] There can be little doubt that the king intended some

---

[26] Ibid. 144, 237; *CPR, 1476–85*, 397, 399, 489, 531.

[27] W. E. Hampton, 'John Hoton of Hunwick', *The Ricardian*, viii, no. 88 (1985), 7–9; see also Horrox, *Richard III*, pp. 195–6, 188–9.

[28] Arnold, 'Commission of the Peace', p. 129; idem, 'West Riding', pp. 200–1.

of his men to play a direct personal part in the rule of the southern counties in 1484 and 1485.[29]

The plantation of northern adherents was a reality; but it is not to be assumed that these three dozen men in receipt of confiscated lands and appointed to royal offices placed the whole of the south under the heel of an alien dictatorship. For a start, as we have seen, not all were willing to play the king's game. The king himself withdrew Sir Thomas Markenfield, whom he made sheriff of Yorkshire in 1484, thus allowing him to enjoy his Somerset lands *in absentia*.[30] And no doubt others contented themselves with being absentee beneficiaries. Sir Richard Ratcliffe, the most liberally rewarded, held so many royal commissions and was employed so frequently in Anglo-Scottish negotiations that it is hard to believe that he spent much time in the west country. It would be wrong too to think that the king called only upon northerners: Sir William Houghton of Birtsmorton, Worcs. was the king's sheriff of Cornwall in 1484/5; Humphrey Stafford of Grafton, Worcs. and his brother Thomas received confiscated lands in Devon and Wiltshire; Morgan Kidwelly was granted lands in Somerset and Dorset; John Howard, duke of Norfolk was liberally rewarded with Hungerford lands in half a dozen counties; and Sir James Tyrell was appointed sheriff of Cornwall in November 1483.[31]

Tyrell is a reminder of another caveat: several men brought in by the king already had connections with the counties in which they acquired land or took up office. Tyrell was married to Anne Arundel of Trevice and Lanherne, over whose inheritance he was in dispute with her half-brother Sir Thomas Arundel, one of the rebels of 1483. Through his wife his connections with Cornwall were long-standing. He had represented the county in 1478, had become a JP in May 1483, and had been a commis-

[29] Cf. Horrox, 'Patronage', p. 155, where a similar distinction is drawn. In her recent discussion of the plantation, Dr Horrox especially stresses the king's need and desire to establish a new royal affinity in the south. In essence the outsiders were to exercise the functions of members of the royal household, normally locally based (Horrox, *Richard III*, pp. 180–2, 197–8, 200–1).

[30] Pollard, 'Tyranny', p. 161. Marmaduke Constable was transferred from Kent to the north midlands in the spring of 1484 (Horrox, 'East Riding', pp. 98–9).

[31] *Harleian MS 433*, i. 136–7; ii. 37; iii. 140, 145, 151; CPR, 1476–85, 453, 528; Hampton, 'Further Comment', p. 47.

sioner of subsidy in April and August, and in August 1484 became steward of the duchy of Cornwall lands in the county.[32] Halnath Mauleverer was another who was no stranger to the west country. He was married to Joan Carminow, widow of Sir Thomas Carew, and had held land in her right in Cornwall, Devon, and Somerset since 1466. He had already served as sheriff of Cornwall in 1470/1 and sheriff of Devon in 1479/80 before serving a second term for Richard III in 1483/4.[33] Similarly Sir Ralph Ashton had married Elizabeth Chicheley early in 1483, and thereby already had an entry to Kentish society.[34] Sir Robert Brackenbury, as constable of the Tower, received the fee of his office by tradition from a group of royal manors in Kent and Essex. He too followed precedent in becoming interested in local society, and his appointment as sheriff of Kent in 1484 was not in itself exceptional.[35] The intrusion of trusted outsiders, even those without existing connections, into a region was not without precedent. Indeed in 1463 Edward IV had anticipated his brother's promotion of Sir Richard Ratcliffe to the earldom of Devon estates in the west country by a very similar grant to William Neville, Lord Fauconberg.[36]

Above all it has to be borne in mind that in every southern county there were large numbers of gentry who did not rebel against the king or flee to Henry Tudor. A glance at the composition of the commission of the peace or array, or at the lists of reliable gentry recorded in the Signet Docket Book, shows that in every county the northern intruders were but a minority of those actively serving the regime.[37] Moreover, some very prominent men who had been members of Edward IV's household threw in their lot with the new king. Among the peers Lord Audley, holding several royal offices in Dorset, and Lords Dinham, Stourton, and Zouche gave Richard III their support.

[32] *Harleian MS 433*, ii. 34; Sutton and Hammond, *Coronation*, p. 304; Wedgwood, *Biographies*, pp. 889–90. Sir William Houghton, his successor as sheriff, was also married to a Cornish heiress.

[33] Hampton, 'Further Comment', pp. 46–7.

[34] Sutton and Hammond, *Coronation*, pp. 304–5.

[35] Horrox, 'Patronage', p. 162; idem, *Richard III*, pp. 190–1.

[36] See above, p. 287. Edward IV had also granted Courtenay lands to Montagu in 1470 in compensation for the loss of the Percy estates in Northumberland (*CPR, 1467–77*, 189).

[37] For the lists of reliable gentry see *Harleian MS 433*, iii. 234–9.

John Sapcote of Elton, Herts. (Dinham's brother-in-law), Sir William Berkeley of Uley, Glos., Sir John Norbury, Sir William Say of Brockbourne, Herts., Thomas Fowler, Edward Hardgill of Mere, Wilts., John Sturgeon of Gatesbury, Herts., John Verney of Claydon, Bucks., John Bamme of Dartford, John Barrantine of Chalgrove, Oxfordshire, John Rogers of Freefolk, Hants, and John Dudley of Ford, Sussex (second son of John, Lord Dudley) formed a cadre of local county leaders throughout the central south and south-east who opted for Richard III rather than Henry Tudor.[38] Furthermore at least two men, Sir John Donne of Horseden, Bucks., and Sir Thomas Fulford of Fulford, Devon, were enticed back into royal service by November 1484.[39] Southern England itself was divided.

Yet, all these reservations notwithstanding, the role of the north-eastern lords and gentry in southern England after the rebellions of 1483 was important. By filling the places of local gentry who had fled to Henry Tudor they reminded the more numerous local gentry to remain loyal to the Crown. The land settlement itself was probably most intrusive in Devon, Somerset, Dorset, and Wiltshire, where a more significant gap had been left by the flight of Sir Edward Courtenay, Sir John Cheyney, Sir Giles Daubeney, Sir Nicholas Latimer, Sir William Berkeley of Beverstone, Sir John St Lo, and Sir Roger Tocotes. The appointment of several north-easterners to the custody of castles along the south coast probably had an equal impact. The king's principal concern was security: the defence of the southern shores of his kingdom against anticipated invasion. Indeed, in the last year of the reign, when there was a series of further disturbances and continuing defections, and Henry Tudor in France secured committed support for a descent on England, the king placed even greater reliance on the northerners, in whom he had an absolute trust. More were pricked as sheriff in November 1484 than in 1483. While Henry Tudor remained a threat a northern presence was necessary to stiffen the resolve of local gentry. It is not surprising that the regime exacerbated resent-

[38] For these men see Sutton and Hammond, *Coronation*, pp. 312 (Berkeley), 378 (Norbury), 391 (Sapcote), 392 (Say); Wedgwood, *Biographies*, pp. 38 (Bamme), 40–1 (Barrantine), 352 (Fowler), 422 (Hardgill), 722–3 (Rogers), 825–6 (Sturgeon), 286 (Dudley), 905–6 (Verney).

[39] *Harleian MS 433*, iii. 61, 70; *CFR, 1471–85*, 300.

ment in some quarters. The very resort to household knights and esquires whose roots lay at the other end of the kingdom stripped bare any pretence that the new regime was generally welcome. Moreover, the victorious return of the exiles in 1485 ensured that the 'tyranny' of the plantation would not quickly be forgotten.

For the beneficiaries of the 'plantation', the three dozen or so northern servants of the king especially, the royal grants of 1483–5 were a generous demonstration of good lordship. Their loyalty and service either 'about the acceptance of the Royal Crown' or 'against the rebels' were amply rewarded. From the northern point of view the flow of lands and offices after the rebellion was a legitimate return for services rendered. The grants of forfeited lands in the south especially benefited younger sons and lesser men, for whom service to the new king had opened enticing prospects. Sir Richard Ratcliffe, once again, is the obvious example. But Sir Robert Brackenbury, Richard Hansard, John Hutton, and Robert Carr are others whose prospects were transformed. For those who settled, the opportunity was created of establishing themselves and their descendants among the élite of their new counties. For those, despite the king's blandishments, who did not, the grants of confiscated estates in the south became a valuable source of income, to be enjoyed from a distance.

The king did not draw only on southern confiscated estates with which to reward his servants; he was equally generous with his largess from his own estates in the north-east. Early in 1484 he began to exploit these as a source of patronage rather than of revenue. Over the next eighteen months at least sixty men and women, great and small, received cash annuities and grants of land for life which cost Richard III well in excess of £1,000 p.a. The king's liberality was remarkable, apparently reckless. From Barnard Castle new grants under the Signet and Great Seal disposed of £143 from an annual revenue which was slightly over £300 p.a.; at Middleham new grants of both land and annuities reduced the annual income by almost £400 p.a.; at Sheriff Hutton by approximately £350. If one takes into account existing fees and annuities which the king had granted as duke of Gloucester it would appear that by the end of his reign as much as three-quarters of the revenues of both Yorkshire lordships had been alienated or were being consumed in fees and annuities.[40] The king's largess was not restricted to his ducal estates. He was generous too with new annuities granted from the duchy of Lancaster lordships in Yorkshire: £118. 13s. 4d. from Knaresborough; £106. 13s. 4d. from Pickering; £318. 13s. 4d. from Pontefract; and £286. 13s. 4d. from Tickhill.[41]

The king's open-handedness began with his own retainers. New annuities of £10 charged to Sheriff Hutton were granted to Geoffrey Frank (the receiver), Robert Constable of Barnby, John Lepton, Robert Gower, Sir John Pickering, and Thomas Asper; £13. 6s. 8d. to Thomas Wrangwysh of York and John Hastings; and £20 to John Harrington, the clerk of the city council and of the king's new Court of Poor Requests.[42] Royal largess extended to many lesser servants, who, as the grants acknowledged, were receiving small sums 'unto the time he be promoted' or 'until promoted to office of better value'. It would appear that in these cases the ducal estates were being used as a reserve fund.[43] In others the king seems merely to have responded to the plea of a persuasive petitioner. At York on 25 June he wrote to Geoffrey Frank, receiver of Middleham, that 'we of our grace, especially for diverse considerations us moving, have given and granted unto our well-beloved Agnes Cowper widow an annual rent of forty shillings' for life.[44]

But at the other extreme the king was so exceptionally generous to a handful of peers and prominent knights of his body as to suggest deliberate policy. The chief beneficiary was Sir John Conyers, who was granted 200 marks from Middleham, and, in addition, the manors of Aldbrough and Catterick and other lands in Swaledale, which in 1488/9 produced a net income of £60 or more. All this was supplementary, it would seem, to the fees of

[40] The above analysis is founded on a computation of grants recorded in *Harleian MS 433* and the Patent Roll, set against the revenues of the estates in 1488/9. (PRO, DL 29/649/10500; 650/10515).

[41] There are at least 33 new grants of annuities charged to these 4 lordships recorded in *Harleian MS 433*. See i. 72, 88–9, 103, 109, 117–18, 126–7, 160, 162, 200, 219–20, 222–3, 231, 239, 258, 260–1, 269, 275–6, 281.

[42] *CPR, 1476–85*, 411, 423, 450, 496, 538, 574, 532, 538.

[43] See e.g. the cases of Thomas Vicars, Robert Robinson, Richard Metcalfe, Otwell Metcalfe, Piers Metcalfe, and Thomas Edwards (*Harleian MS 433*, i. 101; ii. 152, 228).

[44] *Harleian MS 433*, ii. 144.

£32 which he already enjoyed as steward and constable, and to the farm of Rand in Crakehall which he had enjoyed rent-free since 1463, itself worth a further £6. 13s. 4d. p.a.[45] Moreover, two of Conyers's sons were also retained by the king. William of Thormanby was granted an annuity of £20 from Middleham; Richard of Ulshaw and Horden, Co. Durham, an esquire of the body, an annuity of £26. 13s. 4d. from Barnard Castle 'until the king shall provide him with land, an office or something of like value'.[46] Others treated almost as generously as Sir John and his family included Sir Thomas Gower: 200 marks from Sheriff Hutton in two separate grants; Ralph, Lord Greystoke: £100 from Tickhill as his fee as royal councillor; Richard, Lord FitzHugh: a similar fee from Tickhill; Ralph, Lord Neville: £80 from Barnard Castle during the lifetime of Thomas, Lord Stanley, until a reversionary interest in two manors of the countess of Richmond matured; Sir James Strangways: cash and land worth just over 100 marks; Sir Thomas Markenfield: 100 marks from Middleham in December 1484, after he had returned north as sheriff of Yorkshire; Sir Edmund Hastings (sheriff 1483/4): 100 marks from Pickering; and Sir Ralph Bigod: £40 from Sheriff Hutton.[47]

These large annuities to a handful of senior peers and knights of the body suggest a more specific purpose than mere indiscriminate largess; payment for holding specific responsibility. To these men fell the important task of representing Richard's personal authority in the region now that he was king. At first this task was probably exercised by the household of the Prince of Wales. But, after his untimely death in March 1484, the king needed to find an alternative means of maintaining his rule in the region he had dominated as duke. He toured the north-east between the end of April and July, spending most of his time at Pontefract, York, and Scarborough.[48] During this

---

[45] PRO, SC6/1085/20; DL29/649/10500; *Harleian MS 433*, i. 253; *CPR, 1476–85*, 450.

[46] *CPR, 1476–85*, 391, 439. William 'the younger' may alternatively have been Sir John's grandson and heir.

[47] *Harleian MS 433*, i. 102, 117, 126, 169, 171, 199, 220; *CPR, 1476–85*, 424, 428, 470, 482. Bigod was also Master of the Ordnance at the Tower (Horrox, 'Richard III and the East Riding', p. 98). Cf. Lord Dacre, who received 100 marks from the revenues of Cumberland (*CPR, 1476–85*, 388).

[48] Edwards, *Itinerary*, pp. 18–22.

prolonged stay he laid the foundation for his future government of the north. The king kept in his own hands offices which had traditionally been granted to local magnates, and which he himself had enjoyed as duke. Thus he did not appoint a new warden of the west march, but retained Lord Dacre of Gilsland as his deputy.[49] He did not appoint a new steward of the duchy of Lancaster north of the Trent, but appears to have called upon his existing deputy, Miles Metcalfe, to take full responsibility. In Durham, where following the death of Bishop Dudley in November 1483 the temporalities lay in his hands, he reformed the council and made his own man, Richard Danby, steward.[50]

Above all, on the eve of his departure, Richard III established the Council of the North. The articles of the Council are undated; but on 24 July 2,000 marks p.a. were set aside as from Michaelmas 1484 for the expense and wages of a household appointed by the king 'to be holden at Sandal or elsewhere in the County of York'. Moreover, in a memorandum of the same date it was stated that this 'household' began on that same day, 24 July.[51] For household read Council. The articles make it explicit that the Council existed 'for *his* surety and the wealth of the inhabitants' of the region (my italics), in that order. The Council's task, first and foremost, was to keep the king's peace. All its orders were to be issued in the king's name, and all the king's subjects in 'the north parts' were bound to obey them. Under the presidency of the king's nephew and heir presumptive, the earl of Lincoln, it was to be the king's arm in the region.[52] And it was to be funded by the revenues of the royal estates in the region. Thus the new Council's treasurer drew his 2,000 marks p.a. from the remnant of landed revenue after the allocation of fees and annuities from eleven separate lordships and estates in the king's hands. Barnard Castle, for instance, contributed £110 p.a., which would have accounted for practically all the lordship's surplus.[53]

---

[49] Storey, 'Wardens', p. 615.
[50] Pollard, 'St. Cuthbert and the Hog', pp. 121–2.
[51] *Harleian MS 433*, iii. 114–15.   [52] Ibid. 107–8.
[53] Ibid. 115–16. Revenues from Middleham and Sheriff Hutton were not assigned to support the council. But they had been used extensively to support the royal household during its residence in Yorkshire (*Harleian MS 433*, ii. 147–9).

It is not known who the councillors were: the commission issued to them has not survived. But it is clear the *quorum* was to include councillors who were justices of the peace throughout the north.[54] It would seem reasonable to assume that Lord Greystoke, in receipt of a fee of £100 as a councillor, was a member, and that so too were Lord FitzHugh, Sir John Conyers, Sir James Strangways, Sir Thomas Gower, Sir Thomas Markenfield, and Sir Edmund Hastings, all in receipt of annuities of 100 marks or more from the king's northern lordships. These were the fees appropriate to a royal councillor. Thus indirectly, as well as directly, the royal estates were employed to support the new council. The king's largess was not just a reflection of his generosity and his desire to reward his northern retainers now that he was king; it was also part and parcel of his policy, completed in the summer of 1484, of keeping direct control of the north-east by means of a new royal council funded by those estates.[55]

The principal servants of the Council were Miles Metcalfe, whose local influence is reflected in his employment as both Recorder of the city of York and steward of York Minster;[56] John Dawney of Cowick, its treasurer; Geoffrey Frank, the receiver of Middleham and Sheriff Hutton; and, most influential of all, Sir Richard Ratcliffe. The second son of Sir Thomas Ratcliffe of Derwentwater, Ratcliffe had settled at Sedbury in northern Yorkshire after his marriage to Agnes Scrope, sister of John, Lord Scrope of Bolton, and the widow of Sir Christopher Boynton, who held the manor in joint enfeoffment. He came early to the attention of Richard as duke of Gloucester, and was constable of Barnard Castle by 1476—probably by 1475, when he was admitted to the Corpus Christi Guild of York as of Barnard Castle. He was a councillor of the duke by 1477, and one of his feoffees of Middleham at that date. A commissioner of array in both Durham and Northumberland in 1480, he served under the duke

---

[54] Ibid. iii. 107.
[55] For discussion of the role of the new council see Reid, *Council in the North*, corrected by Brooks, *The Council of the North* and Ross, *Richard III*, pp. 182–4, in which the council's administrative and judicial functions, rather than its primary political purpose, are emphasized. Its political purpose explains why 'no such conciliar solution was ever attempted in Wales' (Ross, *Richard III*, p. 183).   [56] Dobson, 'Richard III and the Church of York', pp. 138–9.

in the Scottish wars, being knighted in 1481 and promoted banneret in 1482. It was he who rode north with messages calling for military assistance in June 1483. After his master became king he was one of his closest confidants, created Knight of the Garter with Sir John Conyers. Already steward of Ripon for the archbishop of York, he replaced Sir John Saville as steward of Wakefield late in 1484. Prominent in Anglo-Scottish negotiations throughout the reign, he succeeded William Parr as sheriff of Westmorland for life in August 1484. He held land in Co. Durham, and married his children into palatine families. He may well have held a senior post in the administration of the palatinate while the temporalities were in royal hands. He certainly carried great sway in Durham. At some date during the first year of the reign Prior Robert Ebbchester of Durham wrote apologetically to Bishop Richard Redman of St Asaph explaining that he could not prefer the bishop's nominee to the next vacancy at the vicarage of Merrington, because Sir Richard Ratcliffe had shown him a grant of the nomination by his predecessor (Richard Bell, before 1478), adding that he and his brethren had no choice but to ratify this grant, 'considering the great rule that he beareth under the king's grace in our country'.[57]

Richard III's government of the north through his new council and his knights of the body such as Richard Ratcliffe was a major break with recent practice. His predecessor had been content to surrender authority first to the kingmaker and then to him. As king, with a substantial landed estate in the north-east and an established affinity of his own, he was strong enough to retain his own personal control. In choosing to do so through the vehicle of a specially created standing council, he created a precedent which later kings were to follow. But his decision, since it challenged the authority of the surviving northern magnates, also had immediate political implications, every bit as important as the employment of northerners in the dissident south. The earl of Northumberland in particular, and to a lesser extent Ralph, Lord Neville (who succeeded his uncle as earl of

[57] Durham, Dean and Chapter, Reg. Parv. iii. fo. 188ᵛ. For Ratcliffe's career see Sutton and Hammond, *Coronation*, p. 387 and Pollard, 'St. Cuthbert and the Hog', pp. 122–3.

Westmorland towards the end of 1484) had no doubt hoped and anticipated that the duke of Gloucester's promotion to the crown would have allowed them to step into his shoes in the region. Precedent suggested that this would happen: the reward they would receive for their assistance in the 'acceptance of the Royal Crown' and subsequently 'against the rebels' would surely be the recovery of their pre-eminence as lords of the north. In this they were to be disappointed.

Henry Percy was duly rewarded by Richard III for his support. He recovered the de Brian inheritance, with extensive lands in Devon, Dorset, Gloucester, Kent, Somerset, Suffolk, and Surrey, of which he was the rightful heir; was created Great Chamberlain of England; made warden-general of the marches, although his *de facto* control was restricted to the east and middle marches, of which he was already warden; and granted the lordship of Holderness, confiscated from the duke of Buckingham, for his good service 'in the king's royal right and crown'.[58] Several of his retainers were well rewarded by the king. Sir William Gascoigne received an annuity of £20 from Knaresborough, Sir William Beckwith 20 marks, and Sir William Eure £10 from Pickering. At least nine received forfeited lands in southern England (Sir Marmaduke Constable, Sir John Egremont, Robert Carr, James and William Lilburne, John Hagerston, Gilbert Manners, Sir Christopher Ward, and John Wharton).[59]

It has been suggested that the king poached some of Northumberland's men: that they now transferred their primary commitment from the earl to Richard.[60] This is hard to prove. One or two did remain Ricardians after 1485, notably Robert Carr; which would tend to confirm this hypothesis. Others became knights and esquires of the royal household: Sir Marmaduke Constable and Sir Christopher Ward became particularly active on the new king's behalf. But, as has been pointed out by Dr Horrox, placing his own retainers in the royal household, no less than securing royal rewards for them, was to the earl's

[58] *Harleian MS 433*, ii. 39–40; *Rot.Scot.* ii. 463–4; *CPR, 1476–85*, 409; Hicks, 'Fourth Earl of Northumberland', p. 90.

[59] *Harleian MS 433*, i. 92, 182, 200; iii. 141, 144–5, 146, 148–9, 153.

[60] Hicks, 'Fourth Earl of Northumberland', pp. 91–2.

advantage.[61] Moreover, some men had been serving both duke and earl, or had connections with both, before 1483. John, Lord Scrope of Bolton had been both councillor of the duke and feed man of the earl, and his son Henry was married to the earl's daughter, Elizabeth.[62] Sir Thomas Grey of Wark and Heaton, awarded £10 by the king from Newcastle on 29 November 1484, had been the king's constable of Norham Castle since May. In May 1485 his commission was renewed for seven years. While the earl was one of those who put up surety for Grey's performance of his duty, Sir Thomas came from a line with longstanding associations with the king's family.[63] Sir John Pickering, who was a councillor of the earl, was also the son of a retainer of the king's father. A grant of the farm of Oswaldkirk to Sir John, 'king's servant', in December 1483, and an annuity of £10 charged to Sheriff Hutton in April 1485 represent a continuation of a family connection.[64] Only in Knaresborough did the earl stand to lose local influence to the king, for Richard, as duke of Lancaster, was now its lord. While generous new annuities were granted to the earl's men, and he himself retained his offices, other annuities were granted to the king's men, Sir William Ingleby, John Pullen, John Swale, and Robert Birnand.[65] The king, following in Neville footsteps, had been ambitious to extend his influence into the honour ten years earlier: after 1483 he was free to do so. The earl of Northumberland may have feared that his standing in the north-east would be eroded by the king's superior patronage. But more importantly it became clear that he was not to be allowed to become an independent authority anywhere but in Northumberland and the east marches. He had not helped place Richard III on the throne so as to establish the Council of the North.[66]

Ralph, Lord Neville, the third earl of Westmorland, had even greater ground for disappointment than Northumberland. In his appeal to Neville for assistance on 9 June 1483 Richard wrote:

[61] Horrox, 'Richard III and the East Riding', p. 98.
[62] Ross, *Richard III*, p. 49; Hicks, 'Fourth Earl of Northumberland', p. 89, n. 66.
[63] *CPR, 1476–85*, 535; Durh. 3/56/1,2; and see above, pp. 298–9.
[64] *CPR, 1476–85*, 372, 532; Hicks, 'Fourth Earl of Northumberland', p. 87, n. 52.   [65] *Harleian MS 433*, i. 140, 223, 260, 261; and above, p. 326.
[66] Horrox, 'Richard III and the East Riding', pp. 96–9 comes to a similar conclusion.

'And my lord do me good service as you have always before done, and I trust now so to remember you as shall be the making of you and yours.'[67] Although rewarded with grants of land and an annuity which were worth approximately £200 per annum, he was given no more. This was hardly the making of him. One hope had almost certainly been to secure his claim to a share of the inheritance of his maternal uncle, Henry Holland, duke of Exeter, of whom he was the male heir. Edward IV had allowed this inheritance to pass into the hands of the Woodvilles and Greys in 1483. His support for Richard in the summer may well have been influenced by this. In the event, however, the new king dispossessed his rivals only to resume the Exeter lands for the Crown. Neville might also have hoped that he would be rewarded with the wardenship of the west marches now that its previous holder was king: after all the west march once 'belonged' to his great-grandfather. Instead the king retained control, appointing Humphrey, Lord Dacre as his lieutenant. Thirdly, he could reasonably have anticipated that the king's removal to Westminster would have left the way open for his family to resume its dominance in the county palatine. In fact, while the temporalities lay in his hands, the king continued to exercise control through the bishop's council. It was Sir Richard Ratcliffe, not Neville, who bore the great rule under the king's grace in the country. Indeed, in totally obscure circumstances the king had taken possession, even before the death of the second earl, of the family seat at Raby Castle. As duke of Gloucester Richard had been a frequent visitor. Between 1477 and 1479 the lordship was enfeoffed in the hands of a group of men who were largely his councillors. What terms had been agreed and for what reason are not known, but in July 1484 revenue from Raby was assigned to support the Council of the North, and on 22 February 1485 Geoffrey Frank was appointed the king's receiver of the lordship.[68]

By the summer of 1485 the northern earls had reason to regret their earlier enthusiastic support for Richard III. They had good cause to desert him at Bosworth. Whether they actually did so

---

[67] *Paston Letters, 1422–1509*, ed. J. Gairdner, vi (1904), 71–2.
[68] *Harleian MS 433*, ii. 205; iii. 114–15. For the above paragraph see Pollard, 'St. Cuthbert and the Hog', p. 122.

will never be known. In one of the most confused and confusing accounts of this confused and confusing battle, Diego de Valera recounted six months later how a certain lord of 'Tamorlant' (one of the greatest lords of England) played a decisive role in betraying Richard and securing victory for Henry VII. Tamorlant had assured Henry Tudor of his support before the battle. But afterwards it became known that his real purpose was to make the earl of Warwick king, and so he was arrested and imprisoned until he had given homage and handed over the young earl. In this second- or third-hand account we appear to have the Stanleys and Northumberland confused as one person. 'Tamorlant' is most likely a corruption of Northumberland.[69] Certainly the course of the battle was strange. The Crowland chronicler commented enigmatically that: 'In the place where the earl of Northumberland stood, however, with a fairly large and well-equipped force, there was no contest against the enemy and no blows were given or received in battle.' Later Polydore Vergil implied that Northumberland would have helped Henry if he had been able. The *Great Chronicle of London* commented that the earl took his time to join his king, and that he was murdered in 1489 because 'the commons bore him deadly malice for the disappointing of king Richard at Bosworth Field'.[70] Westmorland's role attracted less attention. The 'Ballad of Bosworth Field' has him present: if he were at the field it would almost certainly have been in Northumberland's company. One record reports that after the battle he, Northumberland, and Surrey were captured and held in custody.[71] Four months later he was required to enter into bonds for his good behaviour, and the king took custody of his son and heir.[72] The evidence is ambiguous for both earls. Distrust of them after

---

[69] E. Nokes and G. Wheeler, 'A Spanish Account of the Battle of Bosworth', *The Ricardian*, 36 (1972), 1–5; and A. E. Goodman and A. McKay, 'A Castilian Report on English Affairs', *EHR* 88 (1973), 92–9. For a recent and judicious discussion of the site and course of the battle see P. J. Foss, 'The Battle of Bosworth: Towards a Reassessment', *Midland History*, 13 (1988), 21–33.

[70] *Crowland Chronicle*, p. 181; *Three Books of Polydore Vergil's English History*, ed. H. Ellis, Camden, os xxix (1844), 224–5; *The Great Chronicle of London*, ed. A. H. Thomas and I. D. Thornley (1938), 242.

[71] H. E. Salter, *Registrum Annalium Collegii Mertonensis*, Oxford Historical Society, 76 (1921), 71. I owe this reference to Bill Hampton.

[72] *CCR, 1485–1500*, 22; Campbell, *Materials*, i. 191, 196.

the battle is hardly consistent with support for Henry VII during it. Moreover, the failure of Northumberland's troops to engage could have been accidental: a consequence of the alignment of the forces and the king's precipitate decision to settle the issue by his own charge at the enemy.[73] Perhaps the earls were themselves ambivalent and undecided.

It is not even certain that the king received more committed support from the remaining northern lords and the gentry whom he had so lavishly rewarded over the preceding two years. True, Henry VII seems to have had little doubt: in his proclamation of 24 September he declared that 'many and diverse persons of the north parts of this our land, knights, esquires, gentlemen and others have done us now of late great displeasure being against us in the field with the adversary of us'.[74] Several of these were named in the later 'Ballad of Bosworth Field' and its prose version: all the peers and 'knights', such as Sir Marmaduke Constable, Sir William Conyers, the Harringtons, Sir Thomas Markenfield, Sir Thomas Mauleverer, and Sir Robert Middleton. Lord Greystoke was said to have brought 'a mighty many' (meinie, or retinue); but the reliability of the list is questionable. It is based on oral tradition, and may be no more than a roll-call of known knights and esquires of the body, rather than a precise list of known participants in the battle.[75] The case of Sir Thomas Markenfield typifies the problem caused by the 'Ballad'. There is no corroborative evidence of his participation in the battle, he was not attainted, and he lived unmolested by the new king for a further twelve years. A *Sir* William Conyers was said in that source to have been killed. If so the casualty was neither William of Marske, *esquire*, brother of Sir John Conyers, nor William, *esquire*, Sir John's grandson and heir, both of whom survived the battle. The only possible candidate is Sir John's youngest son, another William of Thormanby, *esquire*. The evidence of the Act of Attainder of 1485 is not of much greater use either. Only twenty-eight persons were attainted. All the northern peers avoided punishment, and only Ratcliffe,

Brackenbury, John Kendall, John Buck, Sir Robert Middleton, Sir James Harrington, and Sir Robert Harrington were singled out from northern England.[76]

The doubts concerning the reliability of the 'Ballad', as well as Henry VII's failure to attaint a significant number of northerners, have led to the suggestion that few in fact came to the field; or that at best they were in Northumberland's wing, which failed to engage. If they did not reach the field of battle, this could be because they had not had sufficient warning. The city of York had to send to the king to know his mind. Only on 19 August, when their messenger returned from Nottingham, did the city fathers decide to raise eighty men. It is unlikely that they arrived in time for the battle.[77] The same may apply to many others in the north-east. Unfortunately it just is not known whom Richard summoned to his side and when he did so. There were notable names missing even from the 'Ballad': Sir John Conyers, Sir James Danby, Sir Edmund Hastings, Sir William Ingleby, Sir James Strangways among them. It thus remains possible that a significant number of the men in whom he had placed his trust either failed him or were not given sufficient time to demonstrate their loyalty.

Yet there were north-easterners killed at the battle, or who died shortly afterwards, who were neither attainted nor named in the 'Ballad': Sir Robert Percy, controller of the household, Sir Thomas Gower, Ralph Danby (grandson of Sir Richard Conyers of Cowton and son of Robert Danby of Yafforth), Robert Claxton of Thickley, Co. Durham, Alan Fulthorpe of Fulthorpe, Co. Durham, and John Hutton of Hunwick.[78] Robert Morton of Bawtry, Yorks. made his will, which was proved shortly afterwards, on 20 August 1485 'going to serve his most excellent king Richard'.[79] There were surely others who served their excellent king and survived, along with Viscount Lovell, Sir Robert

[76] Rot.Parl. vi. 275–8. Middleton and the Harringtons were victims of Stanley vindictiveness. For them Bosworth was the resolution of a long-standing feud (see Jones, 'The Stanleys', pp. 41–2). Another feud settled at Bosworth was that between Berkeley of Uley and Berkeley of Beverstone (see Arthurson, 'A Question of Loyalty', pp. 404–5).

[77] Richmond, '1485 and All That', p. 174.

[78] Hampton, 'John Hoton', pp. 10–11, 16, nn. 81 and 82.

[79] Hunter, South Yorkshire, i. 75.

Middleton, and the Harrington brothers. One wonders whether pardons issued to Edward Redman on 23 October and Sir Thomas and Halnath Mauleverer on 19 November did not encompass being in the field at Bosworth.[80] The evidence again is frustratingly incomplete. The most likely explanation is that those who died made their own way to Richard's banner, and took part in the last, fatal charge: others, if there, stood by in Northumberland's wing.

The possibility is not to be ruled out, therefore, that many other north-easterners besides the earls of Northumberland and Westmorland were having second thoughts about Richard III by August 1485. The king himself on his part had sought to free himself from too great a dependence on their support. Pardons were offered to many of the rebels of 1483: one or two, as we have seen, came over to him. He made his peace with Elizabeth Woodville, and her daughters were fêted at court.[81] The king's attempts to win back lost support became more hectic after Henry Tudor's escape to France in the autumn of 1484. His desperate masterstroke, after the death of Queen Anne in March 1484, was to propose his own marriage to Elizabeth of York. Such a marriage would have opened the way for the return of the rebels and their restoration. By the same token it would have entailed the loss of land, office, and political influence for those, like Sir Richard Ratcliffe and William Catesby, on whom he had hitherto relied, and have led to a general weakening of his links with the north-east. Thus it was that the royal council blocked the plan, and the king was told to his face by Ratcliffe and Catesby that:

if he did not deny any such purpose and did not counter it by public declaration before the mayor and commonalty of the city of London, the northerners in whom he placed the greatest trust, would all rise against him, charging him with causing the death of the queen, the daughter and one of the heirs of the earl of Warwick and through whom he had obtained his first honour.

The threat was sufficient to force the king to climb down and to make the humiliating denial demanded of him.[82] Richard III had

[80] CPR, 1485–94, 21, 39.
[81] Ross, Richard III, p. 198; Crowland Chronicle, pp. 171, 175.
[82] Crowland Chronicle, pp. 175–7.

become the virtual prisoner of his own support. The lesson he no
doubt learned was that, after he had disposed of Henry Tudor, he
needed to cut himself free of his ducal roots. His northern
household men, like noble kingmakers before them who
threatened revolt, were for their part no doubt beginning to
question the wisdom of continuing an exclusive commitment
to his cause.[83] Whatever the outcome of Bosworth, the relationship between king and northern subject would never be the
same again. The honeymoon was already coming to an end
before the marriage was abruptly terminated on 22 August 1485.

[83] It is to be noted that I am more willing than Dr Horrox to give credence to
the idea that the northern gentry had begun to have second thoughts about
Richard III before his downfall (Horrox, *Richard III*, p. 320).

15

The Triumph of Henry VII, 1485–1502

EVEN if a question mark hangs over the continued commitment of the political élite of north-eastern England to Richard III at the end of his reign, there can be little doubt that in the event defeat at Bosworth left the king's old affinity in disarray. Should those who had once so fervently followed Richard III continue to champion his cause, that of the white rose, in the name of the earl of Warwick, the earl of Lincoln, or even an impostor such as Perkin Warbeck? Or should they come to terms, accept that a brief interlude of exceptional royal grace had come to an end, and make what they could of the new situation? The lords and gentry of the north-east were uncertain, indecisive, and divided. Most sat on the fence to wait on events. The new king, too, was unsure of himself. He was eventually able to take advantage of the wariness of his new subjects to impose his unchallenged authority on the region. But it took Henry VII a long time to feel sure of the north: even in 1497, Polydore Vergil reported, he was greatly afraid that the 'nobles' would declare for Perkin Warbeck.[1] Henry moved hesitantly. At first he tried to rely on lesser lords to hold the region. When after four months this proved unworkable he restored the earl of Northumberland, under constraint. After the earl's death he relied more on his own household men and councillors. But Henry's policy towards the north-east evolved slowly and pragmatically: at all stages he sought to win the support of as many of the established élite as he could. In this he was successful, so that eventually, by the end of the century, he had secured not only the acceptance but also the loyalty of the region.

There can be little doubt that the north-east was a source of considerable anxiety to Henry VII in his early years. The first historians of his reign all reported his fear. In 1486, Polydore

---

[1] Vergil, *Anglica Historia*, p. 89.

Vergil wrote, Henry 'did not know where he could gather a reliable force in a town [Middleham] so little devoted to his interests, which had hitherto cherished the name of Richard'. Edward Hall reminded his readers that Richard III 'more loved, more esteemed and regarded the northern men than any subjects within his realm', and that they 'entirely loved and highly favoured him'. Sixty years later Francis Bacon commented that Richard's memory 'lay like lees at the bottom of men's hearts and if the vessell were once stirred it would rise'.[2] The promptness with which Henry dealt with the risings of 1486, 1487, and 1489, and especially the scale upon which he mobilized to crush an apparently localized tax revolt in 1489, all betoken a man ever mindful that the north-east could be his undoing. Modern historians have tended, with one or two exceptions,[3] to accept that the king's fears were well founded, and to argue that Henry did indeed face a grave risk from the north. While it is indeed true that considerable early discontent was found in northern quarters, it must not be assumed that this was necessarily so sustained, powerful, or determined as to represent a permanent threat to his regime. Nor did it represent the only quarter from which he faced opposition. In the first six months of the reign the west midlands were a source of rebellion; the south-western rebellion of 1497 came near to deposing him; and in all parts of the realm, as Henry's spies from time to time revealed, there were cells plotting in the cause of the white rose.[4] Yet the north-east represented a unique challenge for the king. It was there that Richard III had his roots; it was the north-east that the late king was accustomed to call his home; and it was there Henry VII had quickly to win acceptance if his dynasty were to succeed.

The new king took prompt action immediately after Bosworth to scotch possible resistance. Robert Willoughby was

---

[2] Ibid. 11; Edward Hall, *Union of the Houses of Lancaster and York* (1809), 426, 442–5; Francis Bacon, *The History of the Reign of King Henry the Seventh*, ed. J. Spedding *et al.*, *Works* vii (1858), 88.

[3] See e.g. Dockray, 'Political Legacy', pp. 222–3. I am indebted also to Ian Arthurson, who has expressed similar views in conversation.

[4] Campbell, *Materials*, i. 282; Pollard, *Henry VII*, i. 82–4, 85–7, 89; I. Arthurson, 'The Rising of 1497', in Rosenthal and Richmond, ed. *People, Politics and Community*, pp. 10–11.

despatched to Sheriff Hutton to take possession of Edward, earl of Warwick and escort him to safe keeping in the Tower. One report carried to Diego de Valera by English merchants who left the country at the end of January was that the lord 'Tamorlant' (Northumberland) had intended to take up Warwick's cause after the battle. If it is true, Northumberland quickly abandoned his scheme, and with his fellow earl, Westmorland, submitted to the king.[5] The earls remained in custody until December. But despite these precautions, within a month of his victory Henry heard of disturbances in the north. Commissions of array were issued for the northern counties to suppress rebels 'confederated with our ancient enemies, the Scots'.[6] James III was quick to try to take advantage of the dislocation in England, including the removal of the warden of the east march from his post, to seize his beloved Berwick. The threat to Berwick was known to Henry by 15 October, when the Stanleys were ordered to raise Lancashire levies to defend it. The king feared still that the Scots would have the support of local Northumbrian dissidents, 'divers riotous and evil disposed persons in those parts'. Similar summonses were sent to Henry Vernon and the duke of Suffolk, who in his turn summoned John Paston as sheriff of Suffolk and Norfolk to raise troops.[7] At the same time the king proclaimed a pardon for all those who had offended by being in the field against him, with a few named exceptions, so that they could assist in the defence against the Scots.[8] The combination of Scottish mobilization and northern disturbances clearly caused great alarm, although by 20 October the king was assured that his 'politic and mighty purveyance' had caused the rebels to disperse.[9] Nevertheless, six weeks later Thomas Betanson reported from London to Sir Robert Plumpton that 'here is much speech that we shall have a shift again and no man can say of whom; but they deem of northernmen and welshmen'. The court was evidently jittery: 'there is much running amongst the

[5] Nokes and Wheeler, 'Spanish Account', p. 3; Salter, *Registrum Coll. Mertonensis*, p. 72. It is to be noted that on 23 Aug. the city council of York expected Northumberland, who was reported to be at Leicester 'for the weal of himself and the city', to return to Wressle (*YCR* i. 119–20).

[6] *CPR, 1485–94*, 39–40; Pollard, *Henry VII*, i. 21.

[7] Campbell, *Materials*, i. 579; Pollard, *Henry VII*, i. 19–22.

[8] *YCR* i. 125–6.   [9] Goodman, *Wars of the Roses*, p. 96 n. 58.

lords, but no man wot what it is; it is said it is not well amongst them'.[10]

It was the continuing disturbance in the north which prompted Henry to release the earls of Northumberland and Westmorland early in December. He had tried unsuccessfully to hold the north through the agency of others. Lords FitzHugh and Clifford were given authority in Yorkshire. On 24 September the king's lordships of Richmond, Middleham, and Barnard Castle were committed to FitzHugh's charge. The following day he was instructed to receive the oath of allegiance of a number of neighbouring lords and prominent gentry before they acted as commissioners of array.[11] FitzHugh's authority in these months is confirmed by Miles Metcalfe's desperate attempts, reported on 23 October, to win royal favour by making *daily* 'suit unto my lord FitzHugh and other his good lords, whose favour and labour may profit him in this behalf'.[12] FitzHugh was assisted by the restored Lord Clifford, who with him sent letters to the mayor of York on 8 October commanding him to proclaim his offer of pardons for all but a handful of named men, so that the northern marches could be defended against the Scots. And Clifford on his own authority wrote again on 24 October instructing the city authorities not to allow the sale of arms and armour to outsiders.[13] As far as the east marches were concerned Lord Strange in the mean time had been appointed 'warden of the marches towards Scotland for this turn'.[14] None of these shifts proved satisfactory, and by the end of November the king had reluctantly concluded that he had no choice but to restore the earl of Northumberland, however much he may have privately distrusted him. Northumberland was released under surety, and only when he had given a special oath of allegiance, before 6 December. He was restored to the offices he held under Edward IV, additionally made bailiff of the royal liberty of Tynedale, and restored to the shrievalty of Northumberland *during pleasure* (not for life) in February 1488.[15] He was, however, only restored to the wardenship of the east march on an annual basis. Moreover in 1487 the responsibility for Berwick

[10] *Plumpton Correspondence*, p. 49.   [11] *CPR, 1485–94*, 16, 39–40.
[12] *YCR* i. 128.   [13] Ibid. 125–6, 130.   [14] *CPR, 1485–94*, 40.
[15] Campbell, *Materials*, i. 100; ii. 54; Pollard, *Henry VII*, i. 29; *CPR, 1485–94*, 120, 138, 201; Hicks, 'Fourth Earl of Northumberland', pp. 92–4.

was separated from the wardenship and placed in other hands. Northumberland's power was much curtailed, and he himself was kept on leading strings. He was required to attend at Sheen early in March 1487 to renew his contract as warden; no doubt the occasion, a stay at court for five days, was used by the king to remind the earl where his duty lay.[16] Thus the earl was restored to his accustomed place in the north-east on probation: the king made it abundantly clear that his role was to exercise royal authority and no more. The earl was given even less room for manœuvre by Henry VII than he had been allowed by Richard III. Similarly the earl of Westmorland was released, but placed under immediate surety for his future good behaviour. On 1 December he entered into bonds to pay 1000 marks in three instalments by Michaelmas 1487, and four days later formally conceded the guardianship and marriage of his son and heir to the king.[17] Henceforth he probably resumed his role in the government of the county palatine of Durham, but was given no wider power.[18]

The restoration of the northern earls, especially Northumberland, was still insufficient to stifle trouble. On 15 February 1486 Thomas Betanson wrote again to Yorkshire that the king was planning to come northward himself in strength immediately after the dissolution of Parliament 'to do execution quickly then on such as have offended against him'.[19] The king did indeed set out after Easter, and already had wind that Viscount Lovell and Sir Humphrey Stafford of Grafton, having escaped from sanctuary, were planning to rebel. On his approach to York he was met by a powerful retinue led by the earl of Northumberland, who escorted him into York on 20 April.[20] While Henry was at York, or even before his arrival, Lovell, backed by an ominously named 'Robin of Redesdale', rose in Richmondshire, 'a little

---

[16] *Rot.Scot.* ii. 470–1, 484–5; *Paston Letters*, i. 653. Northumberland received his first commission in Jan. 1486. In Mar. 1487 William Paston reported that he had indented with the king then. It seems that the earl was only granted short-term commissions. Berwick was already in other hands in 1487 (see below, p. 384). The loss of the captaincy of Berwick was a later source of grievance (see M. E. James, *A Tudor Magnate and the Tudor State*, Borthwick Paper 30 York (1966) 36).

[17] Campbell, *Materials*, i. 191, 196; *CCR, 1485–1500*, 22.

[18] Westmorland was a JP from June 1490 at the latest (Durh. 3/58/1).

[19] *Plumpton Correspondence*, p. 50.   [20] Leland, *Collectanea*, iv. 185.

beyond the castle of Middleham', the heartland of Richard III's old support. Either because his rising was ill-planned, or because he himself had scant appeal, Lovell received little help from men of substance. The king's forces, by all accounts few in number, were able to disperse the rebels without much trouble by the promise of pardons.[21] The city of York held firm, most of the northern peers rallied to Henry, and above all the earl of Northumberland repaid the king's judgement in restoring him. One account even suggests that his personal intervention foiled a plot to seize the king in York itself.[22] The king's programme in York, the carefully stage-managed welcome and the conspicuous celebration of St George's day on 23 April, were undisturbed by these alarms.[23] Lovell and other rebels fled westward over the Pennines, and took shelter in the Furness Fells, near the seat of Sir Thomas Broughton; the unidentified Robin of Redesdale was taken by Northumberland in June, and sent south for interrogation by the king.[24] Early in August Sir William Tyler and others were commissioned to receive into the king's grace all rebels in Yorkshire, especially in the lordships of Middleham and Richmond, willing to submit.[25] To those in Furness the king offered pardons. On 20 July 1486 the sheriffs of Northumberland, Cumberland, and Yorkshire were ordered to make proclamation that they were to submit or face forfeiture. A month later, on 17 August, pardons were issued to Sir John Huddleston, Sir Thomas Broughton, Sir Robert Harrington, Geoffrey Frank, Richard Middleton, and others, and on the following day Lord Clifford, Sir Thomas Tunstall, Sir Richard Wortley, and Sir John Conyers were authorized to take their oaths of obedience.[26] With this submission, almost a year to the day after Bosworth, the initial resistance to Henry VII in the north appears to have come to an end.

It is important, however, to appreciate the character of this

---

[21] Pollard, *Henry VII*, i. 21; Leland, *Collectanea*, iv. 186–7; Vergil, *Anglica Historia*, pp. 10–11. See also Michael Bennett, *Lambert Simnel and the Battle of Stoke* (Gloucester, 1987), 37.   [22] *Crowland Chronicle*, 197; YCR ii. 3–5.
[23] Ibid. i. 150, 152–3, 155–9; Leland, *Collectanea*, iv. 188–92.
[24] *Select Cases in the Council of Henry VII*, ed. C. G. Bayne and W. H. Dunham, Selden Society, lxxv (1958), 8.   [25] *CPR, 1485–94*, 112.
[26] Ibid. 119, 132; Campbell, *Materials*, i. 540–2. William Beverley, the rector, and Thomas Otter of Middleham also received pardons (*CPR, 1485–94*, 93, 112).

resistance. It did not come from the lords and principal gentry of the region. As we have seen, although clearly distrusted by Henry VII, Northumberland and Westmorland were restored, and Northumberland in particular took his stand for the new regime. Lord FitzHugh had been quick to rally to the king: perhaps he had hoped to profit from Northumberland's eclipse. But he faded from prominence after Northumberland's return. He was removed from his offices in Richmondshire in February and May 1486, although he appears to have remained steward, constable, and master forester of Barnard Castle until his death on 20 November 1487.[27] Lord Greystoke died in the spring of 1486; but Lords Scrope of Bolton and Masham and Lord Lumley rallied to the king at York in April 1486.[28]

Equally instructive is the reaction of the leading gentry of Yorkshire. Sir John Conyers of Hornby had played a prominent part in local affairs, politics, and civil war since the 1450s. He more than any other had been responsible for the transition of local power from Warwick to Gloucester in 1471. Once more he was to play a critical, if less obvious, role. He was at first replaced in his offices at Richmond and Middleham by FitzHugh. On the other hand he was one of the first to take an oath of allegiance in September 1485 and become a commissioner of array. In February, once more a knight of the body, he was restored to the stewardship of Richmond and constableship of Middleham, in survivorship with his grandson and heir William, with fees of 200 marks.[29] And it is to be assumed that as a Knight of the Garter Sir John participated in the Garter service and feast at York on 23 April. He was not able, however, to prevent the rising which occurred in April, in which the rector William Beverley and Thomas Otter seem to have played a part. Yet he was one of those trusted to receive rebels, including the one-time receiver of Middleham, Geoffrey Frank, back into obedience in August 1486.[30] The endorsement of this

---

[27] CPR, 1485–94, 84, 89–90. FitzHugh's withdrawal might have been due to ill-health, incompetence, or implication in the conspiracy of his brother-in-law, Viscount Lovell.

[28] Leland, *Collectanea*, iv. 186–7.   [29] CPR, 1485–94, 39–40, 84.

[30] Leland, *Collectanea*, iv. 186–7. He attended at least one Garter feast under Henry VII, either in 1487 or 1488, for which he received the customary robe (Campbell, *Materials*, i. 498).

senior statesman of the region, who more than any other could speak for the old Neville interest in Richmondshire, was no doubt influential not only in persuading other members of the local gentry (many related to him) to accept the new regime, but also in containing local opposition. Men until recently associated with the Neville–Gloucester connection, such as Sir Richard Conyers, Sir William Ingleby, and Sir James Strangways[31] were in Northumberland's company when he welcomed Henry VII to Yorkshire in April 1486. Others whose links had been close to Richard III as well as to the earl himself —Sir William Eure, Sir Thomas Mauleverer, Sir John Pickering, and Sir Christopher Ward—were also in his entourage.[32] Sir Ralph Bigod of Settrington was already constable of Sheriff Hutton by 1486, when he too was a knight of the body.[33] And Sir John Saville was quickly restored to the stewardship of Wakefield, and became Henry VII's first sheriff, a promotion in itself unsurprising, bearing in mind his quarrel with Richard III.[34] A list of men who helped suppress the tax revolt of 1489 confirms that Bigod, Strangways, Saville, Eure, and Pickering could be relied upon in a crisis. This heraldic list also adds William Conyers, grandson and heir to Sir John, Sir Thomas Markenfield, and Sir James Danby.[35] In Durham our knowledge is limited by the loss of the palatine patent roll for the years to 1490. We do not know who was trusted as commissioner of the peace or of array, or alternatively who sued for pardon, until the end of the decade. It does seem, however, that the administration remained much as the absentee Bishop Shirwood had inherited it at the end of Richard III's reign. Richard Danby, King Richard's appointee as steward, remained in office, as did the sheriff, Sir Ralph Bowes. There is no reason to suppose that the earl of Westmorland, Lord Lumley, Sir William Eure, Sir Roger Conyers, and William Claxton did not continue to act as JPs, just as Sir Thomas Grey of Wark and Heaton kept his office as

---

[31] Above, pp. 128–9.
[32] Leland, *Collectanea*, iv. 185.
[33] PRO, DL 29/650/10510.
[34] Dockray, 'Political Legacy', pp. 209, 212, and above, p. 349.
[35] I am grateful to Michael Bennett for permission to cite an advance copy of his article on 'Henry VII and the Northern Rising of 1489', which includes this information.

constable of Norham on the border.[36] In Northumberland, after a short interlude, the dominance of Henry Percy was resumed at the end of 1485; and it is to be assumed that the control of the county continued much as it had done until the earl's death in 1489.

Henry VII discovered in the first year of his reign that he had little to fear from a temporizing county élite in the north-east. Yet he was by no means out of the wood. In 1487 a more serious challenge to his throne developed in the Lambert Simnel conspiracy. Co-ordinated by the earl of Lincoln and Viscount Lovell, and parading the innocent Simnel as the boy Edward VI (Edward of Warwick), the rebel force of Irish levies and German mercenaries landed in Furness on 4 June. Dissidents in Cumbria, led by Sir Thomas Broughton, Sir Thomas Pilkington, and Sir James and Sir Robert Harrington, rallied to his cause. But as soon as possible the rebels made for north Yorkshire, where, it was later said, they believed they had friends enough upon the ground.[37]

By 18 June they were at Masham, the seat of Thomas the younger of the two Lords Scrope. They were undoubtedly disappointed by their reception. Relatively few men of Richmondshire rallied openly to their cause. Both Lords Scrope, of Bolton as well as of Masham, declared for them. But few apart from their own tenants and dependants followed their example. The only other man of note from Wensleydale implicated in the rising was Thomas Metcalfe of Nappa, the king's supervisor of Middleham, who later sued for pardon, and was perhaps one of those who 'relieved those that were against the king'.[38] Sir John Conyers, the king's steward in Richmondshire, who in 1469–71 had 'provoked and stirred' the people in his parts, stood aloof; while doing little to assist the invading army, he perhaps did little to oppose it. This probably explains why in August 1487 the grant of February 1486 in favour of him and his grandson was cancelled, and he was replaced by Sir Thomas Wortley, a

---

[36] See above, pp. 163, 360.

[37] For the most recent account of the rebellion see Bennett, *Lambert Simnel*, pp. 70–5; *YCR* ii. 20–1.

[38] While Thomas Metcalfe was implicated, his brother James, master forester, was not. Christopher Lightfoot, appointed bailiff of Crakehall for life on 14 Dec. 1487, was probably another local servant of the Crown who proved his loyalty (Campbell, *Materials*, ii. 213).

Yorkshireman and an ex-Ricardian, but a stranger to Richmond-shire, who remained in office until 1493.[39]

The rebels were more overtly successful in the honour of Knaresborough. At least three men with Ricardian connections, Robert Percy of Scotton, John Pullen of Scotton, and Richard Knaresborough declared for the rebels. Their rebellion, dealt with firmly by Northumberland, harked back to the long rivalry and division in the honour between Neville and Percy followers. It would seem that their making common cause with Lincoln and Lovell was as much a protest against the earl and his local officers, Sir William Gascoigne and Sir Robert Plumpton, as it was against Henry VII.[40] A few other isolated notables scattered throughout the region would seem to have given support, for they were quick to sue pardons from the king when he toured the region two months later. Prior Auckland of Durham, Abbot Heslington of Jervaulx, Archdeacon Booth of York, and William Claxton all came in to the king when he was at Durham on 20 August and at Ripon four days later. A month later Robert Gower of Stittenham took out a pardon.[41] The most remarkable recruit was Sir Edmund Hastings of Roxby, the steward of Pickering, who in September lost the right of presentation to a Yorkshire parish by forfeiture for his treason. The charge of treason—later remitted, for he was not attainted—suggests that he had fought at Stoke rather than remained with the Scropes in Yorkshire.[42] Apart from these men the only known adherents were lesser figures, like Lovell's agent Edward Frank, his bailiff of Bedale John Robinson, Ralph Scrope, the rector of Wensley, or Agnes Scrope, the widow of Sir Richard Ratcliffe.[43]

[39] *CPR, 1485–94*, 192; Hunter, *South Yorkshire*, ii. (1831), 312. Hunter, quoting the family papers, states that Wortley was granted the office early in Henry VII's reign. It is clear from the context this was before 1488. At the same time Wortley became steward of Jervaulx (ibid.). He was a JP in the North Riding from October 1489 to May 1493 (*CPR, 1485–94*, 507). Advancing age (he died in 1490) may also help to explain Sir John's 'retirement'.

[40] *Plumpton Correspondence*, 54–5; *Rot.Parl.* vi. 397; *CPR, 1485–94*, 191; and see also above, pp. 131, 271, 326 and 360.

[41] *CPR, 1485–94*, 191; Campbell, *Materials*, ii. 163, 184, 194.

[42] Campbell, *Materials*, i. 194; Somerville, *Duchy of Lancaster*, i. 534; *CPR, 1485–94*, 194, 534. One source of resentment may have been the loss of Gilling to Sir Charles Somerset in August 1485 (*CPR, 1485–94*, 398).

[43] *CPR, 1485–94*, 191; Campbell, *Materials*, i. 194, 198. See also Dockray, 'Political Legacy', pp. 218–20 for the Yorkshire rebels of 1487.

Perhaps the principal reason why the rebels received so little support in the north-east is that the government was forewarned and forearmed. As early as April the city of York was taking precautions for its defence against invasion, then expected on the east coast. The earl of Northumberland acted promptly on 6 June when he heard of the landing in Furness. The gates of York were shut firmly against the rebels; the mayor and corporation stood solidly behind the king. The rebels therefore decided to march rapidly south to seek a quick engagement with the king. They were followed by Lord Clifford, who on Sunday 10 June attempted an attack on their encampment at Bramham Moor, but was beaten off. The rebels in their turn left the Lords Scrope and their band to attempt an assault on Bootham Bar, the northern gate of York, on 12 June. This failed; but it had the secondary success of drawing Northumberland and Clifford back to hold Yorkshire against further disturbance.[44] But in truth Simnel's rebellion was not primarily a north-eastern rising. At bottom it was a foreign invasion sponsored by Margaret of Burgundy. One wonders what appeal an army of Irish and German mercenaries had to the people of Wensleydale who had no choice but to act as their hosts.

Apart from the few, like the Lords Scrope, Thomas Metcalfe, Sir Edmund Hastings, and William Claxton, who succumbed to the appeal of Lambert Simnel, the political establishment of north-eastern England, typified by Sir John Conyers, once again waited on events. Sustained opposition in the early years of Henry's reign came from other quarters. One group was that of the Furness circle in which Sir Thomas Broughton and the Harrington brothers were prominent. Their quarrel was with the Stanleys. They were pursuing in vain the private feud which had occupied them for several decades. It was this, not commitment to the cause of the white rose, that fired them.[45] Another group was formed by the devoted personal servants of Lovell, de la Pole, and the unfortunate earl of Warwick. Edward Frank,

[44] YCR ii. 22–4. On 14 June Northumberland and Clifford set out 'towards the north parts'. There is nothing necessarily suspicious or ambivalent about Northumberland's role in holding the north-east against possible further rebellion.

[45] See Dockray, 'Political Legacy', pp. 220–1 and Jones, 'The Stanleys', pp. 37–42.

who was attainted after Stoke, and finally captured and executed in December 1489, when a plot to arrange the escape of
the earl of Warwick from the Tower was unearthed, had been
Lovell's right-hand man during the reign of Richard III, to whom
he owed promotion in Oxfordshire and Berkshire. He was a son
of Cuthbert Frank of Kneeton in north Yorkshire, and kinsman
of Geoffrey Frank, the one-time receiver of Middleham who
made his peace with the new regime.[46] Roland Robinson, identified in a Durham pardon of 1490 as of Bradley, Co. Durham,
was perhaps originally of the Bedale family of Robinsons. An
exile, he ultimately attached himself to the cause of Perkin
Warbeck. John Taylor, an inveterate plotter, would seem to
have been a personal servant of the earl of Warwick who
subsequently worked tirelessly in his master's cause. Others,
like Sir Robert Chamberlain, who was captured trying to leave
England in 1490, came from de la Pole circles.[47] The later,
continuing opposition to Henry VII in the name of the white
rose lay in the hands of men like these, not with the established
landed society of northern England.

   The third, and for all landed society the most worrying,
feature of northern opposition to Henry VII was its popular and
plebeian character. From the very early disturbances in the
months after Bosworth the commons were the most persistent
in their refusal to accept the new regime. In his letter to Henry
Vernon on 17 October 1485 Henry VII stressed that the rebels
and traitors in the north parts were 'of little honour or substance'. The king's view would appear to be confirmed by Lord
Clifford's letter to York a week later, in which he warned that
ill-disposed persons who were causing disturbances would wish
to buy harness in the city of York. No man of honour or
substance would need to buy his weapons and armour in such a
way. The rioters took the names of Robin of Redesdale, Jack
Straw, and Master Mendall, common pseudonyms for popular leaders.[48] The commons provided most of the support

---

[46] Pollard, *Henry VII*, i. 84–7; *Harleian MS 433*, i. 265; *Paston Letters*, ii. 456.
[47] For the dedicated opposition of these men to Henry VII see W. E. Hampton,
'The White Rose under the First Tudor', *The Ricardian*, vii, no. 97 (1987),
417–18; and Arthurson, 'A Question of Loyalty', pp. 401–13.
[48] Pollard, *Henry VII*, i. 21; *YCR* i. 130.

for Viscount Lovell in 1486. The ease with which the king's poorly armed retainers dispersed them indicates that Lovell was then at the head of a popular rather than an aristocratic rising. The capture two months later of a 'Robin of Redesdale' whose real identity was never worth recording confirms the character of Lovell's local support as essentially plebeian.[49]

Popular resentment against the new regime burst into the open again in April 1489. The cause of the Yorkshire rebellion, two of whose leaders took the pseudonyms of Master Hobbehirst and Robin Goodfellow,[50] was the levying of taxes to fund the king's campaign in Brittany. In November 1487 Parliament voted two-fifteenths to be raised in 1488 and 1489, followed by an additional grant in January 1489 of a novel levy of a tenth of the value of all lands and goods in country as well as in town. These taxes were to be paid in Yorkshire as well as in other parts of the kingdom. They met with immediate local resistance.[51] Over the preceding decade Yorkshiremen had become accustomed to being remitted royal taxation. Richard III as duke of Gloucester had successfully lobbied his brother the king to exempt them payment of tenths and fifteenths originally voted in 1474 and later raised to pay for the Scottish wars. The exemption was granted in recognition of his labour as well as the expense already sustained in the war.[52] Richard III himself raised no lay subsidies. Of equal significance, perhaps, was that while two clerical subsidies were demanded from the southern province during his reign, the northern was exempted.[53] Yorkshiremen no doubt also felt that they had a genuine case of poverty. The city of York made much of its poverty in 1488 in securing a reduction in the amount demanded of it. But collection of the first instalment had not begun in the neighbouring countryside before mid-1488. It is therefore likely that

---

[49] Bayne and Dunham, *Select Cases*, p. 8, and above, p. 371.

[50] Pollard, *Henry VII*, i. 70.

[51] M. A. Hicks, 'The Yorkshire Rebellion of 1489 Reconsidered', *NH* 22 (1986), 50. I am also grateful to Richard Hoyle for permission to cite an advance copy of his article, 'Resistance and Manipulation in Early Tudor Lay Subsidies: Some Evidence from the North'.   [52] Scofield, *Edward the Fourth*, ii. 361–2.

[53] A. K. McHardy, 'Clerical Taxation in Fifteenth-Century England', in Dobson, *Church, Politics and Patronage*, pp. 181, 188.

collection of the 1487 tax had not been completed before April 1489, when the new tax also had to be paid.[54]

This was the explosive situation met by the earl of Northumberland, instructed by the king to enforce collection, at South Kilvington on 27 April. In the meeting between Northumberland and a group of protesters from Cleveland the earl was killed. As Dr Hicks has suggested, his death was probably unpremeditated: tempers flared when the earl refused to compromise, and his retainers failed to protect him. After the earl's death the rising spread. Gatherley Moor north of Richmond, and Allerton Moor 'in the east' were nominated as meeting points for a general popular rising on 5 May. But the response was disappointing: two hundred or so came in from the East Riding, having gathered at Sheriff Hutton. At this point Sir John Egremont seems to have taken the lead. The rebel force moved south to Doncaster, gathering what support it could, and then returned to York, where it gained entrance with the help of sympathizers in the city. Egremont on 17 May apparently set off for Richmondshire to attempt once more to raise that district; but before long the rebels heard of the advance of the earl of Surrey with the king's vanguard, and quickly dispersed.[55]

There are several enigmatic features to this revolt which have attracted the attention of recent historians. The only known manifesto referred not to taxation, but, cryptically, to the king's breaches of sanctuary. As Dr Hicks has suggested, this may well refer to the manner in which Robin of Redesdale, the leader of popular risings in 1486, was apparently taken from sanctuary in Durham and handed over to the king.[56] If so, the rebellion of 1489 would clearly be linked to the popular disturbances of 1485–6. It is significant too, perhaps, that rebels gathered at

[54] Hicks, 'Yorkshire Rebellion', pp. 50–3; Hoyle, 'Resistance and Manipulation'.

[55] The above is based on Hicks, 'Yorkshire Rebellion', pp. 39–62. Gatherley Moor will be familiar to late-20th-cent. motorists as Scotch Corner; the precise identification of Allerton Moor is unclear.

[56] Ibid. 54–5. Cf. the case in August 1487 in which the king took two other humble rebels, Thomas and Herbert Relshaw, from sanctuary at Hexham. The justification given to Archbishop Rotherham on this occasion was that sanctuary did not extend to high treason. Hinds, *Hexhamshire, vol. i:* 41; *The Register of Thomas Rotherham, Archbishop of York, 1480–1500,* i, ed. E. E. Barker, Canterbury and York Society, lxix (1976), 220; Cox, *Sanctuaries*, pp. 136, 144.

Sheriff Hutton, and that attempts seem to have been made twice to raise men in Richmondshire. Through all this a common thread seems to have been a lingering attachment to the memory of Richard III, who, unlike Northumberland, had successfully remitted taxation on the commons. Substance would then appear to be given to the Great Chronicler of London's view that Northumberland was killed because of the 'deadly malice for the disappointing of king Richard at Bosworth Field', and to the views expressed later by Bacon that the rebellion proceeded not simply out of opposition to the taxation, but 'much by reason of the old humours of those countries where the memory of King Richard was so strong'.[57]

The circumstance whereby Northumberland's retainers were said to have stood back to allow their lord to be killed has led to speculation that many of his own men, who had served Richard III, and only entered the earl's service after 1485, privately shared the old humour, and deserted him. This view originated with Skelton, writing shortly after the event, who hinted darkly at 'false packing', and at Northumberland's escort's being 'linked with a double chain' with the commons 'under a cloak'. The truth of this is unlikely to be known;[58] but in York the plebeian uprising was certainly linked with Ricardian sympathy. Thomas Wrangwysh, who raised armed men to join the rebels who were allowed to enter the city gates under his control, had been Richard III's most committed supporter in the city, and had lost influence since 1485.[59]

Evidently Henry VII himself feared that there was more behind the rising than a popular disturbance. He took no chances. The king called his household together in strength and marched promptly north. The earl of Surrey, released from prison just before the royal force set out, was sent ahead in command of the vanguard; but it was the king himself who dealt

---

[57] Thomas and Thornley, *Great Chronicle*, p. 242; Bacon, *Henry VII*, p. 88. Sir Thomas Wortley seems to have held Richmondshire securely for the king. The one recorded disturbance, the breaking down of the walls of Sunscue park, of which he was keeper, may well have been directed against him (PRO, DL 29/649/10500).

[58] Pollard, *Henry VII*, i. 75; Hicks, 'Fourth Earl of Northumberland', pp. 79–80, 96–100.

[59] Hicks, 'Yorkshire Rebellion', pp. 56–7; Palliser, 'Richard III and York', p. 65.

with the rising, and presided at York as the principal rebels were brought to justice. The king might have feared that popular grievances would be harnessed to a Ricardian rising; but he is likely to have been reassured on this score by the impressive turn-out of Yorkshire lords, knights, and gentry who had helped suppress it.[60] Perhaps he was more concerned about the danger of Scottish intervention, and the possible link between the earl's death, the rising, and the presence of Viscount Lovell, now receiving a warmer welcome from the government of the young James IV, at the Scottish court. The king is likely to have been aware of the plotting against him in Burgundy, Edinburgh, and elsewhere. At the end of the year Edward Frank was revealed to be engaged in a treasonable conspiracy to free the earl of Warwick from captivity; and Frank no doubt was in communication with Lovell.[61] What Henry probably feared most was not a direct connection between the popular rising in Yorkshire and local Ricardian opposition, but the possibility that other conspirators elsewhere would take advantage of disorder unless he dealt with it promptly and firmly.

The commons were not so much a many-headed as a headless monster in the first few years of Henry's reign. Robin of Redesdale was not the assumed name of a local aristocrat. But the various disturbances, riots, and risings which occurred in Yorkshire after 1485, most of which can be linked to lingering popular feeling for Richard III, no doubt helped sway the opinion of the landed élite. Faced with a choice between the public disorder associated with the cause of Warwick or Lincoln and enforcement of law and order under Henry VII, most backed the new king. Self-interest was a powerful incentive to support the new regime. The established élite in town or country had too much to lose to follow any other course.[62] And Henry VII

---

[60] I owe this information to Michael Bennett, 'Henry VII and the Northern Rising of 1489' (see n. 35 above). See also Hicks, 'Yorkshire Rebellion', p. 58.

[61] S. O'Connor, 'Francis Lovell and the Rebels of Furness Fells', *The Ricardian*, vii, no. 96 (1987), 368–9; A. Conway, *Henry VII's Relations with Scotland and Ireland, 1485–1498* (Cambridge, 1932) 26–30.

[62] Dockray, 'Political Legacy', p. 223, makes a similar point. The last recorded popular rising took place in May 1492, the insurrection being crushed by the earl of Surrey at Ackworth, near Pontefract (see *Plumpton Correspondence*, pp. xcix, 96–7).

encouraged aristocratic loyalty by a judicious balance of exemplary severity and calculated clemency. Most north-easterners who offended were pardoned. But there was a price for royal grace. An example was made of the peers at the very top. Both Northumberland and Westmorland were only restored under condition of good behaviour. The Lords Scrope of Bolton and Masham escaped attainder and forfeiture in 1487; but they both compounded with the king, were placed under hefty bonds, and were held under house arrest in Windsor and Wallingford respectively. Scrope of Masham was given licence to live freely in England a year later, and pardoned on 16 February 1489; Scrope of Bolton, pardoned on 31 January 1488, was not given a conditional discharge to reside freely south of the Trent until July 1489.[63] Lesser men escaped with a warning for their transgressions. Sir Edmund Hastings, clearly under threat in late 1487, was restored to favour. He retained his offices at Pickering, and was, early in 1488, entrusted as a tax assessor.[64] Thomas Metcalfe's second career as a Tudor servant was not blighted by being under suspicion in 1487. He continued in his post as supervisor of the king's estates in Richmondshire, was as a king's esquire granted an annuity in 1490, and became a JP from 1493. As Leland later commented, he waxed rich as the king's financial agent in Richmondshire.[65] The king's clemency proved effective policy.

But there were other more fundamental reasons than self-interest and effective royal handling for the ready acceptance of Henry Tudor by the ruling élite of north-eastern England. Henry, it is often overlooked, was earl of Richmond, and therefore mesne lord of Middleham. At Bosworth he not only took the crown from Richard III, but also recovered his earldom from its usurper. One of his standards at the battle carried the Dun Cow, the badge of his earldom.[66] Thus Henry plausibly presented

[63] Campbell, *Materials*, ii. 235, 291, 410, 457.

[64] *CPR, 1485–94*, 194, 209. [65] Ibid. 209, 299, 425, 442, 508 and above p. 138.

[66] Delloyd J. Guth, 'Richard III, Henry VII and the City: London Politics and the Dun Cowe', in Griffiths and Sherborne, *Kings and Nobles*, pp. 196–7, 203, n. 81. Guth draws attention to Henry VII's use of the Dun Cow, but with some ingenuity transforms it into a Neville Bull. Yet the comment he cites from Cavendish's *Life of Wolsey* that the Dun Cow in the early 16th cent. symbolized the earldom of Richmond provides a much simpler explanation of Henry VII's use of the emblem in 1485.

himself as the legitimate lord of north-west Yorkshire. In taking possession of Middleham and Sheriff Hutton he seems in the first instance to have adopted the legal device that they were in his hands by reason of the minority of Edward, earl of Warwick, the heir to the daughters of the Kingmaker.[67] Ultimately, after the attainder of the earl in 1499, they were assimilated to the Crown. No recognition was made of the claim of Richard Neville, Lord Latimer, the male-tail heir. Latimer, who came of age in 1491, seems to have accepted the permanent loss to the Crown without demur. Barnard Castle too was first treated as part of the young earl of Warwick's inheritance. But in Parliament on 17 November 1485 the dowager countess, the earl's grandmother and true possessor of the estate, 'showed a piteous complaint', and delivered a bill presumably for the restoration of her right.[68] The king's initial response was to grant her an annuity of 500 marks, payable from the southern lands of her inheritance. But by an Act of the autumn parliament of 1487 she was restored to her full right on condition, it became apparent, that she granted it, including Barnard Castle, to the king, saving only one manor in Warwickshire for herself. Two years later the king relented to the extent of a large grant of these lands, excluding Barnard Castle, for life. She died in 1492. Thus by gift of the dowager countess of Warwick, Barnard Castle was absorbed into the royal demesne in December 1487.[69]

The new Crown lands in north Yorkshire and south Durham, linked administratively with the duchy of York estates, produced an income of over £2,000 per annum for the king. Whereas Richard III had used this income to reward his followers and to fund his new Council in the North, Henry VII deployed it to pay for the cost of Berwick, separated from the wardenship of the east march and maintained by the Crown. The king's lieutenant was Sir William Tyler; his chamberlain and treasurer of war there from 16 August 1487 was Richard Cholmley, who was also made receiver-general of the king's northern estates, from which he drew the greater part of his budget.[70] Having deter-

---

[67] Campbell, *Materials*, ii. 82.

[68] N. Pronay and J. Taylor, *Parliamentary Texts of the Later Middle Ages* (Oxford, 1980), 186.

[69] Campbell, *Materials*, ii. 211–12; *CPR, 1485–94*, 298; *CP* xii. Part 2, 393.

[70] PRO, DL 29/651/10528; Campbell, *Materials*, ii. 234.

mined that the revenues of his northern lands should be directed to pay for the garrisoning of Berwick, Henry was abstemious with annuities and fees. At Middleham, for instance, by the mid-1490s the total charge was no more than £250, half of which was consumed by William Conyers as steward and constable. Approximately £630 was left every year to be paid over to Cholmley. The contrast with Richard III, who expended three-quarters of the revenue in fees and annuities, could not be more marked.[71]

Although not exceptionally generous in his patronage drawn from his new crown lands, Henry VII did at first use the resources to reward local men. Sir John Conyers, as we have seen, was restored in part to his accustomed place at Middleham after a few months early in 1486, only to be removed again in 1487.[72] William Conyers, who had succeeded his grandfather in 1490, was rehabilitated in February 1493, when he received a grant identical in terms to that made initially to his grandfather and him in 1486.[73] The head of the Conyers family thus success-fully retained for all but a short spell his traditional place in the lordship. Other members of the family, as well as the Metcalfes, made the transition from lord to lord more comfortably. Sir Richard, brother of Sir John, remained farmer of Moulton; Richard, Sir John's younger son, not only retained possession of Ulshaw, but also on 2 May 1486, shortly after Lovell's rising, was granted a life annuity of £8 from the estate.[74] Henry VII found it relatively easy to win the confidence of the officers and tenants of Middleham. He was, when all was said and done, not only king but also earl of Richmond.

At Sheriff Hutton less continuity was possible. Sir Thomas Gower of Stittenham died at Bosworth. His place was taken by another leading ex-Ricardian, Sir Ralph Bigod, who was constable within six months. Moreover, John Dawney of Cowick, one-time treasurer of the Council of the North, happily continued in royal service as receiver there.[75] At Barnard Castle Lord FitzHugh remained steward and constable until his death,

---

[71] PRO, DL 29/649/10505 and above, pp. 353–5.
[72] See above, pp. 373, 375–6.   [73] CPR, 1485–94, 84, 427.
[74] PRO, DL 29/649/10500; CPR, 1485–94, 130.
[75] PRO, DL 29/650/10515; CPR, 1485–94, 54, 259; Dockray, 'Political Legacy', pp. 211–12; Warnicke, 'Lord Morley's Statements', pp. 299–303.

and the formal settlement of the lordship on the king, at the end of 1487. There Henry VII did break with local tradition; perhaps because there was no local candidate of sufficient stature available, he appointed John, Lord Cheyney as steward. Cheyney seems to have carried out some of his duties in person; but by 1493 he had been succeeded by Sir Edward Pickering.[76]

Apart from the employment of household men to command and manage the finances of Berwick, the promotion of Cheyney, and the occasional grant, such as Gilling in Ryedale and the stewardship of Helmsley to Sir Charles Somerset, Henry at first made no significant introduction of trusted courtiers in the north.[77] Until the surely unwelcome death of the earl of Northumberland in 1489 he bent all his efforts, with overall success, to winning over the lords and gentry of the region. But Northumberland's death, at the hands of a mob and with the apparent collusion of some of his own retainers, seems to have led Henry to adopt a different approach. While during the minority of the fifth earl Percy retainers and officers were confirmed in their local posts, control of the comital finances passed in February 1492 to Reginald Bray as receiver-general,[78] and the role of the king's principal representative in the region was given to Thomas Howard, earl of Surrey.

The choice of Surrey was inspired. Like Northumberland he was under a cloud and on probation; he was a man with impeccable Ricardian credentials; but he was without local connections, and could represent the king without a conflict of interests. Left in charge after the king returned south in June 1489, he became steward and constable of Sheriff Hutton, which he made his headquarters, at Michaelmas. In May he was made lieutenant of Prince Arthur as warden of the east and middle marches, and he succeeded Northumberland to the office of chief justice of the forests north of the Trent.[79] As Surrey's deputies the king promoted Sir Henry Wentworth, a man of

[76] PRO, DL 29/651/10528. In 1489 Sir John Cheyney delivered revenues by hand to Richard Cholmley, the receiver-general. He was a Durham JP by 1490 (Durh. 3/58/1).   [77] CPR, 1485–94, 100, 173.

[78] Ibid. 300, 302, for confirmation of Sir Marmaduke Constable as steward of Pocklington, Sir William Eure as steward of Seamer, and Sir John Pickering as Yorks. receiver; p. 368, for the appointment of Bray.

[79] Pollard, Henry VII, i. 81; PRO, DL 29/650/10515; CPR, 1485–94, 322; Leland, Itinerary, p. 65.

Suffolk roots but with West Riding links, and Sir Richard Tunstall. Tunstall had been a royal councillor and steward of Pontefract since the beginning of the reign; he had served every king since Henry VI with distinction; his brothers William and Thomas had put down North Riding roots, William being constable of Scarborough; and the close family relationship with the Conyers ensured that he was not perceived as an intruder.[80]

Tunstall, a royal councillor from the beginning of the reign, died in 1491. Other household men were promoted to assist the earl, particularly three who were among Warbeck's 'caitiffs and villeins of simple birth': Sir William Tyler, Richard Cholmley, and Bishop Fox.[81] Tyler, as lieutenant of Berwick and a deputy warden from 1495, became the king's principal officer in Northumberland, a JP, and its MP in 1491–2.[82] The extent to which Tyler, as the king's lieutenant, stepped into the earl's shoes in Northumberland is shown by fees totalling almost £90 paid to divers gentlemen of the county retained with the king from 1491 to help and assist his lieutenant of Berwick. Fourteen men were so retained, including Sir Thomas Grey of Wark and Heaton, Sir Thomas Grey of Horton, Sir Robert Manners, Thomas Hagerston, John Swinburne, Henry Swinhoe, and Ralph Hebburn, all Percy retainers and probably previously retained by the fourth earl on similar conditions.[83] While no doubt an *ad hoc* response to an unexpected circumstance, such retaining by the king pointed to future practice.

Richard Cholmley was descended of a cadet branch of the leading Cheshire family. If not a villein of simple birth, he certainly came from obscure and humble origins. Tradition has it that he began his public career in the service of Margaret Beaufort, countess of Richmond, the king's mother. There may also have been earlier Stanley connections.[84] His first appearance in the record in the north-east is on 30 June 1487, in the

[80] Campbell, *Materials*, ii. 45; *CPR, 1485–94*, 87, 255; Wedgwood, *Biographies*, pp. 883, 934.   [81] Pollard, *Henry VII*, i. 153.

[82] Wedgwood, *Biographies*, p. 889. He was frequently employed in border negotiations from 1488 (*CDRS* ii. 815, 321–2, 326).

[83] PRO, DL 29/651/10528, 9. In 1500 Tyler was replaced by Sir Thomas Darcy (*CDRS* ii. 333).

[84] See Turton, *Forest of Pickering*, i, p. xxv. He was possibly the yeoman rewarded by Richard III (*Harleian MS 433*, iii. 147).

aftermath of the Simnel rebellion, when as one of the king's gentlemen ushers he was granted an annuity of £20 from the customs of Newcastle. On 26 August following he was promoted chamberlain of Berwick and treasurer of war there, as well as receiver-general of all the king's lordships in Yorkshire and County Durham. In addition he filled the offices of receiver in the constituent lordships. At first he acted in person as receiver of Middleham, being present at the audit for twenty-two days in October and November 1488.[85] Later the lesser offices were all exercised by deputy. He rose rapidly in the king's service after Northumberland's death. He was appointed steward of Cottingham in 1490, and became the receiver of the bishopric of Durham and one of the guardians of the temporalities during the vacancy following the death of Bishop Shirwood. Granted in tail male the manor of Forcett, a member of the lordship of Richmond, in February 1494, he also acquired an estate in Thornton-on-the-Hill. On Yorkshire commissions from 1493, when he became a JP in the East Riding, he was one of those charged to search for concealed wardships in 1494, 1495, and 1496. Knighted by the end of the decade, he became steward of Pickering in 1499; was appointed a commissioner to settle border disputes in 1500; was made constable of Norham for five years in 1500; became lieutenant of Sir Thomas Darcy as captain of Berwick by November 1500, and a deputy warden of the east march in the following year; was steward of York Minster by the early sixteenth century; and finally, in 1502, succeeded Surrey as steward and constable of Sheriff Hutton.[86] Henry VII's Ratcliffe, Sir Richard Cholmley typifies the rising household officer and royal councillor who came to wield great local power in the king's name.

In Durham Henry VII initially faced the problem that Bishop Shirwood was an absentee. He seems only to have resided in his diocese in 1490–1, and died in Rome in January 1494.[87] On 30

---

[85] PRO, DL 29/651/10528. The appointment passed the Great Seal on 24 January 1488, but he initially held the post for 6 years from 26 August.

[86] *CPR, 1494–1509*, 213, 233, 269; Somerville, *Duchy of Lancaster*, i. 534; Allen, *Letters of Richard Fox*, p. 19; J. Raine, *History and Antiquities of North Durham*, (1852), 12; *YCR* ii. 174.

[87] Emden, *Cambridge Register*, pp. 524–5. On 27 Jan. 1490 he 'scribbled in the most haste' to Sir John Paston from Bishop Auckland (*Paston Letters*, ii.

June, Richard Fox, the king's keeper of the Privy Seal and one of his inner council, was provided. He became an active and vigorous bishop, despite all the other calls on his time, until transferred to Winchester in 1501.[88] Tunstall, Tyler, Cholmley, and Fox were all royal councillors. At this time the king had no wish to establish a special council in the north. His needs were the opposite to Richard III's; the late king had been seeking to retain an established influence, Henry sought to impose a new control. Policy and administration were therefore conducted through the king's central council at Westminster or his itinerant council in attendance, to whom his northern lieutenants were answerable.

The degree of direct royal and conciliar intervention in the government of the north-east is evident on several fronts. At the beginning of 1489 a dispute arose between William Scargill of Lead and one of Sir Richard Tunstall's officers at Pontefract, Thomas of Pomfret. Sir Robert Plumpton took Scargill's part. But he was advised by Edward Plumpton after a meeting with Tunstall that Scargill should be persuaded 'not to use his old walks; for if he do he will be taken, and brought to find such surety for the peace and otherwise, as shall be to him inconvenient'. Tunstall himself wrote to Plumpton requesting him to advise Scargill to submit 'for and he will not I intend to show his obstinance to the king and his counsel, which if I so do, I think it will not be for his ease'.[89] Tunstall may not have been impartial in the issue, but he was a frequent attender at council[90] and knew that the king would act firmly against any disturber of the peace reported to him. His was no idle threat.

Public disorder, with its treasonable associations, particularly preoccupied the king. Disturbances and riots at the mayoral election in York were a constant source of concern. In 1489 a riotous election had preceded the tax revolt. The king himself

---

462). He was in England in attendance on the king at the end of 1488 (Leland, *Collectanea*, iv. 244). See also the letter of Prior John Auckland of 25 July 1486: 'I pray to God and Saint Cuthbert bring you soon to us' (*Scriptores Tres*, p. ccclxx).

[88] See, for instance, his correspondence concerning the minutiae of local administration (Allen, *Letters of Richard Fox*, pp. 23–6).

[89] *Plumpton Correspondence*, pp. 59–60.

[90] Bayne and Dunham, *Select Cases*, pp. 8–9, 13, 16, 22.

intervened, and on 10 April appointed a commissioner to deal with the offenders, in defiance of the city's privileges. On this occasion the rioters almost certainly had links with the men who rebelled a few weeks later.[91] Thereafter Henry kept a careful watch on elections. Two years later Tunstall and Cholmley reported to the king that the election had been orderly, and the king wrote to the mayor and council to thank them. But the king and his councillors were brought into a dispute between the weavers and cordwainers in 1493. On this occasion Abbot William Sever of St Mary's and Cholmley came into the city, and informed the mayor that they would settle the matter 'without advice of any other'. Understandably the mayor objected to this open disregard for the liberties of the city, but to no avail. Sever and Cholmley replied that since they had the king's command to settle the issue they had to do so, and begged the corporation to avoid the king's great displeasure. The corporation backed down, having been offered the face-saving formula of being shown the award before it was declared in the council chamber on Ousebridge on 11 May.[92]

But the royal intervention was perhaps most persistent in the matter of his rights as tenant in chief, and the campaign from the mid-1490s onwards to uncover all concealments of reliefs, wardships, and other feudal dues.[93] William Sever became, in 1499, surveyor of the king's prerogative, with the express duty of discovering concealments.[94] A letter of his to Reginald Bray, written on 7 December 1502 when he was bishop of Durham, gives the flavour of his approach to his task.[95] Reporting a dispute between the young earl of Northumberland and Sir William Bulmer over a woman (her wardship?) and land valued at £40 p.a., he commented:

and so it happeneth that when two dogs striveth for one bone the third cometh and taketh the same from them both. Because of the shortness

---

[91] Hicks, 'Yorkshire Rebellion', pp. 56–7; Miller, 'Medieval York', pp. 82–3.
[92] YCR ii. 97–9. The Cordwainers had appealed to the king. Henry VII's intervention was not novel. Edward IV had intervened in 1482 in a disputed mayoral election (YCR i. 48–9, 50–1). See also the discussion in J. I. Kermode, 'Obvious Observations on the Formation of Oligarchies in Late Medieval Towns', in Thomson, Towns and Townspeople, pp. 88–90, 99–101.
[93] S. B. Chrimes, Henry VII (1972), 208–12.
[94] Condon, 'Ruling Elites', p. 117. [95] Westminster Abbey Muniments, 6052.

of the matter my servant shall tell you what I mean herein for the king's advantage.

He further reported on matters which had come to light in consequence of his possession of the estates of the earldom of Westmorland in Durham during the minority of the fourth earl.

Sir, I pray you for the king's letter to be directed to one young John Metcalfe, auditor of the earl of Westmorland's lands in the bishopric, that he may come up with me after Christmas and bring with him three or four accounts in the last year of the earl of Westmorland's, and also all the accounts that was made in the year that my lord of Winchester [Fox] occupied when he was bishop of Durham. My conceit is for the king's advantage for it is showed me that their terms changed of late in the books, which can not be for the king's advantage.

How the books were cooked is not known: the accounts were sent up, for a stray, a list of fees paid by the late earl, has survived with Sever's letter in Bray's papers.[96]

The king himself was personally involved in the administration of the north-east. He was, it appears, almost always present at meetings of council which determined policy and made decisions.[97] In May 1489 all cases were adjourned to the Trinity term because he himself was going north to suppress the Yorkshire rebellion. In 1491–2 two of his principal lieutenants in the north, Lord Clifford and Lord Dacre, were temporarily committed to the Fleet 'for riots'. The king took the case out of the hands of the council and settled it himself alone in Star Chamber by fining the two lords £20 each.[98] But it was not only in matters of grave concern involving his peers that Henry intervened personally. In July 1500 Bishop Fox as Privy Seal drew up the indentures of Sir Robert Darcy and Sir Richard Cholmley as border commissioners. Subsequently the king himself checked the terms 'and at the sight thereof' wrote Fox, 'he hath found divers and many things therein that he hath caused to be amended'. As a result Fox had to draw up new

---

[96] Ibid. 16073. None of the fees was illegal.

[97] Bayne and Dunham, *Select Cases*, pp. xxxii–xxxiv, 22.

[98] Ibid. xxxiv, 58. See also the council's involvement in and efforts to resolve the disputes between Cholmley and Hastings in Pickering, 1498–1503, and Archbishop Savage and the 5th earl of Northumberland in 1501–7 (ibid. cxlix–cxlxx; James, *Tudor Magnate*, pp. 18–19; Turton, *Forest of Pickering*, i. 136–8 and 172 ff.).

indentures 'after the form that he hath now caused they to be devised and made'. He sent the two parts of the new indentures down to the commissioners, with a request to return as soon as possible both their copies of the old contracts and their signed and sealed halves of the new indentures.[99] Perhaps nothing more graphically illustrates both the king's oversight of even the minutiae of government affecting the north-east and his close personal control, even over such trusted personal servants as Bishop Fox.

Of course the north-east was not alone. All England was subjected to the king's personal rule and increasingly heavy lordship, exercised through assiduous councillors and knights of the body such as Fox and Bray, Tunstall and Cholmley. But for the region the king's rule confirmed a major change in royal policy. In refusing to allow a local magnate to exercise quasi-regal power, Henry VII took over where Richard III left off; but by dispensing with even an intermediary council he initially went a stage further. Richard III delegated royal authority to his council in the north: Henry VII, as Fox's letter to Darcy amply demonstrates, kept it in his own hands. Both kings enjoyed the advantage of having succeeded to the estate of the greatest northern magnate, and thus having a substantial landed presence in the region denied to Edward IV and Henry VI. Henry VII additionally benefited from the fortuitous minority of the fifth earl of Northumberland. But ultimately it was Henry's clear-sighted determination to capitalize on his advantages which set him apart even from Richard III, and enabled him, in the face of several obstacles, to bring the north-east under his firm control.

There is no doubt that Henry VII was in command of the north-east by 1500. But the methods he adopted did not necessarily endear him to his subjects. The opportunity to gain more willing acceptance arose through his relations with Scotland. In the very first month of his reign the northern kingdom's potential for disruption by supporting rebels was brought home to him.[100] After 1491, with the development of the Warbeck

---

[99] Allen, *Letters of Richard Fox*, p. 19.

[100] See above, p. 369. On 13 June 1486 the English council determined: 'it is agreed rather wars to be taken with the King of Scots then to lose any foot of the king's possession' (Bayne and Dunham, *Select Cases*, p. 10).

conspiracy, Anglo-Scottish relations became a matter of press-ing concern. Between 1491 and 1495 Warbeck, claiming to be Richard of York, moved between Ireland, France, and the Low Countries, receiving the support of England's enemies and finding a steady stream of willing conspirators in England, most significantly Sir William Stanley, tried for treason on 30 and 31 January 1495. A first attempt at invasion at Deal in July 1495 ended in disaster; but Warbeck found refuge in Ireland, and from there made his way to Scotland, where he was received by James IV in November. The most dangerous stage of Warbeck's conspiracy now began.[101]

Henry VII had managed to preserve the peace with Scotland since 1485. War had been threatened in October 1485 and again in January 1488; but the truce renewed for three years in July 1486 had been maintained, although plans for a longer-term peace had foundered over the issue of Berwick. The truce had survived the death of James III at Sauchieburn on 11 June 1488.[102] But the government of James IV maintained contact with Henry's enemies, and the young king himself enthusiastic-ally seized the opportunity of an alliance with the would-be Richard IV at the end of 1495. In the fevered negotiations of 1496 Bishop Fox of Durham, on his king's behalf, sought to detach James by promise of a marriage treaty with the king's daughter Margaret.[103] But King James could not be shaken, and agreed, at a price, to back an invasion. The price was the surrender of Berwick and repayment of 50,000 marks within two years for the cost of Scottish troops.[104] On 15 September the attack was launched on North Durham. It was a dismal failure. The allies penetrated only four miles, burnt a few houses and peels, and then quickly withdrew on hearing of the approach of Ralph, Lord Neville, son of the earl of Westmorland, with 4,000 troops. Henry VII, Bishop Fox, and Surrey had been forewarned by their Scottish agent, Lord Bothwell, and were prepared. It was put

---

[101] For Warbeck see Gairdner, *Richard the Third*, pp. 263 ff.; Chrimes, *Henry VII*, pp. 88–9.

[102] Conway, *Relations*, pp. 8–22; Macdougall, *James III*, pp. 216–22.

[103] Conway, *Relations*, pp. 25 ff. For Fox's experience in Anglo-Scottish affairs since 1487 see Vergil, *Anglica Historia*, pp. 27–9.

[104] Pollard, *Henry VII*, i. 138–9. In his introduction (p. xxi) Pollard wrongly cites 100,000 marks as the agreed price.

about that Warbeck fled so ignominiously because he had no taste for war. It is as likely, however, that his advisers realized that they had grossly misjudged the reception that they would receive.[105]

Henry VII, at a council held at Sheen early in October, now determined on all-out war.[106] It is possible that Surrey organized a counter-raid early in the new year. A letter dated just 22 December to Sir Thomas Wortley ordered him to join the earl, who was planning to raid 'two moonlights next ensuing' (full moons?);[107] and Lord Dacre remembered in October 1513 how:

in the last war, when my lord of Norfolk [Surrey], my lord of Winchester [Fox] then lying at Alnwick, my lord Conyers [then Sir William], Sir William Bulmer and other captains then lying upon the east and middle marches, with garrisons, to the number of 1,000 soldiers and more, besides the garrisons of Berwick and Norham, it was as much as they might take upon their hand to make a raid into Teviotdale.[108]

Such a raid could only have occurred between Warbeck's attack in September 1496 and James IV's siege of Norham the following August.

In the mean time, between January and April 1497 Henry VII began to mobilize a powerful army, the vanguard of which numbered over 10,000 men, provided substantially by knights and esquires of his household. Although drawn from the length and breadth of England, eight retinues were contributed by Yorkshire men, including Sir William Conyers, who contracted to lead a contingent of 300.[109] These troops were making their way to muster at Berwick in June when the Cornish rebellion broke out and halted the expedition.[110] Thereupon James IV took the initiative, and launched an attack on Norham, which he besieged for fifteen days in August. The defence of Norham

---

[105] Ibid. 136–43; Vergil, *Anglica Historia*, p. 89.

[106] I. Arthurson, 'The King's Voyage into Scotland', in Williams, *England in the Fifteenth Century*, p. 5.

[107] Hunter, *South Yorkshire*, ii. 313.   [108] Raine, *North Durham*, p. vi.

[109] Arthurson, 'King's Voyage', pp. 9–10, 16, 22. The other Yorkshire captains were Sir Marmaduke Constable, Ralph Constable esq., Sir Thomas Darcy, Sir William Gascoigne, Sir Walter Griffith, Sir John Hastings, and Sir Henry Wentworth. One should probably add Sir Thomas Wortley to their number (see Hunter, *South Yorkshire*, ii. 313).

[110] Arthurson, 'The Rising of 1497', p. 313.

was conducted by Bishop Fox himself, before he was relieved by Surrey, who hurried up with reinforcements.[111] Having failed before Norham, and knowing that Warbeck was a spent force, King James was quick to respond to renewed moves for peace. A truce was agreed at Ayton for seven years, and negotiations were begun, conducted on the English side by Bishop Fox, for a permanent peace. The treaty was finally sealed on 24 January 1502, whereby a perpetual peace was established between the two kingdoms which was to include the castle and town of Berwick, against which the king of Scotland would never make war again. In effect Berwick was ceded to England. The new alliance was sealed by the marriage between James IV and Margaret Tudor, which held the prospect of further hopes in England for the Stuarts.[112] Thus, it was hoped, would two centuries of Anglo-Scottish war come to an end.

Perkin Warbeck and James IV could hardly have done Henry VII a better service in the north-east. Warbeck, or more probably his advisers, such as Sir George Neville and Roland Robinson, had assured James IV that the north of England would rise on Warbeck's behalf; James had apparently been convinced, and for this reason had considered Warbeck worth backing; even Henry VII, according to Polydore Vergil, was greatly afraid that the nobility of the north would go over to him.[113] But Warbeck misjudged the north. He was tarred with the brush of being pro-Scottish. In particular, by agreeing to cede Berwick as the price for Scottish aid Warbeck had forfeited any sympathy his cause might have enjoyed. North-easterners did not take kindly to pretenders who were prepared to bargain away their principal border fortress. In fact Henry VII had had nothing to fear. The northern nobility rallied to his cause: Ralph, Lord Neville dispersed Warbeck's raid in 1496; Sir William Conyers, Sir William Bulmer, and other captains garrisoned the border in the following months. Norham was relieved in August 1497 by Surrey and other 'nobles of the area' who 'each according to his resources collected a small or large body of men'.[114] The reverse

[111] Vergil, *Anglica Historia*, pp. 99–101; Pollard, *Henry VII*, iii. 157, 159; Raine, *North Durham*, pp. v–vi; Hutchinson, *Durham*, i. 459.
[112] *CDRS* iv. 336–7; Pollard, *Henry VII*, iii, 37–42, 60–75; Chrimes, *Henry VII*, p. 284.   [113] Vergil, *Anglica Historia*, pp. 87–91, 104.
[114] Ibid. 99; Raine, *North Durham*, p. vi.

of Henry VII's reported fears was the case: the threat from Scotland in the cause of Perkin Warbeck united north-easterners and king as they never had been before against the common enemy. As Bothwell perceptively pointed out to Henry VII, with northern Englishmen in mind (and perhaps remembering the deeds of Richard of Gloucester):

Sir, king Edward had never fully the perfect love of his people until he had war of Scotland; and he made so good diligence and provision therein, that to this hour he is loved; and your Grace may as well, and have as good a time as he had.[115]

In September 1496, on the day that Warbeck with Scottish assistance invaded North Durham, the cause of the white rose in north-eastern England was finally lost. Thereafter Henry VII was assured of as good a time as Richard III.

---

[115] Pollard, *Henry VII*, i. 141.

Conclusion

By no stretch of the imagination was north-eastern England a remote, poor and backward corner of the land in the second half of the fifteenth century. Only the far north, the border dales of Northumberland, which formed a distinctly different society created by the experience of endemic warfare, could possibly be described in these terms. Down from the immediate vicinity of the Scottish border it was, as Piccolomini observed 'a familiar world and a habitable country'. The north-east was not, as has been alleged, an extended frontier zone. The frontier and its marches were of only limited geographical extent. Yet the presence of the Scots to the north, the continuing state of war, and the threat of invasion helped weld the north-east into a region with a common identity. This identity was strengthened by the power of the great magnates who held estates in all three counties, and who customarily led the region in war against the common enemy.

Away from the specialized pastoral country of the Pennines, the north-east shared the mixed arable farming economy which characterized all lowland England in the later Middle Ages. Open-field farming was practised throughout the region as far north as the coastal plain of Northumberland. For most people the way of life was the same as elsewhere in England. The daily lives of the inhabitants of the Tees valley were barely distinguishable from the lives of those who lived along the Warwickshire Avon. In the later fifteenth century they enjoyed, like their southern equivalents, a relatively high standard of living. The gentry of the north-east were numerous and prosperous: their customs and mores the same as those of their cousins from Suffolk or Sussex. All belonged to one lesser landed nobility. Many were as familiar with London and Westminster as they were with York or Newcastle. Equally at home in the courts of Durham, the Court of Common Pleas in Westminster Hall, or the south-east circuit, a busy lawyer like Richard Pigot could attest that the north-east was not cut off

from the rest of the kingdom. Although political divisions with
a regional dimension did appear, especially in the 1480s, and
royal propaganda did its best to magnify these when it suited,
England in the later fifteenth century was not two nations,
north and south, standing in mutual incomprehension and
hostility.

Yet there were certain characteristics of northern society,
especially northern landed society, which would suggest that
there were differences in values and attitudes, as well as contrasts in circumstances and experience, which left the northern
outlook more conservative and more traditional at the close of
the century. These were matters of degree, not of kind. Thus
chivalric enthusiasm and the love of hunting were common to
lords and landed gentry throughout the realm. But one has a
sense that in the north they retained their attraction longer and
for a greater number than in the cosmopolitan south, more
readily influenced by new fashions from abroad. Critics of the
wasteful idleness of traditional pursuits were thinner and fewer
on the ground north of the Humber. Likewise traditional forms
of piety and Christian worship, most notably in the support of
chantries and prayers for the dead, retained their popularity well
into the next century. Educational provision increased in the
later part of the fifteenth century; but in traditional forms and to
serve traditional ends. In Durham city the old schooling remained strong, especially musical education, until challenged
during the Reformation.[1] And, as Professor Dobson has suggested, in both the cathedral cities of the region there was
something of an ecclesiastical revival at the end of the century.[2]
The signs were already visible by 1500 that the north-east,
although not without its Protestants in the next decades, was of
a character more likely than East Anglia or the home counties to
resist the dismantling of the established religious order.

Culturally, therefore, the north-east was probably more conservative than southern England, especially the south-east.
Deep-rooted and far-reaching economic changes were also leaving the region poorer and more dependent on the flourish-

---

[1] J. J. Vickerstaff, 'Schools and Schooling in County Durham, 1400–1640',
(unpublished CNAA M.Phil. thesis, Teesside Polytechnic, 1988), 43–51, 94–5,
100–7, 224–45.   [2] Dobson, 'Cathedral Chapters', pp. 42–3.

ing metropolitan region by the end of the century. It was not poverty or backwardness as such, but economic decline which differentiated the north in the later fifteenth century. The implications of the economic circumstances of the north-east for the political history of both the region and the whole realm should not be overlooked. The conventional view today is that economic circumstances in the mid-fifteenth century had little effect on politics, and in particular little to do with the outbreak of civil war in the 1450s. There are, however, two respects in which one might consider that economic developments may have influenced the behaviour of the political élites of north-eastern England.

The agrarian crisis of 1438–40 led to a 10 to 15 per cent contraction in agricultural output and in rents collected by landlords. Such a reduction was not a loss to be taken lightly by peers and gentlemen who were already conscious of a long decline in their ancestral revenues. In particular men such as Richard Neville, earl of Salisbury and Henry Percy, earl of Northumberland, who desired and were expected to maintain a lavish and flamboyant life-style, would surely not easily have brushed aside a reduction such as this in their income. Indeed, on the contrary, it is likely to have intensified their determination to win and retain favour at court, and to extend, or at least preserve, their landed possessions. Moreover, the very same pressures which affected them also bore on their clients, dependants, retainers, and well-wishers, and is likely therefore to have sharpened the demands on their good lordship. Economic recession, in short, exacerbated political tensions. Rivalry for office and favour at court, sharpened by dispute over property, is precisely what drove Neville and Percy into bitter and bloody feud in the 1450s. One would not wish to suggest that agrarian recession after 1440 alone caused the great Neville –Percy feud; but it was a contributory factor to the conflict for local dominance that consumed the north-east in the last decade of Lancastrian England.

Economic conditions twenty years later may also have had a bearing on the career of Richard III. The special relationship between Richard III, both as duke of Gloucester and as king, and the city of York needs no rehearsing. The citizens looked to him to assist them in their economic plight: not only to place his influence and reputation behind their campaign to clear the navigable waterways of Yorkshire of illegal obstruction, but also to secure a reduction in their fee-farm. High hopes may have been held of the duke in north-west Yorkshire, too, where the local cloth-manufacturing industry was in decline. The enthusiastic support given to Richard III by many sections of north-eastern society may have been reinforced by an awareness that in recent years the north-east had stagnated, while London and many other southern districts seemed to be on the road to recovery. Here was a potential source of resentment between north and south, and a basis for expectation that a king who knew the problems of the region would seek to tackle them. Indeed this is precisely what the city council of York claimed in a petition to the victorious Henry VII on 30 November 1485. Pleading the extreme poverty of the city since 1471, 'which premises of poverty was too evidently known to be true unto the Duke of Gloucester in his days being continuously among your subjects', the council asserted that the duke had recognized the danger not only that York might cease to be a great city, 'but as well the north parts of this your Realm should be greatly dishonoured and hurt'.[3] The very tactlessness of this argument, advanced to persuade the new king to reduce the city's fee-farm, adds to its credibility. Thus there would appear to have been an element of justifiable self-interest behind the local support given to Richard of Gloucester, and good reason for popular support for his cause in the years immediately following his fall.

The appeal of Richard III as a possible saviour of the north depended on the power and influence he wielded as a good lord, both before and after he became king. The economic plight of north-eastern England in the later fifteenth century became politically of significance precisely because of the power concentrated into the hands of its magnates: the Nevilles of Middleham, succeeded by Richard of Gloucester, and the Percies. There were several reasons for the might of the north-eastern magnates. First and foremost was the territorial weakness of the Crown. While the two families of Neville and Percy enjoyed the possession of great estates, the Crown held comparatively little land north of the Ouse until Richard III became king in 1483.

[3] YCR i. 136.

Territorial weakness had a direct bearing on the Crown's capacity to exert immediate and local influence in the region. Secondly, its authority was further diminished by the existence of substantial liberties where the king's writ did not run. Territorial weakness was compounded by constitutional limitation. Instead, in their liberties, the greater subjects of the Crown were free to exercise quasi-regal authority. This was as true of Richmondshire, where the steward of the honour acted as sheriff, as of Durham or Hexham, where a clerical lord held a more extensive franchise. Mesne lordship too retained a social as well as a financial and legal significance in the region which it had apparently lost further south. To this extent, to say that the north-east remained more feudal is strictly accurate.

Thirdly, as heads of old feudal honours and baronies, the magnates, not the Crown, tended to be the focus of local loyalties. Neville and Percy were the leaders of powerful affinities which drew upon this older sense of identity and unity, and which, partly as a result, enjoyed a continuity and solidarity which was possibly lacking in other magnate connections elsewhere in the kingdom. The good lordship exercised by Neville and Percy, acting as a stabilizing bond within the districts each dominated, further enhanced the power each could wield. Fourthly, because the leading knightly families who by birth and status filled the local offices of the Crown were at one and the same time attached to one or other of the great lords by land, office, and tradition, royal administration in the region tended to be conducted through the mediation or according to the interests of the magnates. Fifthly, this situation was institutionalized through the delegation of senior offices, such as master foresterships and stewardships of the duchy of Lancaster, to the magnates themselves. Above all the military authority of the Crown in the region was delegated to the magnates as wardens of the marches. While it remains doubtful whether the wardenship was a source of financial profit, there can be little question that the office was sought, if only for the power and prestige it conferred. The wardens were given partial exemption from the laws controlling retaining; and the requirement to guard the borders allowed them greater scope to expand their retinues and military strength. War itself gave them opportunity to demonstrate their prowess and further enhance their

standing in quarters which valued martial skills. War with
Scotland was an ever-present possibility. For this reason the
north-east remained a society prepared and ready for war.
Leadership fell on the shoulders of the magnates, who thus had
at their disposal an awesome military potential. For good cause
are they known as the princes of the north.

'The north knows no prince but a Percy', elaborated by R. R.
Reid as 'the north of Trent in which men knew no prince but a
Percy and a Neville',[4] is one of the most overworked misquota-
tions in English history. What Lord Hunsdon actually reported
to the Privy Council in December 1569 (when Berwick was
threatened by an attack from the routed northern earls with
Scottish help), was:

If any foreign power should attempt it he knows few in Northumberland he would suffer to enter [Berwick] to help him, for throughout
Northumberland they know no other prince but a Percy.[5]

It was the county of Northumberland in 1569 that knew no
prince but a Percy. The same was undoubtedly the case between
1416 and 1461 and between 1470 and 1489. When Hardyng
earlier wrote of the Percies 'they have the hearts of the people by
north and ever had'[6] he probably had the far north-east in mind
too. Unrivalled Percy power never extended south of the Tyne.
In the North Riding the Nevilles dominated: in Richmondshire
alone, an area as large as Northumberland, they were as great
princes as the Percies in the far north. In the county palatine of
Durham, too, during the middle decades of the fifteenth century, the Nevilles of Middleham and Richard of Gloucester were
often dominant (1437–57, 1462–4, 1476–85). In truth, between
1450 and 1483, if any single family can be said to have been the
princes of the north it was the Nevilles of Middleham, and after
them their heir, Richard III.[7]

---

[4] Reid, *Council in the North*, p. 19. Cf. E. Miller, *War in the North: the
Anglo-Scottish Wars of the Middle Ages* (Hull, 1960), 16, '. . . no prince but a
Percy or a Neville'; Storey, 'North of England', p. 132, '. . . no king but a Percy,
Neville or Dacre'.
[5] *Calendar of State Papers Foreign, 1569–71*, ed. A. J. Crosby (1874), No. 568,
159.　　[6] Hardyng, *Chronicle*, p. 380.
[7] This point was also made by M. Weiss, 'A Power in the North?', pp. 503–4.
Unfortunately in his analysis Weiss failed to distinguish between the two
branches of Neville.

Politically the north-east in the fifteenth century was dominated by its magnates, especially the Nevilles of Middleham. In
mid-fifteenth century the Crown was undermighty. It was
undermighty in the region not because of the personal lack of
fitness of the king, but because of the weakness of the office and
the inadequacy of its local recources.[8] The situation may have
been different in other parts of the realm. But because of the
innate might of its magnates the north-east possessed a potential to disrupt the whole of the kingdom. The concentration of
power into their hands, so much greater than elsewhere in the
kingdom, gave the region a political importance out of all
proportion to its distance from Westminster or its wealth. When
they were divided and in conflict, between 1452 and 1471, the
magnates helped drag the kingdom into civil war; when they
were united in one powerful block, between 1474 and 1485, they
were able, briefly, to dominate the kingdom.

Yet by 1500 this political world had been transformed. The
earls of Salisbury and Warwick were overmighty subjects; by
1500 the independent power of the Nevilles was broken. The
estates of the Middleham line, which by strict law of descent
should have passed to the person of Richard Neville, Lord
Latimer, had been annexed to the Crown in 1483, and were
never surrendered; the senior line of the earls of Westmorland
was never allowed even to consider a restoration. The earls of
Northumberland, who survived with their landed inheritance
intact, were denied by successive kings the chance to recover
the authority fleetingly exercised at the beginning of Henry IV's
reign. The critical turning point for realm and region alike was
the usurpation of the throne by Richard III. As duke of Gloucester, Richard had built up a regional hegemony more powerful
than that enjoyed even by Warwick the Kingmaker. At the
beginning of 1483 he had a hereditary palatinate created for him,
and, had events moved otherwise, it is not inconceivable that a
Burgundian-style dismemberment of the kingdom might have
taken place. The logic of the policy of Edward IV, had he lived,

---

[8] See McFarlane, 'Wars of the Roses', pp. 95–6; 'only an undermighty king
had anything to fear from an overmighty subject; and if he were undermighty his
personal lack of fitness was the cause, not the weakness of his office and its
resources'.

was to allow the creation of a quasi-independent border duchy under the line of the dukes of Gloucester. But the reverse happened. Instead of the realm's integrity and unity being undermined, Richard III's seizure of the throne and his unifying of all his landed inheritance with the Crown ensured that the integrity of the kingdom was strengthened. At a stroke, in 1483, Richard III reversed the trend of recent decades. The way was then open for the Crown to reassert its failing authority over the region.

It was Richard III, not Henry VII, who began this process. With his personal estate and powerful affinity in the region he was able to retain personal control. His chosen vehicle, a council seated in the north and staffed by his household servants, was a logical continuation of his existing authority in the north-east. Under Richard III the north was to be ruled by his councillors and the knights and esquires of his body. No magnate was to be allowed to challenge royal authority. Henry VII developed what Richard III initiated, albeit on a different basis and by different means. While it took time for Henry to win the confidence of the northern political élite, he was able always to exploit to his advantage his acquired position as a powerful landowner in the north. Like Richard III he relied on his councillors and house-hold men; the difference was that they were answerable to his council at Westminster or in attendance, and not to a specially established council in the north. Because he had no existing roots in the region Henry VII had no choice. But his subjection of the region to his direct personal control, without even the intermediary and mitigating role of a northern council, took the exercise of royal authority in the north-east one step further. The magnates, the earls of Northumberland and Westmorland, who had hoped for so much from the promotion of Richard of Gloucester to the throne, found under Henry VII that what had been a cold wind turned to a blizzard. From 1483 the Crown recovered its might in the north: this was not only because of the determination and capacity of the individual monarchs to rule, it was also because the Crown now had the resources and the material strength to overawe all its northern subjects, including the earls of Northumberland and Westmorland.

The balance of power between Crown and mighty subject in the north-east was not necessarily shifted permanently in the reigns of Richard III and Henry VII. The potential still existed for later monarchs to revert to earlier policies. In the reign of Edward VI the ambitious John Dudley, duke of Northumberland sought to make himself an old-style northern magnate. And under Queen Mary, who promoted the staunchly loyal and catholic earls of Northumberland and Westmorland, it might have appeared that the more traditional approach was returning. But in practice the steps taken by Richard III and Henry VII pointed to the future. The principle enunciated by Edmund Dudley in his *Tree of Commonwealth* was the principle finally to be enforced by Queen Elizabeth:

Though it be tolerable for the nobles to desire it [office] when they are meet therefor, yet it is more laudable to have it of the free disposition of their sovereign: but in all cases let them not presume to take it of their own authority, for then it will surely choke them.[9]

One of the principal achievements of the Tudors, if not the chief, was to tame the north-east. It is arguable that this was the critical difference between Tudor success and Yorkist failure. Yet it was not so much Yorkist failure as Edward IV's failure. It was he who in 1471 made the momentous decision to promote his brother Richard in the north when the power of the Nevilles lay shattered. Whether he encouraged Gloucester to take so much power, or whether he merely acquiesced, is of little moment; his was the responsibility. Gloucester as Richard III did not repeat his brother's mistake. Thus in this case the difference lies not between dynasties, but between individual kings. In the north-east Henry VII built on foundations laid, not by the Yorkists in general, but by Richard III in person. The transformation from the old to the new political world began in 1483: perhaps, to adapt Gairdner, it would be true to say that as far as the political history of north-eastern England was concerned the Middle Ages passed away with Edward IV.

[9] E. Dudley, *The Tree of Commonwealth*, ed. D. M. Brodie (1948), p. 57.

Bibliography

PRINTED SOURCES

ATTHILL, W., *Documents of the Collegiate Church of Middleham*, Camden, os xxxviii (1847).

BACON, FRANCIS, *The History of the Reign of King Henry the Seventh*, ed. J. Spedding *et al.*, *Works*, vii (1858).

BENTLEY, S., *Excerpta Historica* (1831).

Bishop Percy's Folio Manuscript, ed. J. W. Hales and F. J. Furnivall, iii (1868).

Bolton Priory Rentals and Ministers' Accounts, 1473–1539, ed. I. Kershaw, YAS, RS, 132 (1970 for 1969).

The Book of Margery Kempe, EETS os ccxii (1940).

British Library Harleian Manuscript 433, ed. R. E. Horrox and P. W. Hammond, 4 vols. (1979–83).

Calendar of Close Rolls 1435–1509 (1937–63).

Calendar of Documents Relating to Scotland preserved in the Public Record Office, ed. J. Bain, 4 vols. (Edinburgh, 1881–4).

Calendar of Fine Rolls, 1422–1509 (1935–62).

Calendars of Inquisitions Miscellaneous (Chancery) preserved in the Public Record Office, 7 vols. (1916–68).

Calendar of Inquisitions Post Mortem, Henry VII (1898–1955).

Calendar of Patent Rolls, 1436–1509 (1907–63).

Calendar of State Papers Foreign, 1509–71, ed. A. J. Crosby (1874).

Calendar of State Papers, Milan, ed. A. B. Hinds, i (1902).

Calendar of State Papers, Venice, ed. R. Brown (1864).

Camden's Britannia, 1695 (Newton Abbot, 1971).

Cartularium Abbathiae de Whitby, ii, ed. J. C. Atkinson, SS, lxxii (1879).

The Chronicle of John Hardyng, ed. H. Ellis (1802).

'The Chronicle of the Rebellion in Lincolnshire, 1470', ed. J. G. Nichols, in *Camden Miscellany*, i, Camden, os xxxix (1847).

A Collection of Ordinances and Regulations for the Government of the Royal Household (Society of Antiquaries, London, 1970).

The Coronation of Richard III, ed. A. F. Sutton and P. W. Hammond (Gloucester, 1983).

The Crowland Chronicle Continuations, 1459–1486, eds. N. Pronay and J. Cox (Gloucester, 1986).

The Customs Accounts of Hull, 1453–1490, ed. W. R. Childs, YAJ, RS, 144 (1986 for 1984).

DE FONBLANQUE, E. B., *Annals of the House of Percy*, i (1887).

Depositions and Other Ecclesiastical Proceedings from the Courts of Durham, ed. J. Raine, SS, xxi (1845).

The Duchy of Lancaster Estates in Derbyshire, 1485–1549, ed. I. S. W. Blanchard, Derbys. Arch. Soc., RS, iii (1971).

DUDLEY, E., *The Tree of Commonwealth*, ed. D. M. Brodie (1948).

DUGDALE, W., *Monasticon Anglicanon*, vol. iii, pt. 2 (1673).

Early English Meals and Manners, ed. F. J. Furnivall, EETS, xxxii (1814).

An English Chronicle of the Reigns of Richard II, Henry IV, Henry V and Henry VI, ed. J. S. Davies, Camden, os lxiv (1856).

The Fabric Rolls of York Minster, ed. James Raine, SS, xxv (1859 for 1858).

FABYAN, R., *New Chronicles of England and of France*, ed. H. Ellis (1811).

Feudal Aids, vi, *Yorkshire* (London, 1906).

Foedarium Prioratus Dunelmensis, ed. W. Greenwell, SS, lviii (1871).

The Fountains Abbey Lease Book, ed. D. J. H. Michelmore, YAS, RS, 140 (1981).

The Fountains Abbey Rental, 1495–6, ed. D. J. H. Michelmore (privately printed, Leeds, 1974).

GALE, R., *Registrum Honoris de Richmond* (1722).

GASQUET, E. A., *Collectanea Anglo-Premonstratensia*, Camden, 3rd ser., vi, i (1904).

The Great Chronicle of London, ed. A. H. Thomas and I. D. Thornley (1938).

HALL, E., *Union of the Houses of Lancaster and York* (1809).

HALLIWELL, J. O., *Letters of the Kings of England* (1848).

Halmota Prioratus Dunelmensis, AD 1296–1384, ed. W. H. Longstaffe and J. Booth, SS, lxxxii (1889).

HANHAM, A., *The Cely Letters, 1472–1488* (Oxford, 1975).

Historiae Dunelmensis Scriptores Tres, ed. J. Raine, SS, ix (1839).

The Historical Collections of a Citizen of London, ed. J. Gairdner, Camden, NS xvii (1876).

Historie of the Arrivall of King Edward IV, ed. J. Bruce, Camden, os i (1838).

HMC, *Report on MSS of Beverley* (1900).

HOLINSHED, R., *Chronicles of England, Scotland and Ireland*, iii (1808).

The Honor and Forest of Pickering, i, ed. R. B. Turton, North Riding Record Series, NS 1 (1894).

HORROX, R. E., 'Financial Memoranda of the Reign of Edward V', in *Camden Miscellany*, xxix, Camden, 4th ser., xxxiv (1987).

'John Benet's Chronicle', ed. G. L. and M. A. Harriss, in *Camden Miscellany*, xxiv, Camden, 4th ser., ix (1972).

LEADHAM, I. S., 'The Inquisition of 1517', *TRHS* NS 6 (1892).

LELAND, J., *Collectanea*, ed. T. Hearne (1774).

—— *The Itinerary of John Leland, in or about 1535–1543, Parts I to III*, ed. L. Toulmin Smith (London, 1907).

LESLEY, J., *History of Scotland* (Bannatyne Club, Edinburgh, 1830).

Letters and Papers, Henry VIII, ed. D. S. Brewer, vol. i, pt. 2 (1920).

The Letters of Richard Fox, 1486–1527, ed. P. S. and H. M. Allen (Oxford, 1929).

The Master of Game, ed. W. A. and F. Baillie-Grohman (1909).

MANCINI, D., *The Usurpation of Richard III*, ed. C. A. J. Armstrong, 2nd edn. (Oxford, 1969).

The Manor and Borough of Leeds, 1425–1662, ed. J. W. Kirby, Publications of the Thoresby Society, lvii (1983 for 1981).

Materials for a History of the Reign of Henry VII, ed. W. Campbell, 2 vols., RS (1873–7).

McCALL, H. B., *The Family of Wandesforde of Kirklington and Castlecomer* (1904).

Memoirs of Ambrose Barnes, ed. W. D. Longstaffe, SS, i (1867 for 1866).

Memoirs of a Renaissance Pope: The Commentaries of Pius II, ed. L. C. Gabel (1960).

Memorials of the Abbey of St. Mary of Fountains, ii, ed. J. R. Walbran, SS, lxvii (1878).

Memorials of the Abbey of St. Mary of Fountains, iii, ed. J. T. Fowler, SS, cxxx (1918).

North Country Wills, ed. J. W. Clay, SS, cxvi (1908).

Northern Petitions, ed. C. M. Fraser, SS, cxciv (1982 for 1981).

The Official Correspondence of Thomas Bekynton, ed. G. Williams, ii (1872).

Original Letters Illustrative of English History, ed. H. Ellis, 1st ser., 3 vols. (1823); 2nd ser., 4 vols. (1827); 3rd ser., 4 vols. (1846).

Paston Letters, 1422–1509, ed. J. Gairdner (1904).

Paston Letters and Papers of the Fifteenth Century, ed. N. Davis, 2 vols. (Oxford, 1971–6).

Percy Bailiff's Rolls of the Fifteenth Century, ed. J. C. Hodgson, SS, cxxxiv (1921).

PERCY, T., *The Northumberland Household Book* (1777).

Placita de Quo Warranto (1818).

Plumpton Correspondence, ed. T. Stapleton, Camden, os iv (1839).

POLLARD, A. F., *The Reign of Henry VII from Contemporary Sources*, 3 vols. (1913).

The Priory of Hexham, i, ed. J. Raine, SS, xliv (1864).

The Priory of Hexham, ii, ed. J. Raine, SS, xlvi (1865).

Proceedings and Ordinances of the Privy Council, ed. N. H. Nicolas, 7 vols. (Record Commission, 1834–7).

The Prologues and Epilogues of William Caxton, ed. W. J. B. Crotch, EETS, os clxxvi (1928).

PUTNAM, B., *Proceedings before the Justices of the Peace in the Fourteenth and Fifteenth Centuries* (1938).

Records of Antony Bec, ed. C. M. Fraser, SS, clxii (1953 for 1947).

The Register of the Guild of Corpus Christi in the City of York, ed. R. H. Scaife, SS, lvii (1872).

The Register of Richard Fox, Lord Bishop of Durham, 1494–1501, ed. M. P. Howden, SS, xlvii (1932).

The Register of Thomas Rotherham, Archbishop of York, 1480–1500, i, ed. E. E. Barker, Canterbury and York Society, lxix (1976).

The Register of Thomas Langley, Bishop of Durham, 1406–37, ed. R. L. Storey, iv, SS, cxx (1961).

The Reign of Henry VII from Contemporary Sources, ed. A. F. Pollard, 3 vols. (1913).

A Relation . . . of the Island of England, ed. L. A. Sneyd, Camden, os xxxvii (1847).

Reports of the Deputy Keeper of Public Records, xliv (1883).

Rotuli Parliamentorum, ed. J. Strachey, 6 vols. (1767–77).

Rotuli Scotiae, 2 vols., (Record Commission, 1814–19).

RYMER, T., *Foedera, Conventiones, Litterae, et Cuiuscunque Generis Acta Publica*, 20 vols. (1704–35).

SALTER, H. E., *Registrum Annalium Collegii Mertonensis*, Oxford Historical Society, 76 (1921).

Sanctuarium Dunelmense et Sanctuarium Beverlacense, ed. J. Raine, SS, v (1837).

Select Cases in the Council of Henry VII, ed. C. G. Bayne and W. H. Dunham, Selden Society, lxxv (1959).

SMITH, THOMAS, *De Republica Anglorum* (Menston, 1970).

Statutes of the Realm, ed. A. Luders, 11 vols., Record Commission (1810–28).

'The Statutes . . . for the College of Middleham', ed. J. Raine, *Archaeological Journal*, 14 (1857).

St. Ingulph's Chronicles, ed. H. T. Riley, (1854).

STEELE, R., *Tudor and Stuart Proclamations*, i (Oxford, 1910).

Testamenta Eboracensia, ed. J. Raine, Parts 2–5, SS, xxx, xlv, liii, lxxxix (1855, 1865, 1869, 1884).

Testamenta Vetusta, ed. N. H. Nicolas, i (1826).

THOMPSON, A. H., 'The Register of the Archdeacons of Richmond, 1422–77', Part 1, *YAJ* 30 (1931); Part 2, *YAJ* 32 (1936).

Three Books of Polydore Vergil's English History, ed. H. Ellis, Camden, os xxix (1844).

Three Fifteenth Century Chronicles, ed. J. Gairdner, Camden, NS xxviii (1880).

VERGIL, POLYDORE, *The Anglica Historia of Polydore Vergil*, ed. D. Hay, Camden, 3rd ser., lxxiv (1950).

'Verses on the Battle of Towton', *Archaeologia*, 29 (1842).

A Visitation of the North of England ca 1490, ed. C. H. Hunter Blair, SS, cxliv (1930).

A Volume of English Miscellanies, ed. J. Raine, SS, lxxxv (1890 for 1888).

WARKWORTH, J., *A Chronicle of the First Thirteen Years of the Reign of King Edward the Fourth*, ed. J. O. Halliwell, Camden, os x (1839).

The Wars of the English in France, ed. J. Stevenson, vol. ii, pt. 2, RS, 22 (1864).

Wills and Inventories Illustrative of the History, Manners, Language etc. of the Northern Counties of England, ed. J. Raine, SS, ii (1835).

WORCESTER, W., *Itineraries*, ed. J. H. Harvey (Oxford, 1969).

York City Chamberlains' Account Rolls, 1396–1500, ed. R. B. Dobson, SS, cxcii (1980).

York Civic Records, ed. A. Raine, i and ii (YAS, RS, xcviii and ciii (1939 and 1941).

Yorkshire Chantry Surveys, ed. W. Page, SS, xli (1894).

Yorkshire Deeds, ed. W. Brown, C. T. Clay, i–vi, YAS, RS, xxxix, l, lxiii, lxv, lxix, lxxvi (1909, 1914, 1922, 1924, 1926, 1930).

Yorkshire Star Chamber Proceedings, ed. W. Brown, YAS, RS, xli (1909 for 1908).

PRINTED, SECONDARY WORKS

ARMSTRONG, C. A. J., 'The Piety of Cecily, Duchess of York', in D. Woodruff (ed.), *For Hilaire Belloc* (1942).

—— 'Politics and the Battle of St Albans, 1455', *BIHR* 33 (1960).

ARNOLD, C., 'The Commission of the Peace for the West Riding of Yorkshire, 1437–1509', in A. J. Pollard (ed.), *Property and Politics: Essays in Late Medieval English History* (Gloucester, 1984).

ARTHURSON, I., 'A Question of Loyalty', *The Ricardian*, vii, no. 97 (1987).

—— 'The Rising of 1497', in J. T. Rosenthal and C. F. Richmond (eds.), *People, Politics and Community in the Later Middle Ages* (Gloucester, 1987).

—— 'The King's Voyage into Scotland', in D. Williams (ed.), *England in the Fifteenth Century* (Woodbridge, 1987).

ATTREED, L. C., 'The King's Interest: York's Fee Farm and the Central Government, 1482–92', *NH* 17 (1981).

—— 'An Indenture between Richard, Duke of Gloucester and the Scrope Family of Masham and Upsall', *Speculum*, 58 (1983).

AUSTIN, D., 'Low Throston II. Excavations of a Deserted Medieval Hamlet, 1972', *Transactions of the Archaeological and Architectural Society of Durham and Northumberland*, NS, 4 (1978).

BARTLETT, J. M., 'The Expansion and Decline of York in the Later Middle Ages', *Econ. HR* 2nd ser., 12 (1958).

BATESON, E., *A History of Northumberland, vol. i: The parish of Bamburgh* (1893).

—— 'Notes on a journey from Oxford to Embleton in 1464', *Arch. Ael.*, NS, 16 (1894).

—— *A History of Northumberland, vol. ii: The parish of Embleton etc.* (1895).

BEAN, J. M. W., *The Estates of the Percy Family, 1416–1537* (Oxford, 1958).

BECKINGSALE, B. W., 'The Character of the Tudor North, *NH* 4 (1969).

BELLAMY, J. G., *Criminal Law and Society in Later Medieval and Tudor England* (Gloucester, 1984).

BENNETT, M., *Lambert Simnel and the Battle of Stoke* (Gloucester, 1987).

BENSON, R. and HATCHER, H., *Old and New Sarum* (Salisbury, 1843).

BERESFORD, M. W., 'The Lost Villages of Yorkshire, Part IV', *YAJ* 38 (1954).

—— and HURST, J. G., *Deserted Medieval Villages* (Cambridge, 1971).

BIRRELL, J. R., 'The Forest Economy of the Honour of Tutbury in the Fourteenth and Fifteenth Centuries', *University of Birmingham Historical Journal*, 8 (1962).

BLAKE, J. B., 'The Medieval Coal Trade of North-East England: Some Fourteenth Century Evidence', *NH* 2 (1967).

BLANCHARD, I. S. W., 'Population Change, Enclosure and the Early Tudor Economy', *Econ. HR* 2nd ser., 23 (1970).

—— 'Seigneurial Entrepreneurship and the Bishops of Durham and the Weardale Lead Industry, 1406–1529', *Business History*, 15 (1973).

—— 'Lead Smelting in Medieval England and Wales', in D. W. Crossley (ed.), *Medieval Industry*, CBA Research Report, xl (1981).

BOLTON, J. L., *The Medieval English Economy, 1150–1500* (1980).

BOSSY, J., *Christianity in the West, 1400–1700* (Oxford, 1985).

Brentano, R., *York Metropolitan Jurisdiction and Papal Judges Delegate, 1278–96* (Berkeley, 1959).

Brooks, F. W., *The Council of the North* (Historical Association, 1966).

Brown, W., *Ingleby Arncliffe and its Owners* (Leeds, 1901).

Buck, G., *The History of King Richard III (1619)*, ed. N. A. Kincaid (Gloucester, 1979).

Burgess, C., 'A Fond Thing Vainly Invented', in S. M. Wright (ed.), *Parish, Church and People: Local Studies in Lay Religion, 1350–1750* (1988).

Butcher, A. F., 'Rent, Population and Economic Change in Late Medieval Newcastle', *NH* 14 (1978).

Cantor, L. M., 'Forests, Chases, Parks and Warrens', in idem (ed.), *The English Medieval Landscape* (1982).

—— and Hattersley, J., 'The Medieval Parks of England', *Geography*, 64 (1979).

Carpenter, C., 'Law, Justice and Landowners in Late-Medieval England', *Law and History Review*, 1 (1983).

—— 'The Duke of Clarence and the Midlands: A Study in the Interplay of Local and National Politics', *Midland History*, 11 (1986).

—— 'The Fifteenth-Century English Gentry and their Estates', in M. Jones (ed.), *Gentry and Lesser Nobility in Later Medieval Europe* (Gloucester, 1986).

—— 'The Religion of the Gentry in Fifteenth-Century England', in D. Williams (ed.), *England in the Fifteenth Century* (Woodbridge, 1987).

Chadwick, H., 'The Arm of St Ninian', *Transactions of the Dumfriesshire and Galloway Natural History and Antiquarian Society*, 3rd ser., 23 (1946).

Chippindale, W. H., 'The Tunstalls of Thurland Castle', *Transactions of the Cumberland and Westmorland Antiquarian and Archaeological Society*, ns, 28 (1928).

Chrimes, S. B., *Henry VII* (1972).

Clanchy, M., 'The Franchise of Return of Writ', *TRHS* 5th ser. 17 (1967).

Clay, J. W., *The Extinct and Dormant Peerage of the Northern Counties of England* (1913).

Cokayne, G. E., *The Complete Peerage of England, Scotland, Ireland, Great Britain and the United Kingdom*, ed. Gibbs *et al.*, 12 vols. (1910–59).

Colper, H. S., 'Millom Castle and the Huddlestons', *Transactions of the Cumberland and Westmorland Antiquarian and Archaeological Society*, ns, 24 (1924).

Condon, M. M., 'Ruling Élites in the Reign of Henry VII', in Charles

Ross (ed.), *Patronage, Pedigree and Power in Later Medieval England* (Gloucester, 1979).

CONWAY, A., *Henry VII's Relations with Scotland and Ireland, 1485–1498* (Cambridge, 1932).

COOPER, J. P., 'The Counting of Manors', in G. E. Aylmer and J. S. Morrill (eds.), *Land, Men and Beliefs* (1983).

—— 'Ideas of Gentility in Early Modern England', in G. E. Aylmer and J. S. Morrill (eds.), *Land, Men and Beliefs* (1983).

—— 'Retainers in Tudor England', in G. E. Aylmer and J. S. Morrill (eds.), *Land, Men and Beliefs* (1983).

COX, J. C., *The Sanctuaries and Sanctuary Seekers of Medieval England* (1911).

CRASTER, H. E., *A History of Northumberland, vol. viii: Tynemouth* (1907).

CRASTER-CHAMBERS, M., 'Penrith Castle and Richard, Duke of Gloucester', *The Ricardian*, v, 86 (1984).

CREIGHTON, C. I., *A History of Epidemics in Britain*, i (Cambridge, 1894, 2nd edn., 1965).

DARBY, H. C., GLASSCOCK, R. E., SHEAILL, J., and VEISEY, G. R., 'The Changing Geographical Distribution of Wealth in England, 1086–1334–1525', *Journal of Historical Geography*, 5 (1979).

DAY, J., *The Medieval Market Economy* (Oxford, 1987).

DICKENS, A. G., *Lollards and Protestants in the Diocese of York, 1509–1558* (Oxford, 1959).

DOBSON, R. B., 'Richard Bell, Prior of Durham (1464–78) and Bishop of Carlisle (1478–95)', *Transactions of the Cumberland and Westmorland Antiquarian and Archaeological Society*, NS, 65 (1965).

—— *Durham Priory, 1400–1450* (Cambridge, 1973).

—— 'The Later Middle Ages, 1215–1500', in G. E. Aylmer and R. Cant (eds.), *A History of York Minster* (Oxford, 1977).

—— 'Cathedral Chapters and Cathedral Cities', *NH* 19 (1983).

—— 'Yorkshire Towns in the Late Fourteenth Century', *Publications of the Thoresby Society*, 59, 1 (1983).

—— 'Richard III and the Church of York', in R. A. Griffiths and J. W. Sherborne (eds.), *Kings and Nobles in the Later Middle Ages* (Gloucester, 1986).

DOCKRAY, K. R., 'The Yorkshire Rebellion of 1469', *The Ricardian*, vi, no. 83 (1983).

—— 'The Political Legacy of Richard III in Northern England', in R. A. Griffiths and J. W. Sherborne (eds.), *Kings and Nobles in the Later Middle Ages* (Gloucester, 1986).

—— 'Why did Fifteenth-Century English Gentry marry? The Plumptons and Stonors Reconsidered', in M. Jones (ed.), *Gentry and Lesser Nobility in Later Medieval Europe* (Gloucester, 1986). ·

DOCKRAY, K. R., 'Richard III and the Yorkshire Gentry', in P. W. Hammond (ed.), *Richard III: Loyalty, Lordship and Law* (Gloucester, 1986).

DODDS, M. H., *A History of Northumberland, vol. xv: Parish of Simonsburn, etc.* (1940).

DONALDSON, G., 'The Bishops and Priors of Whithorn', *Transactions of the Dumfriesshire and Galloway Natural History and Antiquarian Society*, 3rd ser., 27 (1950).

DONKIN, R. A., 'Cattle on the Estates of Medieval Cistercian monasteries in England', *Econ. HR* 2nd ser., 15 (1962–3).

DRAKE, Francis, *Eboracum or the History and Antiquities of the City of York* (1736).

DRURY, J. L., 'Early Settlement in Stanhope Park, Weardale, c. 1406–79', *Arch. Ael.* 4 (1976).

—— 'Durham Palatinate Forest Law and Administration, specially in Weardale up to 1440', *Arch. Ael.* 5th ser., 6 (1978).

DUGDALE, W., *The Baronage of England*, i (1675).

DUNHAM, W. H., *Lord Hastings' Indentured Retainers, 1461–1483*, Transactions of the Connecticut Academy of Arts and Sciences, 39 (1955).

DUNLOP, A. I., *The Life and Times of James Kennedy, Bishop of St Andrews* (Oxford, 1950).

DYER, C. C., 'A Small Landowner in the Fifteenth Century', *Midland History*, 3 (1972).

—— *Lords and Peasants in a Changing Society: The Estates of the Bishopric of Worcester, 680–1540* (Cambridge, 1980).

—— *Warwickshire Farming, 1349–c.1529*, Dugdale Society Occasional Paper 27 (1981).

—— 'Deserted Medieval Villages in the West Midlands', *Econ. HR* 2nd ser., 35 (1982).

EDWARDS, A. J. G., 'The Manuscripts and texts of the second version of John Hardyng's Chronicle', in D. Williams (ed.), *England in the Fifteenth Century* (Woodbridge, 1987).

EDWARDS, R., *The Itinerary of King Richard III, 1483–1485* (Richard III Society, 1983).

EMDEN, A. B., *A Biographical Register of the University of Oxford to AD 1500*, iii (Oxford, 1959).

—— *A Biographical Register of the University of Cambridge to AD 1500* (Cambridge, 1963).

EMSLEY, K., 'The Yorkshire Enclaves of the Bishop of Durham', *YAJ* 57 (1975).

EMSLEY, K. and FRASER, C. M., *The Courts of the County Palatine of Durham from the Earliest Times to 1971* (Durham, 1984).

EVERITT, A., 'Country, County and Town: Patterns of Regional Evolution in England', *TRHS* 5th ser., 29 (1979).

FIELDHOUSE, R., 'Social structure from Tudor lay subsidies and probate inventories', *Local Population Studies*, 12 (1974).

FIELDHOUSE, R. and JENNINGS, B., *A History of Richmond and Swaledale* (Chichester, 1978).

FISHER, J., *History and Antiquities of Masham and Mashamshire* (1865).

FLEMING, P., 'Charity, Faith and the Gentry of Kent, 1422–1529', in A. J. Pollard (ed.), *Property and Politics: Essays in Later Medieval English History* (Gloucester, 1984).

FOSS, P. J., 'The Battle of Bosworth: Towards a Reassessment', *Midland History*, 13 (1988).

FRASER, C. M., *History of Antony Bec* (Oxford, 1957).

——'The Pattern of Trade in North-East England, 1265–1350', *NH* iv (1969).

GAIRDNER, J., *The History of the Life and Reign of Richard the Third* (Cambridge, 1898).

GIVEN-WILSON, C., 'The King and the Gentry in Fourteenth-Century England', *TRHS* 5th ser., 37 (1987).

GOLDBERG, P. J. P., 'Mortality and Economic Change in the Diocese of York, 1390–1514', *NH* 24 (1988).

GOLDTHORPE, L. M., 'The Franciscans and Dominicans in Yorkshire', *YAJ* 32 (1936).

GOODMAN, A. E., 'Responses to Requests in Yorkshire for Military Service under Henry V', *NH* 17 (1981).

——*The Wars of the Roses* (1981).

——'The Anglo-Scottish Marches in the Fifteenth Century: A Frontier Society', in R. A. Mason (ed.), *Scotland and England, 1286–1815* (Edinburgh, 1987).

——and MCKAY, A., 'A Castilian Report on English Affairs', *EHR* 88 (1973).

GOTTFRIED, R. S., *Epidemic Diseases in Fifteenth Century England* (Leicester, 1978).

GRANSDEN, A., *Historical Writing in England ii, c.1307 to the Early Sixteenth Century* (1982).

GRANT, A., *Independence and Nationhood: Scotland, 1306–1469* (1984).

GRAY, H. L., 'Incomes from land in England in 1436', *EHR* 49 (1934).

GREENWOOD, W., 'The Redmans', *Transactions of the Cumberland*

and Westmorland Antiquarian and Archaeological Society, NS, 3 (1903).

GRIFFITHS, R. A., 'Local Rivalries and National Politics: the Percies, the Nevilles and the Duke of Exeter, 1452–55', *Speculum*, 43 (1968).

—— 'Public and Private Bureaucracies in England and Wales in the Fifteenth Century', *TRHS* 5th ser., 30 (1980).

—— *The Reign of Henry VI* (1981).

GUTH, Delloyd J., 'Richard III, Henry VII and the City: London Politics and the Dun Cowe', in R. A. Griffiths and J. W. Sherborne (eds.), *Kings and Nobles in the Later Middle Ages* (Gloucester, 1986).

HAIGH, C., *Reformation and Resistance in Tudor Lancashire* (1975).

HALSTED, C. A., *Richard III as Duke of Gloucester and King of England*, 2 vols. (1844).

HAMMOND, P. W., 'Richard III's Books: III. English New Testament', *The Ricardian*, vii, no. 98 (1987).

HAMPTON, W. E., *Memorials of the Wars of the Roses* (Gloucester, 1979).

—— 'Further comment on *Richard III* by Charles Ross', *The Ricardian*, vi, no. 77 (1982).

—— 'The White Rose under the First Tudor', *The Ricardian*, vii, no. 97 (1987).

—— 'John Hoton of Hunwick', *The Ricardian*, xviii, no. 88 (1985).

Handbook of British Chronology, ed. E. B. Fryde, D. E. Greenway, *et al.*, 3rd edn. (1986).

HANHAM, A., *Richard III and his Early Historians, 1483–1535* (Oxford, 1975).

HARRISON, B. J. H. and DIXON, G., *Guisborough before 1900* (Guisborough, 1981).

HARRISON, B. J. H. and HUTTON, B., *Vernacular Houses in North Yorkshire and Cleveland* (Edinburgh, 1984).

HATCHER, J., 'Mortality in the Fifteenth Century: Some New Evidence', *Econ. HR* 2nd ser., 39 (1986).

HEATH, P. 'North Sea Fishing in the Fifteenth Century: the Scarborough Fleet', *NH* 3 (1968).

HEATON, H., *The Yorkshire Woollen and Worsted Industries*, 2nd edn. (Oxford, 1965).

HEXTER, J. H., 'The Education of the Aristocracy during the Renaissance', in *Reappraisals in History* (1961).

HEY, D., *A Regional History: Yorkshire from AD 1000* (1986).

HICKS, M. A., 'Dynastic Change and Northern Society: The Career of the Fourth Earl of Northumberland, 1470–89', *NH* 14 (1978).

—— 'Descent, Partition and Extinction: The Warwick Inheritance', *BIHR* 52 (1979).

—— *False, Fleeting, Perjur'd Clarence: George, Duke of Clarence, 1449–78* (Gloucester, 1980).

—— 'Restraint, Mediation and Private Justice: George, Duke of Clarence as "good lord"', *Journal of Legal History*, 4 (1983).

—— 'Edward IV, the Duke of Somerset and Lancastrian Loyalism in the North', *NH* 20 (1984).

—— *Richard III as Duke of Gloucester: A Study in Character*, Borthwick Paper 70, (York, 1986).

—— 'Richard, Duke of Gloucester and the North', in R. E. Horrox (ed.), *Richard III and the North* (Hull, 1986).

—— 'The Yorkshire Rebellion of 1489 Reconsidered', *NH* 22 (1986).

—— 'The Last Days of Elizabeth Countess of Oxford', *EHR* 103 (1988).

HILTON, R. H., 'Medieval Market Towns and Simple Commodity Production', *PP* 109 (1985).

HINDS, A. B., *A History of Northumberland, vol. iii: Hexhamshire*, pt. i (Newcastle, 1896).

HOGG, J., 'Mount Grace Charterhouse and Late Medieval English Spirituality', *Collectanea Cartusiensia*, 3 (1980).

HOLMAN, E. C., *The Church of St. Mary the Virgin, Hornby, North Yorkshire* (Bedale, 1978).

HORROX, R. E., 'Urban Patronage and Patrons in the Fifteenth Century', in R. A. Griffiths (ed.), *Patronage, the Crown and the Provinces* (Gloucester, 1981).

—— 'Richard III and Allhallows Barking by the Tower', *The Ricardian*, vi, no. 77 (1982).

—— (ed.), *Richard III and the North* (Hull, 1986).

—— 'Richard III and the East Riding', in idem (ed.), *Richard III and the North* (Hull, 1986).

—— 'The Urban Gentry in the Fifteenth Century', in J. A. F. Thomson (ed.), *Towns and Townspeople in the Fifteenth Century* (Gloucester, 1988).

—— 'The English Court', *The Ricardian*, viii, no. 101 (1988).

—— *Richard III: A Study of Service* (Cambridge, 1989).

HORSFALL, T., *The Manor of Snape and Well* (Leeds, 1912).

HUNTER, J., *South Yorkshire*, i (1828), ii (1831).

HUNTER-BLAIR, C. H., 'Members of Parliament for Northumberland, 1399–1558', *Arch. Ael.* 4th ser., 12 (1935).

—— 'The Sheriffs of Northumberland', *Arch. Ael.* 4th ser., 20 (1942).

HUTCHINSON, W., *The History and Antiquities of the County Palatine of Durham*, 3 vols. (Durham, 1817).

IVES, E. W., *The Common Lawyers of Prereformation England: Thomas Kebell, a Case Study* (Cambridge, 1983).

JACOB, E. F., *The Fifteenth Century* (Oxford, 1961).

JACOB, E. F., 'The Book of St. Albans', in *Essays in Later Medieval History* (Manchester, 1968).

JALLAND, P., 'The Influence of the Aristocracy on Shire Elections in the North of England, 1450–70', *Speculum*, 47 (1972).

——'The Revolution in Northern Borough Representation in mid-fifteenth-century England', *NH* 11 (1976).

JAMES, M. E., 'English Politics and the Concept of Honour', *Past and Present* Suppl. 3 (1978).

——*A Tudor Magnate and the Tudor State*, Borthwick Paper 30 (York, 1966).

——'The First Earl of Cumberland and the Decline of Northern Feudalism', *NH* 1 (1966).

——*Family, Lineage and Civil Society: A Study of Society, Politics and Mentality in the Durham Region, 1500–1640* (Oxford, 1974).

JENNINGS, B. (ed.), *History of Harrogate and Knaresborough* (Huddersfield, 1970).

JOHNSON, P. A., *Duke Richard of York, 1411–1460* (Oxford, 1988).

JONES, M. K., 'Richard III and the Stanleys', in R. E. Horrox (ed.), *Richard III and the North* (Hull, 1986).

JORDAN, W. K., *The Charities of Rural England* (1961).

KEEN, M. H., *Chivalry* (Newhaven, Conn., 1984).

KENDALL, P. M., *Richard III* (1955).

KERMODE, J. I., 'Merchants, Overseas Trade and Urban Decline, York, Beverley and Hull, *ca* 1380–1500', *NH* 23 (1987).

——'Obvious Observations on the Formation of Oligarchies in Late Medieval Towns', in J. A. F. Thomson (ed.), *Towns and Townspeople in the Fifteenth Century* (Gloucester, 1988).

KERSHAW, I., 'The Great Famine and Agrarian Crisis in England, 1315–22', *PP* 59 (1973).

——'A Note on the Scots in the West Riding, 1318–19', *NH* 17 (1981).

KNOWLES, D., *The Religious Orders in England*, ii (Cambridge, 1955).

KNOWLES, D. and HADCOCK, R. N., *Medieval Religious Houses in England and Wales* (1953).

KREIDER, A., *English Chantries: The Road to Dissolution* (Cambridge, Mass., 1979).

LAMB, H. H., *Climate, History and the Modern World* (1982).

LANDER, J. R., 'Attainder and Forfeiture, 1453 to 1509', in *Crown and Nobility, 1450–1509* (1976).

——*Government and Community: England, 1450–1509* (1980).

LAPSLEY, G. T., *The County Palatine of Durham: A study in Constitutional History* (Cambridge, Mass., 1900).

LAWSON TANCRED, T., *Records of a Yorkshire Manor* (1937).

LE PATOUREL, J., 'Is Northern History a Subject?', *NH* 12 (1976).

LLOYD, T. H., *The Movement of Wool Prices in Medieval England*, *Econ. HR* Suppl. 6 (1973).

LOMAS, R. A., 'Developments in Land Tenure on the Prior of Durham's Estate in the Later Middle Ages', *NH* 13 (1973).

—— 'The Priory of Durham and its Demesnes in the Fourteenth and Fifteenth Centuries', *Econ. HR* 2nd ser., 31 (1978).

—— 'A Northern Farm at the End of the Middle Ages', *NH* 18 (1982).

LOMAS, T., 'South East Durham: Late Fourteenth and Fifteenth Centuries', in P. D. A. Harvey (ed.), *The Peasant Land Market in Medieval England* (Oxford, 1984).

McCALL, H. T., *Richmondshire Churches* (1910).

MacCULLOCH, D., *Suffolk and the Tudors* (Oxford, 1986).

MACDOUGALL, N., *James III: A Political Study* (Edinburgh, 1982).

—— 'Richard III and James III', in P. W. Hammond (ed.), *Richard III: Loyalty, Lordship and Law* (Gloucester, 1986).

McFARLANE, A., *Marriage and Love in England* (Oxford, 1986).

McFARLANE, K. B., 'The Wars of the Roses', *Proceedings of the British Academy*, 50 (1964).

—— *The Nobility of Later Medieval England* (Oxford, 1973).

McHARDY, A. K., 'Clerical Taxation in Fifteenth-century England', in R. B. Dobson (ed.), *The Church, Politics and Patronage in the Fifteenth Century* (Gloucester, 1984).

McINTOSH, M. K., 'Local Change and Community Control in England, 1465–1500', *Huntingdon Library Quarterly*, 49 (1986).

—— *Autonomy and Community: The Royal Manor of Havering, 1200–1500* (Cambridge, 1986).

McKENZIE, W. M., 'The Debateable Land', *Scottish Historical Review*, 30–1 (1951–2).

MADDICOTT, J. R., *The English Peasantry and the Demands of the Crown, 1294–1341*, *Past and Present* Suppl. i (1975).

MARSHALL, J. D., 'Why Study Regions (2): Some Historical Considerations', *Journal of Regional and Local Studies*, vi (1) (Spring 1986).

MERTES, K., *The English Noble Household, 1250–1600* (Oxford, 1988).

METCALFE, W. C., *A Book of Knights Banneret, Knights of the Bath and Knights Bachelor* (1855).

MILLER, E., *War in the North: the Anglo-Scottish Wars of the Middle Ages* (Hull, 1960).

—— 'Medieval York', in P. M. Tillott (ed.), *VCH, York* (1961), pp. 25–116.

MISKIMIN, H. A., 'Monetary Movements and Market Structure: Forces for Contraction in Fourteenth and Fifteenth Century England', *Journal of Economic History*, 2nd ser., 24 (1964).

MORAN, J. A. H., 'Clerical Recruitment in the Diocese of York, 1340–1530', *JEH* 34 (1983).

—— *The Growth of English Schooling, 1340–1548* (Princeton, 1985).

MORGAN, D. A. L., 'The King's Affinity in the Polity of Yorkist England', *TRHS* 5th ser., 23 (1973).

—— 'The Individual Style of the English Gentleman', in M. Jones (ed.), *Gentry and Lesser Nobility in Later Medieval Europe* (Gloucester, 1986).

NEF, J. U., *The Rise of the British Coal Industry*, i (1932).

NEWTON, R., *The Northumberland Landscape* (1972).

NICHOLSON, J. and BURN, R., *The History and Antiquities of Westmorland and Cumberland*, i (1777).

NICHOLSON, R., *Scotland: The Later Middle Ages* (Edinburgh, 1974).

NOKES, E. and WHEELER, G., 'A Spanish Account of the Battle of Bosworth', *The Ricardian*, 36 (1972).

O'CONNOR, S., 'Francis Lovell and the Rebels of Furness Fells', *The Ricardian*, vii, no. 96 (1987).

ORME, N., *From Childhood to Chivalry* (1984).

PALLISER, D. M., 'York under the Tudors: The Trading Life of the Northern Capital', in A. Everitt (ed.), *Perspectives in English Urban History* (1973).

—— 'A Crisis in English Towns? The Case of York, 1460–1640', *NH* 14 (1978).

—— 'A Regional Capital as Magnet: Immigrants to York, 1477–1566', *YAJ* 57 (1985).

—— 'Richard III and York', in R. E. Horrox (ed.), *Richard III and the North* (Hull, 1986).

—— 'Urban Decay Revisited', in J. A. F. Thomson (ed.), *Towns and Townspeople in the Fifteenth Century* (Gloucester, 1988).

PALLISTER, A. F. and PALLISTER, P. M., 'A Survey of the Deserted Medieval Village of Newsham', *Transactions of the Archaeological and Architectural Society of Durham and Northumberland*, NS 4 (1978).

Parliamentary Representation of the County of York, 1258–1832, ed. A. Gooder, ii, YAS, RS 91 (1935).

PAYLING, S. J., 'The Widening Franchise: Parliamentary Elections in Lancastrian Nottinghamshire', in D. Williams (ed.), *England in the Fifteenth Century* (Woodbridge, 1987).

—— 'Law and Arbitration in Nottinghamshire', in J. T. Rosenthal and C. F. Richmond (eds.), *People, Politics and Community in the Later Middle Ages',* (Gloucester, 1987).

—— 'The Ampthill Dispute: a Study in Aristocratic Lawlessness and the Breakdown of Lancastrian Government', *EHR* (1989).

Bibliography 421

PAYNE, A., 'The Salisbury Roll of Arms, 1463', in D. Williams (ed.), *England in the Fifteenth Century* (Woodbridge, 1987).

POLLARD, A. J., 'The Northern Retainers of Richard Neville, Earl of Salisbury', *NH* 11 (1976).

—— 'The Tyranny of Richard III', *Journal of Medieval History*, 3 (1977).

—— 'Richard Clervaux of Croft: a North Riding Squire during the Fifteenth Century', *YAJ* 50 (1978).

—— 'The Burghs of Brough Hall, ca 1270–1574', *NYCROJ* 6 (1978).

—— 'The Richmondshire Community of Gentry', in Charles Ross (ed.), *Patronage, Pedigree and Power in Later Medieval England* (Gloucester, 1979).

—— 'Lord FitzHugh's Rising in 1470', *BIHR* 52 (1979).

—— 'Croft-on-Tees in the Later Middle Ages', *Teesside and Cleveland Local History Bulletin*, 39 (1980).

—— *John Talbot and the War in France, 1427–53*, RHS Study in History 35 (1983).

—— *The Middleham Connection: Richard III and Richmondshire, 1471–85* (Middleham, 1983).

—— 'St. Cuthbert and the Hog; Richard III and the County Palatine of Durham, 1471–85', in R. A. Griffiths and J. W. Sherborne (eds.), *Kings and Nobles in the Later Middle Ages* (Gloucester, 1986).

—— 'The North-Eastern Economy and the Agrarian Crisis of 1438–40', *NH* 25 (1989).

—— and ASHCROFT, M. Y., 'Coverham: Some Fifteenth-Century Documents', *NYCROJ* 10 (1982).

POTTER, Jeremy, *Good King Richard?* (1983).

POWELL, E., 'Arbitration and the Law in England in the Later Middle Ages', *TRHS* 5th ser. 13 (1983).

POWELL, E. H. and WALLIS, K., *The House of Lords in the Later Middle Ages* (1968).

POWER, E. E. and POSTAN, M. M., *Studies in English Trade in the Fifteenth Century* (1933).

PRONAY, N. and TAYLOR, J., *Parliamentary Texts of the Later Middle Ages* (Oxford, 1980).

PUGH, T. B., 'The Magnates, Knights and Gentry', in S. B. Chrimes *et al.* (eds.), *Fifteenth-Century England: Studies in Politics and Society* (Manchester, 1972).

—— 'The Southampton Plot of 1415', in R. A. Griffiths and J. W. Sherborne (eds.), *Kings and Nobles in the Later Middle Ages* (Gloucester, 1986).

PYTHIAN-ADAMS, C., 'Urban Decay in Late Medieval England', in J. Abrams and C. T. Wrigley (eds.), *Towns in Societies* (Cambridge, 1978).

RAINE, J., *History and Antiquities of North Durham* (1852).

RAMSAY, J. H., *Lancaster and York*, ii (Oxford, 1892).

RAWCLIFFE, C., *The Staffords, Earls of Stafford and Dukes of Buckingham, 1394–1521* (Cambridge, 1978).

—— 'The Great Lord as Peacekeeper; Arbitration by English Noblemen and their Councils in the Late Middle Ages', in J. A. Guy and H. G. Beale (eds.), *Law and Social Change in British History*, RHS Study in History 40 (1984).

REEVES, A. C., *Lancastrian Englishmen* (Washington, DC, 1981).

REID, R. R., *The King's Council in the North* (1921).

RICHMOND, C. F., *John Hopton: A Suffolk Gentleman in the Fifteenth Century* (Cambridge, 1981).

—— 'After McFarlane', *History*, 68 (1984).

—— 'Religion and the Fifteenth-Century Gentleman', in R. B. Dobson (ed.), *The Church, Politics and Patronage in the Fifteenth Century* (Gloucester, 1984).

—— 'The Pastons Revisited: Marriage and the Family in Fifteenth-Century England', *BIHR* 58 (1985).

—— '1485 and All That', in P. W. Hammond (ed.), *Richard III: Loyalty, Lordship and Law* (Gloucester, 1986).

—— *The Penket Papers* (Gloucester, 1986).

RIGBY, S. H., 'Urban Decline in the Later Middle Ages', *Urban History Yearbook* (Leicester, 1984).

ROSENTHAL, J. T., *The Purchase of Paradise: Gift Giving and the Aristocracy, 1307–1485* (1972).

—— 'The Yorkshire Chantry Certificates of 1546: An Analysis', *NH* 9 (1974).

—— 'Aristocratic Cultural Patronage and Book Bequests', *BJRL* 44, 2 (1982).

ROSKELL, J. S., 'Sir James Strangeways of West Harlsey and Whorlton', *YAJ* 34 (1958).

ROSS, C. D., *Edward IV* (1974).

—— *Richard III* (1981).

—— and PUGH, T. B., 'The English Baronage and the Income Tax of 1436', *BIHR* 20 (1953).

ROSSER, G., 'London and Westminster: the Suburbs in the Urban Economy in the Later Middle Ages', in J. A. F. Thomson (ed.), *Towns and Townspeople in the Fifteenth Century* (Gloucester, 1988).

—— 'Communities of Parish and Guild in the Late Middle Ages', in S. M. Wright (ed.), *Parish, Church and People: Local Studies in Lay Religion, 1350–1750* (1988).

ROUTH, P. E., *Medieval Effigial Alabaster Tombs in Yorkshire* (Ipswich, 1976).

ROWNEY, I., 'Arbitration in Gentry Disputes in the Later Middle Ages', *History*, 67 (1982).

—— 'Government and Patronage in the Fifteenth Century in Staffordshire, 1439–59', *Midland History*, 8 (1983).

—— 'Resources and Retaining in Yorkist England: William Lord Hastings and the Honour of Tutbury', in A. J. Pollard (ed.), *Property and Politics: Essays in Late Medieval English History* (Gloucester, 1984).

RYDER, P. and BIRCH, J., 'Hellifield Peel: A North Yorkshire Tower House', *YAJ* 55 (1983).

SALZMAN, L. F., *Building in England down to 1540* (Oxford, 1954).

SAUL, N., 'The Religious Sympathies of the Gentry in Gloucestershire, 1200–1500', *Bristol and Gloucestershire Archaeology Society Transactions*, 98 (1980).

SCAMMELL, J., 'Robert I and the North of England', *EHR* 73 (1958).

SCHOFIELD, R. S., 'The Geographical Distribution of Wealth in England, 1334–1649', *Econ. HR*, 2nd ser., 18 (1965).

SCOFIELD, C. L., *The Life and Reign of Edward the Fourth* (1923).

SEARLE, W. G., *History of Queens' College Cambridge* (Cambridge, 1867).

SEWARD, D., *Richard III: England's Black Legend* (1983).

SHARP, C., *History of Hartlepool* (Hartlepool, 1851).

SHAW, R. C., *The Royal Forest of Lancaster* (Preston, 1956).

SHAW, W. A., *The Knights of England*, ii (1906).

SHREWSBURY, J. F. D., *A History of Bubonic Plague in the British Isles* (Cambridge, 1971).

SINGLETON, F. B. and RAWNSLEY, S., *A History of Yorkshire* (Chichester, 1986).

SMAILES, A. E., *North England* (1960).

SOMERVILLE, R., *History of the Duchy of Lancaster, 1265–1603*, i (1953).

STILL, L. and PALLISTER, A. F., 'The Excavation of One House Site in the Deserted Village of West Hartburn', *Arch. Ael.* 4th ser., 42 (1964).

STOREY, R. L., 'The Wardens of the Marches of England towards Scotland, 1377–1489', *EHR* 72 (1957).

—— *Thomas Langley and the Bishopric of Durham, 1406–1437* (1961).

—— *The End of the House of Lancaster* (1966).

—— 'The North of England', in S. B. Chrimes, C. D. Ross, and R. A. Griffiths (eds.), *Fifteenth Century England, 1399–1509: Studies in Politics and Society* (Manchester, 1972).

—— 'Gentlemen-Bureaucrats', in C. H. Clough (ed.), *Professions, Vocations and Culture in Late Medieval England* (Liverpool, 1982).

STURGE, C., *Cuthbert Tunstall* (1938).

SUNDERLAND, N., *Tudor Darlington*, i (Durham, 1974).

SURTEES, H. C., *A History of the Parish of Middleton in Teesdale* (Newcastle, 1925).

SURTEES, R., *The History and Antiquities of the County Palatine of Durham*, 4 vols. (1816–40).

SUTTON, A. F., 'A Curious Searcher for Our Weal Public', in P. W. Hammond (ed.), *Richard III: Loyalty, Lordship and Law* (1986).

—— 'The Lord Richard, Duke of Gloucester', *The Ricardian*, viii, no. 100 (1988).

—— and VISSER-FUCHS, L., 'Richard III's Books: IV. Vegetius' *De Re Militari*', *The Ricardian*, vii, no. 99 (1987).

—— and—— 'Richard III and St Julian: A New Myth', *The Ricardian*, viii, no. 106 (1989).

TANNER, N. P., 'The Reformation and Regionalism', in J. A. F. Thomson (ed.), *Towns and Townspeople in the Fifteenth Century* (Gloucester, 1988).

THIRSK, J., *The Agrarian History of England and Wales*, iv, ed. Joan Thirsk (Cambridge, 1967).

THOMPSON, A. H., 'The Clervaux Chartulary', *Arch. Ael.* 3rd ser., 17 (1920).

THOMPSON, E. M., *The Carthusian Order in England* (1930).

TREVOR ROPER, H. L., 'The Bishopric of Durham and the Capitalist Reformation', *Durham University Journal*, 38 (1945–6).

TUCK, J. A., 'War and Society in the Medieval North', *NH* 21 (1985).

TUDOR CRAIG, P., *Richard III*, 2nd edn. (National Portrait Gallery, London, 1977).

—— 'Richard III's Triumphal Entry into York, August 29th, 1483', in R. E. Horrox (ed.), *Richard III and the North* (Hull, 1986).

TUPLING, G. H., *The Economic History of Rossendale* (Manchester, 1927).

TURNER, G., *The North Country* (1967).

VALE, M. G. A., *Piety, Charity and Literacy among the Yorkshire Gentry, 1370–1480*, Borthwick Paper 50 (York, 1976).

Victoria History of the County of Durham, ed. W. Page, ii (1907); iii (1928).

Victoria History of the County of York: East Riding, i, *The City of Kingston upon Hull*, ed. K. J. Allison (1969).

Victoria History of the County of York: North Riding, ed. W. Page, i (1914); ii (1923).

Victoria History of the County of York: The City of York, ed. P. M. Tillott (1961).

WAGNER, A. R., *Heralds of England: A history of the Office and College of Arms* (1967).

—— *Heralds and Heraldry in the Middle Ages*, 2nd edn. (Oxford, 1973).

WAITES, B., 'Medieval Iron Working in Northeast Yorkshire', *Geography*, 49 (1964).

——'Aspects of Medieval Arable Farming in the Vale of York and the Cleveland Plain', *Ryedale Historian*, 2 (1966).

——*Moorland and Valeland Farming in North-East Yorkshire*, Borthwick Paper 32 (York, 1967).

WARNICKE, R. M., 'Lord Morley's Statements about Richard III', *Albion*, 15 (1983).

WARREN, K., *North East England* (Oxford, 1973).

WEDGWOOD, J. C., (ed.), *History of Parliament: Biographies of Members of the Commons House, 1439–1509* (1938).

WEISS, M., '"A Power in the North?", The Percies in the Fifteenth Century', *Historical Journal*, 19 (1976).

WELFORD, R., *A History of Newcastle and Gateshead in the Fourteenth and Fifteenth Centuries* (1884).

WESTLAKE, H. F., *The Parish Gilds of Medieval England* (1919).

WHEATER, W., *Knaresburgh and its Rulers* (Leeds, 1907).

WHITAKER, T. D., *An History of Richmondshire*, 2 vols. (1823).

WILCOCK, D., *The Durham Coalfield: Part One* (Durham, 1979).

WOLFFE, B. P., *Henry VI* (1981).

WOOD, C. T., 'Richard III, William, Lord Hastings and Friday the Thirteenth' in R. A. Griffiths and J. W. Sherborne (eds.), *Kings and Nobles in the Later Middle Ages* (Gloucester, 1986).

WRIGHT, S. M., *The Derbyshire Gentry in the Fifteenth Century*, Derbys. Record Society, 8 (1983).

UNPUBLISHED THESES

ARNOLD, C. E., 'A Political Study of the West Riding of Yorkshire, 1437–1509' (University of Manchester Ph.D., 1984).

BLENKARN, R., 'Mortality in the Diocese of York, 1430–1539' (CNAA MA, Teesside Polytechnic, 1983).

CARDEW, A. A., 'A Study of Society in the Anglo-Scottish Borders, 1455–1502' (University of St Andrews Ph.D., 1974).

COLES, G. M., 'The Lordship of Middleham, especially in Yorkist and Early Tudor Times' (University of Liverpool MA, 1961).

CURRY, A. E., 'Military Organisation in Lancastrian Normandy, 1422–1450' (CNAA Ph.D., Teesside Polytechnic, 1985).

HALL, P. W., 'Tenure and Tenants: Billingham, 1495–1523' (CNAA MA, Teesside Polytechnic, 1985).

HICKS, M. A., 'The Career of Henry Percy, 4th Earl of Northumberland, with Special Reference to his Retinue' (University of Southampton MA, 1971).

HORROX, R. E., 'The Extent and Use of Crown Patronage under Richard III' (University of Cambridge Ph.D., 1975).

LINACRE, R. D., 'The Distribution of Lay Wealth in the North Riding during the Early Fourteenth Century' (CNAA MA, Teesside Polytechnic, 1981).

LOMAS, R. A., 'Durham Cathedral Priory as a Landowner and a Landlord' (University of Durham Ph.D., 1973).

LOMAS, T., 'Land and People in South-East Durham in the Later Middle Ages' (CNAA Ph.D., Teesside Polytechnic, 1976).

ROSS, C., 'The Yorkshire Baronage, 1399–1435' (University of Oxford D.Phil., 1951).

ROWNTREE, C. C., 'Studies in Carthusian History in Later Medieval England' (University of York D.Phil., 1981).

VICKERSTAFF, J. J., 'Schools and Schooling in County Durham, 1400–1640' (CNAA M.Phil., Teesside Polytechnic, 1988).

Index

442   Index